# Contestation and Polarization in Global Governance

LEUVEN GLOBAL GOVERNANCE

**Series Editor:** Jan Wouters, *KU Leuven, Belgium*

The Leuven Global Governance series comprises high-quality monographs and edited volumes dedicated to innovative research on global governance. The series covers a wide range of themes, from the EU and global multilateral governance to trade, sustainable development, peace and security, human rights, democracy and rule of law, private standards, and global commons. In full recognition of the complex issues involved, the series favours studies approaching global governance from a multidisciplinary, multi-level and multi-actor perspective.

Titles in the series include:

Parliamentary Cooperation and Diplomacy in EU External Relations
An Essential Companion
*Edited by Kolja Raube, Meltem Müftüler-Baç and Jan Wouters*

The Belt and Road Initiative and Global Governance
*Edited by Maria Adele Carrai, Jean-Christophe Defraigne and Jan Wouters*

Can We Still Afford Human Rights?
Critical Reflections on Universality, Costs and Proliferation
*Edited by Jan Wouters, Koen Lemmens, Thomas Van Poecke and Marie Bourguignon*

The Rule of Law and Areas of Limited Statehood
Domestic and International Dimensions
*Edited by Linda Hamid and Jan Wouters*

Japan, the European Union and Global Governance
*Edited by Eiji Ogawa, Kolja Raube, Dimitri Vanoverbeke and Jan Wouters with Camille Van der Vorst*

The Nexus Between Organized Crime and Terrorism
Types and Responses
*Edited by Letizia Paoli, Cyrille Fijnaut and Jan Wouters*

EU Industrial Policy in the Multipolar Economy
*Edited by Jean-Christophe Defraigne, Jan Wouters, Edoardo Traversa and Dimitri Zurstrassen*

Contestation and Polarization in Global Governance
European Responses
*Edited by Michelle Egan, Kolja Raube, Jan Wouters and Julien Chaisse*

# Contestation and Polarization in Global Governance

## European Responses

*Edited by*

Michelle Egan

*Professor and Jean Monnet Chair ad personam, School of International Service and Co-Director, Transatlantic Policy Center, American University, Washington, DC, USA*

Kolja Raube

*Associate Professor for European Governance and EU External Action, Faculty of Social Sciences, Director, Centre for European Studies and Senior Member, Leuven Centre for Global Governance Studies, KU Leuven, Belgium*

Jan Wouters

*Full Professor of International Law and International Organizations, Jean Monnet Chair ad personam EU and Global Governance and Director, Institute for International Law and Leuven Centre for Global Governance Studies, KU Leuven, Belgium*

Julien Chaisse

*Professor, School of Law, City University of Hong Kong, Hong Kong SAR and Advisory Board Member, Asian Academy of International Law (AAIL)*

LEUVEN GLOBAL GOVERNANCE

Edward Elgar PUBLISHING

Cheltenham, UK • Northampton, MA, USA

Published by
Edward Elgar Publishing Limited
The Lypiatts
15 Lansdown Road
Cheltenham
Glos GL50 2JA
UK

Edward Elgar Publishing, Inc.
William Pratt House
9 Dewey Court
Northampton
Massachusetts 01060
USA

A catalogue record for this book
is available from the British Library

Library of Congress Control Number: 2022948519

This book is available electronically in the **Elgar**online
Political Science and Public Policy subject collection
http://dx.doi.org/10.4337/9781800887268

Printed on elemental chlorine free (ECF)
recycled paper containing 30% Post-Consumer Waste

ISBN 978 1 80088 725 1 (cased)
ISBN 978 1 80088 726 8 (eBook)

Printed and bound in the USA

# Contents

## PART II CHANGING GLOBAL ORDERS AND EUROPEAN RESPONSES



## PART III CHANGING GLOBAL TRADE ORDER AND EUROPEAN RESPONSES

# Contributors

**Alex Andrione-Moylan** is a PhD candidate at the Faculty of Social Sciences and junior researcher at the Leuven Centre for Global Governance Studies, KU Leuven, Belgium.

**Katja Biedenkopf** is Associate Professor of Sustainability Politics in the Faculty of Social Sciences and Director of Leuven International and European Studies at KU Leuven, Belgium.

**Matthieu Burnay** is Senior Lecturer in Global Law in the Faculty of Law at Queen Mary University of London, UK.

**Julien Chaisse** is Professor in the School of Law at City University of Hong Kong, Hong Kong SAR and Advisory Board Member, Asian Academy of International Law (AAIL).

**Angelos Chryssogelos** is Senior Lecturer in Politics and International Relations in the School of Social Sciences and Professions at London Metropolitan University, London, UK.

**Karol Chwedczuk-Szulc** is Assistant Professor in the Institute of Political Science at the University of Wrocław, Poland.

**Alexandru Circiumaru** is a research assistant in the Faculty of Law at Queen Mary University of London, and European Public Policy Lead at the Ada Lovelace Institute, London, UK.

**Francisca Costa Reis** is a PhD candidate in the Faculty of Social Sciences and junior researcher at the Leuven Centre for Global Governance Studies, KU Leuven, Belgium.

**Nicolas de Zamaróczy** is Lecturer of International Relations at Baylor University, USA.

**Shawn Donnelly** is Assistant Professor for Technology, Resilience & Europe at the University of Twente, Netherlands.

**Michelle Egan** is Professor and Jean Monnet Chair ad personam in the School of International Service and Co-Director of the Transatlantic Policy Center at American University, Washington, DC, USA.

**Doga Ulas Eralp** is Senior Professorial Lecturer in the School of International Service at American University, Washington, DC, USA.

**Emily Gilson** is an Associate Attorney at Pickard Djinis and Pisarri LLP, Washington, DC, USA.

**Magdalena Góra** is Associate Professor in the Institute of European Studies at Jagiellonian University, Poland.

**Terrence Guay** is Clinical Professor of International Business and Director of Center for Global Business Studies at Penn State University, USA.

**Tamar Gutner** is Associate Professor in the School of International Service at American University, Washington, DC, USA.

**Niklas Helwig** is Leading Researcher for European Strategic Autonomy in the Finnish Institute of International Relations and Adjunct Professor at the University of Tampere, Finland.

**Miles Kahler** is Distinguished Professor in the School of International Service at American University and Senior Fellow for Global Governance at the Council on Foreign Relations, Washington, DC, USA.

**Akasemi Newsome** is Associate Director of the Institute of European Studies at the University of California, Berkeley, USA, and Senior Fellow at the Inland School of Business and Social Sciences, Norway.

**Franziska Petri** is a doctoral researcher in the Faculty of Social Sciences at KU Leuven, Belgium.

**Kolja Raube** is Associate Professor for European Governance and EU External Action in the Faculty of Social Sciences, Director of the Centre for European Studies and Senior Member of the Leuven Centre for Global Governance Studies, KU Leuven, Belgium.

**Marianne Riddervold** is Professor in the Inland School of Business and Social Sciences, Norway, and the Norwegian Institute of International Affairs, NUPI, and Senior Fellow in the Institute of European Studies at the University of California, Berkeley, USA.

**Iulianna Romanchyshyna** is an International Trade Consultant based in Brussels, Belgium, and a PhD candidate at the University of Passau, Germany.

**Fernando Dias Simões** is Associate Professor in the Faculty of Law at Lusíada University of Porto and Portucalense University, Portugal.

**Michael H. Smith** is Professor in European Politics in Politics and International Studies at Warwick University, UK.

**Xueji SU** is a Post-doctoral Research Fellow in the School of Law at City University of Hong Kong, Hong Kong SAR.

**Güneş Ünüvar** is a Senior Research Fellow at the Max Planck Institute for International, European and Regulatory Procedural Law, Luxembourg.

**Jan Wouters** is Full Professor of International Law and International Organizations, Jean Monnet Chair ad personam EU and Global Governance, and Director of the Institute for International Law and Leuven Centre for Global Governance Studies at KU Leuven, Belgium.

**Gudrun Zagel** is Assistant Professor in the Department of Legal Theory, International and European Law at Paris Lodron University Salzburg, Austria.

# Introduction to *Contestation and Polarization in Global Governance*[1]

**Michelle Egan, Kolja Raube, Julien Chaisse and Jan Wouters**

The present volume came out of two meetings organized by the Jean Monnet Network "The European Union at the Crossroads of the Global Order" (EUCROSS).[2] The aim of the project was to deepen our understanding of current global trends in times of increased contestation of the international liberal order. Focusing on different issue areas as well as institutions at the global and regional level, our goal was first to examine the contestation and polarization that has characterized global governance and, second, to focus more specifically on how the European Union (EU or Union) has responded to the various challenges confronting the liberal order at the domestic, regional, and international level. While there has been extensive commentary on how to maintain and strengthen the rules-based liberal order, our book focuses on understanding the limits of the international order across different issue areas as well as highlighting how the discourse and values inherent in these long-established political arrangements are facing a backlash. Some of these challenges arise from populist-nationalist movements within the EU itself, where we see attacks on some of the Union's fundamental values and ideals. Other challenges are the product of rising geopolitical tensions which to an extent undermine the foundational values of the current international liberal order: national sovereignty, economic openness, and rules-based multilateralism.



2 For more information see the official website of EUCROSS: https://ghum.kuleuven.be/ggs/research/eucross.

While there is continued academic and policy debate about the state of the liberal international order, our volume acknowledges the transformation of this order in response to greater interdependence and connectivity (Kahler 2022, this volume). With greater dispersion of power and heterogeneity of preferences, Europe must navigate an international system that is characterized by a growing deadlock in major international institutions and a lack of compliance with international rules on global governance.

This volume focuses on the challenges and contestation within international organizations as well as the institutional order itself, where the global balance of power is shifting towards a multipolar system (Acharya 2014). For some, the challenges of the liberal order are domestically anchored in growing inequality, political polarization, and diminishing trust in political institutions. For others, the traditional state-based liberal order is falling short when it comes to addressing global problems, and there needs to be more diversity in governance structures to deal with increased connectivity and interdependence of economies and societies. However, given the continual pull of global competition and rising power politics, there are limitations to multilateral cooperation, even as we see a glaring need to address global challenges that have risen to the top of the international agenda. Indeed, to name just a few, the challenges of public health, climate change, cybersecurity, artificial intelligence, and responsibility to protect illustrate the need to examine new pathways towards international cooperation and governance. Yet, it is not obvious in an environment of rising power politics and illiberal practices to maintain traditional liberal priorities, where multiple centers of power and influence render cooperation much more challenging and contested.

The chapters in this volume recognize that such shifts have generated different policy choices vis-à-vis the international system and its ordering norms. This can be seen in the 'America First' policy of President Trump and his rejection of a "post-war liberal order", President Biden's systemic economic rivalry with China tempered by support for the Western Alliance, Russia's war towards Ukraine and interference in Western elections, and the more ambitious and nationalistic foreign policy and economic coercion practices of China. Europe is navigating its commitment to liberal norms with its internal illiberal pressures, as well as balancing its support for multilateralism and trade liberalization with increased geopolitical ambitions.[3] This raises the key question as

[3] Council conclusions, the Commission and the High Representative presented a Joint Communication on the EU's Indo-Pacific Strategy, September 2021: https://eeas.europa.eu/sites/default/files/jointcommunication_2021_24_1_en.pdf; European Commission and HR/VP contribution to the European Council EU-China Strategic Outlook: https://ec.europa.eu/info/sites/default/files/communication-eu-china-a-strategic-outlook.pdf.

to whether the EU can secure meaningful cooperation on the most consequential global challenges in the twenty-first century when the support for its own liberal order, linked to economic stability and growth and the commitment to individual rights and freedoms, has become increasingly uneven across its Member States (Niblett and Vinjamuri 2021).

At the same time, recent ruptures within the transatlantic community, as well as American disengagement from international leadership, have forced Europe to reflect on how to adapt to the changes in the international order. If anything, the transatlantic partnership that has been a quintessential part of the post-war liberal order has faced tremendous stress with the advent of a protectionist and nativist approach to foreign policy (see the contributions of Chwedczuk-Szulc 2022 and Newsome and Riddervold 2022, this volume). This *America First* strategy differs from the traditional view of the transatlantic alliance as a bipartisan goal in American foreign policy and raises concerns about the degree to which there can still be substantive international cooperation on major challenges. While the Biden Administration has sought political renewal in its transatlantic ties, opening new avenues of cooperation with its European counterparts, the transatlantic partners' strategic visions on economic recovery and investment, their security capabilities and crisis management may continue to differ. The chaotic withdrawal from Afghanistan was an illustration for Europeans that the US is less willing to bear the costs of military engagement. Yet, such tensions are not only the result of actions or inactions within the transatlantic relationship itself, but also of the failure of the multilateral institutions set up by Western allies to address rising concerns over societal polarization, inaccurate information, and threats to democracy and human rights protections. Against this backdrop, the EU and its Member States must develop strategies to adapt their liberal values to deal with a fundamentally changing international liberal order that significantly challenges the cohesion among liberal democracies.

Our book wrestles with challenges such as the contestation of key norms, values, and institutional practices by populist and authoritarian leaders, and the latter's undermining of frameworks of international law that provide the basis for economic liberalism and liberal internationalism. In doing so, this volume recognizes that Europe is at crossroads of a changed global order in which it is difficult to propose solutions when the Union itself faces important internal constraints on collective action. While Europe needs a common strategy, it faces an environment where protectionism, great power rivalry, and ideological competition as well as nationalism are overlaid by the need to address the challenges brought by the global pandemic, migration flows and displacement, climate change, digital and cyber security, and artificial intelligence. In essence, the international liberal order as it was originally construed needs to adapt, rather than resigning itself to its own demise. We highlight how Europe must focus on the aspects it needs to support, in terms of rules, institutions, and processes. In doing so, the volume brings together scholarship in international relations and global governance with that of scholarship in European studies to assess the state of multilateralism and the global (dis)order.

## EUROPE FAILING FORWARD?

While tensions and crises abound in the history of European integration, the EU endures. Jones et al. (2021) argue that its authority continues to strengthen, illustrating a level of resilience in response to external shocks and internal pressures. European policymakers have continually focused on developing policy processes to cope with change and thus, with uncertainty, forging a common response to the crises regarding the euro, migration, security, democracy, and health, even if it was slow to emerge. Such "failing forward" actions have led to an evolving set of practices of reconstituting sovereignty to address crises through incremental adjustment and reflexive deliberation (Jones et al. 2021). However, those processes have not been straightforward or uncontested. On the contrary, the EU struggles to maintain comprehensive regulatory and legislative alignment with significant socio-economic and political reforms in the face of challenges to its legitimacy and authority. As indicated above, European policies and actions face challenges from authoritarian, populist, and nationalist governments within the Union along with external pressures from global power competition contesting the norms of multilateral cooperation (Petri et al. 2020; Biedenkopf et al. 2021; Riddervold and Newsome 2018; Börzel and Zürn 2021; see also Kahler 2022, this volume). Beyond the continued support of liberal institutions, there is a sense that the entrenched expectations of the post-war order may be giving way to the return of great power politics. With concerns over the long-term political reliability of the US, Europe, which built its regional foundation on a stable and lasting political order and resilient architecture, faces increased volatility and change (see, for example, the contributions of Donnelly 2022 and Guay and Smith 2022, this volume).

As the EU acknowledges a changing global order, the linkages between policy actions and outcomes raise questions about its capacity to act effectively and decisively. The past decade has been a challenging one starting with the pending Greek default that sparked pressure on the eurozone and ended with the immense social and human toll of the pandemic. European ambitions have felt somewhat diminished due to internal divisions over multiple crises. With domestic and international pressures from migration, climate, debt, inequality and fiscal austerity, a prime challenge lies in whether the Union can act cohesively across different policy domains (Riddervold et al. 2021). It is not just the content but also the form of the narratives of these multiple crises that invoke foundational challenges to the nature of belonging, inclusion, and integration in the EU. The Union's actions are routinely constructed around crises, leading to a range of responses, and triggering reforms resulting in more integration through incremental adjustments and adaptation. Alternatively, EU actions generate more politicization, resulting in calls for renationalization and protectionism, thereby increasing the prospect of disintegration (Cross 2017). The operational effectiveness of the EU in enforcing and upholding liberal norms and values is, in the end, heavily contingent on European capability, consensus, and political will.

As indicated above, the chapters in this volume focus on the multiple governance challenges that result from a transformation of the liberal order from a specific set of Western institutions based on a framework of international cooperation towards a more fragmented, increasingly polarized and contentious system of global governance. As Europe struggles to situate itself within an environment in which there is a rise of nationalism and loss of commitment towards a broader global society, political extremism and democratic backsliding, and surge of protectionism and adverse social consequences due to rising inequality, the crisis of governance is also a profound crisis of legitimacy. For some, the collection of norms and rules that structure the interactions between governments has been transformed by challenges to the prevailing orthodoxy, whether by the actions of states including China, India, and the US, or by the surge of disinformation and decline in trust in institutions where issues of asymmetric relationships or preferential treatment embody for some the dominance of a liberal paradigm that is more fragile than before. Yet that liberal international order has marginalized as well as advanced specific goals and ideas, creating myriad problems and opportunities which, according to the EU, necessitates greater international cooperation. Such cooperation is difficult as it can generate both functional and dysfunctional effects, which means that institutional design is important for the quality of governance, as well as institutional protection to ensure standards of accountability and participation to avoid the arbitrary exercise of coercion, or authoritative exploitation (Keohane 2002). Europe must find a way to deal with assumptions held by those States marginalized in the international system that the goals and aspirations are not exclusive and imbued with explicit neo-colonial assumptions about the efforts to export European rules and norms, to promote trade agreements, fund investment and infrastructure, and foster good governance and transparency through its new Global Gateway.[4] But the assumption that the EU can convert

4 European Commission, "Statement by President von der Leyen on the Global Gateway", 21 December 2021, Statement/21/6522, https://ec.europa.eu/commission/presscorner/detail/en/STATEMENT_21_6522 (accessed 4 February 2022).

its economic weight to geopolitical power faces considerable constraints, as evident by Russian strategy in the ongoing military crisis over Ukraine, Chinese economic coercion against Lithuania over recognition of Taiwan, and the spat over the American/Australian/British alliance (AUKUS) involving nuclear submarines that created diplomatic friction with France.

## AT THE CROSSROADS: WHICH PATH TO TAKE?

Increasingly, the prominence of liberalism, capitalism, and modernity has faced increased scrutiny. The settled international liberal order for over half a century is now shifting, whereby the major question becomes not whether the order will change, but on whose terms it will change (Cooley and Nexon 2022). Debates about the increasing contestation in international relations among academics and practitioners have focused on power shifts, regional fragmentation, and socio-economic competition, drawing attention to the transformation of what has been a distinctive historical order driven by American power and influence. The post-Cold War context saw the expansion of multilateral institutions, economic liberalization, the promotion of human rights, and the fostering of democratic transition. There was a dominant perspective in which the security and economic framework successfully provided for an extended and expansive liberal order (Ikenberry 2018). Yet many of the authors in this volume point to the fact that the international order led by the US and its partners is now in crisis due to the surge of authoritarian populism, democratic backsliding, trade protectionism, and shifting power relations and struggles over the terms of global order. Those challenges arise from internal dissatisfaction with some of those same proponents of the liberal order in Europe and the US, stirred by nationalist and populist upheavals, that have led to contradictions between liberal norms and their acceptance domestically (see, for example, the contributions of Chryssogelos 2022, Andrione-Moylan and Wouters 2022, and Góra 2022, this volume). The growth and vibrancy of democratic governance has weakened through the surge of right-wing parties and the pressures on mainstream parties, as well as infringements on the rule of law, the surge of misinformation, and rising income inequality that have plagued both the US and Europe.

### Transatlantic Relations and China

The EU Member States have long struggled to agree on a common position towards China primarily driven by the varying degrees of economic dependence on the Chinese market. Although the Union has dramatically sharpened its political stance toward China, various investment deals through the 'Belt and Road Initiative' have continued to sow discord among Member States.

While the EU sought to complete a bilateral investment agreement with China before the Biden Administration took office, the decision was based on the perception that the new administration would continue to focus on Chinese market practices and unfair trade advantages. The rise of China as a security challenge will continue to shape American policy, and as such, Europeans will need to determine what their response will be in terms of economic and political relations with China, as these have not been coordinated and agreed upon by the two allies so far (see also the contributions of SU 2022 and Burnay and Circiumaru 2022 in this volume). The new Technology and Trade Council (TTC) may provide some measure of economic coordination in areas of investment screening, technology transfer, and dual use technologies, all areas where China has taken an essentially state-driven approach so that rising contestation over high technology has pushed the US and EU to cooperate in key strategic areas.[5]

Europe has shifted its orientation in viewing China as a "systemic rival" in 2019.[6] The EU has sought to address some of the challenges through a Comprehensive Agreement on Investment, known as the CAI, now on hold (Chaisse and Burnay 2022). Yet China has targeted European supply chains, and in doing so has challenged the integrity of the single market. As a result, Europe is strengthening its trade defense measures with anti-coercion measures as well as restrictions on foreign subsidies in the single market. The Union has also moved forward with a new strategy in the Indo-Pacific that seeks to have long-term engagement in the region. Such a position in which Europe does not wish to get into an 'open confrontation' with China reflects an ambivalence that puts it squarely at odds with the US' perception of the rising challenge from China. Yet as China continues to remain engaged at the multilateral level during the period of American disengagement, its economic and technological advancement, increased militarization and escalating assertiveness of foreign relations have brought to the fore the challenges to the liberal international order. Though this has escalated into a trade war that has continued from the Trump to the Biden Administration, it reflects a broader geopolitical shift in which the US has not been able to see Europe as a consistent ally. Yet growing discontent over China's market economy status and unfair trade practices has elicited a broadening of allies within the World Trade Organization (WTO)

---

[5] Office of the United States Trade Representative, U.S.-E.U. Trade and Technology Council (TTC), https://ustr.gov/useuttc (accessed 4 February 2022).

[6] European Commission and High Representative/Vice President, *EU-China – A Strategic Outlook*, 12 March 2019, https://ec.europa.eu/info/sites/default/files/communication-eu-china-a-strategic-outlook.pdf (accessed 4 February 2022).

who want stronger enforcement of trade measures as well as greater attention to the nature of Chinese investment in strategic sectors.[7]

## Challenging Western Institutions

For some observers, the foundational values, interests and institutions of the Western liberal order are problematic. Critics argue that non-Western powers are challenging liberal conceptions of global order by building alternative institutions, as the ascent of the US and Europe has privileged the history, intellectual traditions, and agency of Western institutions and policies (Acharya 2014; see the contribution of Gutner 2022, this volume). As a result, the evolving relationship between the post-war international order and major powers has fostered debate about whether this necessitates a change in strategy due to increased great power competition requiring a more assertive foreign policy or whether the vestiges of the liberal order can be modified or expanded so that there is room to work together on common challenges, including public health, climate, and trade/migration (see the various contributions in Parts I and II in this volume).

That said, there is no sense of the structure and content of what might emerge from the increased challenge to liberal international norms. Despite uncertainty about the global or regional architecture that may emerge, the values and norms of democratic peace, economic interdependence, and liberal institutionalism frame European debates. The EU, built on the foundation of universal values and international cooperation, is often viewed as a normative power promoting democracy and human rights as outlined by its founding Treaties and promoting economic integration and market liberalization. Such a premise has been the cornerstone of the political and constitutional paradigm that has underpinned the European model, emphasizing the positive contributions of the architects of the post-war order. That order, whether measured in terms of international institutions, the propensity for multilateral action, or the community of like-minded states, has provided benefits to Europe. Yet this legal and political paradigm has underemphasized key aspects of the liberal experience, including policy choices and outcomes that have not worked. As Staniland notes, the focus on maintaining the liberal order "present[s] a narrow and highly selective reading of history that ignores much of the coercion, violence, and instability that accompanied post-war history" (Staniland 2018). This selective acceptance and promotion of the European experience as part of the liberal order, bracketing racial inequality, violations of human rights, ter-

---

[7] EU Regulation 2019/452 of 19 March 2019; *First Annual Report on Screening of FDI to EU*, https://trade.ec.europa.eu/doclib/docs/2021/november/tradoc_159935.pdf.

ritorial expansion, and diminution of democratic norms, has propelled Europe into a belief that it has upheld constitutionalism and rights, while simultaneously dismissing some of the more profound socio-economic challenges that its actions have posed to former colonies and other markets and polities. This reading is especially important, we argue, because the dominant European legal and political paradigm provides a focus on resilience, and to some degree maintenance, of a Western liberal order at a time when new institutions are emerging, and competing ideas, norms, and institutions are now in play in a changing global context.

## The Need for an Inclusive Liberal International Order

The EU focuses on maintaining its security and prosperity through the consolidation of the liberal order without acknowledging that the view has often been imposed on other states and societies. Though support for democracy, freedom, and human rights are central elements of the Union's foreign policy, the diffusion of such practices is also tied to conditionality. Grappling with successes as well as setbacks – even within the EU itself – is essential to think about whether the core of the liberal order remains transatlantic in orientation and whether it can truly expand its scope and reach to institutionalize specific goals and values in regions where instability, authoritarianism, warfare, and managed economies continue to shape politics and policies. While the liberal order is more contested than ever, simply appealing to the order does not address some of the fundamental challenges and contradictions facing Europe. In other words, at the crossroads of global order, the Union needs to address how it can rebuild resilience based on its liberal paradigm domestically. At the same time, the EU needs to reflect on, and potentially recalibrate, its external approach in the eyes of the other.

Europe's strategic landscape has changed fundamentally since the establishment of the post-war liberal order. In addition, the willingness to integrate allies, support the expansion of membership, and balance threats to peace has forced the EU to expand its territorial scope through successive enlargements and promote its collective security through a more institutionalized set of norms and practices that does not reflect a great power in the traditional sense of international relations. The Union is dealing with threats to the mainstay of the liberal order itself as the effort to promote effective multilateralism has also driven China, Russia, and the US to set aside those rules, whether in terms of respecting territory, markets, or governance. The EU needs to push for effective multilateralism with partners having seen a fall in US support for the multilateral trade system and European integration along with the security guarantee under the Trump Administration (Raube et al. 2021). The withdrawal from Afghanistan as well as the continued focus on China by the

Biden Administration also signal that the capacity and willingness to act independently requires Europe to gear up its external policies. What is important is for Europe to strategize how to work with democratic powers, including Atlantic partners such as the US, Canada, and the United Kingdom, on the political values that underpin the liberal order, especially those that focus on issues such as human rights, democracy, and rule of law (Youngs 2022). However, rather than lofty rhetoric, the Union should also engage in collective action, focusing on specific concrete initiatives with partners that want more global voice and, respectively, reflecting the rebalancing of international power that has occurred over the post-war period. This means that the liberal order would not be so closely tied with the West, but rather that it must adapt or evolve to changing global realities to ensure that some elements of the liberal order are sustained.

## Europe's Strategic Outlook

Europe will have to work within the underlying power configurations where its principles, norms, and rules have seen contradictions and challenges, and where patterns of cooperation and conflict may vary across issue areas. The effect of this differentiation may generate a range of bilateral, multilateral, and plurilateral initiatives and partnerships in areas such as climate change, pandemics, and conflict resolution (Maull 2019). This should fit within the parameters of European integration, which has allowed for a mixture of institutional arrangements that provide varying systems of governance in terms of scope and coverage. If the liberal order is a European strategic interest, the EU needs to marshal resources, actions, and the political will to defend it in ways that avoid strategic ambiguity. Greater conceptual clarity on how the Union wants to address criticism and challenges to the liberal order is not merely a theoretical exercise, but rather forces us to analyze the differences between moral principles and values, the legal framework and institutional effectiveness, and the collective expectations in terms of distributive burdens and payoffs in supporting the liberal order. We tend to focus on what the EU ought to do – often framed in terms of appropriateness – rather than the strategic interests and calculations as/since we use the language of normative power. Yet Europe faces challenges that can be disaggregated into a swathe of different legal, regulatory, social, and prescriptive actions that undermine the liberal order. Traditionally, the EU is very much focused on the legalization of rules to ensure that the values inherent in the liberal order are institutionalized. But even if a group of Western States has internalized such liberal norms, these may not be universally shared social expectations. The problem for Europe is that increasingly there are States – notably Russia, China, Turkey, and others – that operate within the institutional framework of liberal institutions but do not share the same expected behavior leading to problems of compliance and credible commitments.

This raises two fundamental problems for the EU: is the end goal to prevent free-riding where States can access the benefits but not adhere to specific standards and rules? Or is the goal to ensure credible commitments and in this case, address some of the asymmetries of influence and foster cooperation to international norms and agreements by changing the incentive structure? The Union needs to consider how to create conditions conducive to cooperation given debates about the politicization, contestation, and transformation as well as the potential end of the global liberal order. Indeed, international institutions have triggered domestic opposition and public distrust, and the pressures of globalization have fostered greater income inequality, and generated a surge of populism, that has challenged much of the existing left/right political cleavages (Lake et al. 2021).

The EU needs to adapt to the changing global context in which pressure for changes comes from either those who have been weakly institutionalized into the dominant frameworks of cooperation or those who have been excluded from the hierarchies of global governance. Power is shifting to non-Western States who bring their own cultural and economic values, practices, and histories. The Union needs to decide how to expand the benefits as privileged access and resources were initially conferred on the US and Europe, as architects of the liberal order. If those values are now under pressure, as most leading international relations scholars have noted, the EU must be prepared for either contestation and changes that will cause major shocks, so-called 'critical junctures', as realism suggests, or for the transformation of the liberal order that will be incremental, where the role of ideas and norms may lead to system change and institutional transformation (Sinha 2018). The Union will need to consider the shifts in global power distributions, changes in ideological commitments and values as well as beliefs about interests and power, and changes in the working of existing institutions or the creation of new institutions (Sinha 2018, p. 197). The chapters in this volume lead us to look at an increasingly complex system of international governance with multiple sets of rules and institutions, affecting different legal and policy areas, that are both embedded in the international liberal order as well as emerging as a countermovement to that liberal order.

To conclude, the EU needs a broad set of prescriptions and strategies about how to adapt to changes that have evolved in global governance. Policy change may come in two ways. It can be slow, incremental, and oftentimes conservative, which can often lead to efforts to maintain the status quo or engage in minor adjustments. This stability framework has carried significant weight in foreign policy debates but has garnered criticism for not being democratic or responsive enough to those marginalized in the decision-making process, failing to respond to global social and economic changes (Acharya 2014). Preferences were viewed as stable and ordered, around a set of values and principles that converged even if subject to frictions and frustrations at various points. In the current political climate of intense polarization and contestation, it is essential for the EU to embrace a more diverse international order for its continued duration and to reposition itself in that order to promote its foundational values of democracy, multilateralism, and liberalism. Alternatively, policy change can be disjointed, episodic and less predictable, so that challenges to the liberal order are less about mutual adjustment and incrementalism but instead about the lack of collective action and policy equilibrium. The EU faces authoritarian States operating within institutions of the liberal order, refusing to accept existing rules, and undermining the legitimacy and effectiveness of the post-war liberal international order. It must confront the persistence of durable inequalities within global governance to assure support from those that value liberal ideas to deter the attractiveness of alternatives to the existing institutional framework where new regional economic and security organizations openly reject the dissemination of political liberal norms and values.

## ORGANIZATION OF THE VOLUME

In line with the link between changes of global order on the one hand and European strategic responses on the other, this volume assembles the following chapters in three parts. In Part I, *Contestation and Polarization in Global Governance and Changing Global Orders*, authors focus on the key determinants that question the international liberal order as we have known it for the past decades. To this end, the various chapters take different starting perspectives and angles to illustrate the changes global orders undergo. Focusing on the making of global order and its current challenges, Kahler asks whether we are indeed witnessing an "end of the Bretton Woods Moment" given factors of state contestation (China) and popular discontent (populism) which wrench the pillars of the post-war world (Chapter 1). In the subsequent three chapters, Donnelly (Chapter 2), de Zamaróczy (Chapter 3) and Chwedczuk-Szulc (Chapter 4) further explore and explain the prospects of internationalism, regional integration, and cooperation in times of a shifting understanding of world order. In essence, the first four chapters allow us to better understand the ongoing dynamics that global governance has experienced over the last years, and how it has changed accordingly. In her chapter, Gutner (Chapter 5) further shows how emerging alternative international orders, exemplified by the Asian Infrastructure Investment Bank, have changed the way global governance is structured and operated. Next to the Chinese contestation of a Western-led order, it is, however, equally important to show the implications of populism for international cooperation and multilateralism. While Chryssogelos (Chapter 6) studies the effect of US and UK populism on international economic governance, Andrione-Moylan and Wouters specifically zoom in on how populist leadership has changed informal global governance institutions, such as in the context of the G7 and G20 (Chapter 7).

In Part II of this volume, *Changing Global Orders and European Responses*, the contributing authors focus on how especially the EU and other European actors have dealt with and adapted to the current changes in global orders. In the first two chapters of this part of the volume, Newsome and Riddervold (Chapter 8) and Guay and Smith (Chapter 9) discuss European responses to global change in the context of EU relations with the United States and China. Their attention to the US and China as explanatory variables that shape the Union's adaptation to global changes is echoed in subsequent chapters by Biedenkopf and Petri (Chapter 12) and Burnay and Circiumaru (Chapter 15), in which they respectively focus on the effects of US administrations on EU climate policy and China's rise in the context of the area of artificial intelligence. Similarly, Wouters and Costa Reis focus on a specific area of global security governance, the right to protect, and the ways in which European and Brazilian perspectives have mutually shaped each other (Chapter 14). Additional chapters by Góra, Helwig and SU (Chapters 10, 11 and 13) zoom in on domestic European developments and effects upon the EU's global role and other actors, including inner-European contestation (Chapter 10) and leadership (Chapter 11) as well as the Union's projection of normative power (Chapter 13).

In Part III, *Changing Global Trade Order and European Responses*, the chapters focus on one specific area of global governance: trade. Dias Simões analyzes the persistence of the liberal trade order in times of crisis and, more specifically, the EU's role within it (Chapter 16). Zooming in on trade and investment, Gilson explains the different positions of the EU and the US on investor-state dispute reform (Chapter 17). Taking a broader perspective, Eralp (Chapter 18) reminds us how important climate change is in understanding the EU's actorness in global governance, including many trade-related areas. The nexuses between trade and other areas of global governance are taken up in the chapters by Romanchyshyna (Chapter 19) and Zagel (Chapter 20) which demonstrate the role of the EU in establishing links between trade and sustainable development in trade and investment treaties. Finally, Ünüvar (Chapter 21) focuses on the changing nature of investment treaties and argues that the "exclusively investor-centric identity" of investment treaties, including those of the EU, is changing and reflects the interdependent nature of (trade and) investment with areas such as health, sustainable development, and labor rights.

## REFERENCES


Acharya, A. (2014) *The End of American World Order*. Cambridge: Polity Press.

Andrione-Moylan, A. and Wouters, J. (2022) Populists at the G20 and G7: Informal Cooperation in Turbulent Times. In Egan, M., Raube, K., Wouters, J. and Chaisse, J. (eds), *Contestation and Polarization in Global Governance: European Responses*. Cheltenham, UK and Northampton, MA, USA: Edward Elgar Publishing.

Biedenkopf, K., Costa, O. and Góra, M. (2021) Introduction: Shades of Contestation and Politicisation of CFSP. *European Security*, **30**(3), 325–343.

Börzel, T. and Zürn, M. (2021) Contestation of the Liberal International Order: From Liberal Multilateralism to Postnational Liberalism. *International Organization*, **75**, 282–305.

Burnay, M. and Circiumaru, A. (2022) The A.I. Global Order: What Place for the European Union? In Egan, M., Raube, K., Wouters, J. and Chaisse, J. (eds), *Contestation and Polarization in Global Governance: European Responses*. Cheltenham, UK and Northampton, MA, USA: Edward Elgar Publishing.

Chaisse, J. and Burnay, M. (2022) Introduction – CAI's Contribution to International Investment Law: European, Chinese, and Global Perspectives. *The Journal of World Investment and Trade*, **23**, 497–520.

Chryssogelos, A. (2022) Contesting International Economic Governance: The "People" and Trade in the Trump and Brexit Rhetoric. In Egan, M., Raube, K., Wouters, J. and Chaisse, J. (eds), *Contestation and Polarization in Global Governance: European Responses*. Cheltenham, UK and Northampton, MA, USA: Edward Elgar Publishing.

Chwedczuk-Szulc, K. (2022) The European Union and United States in the Era of Shifting Global Order. In Egan, M., Raube, K., Wouters, J. and Chaisse, J. (eds), *Contestation and Polarization in Global Governance: European Responses*. Cheltenham, UK and Northampton, MA, USA: Edward Elgar Publishing.

Cooley, A. and Nexon, D. (2022) Illiberalism on the Rise. *Foreign Affairs*, **101**(1), 103–118.

Cross, M. (2017) *The Politics of Crisis in Europe*. Cambridge: Cambridge University Press.

Donnelly, S. (2022) Recasting World Order: Power Politics, Contestation and International Institutions. In Egan, M., Raube, K., Wouters, J. and Chaisse, J. (eds), *Contestation and Polarization in Global Governance: European Responses*. Cheltenham, UK and Northampton, MA, USA: Edward Elgar Publishing.

Góra, M. (2022) What Role for the EU? Domestic Contestation of the EU's Global Role(s) in its Neighbourhood. In Egan, M., Raube, K., Wouters, J. and Chaisse, J. (eds), *Contestation and Polarization in Global Governance: European Responses*. Cheltenham, UK and Northampton, MA, USA: Edward Elgar Publishing.

Guay, T. and Smith, M. H. (2022) Divide and Conquer? Europe, China, and Policy Coherence. In Egan, M., Raube, K., Wouters, J. and Chaisse, J. (eds), *Contestation and Polarization in Global Governance: European Responses*. Cheltenham, UK and Northampton, MA, USA: Edward Elgar Publishing.

Gutner, T. (2022) Why Create Another Development Bank? China and the Asian Infrastructure Investment Bank (AIIB). In Egan, M., Raube, K., Wouters, J. and Chaisse, J. (eds), *Contestation and Polarization in Global Governance: European Responses*. Cheltenham, UK and Northampton, MA, USA: Edward Elgar Publishing.

Ikenberry, G. J. (2018) The End of Liberal International Order? *International Affairs*, **94**, 7–23.

Jones, E., Kelemen, D. and Meunier, S. (2021) Failing Forward? Crises and Patterns of European Integration. *Journal of European Public Policy*, **28**(10), 1519–1536.

Kahler, M. (2022) Global Governance in the Twenty-First Century: End of the Bretton Woods Moment? In Egan, M., Raube, K., Wouters, J. and Chaisse, J. (eds), *Contestation and Polarization in Global Governance: European Responses*. Cheltenham, UK and Northampton, MA, USA: Edward Elgar Publishing.

Keohane, R. O. (2002) *Power and Governance in a Partially Globalized World*. London: Routledge.

Lake, D. A., Martin, L. L. and Risse, T. (2021) Challenges to the Liberal Order: Reflections on International Organization. *International Organization*, **75**, 225–257.

Maull, W. (2019) The Once and Future Liberal Order. *Survival*, **61**, 7–32.

Newsome, A. and Riddervold, M. (2022) Contesting Transatlantic Relations: How Weaker Relations Influence EU Foreign Policies. In Egan, M., Raube, K., Wouters, J. and Chaisse, J. (eds), *Contestation and Polarization in Global Governance: European Responses*. Cheltenham, UK and Northampton, MA, USA: Edward Elgar Publishing.

Niblett, R. and Vinjamuri, L. (2021) The Liberal Order Begins at Home: How Democratic Revival Can Reboot the International System. *Foreign Affairs*, Snapshot March 2021. https://www.foreignaffairs.com/articles/2021-03-30/liberal-order-begins-home.

Petri, F., Thevenin, E. and Liedlbauer, L. (2020) Contestation of European Union Foreign Policy: Causes, Modes and Effects. *Global Affairs*, **6**, 323–328.

Raube, K., Andrione-Moylan, A. and Wouters, J. (2021) The Commitment to Multilateralism in Times of Contestation: Reshaping EU-Japan Relations? In Ogawa, E., Raube, K., Vanoverbeke, D. and Wouters, J. (eds), *Japan, the European Union and Global Governance*. Cheltenham, UK and Northampton, MA, USA: Edward Elgar Publishing, 20–43.

Riddervold, M. and Newsome, A. (2018) Transatlantic Relations in Times of Uncertainty: Crises and EU-US Relations. *Journal of European Integration*, **40**(5), 505–521.

Riddervold, M., Trondal, J. and Newsome, A. (eds) (2021) *The Palgrave Handbook of EU Crises*. Cham: Palgrave Macmillan.

Sinha, A. (2018) Building a Theory of Change in International Relations: Pathways of Disruptive and Incremental Change in World Politics. *International Studies Review*, **20**, 195–203.

Staniland, P. (2018) Misreading the "Liberal Order": Why We Need New Thinking in American Foreign Policy. *Lawfare*, 29 July. https://www.lawfareblog.com/misreading-liberal-order-why-we-need-new-thinking-american-foreign-policy.

SU, X. (2022) Normative Power Europe in the Belt and Road Initiative: Challenge for Constructing the Self or an Opportunity for Changing Others? In Egan, M., Raube, K., Wouters, J. and Chaisse, J. (eds), *Contestation and Polarization in Global Governance: European Responses*. Cheltenham, UK and Northampton, MA, USA: Edward Elgar Publishing.

Youngs, R. (2022) Re-examining Norms-Diffusion: The EU, Democracy and Rival Powers. *Democratization*, **29**(3), 545–552.

# PART I

# Contestation and polarization in global governance and changing global orders

# 1. Global governance in the twenty-first century: end of the Bretton Woods moment?[1]

**Miles Kahler**

The labels 'crisis' and 'turning point' are used freely to describe international politics. In the decade since the global financial crisis of 2008–2009, and even more frequently in the past four years, arguments that the world is *not* at a turning point have become difficult to find. The debates have often been confusing, however, suggesting both fundamental and sudden ruptures as well as recent recognition of long-term structural changes. Reflecting on a century that began with the Treaty of Versailles and the League of Nations and is closing with a pandemic and the worst economic downturn since the Great Depression, the effects of conflict, peacemaking, and economic turmoil on global order can certainly be identified. Long-term trends and trajectories, inflected by those episodes, have been equally influential: the dissolution of empires – from colonial to Soviet – and the proliferation of sovereign states; the integration of Europe and the rise of military and economic powers outside Europe; and a rapid growth in the institutions of regional and global governance.

Arguments for a break in those trajectories in global governance can be summarized as the end of the Bretton Woods moment, that crucial reordering at the midpoint of the last century. Three distinct candidates can claim identification as this latest turning point: the end of the *liberal* international order; the end of the *dominant position of the United States and its allies* in the global order; and, finally, the relative decline of *formal global institutions* as constituents of contemporary global governance. Those three alleged transformations in the contemporary international order are linked, but they should be evaluated independently. Each has important implications for the future of global governance and the international role of the European Union.

## END OF THE BRETTON WOODS MOMENT: LIBERAL NORMS IN DECLINE?

The most contentious of the three is the claim that the liberal international order (LIO) is on the verge of disintegration, if it has not already collapsed. Assessing that claim requires an agreed definition of the liberal order. For realists, the liberal order, like preceding international orders, is an expression of the interests of dominant powers, specifically the United States (Allison 2018; Mearsheimer 2019). For those who evaluate the LIO positively, a principal concern is not exploitation of the LIO by the United States but disengagement by the United States from an order that relies on the indispensable nation (Kagan 2018). Since the rise of anti-globalization movements in the 1990s, the liberal order has been pilloried from the left as an enabler of economic injustice. It has often been equated with neoliberalism and the Washington Consensus: a harsh, market-based order that magnifies the gap in power and prosperity between rich and poor (Moyn 2018). That critique has been extended to the effects of the LIO on workers in the rich countries. Although elites may have benefited from globalization, those with less political power have seen their positions decline in an increasingly rigged system (Colgan and Keohane 2017). Despite its dilapidated condition, the LIO seems for some to be the source of nearly all ills – global and domestic – in the contemporary world.

### Defining a Liberal International Order

However, before evaluating both the normative content of the existing LIO and its future prospects it must be defined more precisely. In contrast to many of its critics, whatever their political perspective, a LIO must be separated from US foreign policy. As a first approximation, it can be defined using the familiar Kantian triad and a number of corollaries: economic openness and interdependence; international collaboration through law and institutions; and liberal democratic polities characterized by respect for individual rights and the rule of law. Individual rights were recognized as part of the global order in such foundational documents of the LIO as the United Nations Charter and the Universal Declaration of Human Rights. The Kantian triad points to an additional corollary – a bias toward peace and a belief that war is not an inevitable feature of international politics. This belief in the possibilities of progress – a meliorist vision that has contended with the darker foundations of

*Realpolitik* – is inseparable from the idea of a liberal order as one that encourages and adapts to peaceful change.

No international order will perfectly realize any set of normative guides or aspirations, but the liberal characteristics of the existing international order can be evaluated against alternative orders. One alternative, which disappeared rapidly after 1945, was an order populated by colonial empires: mercantilist in economic ideology and practice, hierarchical in political structure, and based explicitly on racial discrimination and denial of political rights. A different imperial structure was created by the Soviet Union as it consolidated control in Eastern Europe after the Second World War. A transnational and hierarchical collective of communist parties provided a political infrastructure; state-directed economic transactions took place under the auspices of the Council for Mutual Economic Assistance (Comecon); human rights were recognized on paper and systematically violated in practice. Throughout the Cold War these orders coexisted, at times uncomfortably, with a LIO.

Critics of the LIO point out its own persistent violations of liberal norms: compromises with imperialism and support of colonial wars, protectionism and restrictions on immigration (often using racialized criteria), violations of international law, and domination of nominally multilateral institutions by a few great powers. Failure to realize liberal norms in practice, however, should be distinguished from inherent tensions within the liberal family of norms, many of which are centuries old. Contestation over reliance on markets rather than state regulation arose as an organizing principle of international economic exchange in the nineteenth century, with the rise of working class and reformist movements. The degree and method of such regulation has remained a core issue of debate among supporters of the LIO.

Another tension with liberalism is built into the international system. Multilateralism and the sovereign equality of states, a principle of LIO institutions, confronts the inequality of countries measured by their military, economic, and cultural power. Institutions have met this tension through bicameral structures (the United Nations Security Council and its P-5, versus the General Assembly), weighted voting, and decision-making by consensus. In a world organized into states with wide variation in population size, the broader issue of democratic deficit represents an even deeper tension in global governance. Finally, rights recognized in the LIO clash. Particularly, the right of self-determination of peoples, which implies non-intervention in domestic affairs, clashes with the rights of individuals and minority populations. The liberal norm of self-determination has infused non-intervention with additional force, beyond claims of state sovereignty. It has done so particularly when intervention collides with an additional liberal aim, the preservation of peace. These tensions are not emblems of hypocrisy or failure in the LIO; they are inherent in its normative foundations.

## Threats to the Liberal International Order: Economic Closure, Rising Illiberalism, Retreat of Liberal Democracies

Three systemic outcomes have been identified as especially consequential for the future of the LIO: the fate of economic liberalization and integration, the rise of a coalition of illiberal political forces, and the retreat of liberal democracy. The evidence for 'slowbalization' – an apparent plateau in international economic integration and measures to promote liberalization – has grown since the global financial crisis of 2008–2009 (The Economist 2019). Once again, however, the evidence is mixed and hardly presents a clear picture of globalization in retreat. In particular, financial globalization has not returned to the peak reached before the global financial crisis. However, the pre-crisis level of inflated cross-border financial flows was driven by an unsustainable financial bubble that preceded the crisis (McKinsey Global Institute 2017).

The pattern of globalization in trade is more complex and has received the most attention. Several explanations have been presented to account for the slowing growth of world trade over the past decade, including a Chinese economy that increasingly sourced inputs domestically, reduction in the importance of global supply chains, and a growing share of services in trade (McKinsey Global Institute 2019). Others have pointed to growing protectionism. The United States under the Trump Administration has wielded tariffs against major trading partners in specific sectors (steel and aluminum) and as part of a larger trade conflict with China. The United States has paralyzed the Appellate Body at the World Trade Organization (WTO), withdrawn from a mega-regional trade agreement, the Trans-Pacific Partnership (TPP), and failed to advance negotiations for the Transatlantic Trade and Investment Partnership (TTIP).

Although these US actions and the US–China trade conflict were perceived as a blow to international trade, conflict between the two largest national economies often displaced trade to other Asian economies, such as Vietnam, rather than reducing trade volume. During the trade conflict with the US, China strategically *lowered* trade barriers to economies producing substitutive goods for those that might have been imported from the United States (Bown 2019). The United Kingdom's exit from the European Union and its Single Market signaled another ambiguous reaction to globalization, since many of its proponents endorsed a 'global Britain' open to world trade.

Despite this evidence of an erosion of liberal norms and practices in the global economy, other developments indicate continued momentum for liberalization. The United States, Canada, and Mexico successfully negotiated a modernized trade agreement that maintained relatively open – if managed – trade and deepened labor rights and environmental requirements. Other major economies proceeded with trade negotiations and agreements, including the Regional Comprehensive Economic Partnership (RCEP), which linked the largest economies in Asia, and the African Continental Free Trade Area (AfCFTA), which had the largest number of members among regional trade agreements. After the withdrawal of the US from TPP, the remaining signatories negotiated a modified successor agreement, the Comprehensive and Progressive Agreement for Trans-Pacific Partnership (CPTPP). Many of the new trade agreements include rules to govern rapidly growing cross-border digital flows (Burri and Polanco 2020). Trade agreements were also modified to accommodate a growing number of stakeholders, who aimed to curb investor-state dispute resolution and incorporate tougher labor and environmental provisions (Young 2016). The EU was the most active major trading power in these liberalization efforts, completing trade and economic partnership agreements with Singapore, Canada, Japan, and Vietnam and engaging in trade negotiations with the Common Market of the South (Mercosur) in Latin America.

The most marked questioning of the liberal economic order occurred in the movement of people across borders, a domain that the LIO had left largely to national governments. Cross-border travel was essential to the management of increasingly intricate global supply chains (Baldwin 2016). Tourism had emerged as a major economic sector in economies from the Caribbean to Europe. International students populated universities, providing a major service export for industrialized economies, particularly in the English-speaking world. These sectors dependent on people crossing borders were less affected than the movement of economic migrants and refugees by the growth in anti-immigration movements and policies in Europe and the United States. Those political movements and their influence on national policies pose a second threat to the liberal content of the existing international order.

## Growing Illiberalism in the Liberal Core?

Since the global financial crisis more than a decade ago, the economic dimensions of the LIO have shown signs of stress. Compared to more autarchic economic orders in the past, however, movements of goods, services, capital, and people across borders in the contemporary global order remain relatively open. Elite attachment and the preferences of many voters remain positive toward the liberal precepts of recent decades. Perhaps the most threatening development for the LIO – and a new source of pressure to close borders to trade and migration – is the growing influence throughout the industrialized world of political movements that attack established elites, promote national sovereignty and ethnonationalist identity, undermine liberal political norms, and criticize the institutions and rules of global and regional governance.

Whether the political influence of these movements derives from conjunctural shocks or from structural changes in the economy and society will determine their significance in the longer term. A series of shocks over the past two decades have undermined confidence in the political elites of industrialized democracies: military interventions in Afghanistan and Iraq by the US and its allies, the global (or Atlantic) financial crisis and subsequent Eurozone crisis, the trade shock that followed China's accession to the WTO, and migration shocks, such as the 2004 UK decision to accept free movement of labor from new members of the EU and the 2015 surge of Middle Eastern refugees to Europe.

These shocks can be linked to the rise of anti-establishment political movements that are highly critical of elements of the LIO. If, however, these movements are also a response to structural changes linked to globalization – an anti-globalization backlash – their political influence will persist. Electoral support for these movements and their opponents, a contest between parochials and cosmopolitans, highlights a new political divide in the industrialized world based on demographic as well as locational characteristics (Kahler 2020a). Voters and activists in these movements, whether supporters of Leave in the UK's Brexit campaign, the Trump Republican base in the United States, or European right-wing populists, such as the *Rassemblement National* in France and the *Alternative für Deutschland* (AfD) in Germany, tilt toward the older and less educated segments of the population. Cosmopolitans are more likely to be younger and better educated.

However, equally striking is a locational divide between those living in vibrant urban agglomerations that have prospered from their links to the international economy and the hinterlands of these global cities, which may be geographically proximate but economically left behind. Globalization – including the economic shocks of the past two decades – has had disparate effects on different locations. In those locales that have not benefited from globalization, attitudes support a narrative of national decline and cultural displacement. Political movements and information environments, such as social media, can reinforce and amplify these effects, transforming parochial attachments and anxieties into declining national support for constituents of the LIO.

Although movements that incorporate parochials are often portrayed as embracing wholesale attacks on the LIO and liberal norms, trade has not been a central mobilizing issue.[2] Instead, the major vulnerability for the LIO in the industrialized countries has been immigration. Given the demographic

---

2 The uneven impact of the China trade shock has been associated with electoral support for parties critical of the LIO. On the political effects in the US, Autor et al. (2016). For the UK, Colantone and Stanig (2018).

futures of these countries and their need to choose between demographic (and economic) decline and higher levels of immigration, the issue is likely to sustain anti-establishment politics in the absence of national consensus on immigration policy. Sustaining an international economy and global order that reflects liberal norms may require a resolution of the persistent conflict over immigration, an issue that has both domestic and international dimensions.

## Democratic Backsliding and the Liberal International Order

Liberal norms in global economic governance have received most attention from those who contend that the LIO has eroded. The fate of liberal democracy, another pillar of the LIO, has also been a source of alarm. The causal link between economic globalization and democratization appears to run in one direction only: liberal democracies support economic liberalization and openness, but economic openness does not appear to produce democratic governance (Milner and Mukherjee 2009). Populist parties and governments in the industrialized world have chipped away at liberal democratic norms – through attacks on the media, efforts to subordinate the courts and law enforcement to political ends, and pervasive corruption. Nevertheless, erosion of democratic institutions and norms has not yet meant a return to authoritarian rule in any established democracy. As in the case of economic globalization, the post-Cold War wave of democratization has crested, but the global proportion of democratic regimes remains stable (Treisman 2022). Important democratizing breakthroughs have continued to occur in recent years, many driven by opposition to official corruption. Even in the Middle East, a region of authoritarian triumph after suppression of the Arab Spring, protesters in Sudan and Algeria have forced concessions on authoritarian governments; and demands to end corruption have erupted in Lebanon.

However, in parallel to the global economy, an overall portrait of stability conceals both a more serious chipping away at democratic rule in transitional democracies and a deepening of authoritarian rule in autocratic regimes. Just as authoritarian rule has been challenged at the edges of the Middle East, illiberal democracy – a phrase used by Hungarian Prime Minister Viktor Orbán – has emerged in Europe and Latin America. Until recent steps taken by the European Commission to sanction Hungary and Poland, clubs of liberal democracies in Europe and Latin America have failed to discipline members who violate the liberal democratic norms of their regional organizations. At the same time, authoritarian regimes – China, Russia, and many Middle Eastern countries – have tightened control over their populations and increased repressive actions. China's recent moves to restrict further the political freedoms of Hong Kong have been met by a fragmented and ineffective response by liberal democracies. Technological advances, such as widespread use of smart phones and new surveillance capabilities, have supported this deepening of authoritarian rule. This trend could signal either confidence in authoritarian immunity to global pressure or rising insecurity as educated populations, open to international influences, bridle at curbs on civil society and political participation.

Using these three crucial benchmarks for a liberal order – economic openness, support for liberal foreign policies in the industrialized core, and the advance of liberal democratic regimes – the liberal advances of the past three decades appear to have halted, if only temporarily, but they have not yet receded. One of the greatest sources of the LIO's resilience is an absence of clear normative alternatives that could mobilize equivalent support. The domestic and international moves toward closure and dictatorship in the 1930s are not yet on the horizon. The only major alternatives today are represented by populist and parochial movements in the liberal core – a chaotic turn toward a nationalist scramble for advantage – or an order more to the liking of China, state-centered rather than market-oriented, a world safe for autocracy, in which claims of sovereignty give free rein to rulers (Weiss 2019). The success of either of those normative alternatives will depend in part on the future configuration of national preferences and power, a second route to the end of the Bretton Woods moment.

## END OF THE BRETTON WOODS MOMENT: RETREAT OF THE UNITED STATES AND ITS ALLIES, RISE OF CHINA AND THE BRICS?

For those who view the liberal order as created and maintained by the United States, the end of the Bretton Woods moment means the twilight of American leadership. This recession originates in US withdrawal from and disruption of that institutional order, illiberal challengers assuming a significant role in setting global rules and influencing international institutions, or both. Furthermore, this explanation for the end of the Bretton Woods moment is state-centric and top-down, focusing on the role of great powers, particularly the United States.

The record of the Trump Administration and the growing assertiveness of China under Xi Jinping lend credence to this narrative. In the name of national sovereignty, President Trump and his administration systematically disparaged and weakened international agreements and institutions by withdrawing from the Joint Comprehensive Plan of Action (JCPOA) that restricted Iran's nuclear program, the Paris Agreement on climate change, the United Nations Economic, Scientific and Cultural Organization (UNESCO), and the United Nations Human Rights Council. The United States also refused to participate in the UN Conference on a Global Compact for Migration, rejecting even a preliminary multilateral discussion of this sensitive issue. Rather than pursuing multilateral solutions to trade disputes and trade liberalization, the Trump Administration wielded unilateral protectionist instruments, particularly tariffs, in bilateral trade negotiations. Instead of aligning with liberal democratic allies, Trump made his personal preference for authoritarian rulers clear and has led an administration that has consistently devalued human rights in its foreign policy program. As Thomas Wright (2016) has observed, Trump's policy preferences were pre-Bretton Woods, situated in an America First nationalist ideology that was last influential in the 1930s. In the Trump Administration longstanding suspicion of global governance institutions among American conservatives was combined with a new/old skepticism toward market-based outcomes in international economic relations.

China's President Xi Jinping presents a mirror image of the US leadership: transactional, supporting the existing order only when it can be conceived as promoting his reading of China's narrow national interest. For example, China has rejected judgments based on the UN Convention on the Law of Sea against its claims in the South China Sea. Although rhetorically embracing global institutions, China under Xi has also established competing institutions and programs in development finance. China remains an active participant in the global economy, but, since accession to the WTO, commitments to liberalize its economy have been few. Whether China's pragmatic and selective support for the existing international order continues or whether it will mount a more fundamental challenge to that order remains uncertain.

Set against this recent record of great power disengagement from the Bretton Woods order are three counter arguments. First, the LIO originated with and is supported by a broad coalition of states, not solely the US and its network of allies. Second, American criticism of the existing order is not unprecedented, given its ideological attachments and history of acting unilaterally. Finally, China – or China and its partners in the BRICS group – are not likely to achieve a dominant role in shaping the future international order.

## The Bretton Woods Moment: Origins and Supporters

The institutional order that has persisted since 1945 is often portrayed as a creation of the United States and its allies, particularly the United Kingdom. However, the history of those international norms and institutions confirms the existence of a broader and more diverse coalition of support. Decades before Bretton Woods, Latin American states provided early support for multilateral norms, such as universal participation and voting rules based on sovereign equality (one nation, one vote) (Finnemore and Jurkovich 2014). Before Bretton Woods, Latin America had reshaped the liberal prescription of free trade and, together with Chinese figures such as Sun Yat-sen, contributed to the norm of international development that would legitimate the formation of the World Bank and other multilateral development institutions (Helleiner and Rosales 2017; Helleiner 2014, 2018). Latin American governments were also proponents of the inclusion of human rights in the United Nations Charter and had agreed to the American Declaration of the Rights and Duties of Man in advance of the Universal Declaration of Human Rights (Sikkink 2014). Despite their criticism of the post-1945 order – and those criticisms, particularly of its economic dimensions, have been sustained and substantial – developing countries and smaller industrialized economies have been among the most stalwart supporters of multilateral institutions and their equalizing and constraining effects on the largest military and economic powers.

## The United States: Uncertain Anchor for the Post-1945 Order

Although the Bretton Woods order is often portrayed as a thin disguise for the power of the United States, the United States has, over time, provided an increasingly uncertain anchor for those institutions. The Bretton Woods moment resulted from a specific alignment of progressive coalitions in the United States, the United Kingdom, and other coalition members that had won the Second World War (Kahler 2002). In the United States, the liberal internationalist vision born during the war was soon challenged by the onset of the Cold War and the Soviet bloc's exit from key global economic institutions. The Cold War also produced compromises in the liberal vision of regulated capitalism, democratization, expanded human rights, and self-determination for colonial peoples. Rather than leading a new global mainstream, the US interpretation of the postwar order and its norms was often a distinctive and controversial one. The United States, driven by anti-communism, deployed liberal universalism to transform developing countries, often through US proxies or direct military intervention. The regulated capitalism of Bretton Woods was eventually replaced by a market-oriented version that awarded a far smaller role to government. US foreign policy was also shaped by the influence of organized religion, giving American foreign policy a moralistic flavor that was largely absent among its allies.

After the Cold War, the LIO deepened and spread, but its hold on American politics, paradoxically, became more tenuous. From the right, a conservative vision – suspicious of international organizations, embracing the stability of deregulated international markets, and promoting unilateral action – grew in influence. International business provided important support for the post-1945 economic order, but it pressed an agenda, including investor-state dispute settlement and protection of intellectual property, that mobilized opposition from civil society organizations. The broad domestic coalition that had supported Bretton Woods narrowed over time: labor had defected from trade and investment liberalization by the 1970s and joined forces in the 1990s with nongovernmental organizations (NGOs) to demand the inclusion of stiff labor rights and environmental provisions in trade agreements. Liberalized trade and the global economic multilaterals became targets of a broader anti-globalization movement, which had avatars on both the left and, by the time of Trump, the right of the political spectrum.

The advent of the Trump Administration seemed a final confirmation of the oscillation in American policy toward central elements of the Bretton Woods order. The swings of the pendulum had become more extreme. The post-Trump United States that seeks to re-engage will need to re-establish its credibility. Any further swing of the pendulum, with Trump or Trumpism resurgent, and the existing order would depend even more heavily on other industrialized and developing economies, the EU prominent among them. Also critical to an extension of the Bretton Woods moment would be the support or opposition offered by rising powers, such as China.

## The Bretton Woods Moment and the Changing Configuration of Power: China and the BRICS

In a state-centric view of the contemporary international order, the stance of rising powers toward the Bretton Woods order could signal either consolidation of a reformed global order or a challenge that brings the Bretton Woods moment to a close. The BRICS group (Brazil, Russia, India, China, South Africa) represents the most prominent emerging powers. Although none have been close allies of the United States, their programs of economic reform over the past three decades have internationalized their economies and led them to more active involvement in global and regional governance. Economic nationalism rather than liberalism is a hallmark of their domestic politics and ideology. Each faces a long and challenging domestic agenda, which limits the resources that can be devoted to their international ambitions. What sets the members of the BRICS group apart from one another are income levels, population, membership in the UN Security Council, and, most important, regime type. As the recent border conflict between India and China illustrates, members of the group are also divided by territorial disputes and economic conflicts.

In the decade since its formation, the BRICS group has held regular summits and cooperated successfully in increasing its influence in the Bretton Woods organizations. They have created parallel financial institutions (New Development Bank and Contingent Reserve Facility) and shifted the international consensus on such issues as capital controls, an agenda that is best described as "moderately revisionist" (Roberts et al. 2018, p. 181). In the WTO's Doha Round of trade negotiations, BRICS economies were able to prevent a final agreement on terms backed by the United States (Stephen

2019). In the Paris Agreement on climate change, emerging economies accepted a qualification ("in light of national circumstances") to the principle of differentiation that had previously prevented agreement. In global governance, the BRICS have adopted the position of conservative globalizers: benefiting from an open international economy, supporting reformed versions of core institutions, but reluctant to undertake additional commitments that would restrict their ability to set national policy.

Rather than a co-equal group of emerging powers, the BRICS group might better be seen as a product of the China boom, a commodity super cycle that linked three major commodity producers – Russia, Brazil, and South Africa – to the Chinese market for their exports. The BRICS group was a site for managing this relationship of economic dependence. Within the BRICS group, Russia and China evinced greater discontent with a global order centered on the United States and Europe; both aimed for a more multipolar distribution of power. Their apparent convergence of interests has led some observers to proclaim a new Beijing–Moscow axis, based on their proclaimed "comprehensive strategic partnership of coordination in the new era" (Shambaugh 2019). The term 'axis' understates barriers to collaboration among authoritarian regimes, since their regimes lack transparency and rely on personal or party ties for credible commitments. Stable authoritarian cooperation often relies on a dominant government or party and more junior partners. In the China–Russia relationship, there is little question which government is junior, a likely source of future instability.

Collective action by China and other emerging powers is of less significance for global governance than China's capabilities and preferences, especially in climate, finance, and trade. Rather than wholesale disruption of the existing order, China's degree of revisionism varies from issue area to issue area (Kastner et al. 2019). China continues to support the Paris Agreement on climate change. Among the UN Security Council's P-5, it contributes the most personnel to UN peacekeeping operations. It has actively sought and obtained leadership in international agencies, among them four of the fifteen UN specialized agencies. At the same time, China has created or supported parallel institutions, such as the Asian Infrastructure Investment Bank (AIIB), which provide it with bargaining leverage in global institutions.

On other issues, particularly those related to its territorial claims and domestic stability, China has become increasingly assertive externally and repressive internally. A core Chinese aim is defensive: warding off a threat to and criticism of its regime. The success of its strategy toward flawed or backsliding democracies has been demonstrated in Cambodia (with the benefit of undermining ASEAN unity on the South China Sea) as well as in Hungary and

Greece.[3] Toward established democracies, defensive strategies have turned offensive, exerting "sharp power" by cultivating allies through economic carrots, both legal and illicit, and punishing critics with sticks that include economic sanctions as well as intimidation of its large diasporic community. As a recent survey summarized, Russia is more intent on "undermining the health and credibility of democratic regimes", while China "aims to portray the country as either a benign foreign influence or a successful example of economic development with democratic political institutions" (Cardenal et al. 2017). The appeal of China's model is economic rather than ideological – aid and investment with no questions asked regarding corruption or good governance.

Counter arguments to claims that US disengagement and Chinese assertiveness signal an end to the Bretton Woods moment rest on estimates of the future aims of the United States, China, and the rest of the world. Political polarization in American politics is not likely to disappear, and swings in US foreign policy between engagement and disengagement could widen over time. Post-Trump US administrations that re-engage with global governance institutions and work to reform the Bretton Woods order must contend with perceptions that a future administration may once again withdraw or disrupt. China's selective collaboration, dependent in part on the response of the United States, may also become more unreliable as declining growth and unrest on its periphery lead to more nationalist assertion.

If one or both of these great powers fails to sustain the Bretton Woods order, could the rest of the world renovate global intergovernmental cooperation on a different model? The recent WTO Multiparty Interim Appeal Arbitration Arrangement, designed to circumvent US paralysis of the Appellate Body, is one example; the renegotiated CPTPP is another. Such a patchwork of institutional fixes may not be an adequate substitute for engagement and leadership on the part of the United States and China. A purely state-centric view of the Bretton Woods moment, however, omits the possibility of another end to that moment, one that creates a model of international cooperation less reliant on national governments, large or small, a format of global governance that awards a larger role to a diverse array of actors. That format has already taken shape in climate change, global health, peacebuilding, and other issue areas.

---

[3] Greece vetoed European Union criticism of China's human rights record at the United Nations Human Rights Council in June 2017. Greece did not admit that Chinese investment had motivated its stance. Hungary had objected to the EU's statement on Egypt, but finally withdrew its objection (*New York Times*, 19 June 2017).

## END OF THE BRETTON WOODS MOMENT: INTERNATIONAL COLLABORATION TRANSFORMED

The end of the Bretton Woods moment is usually defined as a decline in intergovernmental collaboration and a weakening of global institutions. A third meaning of the end of the Bretton Woods moment focuses on the changing format of global governance, rather than its normative content or its support by an evolving group of powerful states. From the vantage point of the twenty-first century, dominance of global governance by intergovernmental, multilateral organizations may be one moment, originating in an expansion of the regulatory state during the Great Depression and the Second World War and a sharp decline in global economic integration during those same decades. Both before and after that Bretton Woods moment, global governance awarded a larger role to more informal, often networked modes of governance that incorporated government agencies, private corporations and financial institutions, and NGOs. Global governance was supplied, but it was supplied differently.

After 1945, as the number of nation-states grew from 51 at the founding of the United Nations, to nearly 200 today, multilateral negotiations grew more difficult. Governments first turned to club-like arrangements with more limited numbers, lowering the transaction costs of negotiation and agreement. These informal intergovernmental organizations (IIGOs) appeared among the industrialized countries as membership in global economic multilaterals expanded: the G10 (founded 1962); the G5, which became the G7 (1975); and, within the GATT, the Quad. IIGOs expanded more rapidly in the 1980s and 1990s, favored for their flexibility, low cost, and lack of binding obligations (Roger 2020). As economic interdependence grew among the industrialized countries and regulatory clashes became more frequent, transgovernmental networks (TGNs) became a favored means for national bureaucracies to negotiate and coordinate in shared domains. The Basel Committee on Banking Supervision was an early example. Other networks met the need for informal security collaboration (Avant and Westerwinter 2016).

During the 1990s and 2000s nongovernmental actors played a larger role in setting agendas and promoting collective solutions in climate change, global health, peacebuilding, WTO-plus trade agreements, and combating illicit financial flows (Kahler 2020b). These institutional complexes shared a common trajectory that distinguished them from legacy IGOs of the Bretton Woods moment. A formal organization with a charter and mandate might serve as the nucleus for the new complex governance, but nonstate actors – NGOs and international corporations – led in widening the issue area's agenda. Underlying agenda-setting and creating new demand for global governance are coalitions of actors, engaged in political conflict and contestation. Counter-coalitions also form, framing the issue differently, for example questioning expert opinion (climate change) or opposing supranational rules and organizations.

National governments and IGOs continue to play important roles in these new forms of complex governance, through orchestration, information provision, legitimation, and, most important, enforcement. Resource flows within these complexes have produced more influence for new actors with substantial endowments and a blurring of lines between different types of actors linked by those resources: NGOs and IGOs may be dependent on private foundations; multi-stakeholder arrangements are funded by corporations. The Bretton Woods model of intergovernmental cooperation was aimed largely at changing the policy trajectories of national governments; other actors were influenced through the international commitments made and enforced by those governments. In contrast, these new governance complexes target a wider array of actors, rather than relying solely on the capacity and willingness of national governments for enforcement. Ideally, these new governance formats will provide "different regimes purpose-built for specific challenges" (Fidler 2010, p. 9). The new model of complex governance exploits different pathways of influence, rather than relying solely on the route of hard treaty law that binds national governments (Bernstein and Cashore 2012).

Complex global governance has produced a twenty-first-century model that diverges from the formal intergovernmental template of the Bretton Woods moment. Whether these institutional complexes provide a more effective and legitimate form of governance is contested. Its proponents argue that complex governance provides for global collective action through a more inclusive and therefore more legitimate institutional coalitions. Complex governance also circumvents the gridlock that results when national governments cannot agree in more formal institutional settings. Critics remark that a beneficial division of labor among national governments, IGOs, and nonstate actors may not emerge in every case. Instead of useful collaboration among a widening array of actors, they find a "governance patchwork" that is "fragmented, inefficient, and incapable of producing a convergence of interests, strategies, and resources, which often makes it difficult for developing countries to participate effectively" (Fidler 2010, pp. 12–13). Beneath a veneer of democratization in agenda-setting and participation, complexity can obscure an absence of accountability and a deficit in achievements, leading to a further erosion of legitimacy.

## COVID-19, PANDEMIC POLITICS, AND THE FUTURE OF GLOBAL GOVERNANCE

The ongoing coronavirus pandemic has only deepened concern over the fraying of liberal norms, the deepening conflict among major powers, and the adequacy of new modes of global governance. Pessimistic appraisals of the LIO during the pandemic have pointed to a scramble for essential medical supplies, often accompanied by export controls; haphazard closure of borders; and limited oversight of national governments by the World Health Organization (WHO). Relations between the world's two largest economies, China and the United States, can be characterized as blame-shifting rather than cooperation.

Moreover, the global pandemic represented the most recent and perhaps the largest of shocks to the global economy. The response of global governance to the economic consequences of the pandemic demonstrated more collaboration and leadership by global institutions than earlier reactions to the global health emergency. The International Monetary Fund (IMF) and the World Bank expanded their lending operations in light of the emergency, and the central bank network, centered on the US Federal Reserve, was activated to counter the sharp and unexpected economic slowdown. The pandemic, which sharply reduced or shut down large swathes of international travel, also brought home the dire economic consequences of rapid deglobalization. Despite the shifting attitudes of governments, transnational civil society has remained robust, as demonstrated by the remarkable spread across national borders of US protests against racism and police violence.

The economic effects of the pandemic may be severe and long-lasting, especially for developing economies. The IMF has labeled the economic downturn "a crisis like no other", warning that the progress made in reducing extreme poverty globally is in peril (International Monetary Fund 2020). Although it is too early to predict the ultimate effects of the coronavirus pandemic on global governance, it must be regarded as a shock that was only in part produced by nature. The consequences of the pandemic – whether measured in loss of life, economic damage, or changes in global governance – depend on human behavior, individual and collective.

Restrictions on travel imposed abruptly during the pandemic, national barriers erected to secure medical supplies, and the questioning of economic globalization and the interdependence that it has created – all appear to predict a bleak future for the liberal economic order. A sharp economic downturn followed by a weak recovery would likely produce calls for further restrictions on trade and immigration, such as those imposed by the Trump Administration. Countering these dynamics, however, is the political importance of economic sectors that are highly dependent on an opening of borders, such as transport and tourism. Strategies aimed at future resilience need not include the disruption of global supply chains or increased protectionism.

More significant for the longer run future of the LIO is the relative balance between illiberal or parochial political forces and more cosmopolitan movements within the advanced industrial democracies. If the record of responding to the pandemic figures in the political future of these movements, more cosmopolitan leaders and parties would appear to be in a stronger position. The divide in country performance during the pandemic is not a clear one between democracies and autocracies. Nevertheless, loss of life has been low in liberal democracies with high social capital, in which populations trust their governments and governments have deferred to public health expertise, among them, South Korea, Taiwan, New Zealand, Norway, and Germany. Even in these successful liberal democracies the imposition of additional restrictions on individual mobility and surveillance of personal behavior during the pandemic – and as part of future public health measures – poses a threat to liberal practice.

On the other hand, "strong man" regimes, whether democracies led by populists or autocracies veering toward personalist dictatorship, have not fared well: Brazil (perhaps worst of all), the United States, Russia, India, the United Kingdom, and China (at least in the early stages of the pandemic). At the onset of the pandemic, all of these governments were headed by leaders who appeared unwilling to defer to experts and reluctant to admit that the virus could defeat their political programs (or re-election). Early warning in such systems is less likely to reach the top of the political hierarchy. The parochial leaders and movements most critical of global governance could enjoy a resurgence as a result of economic hardship and deepening equality that has yet to appear. Nevertheless, if the Bretton Woods moment is defined as a LIO, it is not likely to end because of a resurgence of illiberal ideology and political movements in the wake of the pandemic.

Sustaining the Bretton Woods moment post-pandemic may also rest on the power and engagement of the United States and its democratic allies. The pandemic initially saw further evidence of United States withdrawal from multilateral forums and disengagement from international institutions that demonstrated their value during the global financial crisis of 2008–2009. The WHO was drawn into the China–US conflict, with the United States accusing the organization of being too closely tied to China. The WTO, already weakened by trade conflicts among China, the United States, and the EU, has been unable to restrain the protectionist actions of many of its members. The G20, which had played an important role in the global financial crisis, bringing together the largest industrialized and emerging economies to design a common strategy for recovery, hardly figured in responding to the pandemic, paralyzed by the widening conflict between China and the United States. Other IGOs that remained less hampered by that conflict, such as the IMF and the World Bank were able to act more expeditiously to meet increased demand for financial support from governments confronting both pandemic and recession.

A revival of intergovernmental collaboration will rest on a détente rather than a deepening of the US–China conflict, which has hindered a global response to the pandemic. That détente, in turn, and a revival of cosmopolitan fortunes will depend largely on domestic political developments, particularly in the United States. In the absence of such change, the Bretton Woods order and the effectiveness of its principal intergovernmental forums will depend on the influence of those industrialized and developing country governments that have the largest stake in the existing international order. The Ottawa Group working on WTO reform is an example of this alternative, which excludes both the United States and China. The EU is first among those that represent a strong attachment to multilateralism, an agenda of external economic liberalization, and, so far, little backsliding in its core on liberal democratic practice. Whether the EU, working with like-minded governments, can sustain the foundations of the Bretton Woods order in the face of disengagement or disruption by China or the United States may be the central question that will determine the future of global governance.

A failure to overcome the ideological and political challenges to the Bretton Woods moment is less likely to lead to an overthrow or disintegration of that order than either fragmentation or stagnation. In the first instance, China and the United States could attempt to build parallel and exclusive economic and military spheres and force others to join one or the other. Such a bifurcation of international order is unlikely to be acceptable to the rest of the world, with the exception of the weakest client states on either side. A more likely model of fragmentation, already apparent in global economic governance, is the building of clubs or coalitions of the willing that will forward political and economic agendas that are acceptable to smaller groups of countries or regions. The CPTPP exemplifies this approach, advancing beyond WTO liberalization in certain domains, without the participation of either the US or China. Stagnation at the global level could accompany such fragmentation, if the US–China conflict and the rise of parochial and nationalist movements in major countries paralyzes progress and institutions in the domains of climate, trade, human rights, and cyber security. The Bretton Woods moment would end with a whimper rather than a bang, leaving islands of cooperation in a sea of unilateral action with few constraints on the major powers.

Apart from those liberal democratic governments – including the members of the EU – with a stake in a reformed Bretton Woods order, a post-pandemic reconstruction of global order might utilize the resources and activism of those outside the state and the formal organizations of the Bretton Woods moment. Those fractious coalitions that demand urgent action in global health, climate, and other global domains might create a redefined liberal order, one that emphasizes the "macro-liberalism" of self-determination and experimentation rather than a "micro-liberalism" that aims to harmonize policy and institutions according to a single model. Such an order would be more inclusive, awarding voice to those whose views were inadequately represented in the Bretton Woods order. And, despite the complexity of such a transformed order, it may prove to be the only feasible means for successfully addressing threats to global health, economic inequality and instability, climate change, and other challenges high on the agenda of global governance.

## REFERENCES

Allison, G. (2018) The Myth of the Liberal Order. *Foreign Affairs*, **97**(4), 124–133.

Autor, D. H., Dorn, D., Hanson, G. H. and Majlesi, K. (2016) A Note on the Effect of Rising Trade Exposure on the 2016 Presidential Election. https://economics.mit.edu/files/12418.

Avant, D. and Westerwinter, O. (eds) (2016) *The New Power Politics: Networks and Transnational Security Governance*. New York: Oxford University Press.

Baldwin, R. (2016) *The Great Convergence: Information Technology and the New Globalization*. Cambridge, MA: Harvard University Press.

Bernstein, S. and Cashore, B. (2012) Complex Global Governance and Domestic Policies: Four Pathways of Influence. *International Affairs*, **88**(3), 585–604.

Bown, C. (2019) China is Cutting Tariffs—For Everyone Else. *The Atlantic*. https://www.piie.com/commentary/op-eds/china-cutting-tariffs-everyone-else.

Burri, M. and Polanco, R. (2020) Digital Trade Provisions in Preferential Trade Agreements: Introducing a New Dataset. *Journal of International Economic Law*, **23**(1), 187–220.

Cardenal, J. P. et al. (2017) *Sharp Power: Rising Authoritarian Influence*. Washington, DC: International Forum for Democratic Studies, National Endowment for Democracy.

Colantone, I. and Stanig, P. (2018) Global Competition and Brexit. *American Political Science Review*, **112**(2), 201–218.

Colgan, J. D. and Keohane, R. O. (2017) The Liberal Order is Rigged: Fix It Now or Watch It Wither. *Foreign Affairs*, **96**, 36–44.

Fidler, D. P. (2010) *The Challenges of Global Health Governance*. Working Paper. Council on Foreign Relations.

Finnemore, M. and Jurkovich, M. (2014) Getting a Seat at the Table: The Origins of Universal Participation and Modern Multilateral Conferences. *Global Governance*, **20**, 361–373.

Helleiner, E. (2014) Southern Pioneers of International Development. *Global Governance*, **20**, 375–388.

Helleiner, E. (2018) Sun Yat-sen as a Pioneer of International Development. *History of Political Economy*, **50**(S1), 76–93.

Helleiner, E. and Rosales, A. (2017) Peripheral Thoughts for International Political Economy: Latin American Ideational Innovation and the Diffusion of the Nineteenth Century Free Trade Doctrine. *International Studies Quarterly*, **61**, 924–934.

International Monetary Fund (2020) *World Economic Outlook Update*, June. https://www.imf.org/en/Publications/WEO/Issues/2020/06/24/WEOUpdateJune2020.

Kagan, R. (2018) *The Jungle Grows Back: America and Our Imperiled World.* New York: Alfred A. Knopf.
Kahler, M. (2002) Bretton Woods and its Competitors: The Political Economy of Institutional Choice. In D. Andrews, R. Henning, and L. Pauly (eds), *Organizing the World Economy*. Ithaca, NY: Cornell University Press, 38–59.
Kahler, M. (2020a) Cosmopolitans and Parochials: Economy, Culture, and Political Conflict. In J. P. Singh (ed.), *Cultural Values in Political Economy*. Stanford, CA: Stanford University Press, 87–112.
Kahler, M. (2020b) The Arc of Complex Global Governance: From Organization to Coalition. Unpublished manuscript.
Kastner, S. L., Pearson, M. M. and Rector, C. (2019) *China's Strategic Multilateralism: Investing in Global Governance*. Cambridge: Cambridge University Press.
McKinsey Global Institute (2017) *The New Dynamics of Financial Globalization.* August.
McKinsey Global Institute (2019) *Globalization in Transition: The Future of Trade and Value Chains*. January.
Mearsheimer, J. J. (2019) Bound to Fail: The Rise and Fall of the Liberal International Order. *International Security*, **43**(4), 7–50.
Milner, H. V. and Mukherjee, B. (2009) Democratization and Economic Globalization. *Annual Review of Political Science*, **12**, 163–181.
Moyn, S. (2018) *Not Enough: Human Rights in an Unequal World.* Cambridge, MA: Harvard University Press.
Roberts, C., Elliott Armijo, L. and Katada, S. N. (2018) *The BRICS and Collective Financial Statecraft.* New York: Oxford University Press.
Roger, C. B. (2020) *The Origins of Informality: Why the Legal Foundations of Global Governance are Shifting*. New York: Oxford University Press.
Shambaugh, D. (2019) China-Russia Relations: The New Axis. *China Focus*, 26 June. https://www.chinausfocus.com/foreign-policy/china-russia-relations-the-new-axis.
Sikkink, K. (2014) Latin American Countries as Norm Protagonists of the Idea of International Human Rights. *Global Governance*, **20**, 389–404.
Stephen, M. D. (2019) Contestation Overshoot: Rising Powers, NGOs, and the Failure of the WTO Doha Round. In M. D. Stephen and M. and Zürn (eds), *Contested World Orders*. New York: Oxford University Press, 39–81.
The Economist (2019) The Steam Has Gone Out of Globalisation. *The Economist.* https://www.economist.com/leaders/2019/01/24/the-steam-has-gone-out-of-globalisation.
Treisman, D. (2022) How Great is the Current Danger to Democracy? Assessing the Risk with Historical Data. Unpublished paper, University of California, Los Angeles, March.
Weiss, J. C. (2019) A World Safe for Autocracy? *Foreign Affairs*, **98**, 92–102.
Wright, T. (2016) Trump's 19th Century Foreign Policy. *Politico*, 20 January. https://www.politico.com/magazine/story/2016/01/donald-trump-foreign-policy-213546.
Young, A. R. (2016) Not Your Parents' Trade Politics: The Transatlantic Trade and Investment Partnership Negotiations. *Review of International Political Economy*, **23**(3), 345–378.

# 2. Recasting world order: power politics, contestation and international institutions

**Shawn Donnelly**

## POWER POLITICS, EUROPE AND THE WORLD

This chapter looks at two existential challenges to the EU and European responses through the lens of power politics. In doing so, it seeks to demonstrate that the same mechanisms that drive institutional change at the global level apply to the EU as well, allowing us to use the same theoretical tools for analysis. Institutions are defined here as the organizations, rules, and generally accepted norms that manage interdependence and relations between states. The focus of this chapter is the institutional changes that take place under highly contested circumstances, including ones that alter, steer, and repurpose existing institutions rather than replacing them. In practical terms, I look at how Europe has transformed under contestation, polarization and stress since 2008, how power coupled with institutions has led to outcomes that are unlike those we expect from traditional EU policy studies, and how those outcomes shape Europe's position in the international order. A key part of the chapter's argument is that while contestation and deadlock within the EU have threatened to undermine it in more than one way, power politics has managed to drive institutional innovations that enhance the EU's resilience under difficult conditions. This is surprising because normally the EU either negotiates new arrangements voluntarily in the Council, or in conjunction with supranational institutions that generate consensus, however thin, within the confines of EU decision-making rules. A power politics approach highlights elements of European institutional responses to crisis that overcome divisions in coercive, unilateral ways with non-EU institutions, and providing parameters for EU institutions to do the work that they do, instead of diffusing them. This chapter demonstrates how this has developed in the financial sphere, where Germany has been decisive, and to a lesser degree in the defense sphere, where France has assumed the leadership position.

A realist approach is taken to analyze institutions, order, and governance that stresses how powerful states (1) reshape international affairs by replacing existing arrangements with alternatives, and (2) harness the power of institutions to shape the behavior of other states, other institutions, and private actors in desired ways. The first of these points follows Jupille et al. (2013) and Zürn (2018) to contend that powerful states – those that possess and control a preponderance of material resources critical for other states – should be expected to (1) force changes to the basic principles, values and rules of international institutions, governance architectures, and regime complexes, in order to (2) redistribute material benefits and impose broader policy preferences. Depending on the resistance of others to alter existing institutions, they will (3) use, select, change, or create new institutions as needed to achieve this goal (Jupille et al. 2013). The second point is reflected in the work on the capacity of powerful states to exploit their preponderance of resources to shape the direction of international institutions (Drezner 2009) and the authority those institutionalized preferences can have on connected institutions and their members (Pratt 2018). This strand of realist research, unlike classical realism, sees governments caring deeply about the power implications of institutional settings (He 2006), and actively shaping them where they can. This strand can be distinguished as *realist institutionalism*.

In global affairs, realist institutionalism sheds light on the populist Trump Administration, multilateral institutions undermined by the United States in favor of new agreements, and a demonstrated general preference for executive power politics reminiscent of pre-1945 international relations (Drezner 2019; Destradi and Plagemann 2019). It also fits with the propensity of China's Xi government to challenge international law of the sea as it creates and claims new islands in the Pacific Ocean, and to organize trade infrastructure investment through the Asian Infrastructure Investment Bank as a way to reshape China's environment to its own advantage (Kutlay and Önis 2020). The expected methods include not only negotiated, voluntary changes within existing institutional rules, as expected by liberal intergovernmentalism (Schimmelfennig 2018; Verdun 2015), and neoliberal institutionalism (Keohane and Victor 2011), but also coercive, unilateral ones in the face of polarization, contestation, and deadlock (Donnelly 2021).

In European affairs, this chapter contends that the same dynamics can be seen in the way that Germany has sought to reorder the Economic and Monetary Union (EMU), and in a much weaker form, how France has sought to reorder European defense cooperation. Both make ample use of EU institutions, laws, and programs, but create and leverage resources in institutions outside the EU to steer the EU's work. This allows them to override Council disagreements over policy principles, aligning the EU's work with their own interests. While this violates the normal rules of intergovernmental bargaining, and of neo-functional theory (Niemann and Ioannou 2015; Smeets and Beach 2020), the results have kept the EU together under conditions of extreme stress and nested EU policy-making (Alter and Meunier 2006) within the demands of non-EU institutions led by a powerful state, making it an actor to be reckoned with in the global monetary order. The same may happen in the international security order as well. This constitutes an important and notable transformation of Europe, the EU, and its relationship to Germany and to France.

With regard to the Eurozone, the principles outlined above lead to the following expectations: Germany, as a country with extraordinary financial firepower, will respond to extreme Eurozone stress and deadlock over principles with institutions that reflect its own distributional preferences. Rather than a negotiated solution in the Council, which would favor cross-border transfers, the establishment of a non-EU institution to leverage financial aid should be seen. Finally, conditionality should be leveraged to shape the behavior of member states and EU institutions regarding the single currency. In defense, the chaos surrounding America's NATO-based commitment to European defense, the return of a possible Russian military threat, disagreement between European countries over military strategy, and France's overwhelming importance and distinctiveness in military capabilities and strategy have incited France to take a similar approach – creating a non-EU institution to promote a common strategy and command structure, while promoting and harnessing EU collaboration and initiatives.

The next section analyses Germany's role in keeping the Eurozone together through the establishment of the European Stability Mechanism and using it to set the terms for the EU's economic institutions, programs, and policies from outside of the EU through conditionality. The following section analyses France's role in providing a military command and control facility outside the EU that leverages the EU's own collective efforts in European defense. The final section concludes.

## REORDERING EMU TO GERMAN PREFERENCES

Contestation over EMU between member states is present within Europe regarding how to stabilize the single currency in the absence of a federal budget. Divides between France and Germany, each with their respective allies, have manifested in deadlock over questions of whether the EU should have a federal budget, combined with common debt and grants to national governments. Contestation with the rest of the world is visible between Germany's hard currency preferences, which dominate EU institutions and policy, and those of EU institutions (Commission and European Central Bank), global institutions (IMF and OECD) and the United States government, which would like to see Europe contribute to a more prosperous global economy by being more resilient against economic shocks and enjoying higher growth rates than official EU rules allow.

EMU, the institutional framework governing monetary and fiscal policy for countries participating in the single currency, consists of a centralized monetary policy run by the European Central Bank and a decentralized fiscal and economic policy run by the member states, together with rules, guidelines, and surveillance typical of the open method of coordination.

A key point of EMU conflict is fiscal policy. The original rules and institutions required national governments to balance their budgets over the long term – an aspect that was not realized (Hodson 2011). In the wake of the 2008 Great Financial Crisis, EU government deficits grew substantially. As some governments were unable to raise money from financial markets (Moschella 2017), conflict flared up over whether the Eurozone should institute cross-border transfers to stabilize government finances in hard-hit countries, or whether the individual member states should solve problems themselves by reducing their own borrowing and spending. Germany's governments preferred the latter, arguing that common debt would only discourage badly needed reforms (Laffan 2014; Goodliffe 2019), while France and much of Southern Europe, along with international, EU institutions (IMF, OECD, ECB), and the US government preferred the former. They argued that only transfers could provide necessary automatic stabilizers and compensate for long-term economic declines and short-term capital flight in Southern Europe during economic crises (Donnelly 2018a, 2018c; Matthijs and McNamara 2015). By 2012, when it became clear that the financial health of banks and governments was heavily intertwined, this conflict intensified and extended to government support for banks as well as governments (Howarth and Quaglia 2013, 2016). This home-grown conflict, exacerbated by the crisis, threatened to undermine the EU itself as national governments remained unable to find compromises in the Council that would save the euro, the EU, and its member states.

Rather than let interdependence collapse, or accept fiscal transfers, Germany pursued the European Stability Mechanism (ESM) as a non-EU backstop to Eurozone member states (Howarth and Spendzharova 2019; Fabbrini 2019) and tied access to this fund to countries that had committed to balancing their budgets in a new international Treaty on Stability, Coordination and Governance (TSCG). This meant that the ESM would make loans to national governments in financial distress, providing enough support to the Eurozone's capital market integration to prevent collapse, but simultaneously preventing fiscal transfers. The money would be repaid to the creditor countries that paid into the fund, via the ESM.

The ESM's setup ensured low start-up costs, but large potential for managing a systemic crisis with considerable firepower. Start-up costs of 80 billion euros would be demanded of all Eurozone member states up front, coupled with subscriptions amounting to 700 billion euros that the ESM Board could call on in a crisis situation. Similarly, the ESM could borrow up to a further 300 billion in such a crisis. For a small cost of 80 billion euros, Germany orchestrated a non-EU institution with one trillion euros of potential financial firepower to hold the interdependence of the euro intact in the event of a future Eurozone crisis. In the process, the ESM alternative to a fiscal union preserved the tax bases of well-off states in the North and the fiscal fragility of Southern countries, thereby confirming the attention to relative gains in German proposals.

The ESM would require all Eurozone member states to pay in as shareholders, and issue loans attached to conditions, like the IMF (Woods 2014). In return for assistance, in order to keep the amounts of assistance limited, and to ensure repayment to the greatest degree possible, it reserved the right to set conditions for the national economic policy. From the German perspective, which viewed financial fragility as a consequence of fiscal profligacy and poor overall economic sustainability (Hall 2018; Blyth 2013), ESM conditionality was both essential to ensuring that weak Eurozone member states instituted needed reforms, and compensating for EU institutions that had never applied sanctions to countries that violated the deficit limits of EMU's Stability and Growth Pact (SGP).

The ESM's design further demonstrates German attention to securing and protecting the leadership of the institution. German seed money for the ESM had the quid pro quo of retaining the institution's intergovernmental status – meaning that EU bodies could not interfere in its governance or priorities. By virtue of subscription-based quotas and voting thresholds, only Germany was granted a veto in lending decisions. Finally, Germany used that veto position to demand EU legislation and institutional changes that would push responsibility for financial stability back on to national governments individually, rather than establish a foothold for fiscal federalism.

In line with the TSCG's requirement that all signatories entrench balanced budgets into their constitutions, Germany countered continued calls for fiscal union and other transfers to stabilize EMU with calls for EU programs and legislation to support national risk reduction instead. The Commission complied by proposing the introduction of the European Semester in 2011 to oversee national budgets, the Six-Pack of regulations providing Commission and Council with enhanced rights of budget surveillance, the introduction of a reversed qualified majority vote procedure to increase the likelihood that fines could be levied against countries with excessive deficits in the Excessive Deficit Procedure (EDP), and the introduction of the Macroeconomic Imbalances Procedure, which moved beyond fiscal policy to cover all manner of structural policy, introduced detailed spreadsheets of potential financial stability risks and introduced country-specific recommendations. EU institutions and policies therefore were nested inside the political demands of the ESM, which Germany effectively instituted and led.

In practice, the degree of outside micro-management involved in the conditions could be and was calibrated to match the degree of trust the ESM board had in the prospective recipient. Spain, for example, was lent money in 2012 largely on its own recognizance, while negotiations with Cyprus and Greece proved difficult and contested. The result was that the ESM imposed heavy conditions on disbursement to the point that it intruded greatly into social, economic, and industrial policy as well as fiscal and banking policy (Ioannidis 2014). These measures also demonstrated the degree of coercive power that could be brought to bear on recalcitrant governments through the ESM (and the Troika of ECB, Commission, and IMF that had direct contact with the governments involved) that the EU itself could not accomplish.

## The Banking Union

Banking Union was established to tackle a private sector source of EMU instability, as heralded by a systemic banking crisis in Spain in 2012 that threatened to undermine public finances and the revived contestation of fiscal transfers or national adjustment to hold the EU together. A broader collapse of interdependence in European financial markets was also well underway, as banks terminated their cross-border exposures, and national supervisors coerced them to do so. Germany took the initiative to support ESM loans to finance a bank restructuring and resolution plan at the request of the Spanish government. In the meantime, a discussion started over what further institutions might be needed in Europe to prevent and manage such problems in the future. France, the Commission, and a host of international standard setting bodies (IMF, OECD, the International Association of Deposit Insurers and the US government) agreed that stabilizing European banks required three mutually supporting components at the EU level: independent bank supervision; a strong resolution authority; and a European Deposit Insurance Scheme (EDIS). The latter two innovations would require a common pool of contributions. These in turn needed to be equipped with a public backstop to counter systemic disturbances, effectively a European fiscal union. With this, the conflicts over EMU policy resurfaced, as did Germany's intent to prevent transfers by using the ESM as a substitute.

Of these Banking Union requirements, only supervision became a strong EU institution, as it furthered the goal of risk reduction and Germany demanded its introduction in return for making ESM loans available for banks. In 2014, The EU agreed to install the European Central Bank (ECB) as the lead institution of the Single Supervisory Mechanism (SSM) to enhance risk reduction. The ECB took over supervision of the Eurozone's largest banks from the national supervisors coordinated by the European Banking Authority (established 2011), which had proven weak and ineffective. This step forced systemically important banks to raise capital and reduce their exposure to toxic assets.

Effective bank resolution was also a key German demand in exchange for ESM access for banks, to reduce the impact of a bank's collapse on other banks during the time of crisis. Rather than cross-border transfers, problems had to be tackled and paid for at the point of disruption. It was a further demand in the construction of the Single Resolution Mechanism that banks could be closed or restructured without public money or cross-border transfers. The financial consequences of bank weakness would continue to be borne by the banks themselves, their shareholders and creditors, and their respective national governments. However, limiting bank claims on governments was an essential outcome for the German government. The cost of a bank failure was to be placed on the banks themselves, shareholders, and creditors, but with additional rules to minimize the burden on national taxpayers. Bail-outs, in which national governments supplied capital to banks, would become illegal unless creditors had been forced to accept losses on their investments amounting to at least 8 percent of the bank's liabilities. This adjustment would become known as a bail-in and was designed to alleviate the pressure on government finances for state aid to banks.

In addition to the bail-in rule, the Single Resolution Mechanism, which took effect on 1 January 2016, established a Single Resolution Board (SRB) to supervise national authorities and ensure consistent application. However, the SRB proved much weaker than resolution bodies are expected to be. It does not decide on whether a bank is failing or likely to fail (ECB competence), nor does it draw up resolution plans (national authorities do this), nor does it initiate resolution (Commission competence with the approval of the Council). And while resolution authorities normally have sizable funds with which to prevent a bank's failure from unleashing a domino effect throughout the banking system, the Single Resolution Fund remains small at 55 billion euros, and under intergovernmental control outside the EU. This EU-IGA hybrid (Fabbrini 2014; Asimakopoulos 2018) ensured that Germany's moral hazard concerns about funding would remain contained into the future. But it also undermined the SRB's capacity to wind down banks, as was seen in a series of Italian cases. Other countries accepted supervision and resolution as part of discussions for deposit insurance. However, negotiations failed to reach an agreement on introducing deposit insurance, as Germany demanded ever-increasing regulations to reduce financial risks in banks before opening negotiations (see the Banking Package: Donnelly 2018b, 2018c). Contestation remains effectively suppressed.

In sum, Germany succeeded in (re-)ordering EU institutions in EMU and BU to reflect its priorities, thanks to its initiative on the ESM, its ability to take a leading role in financing that institution, and its ability to leverage access for control over EU programs, institutions, and legislation. This has been possible in the face of enormous resistance by a considerable number of member states, European institutions, and even international standard setting bodies. In the end, there is a consistent pattern of other countries accepting German demands to secure continued access to financial markets, which ESM membership can help restore in an emergency. This has resulted in Germany securing better collective oversight of national fiscal and economic policy, introducing new regulations and regulators for banks, and blocking initiatives it rejects. It has simultaneously been able to break its promises of quid pro quo without consequence, so that the final financial backstop remains the ESM, which it controls. It has further been able to accomplish this in the face of continued conflict over cross-border transfers.

This consistent preference disparity has meant that initiatives to move the ESM into the EU legal structure, or to create alternatives, such as a Eurozone budget, have similarly met with German rejection. In late 2020, instead of EDIS or a robust resolution fund, Germany agreed to a change of the ESM Treaty allowing it to function as a backstop to the SRF. With this, Germany has effectively reordered EMU to its own preferences (Donnelly 2016, 2018a), focusing on steering the EU from outside through the ESM.

The COVID-19 crisis brought about important changes in Germany's insistence on national responsibility, strict adherence to the SGP, and reliance on ESM loans for countries with financial difficulties. Faced for the first time with a monumental economic shock over the course of 2020, hurting domestic demand and export markets, Germany's preferences on economic stimulus became progressively closer to those of France. In March and April, Germany resisted fiscal transfers once again and attempted to sway others to accept ESM loans as assistance. However, by May, worsening economic conditions led the German and French governments to jointly propose a 750 billion euro rescue plan based on collective debt, partially as grants, and managed through the EU. It would add to other investments found in the EU's Multiannual Financial Framework and take over some of the burdens that the ECB had carried to keep money flowing within the Eurozone since 2012.

Fund grants were eventually bargained down to 390 billion in July, and made temporary for four years. This was a monumental shift of position for Germany, which relaxed its realist strategy for the moment. This reminds us that the mechanisms of realist institutionalism are not deterministic but expected choices. It also demonstrates two other things: that European institutional development can happen inside the EU, rather than outside when the policy preferences of powerful states and others are closely aligned rather than polarized; and that when placed under pressure, European governments have risen to the task of preserving their single currency. This has the further implication of ensuring that the euro remains a key global currency capable of holding its own for the foreseeable future. It will continue to be a conservative currency. Equally important, it closes the gap between European preferences for the global economy and those prevailing in the United States and elsewhere. International calls for greater economic resilience and growth have been heeded.

The remarkable experience of Germany's reconfiguration of the Eurozone raises the question of whether it is a single case that will not be repeated. The next section examines a similar pattern taking place under French leadership in the area of European defense. France's more modest experience underlines the conditions required for realist strategies to create alternative institutions to work.

## FRANCE'S ATTEMPT AT REORDERING EUROPEAN SECURITY

Contestation within Europe became particularly acute during the Trump Administration in the United States, which raised questions of American military protection for Europe, and what Europe should do in response. In this context, disagreements were allowed to come to the fore, particularly (but not exclusively) between France and Germany, but also between Western and Eastern European countries within the EU. The two key points of conflict are allegiance to/reliance on NATO and the United States as the primary supplier of strategy, resources and operational support vs. strategic autonomy (in which Europe would develop its own strategy and integrated command, in addition to force generation); and a divide over whether Europe's strategic culture should be principally pacifist (German preference) or more activist in the planning and use of military force (France) (Howorth 2019). In the context of these challenges and divides, France has found it useful to complement general cooperation within the EU on defense and security matters with a European Intervention Initiative that seeks to develop strategy for the rest of Europe, while preserving French control over nuclear weapons in the overall architecture.

Security interdependence in Europe is largely a collective action challenge, which became acute in 2017. Russia's annexation of Crimea, its ongoing destabilization of Ukraine, and its military threats against European countries placed security near the top of the European agenda in 2014. Until the inauguration of the Trump Administration in 2017, however, American protection through NATO was considered a given, and collaboration was organized through NATO. American attacks on the EU and NATO strained relations between the UK after its referendum to leave the EU, German reticence to take an assertive posture toward Russia, and a French desire to refocus European attention toward the Middle East and Africa have raised questions about whether European countries might be too divided to work together militarily.

In this context, France has emerged as the candidate to establish institutions to provide collective security for Europe and achieve what it calls strategic autonomy – the capacity to decide and act robustly enough to protect European territory and its near neighborhood independently of NATO. This goes further than the European Union Global Strategy within the EU, which primarily strengthens Europe within the NATO alliance and in its own neighborhood (Howorth 2018). The European Intervention Initiative (EI2) is a project to organize and direct European security outside of NATO and the EU. At the same time, it not only explicitly seeks to steer EU efforts like the European Defence Agency and the Permanent and Structured Cooperation (PESCO), but these EU institutions now explicitly recognize EI2's mission to "further [our] shared strategic culture" that structures what the EU does (European Defence Agency 2021). Like the ESM's relationship to the EU, the EI2 lies outside the EU but makes use of EU institutions, programs, and initiatives. The French contributions allow it to lead and develop an integrated European command, and a European grand strategy, including the use of critical resources that others lack, particularly nuclear weapons. Until recently, France's primary challenge has been a difference of opinion across Europe about where Europe's primary security threats lie (coupled with how to manage them), and, to date, the absence of an existential threat to the EU's territorial integrity.

In this context, the principles outlined in the introduction translate as follows:

1. France seeks institutions that anchor strategic autonomy/collective action over dependence on the United States or voting and resources within the EU.
2. France works together with other EU member states inside the EU (within the European Defence Agency) to further develop common foundations in research and development, logistics and coordination (EUMC), and ideally the EU's Common Defence and Security Policy (CSDP).
3. In the absence of an acute security threat to the entirety of the EU, the nesting of EU activities within a French-led institution will remain limited.

## EI2 and Strategic Autonomy

Proposed in September 2017, and launched in June 2018, the EI2 is a military force outside of both NATO and the EU, with the ambition to provide for what the French government termed: strategic autonomy. This was widely understood as Europe's capacity to deter and defend itself against a Russian attack without assistance from the United States. France, Germany, Spain, Portugal, Netherlands, Belgium, Denmark, and the UK were on board from the outset. Given the timing and result of the 2016 Brexit referendum, the realities of Norway remaining outside the EU, and the demand for increased deterrence by the non-NATO Nordic countries (Sweden and Finland), EI2 was deliberately construed to permit the inclusion of non-EU member states, who felt a need for collective action (the UK in particular) (McTague and Herszenhorn 2018). The same applied to countries that felt a strong need for defense cooperation but could not formally join NATO. In this light, Finland joined in November 2018 (Nicolas 2018). In September 2019, Italy, Norway, and Sweden joined as well (Brzozowski 2019).

EI2 comes with an (initially) modest organizing infrastructure: a secretariat hosting military liaison officers provided by the French defense ministry, plans to make Paris the place where a common strategic culture and doctrine is developed, and where connections are made to France's nuclear strategy. This is not just about coordinating and planning, but eventually replicating those elements of force generation, operational, and strategic command that the United States supports within NATO, if and when the United States ceases to do so (Ministry of Defence 2019). It is also about generating defense equipment and infrastructure over which Europe has complete control, rather than dependence on the United States through NATO.

To date, France has used EI2 as a vehicle by which the other participants support more traditional foreign policy goals and military actions in Africa and the Levant. This signifies a divergence of opinion between France and its allies, particularly Germany, with its more pacifist tendencies (Siebold 2018), over grand strategy and requirements.

For France, the interdependence in question is France's, and by extension Europe's security relationship with its geopolitical neighborhood. This includes much of Africa, the Middle East, and more explicitly by 2019, Russia (Plucinska and Goclowski 2020). France's understanding of the need to stabilize this area with economic, humanitarian, and military assistance, cooperation and intervention is a core component of France's foreign policy (Yates 2018). Most of the European Union's official military and UN peacekeeping missions are in fact French (-led) missions under a European label. France sees other EU countries free riding with regard to Africa. Moreover, France has been disappointed by past examples where voting within the EU's Common Security and Defense Policy (CSDP) prevented the deployment of EU battlegroups (Barcikowska 2013), including for Congo, Algeria, and Libya. The same disappointment applies to France's desire to see Europe act collectively under its leadership regarding the Middle East, as evidenced by François Hollande's call to European leaders to rally support behind France for air raids after the Paris attacks of 2015, under new provisions of the Lisbon Treaty (Article 42.7) (Biscop 2016).

To date, France has not been successful in overcoming differences within the CSDP (Portela and Raube 2011; Howorth 2019). Instead of giving up, however, EI2 seeks to develop a common strategic culture (Ministry of Defence 2019), which the other signatories have agreed to work toward (Letter of Intent 2018).

## Harnessing the EU from Outside

Considering the second expectation of realist institutionalism, France has indeed sought to use any means available to develop and pool resources that EI2 can use in its strategy, operations, and force generation, including European institutions and activities. This is consistent with the approach taken by Germany through the ESM, in that much of what the EU does takes place within the context of the EI2.

The costs are indeed considerable. A credible European military intervention/deterrent capability in a missile-rich environment toward the east would require Europe to develop its own nuclear deterrent capability, A2/AD (anti-access/area denial) capacity, combat clouds with interconnected joint strike fighters and drone swarms, satellite support, land forces with advanced protection and electronic warfare systems, as well as cyber capacities sufficient to defend European critical infrastructure (Fiott 2017). The FCAS project, launched with France, Germany, and Spain in 2019, is an example of an attempt to provide a credible alternative, or complement to the American F35 (Mickel 2019).

Overall, the magnitude of securing such scientific, technological, and military capability limits France's capacity to credibly replace NATO, leading to two expectations. The first is strategic hedging, in which full European strategic autonomy from the United States and NATO is deferred, perhaps indefinitely, as a means of avoiding containing costs, particularly in the nuclear triad. Indeed, France has pulled back from its initial focus on full autonomy to striking the best balance between self-protection and reliance on the United States (Ministry of Defence 2019). This points to continued EU-NATO cooperation in the medium term, building up EU within the context of the alliance and joint EU-NATO centers of excellence and training, but also generating own (European) core technology and weapons systems. Critical infrastructure and agreements for command and control within EI2 would have to be added for it to have independent capabilities. So far, this stage has not been reached.

The second expectation is that France will support EU initiatives that advance research, development, and training that EI2 can incorporate into its strategic planning, which the EU lacks. Here, EU initiatives are indeed increasing in number, taking place parallel to the EI2 and organized within the European Defence Agency. All are issues that enable EI2 to work.

Within two Directorates, the EDA covers:

- The Industry Strategy & EU Policies (ISP) Unit: research, development, and policy implications engagement of industry in the activities of the Agency, determination of Key Strategic Activities at EU level, defense aspects of EU policies varying from legislation (REACH, procurement) to funding instruments.
- The Critical Enablers (CRE) Unit: supports defense cooperation and interoperability through standards harmonization in all military domains.
- The Single European Sky (SES) Unit: facilitates and coordinates military and civilian use of European airspace with the EU.
- The Operations, Training & Exercises (OTE) Unit: promotes adoption of EDA-coordinated training, operations, projects, and infrastructure in CSDP operations.
- Cooperation Planning Unit: Capability Development, Coordinated Annual Reviews, Defence Data.
- PESCO Unit: PESCO secretariat functions, including support to PESCO projects.
- Plus, specialized units for land, air, sea, and Information Superiority, which covers: Communication & Information Systems, Surveillance & Reconnaissance, Space, Cyber Defense (Source: European Defence Agency).

These elements go beyond the general use of the European Defence Fund and the EDIDP (European Defence Industrial Development Programme) to fund research into basic capabilities. What EI2 adds is strategic direction regarding what is needed and how it is to be used.

Overall, EI2 takes place in an environment where military threat is present, but outright military conflict is absent outside of Ukraine. This appears to be a key missing ingredient for a closing of the gap between France and the rest of Europe over what EI2 is there to do, and what geopolitical priorities it should have. This means that it does not predetermine as much of what Europe does as the ESM does for economic policy. In a more challenging security environment, the existential nature of France's military capabilities for other EU states, and France's own need to share the same security concerns with other EU states would change this calculation. France has moved closer to Poland and the Baltics in particular, but the latter remain firmly committed to NATO, the American security guarantee is stronger under the Biden Administration (making new institutions less compelling to other EU states), and France continues to focus more on Africa than the rest of the EU. The EU and EI2 are, therefore, moving forward alongside one another more than in lockstep.

Notably, France sees PESCO's focus on capabilities folding into the strategic command of EI2, rather than the other way around, as Germany would prefer. Paris rejects any move to bring the initiative into the European Council, where it would be debated and blocked, in ways similar to the actions under the CSDP. However, to date, NATO's Eastern Flank member states remain firmly allied to the United States and outside EI2. In the absence of an existential crisis paralleling that of the Eurozone Crisis, France's EI2 will likely remain a capacity-building and strategy developing project for Europe, but not one that will reorder European security fundamentally (Zandee and Kruijver 2019). This is even more so in the wake of a renewed American commitment to NATO following the 2020 presidential elections.

## DISCUSSION AND CONCLUSIONS

This chapter looked at polarization and contestation between European countries in response to existential threats, and examined how Europe responded. It argued that under conditions of high contestation and strong power differentials, powerful states have strong incentives to build new institutions outside existing ones, that existing and new (EU) institutions and programs are then nested in. This is different than the standard expectation that EU member states force themselves to negotiate solutions to pressing problems within the confines of Council voting rules. By setting up alternative institutions unilaterally, making access to a critical resource conditional on terms of its choosing, and expecting the EU to shape its programs and laws to fit them, a powerful country can exert lasting leverage on the others. Only when the degree of contestation declines does the utility of resorting to non-EU institutions decline. But also, by cutting through intergovernmental conflicts, this means of institution building can set the stage for further contestation at the global level.

We can see this pattern working in the establishment, use and leverage of the European Stability Mechanism to drive reforms to monetary union and an entire Banking Union architecture to suit the needs of Germany and a handful of like-minded states, blocking calls for cross-border financial transfers in the process. Notable is that the outcome of the process increases global polarization and contestation, pitting a German-led Europe with a mission to reduce risk through economic downsizing against a broad international coalition pushing Europe to adopt more growth-friendly economic policies for the benefit of both itself and the global economy.

We can also see this pattern working more weakly in the establishment, use and leverage of the European Intervention Initiative to cut through disagreements over how to provide for European security in a more uncertain world.

While the same patterns can be seen in French ambitions and institutional strategies, and the EU is increasingly tying its defense projects into the strategic culture project of the EI2, the existential threat is not as acute, and therefore France's leverage not as strong. This is one reason why France's notion of strategic autonomy, as independence from the United States, enjoys only limited support, and why EI2 has not generated contestation and polarization between Europe and the US as a result. But the pattern of using an outside institution that offers access to critical resources in an emergency has not been lost on France, or on EU member states, so that France plays a key role in how European defense is formed.

## REFERENCES


Alter, K. J. and Meunier, S. (2006) Nested and Overlapping Regimes in the Transatlantic Banana Trade Dispute. *Journal of European Public Policy*, **13**(3), 362–382.

Asimakopoulos, I. G. (2018) International Law as a Negotiation Tool in Banking Union: The Case of the Single Resolution Fund. *Journal of Economic Policy Reform*, **21**(2), 118–131.

Barcikowska, A. (2013) *EU Battlegroups: Ready to Go?* Brief 40/2013. Paris: EU Institute for Strategic Studies.

Biscop, S. (2016) The European Union and Mutual Assistance: More than Defence. *The International Spectator*, **51**(2), 119–125.

Blyth, M. (2013). *Austerity: The History of a Dangerous Idea.* New York: Oxford University Press.

Brzozowski, A. (2019) Macron's Coalition of European Militaries Grows in Force. *Euractiv*, 24 September. https://www.euractiv.com/section/defence-and-security/news/macrons-coalition-of-european-militaries-grows-in-force/.

Destradi, S. and Plagemann, J. (2019) Populism and International Relations: (Un) predictability, Personalisation, and the Reinforcement of Existing Trends in World Politics. *Review of International Studies*, **45**(5), 711–730.

Donnelly, S. (2016) Expert Advice and Political Choice in Constructing European Banking Union. *Journal of Banking Regulation*, **17**(1–2), 104–118.

Donnelly, S. (2018a) *Power Politics, Banking Union and EMU: Adjusting Europe to Germany*. New York: Routledge.

Donnelly, S. (2018b) Advocacy Coalitions and the Lack of Deposit Insurance in Banking Union. *Journal of Economic Policy Reform*, **21**(3), 210–223.

Donnelly, S. (2018c) ECB-Eurogroup Conflicts and Financial Stability in the Eurozone. *Credit and Capital Markets*, **51**(1), 113–126.

Donnelly, S. (2021) Failing Outward: Power Politics, Regime Complexity, and Failing Forward under Deadlock. *Journal of European Public Policy*, **28**(10), 1573–1591.

Drezner, D. W. (2009) The Power and Peril of International Regime Complexity. *Perspectives on Politics*, **7**(1), 65–70.

Drezner, D. W. (2019) Present at the Destruction: The Trump Administration and the Foreign Policy Bureaucracy. *The Journal of Politics*, **81**(2), 723–730.

European Defence Agency (2021) PESCO Drivers: The Floor Is Yours. *European Defence Matters*. https://eda.europa.eu/webzine/issue15/cover-story/pesco-drivers-the-floor-is-yours.

Fabbrini, F. (2014) On Banks, Courts and International Law: The Intergovernmental Agreement on the Single Resolution Fund in Context. *Maastricht Journal of European and Comparative Law*, **21**(3), 444–463.

Fabbrini, S. (2019) *Europe's Future: Decoupling and Reforming*. Cambridge: Cambridge University Press.

Fiott, D. (2017) A Revolution Too Far? US Defence Innovation, Europe and NATO's Military-Technological Gap. *Journal of Strategic Studies*, **40**(3), 417–437.

Goodliffe, G. (2019) Morality in the Service of Mercantilism: Selective Ordoliberalism and German Economic Governance in Europe. Paper delivered to the European Union Studies Association, Denver, CO, 9–11 May.

Hall, P. A. (2018) Varieties of Capitalism in Light of the Euro Crisis. *Journal of European Public Policy*, **25**(1), 7–30.

He, K. (2006) Does ASEAN Matter? International Relations Theories, Institutional Realism, and ASEAN. *Asian Security*, **2**(3), 189–214.

Hodson, D. (2011) *Governing the Euro Area in Good Times and Bad*. New York: Oxford University Press.

Howorth, J. (2018) Strategic Autonomy and EU-NATO Cooperation: Threat or Opportunity for Transatlantic Defence Relations? *Journal of European Integration*, **40**(5), 523–537.

Howorth, J. (2019) Differentiation in Security and Defence Policy. *Comparative European Politics*, **17**(2), 261–277.

Howarth, D. and Quaglia, L. (2013) Banking Union as Holy Grail: Rebuilding the Single Market in Financial Services, Stabilizing Europe's Banks and 'Completing' Economic and Monetary Union. *Journal of Common Market Studies*, **51**(S1), 103–123.

Howarth, D. and Quaglia, L. (2016) *The Political Economy of European Banking Union*. New York: Oxford University Press.

Howarth, D. and Spendzharova, A. (2019) Accountability in Post-Crisis Eurozone Governance: The Tricky Case of the European Stability Mechanism. *JCMS: Journal of Common Market Studies*, **57**(4), 894–911.

Ioannidis, M. (2014) EU Financial Assistance Conditionality after 'Two Pack'. Max-Planck-Institut für ausländisches öffentliches Recht und Völkerrecht, SSRN 2398914.

Jupille, J., Mattli, W. and Snidal, D. (2013) *Institutional Choice and Global Commerce*. New York: Cambridge University Press.

Keohane, R. O. and Victor, D. G. (2011) The Regime Complex for Climate Change. *Perspectives on Politics*, **9**(1), 7–23.

Kutlay, M. and Öniş, Z. (2020) The New Age of Hybridity and Clash of Norms: China, BRICS and Challenges of Global Governance in a Post-liberal International Order. *Alternatives: Global, Local, Political*, **45**(3), 123–142.

Laffan, B. (2014) Testing Times: The Growing Primacy of Responsibility in the Euro Area. *West European Politics*, **37**(2), 270–287.

Letter of Intent (2018) Concerning the Development of the European Intervention Initiative (EI2). Paris, 25 June.

Matthijs, M. and McNamara, K. (2015) The Euro Crisis' Theory Effect: Northern Saints, Southern Sinners, and the Demise of the Eurobond. *Journal of European Integration*, **37**(2), 229–245.

McTague, T. and Herszenhorn, D. M. (2018) Britain Pulls Out of EU Defense Force. *Politico*, 20 March. https://www.politico.eu/article/theresa-may-uk-military-britain-pulls-out-of-eu-defense-force/.

Mickel, D. J. (2019) A Clouded Future: On Combat Clouds in the US and Europe and their Impact on NATO's Capability Gaps. Master's thesis, University of Twente. http://essay.utwente.nl/79352/.

Ministry of Defence, France (2019) European Intervention Initiative. 26 February. https://www.defense.gouv.fr/english/dgris/international-action/l-iei/l-initiative-europeenne-d-intervention.

Moschella, M. (2017) Italy and the Fiscal Compact: Why Does a Country Commit to Permanent Austerity? *Italian Political Science Review/Rivista Italiana di Scienza Politica*, **47**(2), 205–225.

Nicolas, C. (2018) Finland Becomes Tenth Participant Country in European Intervention Initiative. *Euractiv*, 9 November. https://www.euractiv.com/section/defence-and-security/news/finland-becomes-tenth-country-to-join-the-european-intervention-initiative/.

Niemann, A. and Ioannou, D. (2015) European Economic Integration in Times of Crisis: A Case of Neofunctionalism? *Journal of European Public Policy*, **22**(2), 196–218.

Plucinska, J. and Goclowski, M. (2020) Macron Emphasizes EU Defense in Bid to Warm Ties with Poland. *Reuters*, 2 February. https://www.reuters.com/article/us-poland-france-idUSKBN1ZW0SZ.

Portela, C. and Raube, K. (2011) The EU Polity and Foreign Policy Coherence. *Journal of Contemporary European Research*, **8**(1), 3–20.

Pratt, T. (2018) Deference and Hierarchy in International Regime Complexes. *International Organization*, **72**(3), 561–590.

Schimmelfennig, F. (2018) Liberal Intergovernmentalism and the Crises of the European Union. *Journal of Common Market Studies*, **56**(7), 1578–1594.

Siebold, S. (2018) Berlin und Paris streiten über neue Eingreiftruppe. *Reuters*, 6 November. https://de.reuters.com/article/deutschland-frankreich-verteidigung-idDEKCN1NB2FR?il=0.

Smeets, S. and Beach, D. (2020) Political and Instrumental Leadership in Major EU Reforms: The Role and Influence of the EU Institutions in Setting-Up the Fiscal Compact. *Journal of European Public Policy*, **27**(1), 63–81.

Verdun, A. (2015) A Historical Institutionalist Explanation of the EU's Responses to the Euro Area Financial Crisis. *Journal of European Public Policy*, **22**(2), 219–237.

Woods, N. (2014) *The Globalizers: The IMF, the World Bank, and their Borrowers*. Ithaca, NY: Cornell University Press.

Yates, D. A. (2018) France and Africa. In Nagar, D. and Mutasa, C. (eds), *Africa and the World*. Cham: Palgrave Macmillan, 95–118.

Zandee, D. and Kruijver, K. (2019) *The European Intervention Initiative: Developing a Shared Strategic Culture for European Defence*. Clingendael Report, The Hague.

Zürn, M. (2018) *A Theory of Global Governance: Authority, Legitimacy, and Contestation*. New York: Oxford University Press.

# 3. The era of un-institutionalized regions: explaining the diminished prospects of regional integration in the twenty-first century

**Nicolas de Zamaróczy**[1]

## INTRODUCTION

Regional integration played a major albeit underappreciated role in shaping the second half of the twentieth century for the better. While the case of the European Union is well known, regional organizations (ROs) in other parts of the world also significantly contributed to both the 'Long Peace' and the economic 'Long Boom' that characterized the post-Second World War era. ROs, through their facilitation of state-to-state relations and other kinds of cross-border cooperation, tend to make their members more peaceful, wealthier, and better governed than would otherwise be the case. As the twenty-first century progresses, however, regional initiatives are increasingly being contested across the world: worldwide support for regionalism has fallen in recent years, at both the popular and elite levels. Stakeholders that were previously important in upholding regionalism, such as business lobby groups and national parliaments, are increasingly finding themselves sidelined amid a sea of nationalism and suspicion of cross-border trade deals. Accordingly, major countries are either 'exiting' existing ROs or attempting to renegotiate their terms, typically with an eye towards 'de-institutionalizing' them. Meanwhile, at the behest of some major powers, the small handful of new regional initiatives that are being created are often being deliberately set up in an 'un-institutionalized' fashion that privileges individual state leaders at the expense of permanent secretariats.

[1] I am grateful to Tom Lairson, Mario de Zamaróczy, Paula Donovan, Megha Gupta, and Grace de Zamaróczy for comments on earlier drafts.

This chapter seeks to: (i) explain why the existing web of ROs was historically so significant; (ii) note the importance of having a robust institutional structure for successful regional integration; (iii) document the increasing types of challenges that ROs face, including exit, de-institutionalization, and un-institutionalization; and (iv) suggest several structural factors worldwide that explain why regional integration faces increasing headwinds. Overall, the conclusion is rather grim: ROs are under assault from within, and unlikely to serve as effective guarantors of peace and prosperity in the decades to come.

## Regional Integration between 1945 and 2010: The Successful Rise of Institutionalized ROs

Viewed historically, regional integration has followed clear 'waves' of global activity (Figure 3.1). A first wave occurred in the late 1960s and early 1970s, with several parts of the world establishing formal ROs for the first time (Fawcett 1995). Most of these new ROs emerged in response to three trends: the plethora of newly independent states emerging from decolonization; Cold War era regional security concerns that called for greater security cooperation; and emulation of the ongoing successes of the European Economic Community. This first wave included the Organisation of African Unity (OAU – 1963), the Association of Southeast Asian Nations (ASEAN – 1967), the first East African Community (EAC – 1967), the Caribbean Community (CARICOM – 1973), and others.

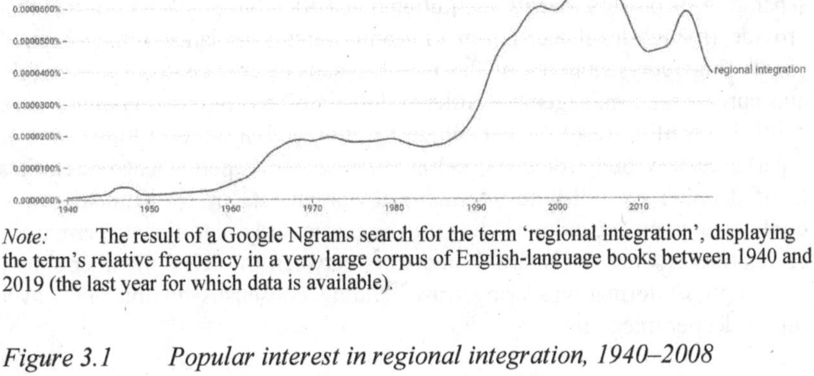


*Note:* The result of a Google Ngrams search for the term 'regional integration', displaying the term's relative frequency in a very large corpus of English-language books between 1940 and 2019 (the last year for which data is available).

*Figure 3.1* *Popular interest in regional integration, 1940–2008*

A second wave took off in the early 1990s. Benefiting from the looser global political environment that followed the end of the Cold War, and more focused on economic goals than the political and security concerns that had characterized the first wave, this second wave truly spanned the globe. It included the Asia-Pacific Economic Cooperation (APEC – 1989), Mercosur (1991), the Central American Integration System (SICA – 1993), the North American Free Trade Agreement (NAFTA – 1994), the second East African Community (2000), and a number of organizations in the former Soviet space, such as the Commonwealth of Independent States (CIS – 1991), the Visegrád Group (1991), and the Organization of the Black Sea Economic Cooperation (1994).

While several of these individual ROs have underwhelmed, International Relations (IR) scholars are increasingly realizing that, when taken collectively, ROs play a major, productive role in global politics. ROs do so by: preventing conflict from emerging between their members (Haftel 2007); serving as mediators if conflict between their members does emerge (Elgström et al. 2003; Gartner 2011); providing important peace-keeping and peace-making services if that conflict then turns into outright warfare (Barnett 1995; Williams 2017); helping to spread and strengthen democratic institutions and norms (Collins 2010; Pevehouse 2005); promoting trade (Mansfield and Milner 1997); establishing forums for increased socialization and knowledge transfers between their member states (Acharya 2011; Agostinis 2019; Börzel and van Hüllen 2015; Checkel 2007); and sending positive investment-related signals to the rest of the world (Haftel 2010).

An important source of strength for ROs in the postwar era has lain in the fact that almost all have been fairly institutionalized. By ‘institutionalized’, I mean that their operations have been structured by codified, regular procedures, as well as by a clear delineation of the roles and responsibilities of the organizational units within the RO. Deeply institutionalized ROs have a permanent headquarters, significant administrative capacity, an annual budget, and full-time employees. More often than not, in keeping with the tradition of separation of powers, deeply institutionalized ROs have distinct entities that provide: (a) high-level decision-making and strategic guidance (often a council comprising representatives of the member states); (b) day-to-day oversight and bureaucratic management (often a full-time secretariat or commission); and (c) a conflict resolution/appellate function (often either a high court or a parliamentary body, or even both). The role of the permanent secretariats (staffed either by full-time international bureaucrats or by national senior civil servants on secondment) has proven particularly significant: permanent secretariats can act as impartial mediators between the ROs’ member states, allowing for information sharing, trust-building, consensus-finding, and – over time – deeper integration.

Consider, for instance, the case of the CARICOM Secretariat in the 1970s:

> The [Secretariat's] senior staff enjoy diplomatic status, and even though recruited from national governments are prohibited from seeking or receiving instructions from 'Any government whether Member States or otherwise' […] Because of its admitted competence the Secretariat enjoys very high prestige in the region. The prestige has resulted in attracting staff from a variety of sources—government, university, other international organizations. The result is that it has been become the principal initiator of proposals advancing integration. […] [The Secretariat] usually convenes the meetings [with Member State representatives], prepares a draft agenda for consideration by governments, drafts most of the papers with proposals and circulates the bulk of the documentation. To some extent this is the result of its right to initiate studies and make recommendations for the advancement of the Community. However, member governments seem to place more reliance on it to initiate proposals because of its technical competence, its considerable prestige and the limited technical capacity of some member governments. (Hall and Blake 1977, pp. 219–220)

The fact that most of the ROs established in the twentieth century have been fairly institutionalized was little noticed until recently, since it was simply assumed to be the norm for ROs (Gray 2018, p. 2). Still, IR scholars working on ROs as well as other types of intergovernmental organizations have helped clarify the benefits conferred on organizations by institutionalization. Institutionalization allows organizations to act impartially, make decisions on rational grounds, and attract higher caliber talent, all of which generate substantial authority; in turn, this authority allows the organizations to more effectively design regional policies, manage negotiations, shape public opinions, and even construct social reality in powerful ways (Barnett and Finnemore 2004; Ruggie 1998).

Some IR scholars continue to discount the importance of such international bureaucracies – perhaps because IR as a field continues to privilege states as the main actors in global politics, or perhaps because 'bureaucracy' remains a dirty word in the United States, where many influential IR scholars are based. But important work by Julia Gray has shone a spotlight on the crucial role that permanent secretariats play in ROs (Gray 2018). Analyzing the effectiveness of 70 ROs over a period of 65 years, Gray empirically demonstrates that an RO's degree of institutionalization affects its overall effectiveness, via two factors: how qualified the secretariat's staff is, and how much autonomy the secretariat is granted by its member states. The higher the quality of an RO's bureaucrats, and the greater autonomy they have, the likelier the organization is to flourish and meet the goals set for it by its member states.

Overall, then, the first two waves of regionalism that marked the second half of the twentieth century made important contributions to world peace, prosperity, and probity, in part because of their high degree of institutionalization.

## The Twenty-First Century Decline of Regional Integration

Unfortunately, regionalism grew increasingly contested over the course of the 2010s. While international cooperation is still seen by most world leaders as desirable, there is markedly less interest in working through established ROs, and instead preference is being given to bilateral cooperation or ad hoc multilateral fora. In part, this is because the deeply institutionalized character of many ROs is now perceived (rightly or wrongly) as a liability instead of an asset: overly rigid, slow, and prone to gridlock. As such, three broad patterns concerning ROs are visible at the global level: (i) member states 'exiting' (or threatening to exit) ROs they are part of; (ii) member states pushing to 'de-institutionalize' existing ROs; and (iii) states setting up new ROs in a deliberately 'un-institutionalized' manner.

Several of the most well-established ROs faced existential crises during the 2010s as some of their members either withdrew or threatened to do so. The United Kingdom withdrew from the EU in 2020 after four years of tumultuous and often acrimonious negotiations. The United States threatened to withdraw from NAFTA in 2017, prompting a renegotiation of the accord from the ground up amidst a climate of mutual mistrust among its members. And the decade-long push to expand the Trans-Pacific Partnership suffered a major setback after the newly installed Trump Administration reneged on its predecessor's promises and withdrew from the agreement. This trend of major powers seeking to exit ROs is part of a broader pattern of major powers unilaterally withdrawing from international organizations of all types (von Borzyskowski and Vabulas 2019).

Perhaps less visible but equally important is a tendency among some member states to seek to de-institutionalize the ROs they participate in, weakening existing procedures and lessening the power of their secretariats. Moreover, member states are increasingly refusing to fund the ROs they participate in, hampering ROs' operations and leaving them ever more dependent on an ever-smaller pool of donors.

There have been few new launches of major ROs since 2010. But the handful that have been established in the past decade have been deliberately 'un-institutionalized'—established in a way that deliberately eschews bureaucratic constraints in favor of more 'flexible' approaches which privilege voluntary agreements among member states.

Overall, in major centers of power around the world, support for deeply institutionalized ROs is at a low point. States which in decades past forcefully advocated the utility of ROs are increasingly pursuing their goals via alternative means. Below, I describe the current mindset of leaders in the United States, Africa, and China. But before turning to them, it is worth quickly considering the state of affairs in the European Union, which has long been a forceful advocate of regional integration. Even the EU's longstanding support for regionalism has been ebbing since the mid-2000s – not only have the EU's recent travails (the sovereign debt crisis, the immigration crisis, Brexit, growing populism, etc.) turned its attention inwards, but critics are increasingly pointing out the flaws in the EU's traditional support for ROs in other parts of the world. Some skeptics have questioned whether the development funds the EU spends on regional integration abroad are well-spent, in effect asking if the EU's money is accomplishing its intended goals (European Court of Auditors 2009). Others have paradoxically suggested that EU support for ROs in the Global South has been too effective, transforming the ROs into neocolonial outposts whose interests align better with those of Brussels than those of their own member states (Bachmann and Sidaway 2010; de Zamaróczy 2016; Söderbaum 2007; Staeger 2016). Lastly, the protracted negotiations over the Economic Partnership Agreements (EPAs) – the EU's most recent set of free-trade negotiations with regions in the Global South – have also taken their toll. Not only do activists see the EPAs as the clearest example of Europe using its overwhelming power disparity to ram a free-trade agenda down the throat of reluctant developing countries (Flint 2009; Girvan 2010; Hurt 2012; Meyn 2008), but the fact that many of the negotiations have dragged on for nearly two decades with still no clear end in sight has sapped energy across the board. It is notable that the European Commission has not issued a major white paper on EU support for regionalism since 2008, and full-throated defenses of regional integration are heard much less often these days in Brussels than in decades past. Accordingly, perhaps the single most significant source of support for highly institutionalized ROs worldwide may be having second thoughts.

## The View from Washington: Choosing between Exit, Voice, and Loyalty

The United States has never been as keen a supporter of regional integration as the EU. Instead, since the Second World War, the US has typically preferred to conduct its relations with other countries either on a bilateral basis, or via multilateral institutions with wide memberships. Indeed, for decades the US sustained the post-Second World War institutionalization of the global order by underwriting important instruments of global governance, such as the UN, the GATT/WTO, the IMF, the WB, and others. This broad support for international institutions was a key element of the 'post-war bipartisan consensus' that historians have argued was a hallmark of the US's late twentieth-century foreign policy (Busby and Monten 2008; Wright 2020). This bipartisan consensus came apart as the twenty-first century began, however, a victim of America's increasing political polarization. Strong partisan reactions to American unilateralism during the George W. Bush administration were an early sign, as was the growing skepticism about the desirability of globalization and free trade within segments of both the Republican and Democratic parties during the 2010s. Ultimately, the advent of the Trump Administration in 2017 made the writing on the wall clear: the United States could henceforth no longer be expected to support international institutions as a matter of course.

Upon taking office, President Trump loudly voiced his skepticism about international institutions as varied as the Intermediate Nuclear Forces (INF) Treaty and the Paris Climate Accords. Sperling and Webber (2019), building on earlier work by Hirschman (1970), have argued that the specific ways in which the Trump Administration approached a given international institution varied substantially. In some cases, the Trump Administration simply withdrew from the institution ('exit'). In other instances, the Trump Administration remained within the institution but stepped up criticism of it in an attempt to shift its inner workings in a direction seen as more favorable to the US ('voice'). In a third, much rarer set of cases, the Trump Administration concluded that the institution actually could advance American goals and continued to support the organization ('loyalty').

Sperling and Webber (2019, p. 515) propose that what usually determined which of these three tactics was adopted by the Trump Administration was the organization's degree of institutionalization:

> The greater the degree of institutionalisation in the foreign policy domain in question, (i) the more historically embedded is the US interest; (ii) the more plentiful are the opportunities for voice rather than exit; and (iii) the more open are the possibilities for compromise with allies. The US under Trump has thus found it easier to renounce commitments where institutionalisation is nascent (as in the Iran and Paris agreements and the aborted Trans-Pacific Partnership) than where it is well developed (as in the WTO, NAFTA, and the UN).

In other words, even for an avowedly 'America First' outfit like the Trump Administration, institutionalization seemed to matter. This held true with regional organizations as well. As was mentioned, although the US does not typically join many regional organizations, it is a member of some, and the Trump Administration handled them quite differently. In the case of the Trans-Pacific Partnership (TPP), a 12-nation free trade agreement negotiated by the Obama Administration, Trump clearly pursued 'exit', announcing America's withdrawal from the burgeoning bloc on his third day in office. In a memorandum announcing the decision, the White House stated plainly its intention to henceforth "deal directly with individual countries on a one-on-one (or bilateral) basis in negotiating future trade deals".

The TPP withdrawal also put NAFTA, America's most important trade agreement, directly in the crosshairs. As a presidential candidate, Trump had often described NAFTA as "the worst trade deal ever made", so it came as little surprise that on May 18, 2017 the US Trade Representative informed Congress of the Trump Administration's desire "to initiate negotiations with Canada and Mexico regarding modernization of NAFTA". Thereafter followed several rounds of negotiations between the three trading partners, with the Americans seeking to put in place measures that would lessen the US' trade deficit with the other two countries, while Mexico and especially Canada sought to maintain as much of NAFTA's existing structures as was politically feasible (see Marcoux 2019). In March 2018, as negotiations were ongoing, the Trump Administration imposed tariffs on Canadian and Mexican steel and aluminum imports, and hinted that further tariffs on automobiles and auto parts might be forthcoming. In retaliation, Canada and Mexico placed their own tariffs on US metals and a wide range of agricultural products.

But just when it seemed that the US was preparing to 'exit' its largest trade agreement, negotiations began bearing fruit. In August 2018, the American and Mexican delegations announced that they had resolved most of their outstanding issues and planned on signing a bilateral free-trade agreement (FTA) within 90 days; the door was left open for the Canadians to attach themselves to this agreement. A month later, the Canadians announced that they too had resolved their outstanding issues with the Americans, opening the way for what had begun as two distinct bilateral negotiations to be concluded with the tripartite signing of the United States-Mexico-Canada Agreement (USMCA) on November 30, 2018. Drama continued even after the signing of the accord – while national legislatures were in the process of ratifying it, President Trump announced in a May 2019 tweet that he was mulling imposing an across-the-board 5 percent tariff on all Mexican imports "until such time as illegal migrants coming through Mexico, and into our Country, STOP". However, this latest proposal was met with strong resistance within the Republican Party, with the Trade Representative, Treasury Secretary, and close Trump advisors all opposing the action. In the end, the proposal was quietly shelved in exchange for Mexico publicizing several border-security measures they had already been planning for several months. Not until ratification of USMCA was completed in all three countries in March 2020 did something resembling normality return to North American trade relations.

Overall then, in the case of NAFTA, the US threatened to unilaterally pull out of a regional organization, but then immediately entered into negotiations to create a successor organization modeled on previous agreements. This approach, lying somewhere between the 'exit' and 'voice' options discussed by Sperling and Webber, could perhaps be termed 'renegotiate'. Why did the Trump administration choose to exit the TPP outright while renegotiating NAFTA? Largely because of the greater degree of institutional constraints surrounding NAFTA, a well-established trading framework that had run for over 20 years, as opposed to the TPP, a treaty which had yet to enter into force.

Militarily, the most important regional organization for the United States is the North Atlantic Treaty Organization (NATO). It too came in for repeated criticism from President Trump, who on several occasions declared it 'obsolete'. Europeans and Americans alike worried that the core principle of NATO – Article 5, which holds that "an armed attack against one or more of [the Parties] in Europe or North America shall be considered an attack against them all" – was de facto being abandoned by the US.[2] Still, despite all its rhetoric, over the course of its four years in office the Trump Administration never made any moves to actually withdraw the US from NATO and instead pursued a 'voice' stance of criticizing NATO from within (Sperling and Webber 2019). Paradoxically, the criticism even led some observers to suggest that NATO was 'thriving' at the time, because "defenders of the alliance are coming out of the woodwork, especially in the US Congress", as well as the US military's senior leadership (Kupchan 2019). In the end, the institutional and normative ties that bind the alliance together were capable of withstanding pressures from the Trump presidency.

Perhaps the most interesting case study of American involvement with a regional organization during the Trump Administration occurred in the Organization of American States (OAS). There, the Trump Administration pursued a clear course of 'loyalty', happily working within a regional body that it deemed sympathetic to its goals. President Trump's appointee as Permanent Representative to the OAS, Carlos Trujillo, worked hand in hand with OAS Secretary General Luis Almagro in supporting right-wing governments and conservative presidential candidates across the region, while also keeping up the diplomatic pressure on America's perceived enemies, most notably Venezuela.[3] The OAS made several questionable decisions during this period, most notably in politicizing its electoral observer missions, including a premature condemnation that the left-wing president of Bolivia, Evo Morales, was attempting to rig the October 2019 presidential election. The OAS' declaration probably contributed to the Bolivian military stepping in to perform a

---

2 Emily Schultheis and Uri Friedman, "Germany Preps a Plan B for Trump's Foreign-Policy 'Zigzag'", *The Atlantic*, February 14, 2019; Steven Erlanger, "Macron Says NATO Is Experiencing 'Brain Death' Because of Trump", *New York Times*, November 7, 2019.

3 Laura Carlsen, "The Organization of American States Shouldn't Be Run by Regime Change Enthusiasts", *Foreign Policy in Focus*, January 23, 2019; Tracy Wilkinson and Patrick McDonnell, "Does Trump Support Democracy in Latin America? Critics Say It Depends Who's in Power", *Los Angeles Times*, January 4, 2020.

'soft coup' and Morales' forced resignation, despite evidence suggesting that Morales won a large plurality of the vote.[4]

Overall, the Trump years reinforced what the rest of the world already knew – that America prefers to deal with countries bilaterally, and engages with ROs reluctantly at best. Still, the degree to which ROs were already institutionalized at the time when Trump took office clearly shaped their eventual fates – less institutionalized ROs like the TPP were exited from, while better institutionalized ones like NAFTA and NATO were the sites of renegotiation and voice. While it is still early, we should broadly expect similar patterns of behavior from the Biden Administration.

## The View from Beijing: The Creation of Un-Institutionalized Regions

The most momentous regional initiative thus far in the twenty-first century is the Chinese-led Belt and Road Initiative (BRI), previously also referred to as 'One Belt One Road'. Begun in 2013, this epic project brings together some 70 countries to significantly upgrade the infrastructure linkages from China to Western Europe, with particular focus on Southeast Asia, West Asia, and East Africa. With over $200 million already spent, and a ceiling in the trillions of US dollars, the financial stakes are astronomical. This large-scale transnational project is clearly 'regional' in scope, but has not yet been widely analyzed by scholars specializing in regionalism (the exception is Mitchell 2021). This is perhaps because BRI looks very different from the regional integration of previous decades – China has chosen to make BRI very un-institutionalized, preferring to keep sole control over the entire enterprise instead of establishing fora which would allow other participants a voice.

BRI is sometimes presented as China's twenty-first century answer to the US' post-war Marshall Plan, but there are profound differences in their internal structures. The Marshall Plan was administered by the Economic Cooperation Administration (ECA), a stand-alone US government body, but one with a fully staffed office in each of the 16 participating European countries. Indeed, ECA employed more Europeans (about 800) than Americans (about 600) at its height.[5] This allowed for genuine shared oversight of the Marshall

---

4 Mark Weisbrot, "The Trump Administration Is Undercutting Democracy in Bolivia", *The Nation*, November 8, 2019; John Curiel and Jack R. Williams, "Bolivia Dismissed Its October Elections as Fraudulent. Our Research Found No Reason to Suspect Fraud", *Washington Post* Monkey Cage Blog, February 27, 2020; Laura Carlsen, "The Organization of American States Is Eroding Faith in Democracy", *Foreign Policy in Focus*, March 4, 2020.

5 Amy Garrett, "Helping Europe Help Itself: The Marshall Plan", *The Foreign Service Journal*, January/February 2018. See also the oral histories available at: https://adst.org/2015/05/the-marshall-plan-the-europeans-did-the-job-themselves/.

Plan between the US and its European partners. Oral histories of ECA confirm that Europeans played a major role in both setting its strategic priorities and managing its day-to-day operations, with some involved in the project going so far as to say "The other thing that people should know about the Marshall Plan was that the Europeans did the job themselves".

This contrasts with the current institutional make-up of BRI, which is dominated by China and organized exclusively on bilateral lines. The 'institutional core' of BRI is the 120+ memoranda of understanding individual states have signed with the Chinese government, each negotiated individually and often vastly different in terms and scope. Overseeing this messy patchwork is a handful of Chinese state officials, assisted by the Asian Infrastructure Investment Bank, the Export-Import Bank of China, and several other Chinese state-owned banks – but without any clear division of roles. So much remains uncertain about BRI that there is not even an official list of BRI's participating states!

Additionally, there are currently no mechanisms whereby BRI's partner states can regularly interact with China in a collective fashion. There is no multilateral forum for all the partners to belong to, except for occasional meetings that take place when, where, and how China chooses. There is no traditional-style permanent secretariat, and no plan to create one – probably because Chinese leaders worry that such a secretariat might turn into an independent voice.[6] Denied a forum in which they might exchange information among themselves and express their views internally, the leaders of unhappy BRI partner states (including top officials in Sri Lanka, Malaysia, the Maldives, Myanmar, and Montenegro) have instead recently begun speaking out to the international media to seek changes in the way BRI is operated.

BRI is the most noticeable example of the Chinese preference for un-institutionalized regions, but it is not the only one. Consider the case of China's recent intervention in South Asian regionalism. For decades, the main RO in South Asia was the South Asian Association for Regional Cooperation (SAARC), which was fairly institutionalized, with a small secretariat located in Kathmandu. SAARC, however, has long been hamstrung by the rivalry between India and Pakistan, two of its founding members, and has been

---

[6] While reluctant to establish a traditional-style permanent secretariat, in recent years China has sought technical assistance from the major multilateral financial institutions, including the World Bank. But, as the *New York Times* reported in April 2019, the Chinese have largely been rebuffed by existing IFIs, which are wary of the lack of transparency that surrounds BRI: Jane Perlez, "China Retools Vast Global Building Push Criticized as Bloated and Predatory", *New York Times*, April 25, 2019. For a more optimistic view on the possibility for cooperation between the World Bank and the new Chinese-run multilateral development banks, see Wang (2017).

effectively dead since India boycotted a scheduled heads of state summit in November 2016 (and pressured other SAARC members to pull out as well). This created an opportunity for China to present a new regional initiative in 2018: the First China-South Asia Cooperation Forum (CSACF).[7] This grouping took the existing SAARC membership (Afghanistan, Bangladesh, Bhutan, Maldives, India, Nepal, Pakistan and Sri Lanka), added Myanmar and Vietnam – and included China itself. China had quietly entertained the notion of becoming a full member of SAARC in the early 2010s, but had been limited to only observer status because of India's objections. Now China is seemingly back, and presenting itself as part of a potential successor regional initiative to SAARC – and one that would be almost completely un-institutionalized.

Similar Chinese efforts to push for looser and more flexible regional configurations can be observed in Southeast Asia,[8] Central Asia,[9] and elsewhere. As China continues to gain global influence, it will likely leave un-institutionalized ROs in its wake.

## Views from the African Continent: De-Institutionalizing Existing ROs

Although the African continent is too diverse to be encapsulated by a single viewpoint, there is emerging evidence that leaders in Africa and elsewhere in the Global South are also moving to de-institutionalize existing regional frameworks. Some of this resistance to deeper regional integration stems from the fact that the EU has been so heavily involved in promoting regional integration schemes on the African continent (as discussed above), but much of it also reflects a renewed homegrown skepticism about the value of regional integration.

Perhaps the preeminent regional organization in Africa is the African Union (AU), established in 2000 as an explicitly more institutionalized upgrade over its predecessor, the Organization of African Unity. Over the course of the 2000s, two core elements of the new AU architecture proved reasonably successful at helping to manage conflicts on the continent: the role of AU Chairperson, who served an important mediating role in conflicts such as in

---

7 Rekha Dixit, "China Launches New Forum to Extend Reach to South Asia", *The Week*, June 14, 2018; N. Sathiya Moorthy, "SAARC in Coma, China Throws Another Challenging Regional Initiative", *ORF Online*, July 10, 2018.

8 China, having declined to become a full member of the 1995 Mekong Agreement, now champions the environmentally focused but loosely institutionalized Lancang-Mekong Cooperative Framework (LMC). Sam Geall, "Why the Mekong Matters", *The Third Pole*, November 1, 2018.

9 Andrey Kortunov, "SCO: The Cornerstone Rejected by the Builders of a New Eurasia?", Russian International Affairs Council, 2018.

Burundi, Comoros, and Guinea, as well as the AU's Political and Security Council (PSC), which emerged as a way for African countries to authorize the use of force on the continent without having to rely upon external actors. The movement to further institutionalize the AU reached a crescendo in 2009, when the then AU Chairperson, Muammar Gaddafi of Libya, proposed upgrading the AU Commission into an AU Authority which would receive executive powers delegated by member states, similar to the EU model (Aggad and Zondi 2009). However, this AU Authority proposal was shot down in 2010, and Gaddafi's execution in 2011 marked the end of a high tide in favor of deepening the institutionalization of the AU.

Since then, a backlash has emerged. African countries have deadlocked on a number of important issues, significantly crippling the AU's overall effectiveness. In 2015, the PSC approved a peacekeeping force of 5,000 soldiers to be sent to Burundi, as the security situation there deteriorated following a controversial election, but its decision was overturned by the full AU General Assembly; having gotten burned, the PSC has since exhibited a newfound tentativeness in authorizing crisis interventions, to the dismay of external observers.[10] In 2016, the AU's membership dramatically failed to elect a new chairperson to head the AU Commission, with several member states boycotting the entire process, forcing the election to be postponed by a year. In 2020, member states eager to see the AU Commission further weakened proposed a broad set of budget and staffing cuts – despite the fact that, for 7 out of the past 12 years for which data is available, foreign donors have footed over half of the AU's budget.[11] Overall, hope is fading that the staff of the AU Commission in Addis Ababa will be able to provide effective and forceful leadership in the years to come.

Elsewhere in Africa, the regional economic communities (RECs) that are the building blocks of the broader AU and typically contain 5 to 15 members have fought their own battles over the degree to which they should be institutionalized. Scholars have written about the tendency of some African leaders to view the RECs less as a venue for collective problem-solving, and more as a forum for pursuing domestic legitimacy through the pageantry and statecraft the RECs embody. According to this 'regime-boosting regionalism' thesis, heads of state are happy to participate in regional bodies for easy photo opportunities and rarely resist a chance to announce new regional initiatives which will show up in newspapers (Söderbaum 2007; Herbst 2007). However,

---

[10] International Crisis Group, "Eight Priorities for the African Union in 2019", ICG Commentary Series, February 6, 2019.

[11] International Crisis Group, "Eight Priorities for the African Union in 2020", ICG Briefing No. 151, February 7, 2020. See also Engel (2020).

leaders draw the line at enacting painful domestic reforms which would further regional integration (for instance, by removing thorny non-tariff barriers to trade), and also tend to resist deeper institutionalization of their RECs, which might allow other power centers to emerge. (This is arguably the case of Africa's latest regional integration scheme, the African Continental Free Trade Area (AfCFTA), which envisions setting up a single FTA across the entire continent. While ratification of the agreement by the currently 54 signatories has moved forward surprisingly quickly, on-the-ground effects will likely take far longer to appear, if ever.)

Illustrative of the tussles over regional integration in African RECs is the saga of the Southern African Development Community (SADC) Tribunal (Hulse and van der Vleuten 2015). Originally called for in the 1992 Treaty establishing the SADC, member states long held off on establishing the Tribunal because of fears that it might imperil their sovereignty. Over the course of the 1990s, however, elite sentiment in the region somewhat shifted, as it was believed that having a regional court that could help settle international commercial and investor disputes might serve as a useful signal to the outside world that Southern Africa was open for business. When the Tribunal eventually began hearing cases in 2007, however, the Tribunal's justices interpreted vague language in the Founding Protocol as giving them jurisdiction over human rights issues in the region. This soon opened the door for private citizens to bring suit against their governments before the Tribunal, as when white Zimbabwean farmers sued their government, alleging inadequate compensation for the seizure of their farms and racial discrimination (*Mike Campbell v. the Republic of Zimbabwe*). Needless to say, this judicial activism did not sit well with the region's governments, who were suddenly confronted with a supranational body in their midst which seemed open to sticking its nose in highly sensitive policy areas and might potentially take them to task over human rights violations. In 2011, the leaders of the SADC countries got together and suspended the Tribunal indefinitely, before entirely disbanding it a year later. Similar battles have played out in other African RECs, as when the East African Court of Justice attempted to push that region's institutionalization forward.

Overall, deepening the institutionalization of African regional bodies remains a fraught matter, with an unclear path moving forward.

## Five Factors Contributing to the Contemporary Decline of Institutionalized Regionalism

I have been arguing that the nature of regional integration is undergoing a fundamental change in the twenty-first century: new ROs are increasingly being set up in an un-institutionalized way, while existing ROs are often being de-institutionalized. Five ongoing trends in global politics help explain this development.

The first major factor is changes in the global balance of power which favor states skeptical of institutionalizing ROs (such as China and Russia) at the expense of entities which have traditionally supported institutionalization (such as the EU and, to a lesser degree, the US). Increasingly, decisions about the degree of institutionalization in new and existing ROs may come down to the preferences of emerging 'middle powers' like Brazil, India, South Africa, and Nigeria, all of which have expressed past concerns about becoming 'entrapped' by their smaller neighbors. Accordingly, these middle powers tend to prize strategic flexibility and prefer keeping their options open, typically only joining lightly institutionalized, informal talk shops like the G-20 or 'the Quad' (which brings together the US, India, Japan, and Australia). Indeed, the BRICS alignment (which brings together Brazil, Russia, India, China, and South Africa) is itself a classic example of a very lightly institutionalized multilateral framework.

The second and perhaps most important factor is the rise of highly personalized foreign policies in many countries. Increasingly, individual heads of state around the world are insisting on conducting foreign relations themselves, instead of relying on their ministries of foreign affairs, or even on trusted lieutenants. This was not only the case of Donald Trump in the US (Goldgeier and Saunders 2018), but remains true of Xi Jinping in China, Narendra Modi in India, Vladimir Putin in Russia, Rodrigo Duterte in the Philippines, and many others. Despite clear limitations, there are likely several reasons for this phenomenon: national leaders increasingly seem to prize greater flexibility in reaching agreements, perhaps as a way of meeting populist demands; national leaders are responding to media incentives, which increasingly frame successful diplomacy as the result of personal rather than state-to-state interactions (Balmas and Sheafer 2013); national leaders are taking advantage of new communication technologies, most notably Twitter, that allow them to directly reach constituents without intermediaries; and national leaders seem less interested than in previous decades about whether or not their policies and reforms will outlive their time in office (which would be more likely if the policies were institutionalized). When national leaders themselves conduct their foreign policies, they are less likely to insist on institutionalizing regional initiatives, and may even actively distrust efforts to institutionalize.

Concurrent with the second factor is a third one: the end of parliamentary ratification as an important aspect of global politics. Legally speaking, international treaties are not considered binding until they are ratified by a certain number of their signatories. But the years it can take for legal ratification to occur in a large number of countries – each with their own ratification procedures and objections to the proposed treaty – no longer fits with contemporary realities of an ever-accelerating global political cycle. Haftel and Thompson (2013, p. 382) report that the average length of time it takes for a basic bilateral investment treaty to be ratified by both parties following the signing ceremony is 3.1 years – and provide many examples where mutual ratification took 5, 10, 15, or even 50 years. Accordingly, there has been a tendency by some national leaders to treat initialing agreements as the de facto start of new international agreements. Here, the precedent set by the US is significant: the US Senate has barely ratified any international treaties over the last three decades owing to a deep-seated aversion by the Republican Party to the very concept of international law. At the same time, however, American presidential administrations have continued to negotiate and sign major international treaty agreements, usually stating that their administrations would enforce the treaty provisions until and unless the treaty was formally voted down in the Senate. While the United States is particularly egregious in its disregard for the parliamentary ratification of treaties, the worldwide decrease in parliamentary ratification has several pernicious impacts on ROs and their institutionalization. For starters, it contributes to the increased power the executive branch is obtaining in many countries around the world. Given the aversion of many heads of state to international institutionalization, it places existing ROs at risk, without the protections they might be afforded by supportive national legislatures. Meanwhile, new ROs are created without the democratic and popular legitimacy that results from successful ratification in the legislatures of member states, crippling them from the get-go (Haftel and Thompson 2013, p. 356).

A fourth factor is a worldwide decline in popular support for regional integration. User data collected by Google Search, the world's largest search engine, confirms that ordinary citizens are less interested in regionalism than in years past. Worldwide, Google searches for the topic of regional integration (in several different languages) have been steadily declining since data collection began in 2004 (see Figure 3.2). The five months when users have searched the least for information on regionalism have all occurred since July 2017, and over the course of 2019 the average of searches for 'regional integration' was only about 18 percent of their all-time peak (back in May 2004). Insofar as there is continued popular curiosity about regional integration, it seems concentrated among citizens located in the Global South, particularly in the Caribbean and sub-Saharan Africa. The list of the top 25 territories whose citizens searched for regional integration, calculated on a per capita basis, does not contain a single country from the Global North. It is difficult to know if this observable decrease in popular support for regional integration is causing states to utilize ROs less, or is instead the consequence of lessened state interest in ROs – probably both simultaneously. What is clear, however, is that the significant amounts of popular support that undergirded many ROs during the first two waves of regionalism have ebbed a great deal since the early 2000s.

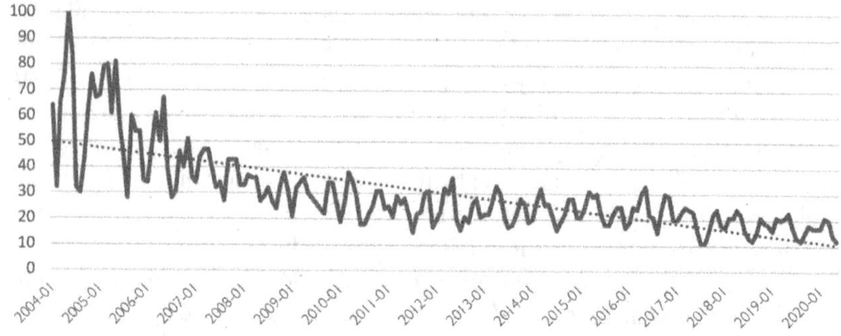


*Note:* The result of a Google Trends search for the topic 'regional integration', displaying the degree to which the topic was searched for across the world using Google every month since January 2004 (the earliest date for which data is available). The chart does not show absolute counts, but is instead normalized so that the month with the most searches – in this case May 2004 – is set to 100 and everything else is scaled in relation to that. The dotted line is a fitted linear trend line. The chart shows worldwide searches across a number of languages.

*Figure 3.2 Worldwide Google searches for the topic of regional integration, 2004–2020*

Lastly, the fifth factor is a decrease in the power of pro-trade business lobbies around the world following the erosion of the Washington Consensus and especially since the 2008 financial crisis. For decades, lobbying organizations representing the private sector – especially those representing multinational firms – played a quiet but steady role in encouraging the formalization of ROs and intergovernmental organization (IGOs). They did so because they believed that institutionalization would lead to clearer rules and greater stability, creating a political environment conducive to making safer long-term investments and business plans. For the most part, this belief has not changed, but their influence has diminished in recent years. Organizations such as the United States Chamber of Commerce or the Federation of Korean Industries in South Korea no longer command the same influence as they used to,[12] and

[12] For journalistic discussions of the decline in business lobby groups in various countries, see among others: Brody Mullins and Alex Leary, "Washington's Biggest Lobbyist, the US Chamber of Commerce, Gets Shut Out", *Wall Street Journal*, May 2, 2019; Christine Kim, "South Korea's Powerful Business Lobby Group Dealt Big Blow by Park Scandal", *Reuters*, December 14, 2016; Ruth Williams, "Are Australia's Business Lobby Groups Past Their Peak?", *Sydney Morning Herald*, December 15, 2017; Mori Kazuo, "How Corporate Japan Lost Its 'Voice': The Plight of Keidanren in the Post-Japan Inc. Era", translated from the original Japanese and posted on Nippon.com, March 10, 2014.

pro-trade business lobbies have struggled in particular to counter a global rising tide of populist nativism. Accordingly, there is currently less opposition to the de-institutionalization of regional and international organizations than there would have been in decades past.

## CONCLUSION: CALCULATING THE COSTS OF UN-INSTITUTIONALIZED REGIONALISM IN THE YEARS AHEAD

The waves of regionalism that marked the second half of the twentieth century depended upon and contributed to a liberal international order championed by the US. As the US retreats from its longtime engagement with global governance and international institutions, as the EU remains entangled with internal problems and struggles to project its influence around the world, and as China and other emerging powers that are skeptical of institutionalized regionalism increasingly take center stage in global politics, what is the likely future of regional integration?

In short, a world of looser, overlapping regional configurations which states will attempt to put on and off to suit their particular interests any given day. Intergovernmental compromise and trust-building, both of which take time and are facilitated by institutionalized ROs, will gradually ebb (perhaps hastened along by the consequences of the coronavirus pandemic). Instead, states will gamble upon the hope that if only they can find the right configuration – the perfect 'Coalition of the Willing' – then their national ambitions might be met. While there will be a few holdouts such as the European Commission, it is increasingly likely that in the coming decades most independent, permanent regional secretariats may slowly become 'zombies', to use Gray's (2018, p. 1) provocative phrase: "Their offices [will] stay open and some minimal activity [will] persist, but they [will] make few meaningful advances in cooperation".

IR scholars and practitioners alike will have to grapple with the diminished ability of countries to work peacefully and pragmatically towards resolving their disputes and accomplishing mutual goals. Ultimately, the end of institutionalized regionalism could even lead to an increased risk of interstate conflict, since there will be fewer meaningful ROs to act as the conflict mediators, knowledge transmitters, service providers, and moral compasses that we take for granted today.

## REFERENCES

Acharya, A. (2011) *Asian Regional Institutions and the Possibilities for Socializing the Behavior of States*. Manila: Asian Development Bank.

Aggad, F. and Zondi, S. (2009) Commission to Authority: Shifting the African Union Balance of Power. *Trade Negotiation Insights*, **8**(2), 1–2.

Agostinis, G. (2019) Regional Intergovernmental Organizations as Catalysts for Transnational Policy Diffusion: The Case of UNASUR Health. *JCMS: Journal of Common Market Studies*, **57**, 1111–1129.

Bachmann, V. and Sidaway, J. (2010) African Regional Integration and European Involvement: External Agents in the East African Community. *South African Geographical Journal*, **92**, 1–6.

Balmas, M. and Sheafer, T. (2013) Leaders First, Countries After: Mediated Political Personalization in the International Arena. Journal of Communication, **63**(3), 454–475.

Barnett, M. (1995) Partners in Peace? The UN, Regional Organizations, and Peace-Keeping. *Review of International Studies*, **21**, 411–433.

Barnett, M. and Finnemore, M. (2004) *Rules for the World: International Organizations in Global Politics*. Ithaca, NY: Cornell University Press.

Börzel, T. A. and van Hüllen, V. (2015) *Governance Transfer by Regional Organizations*. Basingstoke: Palgrave Macmillan.

Busby, J. and Monten, J. (2008) Without Heirs? Assessing the Decline of Establishment Internationalism in US Foreign Policy, *Perspectives on Politics*, **6**(3), 451–472.

Checkel, J. (2007) *International Institutions and Socialization in Europe*. Cambridge: Cambridge University Press.

Collins, S. D. (2010) Regional Trade Agreements and Democracy Promotion: Measuring the Influence of Democracy Requirements in Regional Trade Agreements. *Politics & Policy*, **38**, 737–764.

de Zamaróczy, N. (2016) Taking Orders from Brussels? External Actors and Regional Organizations in the Developing World. PhD dissertation, University of Southern California, Los Angeles.

Elgström, O., Bercovitch, J. and Skau, C. (2003) Regional Organisations and International Mediation: The Effectiveness of Insider Mediators. *African Journal on Conflict Resolution*, **3**, 11–27.

Engel, U. (2020) The Finances of the African Union. In Engel, U. and Mattheis, F. (eds), *The Finances of Regional Organisations in the Global South: Follow the Money*. London: Routledge, 19–34.

European Court of Auditors (2009) *Effectiveness of EDF Support for Regional Economic Integration in East Africa and West Africa*. Special Report No. 18. Luxembourg: Publications Office of the European Union.

Fawcett, L. (1995) Regionalism in Historical Perspective. In Fawcett, L. and Hurrell, A. (eds), *Regionalism in World Politics: Regional Organizations and International Order*. Oxford: Oxford University Press, 9–36.

Flint, A. (2009) The End of a “Special Relationship”? The New EU–ACP Economic Partnership Agreements. *Review of African Political Economy*, **36**(119), 79–92.

Gartner, S. (2011) Signs of Trouble: Regional Organization Mediation and Civil War Agreement Durability. *The Journal of Politics*, **73**, 380–390.

Girvan, N. (2010) Technification, Sweetification, Treatyfication: Politics of the Caribbean-EU Economic Partnership Agreement. *Interventions: International Journal of Postcolonial Studies*, **12**(1), 100–111.

Goldgeier, J. and Saunders, E. (2018) The Unconstrained Presidency: Checks and Balances Eroded Long Before Trump, *Foreign Affairs*, **97**(5), 144–156.

Gray, J. (2018) Life, Death, or Zombie? The Vitality of International Organizations. *International Studies Quarterly*, **62**, 1–13.

Haftel, Y. (2007) Designing for Peace: Regional Integration Arrangements, Institutional Variation, and Militarized Interstate Disputes. *International Organization*, **61**, 217–237.

Haftel, Y. (2010) Conflict, Regional Cooperation, and Foreign Capital: Indonesian Foreign Policy and the Formation of ASEAN. *Foreign Policy Analysis*, **6**, 87–106.

Haftel, Y. and Thompson, A. (2013) Delayed Ratification: The Domestic Fate of Bilateral Investment Treaties. *International Organization*, **67**(2), 355–387.

Hall, K. and Blake, B. (1977) The Caribbean Community: Administrative and Institutional Aspects. *JCMS: Journal of Common Market Studies*, **16**, 211–228.

Herbst, J. (2007) Crafting Regional Cooperation in Africa. In Acharya, A. and Johnston, A. I. (eds), *Crafting Cooperation: Regional International Institutions in Comparative Perspective*. Cambridge: Cambridge University Press, 129–144.

Hirschman, A. (1970) *Exit, Voice and Loyalty: Responses to Decline in Firms, Organizations, and States*. Cambridge, MA: Harvard University Press.

Hulse, M. and van der Vleuten, A. (2015) Agent Run Amuck: The SADC Tribunal and Governance Transfer Roll-back. In Börzel, T. A. and van Hüllen, V. (eds), *Governance Transfer by Regional Organizations*. Basingstoke: Palgrave Macmillan, 84–103.

Hurt, S. R. (2012) The EU–SADC Economic Partnership Agreement Negotiations: 'Locking In' the Neoliberal Development Model in Southern Africa? *Third World Quarterly*, **33**(3), 495–510.

Kupchan, C. (2019) NATO Is Thriving in Spite of Trump: Adversity Has Made the Alliance Stronger. *Foreign Affairs*, March.

Mansfield, E. and Milner, H. (eds) (1997) *The Political Economy of Regionalism*. New York: Columbia University Press.

Marcoux, J. M. (2019) The Renegotiation of NAFTA: The "Most Advanced" Free Trade Agreement? In Bungenberg, M., Krajewski, M., Tams, C., Terhechte, J. and Ziegler, A. (eds), *European Yearbook of International Economic Law 2019*. Cham: Springer, 257–284.

Meyn, M. (2008) Economic Partnership Agreements: A "Historic Step" Towards a "Partnership of Equals"? *Development Policy Review*, **26**, 515–528.

Mitchell, D. (2021) Making or Breaking Regions: China's Belt Road Initiative and the Meaning for Regional Dynamics. *Geopolitics*, **26**(5), 1400–1420.

Pevehouse, J. (2005) *Democracy from Above? Regional Organizations and Democratization*. New York: Cambridge University Press.

Ruggie, J. G. (1998) *Constructing the World Polity: Essays on International Institutionalization*. London: Routledge.

Söderbaum, F. (2007) African Regionalism and EU-African Interregionalism. In Telo, M. (ed.), *European Union and New Regionalism: Regional Actors and Global Governance in a Post-Hegemonic Era*. Aldershot: Ashgate, 185–202.

Sperling, J. and Webber, M. (2019) Trump's Foreign Policy and NATO: Exit and Voice. *Review of International Studies*, **45**(3), 511–526.

Staeger, U. (2016) Africa-EU Relations and Normative Power Europe: A Decolonial Pan-African Critique. *Journal of Common Market Studies*, **54**, 981–998.

von Borzyskowski, I. and Vabulas, F. (2019) Hello, Goodbye: When Do States Withdraw from International Organizations? *The Review of International Organizations*, **14**, 335–366.

Wang, H. (2017) New Multilateral Development Banks: Opportunities and Challenges for Global Governance. *Global Policy*, **8**(1), 113–118.

Williams, P. D. (2017) Global and Regional Peacekeepers: Trends, Opportunities, Risks and a Way Ahead. *Global Policy*, **8**, 124–129.
Wright, T. (2020) The Folly of Retrenchment: Why America Can't Withdraw from the World. *Foreign Affairs*, **99**(2), 10–18.

# 4. The European Union and United States in the era of shifting global order

**Karol Chwedczuk-Szulc**

## INTRODUCTION

The process of European integration is commonly described as being 'in crisis' and 'at the crossroads'. The scope of the EU's problems is so broad that there is a relative consensus among experts, observers, and some politicians that the time has come to take decisions about the future of the European project (see Bevelander and Wodak 2019; Wodak 2020; Eichengreen 2020; Rodrigues 2020; Council on Foreign Relations 2017; Bundesregierung 2018; Dinan 2014). The crisis is clearly visible also in the EU's external relations, namely in the threat of renewed Russian imperialism, migratory pressure, a continuing rise of China to a position of a global power, and the changing character of transatlantic relations. At the same time, the US faced a tumultuous time under Donald Trump's Administration, marked by a change of priorities in foreign policy and a re-evaluation of the US position in the international order. To a large extent, the challenges facing both the EU and the US are the same: large migration flows, Russia conducting a widely perceived hybrid war, the rising power of China, and damaged transatlantic relations.

Facing common challenges, the European Union and the United States, the pillars of NATO, should strengthen their alliance and intensify their multilateral effort. However, that is not occurring. It is a paradox that given the history of close transatlantic relations and the scope of common challenges facing both, the transatlantic ties between the US and the EU seem to be weakening. This chapter's objective is to contribute to solving this paradox. Therefore, the main research question is: why do the positions of the EU and the US seem to diverge, while sharing common interests and having the experience of long-lasting cooperation? I argue that the diverging policies of both actors are, in general, a by-product of globalization and internal dynamics within the EU and the US. Not in the sense that globalization disunites the EU and the US directly, although to some extent it could be explained by the parallel processes of globalization and regionalization (Cooper et al. 2008). In this perspective, globalization, enhancing regional integration of the EU, would reduce intra-European barriers, but would create new ones between the EU and the rest of the world, including the USA. In this chapter, however, I argue that globalization changes the internal dynamics of the EU and the USA which, combined with pre-existing rifts in both systems, results in divergence in transatlantic relations. The rise of populism (mostly right-wing), placing the responsibility for the problems of the EU/US on globalization, would be one example of this. In both polities, the electoral base for extreme, populist politicians comprises people who are on the lower (or missing out) end of rising inequalities, who perceive themselves as paying the price for globalization, instead of benefiting from it.

The second thesis focuses on endemic tendencies, the effect of long-term historical socio-political processes. I argue that decentralist/centrifugal tendencies have been a part of both compound polities since their very beginnings. What I mean by that is that there is a conflict between the federal-level power-centres and member states of the federation/supranational organization. Therefore, the conflict between the elites (centre) and member states (peripheries) is built into both compound polities. I explain this division in detail later. Nevertheless, these tendencies, in combination with negative effects of globalization, lead to the contestation of a widely understood neoliberal global order in international relations. To some extent this may explain why the positions of the US and the EU in a globalized world drifted apart so quickly under US President Trump. The political milieu of Donald Trump and some national governments/societies of member states of the EU (like Poland or Hungary) are challenging the process of integration (also in the US[1]), epitomized by the process of globalization, blaming it for the erosion of nation-state or individual sovereignty and the wealth of nations. I argue that the tensions between globalist and nativist tendencies are a part of the collective habitus in both the EU and the US. Current problems in transatlantic relations stem from the fact that nativist tendencies seem to be gaining a considerable amount of social support.

---

[1] I refer to centrifugal tendencies represented, for example, by so called New Federalism, claiming that federal government went too far in terms of regulating public life in the country (see Lee and Estes 1983).

## THEORETICAL APPROACH: NATIVISTS VS COSMOPOLITANS

Looking at the above-presented theses one can see that the overarching theme is the interplay between internal, endemic tendencies in both compound polities and the process of globalization. What is most intriguing is the paradox expressed at the beginning: the interests, challenges, and the global position of the USA and the EU should poise them for cooperation. Similar internal socio-political tendencies (the rise of populism – especially far right, political polarization), would suggest that there should be even deeper understanding between political elites. Nevertheless, the observable result is that of a divergence.

In the following sections I explore in more detail how long-lasting, domestic tendencies in the EU and the USA are interwoven into today's nativist–cosmopolitan divide and how they result in a transatlantic rift. By no means do I treat the nativist vs cosmopolitan division as a comprehensive description of the world order. These categories are rather Weberian ideal types, analytical categories, within which I place clashing visions of globalization and transatlantic relations. I apply these ideal types as configurations, the way Patrick Thaddeus Jackson describes ideal types (Jackson 2011, p. 114). For the sake of this chapter, I conceptualize 'cosmopolitan' as those who perceive globalization and stronger transatlantic ties as generally desirable. 'Nativists' on the other hand describe those who are disappointed with the effects of globalization (on many levels) and feel that only national or regional polities can guarantee their interests and security.

In this section, I sketch the relevant effects of globalization, understood as a global socio-economic system based on neoliberal rules (Peters 2018). The financial crisis of 2008 made it apparent that the current economic system leads to advancing discrepancies and growing inequalities. As much as the distinction between 'winners and losers' of globalization is not an accurate description of social classes, it does point at one of the most important tendencies of the system: the growing distance between the poorest and the richest. What became a new feature of the last crisis is that the class of the poorest expanded and become more relative. Elections in the US and in most countries of the EU have shown that the electoral base of right-wing populists has broadened and embraced the lower-middle class and middle class. They are not necessarily people who suffered economically in absolute terms, but their situation did not improve in recent years. It generated an impression of shrinking opportunities and the feeling of being left out (OECD 2019).

The relative impoverishment and lack of understanding of the global processes and the reasons for economic crises have left even bigger groups within the societies alienated from public life. It brought a collective feeling of being deprived of influence on public matters and in people's private lives (mostly due to un/underemployment, OECD iLibrary 2019, p. 4). The austerity measures breached the fragile, as it appeared, legitimacy of political systems. It seems especially true in case of the European Union, where the output ('for the people') legitimacy was and still is exercised, whereas in the US input ('by the people') legitimacy is dominant. Irrespective of the modes of legitimacy, the hit was taken by every level of integration, whether regional (European or North American) or global. In the EU, societies started to undermine the process of European integration as illegitimate, burdened with the flaw of democratic deficit.[2] Trust in the EU's institutions remains significantly lower than in national governments of parliaments (Eurobarometer, spring 2018). In the US, protests against global integration took a course towards the tradition of American isolationism, voiced by Donald Trump, aimed against global trade agreements such as the Trans-Pacific Partnership (TPP) or the regional North American Trade Agreement (NAFTA). Trump's moves to impose tariffs on China, and other partners (including the EU) were to satisfy his electoral base. The same rationale lies behind strong anti-migration regulations in the EU and the US.

This dynamic leads to the growing support for right-wing populists. Nominally, this is not a new phenomenon – populism is as old as democracy. What may be new is the form of the populism: xenophobic, hostile towards integration and internationalization, based on a dyadic division of 'us vs them'. Us, 'the (real) folks', and them, 'the elites', hidden behind international institutions, agreements, and procedures that no one understands, operating without democratic oversight. Modern populism aims at empowerment of previously, objectively or subjectively, disenfranchised (Rozwarski 2015), and those newly left out – the middle class. This imagined nativism of 'the folks' (see Anderson 2016) is much more comprehensible, because it is usually anchored in nations, another well-established imagined community. Nationalism enabled modern representative democracy – therefore nation-states – to seem like an essential community for practising democracy. Globalization and regionalization led towards more complicated systems like the European Union, or an abstract global community. International institutions started to erode traditional (national, tribal) loyalties and legitimacies. Following the logic of the functionalist theory of integration (Mitrany 1993, pp. 135–137), it was accepted as long as goods and services were effectively delivered to the people. But market slumps and austerity measures provoked the retreat from

---

2 Growing numbers of Eurosceptic European Parliament members are evidence of this.

output (for the people) towards input (by the people) legitimacy. International or supranational institutions, which according to functionalism, were supposed to attract the loyalty of citizens by fulfilling their needs, did not manage to earn input legitimacy. There are two reasons for this. First, it is due to the characteristic of the global economic system, plagued with recurrent crises, undermining social trust in international institutions. Second, input legitimacy seems to be much stronger, as it is based, again, on the strength of the imagined community. Therefore, in times of crisis, people wend their way back towards the communities they already know and are emotionally attached to – in this case, nations, or religions.

Populists exploit the above-described differences and turn them into an irreconcilable clash of orders: nativist and cosmopolitan. Naturally, this serves as a motivational mechanism for voters, breaking the possibility of coexistence of the two orders, leading to polarization. Populists argue that they bring back agency to the people, who are not fit (educated enough, rich enough, open-minded enough) to benefit from globalization. Mostly by telling them they do not have to: it is enough to frame the underprivileged situation of nativists in terms of the planned policies of cosmopolitan elites. The easy solution is not to let cosmopolitans intimidate 'real people' with epithets like 'xenophobes, racists, primitives', etc. These cleavages were convincingly and empirically scrutinized by Pieter De Wilde, Ruud Koopmans, Wolfgang Merkel, Oliver Strijbis, and Michael Zürn (2019) in their book *The Struggle Over Borders: Cosmopolitanism and Communitarianism*. They argue that the cosmopolitans and communitarians are the new level of political conflict, produced by the alignment of pre-globalization, internal social conflicts (e.g. on secularization in Turkey) and the new global divide, the latter focusing on the accessibility to global, deterritorialized benefits of the global economy. What is relevant to my chapter, is that De Wilde et al. prove that globalization enhances, to some extent, internal conflicts and multiplies them. The effect is an even stronger clash between cosmopolitans and communitarians/nativists. I argue that this is also the case of the EU and USA and ultimately, drives the divergence in transatlantic relations. I use the concept of cosmopolitans, in the juxtaposition of nativists to cosmopolitans, after the authors of *The Struggle Over Borders*.

## HISTORICAL RIFTS OF COMPOUND POLITIES

The divisions described above are visible on a global scale, afflicting every state, every international actor. Global divergencies and inequalities do not function in a vacuum, they occur in political systems, with certain rifts already existing, like the cited conflict over secularization in Turkey. It seems that currently in the EU and the US, global inequalities are aligned with internal pre-existing rifts. In this section I explore and describe some of the most far-reaching divides in the European Union and the United States.

The aim is to prepare a basis for the analysis of the contemporary, aligning interests of transatlantic partners. I wish to show how the cleavages, brought by globalization, enhance pre-existing domestic rifts, and how they negatively play out on EU–US relations.

## Federalists vs Confederalists – Centrifugal Tendencies

The tendencies that I name federal and confederal were present in the EU and the US from the very beginning. As I argue, they were to a large extent responsible for the major crises in both polities (civil war/current crises in the EU), and they are still visible today. In the United States, at the very beginning they took the form of a federalist/anti-federalist dispute. This dispute was the result of poor performance of the US under the Articles of Confederation, especially in the field of economy. The federal government was above all others obliged to guard the sovereignty and independence of the states but could not even levy taxes to repay the debts arising from the Revolutionary War. Moreover, it had no policing forces and no army to effectively implement its decisions, or to defend the states from external or internal threats (rebellions, colonial powers, native Americans, etc.). Nevertheless, as integration advanced under the United States Constitution, the conflict between federalists and confederalists evolved, but did not cease. The division between Northerners living under a commodified, industrializing market economy and Southern farmers and planters led to a strict class-based society, with the extensive use of slavery, and fit mostly into the dividing lines between unionists and proponents of states' rights. Despite the cycles of centralization and decentralization fuelled by the Supreme Court decisions, the union was becoming more integrated. In the end, the failure of the Nullification Doctrine made the Southern states try more decisive actions, namely secession.

Federalists and confederalists in the EU are divided into groups, often referred as federalists/supranationalists vs intergovernmentalists. The essence of the dispute is analogous to the US. Federalists are proponents of stronger integration and transfer of power to the European institutions (expanding majority voting, deeper integrated Eurozone, common army, common fiscal policy, etc.), while intergovernmentalists would like to see the EU as the Europe of Homelands, where the member states retain full control over the process of European integration. The rationale behind progressing federalization in the EU is like the one in the US: economic effectiveness and security of the polity. This division can also be observed right now in the EU and fits more or less a socio-economic/geographic cleavage: well-developed, services-based economy of the western and northern EU and less advanced, more industry- and agriculture-based eastern and southern member states of the EU.

As in the US, the EU has adopted a *de facto* constitution called the Lisbon Treaty, to overcome the institutional shortcomings. And as in the US, this move produced a backlash of European anti-federalists – one can observe attempts to 'nullify' the decisions of the European institutions on the national level. Finally, as in the US, the Court of Justice is viewed as exemplifying "creeping federalism" in the EU, following mostly the rule of *in dubio, pro integration* ('in case of doubt, the principle of integration is to be preferred') in its decisions (Bobek 2014, p. 19).

**Belief in Own Exceptionalism**

To some extent, both polities, their leaders, and societies, are convinced that they are special, like no other before – they see themselves as exceptional. This conviction, about own exceptionalism, stems from the fact that both the US and the EU are entities *sui generis*. They created categories of compound polities, where they were (are) the only examples. It also induced the belief, that because they are something new, the political architecture they build is unique and can bring change to the world (Della Sala 2010, p. 7).

*Sui generis* status is a facilitator of exceptionalism, but for both polities the values they adhere to are the main source of exceptionalist self-identification. Personal and collective freedom, democracy, open-market economy, rule of law, equality – these are the values that Americans and Europeans nominally follow. Even though in the US, the concept of American exceptionalism was early connected with the religious fervour (the concept of 'City upon a Hill'), both polities stress their exceptionality: as Empire of Liberty (Thomas Jefferson) or 'normative power' in case of the EU. Both concepts, and the concept of exceptionalism in general are connected with 'power', *ergo* influence. They also endorse inseparable elements of expansionism (sometimes even messianism), directed at exercising influence on the rest of the world. In case of the US, this is expressed in the doctrine of Manifest Destiny – the nineteenth-century conviction that Americans must expand in order to spread their benign values to all people.[3] In case of the EU, it is explicitly stated in its security strategy that the EU's aim is to promote and expand the zone of

---

[3] This explanation of American expansionism can be found also in modern US policy. One example is the justification of the American invasion of Iraq, when President George W. Bush stated that it was a US obligation to spread democracy. See 'CNN.Com – Bush Pledges to Spread Democracy', 20 January 2005. 2018 edition. http://edition.cnn.com/2005/ALLPOLITICS/01/20/bush.speech/.

stability, freedom, democracy, and wealth among neighbours of the EU and globally (European Union 2017).

The most important element here is the internal dynamic of these compound polities vis-à-vis the myth of exceptionalism. In both cases it has been used as a tool for forging unity between otherwise very different states. Exceptionalism is one of the founding myths for these polities (Tonra 2011; Hodgson 2011).

## Process of Identity Creation

The process of American identity creation and European identity creation share one very important feature, despite the fact that, as in the case of institutionalization, the identity creation in the US was a bottom-process and in the EU, it started rather as a result of top-down design. To understand this feature, one must bear in mind that the European identity, understood more broadly than just the identity of EU citizens, is a much older, long-lasting and patchwork process. Some of the most important elements that influenced the sense of Europeanness are the legacies of ancient Greece, the Roman Empire, the Catholic Church and the eighteenth-century Enlightenment. And just as the European identity is grounded in a long process preceding the creation of the EU, so the process of American identity formation began long before the establishment of the US as a state/national polity. Nevertheless, my units of comparison here are clearly defined polities: a state, the United States of America, and a supranational organization, the European Union. Therefore, I focus on the identities existing within these polities, taking into account the *longue durée* of these political organisms.

One very important difference between Americanness and Europeanness is that the former is already a shaped identity, whereas the status of latter is still contested (Zimmermann and Dür 2012).[4] Both identities are multilevel and nested, consisting of the central (union) level and member states. These levels of identity are, to great extent, not exclusive – one can be a Californian and an American, a German and European at the same time. Both identities can be described as a 'patchwork' identity, created out of many elements (Mendez and Bachtler 2018). On the other hand, the concepts of central identities are officially defined differently on each side of the Atlantic. The US motto is: *E pluribus, unum*, out of many, one. The EU's motto is *In varietate concordia* – the official translation is 'united in diversity', but I think the essence of the motto is better described as 'harmony in diversity'. The difference between these mottos conveys the difference between both polities quite well.

---

4 This difference is potentially beneficial for the comparison because the American case can serve as a possible scenario for European identity development.

American identity is more solidified, established and more unitarian. Out of many elements, we come as one – the emphasis is put more on unity. In contrast, in the EU the emphasis is on diversity – we retain our differences but are harmonious.

The question of identity is strongly connected with the question of legitimacy. Legitimacy, or rather lack of it, is one of the most often noted problems of the EU. The legitimacy of the EU seems to be conditional and depends on the material well-being of the citizens. The better the economic situation, the more support for the EU among citizens. This is because the EU has embraced an output approach to legitimacy (Schmidt 2012). It means that leaders are governing for the good of the people and in this situation, if they are effective, they are legitimized. This model of legitimacy comes directly from the elitist, top-down design of the EU. It evolved over time (through the slowly developing position of the European Parliament), but still maintains its original traits. In the US the dominant type of legitimacy is 'by the people'. Here citizens are responsible for the process of governing, are greatly involved in the process of decision-making and do not condition their support for the whole system only on the positive outcomes of leaders' rules. The effects of the for-the-people and by-the-people approach to governing, in terms of legitimacy, is that the latter proves to be more stable. A polity with this approach seems to be more resilient, as the citizens remain loyal and engaged not only through thick, but also through thin.

## Conflict between Inclusive and Extractive Political Institutions

The division between inclusive/open access and extractive/limited access institutions and orders is another dimension of the diverging tendencies in both compound polities. It goes in general along the division between federalists and confederalists. Both concepts deal with the problems of the societies (nations) on the path to development, a topic that Acemoglu and Robinson (2012) focus on in their book *Why Nations Fail*.

In this conceptual framework, the institutions or orders can be divided into inclusive and open access on one hand, and extractive and limited on the other. In short, inclusive institutions are social regimes where numerous people are involved in the process of governing and can influence the process and benefit from them. Extractive institutions are based on the exploitation of many by few and mobility up the social ladder is very hard (Acemoglu and Robinson 2012, p. 316). Open access orders guarantee the access to governing by the effectiveness of law, safeguarded by state monopoly of violence (nested in the law). Limited access orders are controlled by the stronger: their dominance is safeguarded by the use of violence and the law is subservient to the interests of the stronger (North et al. 2007, pp. 2–3).

I assign extractive/limited access institutions to the antebellum South in the US, and to eastern/southern members of the EU. I think this generalization is mostly justified, but it is still a generalization. Surely, it is easy to produce clear evidence that the Southern US was extractive and with limited access for most of its society, not only enslaved African Americans, but also masses of impoverished white males (not to mention women and Native Americans). The system was elitist and beneficial for few. The same description fits the reality of so called 'new members' of the EU (10 + 2 [Bulgaria and Romania] +1 [Croatia]), with the obvious exclusion of slavery.[5] Social mobility and respect for the rule of law is still much more problematic in the east of the EU than in the west – authoritarian tendencies in Hungary, Poland, and Romania being lately the most apparent examples. Despite these great divisions, it is important to remember that extractive and limited access institutions are visible not only in vertical perspective, but also in the horizontal case. International financial markets and transnational corporations are just one of the examples one can think of, building on Acemoglu and Robinson's concept (Easterly and Levine 2012). The effects of exclusion and limited access in this case can be easily traced also in the west and liberal, blue states of the US, not only in the US south and the EU's east.

Both theories assume that, when these two orders meet within one polity, frictions appear. These frictions appeared and evolved into conflict in both the nineteenth-century US and the modern EU. As North et al. (2007) describe, there are conditions under which institutions and orders can transform, from limited access to open access. And even though the cleavage still holds in the US (even today) and the EU, the transition is also visible. The point is, that this process is not continuous and uninterrupted. Recent political conflicts within the EU, and the history of postbellum US (until today) shows the inclusive/open orders conflict with extractive/limited orders. While clashing within the EU and the US, they also provoke disturbances externally, in transatlantic relations.

## Divergence/Convergence Protocol

In this section I describe some of the most important issues in transatlantic relations that, in my opinion, have tangible effects on the shape of transatlantic relations today. These issues are shared values and political systems, migra-

---

[5] Although one could argue that serfdom, for example in some parts of Poland, was comparable to slavery. It even ended formally about the same time as slavery in the US, by the decree of the Russian Tsar (1867). While serfdom did not exist at the time when European integration started, nevertheless the consequences of serfdom can be identified even today.

tion, relations with Russia and China, and terrorism. All these issues fall into a category of broadly understood security, which emphasizes their importance for both partners. This list is selective and focuses on issues that I perceive as connecting both sides of the Atlantic. In the analysis, I am not looking at a declarative approach to these issues, but rather at recent facts on the ground. Current affairs are analysed from the perspective of long-lasting internal processes and mechanisms in both polities. Therefore, the analytical framework is created, where current divergences are explained by the complex interplay of the cleavages created by globalization and the pre-existing internal rifts.

**Values and political systems and institutions**

The EU and the US jointly are often referred to as the biggest space of freedom, liberal democracy, and the rule of law (see Garton Ash 2005), pointing at the shared values and the political systems resulting from the values. Obviously, the catalogue of values corresponds to both polities, but the way in which these values are understood, operationalized and which dispositions stem from them, differs. It does not change the fact that transatlantic partners share the same cultural roots, which is clear, given the common history and shared (and conflicting) Judeo-Christian and Enlightenment axio-normative systems. The commonalities and differences within the West are nicely encapsulated by the phrase that Americans are from Mars, and Europeans from Venus (Kagan 2003). Sharing the same roots and system of values, they differ in expressing them.

In terms of political systems and institutions both polities also bear resemblance to each other. Not only the beginnings of modern European integration are marked by American influence (the immediate post-war period), but the whole process of institutionalization is quite similar. Both are (were) entities *sui generis*, a federalizing polity, trying to bring separate political units together. Therefore confederal/federal tendencies are visible. The effect is that in both cases, the predominant internal dynamic of the systems is defined by the conflict between the centre (federal government, European institutions) and the elements constituting the compound polity (member states). Institutions represent this tension in their hybridity, representing the federal level (House of Representatives, presidential administration/European Parliament, European Commission) and the level of member states (Senate/ The European Council, the Council of European Union).

All the above-mentioned similarities do not cancel existing differences, in both shared values and political systems of compound polities (Stevens-Finlayson 2019). The differences on the scope of public governance, use of force in international relations, death penalty, legal systems (common law vs civil law), social policy, range of human rights etc. always threatened transatlantic unity and manifested themselves sometimes in political realm (e.g. France withdrawing from NATO military command, conflict over invasion of Iraq 2003). These pre-existing differences, however, are empowered right now by the clash of cosmopolitans and nativists. Weakening of institutionalized rule of law and hostility towards others are not helping to maintain strong transatlantic relations. Centrifugal tendencies are even stronger, making member states lock into their own microcosm. It means also growing distrust towards central governing institutions and juxtaposition of states' interests and federal interests. It means often democratic backsliding, rejection of the rule of law, political corruption, and limiting human rights. Under Donald Trump, these centrifugal tendencies ascended to the federal level, causing conflicts with the EU, where such a stance is still a problem in a minority of member states (particularly Poland and Hungary).

Populism has gained ground on both sides of the Atlantic and is turning the masses against the elites and the transatlantic cooperation is seen as an emanation of this elitist project called globalization. Moreover, confidence in exceptionalism feeds populism, making it more isolationist. We can observe in both polities that values and political systems have become out of sync more within the last few years.

## Migration

Looking at some of the declarations of the politicians on both sides of the Atlantic (like Donald Trump's statement on German immigration – see Oltermann et al. 2018), one could claim that the interests of the EU and the US are opposed in this aspect. Juxtaposing Trump's statements with the security strategy of the EU, it seems that the US is unwelcoming to migrants, whereas the EU is a benign polity, ready to help people in need (see European Union 2017, pp. 10, 11, 17, 24). This picture obviously does not correspond with the world of real politics pursued on both side of the Atlantic. First, historically both the EU and the US benefited from migration greatly, to the extent that one can even assert that migration is a part of American and European identity[6] (especially in the case of the former – see Kennedy 2008). Second, in both cases we currently observe politicians assuming much more assertive positions towards migration. It was not only Donald Trump who has used migration to fuel fear-based management. Viktor Orbán in Hungary and Jarosław Kaczyński in Poland have both used this instrument, generating a considerable rise in public support and electoral wins (Bayer 2019). In effect, the EU and the US have both adopted policy aimed at limiting the number of immigrants and

[6] In the text, the term 'European' refers to the EU, therefore by writing 'Europeans' I mean the citizens of the European Union.

prioritizing security of external borders (Schain 2018).[7] It seems that these policies are mostly successful: migrants' inflow is lower indeed (Human Rights Watch 2019; Anderson 2019) and support for these politicians is considerable.

To sum up, the interest of the EU and the US seems to align on migration. Both rely on migrant labour, but due to anti-immigrant sentiment within societies, they introduce policies to limit and control migration. Nevertheless, the global cosmopolitan/nativist divide interacts with the internal rifts between inclusive and extractive orders of polities and their difference between bottom-up (the US) and top-bottom (the EU) identity building. The US, being much less prone to use social policy to manage inequalities than the EU, seems to operate with more extractive political institutions than the EU (this is not to say that the EU is a perfectly inclusive system). Moreover, in the US, the dominant mode of legitimacy is 'by the people'. Those who are not 'the people' therefore (mostly migrants) are to an extent excluded from the system. EU's 'for the people' seems to accommodate migrants better, as the main aim is to deliver public goods to all the citizens to maintain social stability. The results are diverging migrant policies, with converging interests (Brady 2018).

**Relations with Russia and China**

In the case of relations with Russia, the interests of the EU and the US seem to be in sync. Russia's invasion of Ukraine, its intervention in Syria (and weaponization of migration, by strengthening the migratory pressure, mostly on the EU), weaponization of energy resources trade (Blank 2017), support for right-wing extremism in the West and meddling with Western electoral processes – all these elements of Russian activity abroad go against the national interests of United States and the interests of the European Union. Consequently, the countermeasures to Russian threat should bring partners even closer: stabilizing the region of Middle East, Maghreb, and sub-Saharan Africa; cooperation in the field of cyber-security and intelligence to prevent attacks directed from Moscow; delivery of fossil fuels from the US to the EU (mainly LNG) to diversify supply for the EU vis-à-vis Russian monopoly in this respect; closing ranks, mostly within NATO, against Russia's challenge especially in the eastern region of Europe. The Joint Comprehensive Plan of Action to prevent Iran from acquiring nuclear weapons is a part of the strategic goals in these countermeasures, as it would help to stabilize the Middle East. It was a first step in the process of reintegrating Iran into the international com-

7 The EU seems to do it in a milder form and with the use of a gentler narrative. This may be mainly due to the fact, that the EU decision-making process has many more veto players, and the very strong anti-migrant, even racist, narrative of politicians like Orbán or Kaczyński is sublimated.

munity, and possibly a tool to limit Russian influence in the region – a chance that was lost (Alterman 2019; Serhan 2019), but may be recovered under Biden's Administration. All the above elements constitute as yet unrealized potential of cooperation between the EU and the US.

Donald Trump argued that China was the main target of new tariffs, and the European Union is also subject to these (Noack 2019). Still, Chinese trade policy, with tools like dumping and artificially sustained low value of the yen boosting Chinese exports, hit the EU and US simultaneously (Agence France-Presse 2018). Both transatlantic partners have undertaken actions against Chinese policies for many years now, but separately. It is truly surprising why on this issue, where the EU and the US share the same stance (e.g., vis-à-vis Chinese dumping prices on aluminium or steel), they do not cooperate, failing to reach their goals. It is obvious that the combined economic potential of the US and the EU could nudge the Chinese government to make their trade policies more market oriented.

The damage to EU–US relations in regard to their approach to Russia and China seems to have outlasted Trump's presidency. Joe Biden inherited the effort to finish Nord Stream 2 and a Comprehensive Agreement on Investment (CAI), which the EU signed just three weeks before Biden's inauguration. These conundrums may be mostly attributed to the nativist wave, especially in the US, where Donald Trump skilfully used anti-globalist sentiment to attack its most evident form – global trade. According to the nativist perception, global trade is unfair (Powers et al.2021), therefor e trade wars with China, the EU or anyone else, are justified. Moreover, multilateralism is just a globalist fantasy, hence, the deal-making approach of Donald Trump is an effective way to go. Coincidentally, the same perspective on international relations – bilateral deal-making – is shared by Russian decision-makers (Herbut and Chwedczuk-Szulc 2018). Combining these tendencies with the self-belief in exceptionalism of the EU and the US, the effect is a divergency in international policy making.

## Terrorism

It is quite apparent that the EU and the US share interests in the aspect of combating international terrorism. In 2001, George W. Bush's Global War on Terror brought US and European states together, joined briefly even by Russia and China. International terrorism is a well-recognized threat to citizens and sovereign states all around the world and encourages their cooperation. Unlike Russia or China, the EU and the US mostly share the outlook on international terrorism and domestic far-right terrorism and its sources, and therefore it has been a platform of transatlantic cooperation for many years, especially within the intelligence communities. To some extent this cooperation is a victim of the recent political climate, without any tangible reasons for discrepancy in this respect. Which does not mean, of course, we should ignore differences in tool selection, for example the use of torture.

In the case of terrorism, it is easily connected to nativists' negative perception of the cosmopolitan project of a globalized world with open borders as naïve. Open borders are leading to migration and in effect, the clash of irreconcilable cultures. This global divide overlaps with the rift of inclusive versus exclusive orders. In the US, terrorism is seen rather as an enemy that can be destroyed; in the EU, rather as an effect of polarization and radicalization (Bendiek 2011). Therefore, the major aim in the EU is to combat radicalization, as a source of terrorism. Moreover, the EU is quicker to recognize that extreme-right terrorism is overtaking Islamist terrorism as a main terrorist threat.

## CONCLUSION

The US and the EU are not structurally divergent. They are structurally different. At the same time, in many aspects they are complementary to one another, strengthened additionally by the global division of labour. The complementarity works not only in economy, but also in policy. In terms of economy both the EU and US represent not only a similar level of development, but the structure of trade proves that the division of labour does function well between them (Smith and Sloat 2018). In turn, politically the complementarity is well described by the phrase used earlier: Americans are from Mars and Europeans from Venus.[8] It means that in the global order Americans tend to act and perceive themselves as enforcers and Europeans as rebuilders, providers of public goods – hard power and soft power.

Therefore, as I argued in the chapter, the cleavages between transatlantic partners do not come so much from diverging interests, but rather from the internal rifts in both compound polities. These rifts are used by populists to promote a domestic agenda, sacrificing international relations and interests. This is a tendency observed in the policy of many politicians with authoritarian leanings (Putin, Kaczyński, Orbán, Trump, Erdoğan, etc.). Hence, as argued in this chapter, globalization and the inequalities stemming from it, strengthen internal rifts and damage transatlantic relations. On the one hand globalization strengthens the convergence of states' interests, but on the other hand it empowers internal cleavages, evoking anti-globalist, disintegrationist, and isolationist forces.

---

[8] However, in this case I think the Greek version of the name, Aphrodite, would be more appropriate, as the 'European way' seems to take more from the political culture of ancient Greece, while American culture takes more from ancient Rome.

The internal rifts are an effect of the *longue durée*; they were shaped over a long period of time and constitute a collective experience. The elements of it are, as I presented above: federalists vs confederalists, of identity creation and conflict between inclusive and extractive political institutions. By no means do I reify the dispositions stemming from it. They are obviously dynamic concepts and change over time. Nevertheless, they are still relatively stable and do not change rapidly. That is why the influence of these dispositions on politics in the EU and the US – and therefore on transatlantic relations also – is and will remain significant.

Current trends carry the potential for long-term changes, possibly redefining how Americans and Europeans perceive their interests.[9] This may be especially true in the case of the EU, as it is less integrated than the US. The process of European identity creation is taking placing in an era of rising identitarian movements, so sharp changes in the political climate are plausible. The question remains open, whether the new administration of Joe Biden in Washington and decision-makers in Brussels and the member states will be able to reconcile the global cosmopolitan/nativist divide. For now, it seems that Joe Biden aims at mitigating the conflict instead of using hyper-polarization and conflict between cosmopolitans and nativists, for the purpose of political power games. Many decision-makers in the EU understand the need for this kind of mitigation as well. Nevertheless, Americans were the first to allow the wave of populist nativism to dominate the public sphere of the US, thus disrupting the transatlantic status quo. Now most eyes are on the US. It does not mean that the EU has nothing to do in this respect. Populists, mainly in Poland, Hungary, and lately in Slovenia, must be contained. This is a *sine qua non* for a successful renaissance in EU–US relations.

## REFERENCES

Acemoglu, D. and Robinson, J. A. (2012) *Why Nations Fail*. New York: Crown Publishing Group.

Agence France-Presse (2018) EU Caught in Trade War Crossfire as China Reaches Out for Help against US. *South China Morning Post*. https://www.scmp.com/news/world/europe/article/2140674/eu-feels-heat-china-us-trade-row.

Alterman, J. (2019) Escalating U.S.-Iran Tensions. Center for Strategic and International Studies. https://www.csis.org/analysis/escalating-us-iran-tensions.

[9] One potential example may be the relations with Iran. The current logic of conflict with Iran is deeply embedded in America's knowledge regime and among decision-makers. Path-dependency could lead to growing discrepancy of the EU's and US interests in the Middle East, jeopardizing the current efforts of Joe Biden's Administration.

Anderson, B. (2016) *Imagined Communities: Reflections on the Origin and Spread of Nationalism*. London: Verso.

Anderson, S. (2019) Falling Illegal Immigration Numbers Confirm No Border Crisis. *Forbes*. https://www.forbes.com/sites/stuartanderson/2019/01/17/falling-illegal-immigration-numbers-confirm-no-border-crisis/#4cecec1133fb.

Bayer, L. (2019) The New Communists. *Politico*. https://www.lawandsociety.org/WashingtonDC2019/Washington2019.html.

Bendiek, A. (2011) *At the Limits of the Rule of Law: EU-US Counter-Terrorism Cooperation*. Berlin: Stiftung Wissenschaft und Politik.

Bevelander, P. and Wodak, R. (eds) (2019) *Europe at the Crossroads: Confronting Populist, Nationalist, and Global Challenges*. Lund: Nordic Academic Press.

Blank, S. (2017) Russia Has Weaponized the Energy Sector in War against the West. *The Hill*. https://thehill.com/opinion/international/355742-russias-has-weaponized-the-energy-sector-in-war-against-the-west.

Bobek, M. (2014) The Court of Justice of the European Union. *Research Paper in Law* 02/2013. https://www.coleurope.eu/sites/default/files/research-paper/researchpaper_2_2014_bobek_0.pdf.

Brady, D., (2018) Comparative Study of U.S. and E.U. Experiences with Policies on Immigration Controls. Master's thesis, Springfield: Missouri States University. https://bearworks.missouristate.edu/cgi/viewcontent.cgi?article=4357&context=theses.

Bundesregierung (2018) Europe Is at a Crossroads. *Bundesregierung.de*. https://www.bundesregierung.de/breg-en/chancellor/-europe-is-at-a-crossroads--1141424.

Cooper, A. F., Hughes, C. and de Lombaerde, P. (eds) (2008) *Regionalisation and Global Governance: The Taming of Globalisation?* London: Routledge.

Council on Foreign Relations (2017) *The Future of Europe: The EU at a Crossroads*. https://www.cfr.org/event/future-europe-eu-crossroads.

De Wilde, P., Koopmans, R., Merkel, W., Strijbis, O. and Zürn, O. (2019) *The Struggle Over Borders: Cosmopolitanism and Communitarianism*. Cambridge: Cambridge University Press.

Della Sala, V. (2010) Political Myth, Mythology and the European Union. *Journal of Common Market Studies*, **48**(1), 1–19.

Dinan, D. (2014) *Origins and Evolution of the European Union*. Oxford: Oxford University Press.

Easterly, W. and Levine, R. (2012) *The European Origins of Economic Development*. Working Paper. National Bureau of Economic Research. https://www.nber.org/papers/w18162.

Eichengreen, B. (2020) Europe's Hamilton Moment. *Milken Institute Review*. https://www.milkenreview.org/articles/europes-hamilton-moment.

European Union (2017) *Shared Vision, Common Action: A Stronger Europe – A Global Strategy for the European Union's Foreign and Security Policy*. Luxembourg: Publications Office.

Garton Ash, T. (2005) *Free World: America, Europe, and the Surprising Future of the West*. London: Vintage.

Herbut, M. and Chwedczuk-Szulc, K. (2018) The Trump Effect on Russian Foreign Policy. In Dixon, J. and Skidmore, M. J. (eds), *Donald J. Trump's Presidency: International Perspectives*. Washington, DC: Westphalia Press.

Hodgson, N. (2011) Dialogue and its Conditions: The Construction of European Citizenship. *Policy Futures in Education*, **9**(1), 43–56.

Human Rights Watch (2019) *World Report 2019: Rights Trends in European Union*. https://www.hrw.org/world-report/2019/country-chapters/european-union.

Jackson, P. T. (2011) *The Conduct of Inquiry in International Relations*. New York: Routledge.

Kagan, R. (2003) *Of Paradise and Power: America and Europe in the New World Order*. New York: Alfred A. Knopf.

Kennedy, J. F. (2008) *A Nation of Immigrants*. New York: Harper Perennial.

Lee, P. R. and Estes, C. E. (1983) New Federalism and Health Policy. *The Annals of the American Academy of Political and Social Science*, **468**, 88–102.

Mendez, C. and Bachtler, J. (2018) European Identity and Citizen Attitudes to Cohesion Policy: What do we know?. COHESIFY Research Paper 1, COHESIFY Work Package 2 – Task 2.1: Output 2. http://www.cohesify.eu/downloads/Cohesify_Research_Paper1.pdf.

Mitrany, D. (1993) *The Progress of International Government*. New Haven: Yale University Press.

Noack, R. (2019) Trump Is Threatening Tariffs on Europe's Cheese and Wine. Could This Brie the Start of a Trade War? *The Washington Post*. https://www.washingtonpost.com/world/2019/04/09/trump-administration-threatens-tariffs-eu-wine-cheese-other-goods-europe-has-many-questions/?utm_term=.5b662253ab5b.

North, D. C., Wallis, J. J., Webb, S. B. and Weingast, B. R. (2007) *Limited Access Orders in the Developing World: A New Approach to the Problems of Development*. Policy Research Working Paper 4359. Washington, DC: World Bank.

OECD (2019) *Governments Must Act to Help Struggling Middle Class*. https://www.oecd.org/social/governments-must-act-to-help-struggling-middle-class.htm.

OECD iLibrary (2019) *Under Pressure: The Squeezed Middle Class*. READ online. https://read.oecd-ilibrary.org/social-issues-migration-health/under-pressure-the-squeezed-middle-class_689afed1-en#page3.

Oltermann, P., Borger, J. and Boffey, D. (2018) Trump says Germans 'Turning Against Their Leadership' Over Immigration. *The Guardian*. https://www.theguardian.com/us-news/2018/jun/18/donald-trump-attacks-angela-merkel-saying-her-coalition-is-rocking.

Peters, M. (2018) The End of Neoliberal Globalisation and the Rise of Authoritarian Populism. *Educational Philosophy and Theory*, **50**(4), 323–325.

Powers, K. E., Reifler, J. and Scotto, T. J. (2021) Going Nativist: How Nativism and Economic Ideology Interact to Shape Beliefs about Global Trade. *Foreign Policy Analysis*, **17**(3).

Rodrigues, M. J. (2020) An Historical Breakthrough for the European Union? *The Progressive Post*. https://ppstaging.feps-europe.eu/progressive-page/an-historical-breakthrough-for-the-european-union.

Rozwarski, M. (2015) Poland's Iron Consensus. https://www.jacobinmag.com/2015/11/poland-october-elections-kaczynski-law-justice-party/.

Schain, M. (2018) *Shifting Tides: Radical-Right Populism and Immigration Policy in Europe and the United States*. Washington, DC: Migration Policy Institute.

Schmidt, V. A. (2012) Democracy and Legitimacy in the European Union. In Jones, E., Menon, A. and Weatherill, S. (eds), *The Oxford Handbook of the European Union*. Oxford: Oxford University Press, 661–675.

Serhan, Y. (2019) In an Echo of the Iraq War, the U.S. and Europe Are Split on Iran. *The Atlantic*. https://www.theatlantic.com/international/archive/2019/05/europe-us-escalation-iran-iraq-war/589588/.

Smith, J. and Sloat, A. (2018) The United States and Europe Still Need Each Other. *Brookings*. https://www.brookings.edu/blog/order-from-chaos/2018/06/11/the-united-states-and-europe-still-need-each-other/.

Stevens-Finlayson, B. (2019) *EU vs US Comparing the EU and US Federal Systems: Two Similar Systems of Governance*. London: Gold Mercury International.

Tonra, B. (2011) Democratic Foundations of EU Foreign Policy: Narratives and the Myth of EU Exceptionalism. *Journal of European Public Policy*, **18**, 1190–1207.

Wodak, R. (2020) European Identity Politics: Europe at the Crossroads. In Fomina, J. and Niżnik, J. (eds), *Europe on Test: The Onus of the Past*. Warsaw: Polish Academy of Sciences, 89–103.

Zimmermann, H. and Dür, A. (eds) (2012) *Key Controversies in European Integration*. Basingstoke: Palgrave Macmillan.

# 5. Why create another development bank? China and the Asian Infrastructure Investment Bank

**Tamar Gutner**

## INTRODUCTION

In the fall of 2013, Chinese President Xi Jinping proposed creating a new Chinese-led development bank with a focus on infrastructure development. Many were suspicious of China's intentions. After all, the World Bank, the Asian Development Bank (ADB), the European Bank for Reconstruction and Development (EBRD), and the European Investment Bank (EIB) already operated in Asia. With the exception of EIB, China is a member of all of the above-mentioned banks, warranting the question: Was there a real need for a new Asian Infrastructure Investment Bank (AIIB)? China's prominent bilateral Belt and Road Initiative (BRI), proposed around the same time as the AIIB, also lends significantly larger amounts of money toward infrastructure than the AIIB. China is also the largest official bilateral creditor in the world, having the power to oversee the implementation of projects, control where the money is allocated, and how it is spent. Finally, China's own development banks, the China Development Bank and the Export-Import Bank of China, have assets of \$1.8 trillion, more than the World Bank, ADB, the African Development Bank, the Inter-American Development Bank, EBRD, and EIB combined (EIB 2016, p. 5; Kamal and Gallagher 2016; Hurley et al., 2018). Meanwhile, the BRICS countries, including China, worked on establishing another development bank, which resulted in the opening of the New Development Bank (NDB) in 2016, adding another new development bank to the mix. In the United States, the Obama Administration voiced its concern that the existing development banks would be undermined, while Chinese companies would unfairly benefit, thus urging countries to avoid joining the proposed AIIB altogether.

Nevertheless, the AIIB is an extraordinary development in global governance. As China's first major foray into leading an international organization (IO) with global membership, it may serve as a showcase for China's multilateral leadership. Operational since 2016, today the AIIB has 103 approved members, which makes it the second largest development bank in terms of number of members behind the World Bank, with 189 member countries. It is a medium-sized development bank, with $100 billion in capital, and by mid-2022 it had approved $35.7 billion for 186 projects. The AIIB's membership includes more than 20 European members such as France, Germany, and the UK. Notably absent are the United and Japan. In terms of its policies and norms, the AIIB is cut from the same cloth as other major development banks. Prominent credit rating companies have given the bank their highest ratings, signifying a powerful seal of approval. The bank was initially designed by a number of chief negotiators, amongst them prospective founding members and their teams. The group included former executive directors of the IMF, the World Bank, and the ADB, as well as staff from those institutions as well as the EBRD and the EIB. The Multilateral Interim Secretariat, which included former senior MDB officials, provided support to the negotiators. The proposal to create the AIIB was written under the leadership of AIIB president, Jin Liqun, who had extensive experience in the world of multilateral development banks (MDBs).[1] While the AIIB's birth reflects, in part, China's unhappiness with the institutional character of the liberal order, the AIIB itself is not an institution that challenges the liberal order. Instead, the AIIB reflects the global norms and policies of major development banks.

Yet, this development has taken place as AIIB's creator and largest shareholder, China, already a police state, has become more centralized and authoritarian under Xi. The mass internment of over a million Uyghurs and other Muslim minority groups in Xinjiang, amid reports of torture, forced labor, and sexual abuse, has produced global condemnation. China's tightened grip over Hong Kong has also prompted deep international concern. Undoubtedly, values embedded in the AIIB – including transparency and accountability – do not reflect the ongoing developments in the repressive and authoritarian regime at home. This is a stark reminder that a portrait of China as an actor that either upholds or undermines the global norms and rules is an oversimplification of reality. China supports some aspects and rules of the liberal international order but not others. As Ikenberry and Lim (2017, p. 2) have noted, "American hegemony, liberal internationalism, and the deeper systemic foundations of sovereignty and state primacy are three layers of this existing system, and China has varied orientations toward each".

---

1 Jin spent over a decade at the World Bank, where he served as an alternative executive director for China, and at the Asian Development Bank, where he served as China's first vice president. He spent over two decades in China's finance ministry, including his final position as vice minister. See https://www.aiib.org/en/about-aiib/governance/senior-management/index.html.

This chapter focuses on the factors behind the creation of the AIIB. It argues that three strategic and interconnected political, economic, and institutional factors formed a window of opportunity for the creation of a new MDB. The first factor was Chinese president Xi's expressed desire to turn China into a more outward-looking, actively rising global power. This was translated into China's broader strategy of taking a greater leadership role and reflected its blossoming confidence as a key actor in regional and global politics. Creating a new MDB along the lines of existing MDBs, with global membership, therefore signaled China's desire to follow existing norms and rules and presented China with a means to highlight the legitimacy of its growing leadership. Initially, the AIIB was seen as complementing the BRI. However, the BRI has been criticized for failing to follow international norms and rules on infrastructure lending. BRI lending has been characterized by a lack of transparency and accountability, and criticized for pushing several countries into unsustainable levels of debt. The AIIB, then, presents a more positive version of China's role in global economic governance, and ultimately must be compared and contrasted with the country's other activities for a more comprehensive picture.

The second factor is defined by the enormous unmet demand for infrastructure financing in the region, a gap that China seeks to address through the AIIB and the larger BRI. Without the infrastructure gap there would be no institutional space for an additional MDB in a landscape already filled with institutions.

Third, China for some time had been frustrated by its inability to gain a larger voice in major IOs like the World Bank and IMF, a voice more clearly befitting its status in the global economy as one of the top two economies in the world. This reflects China's dissatisfaction with existing institutional choices.

This chapter proceeds as follows. The next section situates the central argument within major theories that seek to account for the birth of new IOs. Theories of rational choice institutionalism, the USCC theory (**u**sing, **s**electing, **c**hanging, or **c**reating institutions), and historical institutionalism (HI), seek to explain institutional choice and the birth of new IOs. However, they do not entirely accommodate the mix of strategic interests that underlies China's actions in this case study. Therefore, a clear explanation for the creation of the AIIB necessitates a different approach. The argument presented here builds upon these existing theories by accounting for a mix of political, economic, and institutional interests that make up China's strategic choices. The chapter then examines how the three factors shaped an opportunity for China to create its first IO. The chapter concludes by discussing some implications of the theoretical argument.

## WHY CREATE A NEW INTERNATIONAL ORGANIZATION?

In the academic literature on IOs, there are reasons to explore the interaction between why states choose to create new IOs and how those IOs are designed. For example, the United Nations would not have been created to be a collective security organization if the major powers did not have veto power in the Security Council. Similarly, the United States would not have created the World Bank or the IMF if it did not have a weighted vote that reflected its financial contributions and power. Although the 'why' and the 'how' questions are deeply interconnected, one can argue that there is an analytical logic to partially disentangle the two, given that the politics, influential actors, and actor preferences may differ from the decision to create and the process for how the institutions should be designed. In addition, the 'why' decision is typically made before the 'how' decision by participating states, and in the case of the AIIB, the 'how' decision changed over time with the entrance of European powers to the mix of founding member states right before the deadline to join. This chapter focuses on the 'why' question, in terms of why China decided to create a new development bank.

On the 'why' question, there tends to be agreement on the basic and obvious point that states create new international institutions because it is in their interest to do so, although what those interests are vary in individual cases and are viewed differently by different theoretical approaches. Neorealists, for example, argue that great powers will create international institutions as arenas for pursuing their interests (Mearsheimer 1994). Institutionalists observe that states also see welfare-enhancing outcomes resulting from the facilitation of iterative cooperation in ways that reduce transaction costs and incentives to free ride (Keohane 1984). States also find benefits in pooling resources and acting cooperatively to address common interests. They may seek increased political influence and a greater share of resources (Ikenberry and Lim 2017). Although there is a shared basic assumption between realists and institutionalists that functional calculations behind the creation of these institutions exist, there is still a longstanding disagreement about the relevance of these institutions.

Rationalist design accounts offer many important and basic insights into the question of 'why create', focusing on the utility and value of important functions that IOs may serve. IOs can carry out a wide array of functions, including carrying out specific operational activities, organizing negotiations, resolving disputes, and implementing agreements. As Abbott and Snidal (1998, p. 5) put it, "Rational states will use or create a formal IO when the value of these functions outweighs the costs, notably the resulting limits on unilateral action".

Moreover, they observe that states may consider alternative arrangements to creating a new IO, such as the case of China's creation of the bilateral BRI in conjunction with the AIIB.

The USCC bounded rationality framework is a variation on the aforementioned theory. It is more ambitious, seeking to explain the conditions under which states make the choices of using, selecting, changing, or creating institutions (Jupille et al., 2013). Both the earlier iterations and this framework assume that the 'optimal institutional choice' will tend to continue the use of existing institutional frameworks to address new problems. It recognizes the importance of power as a determinant of institutional strategy, but assumes choice is driven by a need to respond to new 'cooperation problems' that are exogenous to the institutions themselves, e.g., trade disputes. For USCC, an important factor that pushes states to remain committed to existing arrangements is the assumption that states look for 'good enough' versus 'optimal' solutions, drawing from the assumptions of bounded rationality. Institutional creation is not seen as the obvious choice facing states if there are existing institutions that can address such cooperation problems.

Several blind spots arise in these explanations. First, the earlier rational design literature tends to privilege efficiency concerns over politics, failing to recognize that politics are deeply present in many creation and design choices. Several development banks are already operational in the region, thus efficiency concerns cannot explain why China would choose to create the AIIB, or participate in creating the NDB. Second, not all 'cooperation problems' that states seek to resolve are exogenous to the institution. To illustrate this example, China's unhappiness with its institutional standing may be seen as a cooperation problem endogenous to the institution. The problem isn't trade tensions, but the power of institutional voice. Third, rationalist accounts typically do not address the question of timing. Scholars Chen and Liu (2018) have tried to get around this through the lens of bargaining theory. They argue that China created the AIIB in this particular moment as a commitment device so rising China could reassure established powers that it was not a threat (Chen and Liu 2018). One can argue that China could have better reassured established powers about its intentions by instead calling for the creation of new infrastructure capacities within existing MDBs, rather than creating an entirely new institution. Certainly, Japan and the United States were not reassured by the creation of the AIIB. The US, in particular, made an explicit effort to ask other countries not to join.

Historical institutionalists directly address the 'why now' issue by adding temporal and regional variation to issues of strategic agency. They examine more closely the dynamics of institutional birth, development, and change, with an emphasis on path dependency and punctuated equilibrium. Critical junctures offer a potentially useful way to identify important moments in these dynamics by emphasizing temporality. Capoccia and Kelemen (2007, p. 343) define such junctures as

> a situation in which the structural (that is, economic, cultural, ideological, organizational) influences on political action are significantly relaxed for a relatively short period, with two main consequences: the range of plausible choices are open to powerful political actors expands substantially and the consequences of their decisions for the outcome of interest are potentially much more momentous.

Alter (2017) applies the concept of critical juncture to the creation and evolution of international courts. Instead of merely being shaped by functional needs, the emergence of international courts at specific times – mainly after the Hague Peace Conference, the Second World War, and the Cold War – reflects "permissive and antecedent conditions" shaped by those junctures (Alter 2017, p. 252). The temporal context may also include factors such as prior institutional choices and ideas (Pierson 2004). The United Nations was modeled on the League of Nations. Even the World Bank, widely viewed as a role model behind the creation of subsequent regional development banks, was in fact modeled on the stillborn Inter-American Bank, first proposed in 1890 (Helleiner 2014, p. 53). In examining the birth of the EBRD in 1990, Weber (1994) argued that instead of being simply a functional solution to a set of problems, or a product of state power, the EBRD was "the product of convergence on a broad set of ideas and purposes shared among a medium-size group of powerful states that remain associated within a set of institutions that survived the end of the Cold War with both their structure and legitimacy intact". Historical context matters, and within that context, so do the ideas and assumptions about "the relationship between institutions, state actors, and the international environment" (Weber 1994, p. 4).

Historical institutionalism is helpful in explaining certain aspects of the timing of the AIIB's birth. For example, the AIIB was ultimately designed to resemble existing development banks, and its genesis happened at a time when the United States was dragging its feet in agreeing to a greater voting share for China at the IMF. Notably, there was no critical juncture as dramatic as the end of a major war. The infrastructure gap is not a new issue, nor is China's dissatisfaction with its role in the governance of the World Bank and the IMF. So, must the junctures be critical? Earlier literature has looked at other, non-critical juncture factors that create a window of opportunity for new policies. Kingdon (1984), for example, argued that 'focusing events', or independent streams of problems, policy options, and politics open as a result of a compelling problem or changes in political factors, and can produce important policy changes as a result (Kingdon 1984). In such a scenario, the problem may arise at a particular moment in time, but it can be driven by independent factors that come together below the radar of major historical events. Strategic choice is important in the case of the AIIB, but is not well addressed in much of the HI literature. Some institutionalist scholars have sought to fill this gap. Ikenberry and Lim (2017), for example, have argued that the degree of complexity in today's international order means that a state can pick and choose where to participate and what to oppose. Additionally, a high degree of institutionalization of the order makes it more difficult for countries to undermine it (Ikenberry and Lim 2017).

The case of the establishment of the AIIB contributes to the literature on the creation of new IOs by highlighting the confluence of political, economic, and institutional challenges that produced a moment of strategic choice for China. This choice was shaped by a change in Chinese leadership, the political interests of that leadership, as well as the underlying economic issues (particularly the benefit of addressing the gap of investment in infrastructure), and China's dissatisfaction with current institutional arrangements. These factors are both independent and interconnected. They offer an explanation as to why China made a choice to create a new MDB, rather than investing in the development of infrastructure in existing banks, or focusing on its bilateral aid.

MDBs may be a special case of international institutions looking at their existing counterparts as role models, because they have banking attributes. For example, the legitimacy and credibility of an MDB to raise money on capital markets comes from the high ratings it receives from credit agencies. States cannot simply create a development bank that does not look credible to major credit agencies. The creation of a new MDB must also involve an assessment of the demand for its loans. If there is no demand from countries to borrow, then there is no need to create a new MDB. Furthermore, if the design of a development bank fails to make its products attractive or competitive, it will also fail to attract borrowers. In the case of China there is an additional point to consider: the AIIB signifies a turning point in China's role. In existing MDBs, China has historically been viewed as a powerful borrower, rather than the most powerful shareholder and source of the largest share of resources.

## THE RISE OF XI JINPING

The rise of Xi Jinping to office is a major factor behind China's initiative to create the AIIB. Xi became Secretary General of the Communist Party in November 2012 and was elected president in March 2013. The 19th Party Congress in October 2017 enshrined his political thoughts into the CPC's constitution. By March 2018, the National People's Congress voted to end presidential term limits, effectively allowing Xi to consolidate his power and remain president for life. Today, Xi is widely seen as the most powerful Chinese leader since Mao Zedong. Upon taking office, Xi had a vision of shaping the world order to better reflect China's political, economic, and security agenda. At present, China is the world's second largest economy standing at $20 trillion, measured in terms of GDP current prices. By comparison, the United States holds the top spot at $24.4 trillion. Japan comes in third place, at $5 trillion.[2] Over the past decade, China benefited from being largely unscathed by the 2008 global financial crisis. Notably, during the coronavirus pandemic, it was the first major economy to rebound, although its growth then weakened.

Xi's vision is, in many ways, drastically differs from that of his predecessors, who followed the ideas of Deng Xiaoping. Deng's approach was a cautious one, embodied in the phrase *tao guang yang hui* or, "hide brightness, nourish obscurity", which encouraged the country to keep a low profile on the global stage (Yang 2011). Scholars have also highlighted the "going out (*zouchuqu*)" strategy first presented by former party secretary Jiang Zemin in 1992. This strategy called for a more involved and competitive Chinese stance in international markets (Yeo 2018).

In numerous speeches, Xi asserted that China should play a more important leadership role in global governance. In his report to the 19th CPC National Congress, Xi said, "China will continue to play its part as a major and responsible country, take an active part in reforming and developing the global governance system, and keep contributing Chinese wisdom and strength to global governance" (Xi 2017). Next to that, he argued that "socialism with Chinese characteristics … offers Chinese wisdom and a Chinese approach to solving the problems facing mankind".

In the fall of 2013, Xi laid out his three visions. The first, in a September 2013 speech in Kazakhstan, was for a new Silk Road Economic Belt. The following month, he presented an idea for a twenty-first century maritime Silk Road. Together the Belt and Road vision developed into what was first known as the One Belt One Road Initiative, later renamed the Belt and Road Initiative (BRI). Initially, the overarching goal of BRI was to expand Chinese trade and investment by building immense infrastructure projects, promoting connectivity and trade across Central Asia, the Middle East, Africa and Europe. It is estimated that Chinese institutions have spent at least $200 billion on BRI-related projects so far, although estimates of this number vary greatly, and many projects were canceled during the pandemic. Over the next decade, this investment is expected to surpass $1 trillion. As the BRI progressed, its scope shifted from focusing only on basic infrastructural projects, to supporting 'green' investments, promoting digital infrastructure, and contributing to an

---

2 IMF Data Mapper, GDP current prices at http://www.imf.org/external/datamapper/NGDPD@WEO/OEMDC/ADVEC/WEO/JPN/FRA.

open world economy. It now includes a Polar Silk Road, a Health Silk Road, and a Green Silk Road, as well as educational and cultural programs. The scope also expanded geographically: BRI has left the boundaries of Eurasia and has expanded into Latin America and Africa.

Xi's third vision was to establish the AIIB, first announced in October 2013. The idea to create a regional development bank led by China had been discussed in Beijing and elsewhere for several years. Zheng Xinli has been thinking about ways for China to address infrastructure gaps in the region since 2009, when he was deputy director of the Policy Studies Office of the Central Committee of the CCP (Perlez 2015). Jin Liqun also started developing ideas on how to design a new MDB for Asia (Jin 2019). In 2013, after Xi became president, Zheng and Jin were involved in writing a proposal to create the AIIB. The proposal circulated around several ministries before finally reaching the State Council and the Premier and Vice Premier. While the proposal was under consideration, there were number of internal government debates between the Chinese Finance Ministry, the Ministry of Commerce, and the China Center for International Economic Exchanges (CCIEE). The discussion was centered around China's capabilities and experience to lead a multilateral development bank, and whether an alternative structure – such as a state investment fund – might be a better choice (Koh 2015).

The possibility of creating the BRICS bank, the New Development Bank (NDB), had also been under discussion since 2012, and leaders had agreed to move forward with the idea in the spring of 2013. But the NDB was seen as a relatively less suitable means to serve China's interests, because there was jostling over who would lead it, and in the end each country had an equal share, so there was no Chinese ownership. The pro-AIIB voices prevailed. Some experts have speculated that the idea that the AIIB would be linked to the BRI helped the AIIB win approval in this period (Koh 2015). Certainly, in the early days of the AIIB's design, it was widely thought that it would directly support the BRI, but this idea was condemned by powerful Western donors who joined the AIIB's group of prospective founding members, and Jin was later vocal about the fact that the AIIB was separate from the BRI.

## UNMET DEMAND FOR INFRASTRUCTURE

Another major factor in the creation of a new regional development bank was the unmet demand and for infrastructure financing in the region While estimates for infrastructure demand vary, they are all quite large. For example, the ADB, which actively funds infrastructure projects, estimated that Asia and the Pacific require infrastructure investments of approximately $1.7 trillion a year, or more than $22.6 trillion in the period through 2030, to maintain growth, eradicate poverty, and better address climate change. At present, annual infrastructure investment in the region totals approximately $880 billion. The ADB also estimated that the MDBs have financed under 3 percent of the infrastructure needs in "developing Asia" (Asian Development Bank 2017). Asia's increasing population, and the fast-paced trend of urbanization, at least pre-pandemic, strongly accentuates the infrastructure gap.

China's emphasis on the infrastructure gap as a rationale for creating the AIIB was a clever move. Contributing to infrastructure does not immediately denote political motives. To develop and grow effectively, countries require electricity, transportation, energy, and communication networks. McKinsey estimated a global infrastructure gap of almost $1 trillion per year through 2030, with emerging economies accounting for 60 percent of the required investments (Woetzel et al. 2016, p. 1). Infrastructure financing is especially important to China, as lagging infrastructure is a source of bottlenecks throughout the region (Ren 2016).

Most of China's traditional infrastructure lending flows through its policy banks, such as the China Development Bank and the China Exim Bank. These banks lack transparency and do not follow global norms on issues such as environmental assessment, corruption, and human rights. Lending under the BRI has raised other red flags. Unsustainable levels of debt in some borrower countries, and financial losses linked to the impact of the pandemic, are just two issues linked to the BRI (Hurley et al., 2018).

## FRUSTRATION WITH THE IMF AND WORLD BANK

While China's economic clout increased, its voice in major IOs did not. This disjuncture became a source of frustration for China, but also for the other major emerging economies. By 2014, the weight in global GDP (PPP basis) of emerging and developing countries had increased from 36.2 percent in 1983 to 56.9 percent.[3] At the same time, their IMF quota remained relatively flat, experiencing a slight increase from 34.5 percent in 1983 to 36.6 percent in 2014. The IMF, as well as the World Bank and the ADB, were all seen as dominated by the G7 countries. The G7 countries were quite resistant to recognizing the imbalance between emerging nations' clout and their voice in the governance of these institutions. For example, before voting reforms agreed to at the World Bank and IMF, China's voting share was 2.9 percent at the IMF and 2.77 percent at the World Bank's International Bank for Reconstruction and Development (IBRD). After the reforms, China's share rose to 6.1 percent at the IMF and 4.42 percent at the IBRD (IMF 2011). The reforms put China in

3 Measured at Purchasing Power Parity (PPP) basis. See Mohan and Kapur (2015).

third place at both institutions, behind the United States and Japan, and ahead of Germany, France, and the UK.

A reform in voting shares at the IMF was especially frustrating to developing countries because it was stalled by five years due to the hesitation of the United States. In April 2008, the IMF's Board of Governors took a step to rectify the issue of 'shares and chairs' by agreeing to a governance reform package that would give stronger voting power to two-thirds of IMF member states. In 2010, the Board of Governors agreed on a more substantive package of reforms, building on the 2008 agreement. This package of reforms gave emerging market economies and other developing countries an additional 6 percent of quota shares. The big European countries on the Board agreed to reduce their combined presence from eight to six of the 24 executive directors. The reforms also called for all board members to be elected, rather than appointed.

Due to the opposition from the conservative Republicans in the US House of Representatives, the second set of reforms was stalled. Under IMF rules, three-fifths of its members representing 85 percent of total voting power must approve the reforms. The US has a 16.74 percent share of total voting power, effectively giving it veto power. In late December 2015, the US Congress approved the reforms, but by that time the train creating the AIIB and NDB had already left the station.

China's choice of creating a new regional institution with open membership was one possible response to its frustration. Alternatively, it could have proposed the expansion of existing infrastructure financing in other development banks working in Asia. It could have supplemented the lending capabilities of its own development banks or other lending and aid mechanisms. It could have been satisfied with just the NDB. Instead, a choice was made to create a new MDB, with China as the largest single shareholder. Creating a new development bank was strategically important for several reasons. First, it highlighted China's intention to move away from acting as a borrower from existing MDBs to a leader and a lender. Second, it created a development bank that could easily be placed within the pre-existing constellation of development banks. Third, by creating an MDB with global membership, China drew in resources from all major donor countries besides the United States and Japan; this means that other major donors were contributing to China's efforts to increase its soft power.

The previous section explained China's dissatisfaction with its own position within the IMF and the World Bank. As mentioned, China is now the third largest shareholder at both institutions. It is also the third largest shareholder at the ADB, behind the United States and Japan. Notably, ever since its establishment, the ADB's presidents have always been of Japanese nationality. Historically, at the World Bank and the ADB, China's role has always been as a borrower, rather than a leading donor country. China's cumulative borrowing from the Bank (both IBRD and IDA) was approximated at $65 billion through June 2020 (World Bank 2020). China borrowed from the IDA until it graduated in 1999. One of the stipulations behind the IBRD's 2018 capital replenishment agreement was that China would reduce its borrowing. China is one of the world's largest official lenders, thus growing criticism centered around whether China's IBRD borrowing is warranted (Morris and Portelance 2019). At the ADB, China is a borrower and a donor. China's cumulative loan and grant disbursements from the ADB totals approximately $45 billion, making China the ADB's second largest sovereign borrower, second only to India. China also contributes to the ADB's Asian Development Fund. In 2005, it created a $90 million PRC Poverty Reduction and Regional Cooperation Fund to offer technical assistance for cooperation initiatives at the sub-regional level.

## CONCLUSION

China's emergence as an increasingly powerful actor in global governance comes at a particularly important time as the world is grappling with multiple crises. The US is recovering from an administration that did not prioritize global leadership and multilateralism, Europe is facing the consequences of Brexit, and countries around the world are coping with the coronavirus health crisis and its lingering impact on the global economy, as well as the many impacts of Russia's war in Ukraine. This chapter analyzes one of China's major strategic moves in the arena of international organizations – the creation and leadership of a new regional development bank, a move that unsurprisingly raised many questions about China's intentions. The political, economic, and institutional factors that created a window of opportunity for China to opt to create the AIIB allowed China to signal its shift from being a major borrower to major multilateral creditor and MDB leader. A new Chinese-led MDB brought in resources from other major donors, skillfully harnessing their financial power to satisfy China's broader goals. Future research would benefit from focusing more closely on the important issue of the relationship between this initiative, an institution created along the lines of an existing category of international institution, and the BRI, a much larger bilateral initiative that has been criticized for operating outside of global norms of transparency and due diligence. An important unanswered question remains: Will the AIIB, in fact, influence the BRI, and perhaps China's own development banks, or will it be the Potemkin Village of Chinese development lending?

The case of the China's creation of the AIIB points to a weakness of existing theories of IO births. Rational choice institutionalism goes too far in removing historical context. It does not generally consider the birth of one institution relative to similar institutions. The literature on rational design privileges notions of efficiency at the expense of politics and timing. Historical institutionalism addresses these issues very well, but 'critical' junctures are not necessarily the key historical junctures that matter. Adding strategic choices and agency back into the equation offers a more nuanced explanation about the complex factors that result in an unusual choice by the states to create a new institution where it is not immediately needed.

## REFERENCES

Abbott, K. and Snidal, D. (1998) Why States Act through Formal International Organizations. *Journal of Conflict Resolution*, **42**(1), 3–32.

Alter, K. J. (2017) The Evolution of International Law and Courts. In Fioretos, O. (ed.), *International Politics and Institutions in Time*. New York: Oxford University Press, 251–273.

Asian Development Bank (2017) *Meeting Asia's Infrastructure Needs*. Manila: ADB.

Capoccia, G. and Kelemen, R. D. (2007) The Study of Critical Junctures: Theory, Narrative, and Counterfactuals in Historical Institutionalism. *World Politics*, **59**, 341–369.

Chen, Z. and Liu, Y. (2018) Strategic Reassurance in Institutional Contests: Explaining China's Creation of the Asian Infrastructure Investment Bank. *Journal of Contemporary China*, **27**(114), 795–810.

European Investment Bank (2016) *2015 Financial Report*. European Investment Bank.

Helleiner, E. (2014) *Forgotten Foundations of Bretton Woods*. Ithaca, NY: Cornell University Press.

Hurley, J., Morris, S. and Portelance, G. (2018) *Examining Debt Implications of the Belt and Road Initiative from a Policy Perspective*. CGD Policy Paper 121.

Ikenberry, G. J. and Lim, D. J. (2017) China's Emerging Institutional Statecraft: The Asian Infrastructure Investment Bank and the Prospects for Counter-Hegemony. Washington, DC: Brookings Institution.

International Monetary Fund (2011) *Quota and Voting Shares Before and After Implementation of Reforms Agreed in 2008 and 2010*. Washington, DC: IMF.

Jin, L. (2019) *The Asian Infrastructure Investment Bank in the MDB System: Reflections from the First Three Years*. Center for Global Development. https://www.cgdev.org/event/asian-infrastructure-investment-bank-mdb-system-reflections-first-three-years.

Jupille, J., Mattli, W. and Snidal, D. (2013) *Institutional Choice and Global Commerce*. New York: Cambridge University Press.

Kamal, R. and Gallagher, K. P. (2016) *China Goes Global with Development Banks*. Bretton Woods Project. http://www.brettonwoodsproject.org/2016/04/20508/.

Keohane, R. O. (1984) *After Hegemony: Cooperation and Discord in the World Political Economy*. Princeton, NJ: Princeton University Press.

Kingdon, J. (1984) *Agendas, Alternatives, and Public Policies*. Boston: Little, Brown.

Koh, G. Q. (2015) How China Decided to Redraw the Global Financial Map. *Reuters*, 15 September.

Mearsheimer, J. (1994) The False Promise of International Institutions. *International Security*, **19**(3), 5–49.

Mohan, R. and Kapur, M. (2015) *Emerging Powers and Global Governance: Whither the IMF?* IMF Working Paper WP/15/219.

Morris, S. and Portelance, G. (2019) *Examining World Bank Lending to China: Graduation or Modulation*. CGD Policy Paper 135.

Perlez, J. (2015) China Creates a World Bank of Its Own, and the U.S. balks. *The New York Times*, 4 December.

Pierson, P. (2004) *Politics in Time*. Princeton, NJ: Princeton University Press.

Ren, X. (2016) China as an Institution Builder: The Case of the AIIB. *Pacific Review*, **29**(3), 435–442.

Weber, S. (1994) Origins of the European Bank for Reconstruction and Development. *International Organization*, **48**(1), 1–38.

Woetzel, J., Garemo, N., Mischke, J., Hjerpe, M. and Palter, R. (2016) *Bridging Global Infrastructure Gaps*. McKinsey & Company.

World Bank Group in China (2020) *Facts and Figures 1980–2020*.

Xi, J. (2017) Secure a Decisive Victory in Building a Moderately Prosperous Society in all Respects and Strive for the Great Success of Socialism with Chinese Characteristics for a New Era. Speech delivered at the 19th Congress of the Communist Party of China. Beijing.

Yang, W. (2011) Diplomatic Words of Wisdom. *China Daily USA*.

Yeo, Y. (2018) China's Policy of 'Going Out' 2.0: Ideas, Interests, and the Rise of the Asian Infrastructure Investment Bank (AIIB). *The Korean Journal of International Studies*, **16**(3), 367–387.

# 6. Contesting international economic governance: the 'people' and trade in the Trump and Brexit rhetoric

**Angelos Chryssogelos**

## INTRODUCTION

Populism is often seen as a 'thin ideology' (Mudde 2004) whose policy content mostly derives from its association with thicker ideologies. Yet populists often invest significant time and resources in developing their own policy proposals. Trade has been a hallmark of populist movements historically and populists have held both pro and anti-free trade positions. North American agrarian populists were pro-free trade in the turn of the twentieth century, while populists in today's US are mostly protectionist. Post-colonial populist leaders from the Global South often demanded protection, whereas today's populists in emerging economies like Turkey and India seek to harness globalization. Given this variety of populist preferences, is there a distinct impact of populism on trade?

Populism is understood here as a discourse that articulates politics as a binary opposition between the system and the people. These discourses emerge at times of severe upsetting of state–society relations due to developments that often have their roots in international politics. Trade is an appropriate area for populism to articulate its opposition between the people and the 'system': as an economic policy, it can address material grievances on the basis of a juxtaposition between 'people' and 'elites'; and as a policy through which the costs and benefits of a state's adaptation to the international system are distributed domestically, trade can help political actors launch appeals for rebalancing society's relationship with the political system (Rodrik 2017, pp. 15–16).

The chapter examines comparatively two populist trade discourses during a period of upheaval in Anglo-Saxon democracies starting in 2016: the election and presidency of Donald Trump in the US and the contestation of Brexit following the EU referendum in Great Britain. Both have been described as populist, yet they represent opposite positions on trade. Contrary to the protectionist Trump, Brexiteers largely support free trade (Rodrik 2017, p. 11). The analysis demonstrates how the distinctiveness of populism is its articulation of preferences as binary opposition between people and official power. If populism is understood in this way as a discourse of international relations, the actual trade policy preferences of populists – whether they support or oppose free trade – are less important than how they are articulated as opposition to the elites and institutions of the international order.

This conceptualization of populism helps explain two other paradoxes of populist trade discourses: the fact that they are often popular despite their expected negative economic impact; and the fact that, in the US and UK, the populist challenge to the international trade regime has emerged from ostensibly pro-market centre-right parties. Taken together, these paradoxes show how the nature of populism and the timing of its emergence are conditioned by a combination of the international political and economic pressures in which a state operates, and the domestic political openings that are created by discontent with these pressures. The chapter closes with a discussion of the implications of the argument for the future of the international order.

## POPULISM AS DISCOURSE OF INTERNATIONAL RELATIONS

The view of populism as a discourse is associated with Ernesto Laclau (2005a, 2005b; see also Panizza 2005; Stavrakakis 2004). According to Laclau, populism is a mode of politics that divides the political field into two blocs, the people and the elites, in fundamental opposition to each other. The populist discourse constructs a political identity based on the *empty signifier* of the 'people' – empty because it is used as a rhetorical vessel to appeal to a variety of excluded groups. Populism binds together various social grievances – economic, cultural, ideological – in a single chain of demands connected by the very fact that they are ignored (Stavrakakis 2004, p. 257). It thus endows a new political subject with the privileged self-conception of the 'real people' (Abts and Rummens 2007, p. 418; Arditi 2010, p. 490; Laclau 2005a, p. 81).

The above means that class differences and social stratification become politically consequential only when they are linked in a chain of equivalence based on their opposition to official power (Stanley 2008, pp. 97–98). In this sense, the purpose of populist policy formulations is less to represent the material preferences of societal interests and more to construct a popular identity on the basis of its exclusion from the system. Much like the 'people', 'trade' can become an *empty signifier* that helps broaden this political identity opposing the system.

As has been shown elsewhere – e.g. in the case of the EU refugee crisis in 2015 (Börzel and Risse 2018) – populist parties can impose new understandings of the identity of the 'people' that challenge the fit between the national political community and the boundaries or character of the supra- or international orders a state belongs to. In cases of worsening, actual or perceived, discrepancy between the national political community and the international order it is subject to, populism articulates the claim for representation as a repatriation of political control from international institutions or governance processes. Therefore, international or regional orders often become the target of populists' critique (Chryssogelos 2020). Consequently, populist positions on trade are part of the discursive articulation of the political identity of the 'people', and, therefore, trade issues matter as part of the antagonism between people and the 'system' rather than for their actual content. Importantly, this approach to populism challenges the standard view of trade preferences as reflecting concrete and elaborated societal interests (Moravcsik 1997).

The precise use of trade positions in the construction of the popular identity confronting official power will reflect the shape of state–society divisions in a state and will, in turn, be context-specific (Hadiz and Chryssogelos 2017). This chapter focuses on a specific pathway that can lead conservative parties – normally reliable supporters of free trade and the international liberal trade regime since the end of the Cold War – to adopt populism: the embrace of liberal economic policies and the internationalization of the economy by formerly working-class, social-democratic mass parties. This opens up new opportunities for centre-right parties to expand their influence towards working-class voters who feel unrepresented by the parties they historically voted for.

In established democracies, societal interests have historically been expressed by mass parties representing the preferences of groups with self-awareness of their ideational and material interests. Typical examples include European labour and Christian-democratic parties mobilizing around the class and confessional cleavages in the nineteenth century (Bartolini and Mair 1990; Lipset and Rokkan 1967). In contrast to these *parties of society*, there emerged parties representing the interests of groups that traditionally had access to political power but decided to adopt methods of mass mobilization of their opponents (Ziblatt 2017). Despite their different origins, both mass and conservative parties aimed to bridge the gap between state and society, either by representing specific societal groups, or by generating popular support for the groups that had hitherto dominated the state (Mair 2000, p. 9).

Rather than *representing* societal interests, populism's aim, on the other hand, is to subsume them in a broad and ideologically loose popular identity that will either challenge the state head-on or, if it manages to occupy it, use it to *incorporate* social demands in a top-down, hierarchical fashion (Mouzelis 1985, pp. 331–332). Paradoxically, while populism promises to emancipate the 'people', it does so by depressing or fusing separate societal demands whose specific programmatic preferences are lost in the general call of opposition to the 'system'. Equally paradoxically, while populism may appear like a disruptive force, it just as often can act as a way to dilute social demands at a time of acute international and domestic pressures on the state.

Such was the provocative argument of Mair (2000), who, after the end of the Cold War, saw a paradoxical overlap between two otherwise different party families: on the one hand, radical far right parties, and on the other hand, Third Way-style, post-ideological 'cartel' parties (Katz and Mair 1995) such as Tony Blair's New Labour. Despite their vast ideological differences, both party types shared the key populist feature of putting forward an appeal to a 'people' composed of atomized citizens, rather than distinct societal groups with separate preferences and interests (Mair 2000, pp. 8–10).

The emergence of both these types of parties during globalization, when the absorption of national elites into transnational or supranational governance networks accelerated (Bickerton 2015, pp. 54–55; Zürn and Deitelhoff 2015, p. 211), points at a more general issue: that populism, either in its consciously disruptive form or as an unforeseen consequence of the de-ideologization of mass parties, is often a by-product of internationally induced upheaval in state–society relations that neither mass parties of society nor conservative parties of traditional power can address. Perhaps unconsciously, but no less due to their unwillingness to address the material demands of their working-class constituencies (Zürn 2014, p. 66), Third Way social-democrats played into the discourse of the populist far-right about society as an amorphous 'people' disgruntled with an increasingly hollowed out state (Bishop and Payne 2019; Della Salla 1997).

The appeal of populism among the declining industrial class in the 'rust belts' of the US Midwest and Northern England is characteristic of how international economic pressures, and the domestic effects created by the representational deficits, upset formerly stable and class-aligned party systems. The work of Justin Gest (2016) in decaying working-class communities in Ohio and East London precisely offers a vivid depiction of this. In both cases, the retreating working class must cope with the corruption or indifference of the parties traditionally tasked with representing them (the Democratic Party in the US and the Labour Party in the UK) amid urban decay, unemployment, and the dismantlement of communal life.

Many accounts of Western politics have discussed how far right populist parties filled the representational gaps created by the move of social-democratic parties to the centre by appealing to working-class voters. Yet, there is also a third potential trajectory for populism to enter a party system from the centre-right: conservative parties seeing an opportunity to broaden their appeal by adopting an anti-system discourse. During tensions in state–society relations, conservative parties, and the traditional elites they represent, may utilize populism as a way to mobilize anew mass support in the form of anti-systemic appeals based on themes of sovereignty, economic protection, and cultural demarcation. As we will see, this is precisely the way that populism penetrated US and British politics, with trade serving as the touchstone of anti-establishment discourses.

## TRADE DISCOURSES AND POPULISM IN THE US AND THE UK

### Trump, Trade and 'Bringing Back Jobs'

There is no external policy area where Trump has had a stronger practical impact than trade. Trump had been calling for the US to adopt protectionist measures since the 1980s, although back then the main source of angst was Japan rather than China (Lamp 2018, pp. 4–5). At the same time, his rhetoric was built on a long-standing tradition of anti-establishment politicians using trade to highlight and encapsulate the costs for broad segments of American society of the external choices of elites. Thus, trade allowed Trump to re-articulate the internationalization of large parts of US economy as a problem of political representation. The contours of US politics since the 1990s explain why there was a shift from the long anti-trade stances emanating mostly from the Democratic left and organized labour, towards a newly emerged anti-trade populist rhetoric from the Republican right.

Trade was the original touchstone of domestic dissent after the end of the Cold War. Early populist upheavals in the 1992 presidential election – Pat Buchanan's challenge to President George H. W. Bush in the Republican primary and the successful third-party candidacy of Ross Perot – focused on trade, especially the ratification of NAFTA (Perot and Choate 1993). Despite sectional opposition coming from organized labour, protectionist sentiments seemed to be most effective when woven around identarian and anti-immigration feelings, such as the ones expressed by Buchanan, or loose anti-elite sentiments like those expressed by Perot.

Free trade was supported by businesses, the establishments of both parties, and the overwhelming majority of academic economists, who largely dismissed anti-trade sentiment as irrational and illiterate (for a characteristic sample of this line of thinking at the time see Krugman 1993). Despite being initiated by pro-business Republicans, NAFTA, the founding of the WTO and the integration of China in the world market were all completed under the auspices of Bill Clinton's Democrats (Skonieczny 2001). Clinton's Democrats functioned like the prototypical 'cartel party' (Katz and Mair 1995) that went from representing sectional mass (labour) interests to manipulating and neutralizing them with the promise of benefits for the whole of society and ad hoc compensation for 'globalization losers' (Shoch 2000).

However, the 2008 financial crisis, along with the debacle of the Iraq War, highlighted the extent to which the US commitment to the post-Cold War multilateral order went against the preferences and interests of large parts of the American society. Together with foreign military entanglements and rising immigration, trade became a symbol of how internationalization undercut the link between a national political community and a political system largely absorbed by considerations of global affairs. Such a political system works towards furthering the needs of strata best positioned to benefit from international economic openness, but ignores those who cannot.

In this context, it is telling that Trump's disruptive 2016 campaign articulated protectionism as an opportunity to castigate the establishment, rather than a well thought out agenda for recalibrating America's political economy (Skonieczny 2018). In Trump's rhetoric, trade was the method by which the 'people' were being 'cheated' by hostile outsiders in collusion with indifferent domestic elites: China (Reuters 2016), Mexico, Japan, and, after he took over the presidency, even long-standing US allies like Canada (Politico 2018) and the EU (CNBC 2019a).

Secondly, the international economic exposure had a relatively concentrated negative economic impact on the decaying post-industrial white working class of the US Midwest, which only exacerbated the support for an anti-trade rhetoric and underpinned Trump's populist strategy (Lamp 2018, pp. 8–9). This allowed him to weave multiple dimensions of exclusion and peripheralization – economic, cultural, regional – and construct a broad and inclusive identity of the 'people', all while pursuing narrower tactical goals, namely, to win the electoral votes of crucial swing states in the 2016 presidential election (Trump 2016).

The potency of Trump's trade policy as an anti-systemic discourse rather than a developed programmatic agenda can be seen also in the way it was applied during his presidency (Lamp 2018, p. 26). He effectively terminated the Trans-Pacific Partnership (TPP), raised tariffs against China, threatened Mexico and Canada into accepting a renegotiation of NAFTA (Gertz 2018), and forced the EU into trade negotiations after threatening punitive tariffs against European exports (especially German cars). He also attempted cross-issue linkages with trade, e.g. threatening Mexico with tariffs if immigration were not reduced (CNBC 2019b). Throughout this time, most economic experts agreed that Trump's policies would fail to achieve their stated economic goals, instead generating costs felt particularly by some of Trump's core supporters (New York Times 2019).

Of course, the line between the applied policies and threats in Trump's trade policy was always blurred. Actual policy mattered less than his ability to display a highly personalistic leadership with little regard for international institutions and negotiation processes (Lamp 2018, pp. 11–12). This was expressed not only in applying tariffs and punishing others for 'cheating' America, but also in trade agreements that he could tout as personal achievements, e.g. the revamped NAFTA (now called USMCA), and the trade truce with China in January 2020. Rather than pursuing economic goals, Trump's trade policy ultimately served as a performance of an elected leader in direct communication with a nationally demarcated 'people' (Boucher and Thies 2019), all while remaining indifferent to the exigencies of the international order (Lamp 2018, pp. 7–8).

It is also interesting how Trump's populist trade discourse was accommodated by the Republican Party although it broke with its economic orthodoxies. Indeed, along with his criticism of the Iraq war, Trump's protectionism was his main anti-system credential in the 2016 Republican primary. However, once he secured power, Trump pursued classical Republican policies such as tax-cuts for the rich and the, ultimately failed, repeal of Obamacare. In the absence of policies that would reassure his newfound supporters, Trump turned to new trade policies to claim that he pursued the interests of the 'people'. Despite difference with their orthodox economic ideas, Trump's trade populism thus dovetailed with the Republicans' broader strategy of presenting themselves as the party of the 'real people'. When Trump's economic protectionism was recast in cultural terms (e.g. in his linkage between immigration and tariffs on Mexico), Republicans found it easier to justify a departure from their economic credos (Associated Press 2019).

Trump's trade policy functioned as a populist discourse rather than a coherent programme of economic recalibration in favour of the parts of American society exposed to international competition. It was interwoven with various other themes of Trump's populism – his attacks on cultural elites, immigration, the political system – while serving as a powerful symbol of reinstating popular control over a policy that had been seen for too long as benefiting other countries rather than US interests (Lamp 2018, p. 37). Protectionism, often expressed as a threat and a sentiment rather than a coherent policy (Skonieczny 2018), mediated between the domestic and the international realms by reinstating the primacy of the former over the latter.

## Brexit, Trade and 'Taking Back Control'

Trade became an unlikely bone of contention of the debate following the British referendum on EU membership in 2016. The success of the Leave campaign in the referendum was widely attributed to its effective and emotional message of the UK 'taking back control' of its borders, especially of immigration. In this sense, the vote for Brexit and the subsequent debate in the UK have been seen as emblematic of the rise of right-wing national populism in Western democracies driven by cultural disaffection (Eatwell and Goodwin

2018; see generally Kriesi et al 2008). To the extent that Brexit was entwined with the immigration debate, it can indeed be seen as the British expression of the same dynamics that have bolstered the populist radical right across Europe.

At the same time, Brexit distilled decades of British Euroscepticism (Forster 2002; Gifford 2014a), especially in one of the UK's two major parties, the Conservatives (Bale 2010). Indeed, its association with an anti-immigration agenda came primarily through the activism of Nigel Farage's United Kingdom Independence Party (UKIP) and the opportunistic adoption of this issue by Conservative leaders of the Leave campaign. Notably, Brexit's origins lie in the long-standing advocacy by a pro-free market, libertarian milieu of the Conservative Party where it was presented as a project of sovereignty and liberation from a 'protectionist' EU that inhibited the UK from harnessing globalization (Baker et al. 2008; Hannan 2012).

As a result, the new Conservative prime minister Theresa May, who assumed power immediately after the 2016 referendum to negotiate the UK's exit from the EU, made trade independence a core criterion of 'delivering Brexit'. In her speeches, both trade and immigration became symbols of 'taking back control', the slogan of the Leave campaign in the referendum (May 2017). However, within the framework of the Brexit debate, 'trade' became intertwined with both national independence internationally and a recalibration of state-society relations domestically. Such free trade discourses in post-referendum Britain revealed a lot about the populist character of Brexit.

When it comes to political economy, the pro-free market Conservatives demanded the UK to be unshackled from the 'protectionist' EU, which is in stark disagreement with the needs of the depressed, post-industrial working class of North England – the constituency largely credited with delivering victory to Leave in the referendum (Rodrik 2017, p. 22). In addition, the economic agenda of the right-wing of the Conservative Party demanding deregulation and the rolling back of the UK's commitment to EU environmental, social, and labour standards (Dromey 2017), was visibly at odds with the material needs of the depressed working class. In the post-referendum period, proposals produced by pro-Brexit groups, such as the Economists for Free Trade, were received with great suspicion by experts and the media. Following initial difficulties to roll over existing free trade agreements it had signed as part of the EU (The Guardian 2019), the new Department for International Trade celebrated the signing of these rolled-over agreements as new 'trade deals', when all they did was largely replicate EU-era provisions (Financial Times 2020). By most objective measures, five years after the referendum, the free trade promise of Brexit was faltering.

Even so, the real value of the call for free trade lay in its populist character. First, the demand for reinstating the UK's independent trade policy was a powerful symbol of regaining national sovereignty, the vision of a confident 'buccaneering' Britain striking out on its own on the international stage and shrewdly making deals for itself without delegating authority to Brussels (Byrne 2017). Free trade was also associated with an emotional image of rediscovering connections with the Commonwealth. Here, Brexiteers' trade discourse often came across as imperial nostalgia, emphasizing ties with countries like Canada, Australia, and New Zealand that would replace economic relations with the EU (Bell and Vucetic 2019). By helping reinstate both national sovereignty and the imperial connection, free trade provided the slogan 'taking back control' with both a sentimental effect and the tangibility of a practical policy (Siles-Brügge 2019).

In turn, this international reorientation reflected the demand of recalibrating state–society relations after decades of widening representational gaps. Since the 1980s, the UK experienced heightened economic deregulation which brought about the material and cultural peripheralization of a once robust working class. State retrenchment initiated by the Thatcherite Conservatives in the 1980s and 1990s was furthered by a new Conservative government elected amid the Great Recession in 2010 and implementing a harsh programme of austerity (Lee 2011). As the centrist wing of the Conservative Party that supported Remain in the 2016 referendum was largely associated with austerity (Vail 2015), in the minds of many the EU became identified with declining welfare.

Euroscepticism had taken over the Conservative Party following its heavy defeat in 1997 at the hands of Tony Blair's New Labour (Lynch and Whitaker 2012). New Labour's post-ideological politics, largely continuing Thatcherite economic policies, was linked with participation in the EU, which Blair strongly supported. For the Blairite project, EU membership was a way to further disentangle public policy from what were seen as parochial sectoral demands (Bulmer 2008). In this way, the absorption of New Labour in the logic of the state (Mair 2000) was interconnected with the absorption of the British state in the EU (Bickerton 2015; Gifford 2014b).

The 1997–2010 tenure of New Labour, however, was also associated with an agenda of social modernization and renewal. Labour's permissive attitudes towards European immigration, opting not to apply transitional limits on the freedom of movement from new EU member states after the 2004 enlargement, matched the party's openness to multiculturalism, but also agreed with an economic mindset that demanded deregulation and welcomed the influx of cheap workers. To this end, representational frustrations with a largely technocratic mode of policymaking, economic discontent and cultural alienation brought about by mass immigration aligned in an explosive mix against a New Labour strongly committed to the EU (Goodhart 2017).

Thus, Brexit as a populist phenomenon constructed a broad chain of frustrations – political, economic, cultural – against the British state. That much was understood by Theresa May who, in her first party conference speech as prime minister, famously admonished internationalized elites as 'citizens of nowhere' (May 2016). More than just a strategy of extending the Conservative Party's appeal to popular strata, the discourse adopted by its pro-Brexit wing struck explicitly populist tones – carrying on from Michael Gove's pre-referendum assertion that 'the people have had enough of experts' (Mance 2016) to Jacob Rees-Mogg's framing of the EU as a project of the 'metropolitan elites' (Logan 2017) and Boris Johnson's warnings of an 'elite conspiracy to thwart Brexit' (Kaonga 2019).

In light of this, Brexiteer free trade advocacy rather crystallized a chain of popular frustrations with the political system than offered consistent policy suggestions of economic policy. Trade became an avatar for 'taking back control', its promise of repatriating powers from Brussels to London a symbol of realigning the policies of the state with the democratic accountability towards the 'people'. Brexit allowed a largely idiosyncratic and unsubstantiated policy proposal – escape 'EU protectionism' and reorient British trade to the 'Anglosphere' – to be accepted by large parts of British society. Especially it was to be accepted by socially, culturally, and geographically peripheralized groups who stood to gain very little from a policy of open trade and market deregulation.

This free trade discourse on the other hand – in conjunction with the anti-immigration one, the other pillar of Brexit– also served an immediate tactical goal of the Conservative Party. Euroscepticism came to dominate the Conservative Party during its time in the political wilderness, when New Labour and its modernizing agenda seemed to have displaced it as the dominant party of British politics. During this period, libertarian Euroscepticism was seen as a problem for the party, thwarting its appeal to moderate voters in a modernizing society. Nonetheless, the populist nature of Brexit helped recast Euroscepticism. This allowed the right wing of the Conservatives to outflank the centrist wing of their party, ultimately leading in 2019 to the emergence of Boris Johnson as leader of the party and prime minister and later, to his crushing victory in the elections of December of the same year.

As with Trump and his revamped trade deals, populist trade discourse in the UK did not go as far as complete rupture between the UK and the EU. If anything, the image of a sovereign government negotiating down to the wire, hours before 'cliff-edge deadlines' were about to expire, agreements with the EU – the exit agreement ahead of formal exit on 31 January 2020 and the future relationship treaty before the end of the transition period on 31 December 2020 – vindicated the populist call for 'taking back control' and fulfilled the promise of 'delivering Brexit', a major symbol of the UK's new ability to strike its own trade deals.

## CONCLUSION: POPULISM AS A NEW EQUILIBRIUM BETWEEN CONTESTATION AND GLOBAL GOVERNANCE

Populism in the US and populism in the UK between 2016 and 2020 presented intriguing analogies. In both cases, populism emerged from within an established conservative party while adopting some of the rhetoric and demands of the left, especially the frustrations of the post-industrial working class; it thrived in the space abandoned by centre-left parties who abrogated their role as representatives of class interests; and it articulated the 'people vs. system' divide in terms of an inside-outside opposition, reflecting the fact that under globalization the 'elites', 'power', and 'system' are not only above the people, but also outside the realm of the nation-state.

Given these analogies, it may appear paradoxical that Trump and Brexiteers expressed opposite attitudes on trade, with the former being protectionist and the latter glorifying free trade. This difference can be accounted for by the differing geopolitical position of the two states, the one – a global superpower that offloaded on its domestic working class the cost of supporting the open system of globalization; the other – a middle-sized state that exited a continental economic and legal order. Both kinds of populism articulated trade as a solution to problems of representation engendered by economic globalization and state internationalization: protectionism in the US and independent trade policy in the UK both promised to reinstate popular control over a state that was no longer responsive.

The articulation of trade policy as a claim to representation explains the appeal of populist trade positions despite their very doubtful validity and questionable benefits to the supporters of these populist movements. US and British populists spoke for a broad and loose identity of the 'people' whose heterogeneous demands were collapsed in the blanket call for recognition and representation, an emotive demand of repatriating 'control' to the territorial state where democratic communities reside. Populism's ability to frame the grievances of left-behind groups as a demand for representation of the 'real people' challenges the norms of openness, efficiency, and rules-based policy-making upon which the legitimacy of international regimes, like the WTO and the EU, lies.

As observed, the practical impact of populist trade discourses is significant, but also has its limits. In practice, the trade policies that result from populist effervescence rarely go as far as initial promises of fully satisfying the material grievance of the 'people'. In the face of tactical considerations – Trump's attempted re-election (which, to many seemed very probable before the COVID pandemic) or the British Conservatives' winning a majority in

Parliament – populists are perfectly capable of pivoting to more pragmatic positions. This often leads to trade truces, like the one the US signed with China in early 2020, or compromise agreements, like the EU–UK exit agreement in early 2020 and the future relationship deal in late 2020 amid the recession caused by the COVID pandemic.

Thinking about the contestation of the international order more broadly, the US and UK cases show the disruptive potential of societal contestation, emerging from grievances among large segments of the population, but also the possibility of it being domesticated in national political systems and, by extension, the structure of the global order. Britain's EU exit and US tariffs were of course a new concerning development for global governance. But despite the uncertainty they created, they also channelled popular discontent towards a new equilibrium between national representational processes and international engagement. In this equilibrium, elements of the international order like the global trade regime do not collapse completely, but become more contingent and uncertain, subject to the ebbs and flows of domestic politics and the varying ability of governments to channel societal contestation.

It is important to note then that the new equilibrium is not one of reinstating the globalization business-as-usual through a populist backdoor. Brexit is a reality and it continues to play out as an acrimonious brinkmanship between London and Brussels over checks and customs in Northern Ireland, endangering peace there. Meanwhile, the new US president Joe Biden does not appear willing to return to the unfettered free trade status quo ante without some conditions being satisfied first. Indeed, in a range of issues, from steel and aluminium tariffs and his 'Buy American' message to vaccine export and foreign travel bans, he has proven to be as sovereignty-minded as his predecessor, if not more. These developments foreshadow bigger fragmentation regardless of whether populists are in power or not, as states instrumentally oscillate between pushes for openness and protectionist retreats depending on the domestic and external pressures they face. As such, contestation is now structurally embedded in the new international order, with a carefully choreographed theatre of contestation between states serving to neutralize societal contestation at home.

In this sense, populism can be understood as both generating and forming part of a new equilibrium between contestation and global governance, absorbing genuine societal contestation into more antagonistic state policies that, however, can always result in bilateral, regional or plurilateral agreements under the right conditions. More than stagnation, but less than return to the old globalization normal, global governance's future seems to be one of fragmentation, unpredictability, and periodical crises bookended by last-moment bargains. Given the intensity of societal contestation witnessed in the US and the UK in 2016, this may well be the best that could be hoped for.

## REFERENCES

Abts, K. and Rummens, S. (2007) Populism versus Democracy. *Political Studies*, **55**(2), 405–424.

Arditi, B. (2010) Populism is Hegemony is Politics? On Ernesto Laclau's On Populist Reason. *Constellations*, **17**(3), 488–497.

Associated Press (2019) Free Traders No More? GOP Warms up to Trump's Use of Tariffs. Associated Press, 7 June.

Baker, D., Gamble, A. and Seawright, D. (2008) Sovereign Nations and Global Markets: Modern British Conservatism and Hyperglobalism. *British Journal of Politics and International Relations*, **4**(3), 399–428.

Bale, T. (2010) *The Conservative Party: From Thatcher to Cameron*. Cambridge: Polity Press.

Bartolini, S. and Mair, P. (1990) *Identity, Competition and Electoral Availability: The Stabilisation of European Electorates 1885–1985*. Cambridge: Cambridge University Press.

Bell, D. and Vucetic, S. (2019) Brexit, CANZUK, and the Legacy of Empire. *British Journal of Politics and International Relations*, **21**(2), 367–382.

Bickerton, C. (2015) A Union of Member States: State Transformation and the New Intergovernmentalism. In Bickerton, C., Hodson, D. and Puetter, U. (eds), *The New Intergovernmentalism: States and Supranational Actors in the Post-Maastricht Era*. Oxford: Oxford University Press, 51–72.

Bishop, M. and Payne, P. (2019) *Is Britain 'Undeveloping' before Our Eyes?* Sheffield: Sheffield Political Economy Research Institute. http://speri.dept.shef.ac.uk/2019/01/29/is-britain-undeveloping-before-our-eyes-part-i/.

Börzel, T. and Risse, T. (2018) From the Euro to the Schengen Crises: European Integration Theories, Politicization, and Identity Politics. *Journal of European Public Policy*, **25**(1), 83–108.

Boucher, J. and Thies, C. (2019) 'I Am a Tariff Man': The Power of Populist Foreign Policy Rhetoric under President Trump. *Journal of Politics*, **81**(2), 712–722.

Bulmer, S. (2008) New Labour, New European Policy? Blair, Brown and Utilitarian Supranationalism. *Parliamentary Affairs*, **61**(4), 597–620.

Byrne, L. (2017) Britain Needs Its Old Buccaneering Spirit Post-Brexit to Lead the World. *The Daily Telegraph*, 9 October.

Chryssogelos, A. (2020) State Transformation and Populism: From the Internationalized to the Neo-Sovereign State? *Politics*, **40**(1), 22–37.

CNBC (2019a) Trump's Tariff Threats on Autos Are Stoking Fears of a German Recession. *CNBC*, 26 April. https://www.cnbc.com/2019/04/26/trump-tariff-threat-on-autos-could-bring-a-german-recession.html.

CNBC (2019b) Trump Says There's a 'Good Chance' that Mexico Averts Tariffs with Deal that Includes Purchase of US Farm Goods. *CNBC*, 7 June. https://www.cnbc.com/2019/06/07/trump-says-theres-a-good-chance-that-mexico-averts-tariffs-by-purchasing-us-farm-goods.html.

Della Salla, V. (1997) Hollowing Out and Hardening the State: European Integration and the Italian Economy. *West European Politics*, **20**(1), 14–33.

Dromey, J. (2017) 7 Times the Tories Let Down British Workers – and Why They Won't Protect You Now. *New Statesman*, 9 November.

Eatwell, R. and Goodwin, M. (2018) *National Populism: The Revolt against Liberal Democracy*. London: Penguin.

Financial Times (2020) UK-Japan Trade Deal Shows Need for EU Pact. *Financial Times* editorial, 13 September.

Forster, A. (2002) *Euroscepticism in Contemporary British Politics: Opposition to Europe in the Conservative and Labour Parties since 1945*. London: Routledge.

Gertz, G. (2018) *5 Things to Know about USMCA, the New NAFTA*. Washington, DC: Brookings Institution, 2 October.

Gest, J. (2016) *The New Minority: White Working Class Politics in an Age of Immigration and Inequality*. New York: Oxford University Press.

Gifford, C. (2014a) *The Making of Eurosceptic Britain: Identity and Economy in a Post-Imperial State*. London: Routledge.

Gifford, C. (2014b) The People Against Europe: The Eurosceptic Challenge to the United Kingdom's Coalition Government. *Journal of Common Market Studies*, **52**(3), 512–528.

Goodhart, D. (2017) *The Road to Somewhere: The Populist Revolt and the Future of Politics*. London: Hurst.

The Guardian (2019) Brexit: UK Has Rolled Over just £16bn out of £117bn Trade Deals. *The Guardian*, 13 February.

Hadiz, V. and Chryssogelos, A. (2017) Populism in World Politics: A Comparative Cross-Regional Perspective. *International Political Science Review*, **38**(4), 399–411.

Hannan, D. (2012) *A Doomed Marriage: Britain and Europe*. London: Notting Hill Editions.

Kaonga, G. (2019) Brexit Conspiracy: Boris Warns Delaying Article 50 Reveals Elite Conspiracy to Stop Brexit. *Express*, 18 January. https://www.express.co.uk/news/uk/1074228/Brexit-News-Boris-Johnson-Brexit-speech-theresa-may-no-deal-brexit.

Katz, R. and Mair, P. (1995) Changing Models of Party Organization and Party Democracy: The Emergence of the Cartel Party. *Party Politics*, **1**(1), 5–28.

Kriesi, H., Grande, E., Lachat, R., Dolezal, M., Bornschier, S. and Frey, T. (2008) *West European Politics in the Age of Globalization*. Oxford: Oxford University Press.

Krugman, P. (1993) The Uncomfortable Truth about NAFTA: It's Foreign Policy, Stupid. *Foreign Affairs*, **72**(5), 13–19.

Laclau, E. (2005a) *On Populist Reason*. London: Verso.

Laclau, E. (2005b) Populism: What's in a Name? In Panizza, F. (ed.), *Populism and the Mirror of Democracy*. London and New York: Verso, 32–49.

Lamp, N. (2018) How Should We Think about the Winners and Losers from Globalization? Three Narratives and their Implications for the Redesign of International Economic Agreements. Kingston: Queen's University Faculty of Law Research Paper 2018-102.

Lee, S. (2011) No Plan B: The Coalition Agenda for Cutting the Deficit and Rebalancing the Economy. In Lee, S. and Beech, M. (eds), *The Cameron–Clegg Government: Coalition Politics in an Age of Austerity*. Basingstoke: Palgrave Macmillan, 59–74.

Lipset, S. and Rokkan, S. (1967) Cleavage Structures, Party Systems, and Voter Alignments: An Introduction. In Lipset, S. and Rokkan, S. (eds), *Party Systems and Voter Alignments: Cross-National Perspectives*. New York: Free Press, 1–64.

Logan, R. (2017) Rees-Mogg Furious at Starmer on Brexit: 'Metropolitan Elite Are Rejecting the Referendum'. *Express*, 3 August. https://www.express.co.uk/news/uk/836465/Brexit-jacob-rees-mogg-remainers-european-economic-area-keir-starmer.

Lynch, P. and Whitaker, R. (2012) Where There is Discord, Can They Bring Harmony? Managing Intra-Party Dissent on European Integration in the Conservative Party. *British Journal of Politics and International Relations*, **15**(3), 317–339.

Mair, P. (2000) *Populist Democracy vs. Party Democracy*. Leiden: ECPR. https://ecpr.eu/Filestore/PaperProposal/56283bba-0e9f-4798-81bf-3a51470ff970.pdf.

Mance, H. (2016) Britain Has Had Enough of Experts, Says Gove. *Financial Times*, 3 June.

May, T. (2016) Speech at Conservative Party Conference. Birmingham, 5 October. https://www.independent.co.uk/news/uk/politics/theresa-may-speech-tory-conference-2016-in-full-transcript-a7346171.html.

May, T. (2017) Speech on Brexit. Lancaster House, 17 January. http://time.com/4636141/theresa-may-brexit-speech-transcript/.

Moravcsik, A. (1997) Taking Preferences Seriously: A Liberal Theory of International Politics. *International Organization*, **51**(4), 513–553.

Mouzelis, N. (1985) On the Concept of Populism: Populist and Clientelist Modes of Incorporation in Semiperipheral Polities. *Politics and Society*, **14**(3), 329–348.

Mudde, C. (2004) The Populist Zeitgeist. *Government and Opposition*, **39**(4), 541–563.

New York Times (2019) Stung by Trump's Trade Wars, Wisconsin's Milk Farmers Face Extinction. *New York Times*, 26 April.

Panizza, F. (ed.) (2005) *Populism and the Mirror of Democracy*. London: Verso.

Perot, R. and Choate, P. (1993) *Save Your Job, Save Our Country. Why NAFTA Must Be Stopped – Now!* New York: Hyperion Books.

Politico (2018) Trump Attacks Canada and Mexico Over Trade. *Politico*, 3 May. https://www.politico.com/story/2018/03/05/trump-canada-mexico-nafta-trade-435820.

Reuters (2016) Trump Targets China Trade, Says Plans Serious Measures. *Reuters*, 24 August. https://www.reuters.com/article/us-usa-election-trump-china/trump-targets-china-trade-says-plans-serious-measures-idUSKCN10Z2JN.

Rodrik, D. (2017) *Populism and the Economics of Globalization*. NBER Working Paper No. 23559, June. Cambridge, MA: National Bureau of Economic Research.

Shoch, J. (2000) Contesting Globalization: Organized Labor, NAFTA, and the 1997 and 1998 Fast-Track Fights. *Politics and Society*, **28**(1), 119–150.

Siles-Brügge, G. (2019) Bound by Gravity or Living in a 'Post Geography Trading World'? Expert Knowledge and Affective Spatial Imaginaries in the Construction of the UK's Post-Brexit Trade Policy. *New Political Economy*, **24**(3), 422–439.

Skonieczny, A. (2001) Constructing NAFTA: Myth, Representation, and the Discursive Construction of U.S. Foreign Policy. *International Studies Quarterly*, **45**(3), 433–454.

Skonieczny, A. (2018) Emotions and Political Narratives: Populism, Trump and Trade. *Politics and Governance*, **6**(4), 62–72.

Stanley, B. (2008) The Thin Ideology of Populism. *Journal of Political Ideologies*, **13**(1), 95–110.

Stavrakakis, Y. (2004) Antinomies of Formalism: Laclau's Theory of Populism and the Lessons from Religious Populism in Greece. *Journal of Political Ideologies*, **9**(3), 253–267.

Trump, D. (2016) Campaign Speech in Milwaukee, WI, 17 August. *Politico*. https://www.politico.com/story/2016/08/full-text-donald-trumps-speech-on-227095.

Vail, M. (2015) Between One-Nation Toryism and Neoliberalism: The Dilemmas of British Conservatism and Britain's Evolving Place in Europe. *Journal of Common Market Studies*, **53**(1), 106–122.

Ziblatt, D. (2017) *Conservative Parties and the Birth of Democracy*. Cambridge: Cambridge University Press.

Zürn, M. (2014) The Politicization of World Politics and its Effects: Eight Propositions. *European Political Science Review*, **6**(1), 47–71.

Zürn, M. and Deitelhoff, N. (2015) Internationalization and the State. Sovereignty as External Side of Modern Statehood. In Leibfried, S., Huber, E., Lange, M., Levy, J. D., Nullmeier, F. and Stephens, J. D. (eds), *The Oxford Handbook of Transformations of the State*. Oxford: Oxford University Press, 193–217.

# 7. Populists at the G20 and G7: informal cooperation in turbulent times

**Alex Andrione-Moylan and Jan Wouters**

## INTRODUCTION

This chapter aims to unravel some of the specific features of the *crisis of multilateralism*, drawing evidence from informal cooperation in the G-format of the G7/8 and G20, particularly during the Trump presidency in the US. In doing so, it will reassess the debates over the efficacy and legitimacy of these informal bodies, in light of domestic developments such as the rise of populism, anti-elitism, and anti-cosmopolitanism and the impact on the conduct of foreign policy and the resilience of global cooperation. By relating both theoretically and empirically domestic and global trends, this analysis will highlight features of the changing nature of (informal) global cooperation, and the new and lasting ways in which domestic politics may be affecting global governance, even as we witness the decline of the 'populist wave'. A brief overview of the inception of Gx cooperation is followed by an assessment of the legitimacy conundrum it raises, its relevance to populism, and how populist leaders behave in international affairs. Some key domestic developments within members of the G7 and G20 are discussed to exemplify the impact of populist leaders on the conduct of foreign policy. Finally, the remainder of this chapter provides an overview of recent summits, highlighting how populist dynamics have played out in the G7 and G20 and underlining the key features of the ever-elusive notion of populism in foreign policy. In this way, the chapter accentuates some key ways in which polarization and contestation occur in the global arena and reveals a greater implication for the role of the European Union as a global actor.

## INFORMALITY, LEGITIMACY AND POPULISM

Since the end of the Cold War, the world has witnessed fundamental changes in the global arena, with the West's predominance gradually giving way to the growing economic and political clout of other world regions, especially

Brazil, Russia, India, China, and South Africa (the so-called BRICS) (Dobson 2006). In addition, the informal nature of the G7 is often associated with unaccountability and lack of transparency. This characterization made the G7 a target of an evolving anti-globalization movement, particularly since the mid-1990s – at the time confined to political activism, not only of anarchists, but also of civil society organizations advocating for greater transparency (Hajnal 2016a). Even so, the G7 and the G20 continue to play an important role in global affairs.

For one, the power wielded by its members combined – US, UK, Germany, France, Italy, Japan and Canada – has not vanished; G7 members cover nearly a third of global gross domestic product. They are uniquely placed to shepherd cooperation towards specific outcomes within formal international organizations, such as the International Monetary Fund or the World Bank. Secondly, though there may be little accountability in terms of whether and how G7 members implement the commitments they sign up to, the yearly summits, along with the lower-level meetings among government officials and ministers, remain key in fostering cooperation (Hajnal 2016a). In an increasingly fractious world, where domestic politics plays an increasing role in shaping how countries behave in global affairs, 'like-mindedness' and a cooperative attitude should not be taken for granted. Although the face of the G7 changed over time to become more inclusive (see e.g. Cooper and Jackson 2008; Kirton 2015), in order to ensure its continuing relevance in a rapidly changing world, its limited membership ultimately fell short of providing a truly global coordination system. Another financial crisis hit, this time in Asia and Latin America, and the G8 recommended the establishment of the finance ministers and bank governors G20 summit, in order to provide targeted solutions and remedy the membership issue. In addition to the G8 countries (G7 and Russia), it includes Argentina, Australia, Brazil, China, India, Indonesia, Mexico, Saudi Arabia, South Africa, the Republic of Korea, Turkey, and the European Union, which here has the status of the twentieth member – together they represent a rather impressive 80 per cent of global GDP (Hajnàl 2016b).

How momentous was the creation of the G20? As noted by Postel-Vinay (2014), what was and remains significant is how the G20 was the first informal setting to overcome the North–South divide. Other Gx-formats, such as the G77 or the G24, along with all the 'outreach' efforts of the G8, had been introduced to give developing countries a voice, but they did not participate on an equal footing with the West (Postel-Vinay 2014). The criterion of 'systemically important' economies was a neutral one, if – and not by chance – vague in its requirements, but that in any case did not rely on the outdated divisions between North and South. In doing so, it also sets the stage for conceiving relations between the West and the Rest not as a zero-sum game, but rather in a world in which sharing influence is possible. The reality remains that there is a degree of arbitrariness in the selection of members, which has triggered significant criticism. In 2009, a *Financial Times* article was famously titled "The Group of 20 Must Be Stopped", where the author argued that it afforded undue influence to a far too limited group of large countries, that compared to the G8 had gained much in terms of self-righteousness because of its veneer of legitimacy (Financial Times 2009).

The analysis of recent G8 and G20 summitry that this chapter seeks to present is an appraisal of possible links between global, transnational and domestic dynamics. Populism can be seen as a 'thin centred ideology', founded on the stark dichotomy between pure people and a corrupt elite (see for instance the seminal work by Mudde and Kaltwasser 2017). As the authors have argued elsewhere (Oldani et al. 2018), particularly among the populist right, the rejection of the establishment, more often than not, for instance, also entails the rejection of the European integration project, of a system that works only for the citizens of nowhere, of cosmopolitan values. Feelings of lack of agency over the direction of one's own destiny are stoked by exclusionary narratives grounded in cultural essentialism, which underpin a worldview in which the effects of the global on the local have largely been negative. In other words, populism may at times fill the legitimacy gaps in global governance – and within Gx-format cooperation they are perhaps more apparent than ever. With globalization affecting the everyday lives of individuals, it appears that citizens' expectations have shifted. When international or supranational institutions fail to deliver on their promise of prosperity and are unable to function as a prevention mechanism in times of crisis, as exemplified by the 2008 global financial and economic crisis, a populist backlash may become more likely (Kriesi 2012, 2014).

## States in Transition, Informal Summitry in Transition

Before delving into key developments during recent summits, it is useful to briefly survey how the domestic political landscape has changed across members of the Gx-format cooperation. There are, one might say, four categories of countries that can help understand the direction of global cooperation. For a time the scales within the membership of the G20 had tipped towards autocratic and populist leaders. In 2016, the election of Donald Trump to the US presidency brought their share of GDP to 60–70 per cent (Bloomberg 2019). The United States were not unique in this group: India, Brazil and, with some caveats, also Italy could be included among these examples of established democracies, which score rather high across democratic indices (see e.g. Freedom House 2020). Yet, they were also among some of the most apparent instances of the recent shifts that are examined in this chapter – below examples of some of these instances are briefly outlined. This was a state of affairs which perhaps lasted less long than some predicted, representing an insightful window into what a world led by populists would look like.

**United States**

The Trump Administration was the initiator of the sharpest US rejection of the post-war liberal institutional pillars, at least in recent history. This included, most notably, the withdrawal from the two major trade agreements, in 2017 and 2018 respectively, in opposition to free trade: the Trans-Pacific Partnership (TPP), which the president described as a "rape of our country" (Politico 2019), and the EU-US Transatlantic Trade and Investment Partnership (TTIP), proposed under the previous administration. In 2017 it was the turn of the United Nations Educational, Scientific and Cultural Organization (UNESCO), an "enemy" of close ally Israel. In the same year, the US ended its participation in the Paris Agreement on Climate Change, signed by the previous administration in 2015, noting that:

> The Paris Agreement handicaps the United States economy in order to win praise from the very foreign capitals and global activists that have long sought to gain wealth at our country's expense. They don't put America first. I do, and I always will. (Trump 2017)

In 2018, the US ended its membership in the UN Human Rights Council (UNHCR), signalling that human rights promotion was no longer a priority. Shortly afterwards, the president withdrew from the hard-won Joint Comprehensive Plan of Action (JCPOA) to limit Iran's nuclear capability. Most recently, in 2020, the US withdrew from the World Health Organization (WHO), in the midst of a global pandemic. At a time when a rapid and coordinated response from the WHO was crucial, the US cited concerns over the organization being "China centric" (CNBC 2020). Finally, as a result of Russian violations of the same treaty, the administration announced the withdrawal from the Treaty on Open Skies aimed at promoting military cooperation among signatories (Washington Post 2020).

This astonishing list is a manifestation of what the Trump Administration would describe as 'America First', which implicitly embraces a realist worldview that interprets international affairs as a zero-sum game and as highly transactional, i.e. entirely driven by short-term output, ostensibly to the direct benefit of the US (Löfflmann 2019). Some note that in many cases Trump's foreign policy showed continuity with existing practice, such as in the case of the US military presence (Afghanistan) and intervention (Syria) in the Middle East. Foreign policy under Trump was far from coherent, and seemed to adhere to the president's campaign promises mainly on issues that were likely to receive greater visibility in the media – as showcased by the trade war with

China (Löfflmann 2019). Yet, Trump's unpredictability and bombastic rhetoric in the global arena, frosty relations with key allies across the EU and NATO, and formal and informal abdication of the United States' role as protector of shared values – multilateralism, democracy, human rights, and the rule of law – did much to entrench a more divided, multipolar world (Macdonald 2018). This is as close as one gets to a populist foreign policy – it is responsive to anti-globalist sentiments among citizens and, crucially, it bypasses the gilded halls of diplomacy and foreign policy elites (Cooper 2019).

**Brazil**

In a similar vein, the case of Brazil also shows signs of a post-diplomatic foreign policy era – one that is no longer dominated by relations with the West and adherence to the global liberal order, and that is "democratised", as a result (Lopes 2020, p. 174). Though this latter notion of the democratization of foreign policy remains rather vague in the current literature, there seem to be signs of how pressures for greater legitimacy have led to expectations that supporters of President Jair Bolsonaro see their worldview – which is anti-globalist and nationalistic – reflected in the country's foreign policy. This has led to further entrenching the presidentialization of foreign policy making, for instance through the strengthened Secretariat for Strategic Affairs (SEA), a body linked to the President's Office, rather than to the once pre-eminent Ministry for Foreign Affairs. The relationship with the West has always been complicated. Over the last decades Brazilian foreign policy has been focused on building autonomy and developing South–South cooperation: today the fault-lines appear to be rather defined by the support or aversion towards the multilateral order, which drove Brazil to form closer ties with Donald Trump and Benjamin Netanyahu (Guimarães 2020). As in the case of the United States, it will be interesting to examine more closely if these developments manifest themselves in recent G20 meetings.

**India**

Under Narendra Modi and the Bharatiya Janata Party (BJP) echoes of similar dynamics can be found, at least in the prevailing rhetoric. There has been a greater emphasis on establishing a powerful role in international affairs, directing the focus on external 'enemies' such as China and Pakistan, and shifting away from the traditional foreign policy goals of the country. Such a shift seeks to build a narrative of the country destined to return to a mythical past of Hindu civilization, marked by economic, political, and military strength. As Wojczewski (2019) argues, foreign enemies that prevent India from returning to its former glory represent a key part of that populist discourse, which in turn is closely connected to his critique of India's elite as corrupt, but also "Westernised" and "English-speaking". This goes hand in hand with wariness of multilateral cooperation, and a professed preference for bilateral settings – though there is little evidence of a dramatic shift towards bilateralism – and a foreign policy that focuses on India's (trade) interests (Plagemann and Destradi 2019). Interestingly, this shapes relations also among the other BRICS members. While they do share some common interests, they also tend to be very nation-focused: competition between India and China remains strong. In the past, Modi has argued against expanding the role of the G20, preferring the more representative United Nations, where India can play the role of a defender of smaller developing countries (Cooper and Farooq 2016; NDTV 2015).

Moreover, the attempts at creating a perception of a people's foreign policy, one that is not per se procedurally more democratic, but that is communicated through social media directly to citizens, are noteworthy. Modi even invites his followers to 'vote' on his policies – an approach different from Trump's *Twitter diplomacy*. This appears to be part of the broader trend towards what has been referred to *disintermediation*, defined as the separation of diplomatic circles from other components of government, as well as citizens in general. It seems germane to understanding the multifaceted phenomenon of populist foreign policy, as it highlights the disconnect between the views of the international elites and citizens. Simply put, it revolves around the idea that intermediaries need to be removed for a more responsive foreign policy – a demand that populist leaders, such as Modi, can translate into support for an executive driven foreign policy. For instance, this has resulted in the downgrading of the Ministry for External Affairs and the increasing influence of Ajit Doval, former police officer and Modi's national security adviser (Ganguly 2017). Here too, we can observe the interplay between centralization and populist governance going hand in hand.

### The European Union

The EU finds itself facing many of the same challenges. While the populist wave of recent years may have subsided, the trends that can be observed in the above-mentioned countries are by no means foreign to the European context, even in the 'old' democracies. The 2018 general elections in Italy ushered in the first populist government in Western Europe, bringing together the right-wing Lega and populist left Movimento 5 Stelle. The ties that this government developed with Russia on the topic of sanctions and China in the context of the BRI were significant. The newly formed relations with the two signalled not so much a radical re-alignment, but a more transactional approach to global affairs (EUobserver 2019). Another example is the Brexit referendum and the eventual exit of the United Kingdom from the EU, raising deeper questions about the European integration project (Bell 2017). The Brexit vote was arguably driven by discontent towards a globalized world, disproportionally benefiting cosmopolitan elites. The promise of 'taking back control', directly and perhaps through oversimplification, plays into the expectations of a *democratized* foreign policy. Undoubtedly, this has significant internal implications for the European project. However, populism and contestation in general, of both supranational institutions and multilateral forums , exposes some of the weaknesses of the global order. This is true particularly in terms of transparency and legitimacy of policy-making processes, as well as geographical representation (Koch 2021). Unlike other actors mentioned here, the EU faces a similar set of challenges within its confines and as a global actor. Issues, such as the current global pandemic, and economic and migration crises, have implications that are transnational in nature.

On the one hand, it could be argued that the EU faces a perfect storm of internal and external challenges, a combination of factors which prevents the EU from becoming an effective global actor. Yet, there is also a window of opportunity. It could be argued that in order to rebuild its domestic legitimacy and respond to the expectations of EU citizens in tackling complex transnational issues effectively, the EU is in need of exerting its influence in a global setting, all while demonstrating the legitimacy, accountability, and rapid responsiveness of the multilateral order towards bottom-up concerns. Such a scenario would render the EU a significantly more proactive actor in challenging outdated aspects of international affairs. Therefore, while the developments discussed in this chapter should be a source of concern, they also offer a new chance for the EU to respond to the demands of citizens and improve global governance rather than undermine its foundations. Some indications of the EU taking advantage of such a scenario can already be observed. In a recent review of its international trade policy, the Commission states that in order to become more "assertive", "competitive" and "resilient" as a global actor, the EU needs to ensure "that the EU's interests are fully met as regards the expected benefits of trade agreements", narrowing the divide between interests and values and focusing on transparency and responsiveness as key principles of its external action (European Commission 2021, pp. 4–5, 22). The EU, particularly as a member of the G20, could find the necessary network of like-minded countries in order to spearhead these efforts. Initiatives presented at the G20, aimed at triggering far-reaching WTO reforms and tackling COVID-19, and the role played by the EU therein, are some indications of the potential of informal governance (Hoekman 2020).

## Gx Cooperation Challenged (2017–2020)

### Trump contained at Taormina and Hamburg (2017)

President Donald Trump first appeared at a G7 summit in 2017, in Taormina, Italy, in a setting where divisions between the US and the other members of the informal club became apparent. German Chancellor Angela Merkel had hoped to bridge the gap on the fight against climate change, identifying a roadmap to keep the US in the Paris Agreement. Trump, however, was less confrontational than might have been expected, ultimately playing ball with his counterparts and agreeing on a compromise, particularly on trade (see leaders' communiqué: G7 2017, p. 4). Though divisions were apparent, the summit benefited from a somewhat cautious newly elected US president. The focus was mainly on terrorism and security – a top priority in the aftermath of terrorist attacks in France and the UK – as well as the new domain of gender equality (Oldani et al. 2018). A closer analysis shows that the G7 was already struggling to make progress on the most difficult global challenges at the time, and arguably those that required most attention – particularly climate change, migration, and the economy.

That year, the G20 summit in Hamburg built on the compromise reached in Taormina, even though struggles to reach a common statement against protectionism were reported. For instance, the reference to "legitimate trade defence instruments" was an addition that was not present in the documents signed at the 2016 summit. This addition can be reasonably assumed to have been a consequence of pressure from the US delegation (Berger 2017). However, in many ways Trumpism was contained and progress was made in other areas, such as the Africa Partnership (G20 2017, p. 13). Another related area of success was the commitments on the 2030 Agenda on the Sustainable Development Goals (SDGs), with leaders committing to "further align our actions with the 2030 Agenda for Sustainable Development" (G20 2017, p. 10).

There were several emerging trends at the time. There was an indication of a shift in the global arena away from a largely uncontested multilateral order, towards a declining consensus. Similarly, there was the opposition of the G20 countries, such as India, against broadening the forum's brief beyond crisis management. It might be argued that the G7 in Taormina served the purpose of stemming the impact of Trump-led disruption, allowing for progress to be made in global cooperation. This tells us something about the complementarity of the two forums , but also how the G20 may indeed be the better setting to push forward commitments on global issues (Berger and Evenett 2017). Finally, the German presidency – a country firmly in the *honest broker* category – played an important role on engaging with the serious legitimacy challenges faced by the G20, by actively supporting the C20, the civil society forum; T20, the forum bringing together Think-Tanks; and the L20, where trade unions and labour organizations meet (Lay 2017).

## Like-mindedness unravels at Charlevoix and the 'RIC' returns at Buenos Aires (2018)

The following G7 summit in Charlevoix, Canada (2018), was notoriously marred by the increasingly uncompromising stance of the Trump Administration, particularly on trade. In March 2018, the US unilaterally introduced 10 per cent import tariffs on aluminium and 20 per cent tariffs on steel. The meeting was dominated by Trump's complaints of the US being "the piggy bank that everybody's robbing" (quoted in Patrick 2018). In the run-up to the meeting, he also provocatively suggested that Russian President Vladimir Putin should once again take part in the informal club's meetings, a position which was widely rejected but interestingly was backed by Italian Prime Minister Conte. Conte noted that Putin's return would be "in the interests of everyone" (Reuters 2018a). Despite tensions running high, with Trump reportedly threatening to end all trade with the G7 economies, given their unfair practices, a common statement was eventually reached (Wouters and Van Kerckhoven 2019). However, following a statement by the Canadian Prime Minister Justin Trudeau warning against possible retaliations in response to US tariffs on Canadian imports, Trump took to Twitter – again a *people's diplomacy* of sorts – to withdraw his support, making it the first instance in the history of the G7 when an agreement was not reached among the leaders:

> Based on Justin's false statements at his news conference, and the fact that Canada is charging massive Tariffs to our US farmers, workers and companies, I have instructed our US Reps not to endorse the Communique as we look at Tariffs on automobiles flooding the US Market! (New York Times 2018)

These events are a reminder of how informality can provide the building blocks for cooperation, all while being more vulnerable to the unpredictability of a *populist foreign policy*: unlike in Taormina the previous year, Trumpism was *not* contained. Its effects were palpable in another informal forum, at the 2018 leader's summit for Asia-Pacific Economic Cooperation (APEC) – in a pattern emerging at recent informal summitry, for the first time since its establishment in 1989, no final communiqué was reached due to the deep differences between the US and China (Glaser and Flaherty 2019). Undoubtedly, this would have far-reaching consequences for the following G20 meeting in Buenos Aires.

If the German presidency of the forum had steered global cooperation towards an ambitious agenda, Argentinian President Mauricio Macri had sought to distance his country from its Latin American neighbours while privileging US support. The weak agenda proposed for the 2018 Buenos Aires Summit was widely interpreted along those lines, even while Macri's outwardly stated aim as "build consensus for an equitable and sustainable development", and direct a "G20 that contributes to the world and humanity" (quoted in Nahón 2018).

However, when it comes to the deepening cooperation between Russia, India and China, the informal 'RIC' trilateral meeting taking place for the first time in twelve years was significant (Reuters 2018b). This was a sign of how an unpredictable and protectionist US had led China to soften its enmity towards India, looking to stabilize relations in the region. Russian President Putin underlined the importance of "jointly protecting the principles of just and honest competition in world trade and finance" and an "open system of international economic relations" (President of Russia 2018).

These comments were echoed also by Prime Minister Modi and President Xi of China (President of Russia 2018; Lee and Lee 2018). China, Russia, and India would generally be placed in the 'disruptor' category of global actors, and yet they are simultaneously eager to be perceived as protectors of the global multilateral order. What can be inferred from the RIC's professed support for global multilateralism and 'open' economic relations, is the rather ad hoc nature of this commitment, dependent on the interests of these countries and therefore volatile or selective. A particular kind of cooperation seems to be prevailing in informal settings, one that some have defined as "competitive cooperation" (Kaul 2019) or "geopoliticization" (Meunier and Nicolaidis 2019). According to this, though cooperation occurs, it primarily seeks to maintain the balance of power and counteract competition.

**Osaka and Biarritz: multilateralism restored? (2018)**

Recent summits seem to have magnified just as much as they have reconciled differences of a fractious global arena. In the run-up to the following G20 summit in Osaka, held in June 2019, President Trump complained at alleged inequalities in the US–Japan defence treaty, noting that "If Japan is attacked, we will fight World War Three ... with our lives and with our treasure ... If we're attacked, Japan doesn't have to help us at all, [Japan] can watch it on the Sony television, okay, the attack" (CNN 2019). On the other hand, President Putin provided his assessment of the populist wave in the West, by noting that "the liberal idea has become obsolete. It has come into conflict with the interests of the overwhelming majority of the population" (Financial Times 2019a). It is a statement that brings home the transnationalization of global fault-lines, as authoritarian leaders seek to develop linkages with populist forces abroad, potentially affecting domestic political outcomes and indirectly undermining the rules-based international order from within. For instance, Russian interference in the 2016 US elections in favour of Trump is a proven fact (Reuters 2016).

The summit in Osaka was the first attended by Jair Bolsonaro, who was beginning to face increasing criticism, especially from EU members of the G20 and notably from Angela Merkel, as deforestation and wildfires ravaged the Amazon rainforest. As a response, during the summit the climate change sceptic president stressed that he would not follow in the footsteps of his predecessors who "came to be reprimanded by other countries [...] We don't accept being treated like in the past" adding that "Brazil can be an example for Germany even in the environment" (Deutsche Welle 2019). This is precisely the rhetoric that flows from his *Brazil first* foreign policy, which was nevertheless combined with Bolsonaro's signing of the agreement for an EU-Mercosur Association Agreement. This agreement provided the basis for concrete steps to be taken after two decades of talks between the European Union and South America. He also participated in the BRICS meeting putting to rest, at least in part, concerns that Brazil under Bolsonaro would become a less enthusiastic member of the informal gathering, given the close ties with Trump (Vianney Freddy et al. 2019).

The summit was closely followed in August 2019 by the 45th G7 summit in Biarritz, France. President Emmanuel Macron's *musclé* chairmanship of the summit was crucial in ensuring relative success in challenging times for multilateral cooperation. The main take away from another 'multilateral broker', Canada's Justin Trudeau, was that if the unpredictability of a foreign policy marked by disintermediation and highly transactional dynamics – originating primarily from the US (cf. *supra*) – was to be overcome, a new approach to the G7 would be taken. This concerned primarily the final leaders' communiqué, the feasibility of which had already been questioned in the run up to the Charlevoix summit in 2018 (Boehm 2019). Donald Trump's last-minute and carefully staged disavowal of the communiqué the previous year, led Macron to opt for doing away with the final statement altogether (France 24 2019).[1]

With a strong voice on the European and global stage, Macron's energetic approach and ambitious agenda was not dampened. Macron invited Iranian Foreign Minister Mohammad Zarif for an unannounced meeting in hopes of saving the Joint Comprehensive Plan of Action. This was followed by bilateral talks with President Trump in a bid to salvage the nuclear non-proliferation agreement with Iran which the US had declared void in May 2018. At the time, there was a hope for a new deal with Iran, which never further materialized (Financial Times 2019b). On the topic of the continuing conflict in the Donbass region, the groundwork was set for new talks in the Normandy

---

1 Macron noted how "these communiqués that no one reads" were the source of "interminable bureaucratic squabbling" deepening the sense that "the G7 had become an enclosure for zooming in on disagreements" (France 24 2019).

Format (France, Germany, Russia and Ukraine). The talks took place later that year and contributed to a ceasefire which took place in the autumn of 2020 (Al Jazeera 2020). Observers also noted how Macron, rather than focusing on the contentious issue of climate change, deftly highlighted the need to fight the fires raging in the Amazon rainforest. He effectively politicized the issue, using the growing domestic sensitivities to foreign policy matters to his advantage, while also championing global cooperation. Macron threatened to withdraw support from the EU-Mercosur trade deal if there was not a guarantee of stronger commitments by Bolsonaro to protect the Amazon. Such a move would be welcomed by both the French voters concerned about climate change, and the farmers uncertain about the consequences of such a trade deal (Financial Times 2019b). Significantly more doubtful is the extent to which any of this had lasting effects on global cooperation.

**Gx cooperation in times of COVID-19 (2020)**

Some populists, such as Modi, have taken advantage of the pandemic to introduce oppressive measures challenging the rule of law; others, like Trump and Bolsonaro, dismissed the threat altogether. For these kinds of leaders multilateral solutions were not the priority (Meyer 2020). Following the election of Barack Obama's right-hand man Joe Biden to the US presidency, it can only be speculated whether in a second Trump-led term, the short-term electoral advantages of a disintermediated *America first* foreign policy would have diminished, once a serious global challenge demanded closer cooperation and multilateral solutions. According to some observers, the global pandemic has ended up being a *circuit-breaker* of sorts, when it comes to the kind of short-sighted populist push to 'go it alone' that Trump and other leaders have promoted in recent years. Trump's perceived mishandling of the pandemic made his re-election far less likely, therefore suggesting that without the outbreak of COVID-19 a second term would have been a strong possibility (Baccini et al. 2021; Politico 2020). This conclusion is consistent with a recent Pew survey: when asked about international cooperation, 58 per cent of US respondents said that when dealing with major international issues, their country should *take into account other countries' interests even if it means making compromises* (Pew Research Centre 2020). The same percentage also agreed with the statement that *if their country had cooperated more with other countries, the number of coronavirus cases would have been lower in their country* (Pew Research Centre 2020). A majority (53 per cent) of respondents also expressed a *favourable view of the WHO's handling of COVID-19* (Pew Research Centre 2020). Finally, even among those US respondents who said that on major issues, *their country should follow its own interests even when other countries strongly disagree*, 40 per cent still had a positive view of the United Nations. Perhaps then it is not global cooperation and multilateralism that is rejected most often, but rather some of its outcomes: greater responsiveness to bottom-up needs and concerns would alleviate such feelings of disconnect. Certainly, improved responsiveness is likely to require greater *throughput* legitimacy, i.e. truly inclusive forums and institutions – no easy task, but an urgent one.

The global pandemic also increased pressure for the G20 to take on a strong leadership role in helping to deal with the consequences of the public health crisis. These difficult circumstances have become the backdrop of the latest example of the kind of hurdles global cooperation faces. In March 2020 the World Bank Group (WBG) and the International Monetary Fund (IMF) issued a statement "calling on all official bilateral creditors to suspend debt payments from IDA countries that request forbearance" adding that "it is imperative at this moment to provide a global sense of relief for developing countries as well as a strong signal to financial markets. The international community would welcome G20 support for this Call to Action" (International Monetary Fund 2020). Following that call for action, the G20 and the Paris Club (an informal grouping of state creditors) set up the Debt Service Suspension Initiative (DSSI), identifying 73 of the poorest countries as eligible applicants to the debt relief. Despite the extremely dire financial outlook, particularly for the developing world, and the clear risks to the resilience of the global economy, the results of these efforts have been underwhelming (Financial Times 2020a). Part of the reason relates to the difficulties in extending the DSSI also to private creditors and the classification of certain official loans as commercial in order to circumvent the debt relief programme. While the details and shortcomings of how the DSSI has been conceived are beyond the scope of this chapter, one key feature relates to the lack of leadership and enduring fractiousness, even when confronted with pressing global challenges. China's share of bilateral loans, second only to that of the US, has increased dramatically over the past decade: the percentage of poor countries owing debt to China has risen from 45 per cent in 2015 to 63 per cent in 2019, and virtually all countries in the African continent have received investments from China (Financial Times 2020b). Much of that debt is held by the China Development Bank (CDB), which Beijing classifies as a commercial lender – therefore, even if China has committed on paper to the DSSI, the CDB is not bound to participate and has not done so thus far, perhaps one of the flipsides to its 'no strings attached' investments (Nee 2020).

It is worth bearing in mind that there was a not-so-distant past – at least until the 1990s – in which the G7 as an extension of US hegemony, was truly capable of *directing global governance*. China's inaction on the issue of debt relief speaks volumes as to the fundamentally different global arena we are confronted with now. The lack of ambition and effectiveness of the debt relief programme, widely criticized for its lack of transparency, should be related to a US foreign policy that is detached from the notion that certain public goods, such as peace, freedom, and prosperity are *indivisible.* This is a cosmopolitan worldview not without its pitfalls, but one in which the US traditionally held an important stake. While the pandemic may have shifted the ground in favour of Joe Biden and "*America is back*" (Biden 2021), many question whether the new administration is in its own way also focusing on domestic crises, rather than global challenges (The Guardian 2020). Richard Haass (2021) recently suggested *America first* represents a new foreign policy consensus in Washington, which in some ways predates but has indeed outlived the Trump presidency. This reveals a new and complex balancing act, whereby the need for *internationalism* in light of global challenges, is tempered by domestic pressures for inward-looking policies. This trend may have even more significant long-term implications.

## CONCLUSION

When it comes to populist parties and governments in established democracies, it is difficult to pinpoint what precisely, if anything, has made their foreign policy 'populist', or discern elusive divides between practice and discourse. This overview of recent G7 and G20 summits, and key domestic developments in certain members, shows some of the ways in which the rise of populist leaders within democratic systems is linked to the turbulence and unpredictability faced by informal cooperation. At the start of this chapter it was suggested that the rise of populism, in its opposition between the *people* and *elites*, can be related to how the lack of accountability, legitimacy, and transparency in global governance – and especially in informal cooperation – has, over time, deepened distrust towards decision-making forums beyond the state level. Examining the behaviour of populist leaders highlighted in this chapter, in settings such as the G7 and G20, there are signs that their success stems in part from how they, at least superficially, seem to mitigate some of those concerns, all while privileging a more personalistic approach to decision-making. *America first*, *Brazil first*, and *India first* all translate into a foreign policy rhetoric that speaks directly to the base of the leader, for instance through online polls or Twitter diplomacy. Though it is a communicative style, and its audience is primarily voters at home, it has a concrete impact on the ability to cooperate both in a predictable manner and beyond short-term transactional goals. This is particularly true for the United States, once the prime mover of global governance initiatives. The recent incessant fluctuations – from cooperative to hostile and back – have undermined any kind of leadership role in global affairs. Unpredictability, disintermediation of diplomatic circles, a diplomacy 'of the People' which conceals a focus on the short-term interests of the nation, rather than the shared goals of a multilateral forum – these are traits common to all of the above-mentioned populist leaders.

What Trump might have criticized as an unfair reliance of multilateral forums on the (financial) support of the US, Bolsonaro might frame as rejecting the interference of European 'colonizers' in domestic affairs – the fundamentals of their worldviews are very similar. Yet, the consequences are different. The leadership gap left by the US is one that affected international cooperation deeply. This may have pushed countries, like the members of the RIC, closer together. However, their willingness to cooperate is also combined with a highly competitive streak, which echoes a propensity for transactional relations. The G20 may – for better or for worse – benefit from a less dominant role of the US even under the Biden Administration. As is apparent in the latest efforts surrounding the DSSI, a more prominent role for China and the other BRICS countries may entail a more ad hoc and indeed competitive approach to cooperation. Ultimately, however, greater public awareness demands greater responsiveness and therefore improved legitimacy – not a rejection of multilateralism and cooperation. Survey evidence shows that international cooperation is still supported by most in 2020 – perhaps also in light of the COVID-19 pandemic, which may prove a circuit-breaker for some populist leaders who have failed to acknowledge the seriousness of the threat. And even as the populist wave seems to ebb, elements of its outlook upon global affairs may well be here to stay. States, either as disruptors or honest brokers, emerge from our analysis as the protagonists of informal governance. While it is true that it is states that more directly are a vessel for populist attitudes in global affairs, we have also indicated that long lasting shifts in multilateralism that take onboard anti-globalist grievances in more positive ways, may be more likely to come from a complex multilevel and supranational actor like the EU.

## REFERENCES

Al Jazeera (2020) Full, Comprehensive Ceasefire Begins in Ukraine. https://www.aljazeera.com/news/2020/7/27/full-comprehensive-ceasefire-begins-in-ukraine.

Baccini, L., Brodeur, A. and Weymouth, S. (2021) The COVID-19 Pandemic and the 2020 US Presidential Election. *Journal of Population Economics*, **34**, 739–767.

Bell, E. (2017) Brexit and the Illusion of Democracy. *Socialism and Democracy*, **31**, 52–73.

Berger, A. (2017) What Remains of the G20 Hamburg Summit? *The Current Column* – German Development Institute.

Berger, A. and Evenett, S. J. (2017) The Trump-Induced G20 Stress Test on Trade: Did the German Presidency Pass? *Global Summitry*, **3**, 124–140.

Biden, J. (2021) Remarks by President Biden on America's Place in the World. The White House. https://www.whitehouse.gov/briefing-room/speeches-remarks/2021/02/04/remarks-by-president-biden-on-americas-place-in-the-world/.

Bloomberg (2019) Populists, Authoritarians Now Oversee Most of G-20 Output. Bloomberg.com.

Boehm, P. M. (2019) The Value of the G7: Reflections of a Sherpa. *Politique étrangère*, Summer Issue, 61–74.

CNBC (2020) Trump Threatens to Permanently Cut Off WHO Funding, Withdraw US Membership. By Christine Wang. https://www.cnbc.com/2020/05/19/trump-threatens-to-permanently-cut-off-who-funding-withdraw-us-membership.html.

CNN (2019) Trump Claims Japan "doesn't have to help" if US Is Attacked. By Zachary Cohen. https://www.cnn.com/2019/06/26/politics/trump-japan-defense-commitments/index.html.

Cooper, A. F. (2019) The Disintermediation Dilemma and its Impact on Diplomacy: A Research Agenda for Turbulent Times. *Diplomacy & Statecraft*, **30**, 799–807.

Cooper, A. F. and Farooq, A. B. (2016) The Role of China and India in the G20 and BRICS: Commonalities or Competitive Behaviour? *Journal of Current Chinese Affairs*, **45**, 73–106.

Cooper, A. F. and Jackson, K. (2008) The Incremental Transformation of the G8 through the Heiligendamm Process. *Studia Diplomatica*, **61**, 79–88.

Deutsche Welle (2019) Bolsonaro: Germany Can Learn "a lot" from Brazil about Environment. dw.com. https://www.dw.com/en/bolsonaro-germany-can-learn-a-lot-from-brazil-about-environment/a-49384095.

Dobson, H. (2006) *The Group of 7/8*. London: Routledge.

EUobserver (2019) Conte to Putin: EU Sanctions on Russia Make Italy "Sad". By Stefano Vergine. https://euobserver.com/foreign/145376.

European Commission (2021) *Trade Policy Review: An Open, Sustainable and Assertive Trade Policy*. https://trade.ec.europa.eu/doclib/docs/2021/february/tradoc_159438.pdf.

Financial Times (2009) The Group of 20 Must Be Stopped. By A. Åslund. https://www.ft.com/content/37deaeb4-dad0-11de-933d-00144feabdc0.

Financial Times (2019a) Vladimir Putin Says Liberalism Has 'Become Obsolete'. By L. Barber, H. Foy and A. Barker. https://www.ft.com/content/670039ec-98f3-11e9-9573-ee5cbb98ed36.

Financial Times (2019b) Macron Uses G7 Summit to Burnish Foreign Policy Ambitions. By Victor Mallet. https://www.ft.com/content/8faeb2ce-c8d2-11e9-a1f4-3669401ba76f.

Financial Times (2020a) G20 Falls Short on Debt Relief For Poor Countries. By Sam Fleming and Jonathan Wheatly. https://www.ft.com/content/e0673a53-7fee-4ef7-baaf-66cc97ee3296.

Financial Times (2020b) African Debt to China: 'A major drain on the poorest countries'. By Jonanthan Wheatley and Joseph Cotterill. https://www.ft.com/content/bd73a115-1988-43aa-8b2b-40a449da1235.

France 24 (2019) No Day at the Beach: G7 Adapts Summit to the age of "America First". By Tracy McNicoll. https://www.france24.com/en/20190823-france-G7-summit-macron-biarritz-adapts-america-first-trump-diplomacy.

Freedom House (2020) *Countries and Territories*. https://freedomhouse.org/countries/freedom-world/scores.

G7 (2017) G7 Taormina Leaders' Communiqué. European Council. https://www.consilium.europa.eu/media/23559/g7-taormina-leaders-communique.pdf.

G7 Finance Ministers (2020a) Chair's Summary: G7 Finance Ministers and Central Bank Governors Virtual Meeting. US Department of the Treasury. https://home.treasury.gov/news/press-releases/sm976.

G7 Finance Ministers (2020b) G7 Finance Ministers' Statement on the Debt Service Suspension Initiative and Debt Relief for Vulnerable Countries. US Department of the Treasury. https://home.treasury.gov/news/press-releases/sm1135.

G7 France (2019) Le Sommet de Biarritz. elysee.fr. https://www.elysee.fr/g7/2019/01/01/le-sommet-de-biarritz.

G20 (2017) G20 Leaders' Declaration: Shaping an Interconnected World. Office of the Federal Government of Germany. https://www.g20germany.de/Content/EN/_Anlagen/G20/G20-leaders-declaration_blob=publicationFile&v=11.pdf.

Ganguly, S. (2017) Has Modi Truly Changed India's Foreign Policy? *The Washington Quarterly*, **40**, 131–143.

Glaser, B. S. and Flaherty, K. (2019) A Deal is Struck in Buenos Aires: *Comparative Connections: A Triannual E-Journal on East Asian Bilateral Relations*, **20**.

Guimarães, F. de S. (2020) The Uneasy 'Well-Placed' State: Brazil within Latin America and the West. *Cambridge Review of International Affairs*, **33**, 603–619.

Haass, R. (2021) The Age of America First: Washington's Flawed New Foreign Policy Consensus. *Foreign Affairs*, **100**, 85–98.

Hajnal, P. I. (2016a) *The G8 System and the G20: Evolution, Role and Documentation*. London: Routledge.

Hajnal, P. I. (2016b) *The G20: Evolution, Interrelationships, Documentation*. London: Routledge.

Hoekman, B. M. (2020) *COVID-19 Trade Policy Measures, G20 Declarations and WTO Reform*. Paris: CEPR Press. https://cadmus.eui.eu//handle/1814/69110.

International Monetary Fund (2020) Joint Statement World Bank Group and IMF Call to Action on Debt of IDA Countries. Press release 20/103. IMF. https://www.imf.org/en/News/Articles/2020/03/25/pr20103-joint-statement-world-bank-group-and-imf-call-to-action-on-debt-of-ida-countries.

Kaul, I. (2019) The G20@10: Time to Shift Gears. *South African Journal of International Affairs*, **26**, 563–582.

Kirton, J. J. (2015) *Advancing G8 and G20 Effectiveness through Improved Accountability Assessment*. Aldershot: Ashgate.

Koch, C. M. (2021) Varieties of Populism and the Challenges to Global Constitutionalism: Dangers, Promises and Implications. *Global Constitutionalism*, **10**(3), 400–438.

Kriesi, H. (2012) *Political Conflict in Western Europe*. New York: Cambridge University Press.

Kriesi, H. (2014) The Populist Challenge. *West European Politics*, **37**, 361–378.

Lay, J. (2017) The G20 under Argentina's Presidency: Time to Deliver on the Hamburg Promises. *GIGA Focus Global – German Institute of Global and Area Studies*, **6**, 13.

Lee, S.-H. and Lee, C. (2018) *G20 in Buenos Aires: End of US-China Trade War?* http://hdl.handle.net/11540/9555.

Löfflmann, G. (2019) America First and the Populist Impact on US Foreign Policy. *Survival*, **61**, 115–138.

Lopes, D. B. (2020) De-Westernization, Democratization, Disconnection: The Emergence of Brazil's Post-Diplomatic Foreign Policy. *Global Affairs*, **6**, 167–184.

Macdonald, P. K. (2018) America First? Explaining Continuity and Change in Trump's Foreign Policy. *Political Science Quarterly*, **133**, 401–434.

Meunier, S. and Nicolaidis, K. (2019) The Geopoliticization of European Trade and Investment Policy. *JCMS: Journal of Common Market Studies*, **57**, 103–113.

Meyer, B. (2020) *Pandemic Populism: An Analysis of Populist Leaders' Responses to Covid-19*. Tony Blair Institute for Global Change. https://institute.global/policy/pandemic-populism-analysis-populist-leaders-responses-covid-19.

Mudde, C. and Kaltwasser, C. R. (2017) *Populism: A Very Short Introduction*. New York: Oxford University Press.
Nahón, C. (2018) Latin America in the G20: Continuities and Ruptures of the Regional Agenda (2008–2018). *International Organisations Research Journal*, **13**, 39–54.
NDTV (2015) At G20, PM Modi Proposes 10-Point Plan to Tackle Terrorism. By Veer Arjun Singh. https://www.ndtv.com/cheat-sheet/g20-summit-begins-as-turkey-sees-suicide-bombing-by-suspected-is-militant-1243584.
Nee, W. (2020) While China and the US Squabble, the World's Debt and Climate Crises Worsen. Amnesty International. https://www.amnesty.org/en/latest/news/2020/09/while-china-and-the-us-squabble-the-world-debt-and-climate-crises-worsen/.
Oldani, C., Wouters, J. and Andrione-Moylan, A. (2018) The G7, Anti-Globalism and the Governance of Globalization: Setting the Scene. In Oldani, C. and Wouters, J. (eds), *The G7, Anti-Globalism and the Governance of Globalization*. London: Routledge, 1–21.
Patrick, S. M. (2018) *At G7 Summit, Trump Takes a Wrecking Ball to the West*. Council on Foreign Relations. https://www.cfr.org/blog/g7-summit-trump-takes-wrecking-ball-west.
Pew Research Centre (2020) *International Cooperation Welcomed Across 14 Advanced Economies*. Global Attitudes Project. https://www.pewresearch.org/global/2020/09/21/international-cooperation-welcomed-across-14-advanced-economies/.
Plagemann, J. and Destradi, S. (2019) Populism and Foreign Policy: The Case of India. *Foreign Policy Analysis*, **15**, 283–301.
Politico (2019) Trump Scuttles Trans-Pacific Trade Pact. By Andrew Glass. https://politi.co/2FQtug.
Politico (2020) 15 Times Trump Praised China as Coronavirus Was Spreading across the Globe. By Myah Ward. https://www.politico.com/news/2020/04/15/trump-china-coronavirus-188736.
Postel-Vinay, K. (2014) *The G20*. New York: Palgrave Macmillan.
President of Russia (2018) Russia-India-China Trilateral – Transcripts. http://en.kremlin.ru/events/president/news/59278.
Reuters (2016) Putin Turned Russia Election Hacks in Trump's Favor: US Officials. Reuters.
Reuters (2018a) Italy's New PM Backs Trump On Re-admitting Russia into the G7. By Crispian Balmer. https://www.reuters.com/article/us-g7-summit-italy-russia-idUSKCN1J41TP.
Reuters (2018b) India's Modi and China's Xi Aim to Build on Thaw in Ties at G20 Meeting. By Sanjeev Miglani and Neha Dasgupta. https://www.reuters.com/article/us-g20-argentina-india-china-idUSKCN1NX0Q3.
The Guardian (2020) US AWOL from World Stage as China Tries on Global Leadership for Size. By Julian Borger. http://www.theguardian.com/world/2020/mar/29/us-awol-from-world-stage-as-china-tries-on-global-leadership-for-size.
The New York Times (2018) Trump's 'Bully' Attack on Trudeau Outrages Canadians. By Dan Bilefsky and Catherine Porter. https://www.nytimes.com/2018/06/10/world/canada/g-7-justin-trudeau-trump.html.
Trump, D. J. (2017) Statement by President Trump on the Paris Climate Accord. The White House. https://www.whitehouse.gov/briefings-statements/statement-president-trump-paris-climate-accord/.
Vianney Freddy, A. B., Sylvestre, A. Y., Aleksandrovich, S. S. and Viktorovna, S. N. (2019) Brazil and South Africa: The Weak Links of the BRICS? *Journal of Politics and Law*, **12**, 15–21.

Washington Post (2020) Trump's Foreign Policy Doctrine? The Withdrawal Doctrine. By Richard Haass. https://www.washingtonpost.com/opinions/2020/05/27/trumps-foreign-policy-doctrine-withdrawal-doctrine/.

Wojczewski, T. (2019) Conceptualizing the Links Between Populism, Nationalism and Foreign Policy: How Modi Constructed a Nationalist, Anti-Establishment Electoral Coalition in India. In Stengel, F. A., MacDonald, D. B. and Nabers, D. (eds), *Populism and World Politics: Exploring Inter- and Transnational Dimensions*. Cham: Springer International, 251–274.

Wouters, J. and Van Kerckhoven, S. (2019) The Role of the EU in the G7. In Oldani, C. and Wouters, J. (eds), *The G7, Anti-Globalism and the Governance of Globalization*. London: Routledge, 68–89.

# PART II

# Changing global orders and European responses

# 8. Contesting transatlantic relations: how weaker relations influence EU foreign policies

**Akasemi Newsome and Marianne Riddervold**

## INTRODUCTION

When Russia invaded Ukraine in February 2022, the EU and the US joined forces in a common, strong response under US lead. At the outset, the relationship hence seems stronger than ever – a claim that is often underlined by actors on both sides of the Atlantic. But is this really telling of the longer-term trends in EU–US relations? In spite of recent developments and strong cooperation between EU and the US in response to Russia, this chapter makes the argument that longer term, due to domestic forces on both sides of the Atlantic, the relationship is under more pressure today than at any other time since the Second World War (Riddervold and Newsome 2018; Newsome and Riddervold 2022). The longstanding partnership between Europe and the US is one in which the US has had a dominant and leading role. As populist movements on both sides of the Atlantic challenge the legitimacy of democracy at home and the post-Second World War international legal order, both Europe and the US face internal challenges from political actors indifferent or even hostile to the transatlantic relationship as such. When Europe or the US is able to overcome internal polarization, the two partners are increasingly at odds with each other both over the course of action to take as well as on the value of working together. Although EU–US divisions intensified under the Trump Administration, they started long before, and are likely to remain under Biden. Even if currently paying much attention to the war in Europe, the US will continue its pivot to Asia, it remains internally divided over the US' international role, and the two allies disagree on issues such as tariffs, 5G and the regulation of tech companies. Indeed, as discussed in the introduction to this volume, numerous observers agree that EU–US ties are more frayed than they have ever been in past decades (see Egan et al. Introduction to this volume; Riddervold and Newsome 2018; Newsome and Riddervold 2022).

This chapter contributes to the volume's aim of understanding how the EU engages with its global partners in a changing global and domestic context by exploring how a weakening of the EU–US relationship has affected EU foreign policies. The chapter makes two main arguments. First, that a weakening EU–US relationship serves to strengthen the EU as a foreign policy actor. In some cases, the EU in fact seeks to provide a counterweight to the US as "an emerging superpower" (Riddervold and Newsome 2018). Second, that the EU has come to act to more pragmatically without US leadership, evidenced by a *changing EU commitment to human rights*.

We first substantiate our claim that the EU–US relationship is weakening by examining the domestic challenge posed by anti-democratic, anti-globalization and anti-Europeanization mobilization by populists on both sides of the Atlantic. While there is already much evidence to suggest that EU–US relations are affected by the US recent withdrawal from multilateral regimes and agreements, there are few overviews of the link to domestic contestation (see, however, Peterson 2018). Looking at previous studies, we examine opposition to international cooperation under Trump by comparing it to previous administrations (Anderson 2018). On the EU side, we examine the impact of Brexit on EU–US relations (Peterson 2018; Martill and Oliver 2021). Then, drawing on our own and other studies, the next section moves beyond the domestic politics roots of weakened EU–US relations to consider how this has impacted EU foreign policies. This analysis comprises two parts. The first explores the resulting transformation of the EU into a *more integrated and independent foreign policy actor*, focusing on its response to a resurgent Russia and how this interacts with a parallel weakening EU–US relationship. Second, we discuss how this has also led to a *more pragmatic EU foreign policy*. We assess the variation in transatlantic responses to refugee crises in Europe by assessing how the EU seems to have emphasized priorities other than human rights in a context absent US leadership as the recent refugee crisis continues to unfold. In the fourth section of the chapter we conduct a first discussion of how the COVID-19 crisis has added to an already weakening relationship. Our conclusion sums up the argument.

## HOW TRANSATLANTIC RELATIONS ARE WEAKENING: THE ROLE OF ANTI-GLOBALIZATION FORCES

An increasing number of studies suggest that EU–US relations are weakening due to a changing US foreign policy, a more uncertain international environment and not least increasingly diverging foreign policy preferences (see the Introduction to this volume; Riddervold and Newsome 2018; Alcaro et al. 2016). Linked to this, a main reason for this weakening that is seldom explored systematically is the growth in populist anti-globalization movements on both sides of the Atlantic. Most importantly, political actors in the United States are no longer as committed to maintaining US global leadership in foreign affairs.[1] Scholars and commentators discussed this change in the US role in the world in a 2019 forum in *Foreign Affairs* and attributed it to a consensus among American citizens about US withdrawal from the world stage as well the absence of foreign contenders for the title of hegemon (Rapp-Hooper and Friedman Lissner 2019, p. 18). Given that US partners such as the EU question their ability to count on US support for the primacy of free trade and democratic systems of government, one of the *Foreign Affairs* essays puts forth the idea of a new motivating ethos for US engagement abroad, namely the "defense of openness". In their view, given that several areas of concern for global governance no longer fit in the traditional postwar liberal international order, such as "AI, biotech and cyberspace" the US ought to redefine how it projects power in its interest. These articles argue in favor of US and EU led overtures to states such as Brazil, India and Russia since these countries have more to gain from an international system organized around openness rather than closure, particularly if these countries have the ability to shape a new order rather than merely acquiesce to it (Rapp-Hooper and Friedman Lissner 2019, p. 25). Another contributor, Walt, underscores the need for internal democratic reforms for the EU and US, not least owing to the need to appear credible in setting up a new international system (Walt 2019, p. 34; Riddervold and Newsome 2021).

While the proposal by Rapp-Hooper et al. is intriguing, the main obstacle to reinvigorated US international engagement around the principle of openness hinges on whether members of the new US federal government will choose to prioritize this principle and based on it, to re-engage. Here, the authors admit that developments in the US, as well as in Europe, suggest that threats to the internal democratic order are not insubstantial. Indeed, since the publication of the *Foreign Affairs* issue in 2019, the subsequent months witnessed an escalation of credible threats to democracy made by then US President Trump and his appointed officials in several areas. First, Trump spent several months trying to undermine election integrity, for example not only stating that he will limit people's ability to vote by mail but that he would restrict funding to the US postal service in order to benefit politically, and proceeded to do so (Levine

---

[1] At the time of writing Antony Blinken was just confirmed as US President Biden's secretary of state and with a mandate from the new administration "to reverse the Trump administration's 'America First' doctrine". See Matthew Lee, "Senate Confirms Antony Blinken as 71st Secretary of State". *AP News*, 26 January 2021. https://apnews.com/article/joe-biden-donald-trump-biden-cabinet-antony-blinken-cabinets-d74929057a9e8e5f74e0ee553a6baced.

2020). Trump and his appointed officials also offered a combative and hostile response to widespread protests across the country by participants of different races and ethnicities against police murders of African Americans (Bump 2020). In response to the COVID-19 pandemic, the Trump Administration also belittled public health recommendations of doctors and the scientific community and encouraged armed protest against state and local government officials implementing science-based policies such as masking mandates or shelter-in-place orders (Burnett and Slodysko 2020). The culmination of these and other events (Bravin and Gurman 2021) in an armed insurrection by Trump supporters on the US Capitol on 6 January 2021, and continued support of a majority of Republican Congress members of former President Trump post-insurrection suggest the US faces considerable obstacles to adopting a strategy in "defense of openness" in the near term. At the same time in the EU, whereas threats to democracy among new member states manifested as populist parties with illiberal tendencies coming to power in Hungary and Poland (Walt 2019, pp. 28–29; see also Brechenmacher 2018; Vachudova 2019), autocratic actors here have also used the global pandemic to consolidate power towards closure rather than openness (Raube and Costa Reis 2021).

Brexit – also at least partly a consequence of anti-globalization and Europeanization forces – may also contribute to a further weakening of transatlantic relations. While the UK exited from its political membership in the EU bloc on 31 January 2020 and a first agreement was reached in December the same year, Brexit remains an unfolding series of interlocking events beyond the agreements delineating the current accepted terms for Britain's political separation from the Union (Martill and Oliver 2021). Cognizant of the dynamic and unpredictable nature of the Brexit process, in other work, we found evidence for potential weakening of the transatlantic relationship as a result of Brexit, in which the absence of the UK could further distance the EU from the US without the UK to act as intermediary on the part of the EU (Riddervold and Newsome 2021). For example, the UK's departure could weaken the EU–US relationship as the UK's special relationship with the US has helped to facilitate economic links given the shared history and English language legacy of the US and the UK (Boffey 2019). Particularly in the banking sector, EU cities with large financial services firms are keen to displace London's primacy as a Europe's finance capital; however, cities such as Paris and Frankfurt may be less attractive to banks based in the US given the dense web of ties already existing between New York and London (Wilson 2017, p. 550). Brexit also means that the EU lacks an internal voice as aligned with US interests as the UK has been. In turn, the EU in the past could rely on the UK to convey European interests to the US through its "privileged access" (Riddervold and Newsome 2021). The remaining EU member states have displayed a willingness to jockey amongst each other for attention from the US, resulting in a weakened position for the EU as a whole in transatlantic relations (Smith 2018).

As it is in the EU's interest to show that there should be a cost to leaving the union, and Boris Johnson's government has contended that a UK outside of the EU is better positioned than within the EU, thus far the EU has been successful in demonstrating that leaving the union puts the UK at a disadvantage. While the UK has concluded a trade deal with Japan, a deal with the United States met a roadblock with the 'Internal Market Bill' introduced by Johnson in the British Parliament in autumn 2020 (Edgington 2020). The suggested 'Internal Market Bill' empowered the British government to nullify common policies in the withdrawal agreement as it sees fit (BBC News 2020b). The Northern Ireland Secretary referred to the bill as illegal given that it "does break international law in a very specific and limited way" (Parliament TV 2020; BBC News 2020b). As several members of the US Congress have expressed their commitment to preserving the Good Friday agreement it seems unlikely that the any free trade deal with the UK would be approved by Congress if breaching with this agreement (Office of Nancy Pelosi 2020; Williams 2020). The EU has remained united and member states support EU Brexit negotiator Michael Barnier's ability to maintain the EU's position. Even with a first Brexit deal signed in December 2020, there are many agreements yet to be reached, not least regarding services. This suggests that the EU remains united in pursuit of its own independent and cohesive path to post-Brexit relations with the UK.

## WEAKENING RELATIONS AND EU FOREIGN POLICY

In sum, although there are many reasons for weakening EU–US relations, anti-globalization and populist forces seem to strengthen this trend. In particular, the increasing lack of US commitment to international regimes and agreements under Trump served to undermine the relationship. However, also domestic trends in Europe such as populism, the drift away from democracy in Hungary and Poland and not least Brexit further fuel what today is a weaker alliance than just a decade or two ago.

In this part of the chapter, we explore how, if in any way, this weakening of EU–US relations has affected EU foreign policy. On the one hand, EU foreign policies seem to be strengthening as a consequence of US withdrawal from international cooperation. On the other hand, however, without US leadership, the EU seems to be less willing or able to promote and uphold human rights.

### A More Integrated and Independent EU Foreign Policy

As EU–US relations worsen, a first observable impact has been that EU member states are more likely to coalesce around foreign policy paths distinctive from and sometimes in opposition to the US. Undoubtedly, the EU often struggles to find common ground in the area of foreign and security policy, for example in Syria and Libya. Recent developments in Belarus also illustrate that EU foreign policy agreement is challenging in a union of states with often different and even conflicting interests. In line with this, Mike Smith (2018) has showed that weakening US engagement with its European partner has led to a fragmentation of EU foreign policy, as EU member states try to establish bilateral special relationships with the US. This, he argues, undermines EU foreign policy unity, suggesting that it may erode over time without US leadership. The growth in populist parties contributes to this development as they seek to limit integration while at the same time establishing favorable connections to the US for their own nations.

A number of studies, however, suggest that EU foreign policy instead might be strengthening in a weakening EU–US relationship in ways that started under previous administrations but accelerated with Trump (Anderson 2018). Since the EU Global Strategy launch, the EU has pursued a stronger and more independent voice on the international stage. Happening in parallel to other foreign policy crises facing the EU (the migration crisis, Brexit and a much more assertive Russia), the US withdrawal from international cooperation, its focus on China rather than Russia as a main security threat and the lack of trust in the US' security guarantee have led the EU to be more concerned with securing this autonomy – something likely to continue under the Biden Administration. According to Drezner (2019) the lack of trust in the US' willingness to respect and uphold international relationships and agreements suggests that US foreign policies will never recover from the foreign policy actions of Donald Trump. This, he argues, will have severe consequences not only for the transatlantic relationship but also the US' role in international system more broadly. As argued by Chancellor Merkel and other European leaders on numerous occasions "It's no longer the case that the United States will simply just protect us" (Merkel in Sharkov 2018); "We can't rely on the superpower of the United States" (Merkel in Reuters 2017), with the consequence that the EU must integrate further, even in security and defense.

The single event that seems to have united the Europeans the most so far is Russian aggression in Ukraine. In spite of the member states' strong and diverging interests vis-à-vis Russia, member states were able to find a common position. For the EU, this was about democracy, about the Ukrainian people's right to self-determination (Sjursen and Rosén 2017). Compared to the crisis in Georgia a few years later, the EU was able to form a common policy (Juncos and Pomorska 2021). These developments in Ukraine led to agreement on a number of difficult to realize foreign policies in other areas. For example, the Ukraine crisis changed reluctant member states' positions from opposition to support of concrete policy initiatives such as the EU's Arctic Policies and the EU Maritime Security Strategy. Both a more assertive Russia and a less engaged US administration pushed the EU member states to be more cohesive in the field of foreign policy (Anderson 2018). The fact that an increasingly assertive Russia runs parallel to reduced US commitments to protect Europe has in other words led to a strengthening of EU foreign policy cooperation both vis-à-vis Russia and beyond.

Relations with China offer another example of newfound EU independence. Here, the EU faces a real dilemma. On the one hand, the US wants the EU to follow its lead and support its stance on China. The EU needs its hegemon, not least for the security guarantee. On the other hand, as the US withdraws from international forums and agreements – most recently the World Health Organization – the EU needs China to help solve international challenges, such as the climate crisis and the COVID-19 pandemic. China is also an important economic partner to the EU. So far, however, the EU seems to be looking for a middle way, seeking to hedge both with the US and China, over explicit US objections and thus suggestive of greater EU independence from the US. The South China Sea conflict is a good illustration. Studying EU–US relations over this crisis, Riddervold and Rosén (2018) found that the two allies have different preferences, with the US being mainly concerned with open sea lines to maintain its regional and global hegemony, and the EU focused on securing free trade passage. What is more – despite US calls for support and for the EU not to engage with China over these issues – the EU is increasingly developing an independent policy towards China even on this highly sensitive issue to the US. As argued also by R. Foot (2016, cited in Riddervold and Rosén 2018), "the China phenomenon is frequently depicted at official and unofficial levels as having put European-US ties under strain ... While Europeans have few strategic assets in the Asia-Pacific region, the US will expect other forms of support, probably to include economic and diplomatic sanctions. In the absence of that support, the strain in ties is likely to evolve into a deep fracture".

A number of different studies also point to the effect of weakening relations on EU unity in multilateral institutions. Cross (2018, pp. 571–572) for example finds that "the climate crisis has ultimately strengthened the EU as an actor independently from, and to some extent in competition with, the US" and that "US recalcitrance in environmentalism has brought Europeans closer together, solidifying the EU's emergence as a leading global power in the realm of climate change policy". Similarly, despite the US' withdrawal from the Iran accords, EU member states have managed to remain united in support of the agreement. Whether or not this is enough is a different question, with many companies fearing US sanctions and thus avoiding investments in Iran, in spite of European guarantees. Focusing in particular on an increasing transatlantic divide over foreign policy preferences and aims, also Smith (2018) suggested that a weakening relationship generates greater efforts within the

EU to integrate further. In addition to a lack of trust, a key factor contributing to the weakening of EU–US relations is their different perspectives on foreign policy, where the EU conducts a distinctive, civilian type of foreign policy that is different from that of the US but that also is better suited to address today's challenges, including in conflicts abroad. Not least, the EU's preference for 'multilateral security cooperation' stands in stark contrast to the isolationist approach many foreign policy elites advocate for in the US.

## The EU's Changing Commitment to Human Rights

While EU foreign policy at least in some areas seems to be strengthening as a result of a less engaged US, another might be that the EU has become less committed to human rights without US leadership. Although more studies are needed to support this, the European refugee crisis has led to a crisis in transatlantic relations and resulted in a weakened commitment to human rights in the EU. Whereas past publications have argued for the important role of the US as the older sibling or 'indispensable partner' in transatlantic relations, to the extent that the EU reacts to and addresses issues of human rights violations in refugee crises after civil war, we are interested in extending these arguments beyond individual and collective rights to questions of support for political regimes committed to protection of human rights and how this overlaps with national sovereignty and democratic reform (Newsome 2018). During the Kosovo crisis, member states in Europe competitively avoided taking refugees into one's national territory while also seeking to pool resources with other member states in order to address the source of migratory flows (Shepard 2009). Yet, with a clear message from then US President Bill Clinton to Europeans that the Americans wanted the Europeans to develop a cooperative solution and host refugees, coupled with a US decision to engage militarily, with NATO support, in the conflict fueling migration, Europeans were able to agree to host large numbers of refugees. This is in contrast to the Syrian civil war, in which US President Barack Obama had little desire to play the leading role in resolving the conflict pushing millions of people out of Syria (Lantis 2021, p. 10; Kwong 2018; Newsome 2018). With the US unwilling to take a leading role in the transatlantic relationship on this particular issue, and to use this war as an arena for promoting human rights, EU member states have not pulled together to take in refugees and have stepped away from the promotion of human rights for refugees. US President Trump has been even more vocal than former President Obama about his distaste for American involvement in the Syrian civil war, announcing a draw-down of American troops on Twitter before consulting with Congress or informing his military personnel and allies on the ground in Syria (Lantis 2021, p. 14; Gearan and Demirjian 2019).

When we examine new developments with the migration crisis that began in Europe in 2015, we find evidence that the human rights of refugees have declined in importance absent US leadership. Rather, material interests such as border security have become prominent priorities. The European Asylum Support Office (EASO) has proposed a refugee allotment system (Newsome 2018) where each member state receives a fair number of refugees based on member state population and economic indicators such as GDP. In response to the 2019 uptick in refugee numbers, the first since 2015, member states have expressed their unwillingness to participate in a refugee allotment system. Commission president Ursula von der Leyen released a new plan to address refugees in September 2020; however, it remains to be seen if member states will comply. In an effort to encourage those countries most hostile to taking in refugees in Central and Eastern Europe, von der Leyen's plan foregrounds a high rejection rate for asylum seekers and both offers funding to member states for taking in refugees and accepts an active member state role in the deportation of rejected asylum seekers as part of shared governance of the refugee issue (European Commission 2020; Chadwick and Monella 2020). Thus far, although Germany is in favor of an allotment system, it has not been able to bring other member states on board (Herszenhorn et al. 2020).

Not only does the refusal of member states to accept the Commission's repeated attempts to forge a common refugee policy signify how human rights has decreased in importance as a priority in this issue area, but also the actions taken by individual member states such as Greece are informative. An illustration of the lower priority of human rights can be seen in responses to the recent fire that destroyed the Moria refugee camp. According to reports, the Moria camp on the Greek island of Lesbos had 12,000 residents and was housing four times the number of people it was designed for. Representatives from NGOs such as *Doctors without Borders* criticized the Greek government for intentionally pursuing overcrowding in order to discourage refugees from coming to Greece. Furthermore, with the onset of the COVID-19 pandemic, NGOs viewed governments as more likely to restrict the movement of refugees ostensibly to prevent virus transmission, but additionally in order to increase the discomfort of refugees: "Coronavirus was, is and is going to be used to increase containment policy and fear and justify inhumane policies" notes Apostolos Veizis, Director of Doctors without Borders' Medical operational support unit in Greece (Herszenhorn et al. 2020).

Further evidence of the EU's receding priority of human rights in refugee policy concerns the agreements the EU concluded with Turkey and Libya. For example, in Libya, the removal of Qaddafi by European and American armed forces resulted in ongoing contestation among different groups for control of the country. The EU partnership with Libya to manage migration does not reflect a desire to achieve high quality governance of the migration issue:

"Rather than cost-savings and efficiency gains … it was the aim to escape legal constraints stemming from the 2012 Hirsi judgement of the European Court of Human Rights (ECtHR) that pushed the EU towards orchestration" (Mueller and Slominski 2021, p. 802). This is part of a growing tendency for the EU to shift execution of migration governance to other actors including states not bound by human rights commitments (Mueller and Slominski 2021, p. 802). Similarly, in Turkey, observers have noted the dire situation of refugees who struggle in crowded camps to limit their own exposure to COVID-19 while struggling to access sanitary food and shelter in addition to also needing to earn money and support themselves (Kirisci and Yavcan 2020).

## EU–US Relations and COVID-19

The onset of the global pandemic in December 2019 placed an already weakening transatlantic relationship under increased stress. Whereas in past global health crises, the EU and indeed other world nations could rely upon the US to provide leadership in multilateral settings to fight infectious diseases, the EU faced a partner missing-in-action (Busby 2020). Firstly, the COVID-19 crisis revealed the continued importance of domestic politics in foreign affairs. Fragmentation and divisions within the US on how to respond to the pandemic were reflected in a similarly chaotic response by the US on the world stage. For example, the Trump Administration refused to act as a 'central buyer' and purchase medical supplies needed by local and state government officials as well as hospitals to combat the virus, urging states to go to the open market. Individual states then turned to wealthy individuals for help locating critical items including ventilators and swabs outside of the United States: "the owner of the New England Patriots football franchise sent his private aircraft to China to pick up and deliver 1.2 million masks that Massachusetts had managed to procure from a Chinese manufacturer" (Bowling et al. 2020, p. 516). States on the west coast and east coast pooled collective resources to fight the virus as there was a lack of decisive action on the part of the federal government. After an initial competitive and uncooperative response from EU member states to address the pandemic, member states turned to already existing tools at the EU level to coordinate their reaction. Greer and De Ruijter note that the past experience of dealing with H1N1 proved informative for member state cooperation in favor of "joint procurement" rather than individual purchasing (Greer and De Ruijter 2020, p. 623).

Not only did the EU and US pursue differing domestic paths in response to the crisis, with the US pursuing a decentered approach absent central direction from the federal government and the EU moving towards greater coordination amongst member states, the EU and the US engaged in competitive behavior with each other. Donfried and Ischinger pointed out that the initial steps taken by governments on both sides of the Atlantic with the onset of the COVID-19 pandemic have been away from international cooperation: "Washington ordered the 3M company to halt its exports of N95 masks and to reroute its overseas production to the United States as part of a broader effort to meet domestic demand, loosening restrictions only in the face of a vocal backlash. The European Union banned the export of face shields, gloves, masks, and protective garments for the same reason" (Donfried and Ischinger 2020). The US also evoked a negative reaction from the EU when it decided to restrict travel from Europe into the US in an effort to reduce transmission of the virus during the spring of 2020 without sufficiently warning the EU (Archick 2020). Later in the summer, the EU also restricted travel from the US into Europe as the infection and death rates spiraled out of control in the US while cases in the EU continued to decrease significantly (Shesgreen 2020).

An additional blow to transatlantic relations during the COVID-19 crisis came with the diverging views the EU and the US displayed on the usefulness of multilateral institutions to deal effectively with the pandemic. President Trump belittled the authority of the World Health Organization and accused WHO's chief Ghebreyesus of mismanaging the health response to the virus and exaggerating its severity (BBC News 2020a). Members of the US Administration both derided WHO for failing to take actions it has no power to enforce, namely to compel Chinese authorities to share data about the extent of the outbreak in their country, and criticized it for bureaucratic overreach. By May 2020, the US Administration took the step of curtailing monetary support for the WHO. EU leaders opposed reducing funding for WHO in the middle of a pandemic and in the months preceding the US withdrawal the EU had pledged $8 billion for a worldwide research effort on immunity to COVID-19 (Busby 2020, pp. 1013–1014).

In this way, the COVID-19 crisis corroborates the findings from our past work (Riddervold and Newsome 2018, 2021) in which EU–US relations continue to weaken as the US and the EU pursue increasingly divergent paths. For both partners, domestic politics within the US and, in the EU, within and among member states, has become polarized. However, for the most part the EU has been able to overcome its divisions among and within member states to mount an effective central response to the pandemic. The US on the other hand remains deeply divided with the federal government in direct conflict with its subnational governments. While newer studies such as Aggestam and Hyde-Price (2019) echo our work in underscoring the cracks in the transatlantic relationship which came before the presidency of Trump, the area of global health provides a case in which the individual aims of President Trump became highly influential for radically changing US commitment to multilateral institutions in global health.

Without the US as a partner in a united transatlantic front to address the global pandemic, the EU is going its own way with COVID-19. In spring 2020, competition among member states to secure and hold medical supplies necessary for COVID-19 had given way to common economic stimulus needed to weather the accompanying contraction in economic activity for shelter-in-place orders. By summer 2020, member states cooperating to cope with the pandemic had agreed to a 25-fold increase in EU funding for public health to be managed at the supranational level. Legal integration of public health as an area under supranational purview changed with the onset of the pandemic (Greer et al. 2021, p. 747). Previously public health regulation occurred as an afterthought or 'by-product' linked to rule-making and enforcement of equality and safety controls for human consumables. In response to COVID-19, the Commission demarcated "public health [as] a 'European concept'" (Greer et al. 2021, p. 750). Economic integration was also a dimension of deeper integration in response to the pandemic. DG for health and food safety (SANTE) pre-COVID-19 had no funds for a pandemic (Greer et al. 2021, p. 756). Once the virus had taken hold, member states moved to empower the European Commission and other supranational actors to administer public health as a policy field for the EU. Similarly, whereas austerity policy had dominated fiscal government without any instruments for social investment, Greer et al. make the case that a new program of shared debt relief without conditions although defined currently as pandemic mitigation seems to be a crucial example of deeper integration (Greer et al. 2021, p. 758).

## CONCLUSION

This chapter discussed how the EU responds and adapts to internal and external challenges by exploring how its changing relations with the US affect EU foreign policies. We argue that the EU–US relationship – in spite the recent, strong cooperation following Russia's invasion of Ukraine – indeed has weakened in recent years, and more so than in previous periods since the Second World War, by focusing on the impact of populist, anti-globalization movements on both sides of the Atlantic. Trump, Brexit and nationalist movements in the EU have all contributed significantly to undermine the belief in a strong relationship, by prioritizing national interests over international cooperation. We then discussed how this weakening of the transatlantic relationship has affected the content and strength of EU foreign policies. Although the picture is somewhat mixed, with many EU member states seeking bilateral relations with the US, we suggest that EU foreign policy is strengthening as a result of three factors: the US pivot to Asia as a foreign policy priority; US disengagement and withdrawal from international obligations; and increasing divergence in US and EU foreign policy preferences and priorities. We also suggest that the EU may be less able or willing to live up to its human rights commitments without US leadership. When comparing the Kosovo and Syrian refugee crises, both times EU member states acted unilaterally to avoid hosting refugees; however, only during the Kosovo crisis did US leadership convince member states to cooperate and find a common solution for taking in refugees. Whether the EU will be able to live up to its human rights obligations also without engaged US leadership will be the true test for an EU foreign policy claiming to be based on such principles. So far, not only our study of the Syrian refugee but also studies of the EU's migration policies more broadly suggest that the EU is not up to this task.

Although its long-term impact remains to be seen, our initial study of the EU and US responses to and lack of cooperation on the COVID-19 pandemic underscores our findings. The pandemic illustrates the growing importance of domestic factors for understanding the relationship more broadly, and it shows the US unwillingness to cooperate let alone take leadership in international crisis management and international organizations. Some of these changes are clearly linked to Trump's nationalism, nativism and racism. But the weakening of EU–US relations goes beyond Trump and it is not likely that the transatlantic relationship will return to its earlier strength even under President Biden. For one, the US seems to be changing its view of the benefits of transatlantic cooperation for American interests more broadly. Undoubtedly, there is still much and close cooperation between Europe and the United States, for example in NATO and in other international organizations. But the United States' perspective on Europe's central position in US foreign, security and defense policy is changing. And although this change was reinforced by Trump, it started before him – not least with Obama and Biden's pivot to Asia strategy. With this pivot, the United States strategic and economic focus shifted from Europe and Russia to the US' real main challenger and threat, namely China.

## REFERENCES

Aggestam, L. and Hyde-Price, A. (2019) Double Trouble: Trump, Transatlantic Relations and European Strategic Autonomy. *Journal of Common Market Studies*, **57**, 114–127.

Alcaro, R., Peterson, J. and Greco, E. (eds) (2016) *The West and the Global Power Shift: Transatlantic Relations and Global Governance*. London: Palgrave Macmillan.

Anderson, J. (2018) Rancor and Resilience in the Atlantic Political Order: The Obama Years. *Journal of European Integration*, **40**(5), 621–636.

Archick, K. (2020) U.S.-European Relations in the 116th Congress. *Congressional Research Service*, 27 May. https://fas.org/sgp/crs/row/IF11094.pdf.

BBC News (2020a) Coronavirus: What Are President Trump's Charges against the WHO? *BBC News*, 8 July. https://www.bbc.com/news/world-us-canada-52294623.

BBC News (2020b) Brexit: Internal Market Bill Clears First Hurdle in Commons. *BBC News*, 15 September. https://www.bbc.com/news/uk-politics-54156419.

Boffey, D. (2019) Boris Johnson to head to Paris and Berlin in Bid to Break Brexit Deadlock. *The Guardian*, 16 August.

Bowling, C., Fish, J. and Morris, J. (2020) Seeking Patterns in Chaos: Transactional Federalism in the Trump Administration's Response to the COVID-19 Pandemic. *The American Review of Public Administration*, **50**(6–7), 512–518.

Bravin, J. and Gurman, S. (2021) Trump Pressed Justice Department to Go Directly to Supreme Court to Overturn Election Results. *Wall Street Journal*, 23 January.

Brechenmacher, S. (2018) *Comparing Democratic Distress in the United States and Europe*. New York: Carnegie Endowment for International Peace.

Bump, P. (2020) Over and Over, Trump Has Focused on Black Lives Matter as a Target of Derision or Violence. *The Washington Post*, 1 September.

Burnett, S. and Slodysko, B. (2020) "Liberate Michigan!" Right-Wing Coalitions Rallying to End Lockdown Restrictions Amid Coronavirus Pandemic. *Chicago Tribune*, 17 April.

Busby, J. (2020) Understanding the Anemic Global Response to COVID 19. *Journal of Health Politics, Policy and Law*, **45**(6), 1013–1021.

Chadwick, L. and Monella, L. (2020) What Is the EU's New Migration Pact and How Has It Been Received? *Euronews*, 25 September. https://www.euronews.com/2020/09/24/what-is-the-eu-s-new-migration-pact-and-how-has-it-been-received.

Cross, M. (2018) Partners at Paris? Climate Negotiations and Transatlantic Relations. *Journal of European Integration*, **40**(5), 571–587.

Donfried, K. and Ischinger, W. (2020) The Pandemic and the Toll of Transatlantic Discord: At a Time of Crisis, the US-European Relationship Can—and Must—be Saved. *Foreign Affairs*, 18 April. https://www.foreignaffairs.com/articles/united-states/2020-04-18/pandemic-and-toll-transatlantic-discord.

Drezner, D. (2019) This Time Is Different: Why US Foreign Policy Will Never Recover. *Foreign Affairs*, **98**(3), 10–17.

Edgington, T. (2020) What Trade Deals Has the UK Done So Far? *BBC.com*, 11 September. https://www.bbc.com/news/uk-47213842.

European Commission (2020) Press statement by President von der Leyen on the new pact on migration and asylum. https://ec.europa.eu/commission/presscorner/detail/en/STATEMENT_20_1727.

Gearan, A. and Demirjian, K. (2019) Trump Vowed to Leave Syria in a Tweet. Now with a Sharpie, He Agreed to Stay. *The Washington Post*, 5 March.

Greer, S. and de Ruijter, A. (2020) EU Health Law and Policy in and after the COVID-19 Crisis. *European Journal of Public Health*, **30**(4), 623–624.

Greer, S., de Ruijter, A. and Brooks, E. (2021) The COVID-19 Pandemic: Failing Forward in Public Health. In Riddervold, M., Trondal, J. and Newsome, A. (eds), *The Palgrave Handbook of EU Crises*. Cham: Palgrave Macmillan, 747–764.

Herszenhorn, D., Barigazzi, J. and Stamouli, N. (2020) Greek Refugee Camp Blaze Highlights EU's Migration Failure. *Politico.com*, 11 September. https://www.politico.eu/article/eu-migration-failure-lit-up-by-greek-moria-lesvos-refugee-camp-fire/.

Juncos, A. and Pomorska, K. (2021) The EU's Response to the Ukraine Crisis. In Riddervold, M., Trondal, J. and Newsome, A. (eds), *The Palgrave Handbook of EU Crises*. Cham: Palgrave Macmillan, 553–568.

Kirisci, K. and Yavcan, B. (2020) As Covid-18 Worsens Precarity for Refugees, Turkey and the EU Must Work Together. Brookings Institution, 11 June. https://www.brookings.edu/blog/order-from-chaos/2020/06/11/as-covid-19-worsens-precarity-for-refugees-turkey-and-the-eu-must-work-together/.

Kwong, J. (2018) Trump vs. Obama: How the Presidents Responded to Syria's Chemical Weapons Attack. *Newsweek*. http://www.newsweek.com/trump-vs-obama-how-presidents-responded-syria-chemical-weapons-attack889191=.

Lantis, J. (2021) Advocacy Coalitions and Foreign Policy Change: Understanding US Responses to the Syrian Civil War. *Journal of Global Security Studies*, **6**(1), 1–20. https://doi-org.libproxy.berkeley.edu/10.1093/jogss/ogaa016.

Levine, S. (2020) Trump Admits He Is Undermining USPS to Make it Harder to Vote by Mail. *The Guardian*, August 13. https://www.theguardian.com/us-news/2020/aug/13/donald-trump-usps-post-office-election-funding.

Martill, B. and Oliver, T. (2021) The EU's Response to Brexit. In Riddervold, M., Trondal, J. and Newsome, A. (eds), *The Palgrave Handbook of EU Crises*. Cham: Palgrave Macmillan, 511–524.

Mueller, P. and Slominski, P. (2021) Breaking the Legal Link but Not the Law? The Externalization of EU Migration Control through Orchestration in the Central Mediterranean. *Journal of European Public Policy*, **28**(6), 801–820.

Newsome, A. (2018) Credible Champions? Transatlantic Relations and Human Rights in Refugee Crises. *Journal of European Integration*, **40**(5), 587–604.

Newsome, A. and Riddervold, M. (2022) Conclusion: Out With the Old, In With the New? Explaining Changing EU–US Relations. *Politics and Governance*, **10**(2). https://doi.org/10.17645/pag.v10i2.5650.

Office of Nancy Pelosi, Speaker of the House (2020) Pelosi Statement on Brexit and Potential U.S.-U.K. Trade Agreement. 9 September. https://www.speaker.gov/newsroom/9920.

Parliament TV (2020) New Brexit Bill Does Break International Law, Says Northern Ireland Secretary – video. *The Guardian*, 8 September. https://www.theguardian.com/politics/video/2020/sep/08/new-brexit-bill-does-break-international-law-says-northern-ireland-secretary-video.

Peterson, J. (2018) Structure, Agency and Transatlantic Relations in the Trump Era. *Journal of European Integration*, **40**(5), 637–652.

Rapp-Hooper, M. and Friedman Lissner, R. (2019) Open World: What America Can Achieve after Trump. *Foreign Affairs*, **98**(3), 18–25.

Raube, K. and Costa Reis, F. (2021) The EU's Crisis Response Regarding the Democratic and Rule of Law Crisis. In Riddervold, M., Trondal, J. and Newsome, A. (eds), *The Palgrave Handbook of EU Crises*. Cham: Palgrave Macmillan, 627–646.

Reuters (2017) Merkel Says Europe Can't Rely on U.S. to Impose World Order. *Reuters*, 20 July. https://www.reuters.com/article/us-germany-merkel-usa-idUSKBN1KA1F9.

Riddervold, M. and Newsome, A. (2018) Introduction: Uniting or Dividing? *Journal of European Integration*, **40**(5), 505–522.

Riddervold, M. and Newsome, A. (2021) EU–US Relations in Times of Crisis. In Riddervold, M., Trondal, J. and Newsome, A. (eds), *The Palgrave Handbook of EU Crises*. Cham: Palgrave Macmillan, 603–618.

Riddervold, M. and Rosén, G. (2018) Unified in Response to Rising Powers? China, Russia and EU–US Relations. *Journal of European Integration*, **40**(5), 555–570.

Sharkov, D. (2018) Angela Merkel: Europe Can No Longer Rely on U.S. Protection. *Newsweek*, 5 October. https://www.newsweek.com/europe-cannot-fully-rely-us-protection-anymore-says-germanys-merkel-919410.

Shepard, A. J. K. (2009) A Milestone in the History of the EU: Kosovo and the EU's International Role. *International Affairs*, **85**(3), 513–530.

Shesgreen, D. (2020) EU Extends Travel Ban on Americans Amid Spike in US Coronavirus Cases. *USA Today*, 16 July. https://www.usatoday.com/story/travel/news/2020/07/16/eu-extends-travel-ban-americans-amid-spike-us-coronavirus-cases/5450198002/.

Sjursen, H. and Rosén, G. (2017) Arguing Sanctions: On the EU's Response to the Crisis in Ukraine. *Journal of Common Market Studies*, **55**(1), 20–36.

Smith, M. E. (2018) Transatlantic Security Relations since the European Security Strategy: What Role for the EU in its Pursuit of Strategic Autonomy? *Journal of European Integration*, **40**(5), 605–620.

Vachudova, M. A. (2019) From Competition to Polarization in Central Europe: How Populists Change Party Systems and the European Union. *Polity*, **51**(4), 689–706.

Walt, S. M. (2019) The End of Hubris. And the End of American Restraint. *Foreign Affairs*, **98**(3), 26–35.

Williams, A. (2020) Pelosi Says "No Chance" of US-UK Trade Deal if Irish Peace Undermined. *The Financial Times*, 9 September. https://www.ft.com/content/fb2e4e0b-de51-49b8-af25-967d4f99e3b6.

Wilson, G. K. (2017) Brexit, Trump and the Special Relationship. *British Journal of Political and International Relations*, **19**(3), 543–557.

# 9. Divide and conquer? Europe, China and policy coherence

**Terrence Guay and Michael H. Smith**

## INTRODUCTION

The European Union (EU) has forged strategic partnerships with ten countries: Brazil, Canada, China, India, Japan, Mexico, South Africa, South Korea, Russia, and the US. Given the global influence of the EU and, collectively Brazil, South Africa, India, and China (BASICs), why have these special relationships largely failed to produce signature accomplishments? We argue that the EU member states have national political and economic interests that are too divergent for the EU to create a unified position toward the BASICs. In other words, bilateral relations between member states and the BASICs are viewed as more valuable by national governments than the benefits derived from a common EU policy. In no case is this more true than that of China: in its most recent China strategy paper, published in March 2019, the European Commission said that China "is simultaneously a cooperation partner with whom the EU has closely aligned objectives, a negotiating partner, with whom the EU needs to find a balance of interests, an economic competitor in pursuit of technological leadership, and a systemic rival promoting alternative models of governance" (European Commission 2019, p. 1). At the same time, differences among EU member states in relation to the impact of Chinese foreign direct investment (FDI), technology such as that provided by Huawei, and the Belt and Road Initiative (BRI) have demonstrated that the hybrid nature of the overall relationship between the EU and China extends beyond Brussels and into the national political economies of all 27 EU members and the UK (Godement and Vasselier 2017). This means that the EU's objective of creating and sustaining a 'strategic partnership' entails not only management of external action but also the balancing of competing member state interests in an interdependent and multi-layered European and global political economy (GPE). In particular, the translation of strategic declarations and frameworks into operational programs, and their adaptation to changes in key strategic partnerships, is a crucial aspect of a successful 'strategic diplomacy' necessitating coordination at several levels, including the allocation of resources at EU level (Smith 2016; Ferreira-Pereira and Smith 2021).

In the first section of this chapter, a broad framework identifies a number of areas of variation and unevenness in the 'domestic political economy' of the EU's strategic partnerships with emerging economies. The second section undertakes a case study of the EU–China relationship with particular reference to the variations between individual member states or groups of member states, focusing on a number of key areas of contention and variation. The final section evaluates the initial evidence and draws conclusions based on the implications for EU policy of the differentiation and variations exposed.

## A FRAMEWORK FOR ANALYSIS

Shifting patterns of economic activity and power have been a central part not only of the broad context facing the EU in its external action, but also of the specific areas in which challengers have emerged and challenges have occurred (Smith 2013). There has been growing awareness of a global power shift, from the established economic powers of Europe and North America to emerging powers in Asia and Latin America; in turn, this shift has put pressure on established institutions and rules, given that emerging powers do not necessarily or completely share the assumptions of a 'Western' liberal economic order (Alcaro et al. 2016; Nye 2017). There is a double challenge: first, from the consequences of Western forms of globalization, and second, from the rise of non-Western responses to globalization and to the institutions and rules created by the established powers (Bremmer 2009).

One way of approaching the analysis of these challenges is to adapt some of the key elements of the 'complex interdependence' framework developed by Keohane and Nye (1977) and since applied in a wide range of cases. Guay and Smith (2017) apply this approach and argue that two sets of analytical demands are pertinent in assessing the EU's responses to the challenge posed by emerging powers: one that emerges from the GPE as a whole and the roles of emerging powers within it, and the second that emerges from the nature and make-up of the EU, and its capacity to respond in a creative, coordinated, and effective way to external challenges. We propose that one way of addressing these material and analytical challenges is to mobilize a number of analytical tools in three areas. First, in order to establish the *significance/salience* of a range of relationships between the EU and emerging powers in the GPE, we adopt a number of criteria. Four elements are important to establishing significance/salience. The first is *scope* – the breadth and depth of the relationship. The second is *scale* – the sheer size of the relationship, and its salience in EU external relations more generally. The third is *intensity* – the extent to which a relationship is persistently, rather than sporadically, present in the EU.

And the fourth element is *centrality* – the extent to which the relationship is concentrated in key areas of EU concern. We examined key indicators of these qualities – the most important being levels of trade, investment, and other commercial activities – and looked at the infrastructure of relations in institutional terms. The aim was to establish a broad measure of significance/salience – to see how large a specific relationship looms in the EU policy process, and conversely how large the EU element is in the perceptions and processes of the relevant partner.

Second, in order to assess the *sensitivity/vulnerability* of the EU in relationships with emerging powers, we draw upon the ideas embodied in the 'complex interdependence' framework (Keohane and Nye 1977). Keohane and Nye argued that the costs of interdependence (and the capacity to adjust to them) could be seen in two ways. Sensitivity interdependence implies that the effects of change in relationships between interdependent actors are transmitted rapidly and can precipitate policy change in order to defray or control the costs. Vulnerability interdependence implies that when confronted with the costs of interdependence, some actors are more vulnerable than others and have fewer alternative responses with which to defray or control the costs. Whilst sensitivity interdependence allows for a range of policy choices by interdependent actors, vulnerability interdependence implies a severely reduced level of autonomy or choice for the more vulnerable actor. In real-world situations a mixture of such components is likely.

Third, we argue that the combination of significance/salience and sensitivity/vulnerability provides us with an indication of the extent to which the EU can respond by developing and applying an effective *strategy* in its relations with emerging powers. The notion of strategy implies an ability to bring interests, commitments, and resources into an effective balance, and to apply relevant instruments in pursuit of policy outcomes. In Keohane and Nye's terms, such outcomes can be pursued in conditions of complex interdependence through linkage strategies, agenda setting, the shaping of transnational and transgovernmental relations, and the use of international organizations as sources of information and arenas for coalition formation and negotiation. In applying such ideas to the relations between the EU and emerging powers, it is clear that the general focus on commercial issues, the lack of direct possibilities of the use of military force, and the growing range of transnational and transgovernmental contacts between the EU and its key emerging-power partners provide at least some basis for pursuing this line of argument. In addition, studies of EU strategic partnerships and of 'strategic diplomacy' provide a firm basis for focusing on the extent to which the EU has been able to muster coordinated and effective action in relation to a range of emerging powers (Renard and Biscop 2012; Smith 2013, 2016).

This set of arguments gives us the building blocks for a set of causal propositions with regards to the EU's relations with emerging powers. First, whilst the *significance/salience* of a specific emerging power for the EU (and of the EU for that emerging power) is a key element in creating the need for EU attention to relations with that power, in establishing the scope of the challenge faced by the EU and in shaping the EU's range of responses to that emerging power, the salience of the power concerned will vary across EU member states in ways that affect the Union's capacity to develop a coordinated strategic partnership at the operational level. Second, the degree of *sensitivity/vulnerability* experienced or perceived by the EU in its relations with an emerging power, when combined with the significance/salience, will condition the ability of the EU to defray or manage the costs of the relationship, but this is also subject to variations in sensitivity/vulnerability among EU member states. These variations will have an effect on the policy instrument choices the EU is willing to employ to manage costs and create positive returns from the relationship. Moreover, this will affect the inclination of individual member states to adhere at the operational level to EU policy prescriptions in light of the potential leverage available to the 'external' emerging power. Third, the combined effects of significance/salience and sensitivity/vulnerability will influence the ability of the EU to develop an effective *strategy* towards a given emerging power, and condition its available strategic responses (linkage, agenda-setting, management of transnational/transgovernmental relations, use of international organizations). Key to this set of influences will be the inclination of member states to pursue bilateral or minilateral strategies in relation to a given emerging power. This chapter applies this analysis to accommodate the variety of member state positions and responses in relation to the growing Chinese presence in the political economy of the Union.

To test this set of propositions, a case study of EU and member state relations with China is presented, using evidence from the period up to 2020. Three outcomes are evident. First, EU–China relations provide a clear example, not only of the significance and salience of their relations in the GPE, but also of the dynamism and evolutionary momentum that are essential to our argument. Second, sensitivities and vulnerabilities in relation to the political and economic costs of the changing relationship are growing, but they are asymmetrically distributed. In other words, the threats and opportunities emanating from China's changing place in the EU's external economic policy, and the potential costs of ignoring them, vary for different regions, sectors of industry and commerce, and member states of the EU. Third, in terms of EU strategy, there is a significant gap between declarations of strategic purpose and the development of day-to-day working relationships between the two partners. There is an observable effort at the EU level to recognize and institutionalize 'the management of difference'. Here the concern is, in particular, with ‘the potential for fragmentation within the EU’ and specifically with the responses of EU member states to China’s presence and actions in a number of key areas of the relationship.

## POLITICAL AND ECONOMIC IMPACT OF CHINA IN EUROPE

In focusing on the economic activities that China has undertaken in Europe, we highlight the variation in interests and positions of member states that has increased Chinese political leverage. The list is not exhaustive, since it examines only three areas: foreign investment; BRI; and Brexit. However, it suggests the range of economic activities that China, including its government, companies, and citizens, engage in, underlines the variation in interests and positions among member states, and potentially increases Chinese leverage over member states (Meunier 2014). As noted above, our detailed evidence relates to EU–China relations up to 2020.

### Foreign Investment

Table 9.1 shows the amount of FDI originating in BASIC countries and invested in Europe and, for comparison, the United States (US) in 2018. According to the Organisation for Economic Co-operation and Development (OECD), Chinese companies had invested about two and one-half times as much in the EU as in the US. Chinese FDI in the UK was an additional $32.3 billion. Indian and South African firms had slightly lower levels of FDI in Europe than in the US in 2018, but slightly higher levels in some prior years. Only Brazilian companies had a consistent preference for investment in the US. This represents a trend in recent years, whereby emerging market multinational corporations have started to become significant investors in Western countries. For example, Chinese FDI accounted for 8.4 percent of all foreign investment in Finland. Table 9.1 almost certainly underestimates Chinese FDI in Europe for two reasons. Data for six countries (including France and Germany) are based on 2017 statistics, and the OECD does not have FDI data for five EU members. It also should be noted that, while Luxembourg’s low corporate taxes have allowed the Duchy to attract more than 40 percent of all Chinese FDI in the EU, most of these ‘phantom funds’ eventually flowed to other member states, although specific destinations and industry sectors are difficult to trace (Damgaard et al. 2019). Additionally, the negative impact of Brexit on London’s dominance in European financial services benefited Luxembourg, which became the European base for at least seven major Chinese banks, and one of the few locations in the world that Beijing has authorized for renminbi trading.

*Table 9.1 Foreign direct investment stock by BASIC firms in Europe, US, and the world (2018, billions US dollars)*

| | Brazil | China plus Hong Kong | India | South Africa |
|---|---|---|---|---|
| Austria | 2.3 | 4.0 | 0.4 | N/A |
| Belgium | −0.8 | 3.5 | 0.4 | −0.1 |
| Finland | N/A | 6.0 | 0.3 | 0.0 |
| France** | 0.8 | 17.3 | 0.5 | 2.3 |
| Germany** | 1.4 | 18.2 | 3.3 | C* |
| Italy | 0.2 | 5.5 | 0.9 | 0.5 |
| Luxembourg | 4.1 | 94.6 | −0.4 | −2.0 |
| Netherlands | −39.6 | 12.5 | C* | C* |
| Portugal | 3.4 | 5.6 | 0.0 | 0.2 |
| Spain | 5.9 | 3.7 | C* | C* |
| Sweden | C* | 9.1 | 0.0 | 0.0 |
| Other EU | −.03 | 16.9 | 2.7 | 0.8 |
| Total EU27*** | −22 | 196.9 | 8.1 | 1.7 |
| UK | 0.3 | 32.3 | 3.0 | 1.9 |
| United States | 39.8 | 77.0 | 13.7 | 5.0 |

*Note:* *Confidential data; **2017 data for Estonia, France, Germany, Hungary, Lithuania, and Slovakia; ***Does not include Bulgaria, Croatia, Cyprus, Malta, Romania.
*Source:* OECD (2020).

In trade, too, the EU's global relations had shifted (European Commission 2020a). While the US was the EU27's primary trade partner in 2019, with €616 billion crisscrossing the Atlantic, China was second at €560 billion (plus €34 billion with Hong Kong). India was tenth (€78 billion), Brazil was thirteenth (€59 billion), and South Africa was nineteenth (€42 billion). Based on FDI and trade statistics, China was the most influential of the BASIC by far, not just in Europe, but globally as well. Yet, this may be just a harbinger of the economic power that emerging market countries more broadly will wield in the coming decades.

There was a corresponding shift in the composition of the world's largest companies. In 2005, only 16 Chinese companies were on the Global Fortune 500 rankings (Fortune 2020). In 2019, there were 119. Over this time period, 45 European multinational corporations dropped off the list, along with 55 US companies and 29 from Japan. Firms from Brazil, India, Russia, and other emerging market countries more than doubled from 17 to 39. As the global economy continues to shift from west to east, technology diffuses, and a global middle class emerges, firms from the BASIC countries and other emerging markets will most certainly continue to increase in numbers.

Based on these measures (investment, trade, and number of large companies) China is the BASIC country most integrated into the global economy. There are several explanations for Beijing's foreign economic strategies (Cheng 2016; Huang 2016; Kashmeri 2019). As the world's second-largest economy, there was an expectation that this attribute could be leveraged into global influence through, first, the 'going out' strategy of the early 2000s and, second, the BRI of the 2010s (to be discussed further below). Part of the rationale for these initiatives was to acquire the natural resources that are essential inputs for China's manufacturing-based economy. Extending China's global economic reach also served the goal of establishing new markets for trade (which supports jobs at home) and investment (which strengthens Chinese companies vis-à-vis other multinationals). There also are geopolitical explanations for China's external strategies in the period under consideration, including expanding relations across Asia, as it competes with the US and, to a lesser extent, Russia and India for influence in the region (Miller 2019).

China's global strategy has extended to all regions of the world, including Europe. A few examples of Chinese investment projects will emphasize this chapter's argument that a key implication of Beijing's strategy in Europe has been to sow internal divisions and curry political influence and support. After years of austerity during its 'Euro crisis', Greece's public finances were strained and the economy was struggling. China's initial foray into Greece consisted of buying toxic government bonds. As the country slowly emerged from a financial crisis, and seeking foreign investment, Greece turned to China. In 2016, Cosco, one of China's state-owned enterprises (SOEs), purchased a controlling (67 percent) stake in the Greek port Piraeus (near Athens) for €385 million (Hoskin and Kasapi 2017; Inman 2017). Now the Mediterranean's busiest port, Piraeus is strategically important, since it is the first major port on the Mediterranean Sea side of the Suez Canal and is deep enough for the largest container ships. Closer Greece–China economic ties spilled over into 'softer' relationships. Athens International Airport aimed to be more China-friendly by offering Alipay (an online platform of China's Alibaba Group) for mobile payments, announcements and signs in the Chinese language, customized food and beverage outlook to accommodate the tastes of Chinese business travelers and tourists, and even Chinese New Year celebrations (Pantziou 2017), although the impact of the COVID-19 pandemic on these measures is yet to be determined.

Whilst Greece's European vocation was not thrown into serious question by such developments, they indicate a significant 'soft power' intervention by China. To a certain extent, Beijing's efforts paid off (Horowitz and Alderman 2017). In summer 2016, Greece helped scuttle efforts by the EU to issue a unified statement against Chinese aggression in the South China Sea. The following year, shortly after then Prime Minister Alexis Tsipras attended a summit in Beijing where he signed billions of euros of investment memorandums with Chinese companies, Greece stopped the EU from condemning China's human rights record, and opposed tighter screening of Chinese FDI in Europe. Hungary, which was expecting a multi-billion euro Chinese investment in its railway, also blocked the EU statement concerning the South China Sea. The lure of closer economic ties with China spanned the political spectrum of most European democracies. Kyriakos Mitsotakis, Greece's prime minister since the country's 2019 election, visited Shanghai and, within about a week, hosted President Xi Jinping in Greece as he sought Chinese FDI and access to Chinese markets for Greek exports (Papadimitriou 2019).

However, some European countries had reservations about the openness to FDI. A UK policy document released in July 2018 aimed to enhance the government's powers to block foreign purchases of security-sensitive assets (Pickard et al. 2018). Concerns arose mainly over a handful of Chinese and Russian acquisitions, and expectations that firms from those countries would continue to seek security-related acquisitions in future years in areas ranging from energy to sensitive technologies under existing rules. Tightening the vetting procedure by, for example, eliminating thresholds for government scrutiny and applying reviews not just to takeovers, but to asset sales and intellectual property as well, put the UK more in line with France and Germany. In 2017, Germany tightened its inward investment rules that, among other things, permitted the government to block acquisitions of 25 percent or more of shares in German companies operating in 'critical infrastructure'. The new policy was widely viewed as a response to Chinese investments in German technology firms, culminating in the Chinese conglomerate Midea acquiring the German robotics manufacturer Kuka in 2016 (Zhang 2018). German Chancellor Angela Merkel, who had become increasingly wary of Chinese SOEs, justified the move as a means to limit China's ability to divide EU members and prevent the bloc from speaking with one voice on human rights and other issues that ran counter to Chinese interests, such as territorial claims in Asia and openness toward investment by Chinese companies in Europe (Horowitz and Alderman 2017).

Another example is Sweden, where Chinese FDI doubled between 2015 and 2018 to $9.1 billion. Of particular concern was the loss of national champions, such as Volvo (Erdbrink and Anderson 2020). Zhejiang Geely Holding Group acquired the automaker in 2010, and announced in 2020 that it would be merged with Geely Automotive, thereby eliminating its Swedish identity. Swedish officials were also concerned about the national security implications of other Chinese acquisitions, particularly of companies producing dual-use technologies that would be shared with the Chinese military, such as the semi-conductor company Silex and satellite positioning firm Satlab Geosolutions. Geely became the second-largest shareholder of Volvo Truck, Sweden's largest industrial company, which makes military vehicles. Although Volvo was previously owned by Ford, Swedish officials were concerned about the close relationships between Chinese companies and the government in Beijing. Eleven Swedish cities cut friendly ties with China, mainly over human rights issues. The combination of economic, security, and identity issues strained relations between the two countries.

At the EU level, there were growing concerns that a unified approach to the screening of inward foreign investment was necessary. France and Germany proposed a joint initiative to introduce more rigorous screening of foreign takeovers of EU companies, especially those with suspected state backing, and French President Emmanuel Macron was a strong advocate for the EU to introduce a screening system (Pickard et al. 2018). In March 2019, Macron claimed that, "China plays on our divisions … The period of European naïveté is over" (Erlanger 2019, p. B3).

Finally, in February 2019, the European Parliament voted overwhelmingly (500 in favor, 49 opposed, 56 abstaining) in favor of a proposal that empowered the European Commission to investigate foreign investments in critical sectors and give its opinion on whether they threatened European interests (Reuters 2019). Backers of the policy, which took effect in October 2020, argued the objective was to give further scrutiny to investments that are more political than economic in nature. Member states would not be required to screen investments in critical industries (including aerospace, health, nanotechnology, media, electric batteries, and food), but they must submit an annual report to the Commission. Significantly, the Commission would not be empowered to block foreign investments. It could only give its opinion on whether vital infrastructure might be compromised or valuable technologies could fall into foreign hands. Thus, the Commission would have no enforcement mechanism. This was a weaker vetting process than, for example, the Committee on Foreign Investment in the United States (CFIUS) – an inter-agency group of the federal government that can block foreign investments outright. The new EU policy reflected a compromise between those member states that were increasingly worried about foreign investment originating in countries with a strong tradition of state capitalism, and those members who stood to benefit at least in the short term from such activities. The COVID-19 pandemic gave investment protection concerns greater urgency, and in March 2020 the Commission issued guidelines to ensure a strong EU-wide approach to foreign investment screening to protect assets in health, medical research, biotechnology, and infrastructures that are essential for security (European Commission 2020b).

This new policy on foreign investment faced further restrictions when international business conflicted with national security sensitivities, as the controversies over Huawei illustrate. Out of concerns that Huawei telecoms equipment may permit the Chinese government to conduct espionage, the US pressured its allies to avoid the company's products, including those related to new 5G networks (Economist 2019). The UK agreed, and announced a new security law in November 2020 that banned telecoms providers from purchasing Huawei equipment from September 2021 and the removal of the company's kit from the entire 5G system by 2027 (BBC 2020). This decision carried risks. As will be discussed in more detail below, the UK would need foreign investors post-Brexit, and following a US hard line on Huawei carried potential economic risks. China's ambassador to the UK reportedly told business leaders that the Huawei decision would be a "litmus test" for the country, with inward investment and trade ties at risk, whilst HSBC's chairman warned of reprisals for the bank if London banned Huawei's equipment (Corera 2020). Germany was more skeptical of US concerns and planned to monitor and test Huawei's equipment. But economic leverage might have been a factor in Berlin's decision. China is Germany's largest trading partner, and one-third of cars sold in that country are German brands (Boston and Woo 2020). Other than Germany and Hungary, other European countries that have made a decision on Huawei opted to ban the company from 5G telecoms contracts. The decisions for most countries came down to US pressure, increasing wariness of China's global ambitions, opposition to Beijing's repressive actions in Hong Kong and against the Uighurs, and (for countries like Italy) few tangible benefits from the participation in BRI. Fearing they might be ostracized by China, some member states sought EU unity on the matter. Caught between the economic incentives for member states to contract with the Chinese technology company and China's vast domestic market, and US pressure to avoid such arrangements, the most that the EU seemed willing to do was encourage member states to limit high-risk 5G vendors (Stevis-Gridneff 2020).

## THE BELT AND ROAD INITIATIVE AND THE 17+1 RELATIONSHIP

China, compared to the other BASIC countries, has done the most this century to expand its global political and economic relations. Beijing's efforts are symbolized in its previously mentioned BRI – an attempt to resurrect the centuries-old Silk Road that traversed central Asia and the Middle East, and facilitated economic and cultural exchange between China, Europe, and the lands in between. The twenty-first century variant goes beyond economics and cultural factors to also include closer political cooperation. The BRI's geography extends to Southeast Asia, Africa, and even to Latin America, encompassing more than 70 countries with the value of all projects estimated to be \$3.67 trillion (Blanchard 2019). A key component of BRI has been funding infrastructure projects in participant countries as an economic development strategy. However, it has also benefited Chinese banks (who finance the deals) and companies (who often do much of the actual construction), as well as Chinese exporters. There also has been an expectation that recipient countries will provide political support to Beijing on a range of international issues. During the period under study, it became increasingly evident that China would seek to expand BRI to Europe as well.

In March 2019, Italy became the first European country to agree to participate in BRI. Twenty-nine deals totaling €2.5 billion, along with the BRI memorandum of intent, were signed by Deputy Prime Minister Luigi Di Maio and President Xi Jinping in Rome (BBC 2019). Although memoranda of intent do not always translate into actual deals, the expectation was that Italian firms would gain greater access to the Chinese market and China, among other accommodations, would be involved in developing the port of Genoa, and its Communications and Construction Company was granted access to the port of Trieste to enable links to markets in Central and Eastern Europe. With Italy entering recession in late 2018 and lacking the funds to improve dated roads, railways, ports, refineries, and other infrastructure, Chinese investment would have been most welcome. The COVID-19 situation added to this urgency.

Until Italy joined BRI, EU officials worried mainly about peripheral and financially desperate countries like Greece, Portugal, and Spain as being the most susceptible to Chinese influence and most likely to undermine Union cohesiveness in global affairs (Horowitz and Alderman 2017). Members further east and countries in the Balkans were also of concern, given the region's geographic advantages. A Chinese company, for example, was building a €280 million bridge on Croatia's Adriatic coast, though the project was funded by the EU (Euractiv 2019a). Chinese companies acquired bankrupt steel mills and copper mines in Serbia, and made them profitable, winning admiration from local communities and Belgrade (Euractiv 2019b).

In April 2019 at a summit meeting in Brussels, EU and China leaders met to discuss areas of cooperation. China agreed to open its market more to European companies and limit forced technology transfers – long-standing demands by EU officials that were unlikely to be fully achieved by the stated date which was the end of 2020. But the next day, a '16 + 1' cooperation meeting was held in Dubrovnik consisting of eleven[1] Central and Eastern

---

[1] Bulgaria, Croatia, Czech Republic, Estonia, Hungary, Latvia, Lithuania, Poland, Romania, Slovakia, Slovenia.

European states (five of which use the euro), five[2] western Balkan countries (four of which have formally applied to join the EU), and China (Erlanger 2019; Euractiv 2019a). Greece joined a month later with the grouping now referred to as '17 + 1'. The region, as previously mentioned, is geographically important to China's economic strategy in Europe, and China formally initiated its efforts in 2012. Between 2007 and 2017 Beijing announced €12 billion in loans for construction projects in 16 of the countries (prior to the inclusion of Greece), with one-third of this amount going to Serbia, followed by Bosnia (21 percent) and Montenegro (seven percent), according to the European Investment Bank (2018). Although not all of these funds had been disbursed by 2020, according to the International Monetary Fund (IMF), China was financing at least €6.2 billion of projects, mainly roads and energy, in the Western Balkans (IMF 2018). With a GDP per capita less than 75 percent of the EU average, the Balkans were eager to accept any foreign funding, regardless of source. Also, the industrial profile of eastern and southeastern Europe differs from western and northern Europe, in that they are in general less technologically advanced and are home to fewer global companies. Thus, whereas companies and investments from China might have been viewed as a threat in more economically developed EU members, they were welcomed in the east and southeast where there was less concern about competition. Yet, in 2020, 75 percent of Chinese FDI in these 17 countries was concentrated in just four countries: Czech Republic, Hungary, Poland, and Slovakia (Karaskova et al. 2020). It was a similar situation with trade, with these four countries importing and exporting more to China than the Baltic and Balkan countries combined, which produced a much higher trade deficit with the Asian country. So the '17 + 1' arrangement was very unbalanced both between Europe and China, and among the 17 European members.

However, in 2019 EU Enlargement Commissioner Johannes Hahn raised "concerns over the socioeconomic and financial effects some of China's investments can have" (Euroactiv 2019b). Montenegro's public debt, for example, increased to more than 70 percent of GDP after borrowing €809 million from China's Export-Import bank to build a highway. Such 'debt-trap' diplomacy, where financially strapped countries handed over assets to Chinese banks and SOEs, had already claimed other countries, including Sri Lanka, Djibouti, and Mongolia (Economist 2018). More broadly, there were concerns that investments sponsored by foreign governments, particularly China, came with little or no consideration for EU values like transparency, press freedom, limitations on state aid, or environmental impact. Chinese funding of coal-fired power plants ran contrary to EU goals of reducing carbon emissions.

[2] Albania, Bosnia and Herzegovina, North Macedonia, Montenegro, Serbia.

European divisions over China's BRI were growing in the period under study. Bulgaria, Greece, Hungary, Italy, Poland, and Portugal had individual agreements with China to be a part of the BRI. Internal EU divisions were further highlighted in April 2019 at a BRI summit in Beijing. The 36 heads of state or government who attended the summit included leaders from Austria, Cyprus, Czech Republic, Hungary, Italy, and Portugal (Tiezzi 2019). In response, German Economic Minister Peter Altmaier urged the EU to join BRI as a bloc, rather than as individual countries, so as leverage the bloc's negotiating position. Officials dismissed this idea, leaving it up to member states to join individually (Valero 2019). At this point, Europe's relations with China appeared to be a classic 'prisoners' dilemma' whereby the gains from individual defections were more tangible and immediate than any greater returns achieved through cooperation.

## Brexit

One of the implications of the UK's withdrawal from the EU was the necessity of forging bilateral trade deals with major countries and regional blocs. Former Prime Minister Theresa May, during a January 2018 trip to Beijing with 50 British business leaders, proclaimed the two countries had entered a 'golden era' – a phrase used frequently by UK leaders to refer to the bilateral relationship since the June 2016 referendum. May said the UK was considering, "how we can build further on that golden era and on the global strategic partnership that we have been working on between the UK and China" (Deutsche Welle 2018). The UK's relationship with China would depend on the implementation of the December 2020 trade agreement between the UK and EU, the full ramifications of which will take time for companies to integrate into their regional operations and strategies. Beijing's increasingly confrontational relations with Hong Kong, a former UK colony, were an additional factor. If the UK–EU trade agreement reduced bilateral trade flows, the UK would become a less attractive target for Chinese investment. However, such an outcome would make the UK even more dependent on investment from China and other emerging markets, thereby reducing any negotiating leverage that London or the UK firms might have on trade, as well as other areas like human rights on the mainland, and threats to political rights in Hong Kong.

While the UK government sought to strengthen relations with China, the European Commission expressed reservations. Budget Commissioner Gunther Oettinger suggested in April 2019 that, "The biggest winner [of Brexit] is China. The Chinese can advance their strategy without disruption and leap everywhere in the world at the opportunities that Europe fails to seize because it's so preoccupied with itself" (Gehrke 2019). This was problematic because there was at the same time an opportunity for the EU and China to strengthen ties, given the tenuous relationship that both have with the US over trade, economic policy, security, and the environment.

There are likely other winners from Brexit besides China. According to the United Nations Conference on Trade and Development (UNCTAD), developing countries could see significant trade gains from a 'hard Brexit' – that is, if negotiations between the UK and EU did not yield an agreement establishing zero or low tariffs on most goods (UNCTAD 2019). This may still be the case for certain goods due to the rules of origin requirements that permit tariff-free trade between the UK and EU. The percentage of required UK content, for example, varies considerably across products (at least 60 percent for automobiles, for example) and if the required threshold is not met then the good faces tariffs. China was estimated to export $10.2 billion more to the UK – an increase of 17 percent. The US would be the second-biggest winner, followed by Japan, Thailand, South Africa ($3.0 billion, or 39 percent), India ($1.3 billion, or 14 percent), Brazil ($1.1 billion, or 35 percent), and Russia. The gains would result from lower UK tariffs on products than what the EU currently has in place, and the fact that many competitors would be taxed at the same rate. Thus, after the UK left the EU, China and other emerging markets should have greater access to the UK market.

## CONCLUSIONS

In terms of the propositions advanced earlier in the chapter, it is possible to draw some preliminary conclusions. Whilst the issue of variation in EU member state attitudes towards China is not a new one (cf. Fox and Godement 2009), and attention to the new challenges in EU–China relations has grown (cf. Godement and Vasselier 2017), the propositions enable us to gain analytical leverage on the issues it has created during the period studied. First, the continuing and growing penetration of the EU's political economy by China over the decade up to 2020 underlined its salience not only to the Union as a whole, but also to individual member states. It is plausible to conclude that this growing salience produced differentiated outcomes, for example in areas such as FDI and the impact of communications technologies. Second, one of the factors that was key to the shaping of differentiated outcomes was the differential sensitivity and vulnerability of member states to Chinese overtures, and we have seen that this varied from the conspicuously defensive to the open and welcoming (cf. Germany and the UK or Italy, and Eastern European member states). Finally, we have seen that whilst the EU was able discursively to generate and reproduce a coordinated strategy towards China, that strategy was subject at the operational level to significant variations in the extent to which it shaped member state responses to China. In a way, the 2019 Commission Communication, with its multiple images of China (cooperating partner, negotiating partner, economic competitor, and systemic rival) showed recognition of this differentiation, but the question was, how might that translate into a policy framework that could contain the differentiated responses on EU member states as well as the 'high diplomacy' of strategic partnership?

Based on the issues and examples discussed above, there appears to be a strong case that the national interests of EU member states have become so increasingly disparate, that they hampered the EU's ability to speak with one voice in global affairs, particularly on issues related to China and other emerging market countries. The Chinese example is clearly the most analytically relevant given its presence in the EU's political economy and thus its potential leverage over individual member states, but in principle a number of the conclusions noted here might be applied to other BASIC countries.

Given current global geopolitical dynamics, the EU has few cards to play in its attempt to appear as a unified global actor. The US historically has been a natural ally for the EU on a wide range of global issues. But under the Donald Trump Administration, the US and Europe moved further apart on trade, the environment, security, and faith in the liberal world order buttressed by regimes and international organizations. Other OECD countries could provide some support, but most either lack global clout or are themselves (like Australia, Japan, and South Korea) gradually falling within the economic sphere of influence of BASICs, especially China. Even Brazil, India, and South Africa, as well as other emerging market countries, are finding links with China too tempting to resist.

It is perhaps appropriate that in December 2020, after seven years of discussions, EU and Chinese leaders agreed on a Comprehensive Agreement for Investment (CAI). The agreement would loosen many restrictions imposed by Beijing on European companies, including obligations to partner with Chinese firms and share sensitive technologies (Ewing and Myers 2020). Although the CAI would improve access to the European manufacturing and energy markets for Chinese companies, the main benefits of the pact were political (Fallon 2021). At a time when Beijing was being criticized around the world for COVID-19, human rights abuses in Hong Kong and Xinjiang Province, and its 'wolf warrior diplomacy', among other reasons, an investment agreement with the EU indicated that China was too important economically to ignore. It also is a geopolitical win for China vis-à-vis the United States – both of which are vying for Europe's allegiance. Nevertheless, it was far from certain that the CAI would become reality. Many members of the European Parliament and some national parliamentarians did not support the agreement, in part because it did not do enough to raise labor standards in China. European public opinion also opposed the deal. According to the Pew Research Center, 71 percent of Europeans surveyed had an unfavorable view of China (Silver et al. 2020). The Biden Administration has tried to persuade Europe to avoid consummating the deal in the hope that a US–EU alliance may produce more concessions by Beijing.

On the other hand, despite the concerns of rising populist parties across many of the world's democracies, one relevant feature here is how economic nationalism is employed as an electoral strategy. Leaders who came to power, in part, by promising to reclaim companies and national assets from foreign (mainly other European and US) companies, have had a hard time explaining why such national treasures were allowed to pass into the hands of SOEs domiciled in China. Perhaps this recognition might make it easier for the EU to find common ground among its members to present a unified and more assertive front against the growing economic threats posed by Beijing.

Russia's invasion of Ukraine in February 2022 suggests that, under certain circumstances, more unified EU action is achievable. In this case, the egregious nature of Russia's action virtually required a common and forceful EU response, that has included financial and economic sanctions, closure of airspace and ports, banning European investment in Russia's energy sector, prohibition of Russian oil and petroleum imports, and even the provision of military equipment to Ukraine. Many member states have gone even further with their own sanctions. It is likely that a coordinated European response was more attainable in this case because it aligned with US interests and preferences, which is often not the case with respect to political economy issues that relate to China and the BASICS. If, for example, a crisis arose over the status of Taiwan (a possibility much-discussed in the wake of the Ukraine invasion), the tension between security, strategy and political economy might take a different form for the EU.

## REFERENCES

Alcaro, R., Peterson, J. and Greco, E. (eds) (2016) *The West and the Global Power Shift: Transatlantic Relations and Global Governance*. Basingstoke: Palgrave Macmillan.

BBC (2019) Italy Joins China's New Silk Road Project. 23 March. https://www.bbc.com/news/world-europe-47679760.

BBC (2020) Huawei Ban: UK to Impose Early End to Use of 5G Kit. 30 November. https://www.bbc.com/news/business-55124236.

Blanchard, B. (2019) China's Xi Touts more than $64 Billion in Belt and Road Deals. Reuters, 27 April. https://www.reuters.com/article/us-china-silkroad-xi/chinas-xi-says-over-64-billion-in-deals-signed-at-belt-and-road-summit-idUSKCN1S308Q.

Boston, W. and Woo, S. (2020) Huawei Gets Conditional Green Light in Germany as Government Approves Security Bill. *Wall Street Journal*, 16 December. https://www.wsj.com/articles/huawei-gets-conditional-green-light-in-germany-as-government-approves-security-bill-11608117504.

Bremmer, I. (2009) State Capitalism Comes of Age. *Foreign Affairs*, **88**, 40–55.

Cheng, L. K. (2016) Three Questions on China's 'Belt and Road Initiative'. *China Economic Review*, **40**, 309–313.

Corera, G. (2020) Huawei Launches Media Blitz as UK Weights its Role in 5G Networks. *BBC*, 8 June. https://www.bbc.com/news/technology-52959644.

Damgaard, J., Elkjaer, T., and Johannesen, N. (2019) The Rise of Phantom Investments. *Finance & Development*, **56**(3), September. https://www.imf.org/external/pubs/ft/fandd/2019/09/the-rise-of-phantom-FDI-in-tax-havens-damgaard.htm.

Deutsche Welle (2018) Theresa May Looks to China for Post-Brexit Future. *Deutsche Welle*, 31 January. https://www.dw.com/en/theresa-may-looks-to-china-for-post-brexit-future/a-42375680.

Economist (2018) Briefing: China's Belt and Road Initiative. *The Economist*, 28 July, 13–16.

Economist (2019) Huawei: Crossed Wires. *The Economist*, 23 February, 66–67.

Erdbrink, T. and Anderson, C. (2020) Fears for Volvo Expose Sour Turn in Sweden's Ties with China. *New York Times*, 14 June. https://www.nytimes.com/2020/06/14/world/europe/sweden-china-volvo.html?searchResultPosition=1.

Erlanger, S. (2019) Europe Holds Summit with China, More Skeptically this Time. *New York Times*, 10 April. https://www.nytimes.com/2019/04/09/world/europe/eu-china-summit.html.

Euractiv (2019a) China Courts Eastern Europe after Key EU Summit. 12 April. https://www.euractiv.com/section/eu-china/news/china-courts-eastern-europe-after-key-eu-summit/.

Euroactiv (2019b) Dubrovnik 16+1 Summit Rolls the Red Carpet for China. 10 April. https://www.euractiv.com/section/enlargement/news/dubrovnik-161-summit-rolls-the-red-carpet-for-china/.

European Commission (2019) Press release, IP/19/1605, 12 March.

European Commission (2020a) Top Trading Partners 2019 – Trade Statistics. http://ec.europa.eu/trade/policy/countries-and-regions/statistics/.

European Commission (2020b) Coronavirus: Commission Issues Guidelines to Protect Critical European Assets and Technology in Current Crisis. Press release, 25 March. https://ec.europa.eu/commission/presscorner/detail/en/IP_20_528.

European Investment Bank (2018) *Infrastructure Investment in the Western Balkans: A First Analysis*, September. https://www.eib.org/attachments/efs/infrastructure_investment_in_the_western_balkans_en.pdf.

Ewing, J. and Myers, S. L. (2020) China and E.U. Leaders Strike Investment Deal, but Political Hurdles Await. *New York Times*, 30 December. https://www.nytimes.com/2020/12/30/business/china-eu-investment-deal.html.

Fallon, T. (2021) The Strategic Implications of the China-EU Investment Deal. *The Diplomat*, 4 January. https://thediplomat.com/2021/01/the-strategic-implications-of-the-china-eu-investment-deal/.

Ferreira-Pereira, L. C. and Smith, M. (2021) Strategic Partnerships in European Union External Action: Evolution and Analysis of a Developing Policy Instrument. In Ferreira-Pereira, L. C. and Smith, M. (eds), *The European Union's Strategic Partnerships: Global Diplomacy in a Contested World*. Cham: Palgrave Macmillan, 69–94.

Fortune (2020) *Global 500*. https://fortune.com/global500/.

Fox, J. and Godement, F. (2009) *A Power Audit of EU-China Relations*. Policy Report. Brussels: European Council on Foreign Relations.

Gehrke, L. (2019) Oettinger: China is the 'Biggest Winner' from EU's Brexit 'Paralysis'. *Politico*, 8 April. https://www.politico.eu/article/china-is-the-biggest-winner-of-brexit-guenther-oettinger-uk-budget-trade-ttip/.

Godement, F. and Vasselier, A. (2017) *China at the Gates: A New Power Audit of EU-China Relations*. Brussels: European Council on Foreign Relations.

Guay, T. and Smith, M. (2017) The European Union and Emerging Powers: The Political Economy of Evolving Relationships. Paper presented at the 16th EUSA Biennial Conference, Miami, 4–6 May.

Horowitz, J. and Alderman, L. (2017) Chastised by EU, a Resentful Greece Embraces China's Cash and Riches. *New York Times*, 26 August. https://www.nytimes.com/2017/08/26/world/europe/greece-china-piraeus-alexis-tsipras.html.

Hoskin, A. and Kasapi, A. (2017) Why is China Investing Heavily in South-east Europe? BBC, 17 October. https://www.bbc.com/news/world-europe-41654346.

Huang, Y. (2016) Understanding China's Belt and Road Initiative: Motivation, Framework and Assessment. *China Economic Review*, **40**, September, 314–321.

Inman, P. (2017) Greece Approves $8bn Chinese-Backed Resort Project Outside Athens. *The Guardian*, 2 June. https://www.theguardian.com/business/2017/jun/02/greece-approves-8bn-chinese-backed-resort-project-outside-athens.

International Monetary Fund (IMF) (2018) *Public Infrastructure in the Western Balkans: Opportunities and Challenges*. February. https://www.imf.org/en/Publications/Departmental-Papers-Policy-Papers/Issues/2018/02/07/Public-Infrastructure-in-the-Western-Balkans-Opportunities-and-Challenges-45547.

Karaskova, I. et al. (2020) *Empty Shell No More: China's Growing Footprint in Central and Eastern Europe*. Policy Paper, Association for International Affairs, April. https://chinaobservers.eu/wp-content/uploads/2020/04/CHOICE_Empty-shell-no-more.pdf.

Kashmeri, S. A. (2019) *China's Grand Strategy: Weaving a New Silk Road to Global Primacy*. Santa Barbara, CA: Praeger.

Keohane, R. and Nye, J. (1977) *Power and Interdependence: World Politics in Transition*. Boston, MA: Little, Brown.

Meunier, S. (2014) A Faustian Bargain or Just a Good Bargain? Chinese Foreign Direct Investment and Politics in Europe. *Asia-Europe Journal*, **12**, 143–158.

Miller, T. (2019) *China's Asian Dream: Empire Building along the New Silk Road*. London: Zed Books.

Nye, J. (2017) Will the Liberal Order Survive? The History of an Idea. *Foreign Affairs*, **96**, 10–16.

OECD (2020) *International Direct Investment Statistics 2018*. Paris: OECD Publishing. https://www.oecd-ilibrary.org/finance-and-investment/oecd-international-direct-investment-statistics-2019_g2g9fb42-en.

Pantziou, E. (2017) Athens Airport Partners with 'Alipay', becomes Chinese-Friendly. *GTP Headlines*, 27 November. https://news.gtp.gr/2017/11/27/athens-airport-partners-alipay-chinese-friendly/.

Papadimitriou, J. (2019) Greece, China Aim to Deepen Ties. *Deutsche Welle*, 3 November. https://www.dw.com/en/greece-china-aim-to-deepen-ties/a-51099654.

Pickard, J., Massoudi, A. and Mitchell, T. (2018) Tight Rules on Foreign Investment Have China in their Sights. *Financial Times*, 24 July. https://www.ft.com/content/9554e45e-8f54-11e8-bb8f-a6a2f7bca546.

Renard, T. and Biscop, S. (2012) *The European Union and Emerging Powers in the 21st Century: How Europe Can Shape a New Global Order*. London: Routledge.

Reuters (2019) With Eyes on China, EU Lawmakers back Investment Screening. 14 February. https://www.reuters.com/article/us-eu-china-investment/with-eyes-on-china-eu-lawmakers-back-investment-screening-idUSKCN1Q31JU.

Silver, L., Devlin, K. and Huang, C. (2020) Unfavorable Views of China Reach Historic Highs in Many Countries. Pew Research Center, 6 October. https://www.pewresearch.org/global/2020/10/06/unfavorable-views-of-china-reach-historic-highs-in-many-countries/.

Smith, M. (2013) Beyond the Comfort Zone: Internal Crisis and External Challenge in the European Union's Response to Rising Powers. *International Affairs*, **89**(4), 653–672.

Smith, M. (2016) The EU, Strategic Diplomacy and the BRIC Countries In Smith, M., Keukeleire, S. and Vanhoonacker, S. (eds), *The Diplomatic System of the European Union: Evolution, Change and Challenges*. London: Routledge, 115–128.

Stevis-Gridneff, M. (2020) E.U. Recommends Limiting, but not Banning, Huawei in 5G Rollout. *New York Times*, 29 January. https://www.nytimes.com/2020/01/29/world/europe/eu-huawei-5g.html.

Tiezzi, S. (2019) Who is (and Who isn't) Attending China's 2nd Belt and Road Forum. *The Diplomat*, 27 April. https://thediplomat.com/2019/04/who-is-and-who-isnt-attending-chinas-2nd-belt-and-road-forum/.

UNCTAD (2019) *Brexit: Implications for Developing Countries*. UNCTAD Research Paper No. 31, April. https://unctad.org/en/PublicationsLibrary/ser-rp-2019d3_en.pdf.

Valero, J. (2019) European Bloc not Considering Joining China's Belt and Road Plans. *Euractiv*, 26 April. https://www.euractiv.com/section/eu-china/news/european-bloc-not-considering-joining-chinas-belt-and-road-plans/.

Zhang, D. (2018) Exit the Dragon? Chinese Investment in Germany. *Deutsche Welle*, 5 February. https://www.dw.com/en/exit-the-dragon-chinese-investment-in-germany/a-42457712.

# 10. What role for the EU? Domestic contestation of the EU's global role(s) in its neighbourhood

**Magdalena Góra**

## INTRODUCTION[1]

Contestation has sharply increased in the global context. The liberal global order has been progressively affected by contestation from actors such as Russia, China, and the US (Haukkala 2015; Thies and Nieman 2018). Likewise, the domestic arena has experienced a similar effect (Góra et al. 2019). In many societies political conflicts have been restructured along new lines – between proponents and opponents of globalization (de Wilde et al. 2019). Such an increased contestation and the growing salience of international affairs in domestic debates have a lasting impact on the EU foreign and security policy leading sometimes to its politicization (Biedenkopf et al. 2021). The aim of this chapter is to examine shifting discourses in the EU's foreign and security policy. To this end, the focus will be dedicated to the relationship of the EU to its neighbourhood.

The analysis will apply the role theory approach to grasp domestic contestation and shed light on whether political actors in the European Parliament (EP) are contesting the involvement and the role of the EU in the neighbourhood, and to what extent these contestation patterns change. The analysis is based on empirical data from the European parliamentary debates on relations with the neighbourhood countries between 2004 and 2019.

The chapter is structured as follows. First, it provides a theoretical framework on the conceptualization of role contestation and outlines the contestation process. Next, the case study of the EU's role in the neighbourhood is

[1] I would like to thank Dr Marcin Zubek for his conceptual contribution to this research on the EU's role in neighbourhood conflicts. I would also like to thank Alex Andrione-Moylan and the editors of this volume for their comments and suggestions for this chapter.

discussed. Subsequently, the analysis focuses on patterns of role contestation in the EP.

## DOMESTIC CONTESTATION OF THE EXTERNAL ROLE OF THE EU: THEORETICAL PERSPECTIVES

In international relations, contestation is mostly encapsulated in literature through the norm contestation approach (Wiener 2014). Recently, this approach has also been tested in internal settings, for instance, regarding contestation by populist parties (Buzogány et al. 2021; Van Berlo and Natorski 2020).

The contestation of foreign policy is prominently examined by scholars employing role theory (Cantir and Kaarbo 2016). Originally, it focused on role contestation by other actors in international relations (Holsti 1970). However, this chapter moves away from the international towards the domestic (European) realm. Role conceptions are derived domestically (Wish 1980). They are contested (criticized) within the domestic context horizontally among political elites, vertically between elites and ordinary citizens, and also from the outside by various other actors. This forms an interactive, relational model where the domestic and international realms interconnect (Harnisch 2014). It is important to stress that the practice of contestation is discursive aiming at undermining established intersubjective meanings and norms (Contessi 2010). Scholars note that a direct impact of contestation on foreign policy practice is not always implied and it depends on who is the contester, what is contested, and how the roles are established and nested (Cantir and Kaarbo 2012). However, it could be said that growing contestation by mainstream actors can lead to reconceptualization of an actor's role(s).

Scholars have applied role theory to the EU's global activities. Aggestam (2006) clarifies that "role conceptions thus refer to images that foreign policy-makers hold concerning the general long-term function and performance of the EU in the international system" (Aggestam 2006, pp. 19–20). However, the EU's roles are more dynamic compared to the national ones because the EU has been developing some of its actions in its foreign affairs capacity for a relatively short period. Additionally, Koenig argues, "national role conceptions demonstrate a higher degree of social embeddedness and legitimacy than the more removed European ones" (Koenig 2016, p. 158). European role conceptions are understood as a "coherent European position deriving out of shared positions/conceptions in the process" (Schmitt 2017, p. 254). This is due to the nature of the construction of the EU's foreign policy, in which the national positions continue to be preserved, and at most Europeanized (Chelotti 2016). At the national level, on the other hand, political actors struggle to "balance international, European, and domestic expectations in the formulation and enactment of national and European roles" (Koenig

*Table 10.1* *Multilevel role contestation system in the EU*

| | |
|---|---|
| Horizontal contestation (type 1) | Horizontal contestation over the EU's role between different national elites at the EU level |
| Horizontal contestation (type 2) | Horizontal contestation over the EU's role among national elites within member states |
| Horizontal contestation (type 3) | Horizontal contestation over the national role in the EU or international contexts among national elites in member states |
| Vertical contestation (type 4) | Vertical contestation over the national role in the EU or international contexts between national elites and citizens within member states |
| Horizontal contestation (type 5) | Horizontal contestation over EU's role between the elites of the EU (and its supranational institutions) and member states' elites |

*Source:* Own compilation, based on Koenig (2016, p. 160), and Niemann and Hoffmann (2019).

2016, p. 159). At the European level, the roles are predominantly "European decision makers' perceptions of the responsibilities, long-term functions, and performance of the Union" (Koenig 2016, p. 160). Roles are also distinguished depending on the context, and could be meta-roles, understood as the generalized role of an actor based on power resources and context-specific roles that are particular to a certain policy or geographical direction (Bengtson and Elgström 2011, p. 114). The two types of roles will be described in detail in the next section.

Domestic role contestation is defined as criticism or disagreement with role conceptions promoted by elites, specifically executive actors. Such contestation is observed horizontally among political elites and vertically between elites and public opinion (Cantir and Kaarbo 2012). Studies show that within the EU, domestic role contestation is even more complicated. The EU roles are less established, and there are multiple actors involved in role conceptualization on the EU level. Notably, contestation of the role(s) of the EU takes place within member states, but also between them. The result is a multilevel role contestation system, which is summarized in Table 10.1 (Koenig 2016, p. 160).

The main focus of this chapter is horizontal contestation type 1, regarding the Union's role among different national elites at the EU level. Within the member states, horizontal role contestation between governing elites and the political opposition mostly occurs in national parliaments (Brummer and Thies 2015; Cantir and Kaarbo 2016; Thevenin 2021; Góra 2021; Wunsch and Olszewska 2022). On the EU level the contestation can be observed in the European Parliament.

In the process of European integration, the EP expanded its competences considerably, including in the area of foreign policy (Irrera 2015; Kamińska 2015; Lord 2017; Góra 2019a). Researchers are observing a growing parliamentarization of EU foreign policy, signifying an increase in the formal powers of parliaments, but also the development of informal practices aimed at legitimizing the EU's external action (Rosén and Raube 2018). The EP remains the main forum for exchange of opinions on international issues and challenges (Chryssogelos 2015; Raunio and Wagner 2017; Falkner and Plattner 2018; Wagner et al. 2021). Simultaneously, such an exchange provides a space for the expression of national preferences with regards to foreign policy ambitions.

## THE EU'S META-ROLES AND SPECIFIC ROLES IN THE NEIGHBOURHOOD

Scholars working within the paradigm of role theory distinguish several crucial roles of the EU in international relations. They treat roles as deriving from normative debates on EU actorness. There are three main conceptualizations of meta-roles of the EU: civilian power, normative power, and comprehensive power. The EU as a civilian power (Duchêne 1973) is chronologically the first attempt to conceptualize the EU's actorness (Sjursen 2006). Civilian power stresses the non-military involvement of the EU in global affairs and non-military methods of conflict resolution. It identifies economic and political influence as a major instrument of power. Normative power is the second meta-role that became popular at the beginning of the 2000s, rooted in the idea of normative infusion into civilian power (Manners 2002). Normative power "influences the thinking of other actors in the international system, rather than acting through coercive means to achieve its goals" (Bengtson and Elgström 2011, p. 115). In reference to the EU's military edge, authors stress that there are at least two main variations in normative power reflection – a pacifist variation that limits the EU's capabilities in military aspects, and another variation that internalizes the possibility of military interventions in order to protect fundamental values (Palm and Crum 2019).

Comprehensive power, the third meta-role, is a combination of "civilian and military instruments in a strategic and coherent fashion" (Koenig 2016, p. 157). In conjunction with greater investments in EU missions, this meta-role has been in development since the beginning of the twenty-first century. If necessary, such powers could include a military or securitized means completing the civilian power toolbox – creating a "robust military edge" (Koenig 2016,

p. 171). The comprehensive power role opens tensions regarding the nature of relations with NATO (a crucial alliance for many member states).

Finally, scholars have recently focused their attention on the EU's norm-setting features in a dramatically changing international system (European Commission 2019). Schmitt (2017) argues that the EU is developing a role as an ordering power (Schmitt 2017, p. 256). From an alternative viewpoint, there is growing attention drawn to the EU's regulatory potential in the global arena. The idea that the EU is a norm setter is not new, and scholars have already noticed the trade potential of the bloc (Meunier and Nicolaïdis 2006). Such considerations were also observed in the previously described roles. However, scholars' attention has shifted towards focusing on whether this specific strength of the EU as a global actor is translating into its dominant international identity. Damro (2015) proposed conceptualizing the EU as a market power, focusing on the strength of its market, regulatory capacities, and domestic interests in exporting regulations (see also Damro 2012). It is also this role that coincides with studies on the regulatory capacity of actors, defined as "the capacity to formulate, implement and uphold international rules, [which] facilitates rule projection even in the absence of overwhelming market power" (Lavenex et al. 2017, p. 2). As Bradford stated: "These five determinants of unilateral global regulatory power – market size, regulatory capacity, preference for strict standards, immobile targets, and non-divisibility of production – explain why the EU has become a predominant regulator of global commerce" (Bradford 2016, p. 134). More recently, this debate has also been channelled under the "liberal power Europe" headline, emphasizing the combination of the promotion of democracy and human rights with market economy and free trade (Wagner 2017, p. 1404). The overlaps with previous conceptualizations – particularly with normative power – are clear, yet Wagner stresses the role of market economy and free trade in his proposal (Wagner 2017, p. 1404). It is not the aim of this chapter to focus solely on the meta-roles, as they serve as a background for specific EU roles in particular regions discussed in the next section.

Departing from meta-roles, scholars have analysed the EU's specific roles in its key area of interest – the close neighbourhood. Most studies confirm that the EU develops a broad set of roles depending on its own resources and tools in specific regions (Kaya 2009, p. 109; Zając 2010). Within the European Neighbourhood Policy (ENP), the Union has frequently stated that the three main aims are the key axes of its involvement: economic prosperity, democracy and democratization, and security and stability. This coincides with such strategic frames as democracy promotion, rule of law, and human rights; economic cooperation and security, conflict resolution and stability that characterize the EP discourse (Nitoiu 2017). Comparably, Cianciara (2017), using the narrative approach, demonstrates shifts in the EU narrative regarding neighbourhood in different periods: "(1) 2003–2010: stability, good governance and prosperity; (2) 2011–2013: democratisation and inclusion; (3) 2015 (in)stability and security" (Cianciara 2017, p. 53). Wunsch and Olszewska (2022) in reference to EU enlargement demonstrate persistence in time of three discourses: "normative discourses comprise an emphasis on democracy promotion and historical commitment; pragmatic discourses address issues of conditionality and stabilisation; and institutional discourses focus on internal consolidation and administrative efficiency" and highlight the dominance of the pragmatic discourse on enlargement (Wunsch and Olszewska, 2022, p. 3). Seemingly, the EU's roles towards its neighbours are changing in response to both external circumstances and the domestic need of political actors.

As a result, this chapter will focus on patterns of contestation of the four specific roles that the EU performs in the neighbourhood: the EU as a pacifier, focusing on conflict management, promotion of security and cooperation (Zubek 2019); the EU as a promoter of democratization, focusing on support for civil society and fundamental values; and the EU as a prosperity builder, focusing on economic cooperation, reforms, and overall development. Additionally, in order to discern its possible new role as a norm setter through norm promotion and regulatory exportation, an additional category will be introduced in this chapter – the EU as a regional regulator (Damro 2015). These four specific roles derived from empirical research and EU official documents analysis – as will be discussed below – correspond with the aforementioned meta-roles.

The analysis presented in this chapter is based on the assumptions of a constructivist approach to international relations, with the sources of behaviour of international actors derived from their experiences, identity, and collective memory. In that vein, contestation is understood here as a discursive practice and "an instance of strategic social construction that aims at undermining or displacing an accepted or emerging intersubjective meaning through the formulation by actors of competing discursive interventions that challenge the meaning of norms that embody conflictive interpretations of values" (Contessi 2010, p. 326).

This chapter examines literature regarding the EU's roles in the neighbourhood, as well as carrying out a qualitative discursive analysis of plenary debates in the EP. Overall 30 debates from the period 2004–2019 were selected and analysed covering three terms in office of the sixth, seventh and eighth EP. The debates cover major issues of the policy dealing with general topics and reviews of ENP, as well as issue- and country-specific debates. Firstly, from this material, the specific roles were inductively extracted and afterwards qualitative discourse analysis was employed as the main research method for examining MEPs' discursive practices of the EU's role contestation and the observed change over time.

## CONTESTING THE EU'S ROLES IN ITS NEIGHBOURHOOD

### The EU as a Pacifier

The EU, with a special focus on conflict resolution as outlined in the European Security Strategy in 2003 and the EU Global Strategy of 2016, prominently plays the role of a pacifier in its neighbourhood. Gradually the development of the hard power aspects of the EU's engagement became more robust. The main role of the EU as a security actor is civilian engagement in conflicts. Its core elements built on multilateralism, institution building and enabling, and a connective and constructive impact on conflicts (Diez et al. 2006). The central element that is contested in reference to conflicts in the neighbourhood is what tools the EU uses. Civilian engagement usually employs two types of activities (Zubek 2019). The first is predominantly economic, where the strong incentive is withdrawal or rejection of an upgrade in economic relations, especially within the ENP. While the second could include political means positively bringing parties together through peace conferences, incentives for complying with the international community expectations, and political sanctions (e.g. the classification of an organization in a list of terrorist organizations).

Initially, the dominant role conception was encapsulated within the civilian power paradigm. In the sixth EP, the dominant narrative referred to the EU's soft power – especially economic and diplomatic means. In that period, the contestation of the dominant role mostly concerned whether to use more coercive instruments of influence rather than conditionality. During the sixth EP, MEPs mostly refer to the greater need to use economic means to influence parties (also those involved in conflicts). This was predominantly about providing better incentives for cooperation and putting more pressure on conditionality. In the next term in office – facing more turbulent events in the neighbourhood – the focus was placed especially on political means. MEPs referred to a variety of instruments, including sanctions, that could be used to impact the behaviour of parties involved in conflict-ridden situations. In view of these circumstances, from the analysed debates, the role conception of comprehensive power almost exclusively appeared in the period of 2009–2011. However, even if the significance of the comprehensive power conceptualization decreased, particularly after the intervention in Libya what remained were calls to increase the security dimension within the ENP.

Traditionally, the main party groups tend to agree on civilian engagement. Interestingly, the reconceptualization of the role of the EU's more direct involvement in conflicts mostly came – apart from the two major party groups – from liberal and left-wing parties. The analysis shows that specifically the demand for a more decisive stance on the use of civilian power instruments was important for the left-wing party groups.

During the ENP debates, a number of conflicts were up for debate amongst MEPs. In the analysed period, the EU's involvement in the Middle East conflict was framed by MEPs predominantly as civilian engagement. Where there was demand for more action, political engagement was used. MEPs were critical of the lack of use of existing tools at the EU's disposal. In contrast, the Lebanon crisis during the sixth EP mostly provoked MEPs to demand more economic tools to be activated by the EU.

The Arab Spring in the early 2010s, and its aftermath across the region, intensified this role contestation. Its turbulent consequences in the North Africa region not only created circumstances that demanded a more active role for the EU, but also stirred up debate on the EU's involvement. This resulted in more frequent references to the active use of power in reaction to conflicts. They were used predominantly in the context of the Libyan conflict. This is in line with the analysis of debates within member states regarding Libya (Koenig 2016).

In the analysed period of 2004–2019, Eastern Europe was plagued with conflicts as well. However, in contrast to the southern neighbourhood, the MEPs initially paid less attention to the conflicts in Eastern Europe and the Caucasus, framing the EU's involvement in predominantly civilian terms. If there was a demand for more action on the EU's behalf, it was mostly about providing more economic incentives for cooperation. This was especially remarkable in the context of the Ukraine crisis in 2014. However, after 2014, the growing military threats and hostile actions by Russia made a significant difference for political actors in the way they constructed the EU's role in the region. In the long run, Russian aggression on Ukraine in 2014 changed the view on the Eastern neighbourhood in general, and on the role of the EU as a pacifier in particular. With the increased demand for an EU response, MEPs' attention was drawn to hybrid threats. In reference to both regions, MEPs from major party groups called for an increase of competences of the EU in crisis management in the form of a more thorough political and diplomatic toolbox, but also increased military capabilities. Most party groups strongly supported more decisive EU actions, supporting its partner countries in fighting against Russian aggression. The analysis covers debates before the unprovoked and unjustified Russian aggression on Ukraine in February 2022. However, the unprecedented decisions by the EU leaders in support for Ukraine including financing military supplies clearly demonstrate the continuation of a trend to increase the EU's pacifying abilities.

Traditionally, the main contesters of the role of the EU as a pacifier came from radical parties, on both the left and the right wing. The European United Left/Nordic Green Left (GUE/NGL) opposed any increase of military means in the EU's repertoire, accusing the Union of imperialist actions. For right-wing parties, it has always been a question of the cost and the intended outcome of the intervention. In the eighth EP, right-wing formations were critical of the sanctions against Russia, and their cost for the EU and its citizens.

## The EU as a Democratizer

The second EU role, that of a democratizer, is in line with the idea of normative power, and assumes that the EU is an important democracy promoter. Initially, democracy promotion was a significant element of the ENP. Its role increased over time – especially during the Arab Spring period. However, despite the centrality of democracy promotion in the EU narrative, problems in achieving lasting effects in this field diminished the significance of that role over time.

The role of the EU in democracy promotion dominated the debates on the ENP immediately from the time of its inception in the sixth EP, and was equally valid for both the southern and the eastern neighbourhoods. The key event changing the role conceptualization in this area was the Arab Spring. Initially the democratization efforts of the revolts were viewed positively by most political actors. As the concern for the adverse changes in the region increased, the democratizer role became progressively contested. In the turbulent times following 2011 in the southern neighbourhood, and 2014 in eastern regions, the EU's role as a democratizer became gradually less significant and less central in the analysed debates. It became clear for many political actors that democracy can only be successfully promoted under certain conditions and that achieving security and stability first was necessary.

The democratizer role was mainly contested based on the question of who qualifies for full democratization. Right-wing parties' representatives, for instance, stated that belonging to the European culture and value system was a precondition for full democratization. This contributed to the more general, ongoing debates on differentiation between partner countries of ENP. In reference to the Eastern Partnership countries there was an ongoing debate on the proper conditions under which democratization can be sustainable. In debates concerning the Southern neighbourhood countries, the topic of democratization was rather limited to only a few qualifying countries (such as Tunisia). The theme for the rest of the region concerned the assurance of security and the protection of fundamental human rights. It seems that the EU's role as a democratizer underwent the most significant transformation in period 2004–2019. With time, the attention on exporting EU values shifted to a greater focus on regulating the existing relations and developing access to specific policies, which will be discussed in the following section.

Vivid disputes in the EP concerned the potential conflicts between the EU as a democracy promoter and the security threats in the neighbourhood.

The growing significance of the latter demonstrated that revisiting the EU's involvement in the close neighbourhood required better balancing of the various roles the EU wanted to play. There were voices amongst political actors that the gradual departure of normatively grounded roles was devastating for the EU. A way to deal with these tensions was, for instance, to introduce the concept of resilience in relation to neighbouring regions that was stressed in the EU Global Strategy of 2016 as a response to the changing and demanding environment with old and new powerful contesters of the EU's role (Juncos 2016; Wagner and Anholt 2016). Juncos (2016) further argued, in the context of the ENP, that "In the area of foreign policy, resilience has thus been preferred over more 'tainted' and politically riskier concepts such as democratisation" (Juncos 2016, p. 3).

## The EU as a Prosperity Builder

The EU's role as a prosperity builder in the neighbourhood was primarily conceptualized in reference to the Eastern enlargement. Economic tools are among the strongest elements of the EU's engagement with its neighbours. Additionally, the EU acting as the most important donor of development aid is specifically significant for ENP partner countries, thus strengthening the economic profile of its actions. In recent years, with the new comprehensive tools of Deep and Comprehensive Free Trade Areas (DCFTAs), the EU's economic capacity to act has increased. Finally, this aspect of the EU's activities is traditionally the least contested by external actors (Góra 2019b).

The classic modernizing argument states that increased prosperity and welfare in the neighbourhood increases stability, helps democratization, and consequently contributes to the safety of the region. The EU primarily defines itself as an economic actor, and tools such as association agreements, free trade agreements, and access to the EU policies were perceived as one of the bloc's main strengths (i.e. European Commission 2015). Interestingly, the EU as a prosperity builder is a role that applied equally to the southern and eastern neighbourhoods. However, in some of the eastern neighbours – primarily Ukraine, Moldova and Georgia – the prospects for economic integration were more advanced.

A significant aspect of the initial role conception of a prosperity builder was making use of the EU's full potential, relying on policies that were tailor-made for partner countries to adhere to and benefit from. Recently, one can detect a change in how the EU, as a prosperity builder, is questioned in terms of costs, content, and form of the provided aid (Hackenesch et al. 2021). Moreover, the debates focused on how to finance the EU foreign policy, including new instruments for the neighbourhood (AFET 2019; European Commission 2020). With that in mind, it is clear that the role of the EU as a prosperity builder is connected to security and stability. To an extent, the role of a prosperity builder is an answer to a need for coherent external relations instruments.

The utilized tools and the logic behind economic development promotion were criticized when discussing the EU as a prosperity builder. Especially left-wing parties – Party of European Socialists (PES), the Greens, and GUE/NGL – were concerned about the possible impact of free trade instruments and the overall impact on the sensitive economies of partner countries. In a radical manner, the GUE/NGL accused the EU's external activities of imperialism, while right-wing MEPs considered them a waste of valuable resources. Notably, the right-wing contestation of the spending on the neighbourhood increased in the eighth EP in comparison to the two previous terms. The role of regional regulator seems to derive from (and possibly replace) the role of the EU as a prosperity builder.

## The EU as a Regional Regulator

The role of a regional regulator is linked to the EU's abilities to globally export regulations derived from intra-European policies and the strength of its market. Scholars argue that "ordoliberal principles and practices are an integral part of the EU's promotion of regulatory reforms in ENP partner countries" (Roccu 2018, p. 1071).

Initially, within the ENP there was a strong multilateral dimension inherited from the Barcelona process, including a strong regulatory component. On the one hand, the ENP strengthened the regulatory aspect, but it also merged it with initiatives from other international organizations, such as the WTO. Regulatory norms were imprinted in Action Plans, as well as promoted association agreements and DCFTAs. Overall, within the ENP partner countries are linked with the EU through a dense network of sectoral policies (Müftüler-Baç and Luetgert 2016). The idea of norm export is a constituent part of the normative power Europe, specifically in its role as a democratizer. However, as proposed here, this role is less about exporting values, and more about keeping a certain order in place.

Interestingly, the EU as a regional regulator was only recently clarified in response to the shifts in the global order. Initially there was limited interest in the broader context where relations with the neighbourhood were located. It was taken for granted that the international environment is guided by liberal norms. The only exception was attention to Russian actions in the regions under investigation. Russia was perceived as an actor undermining regulatory transformation, particularly in the eastern neighbourhood (Langbein 2015). However, over time political actors started to discuss the growing contestation of the EU's actions by third actors. Therefore, the perception of the EU became that of a protector of the liberal international order.

The role of the EU as a regulator is even more apparent when looking at its relations with close neighbours such as Norway or Switzerland (Fossum et al. 2020). By the same token, the upgraded offer was promoted for the most integrated partner countries, including their participation in customs union, digital and energy union. In a bid to compete with other key actors, and to find incentives and rewards for advanced partner countries, the MEPs considered expanding regulatory regimes to include non-members as well. Additionally, the idea emerged of opening the Schengen area and involving more multinational or multilateral financial institutions, such as the European Investment Bank. Interestingly, in December 2021 the EU launched a new initiative – EU's Global Gateway (EUGG) – meant to create a counterbalance for Chinese presence and Russian destabilizations. EUGG is an attempt to build new regional interlinked chains and (redesigned) communities of interest that will focus on efficient solutions to global problems enhancing EU's regulatory impact in neighbourhoods and beyond.

In addition, there was a growing tension between conceptualization of the EU as a regional regulator and the EU as democratizer. It appears that when facing significant obstacles in progressing with promotion of democracy, the political elites reshaped their perceived own role to become guardians of the liberal order. Since this role was only emerging some elements of previous roles of democratizer or prosperity builder were included. Finally, the role of the EU as a regional regulator has not yet became strongly contested in the EP as this is not a fully consolidated role. However, as it potentially will replace or incorporate previous roles – primarily as prosperity builder – it will most likely gain more attention.

## CONCLUSIONS

At the start, this chapter observed a gradual shift in the EU foreign policy away from the concept of normative influence, aimed at promoting European values (Manners 2002). It is replaced by the concepts of the EU as a pragmatic actor promoting "resilience" in its neighbourhood (Blockmans 2017, p. 7; Juncos 2016; Wagner and Anholt 2016). This results from the fact that the situation in many ENP partner countries deteriorated over time and there were attempts to reform ENP to adapt to these changes. An analysis of EU roles contestation in the 15 years between 2004 and 2019 in the EP shows that, indeed, in relations with the neighbouring countries the focus on promoting values is decreasing in favour of a more pragmatic evaluation of the EU's engagement. This is in sync with scholars' findings on EU enlargement (Wunsch and Olszewska 2022). These are shifts in how the EU's roles are narrated. Further research could benefit from studying their impact on policy practice. The central theme for political actors in the EU's relations with its neighbours is security, for the bloc and its citizens. Values in the EU foreign policy continue to be an important element, but they seem to be used mostly instrumentally. Stability and security are the main goals of the EU acting as a pacifier, and gradually the other roles of democracy promoter and prosperity builder became less significant. The Russian aggression Ukraine in February 2022 proved that this topic will dominate the EU's actions in the future.

Additionally, value promotion, which is encapsulated in the EU as a democratizer and remains key in political actors' rhetoric, was narrowed down, with the argument that such activities should be centred on specific actors. In searching for incentives and benefits to attract partner countries to cooperate, there was debate on expanding the regulatory regimes and accepting non-members. The EU's role as a regional regulator is not only to use its market power and attractiveness of regulatory solutions. It expands into the Union as an ordering power, in the sense of guarding the global liberal order in times of contestation and uncertainty, even from its closest allies such as the US under the Trump Administration. It is further pursued within EUGG initiative.

There are the usual suspects in internal contestation of EU roles – surging populist and Eurosceptic radical parties (Balfour et al. 2019; Buzogány et al. 2021). With time we observe an increase in the number of radical left-, and right-wing formations in the EP that are critical toward EU's actions. The most contested role was the EU as pacifier – especially the left-wing GUE/NGL criticism on the topic of the militarization of the EU. Nevertheless, the radical right-wing parties also became strong contesters in reference to Russia, criticizing, for instance, EU sanctions. The role of the EU as a democratizer is the second most contested EU role. However, it was criticized from a different angle, focusing on the fact that efforts in that domain did not result in an overwhelming success for the EU. The criticism concentrated on searching for differentiation among partner countries, so that countries that respond to the democratization receive more incentives, while those that respond negatively receive less and are handled by altogether different instruments. It seems that the ultimate departure from the 'one fits all' democratization is unavoidable. The least contested EU role was that of regulator, mostly as this is a relatively new conceptualization for the EU (even if the regulatory activities are not new at all, but were previously connected with other roles). It also appears as though this new role conception will replace that of the EU as a prosperity builder.

What do the EU's changing roles in the neighbourhood tell us about its global role? The relations with its neighbours serve as a litmus test for the EU's global presence. It clearly demonstrates that the changing external context, in which the bloc operates, requires the EU to better interconnect its own actions and maximize their use. Moreover, the analysis shows that two roles of the EU are key for political actors – as a pacifier focusing on stabilizing and security;

and as a regional regulator reinvigorating the efficient utilization of the market power that the bloc possesses. Scholarly attention of the new conceptualization of the EU as a regulator, guardian of liberal order, and ordering power is already indicating this tendency. It remains to be seen, however, if this new role conceptualization will prove to be significant in the future.

## REFERENCES

AFET (2019) *Report on the Proposal for a Regulation of the European Parliament and of the Council Establishing the Neighbourhood, Development and International Cooperation Instrument*. 11 March. https://www.europarl.europa.eu/doceo/document/A-8-2019-0173_EN.html.

Aggestam, L. (2006) Role Theory and European Union Foreign Policy. In Elgström, O. and Smith, M. (eds), *The European Union's Roles in International Politics*. London: Routledge, 11–29.

Balfour, R., Basagni, L., Floth-Liersch, A., Fusaro, P., Gelhaus, K., Groenendaal, L., Hegedus, D. et al. (2019) Divide and Obstruct: Populist Parties and EU Foreign Policy – Strengthening Transatlantic Cooperation. https://www.gmfus.org/news/divide-and-obstruct-populist-parties-and-eu-foreign-policy.

Bengtson, R. and Elgström, O. (2011) Reconsidering the European Union's Roles in International Relations: Self-Conceptions, Expectations, and Performance. In Harnisch, S., Frank, C. and Maull, H. W. (eds), *Role Theory in International Relations: Approaches and Analyses*. Abingdon: Routledge, 113–130.

Biedenkopf, K., Costa, O. and Góra, M. (2021) Introduction: Shades of Contestation and Politicisation of CFSP. *European Security*, **30**(3), 325–343.

Blockmans, S. (2017) *The Obsolescence of the European Neighbourhood Policy*. CEPS. https://www.ceps.eu/ceps-publications/obsolescence-european-neighbourhood-policy/.

Bradford, A. (2016) The EU as a Regulatory Power. In Leonard, M. (ed.), *Connectivity Wars: Why Migration, Finance and Trade Are the Geo-Economic Battlegrounds of the Future*. London: European Council on Foreign Relations, 121–128.

Brummer, K. and Thies, C. G. (2015) The Contested Selection of National Role Conceptions. *Foreign Policy Analysis*, **11**(3), 273–293.

Buzogány, A., Costa, O. and Góra, M. (2021) Contesting the EU's External Democratization Agenda: An Analytical Framework and Application to Populist Parties in Power. *Cambridge Review of International Affairs*. https://doi.org/10.1080/09557571.2021.2002264.

Cantir, C. and Kaarbo, J. (2012) Contested Roles and Domestic Politics: Reflections on Role Theory in Foreign Policy Analysis and IR Theory. *Foreign Policy Analysis*, **8**(1), 5–24.

Cantir, C. and Kaarbo, J. (eds) (2016) *Domestic Role Contestation, Foreign Policy, and International Relations*. Abingdon: Routledge.

Chelotti, N. (2016) *The Formulation of EU Foreign Policy: Socialization, Negotiations and Disaggregation of the State*. London and New York: Routledge.

Chryssogelos, A.-S. (2015) Patterns of Transnational Partisan Contestation of European Foreign Policy. *European Foreign Affairs Review*, **20**(2), 227–246.

Cianciara, A. K. (2017) Stability, Security, Democracy: Explaining Shifts in the Narrative of the European Neighbourhood Policy. *Journal of European Integration*, **39**(1), 49–62.

Contessi, N. P. (2010) Multilateralism, Intervention and Norm Contestation: China's Stance on Darfur in the UN Security Council. *Security Dialogue*, **41**(3), 323–344.

Damro, C. (2012) Market Power Europe. *Journal of European Public Policy*, **19**(5), 682–699.

Damro, C. (2015) Market Power Europe: Exploring a Dynamic Conceptual Framework. *Journal of European Public Policy*, **22**(9), 1336–1354.

De Wilde, P., Koopmans, R., Merkel, W., Strijbis, O., and Zürn, M. (eds) (2019) *The Struggle Over Borders: Cosmopolitanism and Communitarianism*. Cambridge: Cambridge University Press.

Diez, T., Stetter, S. and Albert, M. (2006) The European Union and Border Conflicts: The Transformative Power of Integration. *International Organization*, **60**(3), 563–593.

Duchêne, F. (1973) The European Community and the Uncertainties of Interdependence. In M. Kohnstamn and W. Hager (eds), *A Nation Writ Large? Foreign Policy Problems before the European Community*. London: Macmillan, 1–21.

European Commission (2015) *Joint Communication to the European Parliament, the Council, the European Economic and Social Committee and the Committee of the Regions. Review of the European Neighbourhood Policy*. SWD (2015) 500 Final. https://ec.europa.eu/neighbourhood-enlargement/sites/near/files/neighbourhood/pdf/key-documents/151118_joint-communication_review-of-the-enp_en.pdf.

European Commission (2019) *Preparing for a More United, Stronger and More Democratic Union in an Increasingly Uncertain World*. https://ec.europa.eu/commission/sites/beta-political/files/comm_sibiu_06-05_en.pdf.

European Commission (2020) Neighbourhood, Development and International Cooperation Instrument. https://doi.org/10.2761/739555.

Falkner, G. and Plattner, G. (2018) Populist Radical Right Parties and EU Policies: How Coherent Are Their Claims? *SSRN Electronic Journal*, December. https://doi.org/10.2139/ssrn.3293855.

Fossum, J., Garcia Quesada, M. and Zgaga, T. (2020) The Key Principles, Underlying Logic(s) and Types of Affiliation for EU Non-Members, Including Post-Brexit UK. *EU3D Report 1*. https://www.sv.uio.no/arena/english/research/publications/arena-reports/2020/report-1-20-fossum-et-al.pdf.

Góra, M. (2019a) The European Parliament as an Agenda Setter of EU Policy toward Its Neighbourhood. In Raube, K., Müftüler-Baç, M. and Wouters, J. (eds), *Parliamentary Cooperation and Diplomacy in EU External Relations*. Cheltenham, UK and Northampton, MA, USA: Edward Elgar Publishing, 289–305.

Góra, M. (2019b) Allied Constructive Criticism? The EU and Crises in its Immediate Neighbourhood from the American Perspective. *Politeja*, **16**(6(63)), 27–42. https://doi.org/10.12797/Politeja.16.2019.63.02.

Góra, M. (2021) It's Security Stupid! Politicisation of the EU's Relations with Its Neighbours. *European Security*, **30**(3), 439–463.

Góra, M., Styczyńska, N. and Zubek, M. (eds) (2019) *Contestation of EU Enlargement and European Neighbourhood Policy: Actors, Arenas and Arguments*. Copenhagen: Djøf Publishing.

Hackenesch, C., Bergmann, J. and Orbie, J. (2021) Development Policy under Fire? The Politicization of European External Relations. *Journal of Common Market Studies*, **59**(1), 3–19.

Harnisch, S. (2014) Full-Spectrum Role-Taking: A Two-Level Role Theoretical Model. Paper prepared for the annual conference of the International Studies Association.

Haukkala, H. (2015) From Cooperative to Contested Europe? The Conflict in Ukraine as a Culmination of a Long-Term Crisis in EU–Russia Relations. *Journal of Contemporary European Studies*, **23**(1), 25–40.

Holsti, K. J. (1970) National Role Conceptions in the Study of Foreign Policy. *International Studies Quarterly*, **14**(3), 233–309.

Irrera, D. (2015) Introduction: The European Parliament as an International Actor. In Stavridis, S. and Daniela, I. (eds), *The European Parliament and Its International Relations*. London: Routledge, 1–14.

Juncos, A. E. (2016) European Security Resilience as the New EU Foreign Policy Paradigm: A Pragmatist Turn? *European Security*, **26**(1), 1–18.

Kamińska, J. (2015) The European Parliament and the Revised European Neighbourhood Policy. In Bouris, D. and Schumacher, T. (eds), *The Revised European Neighbourhood Policy: Continuity and Change in EU Foreign Policy*. Basingstoke: Palgrave Macmillan, 135–154.

Kaya, T. (2009) Identifying the EU's Foreign and Security Policy Roles. *Review of International Law and Politics (Uluslararası Hukuk ve Politika)*, **17**, 107–131.

Koenig, N. (2016) Multi-Level Role Contestation: The EU in the Libyan Crisis. In Cantir, C. and Kaarbo, J. (eds), *Domestic Role Contestation, Foreign Policy, and International Relations*. Abingdon: Routledge, 157–173.

Langbein, J. (2015) *Transnationalization and Regulatory Change in the EU's Eastern Neighbourhood: Ukraine between Brussels and Moscow*. Abingdon: Routledge.

Lavenex, S., Krizic, I. and Serrano, O. (2017) EU and US Regulatory Power Under Strain? Emerging Countries and the Limits of External Governance. *European Foreign Affairs Review*, **22** (Special Issue), 1–18.

Lord, C. (2017) Legitimate and Democratic? The European Union's International Role. In Hill, K., Michael, S. and Vanhoonacker, S. (eds), *International Relations and the European Union*. Oxford: Oxford University Press, 186–206.

Manners, I. (2002) Normative Power Europe: A Contradiction in Terms? *Journal of Common Market Studies*, **40**(2), 235–258.

Meunier, S. and Nicolaïdis, K. (2006) The European Union as a Conflicted Trade Power. *Journal of European Public Policy*, **13**(6), 906–925.

Müftüler-Baç, M. and Luetgert, B. (2016) The European Union's Alternative Models for Maximizing Its Integration Strategy for Candidates and Neighbour States: A Process of External Differentiation. https://www.maxcap-project.eu.

Niemann, A. and Hoffmann, N. (2019) Conceptualising and Analysing the Contestation of the EU as an Actor in the ENP: Actorness, Effectiveness and Beyond. In Góra, M., Styczyńska, N. and Zubek, M. (eds), *Contestation of EU Enlargement and European Neighbourhood Policy: Actors, Arenas and Arguments*. Copenhagen: Djøf Publishing, 31–52.

Nitoiu, C. (2017) Framing the EU's Policy towards the Neighbourhood: The Strategic Approach of the Seventh European Parliament (2009–2014). *Cambridge Review of International Affairs*, **30**(1), 87–104.

Palm, T. and Crum, B. (2019) Military Operations and the EU's Identity as an International Security Actor. *European Security*, **28**(4), 513–534.

Raunio, T. and Wagner, W. (2017) Towards Parliamentarisation of Foreign and Security Policy? *West European Politics*, **40**(1), 1–19.

Roccu, R. (2018) Ordoliberalizing the Neighbourhood? The EU's Promotion of Regulatory Reforms in Egypt. *JCMS: Journal of Common Market Studies*, **56**(5), 1070–1086.

Rosén, G. and Raube, K. (2018) Influence beyond Formal Powers: The Parliamentarisation of European Union Security Policy. *The British Journal of Politics and International Relations*, **20**(1), 69–83.

Schmitt, E. M. (2017) Between European and National Role Conceptions: The EU3 Initiative Regarding the Iranian Nuclear Programme. *European Security*, **26**(2), 253–272.

Sjursen, H. (2006) The EU as a 'Normative' Power: How Can This Be? *Journal of European Public Policy*, **13**(2), 235–251.

Thevenin, E. (2021) Between Human Rights and Security Concerns: Politicisation of EU-Turkey and EU-Libya Agreements on Migration in National Parliaments. *European Security*, **30**(3), 464–484.

Thies, C. G. and Nieman, M. (2018) *Rising Powers and Foreign Policy Revisionism: Understanding BRICs Identity and Behavior through Time*. Ann Arbor: University of Michigan Press.

Van Berlo, M. and Natorski, M. (2020) When Contestation Is the Norm: The Position of Populist Parties in the European Parliament Towards Conflicts in Europe's Neighbourhood. In Johansson-Nogués, E., Vlaskamp M. C. and Barbé, E. (eds), *European Union Contested: Foreign Policy in a New Global Context*. Cham: Springer, 191–211.

Wagner, W. (2017) Liberal Power Europe. *Journal of Common Market Studies*, **55**(6), 1398–1414.

Wagner, W. and Anholt, R. (2016) Resilience as the EU Global Strategy's New Leitmotif: Pragmatic, Problematic or Promising? *Contemporary Security Policy*, **37**(3), 414–430.

Wagner, W., Pelaez, L., Raunio, T. and van de Koppel, M. (2021) The Party Politics of the EU's Relations with the USA: Evidence from the European Parliament. *European Security*, **30**(3), 418–438.

Wiener, A. (2014) *A Theory of Contestation*. Dordrecht: Springer.

Wish, N. B. (1980) Foreign Policy Makers and Their National Role Conceptions. *International Studies Quarterly*, **24**(4), 532–554.

Wunsch, N. and Olszewska, N. (2022) From Projection to Introspection: Enlargement Discourses since the "Big Bang" Accession. *Journal of European Integration*, 1–21. https://doi.org/10.1080/07036337.2022.2085261.

Zając, J. (2010) *Role Unii Europejskiej w Regionie Afryki Północnej i Bliskiego Wschodu*. Warsaw: Warsaw University Press. https://doi.org/10.31338/uw.9788323510109" https://doi.org/10.31338/uw.9788323510109.

Zubek, M. (2019) The European Parliament and the Conflicted EU Neighbourhood: Extinguishing the 'Ring of Fire', or Letting It Burn? In Góra, M., Styczyńska, N. and Zubek, M. (eds), *Contestation of EU Enlargement and European Neighbourhood Policy: Actors, Arenas and Arguments*. Copenhagen: Djøf Publishing, 209–230.

# 11. “Don’t stop believin’”: Germany’s turn from reflexive to strategic multilateralism

**Niklas Helwig**

## INTRODUCTION: GERMANY IN THE CENTER OF GLOBAL TRANSFORMATIONS

Germany’s view on the international order is closely linked to its multilateral vision of global governance. Next to European integration and the transatlantic alliance, the promotion of multilateralism is one of the key tenets of German foreign policy and crucial in its realization of security and economic interests. Consequently, the current contestation of the international order has a strong effect on the German discourse and policy practices. This chapter aims to analyze to what extent the current transformation in the international order causes a readjustment of Berlin’s foreign policy approach and its promotion of multilateralism.

A look at German history and its current position in international politics reveals that the era of international competition has the potential to rock Germany at its foundation. For Germany – a country in the center of Europe, one of the closest transatlantic allies, and a major export power – the contestation of the international order directly results in the contestation of its foreign policy approach. In particular, Germany’s approach to international cooperation has traditionally been based on “reflexive multilateralism”. Based on its post-war identity, it was in Germany’s “DNA” (Steinmeier 2015, p. 1) to support multilateral solutions and formal international integration without the explicit need to consider its strategic interests, which it undoubtedly had. To this end, this chapter explores how Germany adapts to the increasing international competition, and acts strategically in its pursuit of multilateral solutions.

The consequences that Germany draws from the changes in its strategic environment are indicative of the broader reaction of the European Union as an international actor. As a “power in the middle” (Münkler 2015, p. 137) or a global “network power” (Flemes 2013, p. 1016; Raik 2018, p. 4), Germany’s foreign policy has the potential to be both a subject and a driver of the current transformation of the world order and therefore deserves close attention.

The chapter is divided into three parts. First, the chapter discusses the drivers of Germany's multilateral approach to international politics. While the roots of Germany's multilateral devotion lie in its post-Second World War identity and the experiences of reunification, the country's prosperity and security have also greatly benefited from the European and international order. This has further solidified Germany's investment into the system. Second, the chapter turns to a discussion of growing international competition as a major challenge to the current order and discusses the potential consequences for Germany. The growing US–China competition has the potential to seriously harm Germany's economic and security interests – interests that have so far thrived under the multilateral order. Finally, the chapter offers an initial assessment of the qualitative change of Germany's multilateralism. It argues that certain nuanced changes in Germany's foreign policy – a stronger emphasis on interests, a more flexible approach to institutions, as well as a more functional choice of partners – suggest that Germany's multilateralism has become less 'reflexive' and more 'strategic'.

## THE SIGNIFICANCE OF THE MULTILATERAL ORDER FOR GERMANY

The multilateral order is a key element of Germany's approach to international relations. The German government (2016, p. 24) went as far as to define "maintaining the rules-based international order on the basis of international law" as one of Germany's main security interests in the 2016 white paper on security policy. Of course, Germany shares its commitment to the multilateral order with its European partner countries. The EU as an entity is also committed to the promotion of the international cooperation and the rules-based order. Nevertheless, more than other larger nation states, Germany has been recognized as a "civilian power" (Maull 1990, p. 91), which prefers multilateral institutions and diplomatic engagement over other more coercive forms of foreign policy conduct, such as military engagements or even economically restrictive measures. In the following section, three drivers of Germany's traditional devotion to multilateralism will be suggested.

### Order as Identity

Germany's dedication towards the promotion of the multilateral order is deeply shaped by its foreign policy developments since the Second World War. Scholars from the social constructivist tradition, such as Ruggie (1998), presume that the international order that emerged after the war was to a large degree a product of state identities. According to Katzenstein (1997), this ordering effect of national identity is especially strong in the case of Germany, which gave up its powerful position in Europe in favor of integration on the continent. West Germany's two main foreign policy goals were to re-establish itself as a trusted international partner after the horrors of the Nazi regime and to achieve reunification. It achieved both aims through a consequential pursuit of multilateralist strategies. The policy of 'Westbindung' – integration into the West – was pursued by the Konrad Adenauer government. It aimed at closely tying the fate of West Germany to the US and promoting multilateral integration into the emerging European Communities and NATO. German Chancellor Willy Brandt's 'Ostpolitik' of the early 1970s sought to normalize relations with Eastern Europe and the German Democratic Republic. At the end of the Cold War, Chancellor Helmut Kohl and his foreign minister Hans-Dietrich Genscher successfully leveraged multilateral reunification diplomacy to reunite Germany without major opposition from Moscow or the allied capitals (Krause 2004). West Germany's approach of constant diplomatic and multilateral engagement paid off and promised potential also for the post-Cold War period.

The experience of peaceful reunification had a strong impact on the German policymakers' self-conceptions and expectations towards international politics. Because of its individual experience during the fall of the iron curtain, Germany more than any other nation, assumed that countries around the world would transform into liberal democracies and military confrontation would eventually lose significance as a means of settling differences between nation states (Bagger 2019). With Germany at the geographical and historic center of European integration, German policymakers began "to see themselves as Europe's unifiers" (Hamilton 1991, p. 131). While realists feared that a reunited and strengthened Germany might become a liability for the European project (Mearsheimer 1990), it turned out that their historical experience had turned them into a "tamed power" (Katzenstein 1997).

It has been argued that in the decade following reunification, Germany's promotion of the international order has changed its connotation. The German discourse started to increasingly emphasize German interests and alliance responsibilities as a major reason to support the multilateral order (Baumann 2005). Nevertheless, even thirty years after reunification, multilateralism continues to shape Germany's foreign policy identity (Maull 2020).

## Order as Prosperity

It would certainly underestimate Germany's foreign policy skills to assume that its multilateral outlook would be solely driven by a belief in a utopian post-1989 world order. Instead, international order can be analyzed as a product of states' economic interests, which through their rivalry and cooperation "create the framework of political relations within which economic forces operate" (Gilpin 2001, p. 24). In this case, it is a fact that the rules-based international order has been a source of economic prosperity for Germany. While that is the case also for other Western economies, Germany's export-oriented economic model was well-suited to the rules-based and liberal trading environment.

By way of example, a recent study concluded that Germany, alongside China and the US, benefited most from the membership in the World Trade Organization (Felbermayr et al. 2019). However, despite Germany's export interests, its approach to the WTO is not singularly focused on promoting a trade-liberalization agenda. Instead, Germany has traditionally protected its agricultural interests and in the formulation of its positions considered the close partnerships with France and the US (Stahl and Luetticken 2007). In recent years, Germany has increasingly recognized the need to reform the WTO to make it better suited for an environment in which digital services and state subsidies play a substantial role (Schneider-Petsinger 2020). However, while there are concerns about the ability of the WTO rulebook to deal with the current transformation in the global economy, the multilateral approach as such is not disputed and is seen as the most efficient way to address shortcomings (von Daniels et al. 2019; Fabry and Schmucker 2019).

The economic benefits of Germany's multilateral approach are even more apparent with regard to the European integration project. While certain methodical difficulties exist in measuring the economic benefits of the EU, recent studies have shown that Germany has been one of the main beneficiaries of the barrier-free single market. In the twenty years following the 1993 Maastricht Treaty, the single market added 0.5 percentage points to Germany's GDP growth year after year (Dreger 2017). Not all EU countries benefited to the same extent, with only limited additional gains in Southern Europe and the UK (Petersen et al. 2014).

## Order as Security

Security is another objective that Germany pursues through a multilateral agenda. From a liberal institutionalist perspective (Keohane 1984) alliances and international institutions introduce hierarchies and cooperation into an otherwise anarchic international environment. The creation of such interdependencies has the potential to mitigate conflict. This might partly explain German preferences for international cooperation in various institutional settings. European integration within the EU and NATO has been important for a German sense of security (Helwig 2020a). Considering the instability and violence around Germany's borders in the previous centuries (Münkler

2015), the creation of these multilateral frameworks and their enlargement in the early 2000s have shaped a geographical constellation in which Germany is surrounded by friends. In addition, the OSCE was an important multilateral framework in Germany's Eastern policy during the Cold War and played an essential function in the policy towards the Eastern neighborhood also after reunification, albeit sharing its function with the EU's neighborhood policy (Roloff 2007).

Since the 2000s Germany's multilateral approach to security has widened its institutional and geographical scope. A prime example is Germany's engagement in the P5+1 nuclear non-proliferation negotiations with Iran. What started in 2003 as a Franco-German-British diplomatic initiative to curb Tehran's nuclear ambitions, transformed over the years into a multilateral embedded negotiation format under the leadership of the EU High Representative, together with the five permanent members of the UN Security Council. In 2015, under the pressure of UN and EU sanctions, Iran agreed to a roadmap that would restrict its program in compensation for economic relief. Germany was a major proponent of the format and contributed to its success through stable trade relations with Tehran, its civilian nuclear expertise, as well as through the maintenance of well-developed partnerships in the Middle East, especially with Israel as one of the main skeptics of a diplomatic containment (Helwig 2020b).

The German preference for multilateral diplomatic initiatives materialized again in the Ukraine crisis, when the Normandy format (including Germany, France, Russia and Ukraine) was established as the main platform to decide on conflict mitigating measures. Another recent example was the German engagement since 2019 to end the Libyan Civil War. In close cooperation with the United Nations, Germany initiated the so-called 'Berlin process' which seeks to bring together the relevant actors in and outside Libya to find a peaceful solution to the conflict.

The question whether Germany can act outside the formal UN and NATO multilateral structures is especially relevant with regards to the authorization of the use of force. A 1994 ruling of the German Constitutional Court decided that a German out-of-area military engagement is constitutional if it is conducted within a system of collective security (Peters 2018). In addition, the legitimate use of military force can be authorized through a UN resolution. Accordingly, the German participation in the so-called 'coalitions of the willing' repeatedly led to intense discussion and legal controversies. In a recent example, the German parliament mandated a military contribution to the anti-ISIS coalition in Northern Iraq, despite concerns over a missing international legal basis for a military intervention (Bundestag 2018). In general, the German Basic Law and jurisdiction dictates a multilateral approach to international military engagements.

## GREAT POWER COMPETITION AND THE CHALLENGE TO GERMAN MULTILATERALISM

Following the Second World War and reunification, Germany built its economic and foreign policy model on the foundation of a functioning multilateral order. As a consequence, Germany is strongly affected by the contestation of international norms and governance processes that are analyzed in this book. In particular, the contestation of the global order has led to an increase in international competition between great powers in recent years. To some extent, the current competition between the US and China is a byproduct of the continuous contestation that, in recent decades, the international order has fallen victim to. There is a limited consensus on the reform of global governance processes, producing a rapidly accelerating rate of "fragmentation" of the international order into regional systems (Kahler 2018, p. 240). In turn, this provides a basis for a possible decoupling of the US and China in the global system and increases the risk of great power competition.

In the late 2010s, the idea of an emerging great power competition entered the foreign policy debate. The publication of the first National Security Strategy under US President Donald Trump (2017) elevated the notion of a competitive relationship between the US and other major powers, in particular China and Russia. In comparison to the Cold War, the competition seemed less focused on military confrontation and rather concerned with "status grievances or ambitions, economic prosperity, technological advantage, and regional influence" (Mazarr et al. 2018, p. 34). While Russian actions in the 2014 Ukraine crisis and interference in the 2016 US elections underlined the unresolved tensions between Washington, DC and Moscow, rare US bipartisan agreement emerged, rather, on the threat of a rising China (Gaens and Sinkkonen 2020). This threat perception was centered around China's regional influence through the Belt and Road Initiative (BRI), state subsidies and a control of new technologies, aggressive maritime presence in the South and East China Seas, disadvantageous trade practices, as well as human rights practices.

While the current competition arose from decades of contestation of the international order, the geopolitical strategies of great powers run the risk of undermining the rules-based order even further. It is fair to argue that the emergence of great power competition is detrimental to an effective multilateral order (Biscop 2018). Notably, the US used to be the main initiator and a champion of the multilateral system. Recently, a more negative assessment of the costs and benefits of the international order for the US started to gain traction in Washington, DC. Particularly the Trump Administration, but also large segments of the US foreign policy establishment, harbored views that China, Russia and other emerging powers take unfair advantage of the international rules at the cost of the US. Many of the US foreign policy actors still prefer to adapt to the existing rules (Morrison 2018). The Trump Administration has taken a different approach by blocking or withdrawing from major international arrangements. For example, the US blocked the highest conflict resolution mechanism of the WTO – the appellate body – and withdrew from international agreements, such as the INF treaty with Russia, or the nuclear agreement with Iran.

Germany's multilateral foreign policy is negatively affected by the rise of great power competition. First and foremost, Germany stands to lose a lot from a looming trade war between the US and China, as it has major economic links to both countries. China is Germany's biggest trading partner. In 2019, it ranked as the first origin country for German imports and third for the destination of its exports (Destatis 2020). In recent decades, the *Mittelstand* – Germany's industrial sector made up of medium-sized companies – owes its growth to the successful exploration of export markets in the Far East (Karnitschnig 2020). At the same time, outside of Europe, the US is the second most important trading partner for Germany. A nightmare scenario would play out in Berlin if German businesses had to make a choice between the US and China (Barkin 2020).

However, it is not only the increasingly assertive policies of the US that are putting Germany's multilateral foreign policy model under pressure. Russia's revisionist foreign policy, which challenges the rules in the post-Soviet space, exploits 'Western' openness to create divisions in the Euro-Atlantic area, all while forging alliances with strongmen regimes from Belarus to Syria (Götz and Merlen 2019). Such a challenge from Russia is causing Berlin to reassess its approach (Forsberg 2016). Until the Russian invasion of Ukraine in 2022, a multilateral diplomatic engagement with Russia was still the most favorable choice. From a German perspective, diplomatic solutions to conflicts such as the ones in Iran, Libya, or Ukraine promised to be less successful without some sort of Russian involvement (Trenin 2018). However, long gone are the days when Germany hoped to achieve a transformation of the Russian economic, social, and political life through multilateral and economic engagement (Siddi 2016).

The trend towards international competition coincides with a rise of what is sometimes referred to as geo-economics. It describes a trend in international relations by which "states use economic power to pursue strategic aims" (Scholvin and Wigell 2018, p. 4). The most prominent examples are economic sanctions to address security problems, Chinese infrastructure projects in the Asian-European corridor, or the coercive use of raw material and energy dependencies (e.g., by Russia). Geo-economics represents a trend in international relations in which economic and political spheres get entangled. Previously, the global economic agenda was, to an extent, unaffected by political questions; however, economic interdependencies get progressively more and more weaponized (Leonard 2016).

While geo-economics can work within the multilateral order (e.g., UN sanction regimes), unilateral decisions and strategies put the system increasingly under pressure. A prominent recent example is the withdrawal of the US from the Iran nuclear agreement and the reinstatement of US sanctions on Tehran. Due to the ability of the US to enforce sanctions and the dominance of the US dollar and financial system, the US sanctions on Iran have an intended extraterritorial effect, as well as a restrictive effect on European commercial activity. Without economic relief through trade, the Iran nuclear deal seemed on the brink of collapse in summer 2020.

China's use of economic means to further its geostrategic interests can also be illustrated by its BRI, or by observing the activities of the state-subsidized tech giant Huawei. There is an ongoing debate on whether Chinese economic statecraft is harmful to multilateralism, or whether Beijing is simply an opportunistic player in the international order (Kastner et al. 2020). However, China's more assertive foreign economic policy indicates that a global order in which economic interdependencies are pursued without a concern for security assessments is further moving out of sight.

Arguably, Germany follows its own version of geo-economics. It often gives priority to economic relationships, in particular with Russia, over political and security considerations (Kundnani 2011; Szabo 2015). Consideration could be given to the idea that Germany has, for a long time, assumed that it can build its trade relationship uninfringed by security or policy concerns. It did not expect that the US would use its financial and economic dominance to force European partners to rally behind its foreign policy. Furthermore, there was seldom any worry about Chinese direct investments into crucial German and European industries. Only in recent years, Germany awoke to the more malign elements of global economic dependencies, moved to protect European industries through an investment screening mechanism, and devised a European instrument to circumvent the US financial system for global payments (Leonard et al. 2020).

Given the fact that Germany's identity, prosperity, and security are to a large extent based on the multilateral order on the European continent, the biggest concern for Germany is a situation in which great power competition becomes harmful for the regional integration project. While the EU seemed rather resilient in this respect. The Chinese 17+1 economic cooperation initiative with central European countries is a prime example of the receptiveness of some EU countries to Chinese influence. In addition, the US Administration under President Trump had been preferring bilateral relationships with some member states over dealing with the EU as a bloc, including advertising a closer post-Brexit economic relationship with the UK, or closer bilateral defense ties with Poland.

Two decades into the twenty-first century, Germany finds itself in a situation where it has to adjust its foreign policy approach to the new international realities. Reconsidering its approach to multilateralism is just one piece of this puzzle.

## GERMANY: FROM REFLEXIVE TO STRATEGIC MULTILATERALISM?

Traditionally, Germany's multilateral orientation has been described as "reflexive" (Smith 1996; Baumann 2000). Whether based on Germany's post-war identity, its strategic culture, or its constitutional imperatives, Germany's conduct of foreign policy is first and foremost based on multilateral engagement. In particular, the cooperation within the EU framework and the transatlantic security arrangements of NATO are often described as being in the "DNA" of German foreign and security policy (Steinmeier 2015, p. 1). While this continues to be the case, Germany too, has resorted to a "leaner and meaner" approach to multilateral institutions in order to protect national interests (Hellmann 2016). The European sovereign debt crisis perfectly illustrates this new approach. Some onlookers go as far as to say that with Germany's interest-based approach to the EU, "we are witnessing a hollowing out of 'reflexive multilateralism'" (Hofhansel 2005, p. 121).

How can Germany's emerging policy towards the global order be described instead? Due to the adaptations that Germany is currently undergoing in its foreign policy as a reaction to growing international competition, its approach can best be described as "strategic multilateralism" (Klein et al. 2010, p. 23; Kastner et al. 2018). Reflexive and strategic multilateralism represents constructed ideal types of approaches to international institutions in order to showcase the transformation of German foreign policy. In reality, German multilateralism has always combined elements of both. Nevertheless, as argued below, a trend from reflexive to strategic multilateralism can be observed. Reflexive multilateralism is based on the premise that German foreign policy is primarily driven by its post-war identity and the deeply ingrained institutional and societal norms that set an imperative for multilateral foreign policy conduct. In contrast, strategic multilateralism presumes that German foreign policy is rather driven by strategic considerations during the pursuit of its interests in the international environment. This fundamental difference has several implications. Firstly, it creates repercussions on the way that Germany justifies its activities. Next, it dictates which cooperation framework Germany sees as legitimate. Finally, it plays a role in determining which political ideology Germany subscribes to in the area of international

*Table 11.1* *Reflexive versus strategic multilateralism*

| | Reflexive multilateralism | Strategic multilateralism |
|---|---|---|
| Determinants | Identity | Interests, strategic environment |
| Justification | Historical responsibility, (Perceived) Universal interests/ norms | National interests, Promotion of distinct values |
| Frameworks | Formal multilateral institutions | Temporary, issue-based collaboration |
| Cooperation basis | Ideological (Centrality of human rights, rule of law, democracy) | Functional (Centrality of problem-solving capacity) |

*Source:* Own compilation.

cooperation (see Table 11.1). Three aspects of Germany's adaptation towards a more strategic approach are briefly outlined below.

First, Germany's approach to multilateralism is increasingly focused on the promotion of its interests and values. It could be argued that an interest-based approach is nothing new. In the past, Germany has promoted clear national interests through multilateralism, including German reunification, security in the neighborhood, or economic prosperity. However, a nuanced change is discernible. Germany's previous reflexive multilateralism, fueled by the historical experiences that shaped Germany's pacific and cooperative foreign policy approach, did not need to resort to the language of national interests or distinctive values to justify global cooperation. However, Germany adjusted to an environment in which the existence of shared norms is contested, and international governance structures became as much ground for competition as a forum for cooperation. As Baumann (2005) observed, Germany is increasingly comfortable in justifying its multilateral engagement by pointing towards the preservation of its national interests. The position that Germany needs to shape the international agenda based on a distinct set of values and interests overshadowed the previous arguments that the agenda should be rooted in historical lessons, possible benefits of international interdependence, or the universal adoption of norms. The more interest-based approach was also discernible in the process leading up to Germany's 2021 white paper on multilateralism (not yet published at the time of writing). The consultation process took the difficulties of Germany in realizing its economic and security interests in a more competitive international environment as the starting point to explore options for Germany to shape the multilateral order together with partners (Annen 2020).

Indeed, the environment of international competition accelerated strategic reorientation. This is only natural. The US and China did not hide their ambition to shape global politics in line with their interests, Germany and its neighbors came to realize that these ambitions were not always in accordance with European perspectives. Policy areas in which these distinct German or European positions exist – in discrepancy to the US or China – include, for example, data protection or the green transformation. The German discussion is, thus, very much in parallel with the debate on the European level. Similarly, arguments are being made that the EU needs to achieve 'strategic autonomy' to better defend its positions in international politics, as well as a reform of multilateral institutions that could work towards achieving such a goal (Grevi 2019; Helwig 2020c).

Second, Germany has become increasingly flexible regarding the use of multilateral structures. Reflexive multilateralism is linked to the primacy of formal multilateral frameworks, as only they provide the international legitimacy and, in many cases, the internal legal basis in the German Basic Law (military engagement) to get internationally active. The major multilateral institutions – the UN, the EU, and NATO – still remain the bedrock of Germany's multilateral engagement. However, adjacent to these major multilateral structures, Germany increasingly started to engage in smaller and more issue-specific frameworks. The basis of that change was the acceptance of a much more complex international reality to which rigid consensus-based multilateral institutions could not provide effective solutions. An early indication was the German involvement in the Western Balkan Contact group in the 1990s when the US had little appetite to include the EU in the conversations as a whole, but nonetheless needed European participation (Schwegmann 2000). The Iran nuclear talks and the Normandy format in the Ukraine crisis are the most prominent recent examples of a trend in which Germany and other states circumvent the inflexible and slow structures of multilateral institutions and tackle a specific issue head-on. 'Coalitions of the willing' are the military equivalent of groups of states acting together only loosely attached to NATO or the UN. While the use of smaller negotiation formats, contact groups, or coalitions raises legitimacy questions and causes concerns of "diminished multilateralism" (Rüland 2012), in theory, it offers Germany new possibilities of engagement, while still acting in conjunction with the wider multilateral system (Masala 2020).

Third, as post-1989 hopes of a global liberal transformation are fading and authoritarian systems are proving to be resilient in the crises of the recent decades, Germany becomes more open to cooperation with non-democratic and non-market-capitalist countries in upholding the international rules-based order (Benner 2019). The crises of the 2010 – Arab Spring, Crimea annexation, migration crisis – caused a strategic change in Europe towards "principled pragmatism" (Juncos 2017). This approach is based on the acceptance of global power politics, rather than maintaining the hope to fundamentally change it (Biscop 2016). As a consequence, the promotion of values became conditioned by what was seen as a realistic possibility. While the EU's approach to its neighborhood was formerly presented as an attempt to foster normative change in the often authoritarian-led countries, it started to focus on 'resilience' as an important goal. These changes on a European level also reflected a similar change in German thinking (Fröhlich 2019).

The strategic change was apparent not only on the regional level, but also on the global level. While 'reflexive multilateralism' worked best in the context of an overlapping liberal ideology – or at least with a hope that the acceptance of liberal values is just a matter of time – 'strategic multilateralism' works independently of these concerns. The argument states that, when discussing global challenges, such as climate change or pandemics, global cooperation is necessary regardless of the domestic political systems. On the contrary, the coronavirus pandemic prompted a discussion of whether some democracies under the strain of populism have been less effective in managing the crisis through multilateral engagement (Zürn 2020). While Germany still keeps its closest multilateral ties with democratic partners within the EU and NATO, the engagement with non-democracies such as China has become more important on issues ranging from climate change, pandemics, and digitalization, to nuclear non-proliferation.

Germany's adjustments in its multilateral approach are mostly a reaction to the more competitive international environment. In an international political environment, in which national interests are highlighted, multilateral institutions are blocked, and authoritarian regimes demonstrate more resilience. 'Business as usual' becomes less of an option for Germany. Instead, there are indicators that Germany becomes more strategic about its multilateral engagement.

## CONCLUSIONS: A THIRD WAY FOR THE EU IN MULTILATERALISM

In twentieth-century politics, it can be argued that Germany has consistently been at the core of the global order transformations. The current multilateral order is a reaction to the Second World War and the horrors of the Nazi regime. This is especially true for the far-reaching integration on the European continent, initially used as a tool to tame German power. Moreover, the second major change of the world order in the last century, from a bipolar stand-off between the US and the Soviet Union to a 'unipolar moment' with the US at its core, ran through the middle of a previously divided German nation.

At first sight, the current transformation of the world order, marked by growing competition between the US and China in the economic and technological sphere, bypasses the European continent and centers around the Asian-Pacific region. However, this chapter aimed to show that Germany's position in the world is once more affected in major ways by the international tidal shifts. On the back of the European Union and despite its lack of military muscle, Germany has, in recent decades, developed into a global power that can shape the economic and diplomatic realm (Szabo 2017). As much as this status was built on the rise of multilateralism, Germany's fall from rank could be the result of its demise.

As a consequence, Germany shows signs of becoming more strategic about its approach to multilateralism in order to safeguard a key pillar of its international engagement. By way of example, the German federal ministry of foreign affairs is preparing a white paper on multilateralism at the time of writing. However, beyond the insightful snapshot that this strategy paper might deliver, one can already discern a more strategic approach in Germany's multilateralism. In this emerging approach, the multilateral system is more a means to realize Germany's interests, and less of an idealistic end of an interdependent and conflict-free world order. Berlin's policies are less concerned with the order as such than with the results that the order can achieve, which allows also for a stronger engagement in issue-specific, temporary coalitions, or groupings. Finally, the idea of achieving democratic change through international dependencies and multilateral engagement has lost its shine even in Germany, all while global challenges increasingly call for global cooperation. A rules-based and multilateral order is not an exclusive liberal project anymore.

Germany's change to multilateralism is nuanced, as it does not put the system as such in question. Yet it is significant, as it has the potential to preview a distinct multilateral approach of the EU. While the US increasingly focuses on the negative distributive effects of the global order, and China makes opportunistic use of international rules, Europe might attempt to look for a third way in multilateralism. This third way is neither guided by overly ambitious ideals of liberal transformation, which gained currency again under the new Biden Administration in the US and their proposal of calling in a 'summit for democracy'. Nor is it guided by a thin, status-driven, interest-based approach that increasingly comes to the forefront in the growing competition between China and the US. Instead, "Don't stop believin'" might be the EU's soundtrack on its journey towards a multilateral order that puts rule-based cooperation and problem-solving capacity at the center of its efforts. The EU approach might highlight the need for multilateral cooperation in order to tackle the global challenges of our time without compromising distinct values and interests. To what extent we will see a more strategic European approach to multilateralism, not only on paper but successfully implemented on the international stage, needs to be studied in greater detail.

## REFERENCES


Annen, N. (2020) *Ein Weißbuch Multilateralismus*. Peacelab.blog.

Bagger, T. (2019) The World According to Germany: Reassessing 1989. *The Washington Quarterly*, **41**(4), 53–63.

Barkin, N. (2020) *Germany's Strategic Gray Zone with China*. Washington, DC: Carnegie Endowment for International Peace.

Baumann, R. (2000) Understanding Multilateralism in German Foreign and Security Policy: The Participation of the Bundeswehr in Multinational Military Units. Paper prepared for delivery at the 41st Annual Convention of the International Studies Association in Los Angeles, CA.

Baumann, R. (2005) *Der Wandel des deutschen Multilateralismus. Konstruktivistische Analysen der internationalen Politik*. Berlin: Springer.

Benner, T. (2019) *What's Left of Multilateralism? Putting Six Hypotheses to the Test*. Berlin: Global Public Policy Institute.

Biscop, S. (2016) *The EU Global Strategy: Realpolitik with European Characteristics*. Security Policy Brief 75. Brussels: Egmont Institute.

Biscop, S. (2018) The EU and Multilateralism in an Age of Great Powers. In Echle, C., Rueppel, P. and Sarmah, M. (eds), *Multilateralism in a Changing World Order*. Bonn: Konrad-Adenauer-Stiftung, 39–48.

Bundestag (2018) Research Service of the German Parliament. *Wissenschaftliche Dienste des Deutschen Bundestages. Rechtsfragen einer etwaigen Beteiligung der Bundeswehr an möglichen Militärschlägen der Alliierten gegen das Assad-Regime in Syrien*. WD 2–3000–130/18.

Destatis (2020) Ranking of Germany's Trading Partners in Foreign Trade (Preliminary Results). 2019 Statistisches Bundesamt.

Dreger, C. (2017) Der wirtschaftliche Nutzen Europas für Deutschland. In Böttger, K. and Jopp, M. (eds), *Handbuch zur deutschen Europapolitik*. Bonn: Bundeszentrale für politische Bildung.

Fabry, E. and Schmucker, C. (2019) International Trade. In Demesmay, C. and Kunz, B. (eds), *Sustaining Multilateralism in a Multipolar World: What France and Germany Can Do to Preserve the Multilateral Order*. Notes du Cerfa No. 148. Paris: IFRI, 12–15.

Felbermayr, G., Larch, M., Yotov, Y. and Yalcin, E. (2019) *The WTO at 25: Assessing the Economic Value of the Rules Based Global Trading System*. Gütersloh: Bertelsmann Stiftung.

Flemes, D. (2013) Network Powers: Strategies of Change in the Multipolar System. *Third World Quarterly*, **34**(6), 1016–1036.

Forsberg, T. (2016) From Ostpolitik to 'Frostpolitik'? Merkel, Putin and German Foreign Policy towards Russia. *International Affairs*, **92**, 21–42.

Fröhlich, S. (2019) *Das Ende der Selbstfesselung: Deutsche Außenpolitik in einer Welt ohne Führung*. Berlin: Springer.

Gaens, B. and Sinkkonen, V. (2020) *Great-Power Competition and the Rising US–China Rivalry: Towards a New Normal?* FIIA Report 66. Helsinki: Finnish Institute of International Affairs.

German Federal Government (2016) *White Paper on German Security Policy and the Future of the Bundeswehr*. Berlin.

Gilpin, R. (2001) *Global Political Economy: Understanding the International Economic Order*. Princeton, NJ: Princeton University Press.

Götz, E. and Merlen, C.-R. (2019) Russia and the Question of World Order. *European Politics and Society*, **20**(2), 133–153.
Grevi, G. (2019) *Strategic Autonomy for European Choices: The Key to Europe's Shaping Power*. Discussion Paper. Brussels: European Policy Centre.
Hamilton, D. (1991) A More European Germany, a More German Europe. *Journal of International Affairs*, **45**, 127–149.
Hellmann, G. (2016) Germany's World: Power and Followership in a Crisis-Ridden Europe. *Global Affairs*, **2**(1), 3–20.
Helwig, N. (2020a) Out of Order? The US Alliance in Germany's Foreign and Security Policy. *Contemporary Politics*, **26**(4), 439–457.
Helwig, N. (2020b) Germany in European Diplomacy: Minilateralism as a Tool for Leadership. *German Politics*, **29**(1), 25–41.
Helwig, N. (2020c) *EU Strategic Autonomy: A Reality Check for Europe's Global Agenda*. FIIA Working Paper 2019. Helsinki: Finnish Institute of International Affairs.
Hofhansel, C. (2005) *Multilateralism, German Foreign Policy and Central Europe*. Abingdon: Routledge.
Juncos, A. E. (2017) Resilience as the New EU foreign Policy Paradigm: A Pragmatist Turn? *European Security*, **26**(1), 1–18.
Kahler, M. (2018) Global Governance: Three Futures. *International Studies Review*, **20**, 239–246.
Karnitschnig, M. (2020) *How Germany Opened the Door to China – and Threw Away the Key*. Brussels: Politico Europe.
Kastner, S. L., Pearson, M. M. and Rector, C. (2018) *China's Strategic Multilateralism*. Cambridge: Cambridge University Press.
Kastner, S. L., Pearson, M. M. and Rector, C. (2020) China and Global Governance: Opportunistic Multilateralism. *Global Policy*, **11**, 164–169.
Katzenstein, P. (1997) *Tamed Power: Germany in Europe*. Ithaca, NY: Cornell University Press.
Keohane, R. (1984) *After Hegemony*. Princeton, NJ: Princeton University Press.
Klein, N., Reiners, W., Zhimin, C., Junbo, J. and Slosarcik, I. (2010) Diplomatic Strategies of Major Powers: Competing Patterns of International Relations? *MERCURY E-paper No. 2*.
Krause, J. (2004) Multilateralism: Behind European Views. *The Washington Quarterly*, **27**(2), 43–59.
Kundnani, H. (2011) Germany as a Geo-economic Power. *The Washington Quarterly*, **34**(3), 31–45.
Leonard, M. (2016) *Connectivity Wars: Why Migration, Finance and Trade are the Geo-economic Battlegrounds of the Future*. Berlin: European Council on Foreign Relations.
Leonard, M., Pisani-Ferry, J., Ribakova, E., Shapiro, J. and Wolf, G. (2020) *Redefining Europe's Economic Sovereignty*. Policy Contribution 9. Berlin: Bruegel.
Masala, C. (2020) Von Freundesgruppen bis zu Koalitionen der Willigen: Den 'neuen' Multilateralismus aktiv mitgestalten. *PeaceLab*, 20 October.
Maull, H. W. (1990) Germany and Japan: The New Civilian Powers. *Foreign Affairs*, **69**(5), 91–106.
Maull, H. W. (2020) *Multilateralismus und deutsche Außenpolitik: Ein Syllogismus?* Berlin: SWP Studie 18.

Mazarr, M. J., Blake, J., Casey, A., McDonald, T., Pezard, S. and Spirtas, M. (2018) *Understanding the Emerging Era of International Competition*. Research Report 2726. Santa Monica, CA: RAND Corporation.

Mearsheimer, J. (1990) Back to the Future: Instability in Europe after the Cold War. *International Security*, **15**(1), 5–56.

Morrison, C. E. (2018) Tradition, Trump, and the Future of US Participation in Multilateralism. In Echle, C., Rueppel, P. and Sarmah, M. (eds), *Multilateralism in a Changing World Order*. Bonn: Konrad-Adenauer-Stiftung, 27– 38.

Münkler, H. (2015) *Macht in der Mitte: Die neuen Aufgaben Deutschlands in Europa*. Hamburg: Körber Stiftung.

Peters, A. (2018) Between Military Deployment and Democracy: Use of Force under the German Constitution. *Journal on the Use of Force and International Law*, **5**(2), 246–294.

Petersen, T., Böhmer, M. and Weisser, J. (2014) *20 Jahre Binnenmarkt – Wachstumseffekte der zunehmenden EU-Integration*. Policy Brief 2014/4. Gütersloh: Bertelsmann Stiftung.

Raik, K. (2018) *EU Foreign Policy in a Networked World: Webs against Power Politics*. FIIA Analysis 9. Helsinki: Finnish Institute of International Affairs.

Roloff, R. (2007) Organisation für Sicherheit und Zusammenarbeit in Europa. In Schmidt, S., Link, W., and Reinhard, W. (eds), *Handbuch zur deutschen Aussenpolitik*. Berlin: Springer, 779–787.

Ruggie, G. (1998) *Constructing the World Polity: Essays on International Institutionalisation*. New York: Routledge.

Rüland, J. (2012) The Rise of 'Diminished Multilateralism': East Asian and European Forum Shopping in Global Governance. *Asia Europe Journal*, **9**(2–4), 255–270.

Schneider-Petsinger, M. (2020) *Reforming the World Trade Organization: Prospects for Transatlantic Cooperation and the Global Trade System*. London: Chatham House.

Scholvin, S. and Wigell, M. (2018) Geo-Economics as Concept and Practice in International Relations: Surveying the State of the Art. FIIA Working Paper 102. Helsinki: Finnish Institute of International Affairs.

Schwegmann, C. (2000) *The Contact Group and its Impact on the European Institutional Structure*. Occasional Paper 16. Paris: European Union Institute for Security Studies.

Siddi, M. (2016) German Foreign Policy towards Russia in the Aftermath of the Ukraine Crisis: A New Ostpolitik? *Europe-Asia Studies*, **68**(4), 665–677.

Smith, M. (1996) Sending the Bundeswehr to the Balkans: The Domestic Politics of Reflexive Multilateralism. *German Politics & Society*, **14**(4(41)), 49–67.

Stahl, B. and Luetticken, F. (2007) Welthandelsorganisation. In Schmidt, S., Link, W., and Reinhard, W. (eds), *Handbuch zur deutschen Aussenpolitik*. Berlin: Springer, 788–801.

Steinmeier, F.-W. (2015) *The DNA of German Foreign Policy*. Brussels: Politico Europe.

Szabo, S. (2015) *Germany, Russia, and the Rise of Geo-Economics*. London: Bloomsbury.

Szabo, S. (2017) Germany: From Civilian Power to a Geo-Economic Shaping Power. *German Politics & Society*, **35**(3), 38–54.

Trenin, D. (2018) *Russia and Germany: From Estranged Partners to Good Neighbors*. Moscow: Carnegie Moscow Center.

Trump, D. J. (2017) *National Security Strategy of the United States of America*. Washington, DC: White House.

Von Daniels, L., Dröge, S. and Bögner, A. (2019) *Ways Out of the WTO's December Crisis*. SWP Comment 2019/C 46. Berlin: Stiftung Wissenschaft und Politik.

Zürn, M. (2020) Die Zukunft des Multilateralismus und der Wettbewerb der Systeme. Berlin Social Science Centre. https://www.wzb.eu/de/forschung/corona-und-die-folgen/die-zukunft-des-multilateralismus-und-der-wettbewerb-der-systeme.

# 12. A Trump effect on European Union climate ambitions? The European Council and Council of the EU's responses to US climate contestation

**Katja Biedenkopf and Franziska Petri**[1]

## INTRODUCTION[2]

In December 2015, several key governments' active diplomatic efforts and leadership drove the adoption of the Paris Agreement on climate change. The European Union (EU), the United States of America (US), China and Brazil, among others, were central players, contributing to the negotiation success (Biedenkopf and Walker 2016; Cross 2018; Parker and Karlsson 2018; Parker et al. 2017). Shortly after the entry into force of the Paris Agreement in 2016, the global political landscape on climate action underwent substantial changes: Previously a driving force behind the negotiations of the Paris Agreement, the US, under then-President Donald J. Trump, started to dismantle not only domestic, but also international climate action by announcing, in 2017, the withdrawal from the Paris Agreement (White House 2017), which took effect in November 2020. The withdrawal of the world's second-largest greenhouse gas (GHG) emitter (Global Carbon Atlas, n.d.) fundamentally challenged the global consensus on which the Paris Agreement was based and contested the underlying norm of global climate governance that urgent and ambitious climate action is needed (Pickering et al. 2017; Saad 2018; Schreurs 2017; Urpelainen and Van de Graaf 2018).

[1] This work was supported by the University of Leuven's C1 Project CONNECTIVITY and the Research Foundation Flanders (FWO) under Grant 11H3120N.

[2] This chapter and its empirical findings are based on a larger research project conducted by the authors on EU climate ambitions and the European Council/Council of the EU. It presents the extended findings of the coding performed, parts of which have been included in Petri and Biedenkopf (2020), published in the journal *Global Affairs*.

President Trump's open and radical contestation of international climate policy raised the question of how the EU, as a key actor in international climate politics and promoter of high climate ambitions (Oberthür and Groen 2018; van Schaik and Schunz 2012; Walker and Biedenkopf 2018), reacted to the renewed contestation of the norm of global climate action (Petri and Biedenkopf 2020). Strong contestation of global climate action, as exercised by the Trump Administration (De Pryck and Gemenne 2017), is likely to exert a negative influence on the transatlantic relationship (Aggestam and Hyde-Price 2019; Hill and Hurst 2020; Riddervold and Newsome 2018). Furthermore, weakening or strengthening the norm of ambitious climate change can also affect the overall robustness of the international consensus embedded in the Paris Agreement (Deitelhoff and Zimmermann 2018; 2019, p. 4; Schmidt and Sikkink 2019). This contestation by the Trump Administration could have triggered two possible effects on the EU: either (a) reinforce the EU's commitment to ambitious climate policy, in line with the Paris Agreement's goal to keep the global temperature increase to well below two degrees Celsius, attempting to safeguard international climate norms and limiting possible contestation effects internally and externally, or (b) cause or strengthen existing doubts on the norm within the EU, leading to the adoption of the contester's views and weakening the EU's climate ambition.

This chapter systematically analyzes the European Council and Council of the European Union's responses to the international climate policy contestation by the Trump presidency. These two institutions are two of the EU's main decision-making bodies and institutional fora where growing domestic contestation within the EU and among its Member States could become evident. The European Council decides the overall political direction of internal and foreign EU policy. The Foreign Affairs Council (FAC) determines, together with the European Commission and the European External Action Service, foreign climate policy. The Environment Council (ENV) is central, together with the European Parliament, in deciding internal climate policy and also is involved in foreign climate policy (Delreux 2018). To trace the changes in their positions, this chapter presents a systematic analysis of publicly available documents of all meetings in formal settings of the European Council and the two Council formations, FAC and ENV between January 2014 and May 2019, using qualitative content analysis and the qualitative data processing software NVivo (total: 212 meetings, 405 documents). Next, a comparison is made between the EU positions during the pre-Trump (2014–2016) and the Trump period (2017–2019), investigating whether the two Councils explicitly addressed and reacted to aspects of the Trump Administration's climate skepticism.

The analysis shows that the EU countered President Trump's climate-skeptic positions and signaled its strong commitment to the norm of ambitious global climate action. Both the European Council and Council of the EU continuously reaffirmed their commitment to the Paris Agreement and explicitly reacted to Trump's climate-skeptic arguments in their internal rhetoric, as well as their outreach to third parties. These rhetorical actions aimed at limiting the potentially contagious effect of US climate contestation on the EU and other international actors. As such, this chapter offers nuanced empirical insights that advance our understanding of the effect that the former US Administration exerted on the international climate order, in general, and the European role within it, in particular (Petri and Biedenkopf 2020).

The next section provides a short overview of US climate politics before and during the Trump Administration. Section three presents the results of the empirical analysis of Council documents and is followed by a short discussion of these results. Finally, the concluding section suggests avenues for future research on the effect of US contestation on the EU.

## US EXTERNAL CLIMATE POLITICS: FROM OBAMA TO TRUMP

The US took a fundamental turn from supporting ambitious multilateral climate policy to renewed climate contestation when President Obama handed over the presidential role to Donald J. Trump. This section provides an overview of the Obama Administrations' (2009–2017) climate action, before outlining climate politics under President Trump (2017–2021). It builds on secondary literature and speeches of both presidents.

### The Obama Administration

Barack Obama held the presidential office between 2009 and 2017. His presidency represented "a significant departure from the obstructionist policies of the George W. Bush era" (Atkinson 2018, p. 91), with Obama actively pushing for domestic and international climate policies and – in particular during his second term – explicitly embracing an active US role in global climate politics (Bomberg and Super 2009). However, President Obama's climate policy track record is more nuanced: On the one hand, Bailey (2019) finds an overall high climate action commitment from President Obama during his campaigns that promoted a multi-pronged approach, which translated, for example, into his 2013 Climate Action Plan and a number of executive orders on climate matters (Bailey 2019, pp. 856–860). On the other hand, this activism was met with a number of challenges, such as the economic recession following the 2008 global financial crisis and deep partisan divisions on climate action, including the critical role of the Tea Party movement within the Republican Party obstructing climate initiatives. As such, examples like the failure of the American Clean Energy and Security Act in Congress during President Obama's first term illustrate the limits of legislative action on climate change.

His second term was marked by a renewed commitment to climate action. Crucial domestic initiatives, such as the Clean Power Plan, were launched. Moreover, the US took up a more active international role in the United Nations Framework Convention on Climate Change (UNFCCC) negotiations leading to the 2015 Paris Agreement, including active US–China bilateral engagement on climate change (Parker and Karlsson 2018). President Obama's remarks upon joining the Paris Agreement in September 2016 serve as an illustration of the US' strong position towards climate action: "Over the past seven and a half years, we've transformed the United States into a global leader in the fight against climate change. But this is not a fight that any one country, no matter how powerful, can take alone" (White House 2016). Bailey (2019, p. 848) concludes that "faced with unpromising circumstances, Obama displayed considerable leadership skills by taking a number of seemingly small steps to address climate change during his time in office that cumulatively add up to a major change in policy". In sum, despite failed domestic legislative initiatives, when President Obama left office, he showcased the US' renewed commitment to ambitious global climate action, thereby constituting a climate ally for the EU.

## The Trump Administration

Half a year into the Trump presidency, the 45th US president followed up on his campaign promise of putting 'America First' and stated in a speech in the White House's Rose Garden (2017): "[I]n order to fulfill my solemn duty to protect America and its citizens, the United States will withdraw from the Paris Climate Accord ... but begin negotiations to re-enter either the Paris Accord or a really entirely new transaction on terms that are fair to the United States, its businesses, its workers, its people, its taxpayers". On 4 November 2019, the US submitted a formal notification to the United Nations. A year later, the withdrawal from the Paris Agreement took effect. Neither was a process of renegotiating the Paris Agreement initiated, nor did the US adapt its Nationally Determined Contribution (NDCs). On the domestic level, the US Administration took steps that demonstrated its lack of climate ambition, including a number of executive orders taken during the first months of the Trump presidency aiming at dismantling key climate measures previously implemented by the Obama Administration (Bomberg 2017).

With the aim to understand the Trump Administration's views on climate change, we analyzed the 2017 Rose Garden speech and 20 additional speeches by President Trump and Vice-President Pence (8 in 2017, 12 in 2019; 4 by Pence, 16 by Trump; cut-off date: June 2020), listed on the White House's official website (category: energy and environment). Overall, four different arguments against the Paris Agreement were used: (1) Unfairness of the Agreement, arguing that it would put the US at a disadvantage vis-à-vis other countries ("The Paris Climate Accord is simply the latest example of Washington entering into an agreement that disadvantages the United States to the exclusive benefit of other countries", Trump, 1 June 2017); (2) Negative economic impact of the Agreement ("The agreement is a massive redistribution of United States wealth to other countries", Trump, 1 June 2017); (3) Extensive financial burdens put on the US through the Agreement, e.g. the Green Climate Fund ("I saved $1 trillion by not going with the Paris Accord", Trump, 14 May 2019); and (4) Weakened US sovereignty by the climate agreement ("And exiting the agreement protects the United States from future intrusions on the US' sovereignty and massive future legal liability", Trump, 1 June 2017).

Neither Trump nor Pence explicitly refer to 'climate change' or 'global warming'. They instead talk about US environmental leadership: "[T]he United States … [is] the world's leader in environmental protection" (Trump, 1 June 2017). Climate change is only indirectly used in reference to the Paris Agreement, which generally is described in a negative tone throughout all speeches: "the one-sided Paris Climate Accord" (Trump, 10 April 2019), "the disastrous, job-killing Paris Climate Accord" (Pence, 17 April 2019) or "the terrible, very expensive, one-sided Paris Climate Accord" (Trump, 14 May 2019). Overall, the emphasis in White House-recorded speeches is much more on energy than on environmental issues, with the US energy resources being closely linked with a narrative of economic growth.

In conclusion, the Trump Administration had a clear climate-skeptic position, contesting the Paris Agreement and its embedded norm of ambitious global climate action. Undoubtedly, this represents a strong deviation from Obama's previous climate-ambitious course. In the Trump era, climate policy is fundamentally marginalized and contested in abstract as well as concrete terms. Environmental protection, while mentioned more often than climate change, remains a side-lined topic in US rhetoric. In stark contrast, the main theme in the statements analyzed was the American energy sector development, which constituted a key component of President Trump's America First economic strategy. This builds on the trend of growing polarization of climate policy, which started long before Trump's presidency. While moderate Republicans like John McCain supported certain climate policies, the rise of the Tea Party movement shifted the politics towards stronger opposition, which can explain the failure of the climate law that was proposed in Congress during Obama's first term.

## THE EU'S RESPONSE: A TRUMP EFFECT?

US contestation of ambitious international climate action and the Paris Agreement ran counter to the European Union's domestic and international climate efforts (Oberthür and Groen 2017; van Schaik and Schunz 2012). The fact that climate change has become a strong EU-level policy domain suggests that the EU does not easily change course and rather responds to US contestation by reaffirming its own climate ambition. Yet, its strong economic interdependence and trade with the US could weaken EU climate ambition by strengthening climate-skeptic voices within the EU. The analysis suggests that Trump's actions triggered a rhetorical response from the European Council and the Council of the European Union. Mainly, the EU countered Trump's climate-skeptic arguments and reaffirmed its climate ambition, defending international climate norms.

Our analysis and comparison of the Council documents from the pre-Trump (2014–2016) and the Trump period (2017–2019) investigates whether the two institutions explicitly addressed the climate skepticism spread by the Trump Administration. In particular, we address whether the Councils' climate ambitions have changed and whether direct responses to Trump's contestation can be found in their rhetoric. We focus on the two intergovernmental institutions: the European Council and the Council of the European Union's Foreign Affairs Council (FAC) and Environment Council (ENV) formations. These institutions are a direct representation of the overall level of unity within the EU, and consequently give an indication of the Council and EU Member States' sentiments towards climate policy ambitions.

The qualitative analysis of Council statements followed several steps: First, a database of documents from all meetings of the European Council and the two Council of the European Union formations (FAC and ENV) between January 2014 and May 2019 was built (Consilium n.d.). The database encompasses all European Council (40) and Council meetings (172) with the respective documents accompanying each meeting (total: 212 meetings, 405 documents). Second, the Council outcome documents were coded according to whether the theme 'climate change' was mentioned (dichotomous coding). Third, all documents with references to climate policy were further inductively coded using Qualitative Content Analysis (Mayring 2014) with the qualitative data analysis software NVivo 12. The main emerging coding categories were: (1) ideas about the design of climate action and on the Paris Agreement, (2) EU ambition, and (3) themes of climate action (climate science, economic growth, climate finance, multilateral climate action). In order to test whether a 'Trump effect' could be found in the Councils' reasoning, the data was then split in a pre-Trump (2014–2016) and Trump (2017–2019) period, to enable a comparative perspective on EU positions before and after Trump's assumption of office in order to assess whether there was a change and if so, to characterize that change.

## A Trump Effect on the Salience of Climate Change

In a first step, we assessed whether there is a general difference in the salience of climate policy during (European) Council meetings. While this quantitative overview only offers preliminary insights on potential changes in the policy debates, it nevertheless provides an initial overview of general issue developments in the policy debate.

In the period of 2014–2019, overall, 40 European Council meetings took place. During 42.50 percent of them climate policy was debated. To determine a potential effect of the growing US climate contestation, we compared the salience of climate policy between the pre-Trump and Trump periods. In the pre-Trump period (2014–2016), 8 out of a total of 21 European Council meetings (38.10 percent) discussed climate change. During the Trump period (2017–2019), the share of meetings discussing climate issues slightly increased to 42.11 percent (8 out of 19 meetings). This points to a somewhat higher salience of climate-related discussions during European Council meetings and summits in the Trump era.

Turning to the FAC and ENV Council formations, during the 2014–2019 period, climate was discussed in 90 out of the total 172 meetings (82 FAC, 12 informal FAC, 21 ENV, 6 informal ENV, 51 other meetings, including mostly bilateral Cooperation and Association Councils with third countries, e.g., Moldova, Ukraine, Jordan). This represents somewhat more than half of all Council meetings (52.33 percent). This number is slightly higher in the Council, compared to the European Council meetings. However, the share of meetings that addressed climate policies varied considerably between Council formations, as did their total number of meetings: In 44 out of 82 total FAC meetings (53.65 percent) climate policy was discussed. In stark contrast, but unsurprisingly, during each of the 21 ENV meetings climate change was discussed. Similarly, the discrepancy between the salience of climate issues is high between informal meetings: Climate issues were mentioned in only one out of 12 informal meetings of foreign ministers, compared to 3 out of 6 informal meetings of environmental ministers (partly explained by limited data availability for the informal meetings).

The share of ENV meetings addressing climate change remained stable during the pre-Trump and Trump periods. The picture is different in the FAC, where the salience of climate issues increased: During the pre-Trump period, 20 out of 44 meetings dealt with climate issues (45.45 percent), whereas in the Trump period the share went up to 24 out of 38 meetings (63.16 percent).

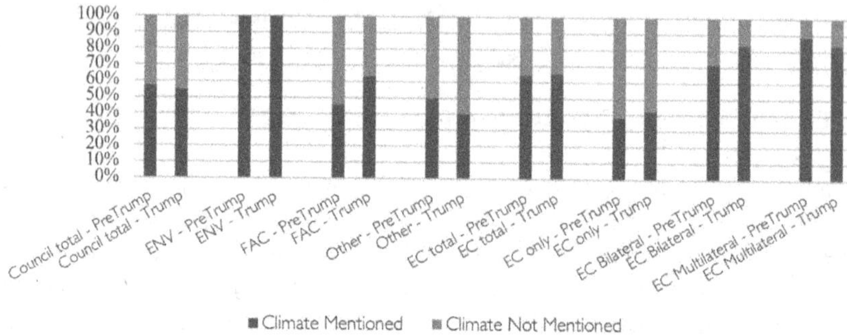


*Figure 12.1* *Salience of climate issues during Council of EU (Council) and European Council meetings (2014–2016 vs. 2017–2019)*

During informal and 'other' Council meetings, the salience of climate change decreased (from 50 to 40 percent). Taking all meetings (FAC, ENV, informal and others) together, the salience remained overall stable (2014–2016: 52.86 percent vs. 2017–2019: 51.96 percent).

Figure 12.1 summarizes the findings of salience of climate discussions in the European Council and Council of the European Union meetings between 2014 and 2019, divided in the pre-Trump and Trump periods. For both EU institutions, a tendency towards greater climate change salience could not be identified. For the European Council, the salience of climate issues was marginally higher during the Trump period (42.11 percent) compared to the pre-Trump period (38.10 percent). For the Council of the European Union, the environmental formation shows stable salience. However, we find a sharp increase in the foreign affairs formation (45.45 vs. 63.16 percent), pointing to the increased perception of climate action as an externally relevant policy topic.

## A Trump Effect on EU Climate Positions

To further explore the increase of climate salience in the (FAC) Council meetings and a possible link to US contestation we conducted a qualitative analysis of Council meetings. We focused on specific aspects of President Trump's criticism and how it is reflected in EU documents. The results reveal that in the context of growing US contestation of ambitious climate action, the EU responded by reaffirming its commitment to the Paris Agreement. The (European) Council explicitly reacted to Trump's climate-skeptic arguments in internal as well as external settings. Thereby, the EU clearly signaled its continued strong commitment to ambitious global climate action.

**Questioning the Paris Agreement?**

The Paris Agreement represents an ambitious global attempt to combat climate change, yet President Trump fundamentally questioned its validity. He not only withdrew his country from the Agreement, but also – at least in the beginning of his mandate – announced the renegotiation of the Agreement (which was never initiated). The European Council and Council of the European Union responded to this contestation with three main arguments, underlining continued support of the Agreement: the importance, active implementation, and the indisputability of the agreement.

First, ahead of the Paris COP21, both Councils repeatedly expressed explicit support for concluding a new global, legally-binding agreement at the Paris climate conference (total: 19 references), e.g.: "Our goal is a fair and ambitious global agreement" (ENV, 28 October 2014). After the successful conclusion of the Paris Agreement, statements by both Councils stress the overall importance of the Paris Agreement, e.g.: "The Paris Agreement is seen as a landmark instrument in climate action" (ENV, 4 March 2016), "the landmark Paris Agreement" (FAC, 25 June 2018) or "leaders were univocal in their *determination to tackle climate change with urgency and ambition* … to implement the goals set down by the Paris Agreement" (European Council, 21 March 2019, emphasis added). All in all, there were 65 coded statements in this category, among these 17 references in the pre-Trump and 48 references in the Trump era. This increase over time can partly be explained by the fact that the Paris Agreement only came into force in 2016. Yet, it can also be a response to the unprecedented contestation of the Agreement by President Trump since the negotiation of the Paris Agreement had been on-going for years before its eventual adoption in 2015.

Second, another prominent narrative is the need for the active and ambitious implementation of the Paris Agreement, e.g.: "Reiterate our commitment to build on our joint efforts that support ambitious climate action … towards the *full and effective implementation* of the UNFCCC and its Paris Agreement" (EU-ACP, 31 May 2018, emphasis added). Coded statements for this narrative were equally more prominent in the Trump period (29 out of 32 references), in line with the Agreement entering into force in 2016. The Paris Agreement is used as a point of reference for ambitious EU and multilateral action, for example, in Council positions on biodiversity or development aid (FAC, 12 May 2016). These references (total: 45, out of which 37 in the Trump period) offer examples of the EU's widespread efforts to stress the Agreement's importance and to mainstream climate objectives into a variety of policy areas.

The third narrative can be connected to Trump's contestation in the clearest way. It is the narrative of indisputability or non-renegotiability of the Paris Agreement. Although this narrative has comparatively fewer coded statements (total: 10), there are explicit references to the claims made by President Trump, including: "The Agreement demonstrates that *countries all over the world with very different interests* can come together to address *shared concerns* that will affect the entire world" (EU-Jordan, 10 July 2017 emphasis added), "STRESSES that the Paris Agreement is *irreversible*" (ENV, 13 October 2017, emphasis added), "l'accord de Paris, pierre angulaire d'une lutte efficace contre le changement climatique, est *irreversible*" (EU-Canada, 4 December 2017, emphasis added). The fact that these statements could be found in a diverse set of outcome documents – both in European and in bilateral meetings – underlines the active outreach of this EU message.

In conclusion, there was an increased emphasis on the Paris Agreement, as well as stronger language on its indisputability. This suggests that the EU reacted to the increased external contestation by defending and strengthening its commitment to the Paris Agreement. This holds particularly true in Council meetings with third parties, where references to the Paris Agreement were made in approximately one-third of meetings (13 out of 41) – all of which during the Trump era.

### Questioning the role of climate action for economic growth?

A second point of contestation raised by the US Administration was the compatibility of climate action with economic growth. President Trump repeatedly argued that the Paris Agreement substantially harms the US economy. This discussion is not new to climate politics. The EU opposed this view by making a 'business' case for climate action by arguing for the compatibility of markets with climate action. These arguments were already in use before Trump came into office, for example: "*actions to cut greenhouse gas emissions can also improve economic performance, spur investment, create jobs* and have *positive co-benefits* in areas such as health and energy security in *all types of economies*" (ENV, 28 October 2014, emphasis added).

While this argument was found in both periods, the number of such statements was particularly high in the Trump period (23 out of 34 references), e.g.: "The Agreement is a key element for the modernization of the European industry and economy" (European Council, 22 June 2017) or "the implementation of the Paris Agreement objective offers *significant opportunities and potential for economic growth,* new jobs and technological development and for *strengthening European competitiveness*" (European Council, 21 March 2019, emphasis added). Overall, 34 statements regarding the relationship between economic growth, innovation, and competitiveness demonstrate the EU's effort to counter the narrative that ambitious climate action is harmful to the economy. Instead, the EU argued that it would be beneficial to "seize economic opportunities offered by the green transition" (European Council, 9 May 2019). This position can be interpreted as a direct reaction to Trump's contestation, but other factors, such as parallel EU internal contestation and technological innovation, are likely to be additional triggers.

**Questioning climate finance?**

The Trump Administration raised concerns about the terms of financial obligations set out by the Paris Agreement and criticized global climate finance. In contrast, arguments emphasizing the need for financial support for developing partners played a crucial role within the EU's positioning on climate action (70 references). There is a substantial increase in references to climate finance in the Trump period (47 out of 70 references). This includes more explicit references to the EU's crucial role in providing climate finance, e.g. "The EU and its Member States are the *largest contributors* of climate financing" (FAC, 19 June 2017, emphasis added). Calls for others to fulfill their commitments and to follow the EU's lead in climate finance could also be seen, e.g.: "The Council recalls the *global commitment* to jointly mobilise USD 100 billion for climate finance per year by 2020 … The Council *urges other developed countries to meet their commitments*" (FAC, 22 May 2018, emphasis added) and "The EU and its Member States *remain committed* to continue scaling up the mobilization of international climate finance, as part of the *collective developed countries' goal* to jointly mobilise USD 100 billion per year by 2020" (FAC, 18 February 2019, emphasis added).

Climate finance has always been a key narrative in the EU's position; however, during Trump's presidency the emphasis on the topic has substantially increased. This suggests that EU Member States aimed to counter US contestation of global climate finance. Other factors, such as the implementation of the Paris Agreement (and its financial provisions), could also have contributed to the increased emphasis of climate finance.

**Questioning multilateralism?**

President Trump criticized the Paris Agreement for weakening US sovereignty, which – also when looking at other statements by the former US President – can be interpreted as a sign of his Administration's shift away from multilateral solutions and the 'liberal order' (Ikenberry 2018; Luce 2017). By contrast, references to the crucial role of multilateralism, the United Nations, and the rules-based order were a cornerstone of the EU position. Council Conclusions often contained statements such as: "The Council reiterates the European Union's steadfast support for the *United Nations as the core of a rules-based multilateral system*" (FAC, 19 June 2017, emphasis added). There was an increase of such statements in Council documents in the Trump period (35 out of total 54), which can be seen as an EU defense strategy against the US challenge. At the same time, such statements increased around the years 2016 and 2017, the moment at which the EU Global Strategy (European

Union 2016) was published, which also contributed to the renewed emphasis on the EU's role in multilateralism.

Strongly related to the support for multilateralism, there is also an increase in the EU's outreach to external actors in 2014–2019: Climate policy was increasingly addressed during bilateral (32 out of 40 references during Trump period), interregional (22 out of 37), and multilateral/international (36 out of 49) meetings and summits. The increased emphasis on climate change in regular interactions with third parties (e.g. association meetings) points to a strengthened mainstreaming of climate policies in EU external relations. Nevertheless, it could represent an attempt to build alliances to respond to the US retreat from international climate politics. The latter interpretation corresponds with the final paragraph of the Council Conclusions on the US withdrawal from the Paris Agreement, which state: "Together, we will implement the Paris Agreement because it is our common interest and responsibility. … *The EU stands ready to cooperate with all parties to this end*" (FAC, 19 June 2017, emphasis added). As such, the Councils (European Council, FAC, ENV) do not directly refer to questions of sovereignty, but thc strong support for multilateralism could be interpreted as an attempt to counter Trump's strong anti-multilateral, sovereignty-centered 'America First' agenda.

**Questioning environmental and climate leadership?**

President Trump claimed that the US was a leader on environmental matters. As expected, no clear references with regards to such a US leadership status can be found in Council documents. Instead, there is a considerable number of statements referring to EU leadership across all Council formations, expressing the willingness to lead on addressing climate change (total: 59 references). Examples include: "pave the way for Europe to take a leading role on climate challenges" (ENV, 28 October 2014), "the EU intends to continue its leadership in nurturing multilateral climate action" (FAC, 18 July 2016), or "exercise global leadership in the fight against climate change" (European Council, 9 May 2019).

A proactive EU leadership stance towards global climate politics is not a new narrative in all three Council formations. The number of documents in which climate leadership is evoked differs only slightly in the pre-Trump and Trump periods (18 vs. 19 outcome documents). However, there is a clear increase in explicit references to climate leadership in outcome documents over time up until 2017 (2014: 4 references; 2015: 9; 2016: 11; 2017: 14; 2018: 11; 2019: 10). The tipping point (2017) coincides with the US announcement to withdraw from the Paris Agreement. This tipping point can be explained by the fact that the Councils (European Council, FAC, ENV) passed Conclusions on or relating to Trump's withdrawal announcement in June 2017. All Conclusions strongly emphasize EU leadership: "The world can *continue to count of the EU for leadership* in the global fight against climate change" (FAC, 19 June 2017, emphasis added), "sent a strong message to the international community about the *EU's global leadership* in taking action against climate change" (ENV, 19 June 2017, emphasis added), and "The European Council strongly reaffirms the commitment … to *continue to lead* in the fight against climate change" (European Council, 22 June 2017, emphasis added).

## CONCLUSIONS

Since the successful adoption in December 2015 and entry into force of the Paris Agreement in November 2016, the global political landscape on climate underwent substantial changes. The open and radical contestation of international climate policy by former US President Trump raised the question of how the EU, as a key actor and promoter of ambitious international climate governance, reacted to the contestation of the norm of ambitious global climate action. This chapter provided a systematic analysis of changes in the EU's position on external climate policy between 2014 and 2019. As such, the findings suggest that the European Council and the Council of the European Union shifted in its rhetoric in a way that suggests a response to Trump's climate contestation. The EU countered the Trump Administration's criticism of ambitious international climate action to ensure the norm's robustness (Petri and Biedenkopf, 2020).

The EU reacted by reaffirming and defending the Paris Agreement and by explicitly addressing Trump's climate-skeptic arguments (economic growth, sovereignty, multilateralism, climate finance). The EU not only directly opposed Trump's criticism, thereby distancing itself from the US position on climate action, but also clearly signaled the EU's strong commitment to ambitious global climate action to counteract potential contagious effects of the US climate contestation on other international actors. As such, the empirical results suggest a differentiated picture of how EU narratives on climate leadership and climate policies evolved over time.

Considering the intensity of US climate-skeptic rhetoric on the Paris Agreement, one can wonder why the EU's response was not harsher. The US plays a significant and far-reaching role in climate policies, not the least since it is the second-largest GHG emitter. Yet, the transatlantic partnership – despite hard hits from the other side of the Atlantic – might have seemed too important for the European partners to abandon in its entirety. Notably, the EU has little leverage over the US in economic or other terms, therefore a coercive response pressuring the US government into policy change was not a feasible option.

This chapter shows that several (European) Council statements can be seen as a response to Trump's climate contestation. For example, the EU statements following the 2017 US announcement to withdraw from the Paris Agreement can be understood as directly aimed at the events in the White House. It is, however, essential to keep in mind that other factors also play a role in influencing the EU position. A combination of US contestation, the need to keep other countries committed to the Paris Agreement, increased public pressure from within Member States through, for example, the Fridays for Future movement, and an increased sense of urgency to act on climate change among EU Member States can more comprehensively explain the positions of the European Council and the Council of the European Union. Future research would benefit from broadening the scope of this study and incorporating internal and external variables that could potentially influence the policy process.

This study did not analyze the actual change of EU behavior, but only changes in rhetoric. Leadership ambition and strong commitment to external climate policies do not necessarily need to be reflected in EU policy implementation. As such, further research could delve into the implementation of the changes found in the Councils' climate positions. Furthermore, similar in-depth analysis of other EU institutions (such as the European Commission and the European Parliament) and EU Member State governments' positions over time could be a fruitful addition to the analysis provided here. The latter could be particularly crucial to understand the dynamics of Council meetings since all outcome documents analyzed represent a compromise reached among very diverse European states.

In January 2021, a new US president was sworn into office, changing the previously climate-skeptic and critical tone in the White House and promising a re-emergence of the US as an ally to EU climate ambitions. At the same time, the contagious effect of Trump's hard contestation of climate norms might outlast his presidency, since other international actors, such as Brazil under President Jair Bolsonaro, still use climate-skeptic narratives. In conclusion, contestation in global climate politics is likely to continue, creating a demand for a stronger EU stance on climate policy, as well as increased pressure on the EU's internal cohesion. Another recent pressure on this stance is the global COVID-19 pandemic, which put new heavy social and economic burdens on the EU. The EU's Recovery and Resilience Facility that aims to counter the pressure from this crisis is specifically intended to take a 'green' approach towards recovery, for example through investments in sustainable industries. Yet, it remains to be seen to what extent implementing the EU's high climate ambitions and the post-pandemic economic recovery will go hand in hand.

## REFERENCES

Aggestam, L. and Hyde-Price, A. (2019) Double Trouble: Trump, Transatlantic Relations and European Strategic Autonomy. *JCMS: Journal of Common Market Studies*, **57**(S1), 114–127.

Atkinson, H. (2018) *The Politics of Climate Change under President Obama*. London: Routledge.

Bailey, C. J. (2019) Assessing President Obama's climate change record. *Environmental Politics*, **28**(5), 847–865.

Biedenkopf, K. and Walker, H. (2016) *Playing to One's Strengths: The Implicit Division of Labor in US and EU Climate Diplomacy*. http://www.aicgs.org/site/wp-content/uploads/2016/12/PR-64-DAAD-Climate-Diplomacy.pdf.

Bomberg, E. (2017) Environmental Politics in the Trump Era: An Early Assessment. *Environmental Politics*, **26**(5), 956–963.

Bomberg, E. and Super, B. (2009) The 2008 US Presidential Election: Obama and the Environment. *Environmental Politics*, **18**(3), 424–430.

Consilium (n.d.). European Council / Council of the European Union Meetings Calendar. https://www.consilium.europa.eu/en/meetings/calendar/.

Cross, M. D. (2018) Partners at Paris? Climate Negotiations and Transatlantic Relations. *Journal of European Integration*, **40**(5), 571–586.

De Pryck, K. and Gemenne, F. (2017) The Denier-in-Chief: Climate Change, Science and the Election of Donald J. Trump. *Law and Critique*, **28**(2), 119–126.

Deitelhoff, N. and Zimmermann, L. (2018) Things We Lost in the Fire: How Different Types of Contestation Affect the Robustness of International Norms. *International Studies Review*, **22**(1), 51–76.

Deitelhoff, N. and Zimmermann, L. (2019) Norms under Challenge: Unpacking the Dynamics of Norm Robustness. *Journal of Global Security Studies*, **4**(1), 2–17.

Delreux, T. (2018) Multilateral Environmental Agreements: A Key Instrument of Global Environmental Governance. In Adelle, C., Biedenkopf, K. and Torney, D. (eds), *European Union External Environmental Policy: Rules, Regulation and Governance Beyond Borders*. Cham: Palgrave Macmillan, 19–38.

European Union (2016) A Global Strategy for the European Union's Foreign and Security Policy. Press release. https://eeas.europa.eu/topics/eu-global-strategy/17304/global-strategy-european-unions-foreign-and-security-policy_en.

Global Carbon Atlas (n.d.) Global Carbon Atlas – CO2 emissions 2019. http://www.globalcarbonatlas.org/en/CO2-emissions.

Hill, M. and Hurst, S. (2020) The Trump Presidency: Continuity and Change in US Foreign Policy. *Global Affairs*, **6**(1), 1–3.

Ikenberry, G. J. (2018) The End of Liberal International Order? *International Affairs*, **94**(1), 7–23.

Luce, E. (2017) *The Retreat of Western Liberalism*. London: Grove Atlantic.

Mayring, P. (2014) Qualitative Content Analysis: Theoretical Foundation, Basic Procedures and Software Solution. *Social Science Open Access Repository*. http://nbn-resolving.de/urn:nbn:de:0168-ssoar-395173.

Oberthür, S. and Groen, L. (2017) The European Union and the Paris Agreement: Leader, Mediator, or Bystander? *Wiley Interdisciplinary Reviews: Climate Change*, **8**(1), e445.

Oberthür, S. and Groen, L. (2018) Explaining Goal Achievement in International Negotiations: The EU and the Paris Agreement on Climate Change. *Journal of European Public Policy*, **25**(5), 708–727.

Parker, C. F. and Karlsson, C. (2018) The UN Climate Change Negotiations and the Role of the United States: Assessing American Leadership from Copenhagen to Paris. *Environmental Politics*, **27**(3), 519–540.

Parker, C. F., Karlsson, C. and Hjerpe, M. (2017) Assessing the European Union's Global Climate Change Leadership: From Copenhagen to the Paris Agreement. *Journal of European Integration*, **39**(2), 239–252.

Petri, F. and Biedenkopf, K. (2020) 'United We Stand, Divided We Fall'. The Effects of US Contestation on EU Foreign Climate Policy Ambition. *Global Affairs*, **6**(4–5), 381–397.

Pickering, J., McGee, J. S., Stephens, T. and Karlsson-Vinkhuyzen, S. I. (2017) The Impact of the US Retreat from the Paris Agreement: Kyoto Revisited? *Climate Policy*, **18**(7), 818–827.

Riddervold, M. and Newsome, A. (2018) Transatlantic Relations in Times of Uncertainty: Crises and EU-US Relations. *Journal of European Integration*, **40**(5), 505–521.

Saad, A. (2018) Pathways of Harm: The Consequences of Trump's Withdrawal from the Paris Climate Agreement. *Environmental Justice*, **11**(1), 47–51.

Schmidt, A. and Sikkink, K. (2019) Breaking the Ban? The Heterogeneous Impact of US Contestation of the Torture Norm. *Journal of Global Security Studies*, **4**(1), 105–122.

Schreurs, M. (2017) The European Union and the Paris Climate Agreement: Moving Forward without the United States. *Chinese Journal of Population Resources and Environment*, **15**(3), 192–195.

Urpelainen, J. and Van de Graaf, T. (2018) United States Non-Cooperation and the Paris Agreement. *Climate Policy*, **18**(7), 839–851.

van Schaik, L. and Schunz, S. (2012) Explaining EU Activism and Impact in Global Climate Politics: Is the Union a Norm- or Interest-Driven Actor? *Journal of Common Market Studies*, **50**(1), 169–186.

Walker, H. and Biedenkopf, K. (2018) The Historical Evolution of EU Climate Leadership and Four Scenarios for its Future. In Minas, S. and Ntousas, V. (eds), *EU Climate Diplomacy: Politics, Law and Negotiations*. Abingdon: Routledge, 33–46.

White House (2016) President Obama: The United States Formally Enters the Paris Agreement. https://obamawhitehouse.archives.gov/blog/2016/09/03/president-obama-united-states-formally-enters-paris-agreement.

White House (2017) Statement by President Trump on the Paris Climate Accord. https://www.whitehouse.gov/briefings-statements/statement-president-trump-paris-climate-accord/.

# 13. Normative power Europe in the Belt and Road Initiative: challenge for constructing the self or an opportunity for changing others?

**Xueji SU**

## INTRODUCTION

Since its launch in 2013, the Belt and Road Initiative (BRI) has been the plank of China's new foreign policy (Chaisse and Matsushita 2018). The BRI investment projects are estimated to add over $1 trillion of outward funding for foreign infrastructure by 2027; at maturity, the BRI will be backed by investments expected to hit around $4 trillion (PwC's Growth Markets Centre 2016; OECD 2018). Because the portfolio of the initiative is massive, regional and international cooperation is entrusted with a vital role since the outset. The BRI strategic landscape now includes, in one form or another, almost all the Member States of the EU as well as several countries in the EU's immediate neighborhood.

On the European side, there is an implicit consensus that the BRI "offers an opportunity that Europe cannot afford to lose" (Liu 2015). However, debates among policy-makers and experts persist over the means by which and the extent to which the EU should be involved (Pantucci 2014). Fundamentally, the concerns stem from the fact that the EU and China differ in their key preferences for and approaches to a desirable world order (Pan 2012; Chen 2016). As a China-led global governance model, the BRI is no doubt a novel external variable for the EU's normative ambition, especially in its immediate and wider neighborhood (Jones 2019). Much ink has already been spilled on this caveat. But the mechanism through which the BRI impacts the EU's normative presence merits closer inspection.

To this end, this chapter draws on the conceptual framework of the constructivist notion of 'Normative Power Europe' (NPE). This chapter begins with a reappraisal of the conceptual framework of NPE. In section two the behavior of the EU and recognition of NPE in the realm of BRI-related regions in the 'pre-BRI' period (before 2013) are examined. Section three proceeds with a discussion regarding the normative foundation and the distinctive governance model of the BRI. Finally, the chapter concludes that the BRI, led by China and constructed upon normative grounds of non-intervention and unconditionality, should not contradict NPE directly. However, it might exacerbate cacophony among the EU Member States and impinge on the already problematic actorness of the EU in regional affairs; if dealt with poorly, it might undermine the EU's normative presence and power in the regions, which consequently would hinder its regional harmonization agenda. This chapter does not deal with the question of whether or not the EU and China are normative powers as such. Rather, it seconds the opinion of Kavalski (2008) that normative power is to be viewed in a perpetual dynamism. Therefore, this work is concerned with how the BRI affects identity construction of the EU as a normative power.

## CONCEPTUAL CLARIFICATION OF 'NORMATIVE POWER EUROPE'

Ian Manners (2002), on the basis of his works on EU foreign policy, advanced that the EU has 'evolved' into a form of governance which transcends Westphalian norms. This feature distinguishes the EU as a normative power from other state actors (Manners 2002). In its simplest terms, what makes the EU a normative power is that it possesses the "ability to shape conceptions of what 'normal' is in international relations" (Manners 2002, p. 236). Apart from pointing out this "greatest power of all", Manners' (2002, p. 253) greater ambition was to bridge and merge several vital elements of EU external policy – identity construction, self-perception, actions, impacts and responses of international society – into an overarching concept. Upon this consideration, the term NPE emerged. In return, the theoretical pursuit underpinning this notion renders it particularly useful in deciphering the EU's external policies and actions; NPE has hence quickly risen to prominence (Forsberg 2009).

Its apparent popularity notwithstanding, the conception of NPE is riddled with controversies. Criticisms mainly concentrate on two aspects – its less coherent theoretical foundation and dissociation from the praxis. The term as such is also often misconstrued and misused. In voluminous literature that employs NPE, the term could refer to various notions: international identity, interests, behavior, adopted means of influence, and normative achievements, solely or jointly (Forsberg 2009). Therefore, prior to substantive analysis, it is of great importance to appreciate the make-up of NPE.

NPE was initially informed by social constructivism, which harbors the view that the study of interests should be done with due regard to the interactions in a society. It argues that "identity formation is relational and prior to interest formation; interests are defined both in material and non-material terms" (Brunnée and Toope 2000, p. 20; Ruggie 2002). Closely following this constructivist root, NPE is, in the words of Manners (2002), an attempt to refocus the analysis away from the empirical emphasis on the EU's institutions or policies and towards including cognitive processes, with both substantive and symbolic components (Manners 2002). Manners (2009) demonstrated that "conceptualising normative power as ideational non-material justification involves a three-part understanding of its use and analysis linking principles, actions, and impact" (Manners 2009, 3). Proceeding from this point, Kavalski (2008) stressed the importance of inter-subjective recognition from the international society for the construction of the normative power concept. According to him, the right question is not whether a country 'is' a normative power, but whether it 'represents' itself as a normative power. Countries that represent themselves as normative powers will always strive to earn recognition for being that (Kavalski 2008). Hence, despite the significance of material aspects in the study of normative power, such analysis should focus mainly on the cognitive effects (identity and normative impacts).

At this point, we might need to bring back the "neo-normative turn in theorizing the EU's international presence", which advocates the interrelations between cognitive processes and the material grounds (Whitmann 2013). Idealistically, NPE excludes material elements such as socio-economy, labor, and environment. But, in practice, some of these grounds may also be taken into account in examining NPE (Gerrits 2009). What is under question is the extent to which normative power is premised upon economic resources and political clout (Whitmann 2013). To be precise, from an idealist perspective, in order to be recognized as a normative power, an actor needs primarily to ensure "clarity of principle, simplicity of action space, consistency of promotion, 'joined-up' thinking in the broader promotion of principles through the multilateral system, partnership and timescale" (Manners 2009, pp. 5–6). These are inward-looking parameters. But if the construction of NPE also relies on material power, resources, and instruments, then an outward-looking contemplation is unavoidable. On this view, any external variables which might reduce the attractiveness of the instruments for socialization would also constitute a bane for NPE.

Although theoretical debate is not within the contours of the chapter, this question is particularly relevant to our inquiry. If NPE is to be understood from this 'neo-normative' lens, the economic rise of China and the BRI are more likely to be regarded as a threat to the EU's normative presence. After all, it represents an alternative, if not competing, exemplar for other countries to duplicate. Besides, the BRI, through its investment repertoire, may reduce the reliance of third countries (and, sometimes, EU Member States) on trade and investment deals and financial supports from the EU. Through this mechanism, the EU's approximation and socialization processes might be placed at risk (Kavalski 2019). Taking a look at the works of Manners, finds that the material factors, despite being secondary, are not explicitly excluded. This chapter follows suit: it will take into account the material factors but remain mindful of overemphasizing their importance in analysis.

## Before the BRI: Normative Power Europe in the Regions

For the purpose of comparison, it is necessary to take a cursory look at the normative presence of the EU in the BRI-related regions prior to the BRI.

As mentioned, the EU is a neo-Westphalian normative actor. It firmly adheres to democratic state apparatus, justified mutual interference in domestic affairs, and significant transfer of sovereignty. For one thing, the EU promotes all the legal, economic, social, political, and cultural norms and standards entrenched in the course of European integration. They are ruled by the following principles: respect for human dignity, liberty, democracy, equality, the rule of law, and respect for human rights.[1] Yet in the realm of European studies a clarification is wanting in respect of what norms 'the normative' concept entails in general (Forsberg 2009). Manners (2002) also does not differentiate between the 'normal' and the 'normative (moral)'. In fact, although norms need not always be viewed as normative, the EU's 'norm package' is by and large value-added.

The EU is a leading power that takes great interest in interpreting what 'normal' is in the international community. This power, in return, helps the EU justify its conduct and diffuse its norms. The process subsumes two parts: actions reinforcing normative power (norm diffusion) and actions mobilizing normative power. In the process of norm diffusion, the EU not only promotes norms, but also should do so in a normative manner (Forsberg 2009). This occurs primarily through the following channels: spontaneous diffusion; the use of communication strategies; procedural activities; transference of mutual benefits; the presence of the EU in third states; cultural diffusion; and the process of internalization by third states (Manners 2009).

Besides these immaterial instruments, the EU's norm promotion toolkit also comprises material instruments such as financial aid and trade/investment agreements (Whitmann 2013; Tocci 2008). In line with the objectives and the principles enshrined in the Treaty of Lisbon,[2] imposition and invocation of social and political requirements on the recipient countries are commonplace in the EU's financial assistance agreements and trade deals. Evidence of this

---

1 TEU, Article 21.
2 Ibid.

is provided by a great number of partnership and cooperation agreements (PCAs) signed by the EU with Russia, the New Independent States of Eastern Europe, the Southern Caucasus, and Central Asia. All of these PCAs feature similar axioms speaking of democracy, human rights, and international law. In the same vein, a standardized human rights clause can also be found in its aid agreements with Africa, the Caribbean, and the Pacific countries. This clause entitles the EU to withdraw or suspend its aid when human rights violations in the recipient countries are detected (Cotonou Agreement 2010), (Peng and Tok 2016).

The EU promotes norms; in return, the socialization process is expected to shape a stable external environment for the EU. More importantly, the EU is empowered by being the 'authority' in defining and interpreting what 'normal' is (Schunz et al. 2012). At least this is how the mechanism is meant to work. But, in reality, the effect of the EU's norm diffusion exercise is contestable, especially when it comes to regions beyond its immediate neighborhood, such as Central Asia. Notwithstanding the paramount principle of 'universality', the EU has established differing external policies with diverse goals "tailored to the needs and context of each society". Accordingly, its actions and impacts vary substantially from region to region. In its neighboring countries, the EU has at its disposal effective policy tools such as the European Neighborhood Policy and the Copenhagen criteria, aided by its strong political and cultural influence there. Naturally, in these countries, the EU has its normative power most grounded. But beyond that, the Brussels bloc has no clear agenda in formulating its normative presence in other regions (International Crisis Group 2006; Kavalski 2007, 2014). Resemblance is evident between the EU's foreign policy towards Central Asia and towards the Balkans with little regard for the peculiarities of the former (Kavalski 2012). Compared to other preeminent 'super-executioners' such as China and the US, the EU has long been rebuked for being slow in forming its own Asian strategy (Manners 2002). It is therefore submitted that in Central Asian countries the EU does not possess normative power. As Kavalski (2014) pointed out, "[t]he overwhelming attention to the Europeanization of candidate states appears to have undercut the operational effectiveness of EU's normative power in 'out-of-Europe' areas" (Kavalski 2014, p. 310). The case of Central Asia does not stand alone (Hyde-Price 2006; Bicchi 2006). A study of Chinese official media coverage of the EU indicated that other Asian countries also perceive the EU as distant and ineffective, resulting in a clear "expectation deficit" (Tsuruoka 2008, p. 107; Zhang 2016).

Apart from the lack of clear strategies, another issue, as pointed out by Nicolaïdis and Howse (2002), is that the true identity of the EU and the image that it wishes to project in international relations are not always consistent. As a result, its image and credibility among political elites and across societies are undermined (Nicolaïdis and Howse 2002).

To recapitulate, even before the BRI came into being, normative actions and the impacts of the EU across the regions were already precarious. Despite the EU's willingness to diffuse norms in its external interactions, the dearth of clear "awareness of a particular kind of self" (Kavalski 2007, p. 842; Diez 2005, p. 614) and tailor-made instruments for socialization has rendered the results rather disappointing (Kavalski 2013).The following section will set forth the new challenges and opportunities the BRI has brought about, starting first with the normative foundation and the characteristics of the BRI.

## Normative Foundation and Characteristics of the BRI

### Normative foundation of the BRI

The BRI serves more than one policy objective for China. On the one hand, it is expected to engender new economic stimulus and market opportunities and to alleviate, if not absorb, domestic overcapacity. On the other hand, it aims to shape an international environment that could enable China to "assume commeasurable responsibilities and have the corresponding influence and voice in determining international affairs and rules" (Liu 2015, p. 588). The initiative is underpinned by six crucial principles: peace, cooperation, openness, inclusiveness, knowledge exchange, and other mutual benefits. These principles characterize a Chinese approach to jointly constructing the initiative with other actors (Shahriar et al. 2018). Up until July 2019, China has signed 194 cooperative agreements with 136 countries, 30 international organizations and institutions under the umbrella of the BRI.[3] The overwhelming majority of these international documents can be categorized as so-called 'soft law' instruments (extra-legal agreements).

The BRI lacks, in the view of many, normative aspects and an overarching legal design (Wang 2019). It is devoid of a treaty-based structure or any systematic BRI-wide multilateral arrangements; it falls outside the conventional typology of international organizations. And China appears to be uninterested in diffusing alternative international norms through the BRI, as with its other external policy strategies. However, as the plank of China's new geopolitical strategy and its contribution to global governance, does the BRI really lack normative grounds?

As Pan (2012) explains, the paramount aim of foreign policies of China and its people, stemming from an enduring history of colonialism, is to acquire an equal sovereign state status. China identifies and presents itself as a responsible international actor and, more importantly, an alternative to the 'Western

---

[3] List of countries signed cooperation documents with China, Belt and Road Portal. https://www.yidaiyilu.gov.cn/xwzx/roll/77298.htm.

solutions'. It is not the neo-liberal values per se that China has been opposing but rather the hegemonic 'universality' approach embedded in neo-liberalism (Jones 2019). China constantly laments that the rights to interpret international norms are captured and wielded by the Western powers for their self-interests and preferences. Kavalski (2013) posited that China's norms appear to be an antithesis to the Western neo-liberalist values. He then went on to submit that attention should be paid to what it is not rather than what it is (Kavalski 2013). His observation sheds light on the search for the guiding principles of China's foreign policies. It is those principles which characterize the political philosophy of China that should be singled out. In this context, the norms 'non-intervention' and 'sovereignty' come to the fore.

Chief of these norms are the "Five Principles of Peaceful Coexistence", which have served as the normative basis of China's external affairs for decades. They are also manifest in the portfolio of the BRI. In addition, within China's foreign aid policy framework and other thematic programs, a practical norm of 'unconditionality' emerged (Jepperson et al. 1996; Florini 1996). The "Eight Principles of Foreign Aid" were put forward in the 1960s when China started to provide foreign aid to African countries (Björkdahl 2002). The first principle proclaims that China "never considers its assistance as a type of unilateral charity but rather as mutual aid", while the second stresses that it "never asks for any privilege and never poses conditions in its foreign aid program" (Peng and Tok 2016, p. 740).[4] The later promotion and diffusion of these norms indicate continuity (Wang 2008). One prominent example is the establishment and operation of the Asian Infrastructure Investment Bank (AIIB). The rules of the AIIB inherited the traditional principles of external assistance, including 'no strings attached', 'mutual benefit', and 'non-intervention'. That was confirmed in a series of official foreign aid policy reviews, in which the Chinese government stated that the AIIB refrains from tying aid (Reuters 2015; Peng and Tok 2016). A similar approach can also be found in the New Development Bank established by the BRICS countries (Svetlicinii 2020).

In this regard, one should not conflate normative principles with developmental models (Vangeli 2018). Indeed, the remarkable economic success achieved domestically equips China with assurance and political clout to promulgate its development model in international affairs; over the past years, China has shifted from "a passive recipient of the world order" (Odgaard 2013) to an assertive rule-maker. This fact led some commentators to argue that China is selling its state-interventionist governance pattern as an example for other countries to emulate. However, it is first contestable whether an economic developmental model could be regarded as a norm, considering

4 Zhou Enlai, Speech in Accra, Ghana, 15 January 1964.

that it lacks normative (moral) imperative and prescriptive orders (Florini 1996; Axelrod 1986; Raymond 1997). That might be the case of the EU. As mentioned above, since European integration as such is value-laden, when it promotes its experience of governance, it exports simultaneously values. However, hardly could this hold true when it comes to China. The promotion of norms and of practical standards is separated – this is what among others distinguishes China's approach to norm diffusion from the EU's.

Another difference lies in the ultimate aim of norm diffusion. The principles of 'non-interference' and 'unconditionality' determine that China embraces the relational-based norm promotion paradigm without the purpose of socialization (Kavalski 2019). The BRI amplifies the merits of China's developmental and reformist experience, but only promulgates it – without coercion – as an example for others to learn, yet voluntarily (Vangeli 2018). As Vangeli (2018, p. 70) notes:

> China does not challenge the domestic circumstances of the participant countries but adjusts to them – by jointly communicating with the national governments ... Similar adaptation of the participant countries, towards the Chinese framework and practice, is expected in return.

In this process, "China sees itself as an instigator, animator and contributor – but not the developer of other nations" (Vangeli 2018, p. 67).

## The governance model of the BRI

Among academics, the BRI is widely labeled as a buzzword. This perhaps results from the idiosyncratic presence of the initiative. The BRI is participatory, decentralized, and developed inductively; it is in a flux – informed by various practices on the ground, flexible to changing circumstances, and open for comments and proposals (Vangeli 2018).

One of the core objectives of the BRI in the rudimentary phase is to create regional connectivity. To this end, Beijing has committed that the construction of BRI will adhere to extensive consultation, joint contribution, and shared benefits.[5] Besides, it is said that the initiative also remains flexible and open to collaborating with existing regional and multilateral platforms (Svetlicinii 2018). Both the objective and approaches, however, are often called into question as liaisons and arrangements under the BRI remain mostly bilateral, taking place only between China and each participant country.

Given the difficulty of proposing multilateral arrangements, this 'partnership-based relational approach' might be China's deliberate policy choice. Theoretically, the more rigid and more focused a cooperation mech-

---

5 The Belt and Road Initiative Progress, 2019.

anism is, the fewer members it could accommodate. As Guzman and Meyer (2010, p. 202) advanced: "in the multilateral context, states that prefer a deeper level of cooperation can be hindered by states that prefer only shallow cooperation". If this postulate holds true, the BRI-related cooperation documents are endowed with two major objectives – branding BRI and pinpointing the focal point for cooperation. The first objective is more self-evident. A variety of 'soft law' instruments signed under the name of BRI are expected to lend legitimacy to the BRI at the international level (Wang 2019).

But normative instruments can also be used to resolve coordination matters (Guzman 2008). For instance, potential collaborations between China and countries like France, Germany, India, and Japan involve complicated variables. In this situation, individual parties may strongly prefer one focal point for cooperation over another. Here, the question is how to spot a focal point that the parties concerned would be most likely to conform with later. This question points to the second important structural design of the normative documents of the BRI – numerous thematic communication platforms. They are established to improve the lines of communication among regulators and to lay out guidelines for interactions. Indeed, the results of the communications are not always binding. But, in this regard, Baird et al. (1994) noted that even 'cheap talk' in liaison could align reconciliation and thereby facilitate coordination. One such example is the establishment of a national standards information platform among the BRI partner countries, initiated by the Standardization Administration of China in order to strengthen the exchange and sharing of standards information.[6] Once points of convergence are found, there are few reasons to defect from the requirements of the agreements. Therefore, it may not make much sense to have binding agreements that demand resources and time that would otherwise have been needed for obtaining domestic approvals. Therefore, at this stage, legalization of the BRI could be considered unnecessary, if not altogether superfluous. This resonates with an observation of Kavalski (2019, p. 407) that "rules, norms, and values are merely contingent figurations – not the embodiment – of China's promotion of regional communities of practice".

The mechanism also explains why so many countries, even those that are skeptical about the BRI, voluntarily participate in its construction in one form or another – for instance, tripartite cooperation, the AIIB, and financing BRI-related projects through other channels.

---

6 The Second Belt and Road Forum for International Cooperation. http://www.beltandroadforum.org/.

## Normative Presence of the EU vis-à-vis the BRI

Arguably, this cooperative pattern poses new challenges to the actorness of the EU and its internal effectiveness and legitimacy in general. As Moravcsik (2017) aptly summarized, the EU regularly applies three paradigms of coordination: common policies, policy coordination, and tacit policy convergence. First, in policy areas where common policies are formed, the actions of Member States are subject to EU laws and policies. Significant contentions can be dealt with through constructive abstention. In principle, this mechanism allows EU decisions to be implemented, while the Member States can signal their concerns. Second, on issues where the EU does not have exclusive competence, a framework for 'coalitions of the willing' established by the *acquis communautaire* applies, which encourages policy coordination among the Member States. This allows for a rapid and consistent response even without the imprimatur and involvement of the EU. Lastly, Moravcsik sets forth that throughout the discourse of integration, in most policy areas Member States share relatively convergent domestic laws, policies, and norms, which would work to preclude national governments from straying too far away from existing norms (Moravcsik 2017).

Conceivably, the way in which the BRI functions could severely undermine the effectiveness of the first and the second coordination methods. For one thing, BRI-related programs are wide-ranging, flexible, and dispersed. It spans various policy areas where the distribution of competences within the EU differs; it requires swift reaction that the EU is unable to produce. Second, the BRI is not an international organization to which countries could accede. In practice, EU Member States have reached various sectoral arrangements with China which may not fall under the heading of BRI, but nonetheless contribute to its construction. These actions could not be interpreted as an 'accession' to the BRI from a legal perspective, but might be read as acceptance or recognition of the BRI and the Chinese approach. Third, the cooperative agreements widely signed between China and European countries as 'soft law' instruments could evade domestic scrutiny or be subject to less stringent rules in the ratification phase.

As a result, the Member States are involved in the BRI in diverse forms. This landscape has deepened the disparities in preferences and methods in dealing with the BRI. The lack of uniformity between the Member States inevitably entraps the EU, undercutting its efforts in forming a single voice and a fully-fledged strategy in respond to China's new proposal (Ekman 2016).

Faced with the BRI, the EU's indeterminacy in its policy-making is apparent. On the one hand, the EU has been relentlessly criticizing the unconditionality and non-intervention principles that China practices in its foreign aid and investment programs and especially in those targeting African countries

(Bräutigam 2011). The omission of social, environmental, and governance standards was described by the president of the European Investment Bank as the 'unscrupulous' behavior of China (Condon 2012). But, on the other hand, individual Member States have demonstrated strong pragmatic interests in engaging in or even joining the BRI (Lanteigne 2016). For instance, Germany and France were pledged to provide financial supports to AIIB aid projects. The United Kingdom was interested to house the European center of the AIIB in its territory (The Diplomat 2015; Gabusi 2019). In the end, the startling contrast between the aloof political discourse and proactive engagement of European countries could undermine the EU's normative image.

From here, we might take a step further to ask how this would impact the EU's normative power. In itself, the conception of NPE does not offer any quantitative gauge to evaluate the capability of normative power and the changes thereof. However, the make-up of NPE may help navigate an analysis. The following analysis examines the implications of BRI by breaking down its impacts on each component of NPE. Normative norms are the first elements that will be discussed. Following that are normative actions and normative impacts. Going beyond the idealistic perspective, certain prominent practical issues will also be taken into account.

To begin with, the legitimacy of normative power derives from well-acknowledged international norms, drawing upon the principles of the United Nations Charter, the Helsinki Final Act, the Paris Charter, the Universal Declaration of Human Rights and the United Nations Covenants, and the Council of Europe/European Convention on Human Rights.[7] As mentioned, the BRI lacks an institutional structure and is not devised to generate and socialize contending international norms and values. In this respect, it does not dismantle the legitimate basis of European norms and values.

But China does set the principles of 'non-intervention' and 'sovereignty' as guiding norms for the BRI. These principles do not shape so much the goals, as the means. The rule of thumb is that other BRI countries should not be coerced into following China's own developmental approach or transforming their domestic governance apparatus. Therefore, regardless of the degree of involvement, the participating countries are not precluded by the BRI from following the values and models promoted by the EU. An opinion poll conducted by the BBC World Service indicated that from 2014 to 2017, positive views of the EU's influence in the world rose from 45 percent in 2014 to 48 percent in 2017 – after the BRI was proposed (Globescan 2017). A recent survey by the Pew Research Center shows a similar result. The report demonstrates that while concerns over the EU's financial issues persist, European citizens none-

---

[7] TEU, Article 21.

theless credit the EU for promoting peace, democratic values, and prosperity, albeit inefficiently (Pew Research Center 2019). This resonates well with the aforementioned issue of consistency in the EU's strategy towards the BRI.

Conversely, the construction of BRI, which is constrained by the principles, may even become a novel opportunity for the EU to promote its norms. First of all, China views involving developed countries into the BRI as a means to advance "production capacity cooperation", a strategy of pooling resources so as to maximize the outcomes and potentially to create a path to a "triple win" (Vangeli 2018, p. 67). For one thing, China has its hands tied in influencing the reformist process of the BRI countries. But now as an emerging capital-exporting country, China needs the host countries to provide stable domestic environments and a level playing field (Vangeli 2018). Thus far, it is less satisfied with the investment environments in many BRI countries. Additionally, the norm of 'unconditionality' limits the degree to which the recipient countries' economic and political regimes can be assessed when providing financial aid. Liu Guijin, China's special envoy for Africa, noted that, "We don't attach political conditions, but we have to realize the political and economic environments are not ideal …" (Financial Times 2008). Economic development which the BRI has claimed to improve depends very much on the national governance and social components. Eventually, the Chinese approach which does not bring in solutions for domestic issues might undermine the BRI's normative profile and China's material interests. Trapped in this dilemma, China is in need for external forces.

On the EU side, to promote transparent, rule-based governance, liberalized domestic and regional markets, and strong civil countries is an inherent requirement of normative power. China by and large benefits from these undertakings of the EU. Li Keqiang, the Chinese Premier, made clear that, "China has been a beneficiary of the current international system in terms of both peace and development". Therefore, "there is no such thing as breaking the existing order" (Financial Times 2015). Therefore, the BRI should not only embrace the participation of European countries, but also the values. One telling example is the AIIB, which incorporated a series of European norms such as transparency, and environmental and social standards (Danner 2019; Gabusi 2019; SU 2022). Besides, in a wide array of cooperative documents signed between China and the EU Member States, the fundamental EU values could be easily identified.

That notwithstanding, most concerns concentrate on a pragmatic question – will the BRI as an alternative to EU projects and integration plans render the latter less attractive? As mentioned, if NPE is to be viewed from a pure idealistic lens, this question is irrelevant. Given that the BRI follows a relational-based approach, it should not diminish the EU's norm diffusion which is done through interstate interactions. But, in practice, it also appears to be true that several Central and Eastern European countries have taken advantage of their involvement in the BRI as a bargaining chip confronting the EU. It is held that both Hungary and Serbia have been deflecting the rules and demands of the EU on these grounds (Kavalski 2019). This phenomenon constitutes a major source of fear of a 'BRI threat' among European officials and experts. But we must note that underneath this question what is challenged is not normative power as such but the very conception of NPE – does the EU really have that great power of mind influencing? Or what we see to date is yet another form of material power that depends on economic advantages and forces.

But this is not to suggest that there should be no normative concern at all. By all means, the identities of the EU and of China are based on contradicting norms – 'universality' and 'unconditionality' respectively. With China, the EU has been grappling for a cooperation paradigm by which it could fully tap into the economic potential, on the one hand, while maintain its normative image, on the other. One example is the cooperation between the EU and China on sustainable connectivity: despite the lack of a clear voice, the EU has also 'joined' the BRI by establishing the Connectivity Platform with China. The objective of this platform is to enhance synergies between the EU's approach to connectivity, with particular reference to the Trans-European Transport Network, and the BRI (Joint Statement of the 21st EU-China Summit 2019). The platform is expected to allow the EU and its Member States to develop infrastructure and transference projects in the regions. From a practical perspective, joining hands with China on connectivity and infrastructure projects is financially beneficial for both sides, especially considering the massive infrastructure gap in Eurasia (Peel 2018). What is interesting is how the EU and China, on the normative grounds, have somehow settled on a rather ubiquitous and elusive soft norm (Whitmann 2013) – 'sustainability'. On this norm, the EU and China in fact diverge in conceptual interpretations. First of all, sustainable development is an elusive concept that comprises multiple dimensions. In the praxis of the EU, the promotion of sustainable development usually embodies the values it is committed to fostering (Beringer et al. 2019; Wissenbach and Wang 2016). But in the framework agreement for the Connectivity Platform, 'sustainability' appears in a value-free manner. A closer look at the documents reached by the two parties shows tacit removal or adjustments of some contending aspects including, for instance, human rights and democracy. This strategy – agreeing upon certain ambiguous yet universally accepted norms – might enable smooth cooperation between the EU and China, in a manner that does not undermine their images as 'good' but distinctive forces (SU 2022).

## CONCLUSION

In contrast to the EU's foreign policies which rest on universality and conditionality, those of China find its normative roots in the norms of non-intervention and sovereignty. These norms have characterized and guided China's external policies for decades and now also the construction of the China-led BRI.

That the BRI offers a value-free option led many to perceive it as a peril to the EU's harmonization agenda in the regions. This chapter, drawing upon NPE theory, seeks to inquire into the mechanisms through which such threats may occur. The constructivist perspective of the theory reminds us that the normative power of the EU, if that exists, should primarily derive from the legitimacy and attractiveness of its norms, rather than material, hard economic strengths.

Bearing that in mind, the chapter finds, first, the EU has been grappling with its normative power identity in the regions even predating the BRI. The crux of the issue is the EU's incapability to form comprehensive region-specific strategies. Its normative image in the regions is blurry and inconsistent, which undermines its normative power. Second, the way in which the BRI functions may exacerbate the long-standing issue of coherence within the EU. Without a strong and clear voice, its normative power might wane. Third, the BRI does not directly bring about normative confrontation or threats to the EU's normative agenda as it stands now. Due to the principles of non-interference and unconditionality, BRI does not export a governance model. Neither does it preclude the participating countries from following the EU's approach. On this account, a potential risk for the EU stems not so much from normative confrontation as from identity construction.

On the other hand, the BRI embraces the participation of EU Member States, if not necessarily the EU as a whole, and also the fundamental values. Not only because they could contribute substantive resources, but also they bring BRI countries in line with norms and values that would lead to good governance. In this way, the EU and China complement rather than supplant each other in the regional governance (van der Meulen et al. 2009). Meanwhile, a profound change of global order is underway, which calls for a paradigmatic shift from a "Western-led governance" model to a more inclusive "East-West co-governance" model (He 2015). If the divergences could be managed rationally, the BRI might be able to set an example in this regard.

## REFERENCES

Axelrod, R. (1986) An Evolutionary Approach to Norms. *American Political Science Review*, **80**, 1095–1111.

Baird, D. G., Gertner, R. H. and Picker, R. C. (1994) *Game Theory and the Law*. Cambridge, MA: Harvard University Press.

Beringer, S. L., Maier, S. and Thiel, M. (2019) Introduction. In Beringer, S. L., Maier, S. and Thiel, M. (eds), *EU Development Policies: Between Norms and Geopolitics*. Cham: Palgrave Macmillan, 1–16.

Bicchi, F. (2006) 'Our Size Fits All': Normative Power Europe and the Mediterranean. *Journal of European Public Policy*, **13**(2), 286–303.

Björkdahl, A. (2002) Norms in International Relations: Some Conceptual and Methodological Reflections. *Cambridge Review of International Affairs*, **15**(1), 9–23.

Bräutigam, D. (2011) Chinese Aid to Africa: What, Where, Why, and How Much? *China Update*. Australia National University, Canberra.

Brunnée, J. and Toope, S. J. (2000) International Law and Constructivism: Elements of an International Theory of International Law. *Columbia Journal of Transnational Law*, **39**(1), 19–74.

Chaisse, J. and Matsushita, M. (2018) China's 'Belt and Road' Initiative: Mapping the World Trade Normative and Strategic Implications. *Journal of World Trade*, **52**(1), 163–185.

Chen, Z. (2016) China, the European Union and the Fragile World Order. *JCMS: Journal of Common Market Studies*, **54**(4), 775–792.

China, People's Republic of (2016) Appendix: Vision and Proposed Actions Outlined on Jointly Building Silk Road Economic Belt and the 21st-Century Maritime Silk Road. In Ji, L., Peng, F. and Jiliang, D. (eds), *A Guide to the Belt and Road Initiative*. Gansu: Gansu Culture Press, 369–387.

Condon, M. (2012) China in Africa: What the Policy of Nonintervention Adds to the Western Development Dilemma. *PRAXIS: The Fletcher Journal of Human Security*, **27**, 5–25.

Danner, L. K. (2019) European Involvement in China's Asian Infrastructure Investment Bank: Geopolitical Pragmatism or Normative Engagement? In Beringer, S. L., Maier, S. and Thiel, M. (eds), *EU Development Policies: Between Norms and Geopolitics*. Cham: Palgrave Macmillan, 79–94.

Diez, T. (2005) Constructing the Self and Changing Others: Reconsidering 'Normative Power Europe'. *Millennium: Journal of International Studies*, **33**(3), 613–636.

Ekman, A. (2016) A Multilateral Agenda for the EU: Taking China's Activism into Account. In Ujvari, B. (ed.), *The EU Global Strategy: Going Beyond Effective Multilateralism*. Brussels: European Policy Centre.

European Commission (2018) *Joint Communication to the European Parliament, the Council, the European Economic and Social Committee, the Committee of the Regions and the European Investment Bank: Connecting Europe and Asia – Building Blocks for an EU Strategy*. JOIN/2018/31 final.

Financial Times (2008) China Defends Africa Aid Stance. http://www.ft.com/intl/cms/s/0/28a69bd4-479a-11dd-93ca-000077b07658.html#axzz3qte3ef2w.

Financial Times (2015) Interview: Li Keqiang on China's Challenges. https://www.ft.com/content/38307b3e-e28d-11e4-aa1d-00144feab7de.

Florini, A. (1996) The Evolution of International Norms. *International Studies Quarterly*, **40**(3), 363–389.

Forsberg, T. (2009) Normative Power Europe (Once More): A Conceptual Clarification and Empirical Analysis. Presentation at the Annual Convention of the International Studies Association, New York.

Gabusi, G. (2019) Global Standards in the Asian Infrastructure Investment Bank: The Contribution of the European Members. *Global Policy*, **10**(4), 631–638.
Gerrits, A. (ed.) (2009) *Normative Power in a Changing World: A Discussion*. The Hague: Netherlands Institute of International Relations.
Globescan (2017) *Sharp Drop in World Views of US, UK: Global Poll*. https://globescan.com/sharp-drop-in-world-views-of-us-uk-global-poll/.
Guzman, A. T. (2008) *How International Law Works: A Rational Choice Theory*. Oxford: Oxford University Press.
Guzman, A. T. and Meyer, T. L. (2010) International Soft Law. *Journal of Legal Analysis*, **2**(1), 171–225.
He, Y. F. (2015) 从 "西方治理" 到 "东西方共治" [From 'Western Governance' to 'East-West Co-governance']. Caixin.com, 6 April. http://weekly.caixin.com/2015-04-03/100797317.html.
Hyde-Price, A. (2006) 'Normative Power Europe': A Realist Critique. *Journal of European Public Policy*, **13**(2), 217–234.
International Crisis Group (2006) *Central Asia: What Role for the European Union?* Asia Report 113. https://www.crisisgroup.org/europe-central-asia/central-asia/central-asia-what-role-european-union.
Jepperson, R. L., Wendt, A. and Katzenstein, P. J. (1996) Norms, Identity, and Culture in National Security. In Katzenstein, P. J. (ed.), *The Culture of National Security: Norms and Identity in World Politics*. New York: Columbia University Press, 33–75.
Joint Statement of the 21st EU-China Summit (2019) 12642/0611, Brussels.
Jones, L. (2019) Does China's Belt and Road Initiative Challenge the Liberal, Rules-Based Order? *Fudan Journal of the Humanities and Social Sciences*. https://doi.org/10.1007/s40647-019-00252-8.
Kavalski, E. (2007) Partnership or Rivalry between the EU, China and India in Central Asia: The Normative Power of Regional Actors with Global Aspirations. *European Law Journal*, **13**(6), 839–856.
Kavalski, E. (2008) *Extending the European Security Community: Constructing Peace in the Balkans*. New York: I. B. Tauris.
Kavalski, E. (2012) *Central Asia and the Rise of Normative Powers: Contextualizing the Security Governance of the European Union, China, and India*. New York: Bloomsbury.
Kavalski, E. (2013) The Struggle for Recognition of Normative Powers: Normative Power Europe and Normative Power China in Context. *Cooperation and Conflict*, **48**(2), 247–267.
Kavalski, E. (2014) The Shadows of Normative Power in Asia: Framing the International Agency of China, India, and Japan. *Pacific Focus*, **29**(3), 303–328.
Kavalski, E. (2019) China in Central and Eastern Europe: The Unintended Effects of Identity Narratives. *Asia Europe Journal*, **17**(4), 403–419.
Lanteigne, M. (2016) *Chinese Foreign Policy: An Introduction*, 3rd edition. Abingdon: Routledge.
Liu, Y. F. (2015) "One Belt and One Road" and Free Trade Zones: China's New Opening-up Initiatives. *Frontiers of Economics in China*, **10**(4), 585–590.
Manners, I. (2002) Normative Power Europe: A Contradiction in Terms? *JCMS: Journal of Common Market Studies*, **40**(2), 235–258.
Manners, I. (2009) The EU's Normative Power in Changing World Politics. In Gerrits, A. (ed.), *Normative Power Europe in a Changing World: A Discussion*. The Hague: Netherlands Institute of International Relations, 9–24.

Moravcsik, A. (2017) Europe is Still a Superpower. *Foreign Policy*, 13 April. https://foreignpolicy.com/2017/04/13/europe-is-still-a-superpower/.

Nicolaïdis, K. and Howse, R. (2002) 'This is my Eutopia …': Narrative as Power. *JCMS: Journal of Common Market Studies*, **40**(4), 767–792.

Odgaard, L. (2013) China's Coexistence Strategy and the Consequences for World Order. *China Brief*, **13**(11), 7–9.

OECD (2018) *China's Belt and Road Initiative in the Global Trade, Investment and Finance Landscape*. OECD Business and Finance Outlook.

Pan, Z. (ed.) (2012) *Conceptual Gaps in China-EU relations: Global Governance, Human Rights and Strategic Partnerships*. Basingstoke: Palgrave Macmillan.

Pantucci, R. (2014) China's Inexorable Drive Into Central Asia. *China Outlook*. https://raffaellopantucci.com/category/electronic-journals/china-outlook/.

Peel, M. (2018) Europe Unveils its Answer to China's Belt and Road Plan. *Financial Times*. https://www.ft.com/content/bbcda96a-bc1b-11e8-8274-55b72926558f.

Peng, Z. Z. and Tok, S. K. (2016) The AIIB and China's Normative Power in International Financial Governance Structure. *Chinese Political Science Review*, **1**(4), 736–753.

Pew Research Center (2019) Europeans Credit EU with Promoting Peace and Prosperity, but Say Brussels Is Out of Touch With Its Citizens: Many Worried about Long-Term Economic Forecast, Impact of Immigration. https://www.pewresearch.org/global/2019/03/19/europeans-credit-eu-with-promoting-peace-and-prosperity-but-say-brussels-is-out-of-touch-with-its-citizens/.

PwC's Growth Markets Centre (2016) *China's New Silk Route: The Long and Winding Road*. https://www.pwc.com/gx/en/growth-markets-center/assets/pdf/china-new-silk-route.pdf.

Raymond, G. A. (1997) Neutrality Norms and the Balance of Power. *Cooperation and Conflict*, **32**(2), 123–146.

Reuters (2015) China's AIIB to Offer Loans with Fewer Strings Attached. http://www.reuters.com/article/us-aiib-china-loans-idUSKCN0R14UB20150901.

Ruggie, J. G. (2002) *Constructing the World Polity: Essays on International Institutionalization*. London: Routledge.

Schunz, S., Basu, S., Bruyninckx, H., Keukeleire, S. and Wouters, J. (2012) Analysing the Position of the European Union in the United Nations System: Analytical Framework. In Wouters, J., Bruyninckx, H., Basu, S. and Schunz, S. (eds), *The European Union and Multilateral Governance*. Basingstoke: Palgrave Macmillan, 25–45.

Shahriar, S., Qian, L., Saqib Irshad, M., Kea, S., Muhammad Abdullahi, N. and Sarkar, A. (2018) Institutions of the Belt & Road Initiative: A Systematic Literature Review. *Journal of Law, Policy and Globalization*, **77**, 1–13.

SU, X. (2022) EU-China Cooperation on Promoting Sustainable Development under the Belt and Road Initiative – Consensus Built on Divergence. In Ntousas, V. and Minas, S. (eds), *The European Union and China's Belt and Road: Impact, Engagement and Competition*. Abingdon: Routledge.

Svetlicinii, A. (2018) China's Belt and Road Initiative and the Eurasian Economic Union: 'Integrating the Integrations'. *Public Administration Issues*, **5**, 7–20.

Svetlicinii, A. (2020) Sustainable Development and the New Development (BRICS) Bank: The Contribution of the BRICS Countries. In Puppim de Oliveira, J. A. and Jing, Y. (eds), *International Development Assistance and the BRICS*. Singapore: Palgrave Macmillan, 119–147

The Diplomat (2015) The AIIB Is Seen Very Differently in the US, Europe, and China. http://thediplomat.com/2015/05/the-aiib-is-seen-very-differently-in-the-us-europe-and-china/.

The National Development and Reform Commission, Ministry of Foreign Affairs, and Ministry of Commerce of the People's Republic of China, with State Council authorization (2015) *Vision and Actions on Jointly Building Silk Road Economic Belt and 21st-Century Maritime Silk Road.*

Tocci, N. (ed.) (2008) *Who is a Normative Foreign Policy Actor? The European Union and its Global Partners*. Brussels: Centre for European Policy Studies.

Tsuruoka, M. (2008) "Expectations Deficit" in EU-Japan Relations: Why the Relationship Cannot Flourish. *Current Politics and Economics of Asia*, **17**(1), 107–126.

Van der Meulen, E., Van der Putten, F. P. and Morris, P. (2009) *Great Powers and International Conflict Management: European and Chinese Involvement in the Darfur and Iran Crises*. The Hague: Netherlands Institute of International Relations.

Vangeli, A. (2018) The Normative Foundations of the Belt and Road Initiative. In Shan, W., Nuotio, K. and Zhang, K. (eds), *Normative Readings of the Belt and Road Initiative*. Cham: Springer, 59–83.

Wang, G. (2008) China and the International Order: Some Historical Perspectives. In Wang, G. and Zheng, Y. (eds), *China and the New International Order*. Abingdon: Routledge, 21–31.

Wang, H. (2019) China's Approach to the Belt and Road Initiative. *Journal of International Economic Law*, **22**(1), 29–55.

Whitmann, R. G. (2013) The Neo-Normative Turn in Theorising the EU's International Presence. *Cooperation and Conflict*, **4**(29), 171–193.

Wissenbach, U. and Wang, Y. (2016) Development Policy: Alternatives, Challenges, and Opportunities. In Wang, J. and Song, W. (eds), *China, the European Union, and the International Politics of Global Governance*. New York: Palgrave Macmillan, 251–269.

Zhang, L. (2016) "Reflexive Expectations" in EU–China Relations: A Media Analysis Approach. *JCMS: Journal of Common Market Studies*, **54**(2), 463–479.

# 14. Localizing the responsibility to protect: European and Brazilian perspectives

**Jan Wouters and Francisca Costa Reis**

## INTRODUCTION

Cooperation and multilateralism have become increasingly challenged in a world order that is more and more characterized by polarization and contestation. Competing ideas about previously internationally agreed norms and structures have revealed deep fragmentations in the acceptance and viability of the post-Cold War liberal order, putting the European Union (EU) – a regional order itself dependent on liberal norms and values – under pressure. On the one hand, emerging powers like Brazil, China or India contest the assumption of universal values and an unequally distributed global order. On the other hand, competing ideas increasingly stem from the core of the order, not only within the EU, but also more distinctly from the previous Trump Administration in the United States. Despite being a traditionally reinforcing vehicle of the global order, the EU's capacity to lead multilateralism has suffered both external and internal blows in recent decades, which has cast doubts on how enduring its cooperation agenda might be in the midst of a polarized reality.

One notable multilateral milestone achieved in the post-Cold War era that marked the zenith of liberal order and politics was the promotion and endorsement of the responsibility to protect (R2P) victims of mass atrocities (Crocker 2015). Reconceptualizing state sovereignty and humanitarian intervention, the responsibility to protect norm was endorsed by UN members at the 2005 World Summit, making the principles needed for a stronger prevention of and response to mass atrocities operational. Despite this wide and momentous endorsement at the turn of the millennium, R2P too, has become the target of increasing contestation and polarization, particularly after its disputed application in the 2011 conflict in Libya, which divided the international community and raised concerns about an overstretch of the UN Security Council's use of coercive measures. These events, alongside the disorder that today characterizes global governance and cooperation, have called the responsibility to protect into question, threatening its application and continued relevance. At the same time, it has become increasingly clear that it is R2P's preventive dimension – that seeks to protect populations by preventing future crimes from happening in the first place – that garners overwhelming support and has been deemed as its "single most important" constitutive element (Sharma and Welsh 2015, p. 2). As many have argued, it has long been clear that preventing atrocities is far more preferable than responding to them, particularly as it can be more conducive to international peace and security than post-conflict reaction, which often faces barriers and high costs (Welsh 2016).

It is against this background of increasing contestation and a changing international liberal order, that the present chapter explores the discourses and practices regarding R2P, particularly after the events in Libya, of two key players: Brazil and the European Union. Both Brazil, as the proposer of the 'Responsibility while Protecting' (RwP), and the EU, as a staunch defender of R2P, provide interesting cases to understand variations of support for R2P in challenging times. Moreover, as two actors on the global stage that have historically supported prevention and partnered in favour of supporting the multilateral order, focusing on Brazil and the EU allows us to better understand how atrocity prevention is promoted in both the Global South and Global North. Building on the idea of norm localization (Acharya 2004) in the case of R2P by a traditional leader in global governance (the EU) and a country often placed in the 'contesting field' of international affairs (Brazil), this chapter tries to add nuance to discussions on contestation and draw attention to potential synergies between players often placed in opposing normative camps. Finally, by focusing particularly on R2P's preventive dimension, this chapter addresses a topic which has garnered great support especially in the wake of events in Libya, yet it has received meagre academic attention (Sharma and Welsh 2015). To this end, this chapter provides, first, a contextualization of the responsibility to protect and its development, followed by a theoretical discussion on the study of norms and contestation in a polarized world order. Subsequently, it analyses the EU's and Brazil's localizations of R2P as well as their contributions towards its implementation, particularly with regard to the preventive dimension of the responsibility to protect. In doing so, it illustrates how different contributions to the same underlying objective, the prevention of atrocities and crimes against humanity, have been advanced by different players on the global stage, showing overlapping normative goals. More so, this chapter's analysis of both actors' localization of the responsibility to protect identifies possibilities for synergetic action amidst what has been characterized as a changing world order, pointing towards avenues for the EU to respond to a fragmented order and potentially lead global cooperation in this field.

## THE RESPONSIBILITY TO PROTECT: BIRTH AND DEVELOPMENT

> … if humanitarian intervention is, indeed, an unacceptable assault on sovereignty, how should we respond to a Rwanda, to a Srebrenica – to gross and systematic violations of human rights that affect every precept of our common humanity? (Annan 2000)

It was with these words that then United Nations (UN) Secretary-General Kofi Annan succinctly formulated the difficult dilemma that had beset the international community since the humanitarian tragedies in Rwanda and Srebrenica and, eventually, led to the birth of the responsibility to protect norm. Mentioned for the first time in the International Commission on Intervention and State Sovereignty's (ICISS) famous 2001 report, *The Responsibility to Protect*, R2P was introduced in an attempt to reconceptualize the problématique of state sovereignty and humanitarian intervention, which had been widely debated in various political and intellectual circles following the international community's failure to address the tragedies in Rwanda and Srebrenica. These massacres reminded the international community of the need to develop mechanisms to deal with mass atrocities and gave an impetus to efforts of reconciling what are often considered as competing norms about non-intervention, sovereignty, and collective security (Stuenkel and Tourinho 2014). Articulating the relationship between sovereignty and responsibility, the ICISS put forward the concept of R2P, whereby states have the responsibility to protect their populations from suffering serious harm, or if states fail or are unwilling to do so, the responsibility falls towards the international community (ICISS 2001). Sovereignty was, according to the ICISS, to be conceived of as responsibility, not control, and intervention not as a right, but as a responsibility of the international community when faced with situations similar to the ones in Rwanda or Srebrenica. Additionally, while R2P was presented as possessing three dimensions of responsibility – the responsibility to prevent, to react, and to rebuild – the ICISS report placed prevention at the forefront. It was described as "the single most important dimension of the responsibility to protect" – an option to be exhausted before invoking other means, such as military interventions, to halt atrocities (ICISS 2001, p. xi).

Hailed by some as "one of the most important developments in world politics in the last decade" (Thakur and Maley 2015, p. 3), the release of the ICISS's report on R2P was followed by years of advocacy and negotiations until the norm was finally unanimously endorsed by UN Members at the 2005 World Summit (Bellamy and Dunne 2016, p. 7). The Summit's Outcome Document, adopted as a General Assembly resolution, signalled the acceptance by more than 170 heads of state and government of the three interlinked responsibilities, which, taken together, form the principle of R2P, and are now commonly referred to as the three pillars of the responsibility to protect (UNGA 2005, 2009). Particularly, paragraphs 138–140 set out, first, the primary responsibility of states "to protect [their] populations from genocide, war crimes, ethnic cleansing and crimes against humanity" as well as to prevent the occurrence of such crimes; second, the duty of states to assist each other in building the necessary capacities to fulfil their protection responsibilities, especially before crises occur; and, finally, the international community's responsibility to take timely and decisive collective action, through the Security Council, in accordance with the Charter (Chapter VII), on a case-by-case basis and in cooperation with relevant regional organizations as appropriate, should peaceful means be inadequate and national authorities manifestly fail to protect their populations from the four crimes mentioned above (UNGA 2005). As various observers have noted, such a commitment to protection and a global governance of human security made by the members of the United Nations gained more traction than possibly anticipated, resulting in the establishment of a new joint office for R2P and the prevention of genocide, as well as the continuous public reaffirmation of R2P since the 2005 World Summit (Bellamy and Dunne 2016; Welsh 2019). As Jennifer Welsh (2019), a former Special Adviser to the UN Secretary-General on R2P, emphasizes, "all of the key intergovernmental bodies of the United Nations have discussed and affirmed RtoP in several instances – both in principle and in relation to specific country situations" (p. 55).

A watershed moment in the life of R2P was marked by Security Council (UNSC) Resolution 1973 (UNSC 2011a), which used the responsibility to protect to justify the coercive use of military force in Libya for the protection of civilians from imminent atrocities in 2011. For the first time since the failures of Rwanda and Srebrenica, the UNSC actively addressed a rapidly deteriorating crisis. And yet, what seemed to be a consensus surrounding R2P and its activation in Libya was short-lived and quickly challenged through an enormous backlash and "buyer's remorse" to the intervention (Powers 2015, p. 1258). Accusations by countries like Brazil of an over-stretch of the UNSC mandate and undue use of military force to foster regime change in Libya prompted many to declare R2P dead (Rieff 2011) or under serious challenges due to the contestation directed at it (Kenkel and Destradi 2019). If the preventive dimension of the responsibility to protect was already seen as one of the main reasons for its broad international acceptance in 2001 (Evans 2016), it became even more important in the aftermath of events in Libya, which saw enormous backlash against R2P's third pillar foreseeing coercive action (Hofmann and Suthanthiraraj 2019). At the same time, while R2P was subjected to great scrutiny and contestation after its activation in the case of Libya, profound structural transformations at the international level started generating concerns about the viability of an international order built on liberal values. The rise of alternative voices in international affairs and a certain withdrawal of traditional leaders from an active role on the global stage sparked renewed discussions on the future of global governance and international cooperation (see the introduction to this volume) and, with it, the viability of norms such as R2P.

## Norm Localization, R2P and a Contested World Order

The emergence and intensification of the contestation of the liberal world order has generated great concerns and debates about the future of international cooperation and multilateralism as we know it. While the prevalence of Western influence, particularly after the fall of the Soviet Union, denoted a shift towards an increasing interdependence and intensification of globalization, such developments also created tensions by reshaping traditional conceptions like sovereignty and its boundaries (Zürn 2010). As a new paradigm of collaboratively managing international affairs and trans-border problems emerged – drawing global attention to issues such as international institutions, human rights, and democracy promotion – the regulatory reach and capacity of global governance structures greatly expanded too (Stephen 2017). Notwithstanding the important achievements of such growing institutionalization of the international system, today this idea is under pressure and increasingly subject to debates and contestation (Morse and Keohane 2014). Multilateralism and the fundamental norms in international relations, such as human rights, that resulted in several global cooperative arrangements, have taken a hit. Meanwhile, notions like autonomous decision-making, sovereignty, and national interest are on the rise, increasing the salience of value conflicts among different players on the global stage (Stephen 2017).

Next to factors such as the rise of nationalism and populism and various crises that have shaken the international liberal order, the rise of new and emerging global actors – like the BRICS – is considered as one of the main catalysts of the increasing contestation and resistance this order is subjected to (Destradi and Jakobeit 2015; Newman and Zala 2018). Disputing the legitimacy of the rules and norms underpinning global governance and, more broadly, the liberal world order, non-Western voices, histories, and philosophies have made their way into global conversations, which were often dominated by Western countries and their normative structures (Stuenkel 2016; Acharya and Buzan 2019). Unwilling to merely stand at the receiving end of norm diffusion processes, emerging powers and non-Western countries have, since the beginning of the millennium, increasingly voiced their normative differences. They challenged the nature of the global order, often taking issue with what is seen as a continuous Western encroachment on sovereign equality and a type of interventionism disguised under human rights and democracy promotion (Newman and Zala 2018). The rise of new voices from outside of the dominant core of the liberal order alongside new challenges coming from within it – embodied by the election of President Trump in the United States – have put a strain on the international order. As a consequence, the liberal order is faced with a plethora of new voices and ideas on how to best manage and discuss it. These voices no longer emerge from a single source, but rather from multiple points of origin which intersect and interact (Acharya 2014). Therefore, recognizing the multiple poles and voices of the international order involves investigating different local understandings and interpretations of norms, an agenda which authors like Acharya (2004) have argued for.

It is within this context of increasing contestation and a wider set of contributions to defining and managing the global world order that a burgeoning research agenda on norms and contestation has arisen. Research has recognized the importance of norms and their impact on guiding interactions among and behaviour of states. However, more recently it has drawn attention to the dynamic and often contested nature of norms, affording local actors greater importance (see Acharya 2004; Wiener 2014). Criticizing what was an initially static and moral cosmopolitan research agenda on norms, often focusing on transnational actors as key agents of normative change and on local ones as barriers to norm diffusion, Acharya (2004) proposed the concept of norm localization as an alternative frame of analysis. Breaking with the rather Western-centred research agenda on norm dynamics, Acharya advanced localization as a way to capture the life of international norms and how they often go through processes of adaptation and contestation that may alter their original meaning and scope and reveal domestic actors' normative priors. According to the author, local actors take an active role in the construction of foreign ideas, often advanced by transnational moral actors (e.g. the United Nations), incorporating these into their cognitive priors and fitting them to pre-existing local beliefs and values. Instead of seeing local actors as a barrier to norm dynamics, Acharya affords them a critical role in the development and life of global norms. More specifically, the author emphasizes how local actors translate and fit foreign norms into the local level, subsequently feeding them back into the wider global context, with the potential to modify, defend, or strengthen normative debates (Acharya 2013).

As a norm subject to contestation and resistance, particularly in the aftermath of the events in Libya, R2P has been often analysed through the prism of localization. While localization can be used as a framework to analyse any actor's engagement and adaptation of global norms, research on R2P localization has mostly focused on non-Western actors and their normative behaviour (Docherty et al. 2020). Such a focus runs the danger of exclusively associating localization to non-Western actors and, consequently, equating Western actors' engagement with the norm as the generic interpretation thereof. Additionally, the dichotomous focus of scholarly analysis on either Western or non-Western actors and their engagement with R2P risks constructing these views as incompatible and necessarily different. In an attempt to address these shortcomings, the remainder of this chapter analyses how both the European Union and Brazil have localized the responsibility to protect. By building on Acharya's localization concept, this chapter uses the author's important work on contestation to reveal how behind contestation there may still be normative common ground.

## The Importance of Prevention: R2P Localization in the European Union and Brazil

R2P's preventive dimension is one of the reasons for its broad international acceptance and widespread support (Paris 2014). To better understand the understudied preventive dimension of R2P, this section traces back how the EU and Brazil, two actors traditionally supportive of conflict prevention, have localized R2P in their discourses and practices. As we will show, while both players have rhetorically engaged with R2P differently since its early days, their practices, albeit different in nature, show that both have localized R2P to fit their local preference for prevention.

### Norm contestation and localization in the European Union

Despite being often characterized as a 'normative' or 'ethical' power (Manners 2002), the EU has been, more recently, the subject of extensive research on its external human rights policies (Brummer 2009), revealing the often uneasy tensions faced by EU member states and institutions between confrontation or engagement of governments over their human rights records, as well as the priority assigned to human rights in the EU's foreign policies (Smith 2018). As an emblematic, yet contested, norm, R2P has been no exception to this. In the following, we trace back the positions taken by the Union as well as its practices regarding the development and implementation of R2P.

Despite the involvement of some European diplomats both in the ICISS and, later, in the UN High-Level Panel on Threats, Challenges and Change, which endorsed R2P, it was not Europe, but rather actors like Canada who played a pivotal role in moving these initiatives forward (UNGA 2004). A more prominent role for the EU, however, arose in the run-up to and aftermath of the 2005 World Summit, when the Union became one of the most fervent advocates of the concept of R2P, signalling its support on various occasions in diverse multilateral fora and calling for a strong response to acts of genocide and human rights violations (De Franco et al. 2016). In communications by the Commission and conclusions of the European Council, the

EU also reaffirmed its support for the endorsement of the concept of R2P and its importance before the 2005 Summit (Council of the European Union 2005). Finally, at the Summit itself, various governments of EU member states formulated their backing of the UN and multilateralism. Some particularly declared their support for the responsibility to protect in their speeches, such as the United Kingdom, observing that "states do not have the right to do what they will within their own borders, but that we, in the name of humanity, have a common duty to protect people where their own government will not" (International Coalition for the Responsibility to Protect, n.d.).

Following the 2005 Summit, the EU Council welcomed the adoption of the Outcome Document mentioning R2P, reckoning it would "be an important tool of the international community" (Wouters et al. 2012, p. 259). In the following years, the concept of R2P continuously appeared in a growing number of EU documents. In fact, one could argue that the EU increasingly became an active actor in supporting R2P as an international norm. For example, a few months after the World Summit, the European Consensus on Development contained the Union's strong support for R2P, stressing its intention to enhance international peace and security by contributing to a "strengthened role for the regional and subregional organizations" (European Consensus on Development 2006). Some years later, the 2008 report on the implementation of the 2003 European Security Strategy confirmed the shared responsibility of governments in protecting populations from the four crimes of genocide, ethnic cleansing, war crimes, and crimes against humanity, stating that "with respect to core human rights, the EU should continue to advance the agreement reached at the UN World Summit in 2005" (European Council 2008).

Despite the EU's overall rhetorical commitment and support, the events triggered by the Libyan crisis, particularly the Security Council resolution authorizing the use of force in Libya, exposed internal divisions among EU member states over the scope and operationalization of R2P (Newman and Stefan 2020). While France and the United Kingdom led efforts to advocate for a no-fly-zone in Libya and actively supported military action, this gathered limited support in the EU, with Germany being particularly vocal about its reservations concerning any possible intervention in the conflict and abstaining from the UNSC resolution authorizing the use of force. Despite these deep ambivalences, the EU continued showing its support for the responsibility to protect in the aftermath, particularly by framing it in terms of its preventive dimension. In 2013 the European Parliament's call on the EU institutions to adopt a "consensus on R2P" did not crystalize (De Franco et al. 2016). Nevertheless, the EU's commitment to the responsibility to protect was subsequently mentioned in the 2016 Global Strategy – "the EU will also promote the responsibility to protect" (EEAS 2016, p. 42) – as well as the New European Consensus on Development (2017), recognizing the EU and its member states' continued support for R2P and the prevention of atrocity crimes. In the latest debate on R2P at the UN General Assembly in 2021, the statement on behalf of the EU and its Member States, noted that "R2P forms an integral part of the EU's foreign and security policy and prevention is a key priority" (UNGA 2021).

The EU's endorsement of R2P has been consistently featured in its speeches, list of priorities, and frameworks for action, particularly focusing on prevention as a core element (Staunton and Ralph 2020). This focus, however, becomes even more evident when analysing the EU's effort in implementing R2P, a priority which has consistently been featured in the EU's agenda at the United Nations. The agenda at the UN has highlighted the role of regional organizations' mechanisms and capacities in the prevention of atrocity crimes (Wouters et al. 2012). As Gareth Evans (2016), co-chair of the ICISS and one of the intellectual fathers of R2P, has remarked, the EU has the greatest potential to fully operationalize R2P, both because of its standing as a normative power and model for conflict prevention across its own territory, and because of the Union's possession of a large set of practical instruments and policies in the realm of prevention and rebuilding.

Unlike the African Union, whose Constitutive Act includes a right to intervene in a member state in grave circumstances, the EU Treaties contain no clear commitment to preventing mass atrocity crimes in the Union's member states. Instead, the Union has focused on emphasizing the implementation of R2P through external rather than internal policies, particularly through existing conflict prevention structures. As mentioned above, the R2P label has specifically been referenced in various recent policy documents, including the 2016 Global Strategy, which captures the EU's vision for its engagement in the world and reflects the EU's normative commitments in its action on the global stage. However, R2P is only directly referred to once in the Global Strategy and alongside other priorities (EEAS 2016). Yet, as Newman and Stefan (2020) argue, the EU's commitment to R2P is not always framed in these terms and is often shown through a localized lens of the EU's work on conflict prevention, development cooperation, and human rights.

As a global actor informed by its values of the respect for human rights, democracy, and the rule of law, the EU is guided by, and places a solid emphasis on, conflict prevention and sensitivity in its external action (EEAS 2016). From its conflict Early Warning System (EWS) to its CSDP missions focusing on a comprehensive approach towards crisis management and the mitigation of risks of conflict, the Union's coordinated action has placed prevention as a key dimension of its foreign policy and, consequently, associated R2P to this localized preference. At the same time, the EU's action on development, aid, and trade matters endows it with great capabilities in the prevention of mass atrocities, with programmes and policies creating positive incentives and compliance standards for the respect of fundamental values like human rights and the rule of law (De Franco et al. 2016). While such programmes and policies are not placed under an explicit "R2P umbrella" and are not necessarily systematically used in mass atrocity prevention efforts (De Franco et al. 2016, p. 400), the more recent Atrocity Prevention Toolkit released by the EU represents the most comprehensive policy effort to date referencing action in the framework of R2P (Newman and Stefan 2020). The Toolkit describes structural risks and imminent warning signs of atrocities, and provides guidance on how EU delegations within third countries can respond to warning signs and address mass atrocity risks in a preventive manner (Global Centre for the Responsibility to Protect 2019). With such a focus on proactive rather than reactive action, the Toolkit holds the potential of addressing weaknesses in the EU's capacity to respond to mass atrocities (Smith 2018) and strengthening its overall action in the framework of R2P (Newman and Stefan 2020). Overall, an analysis of the EU's localization of R2P's reveals its focus on the norm's constitutive preventive elements, in line with European Union's historic preference and prioritization of preventive and non-coercive action over the use of force.

**Norm contestation and localization in Brazil**

Brazil's initial positioning on R2P was characterized by its concern about the abuse of the responsibility to protect for non-humanitarian purposes, fearing that it may merely reflect a colonial agenda in a new disguise (Stuenkel and Tourinho 2014). With its tradition of pacific diplomacy, Brazilian foreign policy has, since the end of the military dictatorship, identified the respect for state sovereignty, the principle of non-intervention and the peaceful settlement of conflicts as cornerstones of both its action and the UN Charter, concerns which have informed its initial scepticism towards R2P (Alsina Jr 2003). In 2004, however, "Brazil evinced an emerging support for interventions to ensure democratic order" (Saliba et al. 2015, p. 39) by agreeing to deploy Brazilian forces in Haiti and commanding the respective UN Peacekeeping Operation (MINUSTAH) authorized by the Security Council, partially,[1] under Chapter VII of the UN Charter (UNSC 2004). While before this event Brazil had only participated in UN peace operations under the auspices of Chapter VI of the UN Charter, which refers to the pacific settlement of disputes, 2004 represents somewhat of a shifting point, which the country's leadership justified by referring to the ideas of 'solidarity' and 'non-indifference' to other peoples'

[1] One of the main justifications by Brazil's leadership for its change of stance towards peace operations under Chapter VII of the UN Charter consists in reinforcing that only §7 of the resolution referred to the Chapter, and not MINUSTAH's core mandate.

plights (Brockmeier and Rotmann 2015). Notwithstanding this change, the meaning attributed to 'non-indifference' in Brazilian foreign policy rather than linked to situations of mass atrocities, as in its African usage, was more related to "socioeconomic development, humanitarian cooperation and the fight against inequality" (Brockmeier and Rotmann 2015, p. 16), placing emphasis on addressing root causes of crises in collaboration with the state asking for help (Soares de Lima 2005; Kenkel 2012). Yet, as will become clear, this is closely tied to the preventive dimension of R2P, which involves addressing root causes of conflicts and other factors putting populations at risk (ICISS 2001).

As already mentioned, Brazil's initial response to the emergence of the responsibility to protect was one of repudiation, questioning the permissiveness of granting countries the right to intervene in the affairs of others. As noted by Kenkel (2012), however, Brazilian officials did, gradually and noncommittally, signal their willingness to debate the R2P concept within the UN system in the run-up to the 2005 World Summit and, eventually, at the negotiation process of the Summit itself. Such a shift in attitude is often attributed to both the increasing institutionalization of the responsibility to protect within the UN, and Brazil's aspirations to global influence under Lula's presidency. Moreover, the Summit Outcome Document's narrowed version of R2P – limited to the four crimes of genocide, war crimes, ethnic cleansing, and crimes against humanity – unlike the ICISS report, as well as subsequent efforts by the Secretary-General at broadening the R2P debate beyond the use of force and towards the importance of helping states meet their responsibilities (UNGA 2009), resonated with Brazil and its foreign policy elite. Gradually, Brazil came to show a stronger willingness to engage in the R2P debate, particularly by localizing the debate and fitting it with the country's support of development-oriented and capacity-building strategies in line with the principle of 'non-indifference' (Kenkel 2012).

It was, however, not until 2011 that Brazil's engagement with R2P and intervention norms reached its high point and its localization translated into a concrete policy proposal. Brazil, a non-permanent member of the Security Council at the time of the Libyan crisis, abstained in the voting of UNSC Resolution 1973 authorizing the use of force in Libya, expressing its concerns with the possible unintended consequences and overreach of such measures (UNSC 2011b). In response, Brazil proposed the concept of 'Responsibility while Protecting' (RwP) calling for more responsible and cautious intervention under Pillar III of R2P as well as advocating for the commitment to negotiation and conflict prevention strategies as the best avenue to pursue (UNGA 2011; Kotyashko et al. 2018). To avoid the misuse of protection mandates, RwP suggests that certain guidelines prior to the authorization of the use of force by the UN Security Council (encompassing last resort, proportionality, and balance of consequences) should be upheld. By the same token, it further underlines the need of adopting monitoring mechanisms to ensure the appropriate interpretation and implementation of Security Council resolutions. The traumatic implementation of Resolution 1973 in the situation of Libya seems, in fact, to have inspired Brazil to devise a new approach to R2P, one that was not meant to restrain the development of R2P, but to move it forward.

The Brazilian initiative of RwP attests to the working of norm localization and its feedback into the global system. Having localized R2P since its inclusion in the World Summit Outcome Document, underscoring the role of development as a means to prevent the eruption of conflict (Kenkel and De Rosa 2015), the events in Libya motivated Brazil to feed-back such local interpretations of R2P into the wider global context through its RwP proposal, which placed much emphasis on the need to exhaust all peaceful means for conflict resolution before considering the use of armed force to protect populations. While not ultimately putting aside the possibility of military intervention, RwP, as President Dilma Rousseff stated, expresses a preference for efforts of conflict prevention through diplomacy and development. As noted by Minster of Foreign Affairs António de Aguiar Patriota, the main rationale behind RwP was fostering a more inclusive debate around R2P in an attempt to rebuild consensus after the events in Libya (Kotyashko et al. 2018). By elaborating on the seriousness of the use of force and the importance of using it as a last resort, the Brazilian proposal was characterized as "marking a new stage in the development of the global standard in prevention and action" against mass atrocities with the intention of strengthening the commitment to peaceful solutions for situations of R2P (Welsh et al. 2013). Indeed, as has been suggested, RwP shifted the conversation on R2P away from debates on whether it should be invoked to the issue of implementation, which had never before been so explicitly addressed by a broad audience.

Unlike the EU, in possession of various strategies and policies related to the prevention of conflicts, even if not necessarily fully adapted to mass atrocity prevention yet (see above), Brazil, as an arguably less internationally oriented actor, has contributed mostly to the implementation and discussion of R2P's preventive dimension through its articulation of the RwP concept. Concrete efforts have previously been observed that indicate Brazil's local preference for atrocity prevention, as exemplified by its leading role in the creation of the Latin America Network for Genocide and Mass Atrocity Prevention (2018). However, it has been its RwP proposal that most clearly laid out the prioritization of prevention over reaction in situations of imminent mass atrocities in line with Brazil's local normative preferences.

## CONCLUDING REFLECTIONS: OVERLAPPING LOCALIZATIONS AND THE FUTURE OF R2P

In an attempt to better understand how different actors have localized and contested the responsibility to protect, we traced back the EU's and Brazil's localized views and practices on R2P and their engagement with the norm. Both actors were selected based on their traditional support towards conflict prevention, yet often different normative backgrounds and orientations. Despite different trajectories in how they have supported R2P – Brazil's initial reluctance towards the concept and subsequent acceptance, versus the EU's continuous and stable support thereof – both actors have localized the norm to fit their pre-existing preference of conflict prevention and, more broadly, preventive action. Based on the preceding analysis, some concluding reflections can be made.

Regarding the EU, a rhetorically staunch proponent of R2P since its inception, our analysis shows how the Union has discursively and practically localized the meaning of the responsibility to protect by grafting it on to other central norms in its global presence, such as conflict prevention, good governance, and democracy promotion. While it is true that the EU possesses various strategies, policies and diplomatic resources aimed at preventing conflicts and advancing the respect for core values as human rights, critics have cautioned that these have not necessarily acquired a mass atrocity prevention focus yet and are, thus, not systematically employed in R2P relevant activities. However, the recent elaboration of an Atrocity Prevention Toolkit represents an important step in the EU's capacity to contribute to R2P's preventive dimension and, consequently, the doctrine's continuous relevance in global affairs.

Brazil, on the other hand, has voiced its local preference for prevention and consequent reluctance vis-à-vis R2P's interventive nature since the norm's early days. Yet, despite its initial reluctance, Brazil soon localized the meaning of R2P by fitting it on to other priorities in its foreign engagement, such as non-indifference and the importance of development. More specifically, its major contribution to the debate on R2P and conflict prevention came in the form the RwP proposal, which fed back to the global level how Brazil locally perceived R2P and its future after the events in Libya. Such a local contribution infused the R2P debate with renewed emphasis on the importance of prevention, key to Brazil, and the necessity to limit interventions under Pillar III to stricter guidelines. The country's main contribution to the endeavour of further advancing mass atrocity prevention has been through RwP and the subsequent debates it catalysed. It is, however, important to remark that for the past years, particularly since the outbreak of Brazil's internal political crisis, the country's activism with regard to the RwP proposal has lost its momentum and place in Brazil's foreign policy agenda. Accordingly, if not picked up by other actors, this contribution to prevention debates may lose much of its salience in the future.

R2P has frequently been viewed as peripheral to states' interests, a doctrine doomed to die after the Libyan intervention's disastrous effect on its credibility and given the current challenges to the rules-based system. Yet, its importance is likely to continue to grow in a world where conflict, human rights violations, and other, new, challenges keep putting populations at risk, making it imperative to reinvigorate R2P. Recognizing synergies between the EU's and Brazil's localization of R2P might be a way forward. Different discursive and practical engagements of Brazil and the EU with regard to R2P and its implementation illustrate how actors can pursue different strategies while still contributing, in their own way, to the same shared goal. As Gareth Evans (2016) remarked, the EU has the greatest potential to fully operationalize R2P, both because of its standing as a normative power and as prime example of conflict prevention across its own territory, and because the Union already has a large set of practical instruments and policies in the realm of prevention and rebuilding. Brazil, an arguably less equipped actor in the international arena, but an important voice as a regional and emerging power, has, in turn, accorded R2P's preventive dimension with a deep and serious debate about the use of force and the importance of relying on proactive and preventive strategies before resorting to it. While both actors have walked different trajectories in how they have related to the conversations and debates on R2P, these variations should not be seen as an obstacle to their cooperation. Indeed, their local normative preferences are ultimately the same: focusing on and strengthening prevention. In current times characterized by an increasing contestation and polarization in global affairs, synergies between different players may be fundamental to the continuation of R2P's relevance and implementation. While Brazil's current administration has a rather questionable attitude to the rules-based international order and the EU's normative leadership is increasingly under strain, the latter, as a diplomatically stronger and credible actor, could take the lead in taking the discussion initiated by Brazil's RwP proposal further and help advance discussions on the importance of R2P's preventive dimension. In doing so, the Union would not only honour its values and contribute to upholding the rules-based order, but also bridge the West/non-West divide, which often casts a shadow over normative debates and, by recognizing synergies in both actors' localizations of R2P counter the charges that R2P merely reflects the Western world's agenda.

# REFERENCES

Acharya, A. (2004) How Ideas Spread: Whose Norms Matter? Norm Localization and Institutional Change in Asian Regionalism. *International Organization*, **58**(2), 239–275.

Acharya, A. (2013) The R2P and Norm Diffusion: Towards a Framework of Norm Circulation. *Global Responsibility to Protect*, **5**(4), 466–479.

Acharya, A. (2014) Global International Relations (IR) and Regional Worlds: A New Agenda for International Studies. *International Studies Quarterly*, **58**(4), 647–659.

Acharya, A. and Buzan, B. (2019) *The Making of International Relations: Origins and Evolutions of IR at its Centenary*. Cambridge: Cambridge University Press.

Alsina Jr, J. (2003) A síntese imperfeita: articulação entre política externa e política de defesa na era Cardoso. *Revista Brasileira de Política Internacional*, **46**(2), 53–86.

Annan, K. (2000) *We the Peoples*. New York: United Nations.

Bellamy, A. and Dunne, T. (2016) R2P in Theory and Practice. In Bellamy, A. and Dunne, T. (eds), *The Oxford Handbook of the Responsibility to Protect*. Oxford: Oxford University Press, 3–18.

Brockmeier, S. and Rotmann, P. (2015) *Debating the Responsibility to Protect?* Policy Paper, Global Public Policy Institute.

Brummer, K. (2009) Imposing Sanctions: The Not So Normative Power Europe. *European Foreign Affairs Review*, **14**, 191–207.

Council of the European Union (2005) *Brussels European Council 16 and 17 June 2005*. http://data.consilium.europa.eu/doc/document/ST-10255-2005-REV-1/en/pdf.

Crocker, C. A. (2015) The Strategic Dilemma of a World Adrift. *Survival*, **57**(1), 7–30.

De Franco, C., Meyer, C. and Smith, K. E. (2016) Europe and the European Union. In Bellamy, A. and Dunne, T. (eds), *The Oxford Handbook of the Responsibility to Protect*. Oxford: Oxford University Press, 391–408.

Destradi, S. and Jakobeit, C. (2015) Global Governance Debates and Dilemmas: Emerging Powers' Perspectives and Roles in Global Trade and Climate Governance. *Strategic Analysis*, **39**(1), 60–72.

Docherty, B., Mathieu, X. and Ralph, J. (2020) R2P and the Arab Spring: Norm Localisation and the US Response to the Early Syria Crisis. *Global Responsibility to Protect*, **12**(3), 246–270.

EEAS (2016) *A Global Strategy for the European Union's Foreign and Security Policy*. https://eeas.europa.eu/sites/eeas/files/eugs_review_web_0.pdf.

European Consensus on Development (2006) *Joint statement by the Council and the representatives of the governments of the Member States meeting within the Council, the European Parliament and the Commission on European Union Development Policy: 'The European Consensus'*. https://eur-lex.europa.eu/LexUriServ/LexUriServ.do?uri=OJ%3AC%3A2006%3A046%3A0001%3A0019%3AEN%3APDF.

European Council (2008) *Report on the Implementation of the European Security Strategy – Providing Security in a Changing World*. https://www.consilium.europa.eu/uedocs/cms_data/docs/pressdata/en/reports/104630.pdf.

Evans, G. (2016) R2P: The Next Ten Years. In Bellamy, A. and Dunne, T. (eds), *The Oxford Handbook of the Responsibility to Protect*. Oxford: Oxford University Press, 913–931.

Global Centre for the Responsibility to Protect (2019) *Summary of the 9th Annual Meeting of the Global Network of R2P Focal Points*. https://www.globalr2p.org/wp-content/uploads/2019/07/2019-9th-annual-r2pfps-summary.pdf.

Hofmann, G. and Suthanthiraraj, K. (2019) Norm Contestation and Norm Adaptation: R2P's Reframing over Time. *Global Responsibility to Protect*, **11**(2), 226–253.

ICISS (2001) *The Responsibility to Protect*. Ottawa: International Development Research Centre.

International Coalition for the Responsibility to Protect (n.d.) *Government Statements*. http://responsibilitytoprotect.org/index.php/document-archive/government?view=fjrelated&id=2409.

Kenkel, K. M. (2012) Brazil and R2P: Does Taking Responsibility Mean Using Force? *Global Responsibility to Protect*, **4**(1), 5–32.

Kenkel, K. M. and De Rosa, F. (2015) Localization and Subsidiarity in Brazil's Engagement with the Responsibility to Protect. *Global Responsibility to Protect*, **7**(3–4), 325–349.

Kenkel, K. and Destradi, S. (2019) Explaining Emerging Powers' Reluctance to Adopt Intervention Norms: Normative Contestation and Hierarchies of Responsibility. *Revista Brasileira de Política Internacional*, **62**(1).

Kotyashko, A., Ferreira-Pereira, L. C. and Vieira, A. V. G. (2018) Normative Resistance to Responsibility to Protect in Times of Emerging Multipolarity: The Cases of Brazil and Russia. *Revista Brasileira de Política Internacional*, **61**(1).

Latin America Network for Genocide and Mass Atrocity Prevention (2018) *An Effective Coalition for Prevention*. http://www.auschwitzinstitute.org/wp-content/uploads/2018/04/RedLatAm-Informe-2018-EN.pdf.

Manners, I. (2002) Normative Power Europe: A Contradiction in Terms? *Journal of Common Market Studies*, **40**(2), 235–258.

Morse, J. C. and Keohane, R. O. (2014) Contested Multilateralism. *The Review of International Organizations*, **9**(4), 385–412.

New European Consensus on Development (2017) *Joint statement by the Council and the representatives of the governments of the Member States meeting within the Council, the European Parliament and the Commission*. https://ec.europa.eu/europeaid/sites/devco/files/european-consensus-on-development-final-20170626_en.pdf.

Newman, E. and Stefan, C. G. (2020) Normative Power Europe? The EU's Embrace of the Responsibility to Protect in a Transitional International Order. *Journal of Common Market Studies*, **58**(2), 472–490.

Newman, E. and Zala, B. (2018) Rising Powers and Order Contestation: Disaggregating the Normative from the Representational. *Third World Quarterly*, **39**(5), 871–888.

Paris, R. (2014) The 'Responsibility to Protect' and the Structural Problems of Preventive Humanitarian Intervention. *International Peacekeeping*, **21**(5), 569–603.

Powers, M. (2015) Responsibility to Protect: Dead, Dying, or Thriving? *The International Journal of Human Rights*, **19**(8), 1257–1278.

Rieff, D. (2011) R2P, R.I.P. *The New York Times*, 7 November.

Saliba, A. T., Lopes, D. B. and Vieira, P. (2015) Brazil's rendition of the 'Responsibility to Protect' Doctrine. *Journal for Brazilian Studies*, **3**(2), 32–55.

Sharma, S. K. and Welsh, J. (2015) Introduction. In Sharma, S. K. and Welsh, J. (eds), *The Responsibility to Prevent: Overcoming the Challenges of Atrocity Prevention*. Oxford: Oxford University Press, 1–20.

Smith, K. (2018) *The EU and the Responsibility to Protect in an Illiberal Era*. Dahrendorf Forum IV Working Paper No. 03.

Soares de Lima, M. R. (2005) Autonomia, Não-Indiferença e Pragmatismo: Vetores Conceituais da Política Exterior. *Revista Brasileira de Comércio Exterior*, **19**(83), 16–20.

Staunton, E. and Ralph, J. (2020) The Responsibility to Protect Norm Cluster and the Challenge of Atrocity Prevention: An Analysis of the European Union's Strategy in Myanmar. *European Journal of International Relations*, **26**(3), 660–686.

Stephen, M. D. (2017) Emerging Powers and Emerging Trends in Global Governance. *Global Governance*, **23**(3), 483–502.

Stuenkel, O. (2016) *Post-Western World: How Emerging Powers Are Remaking Global Order*. Cambridge: Polity Press.

Stuenkel, O. and Tourinho, M. (2014) Regulating Intervention: Brazil and the Responsibility to Protect. *Conflict, Security & Development*, **14**(4), 379–402.

Thakur, R. and Maley, W. (2015) Introduction: Theorising Global Responsibilities. In Thakur, R. and Maley, M. (eds), *Theorising the Responsibility to Protect*. Cambridge: Cambridge University Press, 3–15.

UNGA (2004) *Follow-up to the outcome of the Millennium Summit.* https://www.securitycouncilreport.org/atf/cf/%7B65BFCF9B-6D27-4E9C-8CD3-CF6E4FF96FF9%7D/CPR%20A%2059%20565.pdf.

UNGA (2005) *Resolution adopted by the General Assembly on 16 September 2005*. https://www.un.org/en/development/desa/population/migration/generalassembly/docs/globalcompact/A_RES_60_1.pdf.

UNGA (2009) *Implementing the Responsibility to Protect: Report of the Secretary-General*. https://undocs.org/A/63/677.

UNGA (2011) *Letter dated 9 November 2011 from the Permanent Representative of Brazil to the United Nations addressed to the Secretary-General*. https://undocs.org/A/66/551.

UNGA (2021) *Statement on behalf of the European Union and its Member States*. https://journal.un.org/en/meeting/officials/bb354fcd-eaa7-eb11-911e-0050569e8b67/2021-05-17.

UNSC (2004) *Resolution 1576 (2004)*. https://undocs.org/S/RES/1576(2004).

UNSC (2011a) *Resolution 1973 (2011)*. https://www.undocs.org/S/RES/1973%20(2011).

UNSC (2011b) *The situation in Libya*. https://undocs.org/S/PV.6498.

Welsh, J. (2016) The Responsibility to Prevent: Assessing the Gap between Rhetoric and Reality. *Cooperation and Conflict*, **51**(2), 216–232.

Welsh, J. (2019) Norm Robustness and the Responsibility to Protect. *Journal of Global Security Studies*, **4**(1), 53–72.

Welsh, J., Quinton-Brown, P. and MacDiarmid, V. (2013) Brazil's 'Responsibility While Protecting' Proposal: A Canadian Perspective. Canadian Centre for the Responsibility to Protect.

Wiener, A. (2014) *A Theory of Contestation*. Dordrecht: Springer.

Wouters, J., De Man, P. and Vincent, M. (2012) The Responsibility to Protect and Regional Organizations: Where Does the EU Stand? In Hoffmann, J. and Nollkaemper, A. (eds), *Responsibility to Protect: From Principle to Practice*. Amsterdam: Pallas Publications, 247–270.

Zürn, M. (2010) Global Governance as Multi-Level Governance. In Enderlein, H., Walti, S. and Zürn, M. (eds), *Handbook on Multi-Level Governance*. Cheltenham, UK and Northampton, MA, USA: Edward Elgar Publishing, 80–99.

# 15. The AI global order: what place for the European Union?[1]

**Matthieu Burnay and Alexandru Circiumaru**

## INTRODUCTION

Beyond living through a technological revolution, we now live in the age of Artificial Intelligence (AI) (Scherer 2016). While this idea is not new, it is easier than ever before to account for the concrete manifestations and impact of AI on our contemporary societies, ranging from rather innocuous applications, such as navigation systems and online translation services, to those that can have serious consequences for individual rights, such as the use of facial recognition for policing purposes (BBC 2020), risks assessment instruments in criminal justice (Gless 2020), and intelligent systems and big data for dispute resolution (Lozada-Pimiento 2019). Against this background, the focus of the response of global players in the face of this new technology has been two-fold: (1) capitalizing on it and (2) regulating it. While the ways in which both state and non-state actors can capitalize on this technology are relatively straightforward, the same cannot be said about finding ways to regulate it. In fact, the rapid pace of AI technology development, along with the problems inherent to imposing liability for decisions reached by algorithms, all make it difficult to use the traditional governance toolbox (Scherer 2016). Most of the specialized literature on AI published so far focuses on these points (see, for example, Buiten 2019) as well as on the impact of AI on other areas of law, specifically consumer or competition law (Ezrachi and Stucke 2019). The transnational nature of AI development and its implications call for international cooperation and the involvement of non-state actors (Ala-Pietilä and Smuha 2021). It is in recognition of the transnational nature of AI that a number of states (i.e., United Kingdom, the US, Canada, Japan, and the EU) launched the Global Partnership on Artificial Intelligence in June 2020

[1] This research took place in the context of the Jean Monnet Network EUPLANT (EU-China Legal and Judicial Cooperation) financed by the Erasmus+ Programme of the European Union (Ref.: 599857-EPP-1-2018-1-UK-EPPJMO-NETWORK).

to support "the responsible and human-centric development and use of AI in a manner consistent with human rights, fundamental freedoms and … democratic values" (Global Partnership on Artificial Intelligence 2020).

Despite recent attempts to coordinate, state and non-state actors alike have come up with their own agendas on AI, all putting a relative emphasis on its development and regulation aspects. China and the United States have primarily focused on capitalizing on AI, the former announcing as early as 2017 its intention to lead the world in new trends in the development of AI (Creemers 2017) while the latter expressed its commitment to "maintain American leadership on AI" (The White House 2019). On the other hand, the European Union (EU) has attempted to project its normative identity by establishing itself as a leader of 'ethical AI' (Renda 2020), being the first to put forward a proposal on the regulation of Artificial Intelligence, in April 2021 (European Commission 2021b). While the EU is the only one so far to have put together a legislative proposal in this area, all of the abovementioned actors have interestingly come up with ethical guidelines for the development and deployment of AI, therefore recognizing its risks and taking a more holistic approach to it. In light of this, one can certainly speak of the emergence of a complex, multi-level AI global order, currently defined by an ongoing race for both technological and regulatory leadership. This chapter considers the EU's position in the AI global order with reference to its Digital Strategy (European Commission 2020a), White Paper on Artificial Intelligence (AIWP) (European Commission 2020b), and finally the Artificial Intelligence Act Proposal (AIA) (European Commission 2021b). It focuses on the EU countries' commitment to take a leadership position through regulatory activism and ensure that its values and principles are successfully internationalized through collaborations in the area of AI. It interrogates the extent to which one can currently identify a 'Brussels effect' in making the governance of AI by focusing on the specific case of EU–China cooperation on AI (Bradford 2020).

In the first place, this chapter closely looks at the emerging AI global order and its defining characteristics and compares the positioning of the EU through its regulatory activism and technological development, relative to China and the US. It then assesses the viability of the EU plans to transform its values and rules into a 'global rule book' on AI. The second part discusses the prospects and challenges for the EU to recognize China as a 'like-minded' partner in the field of AI, shedding light on the conceptual, normative, and policy gaps that still characterize the relationship between EU and China, from the perspective of human rights, algorithmic citizenship, and right to privacy and data protection. The chapter concludes that despite many similarities related to broad, lofty objectives such as that AI should be 'human-centred', it is clear that current developments in the governance of AI will most likely lead to a severe fragmentation of the AI global order in which the EU might not have its desired role.

## A EUROPEAN-MINDED AI GLOBAL ORDER?

Living in the age of AI is no longer a sci-fi premise or vision for the future (Erdélyi and Goldsmith 2018) but a reality that all of us are experiencing, albeit to different degrees. In the last four years, not only national or supranational institutions but also, following a wider trend, various stakeholders (Abbott and Snidal 2009), corporate actors (Moore 2016), and civil society organizations (CSOs) have outlined their vision for how AI should be developed and deployed. Corporations, in particular those who play an important role in the development of this technology, have taken a proactive stance, either by drafting their own guiding principles on AI, for example, Google and Microsoft,[2] or by participating in the process of drafting national-level principles, as is the case for Alibaba and Baidu[3] in China. This signals the move of big tech from lobbying to effectively being part of the policy-making process, as well as influencing the opinion of the general public. One example of how this is done is the release of ethical guidelines by various tech companies, which are then used by policy-makers. One concrete example is Microsoft, offering its own ethical principles as feedback for the Commission's consultation on a legislative proposal on AI.[4] CSOs are adopting a new approach too, seeking to play a more important part in regulatory processes. A notable example is The Toronto Declaration, signed by a coalition of NGOs, which calls for the protection of the rights to equality and non-discrimination in machine learning systems.[5]

At the EU level, the European Parliament was the first institution to draw attention to the need for developing a set of principles guiding the devel-

---

[2] "Artificial Intelligence at Google: Our Principles" (https://ai.google/principles/) and "Microsoft AI principles" (https://www.microsoft.com/en-us/ai/responsible-ai?activetab=pivot1%3aprimaryr6).

[3] Alibaba, Baidu and Tencent have all been involved in drafting the Beijing AI Principles. See also the speech of Baidu's CEO during the 13th Chinese People's Political Consultative Conference (CPPCC) National Committee, in which he stressed the need for ethical principles for AI: http://www.xinhuanet.com/english/2019-03/10/c_137883996.htm.

[4] See, for example, the response provided by Microsoft to the European Commission's public consultation on AI ethical and legal requirements, available here: https://ec.europa.eu/info/law/better-regulation/have-your-say/initiatives/12527-Requirements-for-Artificial-Intelligence/F551021.

[5] See https://www.torontodeclaration.org/.

opment of AI. It did so through the 2017 Resolution[6] concerning civil law rules for robotics and AI. In this Resolution, the Parliament recommended to the Commission, among others, the creation of an EU agency dedicated to robotics and AI. In 2018, the baton was passed to the European Commission ('the Commission') which released its "Communication on AI" (European Commission 2018) calling for a unitary approach of all EU Member States (EUMS) on this technology. The EUMS signed the Coordinated Plan on AI (Stupp 2018) the same year and, through an open call, the High Level Expert Group on Artificial Intelligence (AIHLEG) (European Commission 2021a), made up of 52 representatives from academia, civil society, and industry, was assembled. The AIHLEG went on to prepare two deliverables: The Ethics Guidelines for Trustworthy AI ('the Ethics Guidelines') (European Commission 2019a), and the Policy and Investment Recommendations for Trustworthy AI (European Commission 2019b), both containing recommendations for potential policy changes. The year 2019 marked the European Parliament elections and a new Commission. The then President-Elect noted in her Agenda for Europe that AI is a technology that is "changing the world at an unprecedented speed" (von der Leyen 2019), promising to deliver a legislative proposal on AI in the first one hundred days of her mandate (von der Leyen 2019, p. 13), reaffirming EU's bid to lead the world in 'ethical AI'.[7]

Once confirmed, the new Commission included a newly created portfolio, "A Europe fit for the Digital Age". In charge of this portfolio is the Competition Commissioner Margarethe Vestager, who, other than coordinating the EU's work on AI, also leads the creation of Europe's Digital Decade (von der Leyen 2020). In 2020 alone, her cabinet has overseen the release of a new Cybersecurity Policy, the Digital Services Act, and the Digital Markets Act, both directed at the operation of digital platforms and the Data Governance Act that is meant to ensure freedom of movement for non-personal data used to develop AI. However, the bid to lead the world in 'ethical AI' was off to a rocky start. The promised legislative proposal was instead turned into the White Paper on AI (AIWP) (Kayser-Bril 2020). The AIWP, which is part of the broader digital strategy (Brattberg et al. 2020) presented in February 2020, aims to provide a rough, yet indicative sketch of the approach of the EU to the promised legislation and give a chance to relevant stakeholders to voice their

6 European Parliament Resolution of 16 February 2017 With Recommendations to the Commission on Civil Law Rules on Robotics (2015/2103(INL)).

7 This goal can be traced back to the Coordinated Plan on the Development and Use of Artificial Intelligence Made in Europe – 2018, which states that overall, "the ambition is for Europe to become the world-leading region for developing and deploying cutting-edge, ethical and secure AI, promoting a human-centric approach in the global context".

opinions.[8] It is worth mentioning that the AIWP, to a great extent based on the Ethics Guidelines and Policy and Investment Recommendations, has elicited numerous mixed reactions. Critics have claimed that the emerging strategy of the EU will have a negative impact on start-ups, lacks real enforcement mechanisms, and is less bold and ambitious than initially anticipated (Cath-Speth and Kaltheuner 2020).

Section H of the AIWP, dealing with the external dimension of the EU's proposed AI policy, clearly highlights the contribution of the EU to the emergence of an AI global order. Three points are particularly worthy of attention: (1) The Commission argues that the EU is well placed to play a leading role in building alliances around shared values and promote the ethical use of AI. (2) The EU intends to continue collaborating with like-minded countries and other global players on AI following an approach rooted in its rules and values. (3) The Commission emphasizes that international cooperation on AI *must* (emphasis added) be based on an approach that promotes the respect of fundamental rights, including human dignity, pluralism, inclusion, non-discrimination, and protection of privacy and personal data, and distinctly expresses its intention to export its values across the world. The narrative is different when it comes to development and investment. The differences in investments in AI have been highlighted by the Commission in its Communication on AI, where it presented the levels of investment in AI. In 2016, the investment was around EUR 2.4–3.2 billion in Europe, compared to EUR 6.5–9.7 billion in Asia and EUR 12.1–18.6 billion in North America (European Commission 2018). These numbers reveal a bigger picture of the position of the EU within the AI global order, and the Commission has often used these numbers to encourage further investment in AI (Sullivan 2018).

On 21 April 2021, the Commission released a proposal for the AIA, which draws heavily upon the AIWP and the work of the AIHLEG, and suggests a risk-based approach to AI. One of the declared goals of the Commission within the framework of this proposal is to make the EU the leader in regulating AI. The proposal is currently under discussion in the Parliament and optimistic predictions indicate that a final version will be adopted sometime in 2023.

By contrast, since the 'New Generation Artificial Intelligence Development Plan' (Creemers 2017), China has been focused on being the world leader in AI development. While the feasibility of this goal has been called into ques-

[8] After the release of the AIWP the Commission started a consultation period during which it invited a number of stakeholders, including civil society organisations, academics and citizens, to respond to a questionnaire (https://ec.europa.eu/info/law/better-regulation/have-your-say/initiatives/12270-White-Paper-on-Artificial-Intelligence-a-European-Approach/public-consultation).

tion, China has certainly been very active in transforming local companies working on AI into national champions, each tasked with the development of a different branch. For example, Baidu has been tasked with the development of autonomous driving, Alibaba with the development of smart cities, and Tencent with medical diagnoses. As highlighted by Creemers (2017), China's plan to lead in the domain of AI aims to serve both the domestic and foreign policy agenda of the party-state (Creemers 2017). At the domestic level, the leadership has to support the creation of new social management and governance instruments. At the international level, it has to be a strong driver of the export of Chinese technologies and other contributions to the global governance of cyberspace. From an economic point of view, the large-scale investments in AI and innovative technologies should be seen as an important vehicle to avoid the middle-income trap: For China, "the greatest immediate need is to create, absorb, and disseminate the new technologies required to increase the productivity of China's capital stock" (Jiang et al. 2020, p. 520). China has also engaged in drafting its own principles on AI, with the help of its tech giants and researchers, calling the final set "the Beijing AI Principles" (Beijing Academy of Artificial Intelligence 2019). These principles cover aspects of research, development, use, and governance of AI, and call for "its healthy development to support the construction of a community of common destiny, and the realization of beneficial AI for mankind and nature" (Beijing Academy of Artificial Intelligence 2019).

While both the EU and China have ambitious visions for their work on AI, the US remains the global leader in the field, not least thanks to the work of tech giants such as Google, IBM, and Microsoft, as well as the vivacity of the ecosystem of start-ups present in the Silicon Valley (Antonov and Kerikmäe 2020). When it comes to regulation, however, the USA's path has been less straightforward. In a presidential order from 2019 'Maintaining American Leadership in Artificial Intelligence' (The White House 2019), the idea put forward was to adopt a light-touch approach to regulation. The very title of this presidential order was telling, and immediately put the USA's approach in conflict with the those of China and the EU. The presidential order identified five principles[9] that were to guide the American strategy on AI. The second principle – "developing appropriate technical standards and reduce barriers

[9] The five principles are: 1. Driving technological breakthroughs in AI; 2. Driving development of technical standards and reducing barriers to the safe testing and deployment of AI technologies; 3. Training current and future generations of workers to develop and apply AI technologies; 4. Fostering public trust and confidence in AI technologies and protect civil liberties, privacy, and American values in their application; and 5. Promoting an international environment that supports American AI research and innovation and opens markets for American AI industries.

to the safe testing and deployment of AI" – in particular was in stark contrast to the EU's vision. It was meant to serve as a call to action, establishing six strategic objectives, recognizing the impact of AI on the work of all executive departments and agencies, and calling upon some of them to take action. To illustrate, within 180 days after the order was published, executive departments and agencies were encouraged to consider methods of improving the quality, usability, and ensure appropriate access to priority data identified by the AI research community. In 2020, this Presidential Order was followed up by a list of binding principles that must be taken into account by agency regulators (The White House 2020). The USA's position has since changed somewhat, with the new presidential administration taking a different approach. Indeed, a series of regulatory changes and new hires, as well as the inclusion of AI issues in the agenda of the recently established EU–US Trade and Technology Council point to a change in approach which could lead to a better alignment with the EU (Engler 2022).

It is this US advantage combined with China's ambitious vision that led commentators to suggest that the race of AI development is a two-horse race in which the EU does not participate (Minsky 2018). The EU finds itself trying to catch up with China and the US in both investment and AI development. However, it does so without having the benefit of some key assets, such as access to China's large amounts of data, or the robust start-up environment in the US.[10] In contrast, the EU attempts to establish its leadership position in regulating AI,[11] therefore finding itself in a good, but arguably difficult position to maintain within the AI global order. What comes next is the process of turning the relatively ambitious proposal for the AI Act into a final text that the Council and the European Parliament can pass (Boranbay-Akan et al. 2017). This could be a lengthy and difficult process taking into account the different national strategies on AI released so far by EUMS (Moltzau 2019; OECD 2020) as well as the difficult issues to be regulated – including the use of AI in national security. For example, the General Data Protection Regulation (GDPR) took over four years to be realized (European Data Protection Supervisor 2021). While this is, by no means, a perfect comparison, especially since a data protection directive was already in place before (European Parliament and the Council 1995), it could be informative of the expected timeframe. While there

10 This was also suggested by Commissioner Vestager during her hearing in the European Parliament when she argued that "And some say that the Chinese have all the data and the Americans have all the money. But when I see what we have going for us in Europe, it's that we have purpose", Hearing of Margarethe Vestager, European Parliament, Verbatim Report, https://www.europarl.europa.eu/resources/library/media/20191009RES63801/20191009RES63801.pdf.

11 As mentioned above, this goal can be traced back, to some extent, to 2018.

is certainly political will to adopt the AI Act faster, one year and a half after the proposal was published neither the Parliament nor the Council are close to having a final position that would allow for the beginning of the trialogue.

## THE NEW GLOBAL ORDER AND COOPERATION: THE CASE OF EU–CHINA RELATIONS

Cooperation is yet another dimension to this complex emergent global order. AI has no respect for national boundaries and can have serious transnational implications regardless of its place of deployment. This necessitates a strong and stable practice of cooperation (Ala-Pietilä and Smuha 2021). The AIWP suggests that the EU is hoping to play a leading role here too and, undeniably, it seems to have taken steps in that direction by becoming a founding member of The Global Partnership on Artificial Intelligence. However, as previously discussed, the AIWP draws a distinction between the collaborations the EU envisages on AI – with "like-minded countries", such as the other founding members of The Global Partnership on Artificial Intelligence – and "other global players". At this stage, it remains difficult to establish which states, other than the ones mentioned above, will fall in either category. The main challenge is that key players in the AI global order seem to agree on a number of broad and vague objectives such as, "AI should be used for good"[12] that is to say, to help rather than harm humanity. Such ethical principles are typically ill-defined and often remain unclear as to how they can be translated into effective policies rather than "ethical washing" (Yeung et al. 2020). Such lofty goals are also pursued by the Beijing Principles,[13] fifteen in total and divided into three categories – Research, Use, and Governance. One can find numerous similarities between them and the Ethics Guidelines, both in terms of the objectives pursued and the language used. Similar to the Ethics Guidelines, the Beijing Principles also talk about the need for ethical AI, which is kept under control and used for the overall benefit of all human beings. If the analysis were to stop at this rather superficial level, one could reasonably assume that China falls within the "like-minded" category.

However, when taking a closer look, China's status as a like-minded country is seemingly an impossible perspective. In practice, conceptual, normative,

---

[12] See the first principle in the Beijing AI Principles "Do Good" and "Societal and environmental wellbeing" as a requirement for trustworthy AI.

[13] The Beijing Principles were released by a multistakeholder coalition including the Beijing Academy of Artificial Intelligence (BAAI), Peking University, Tsinghua University, Institute of Automation and Institute of Computing Technology in Chinese Academy of Sciences, and an AI industrial league involving firms like Baidu, Alibaba and Tencent in May 2019.

and policy gaps still characterize its relationship with the EU on questions of AI. Numerous discussions are taking place, such as the 2019 EU-China Legal Affairs Dialogue focusing on AI and the legal and ethical challenges that derive from it (European External Action Service 2019).

The first and perhaps most important difference between the EU and the Chinese approach to AI relates to their different views on human rights in relation to AI. While it is clear that the relevance of AI for human rights is still an emerging field (Livingston and Risse 2019), it has now become clear that a number of human rights can be impacted by the increasing reliance on algorithmic systems. According to the Committee of Ministers of the Council of Europe, these include both civil and political rights, as well as economic, social, and cultural rights (Council of Europe 2020).

The Commission's approach in the AIA is heavily based on, and inspired by, the protection of fundamental rights. Evidence of this is found in the defined risk categories. The risk categories range from no or minimal risk to "unacceptable", covered in Article 5 (with biometric surveillance and public social scoring as examples). In between are high-risk systems, a category which can be expanded with reference to the potential negative impact of a certain system on fundamental rights (Article 6). Therefore, the proposal brings together the ideas mentioned in the previous document to the forefront, such as the Ethics Guidelines and the AIWP that call for an approach deeply rooted in the fundamental rights protection. Consequently, the AIA proposal confirms the position taken in the AIWP, namely that the EU will seek international collaboration in line with its own vision and values. This approach highly fits into the centrality of human rights as part of the EU's normative identity projected by the Lisbon Treaty (see Wouters 2020).

In their last joint communication on China to the European Council, the European Commission and High Representative for Foreign Affairs and Security Policy ('the joint communication') emphasized cooperation with China in the area of human rights acts as a "measure of the quality of the bilateral relationship" (European Commission 2019c). Nevertheless, the EU's normative policy vis-à-vis China suffers from a lack of internal and external coherence, thereby impeding the legitimacy and effectiveness of the EU's external action with respect to China (Raube and Burnay 2018). Issues pertaining to internal coherence – the EU's ability to consolidate its own values at home – have negatively impacted the legitimacy and effectiveness of the EU's value promotion towards China (Lai 2019). For instance, the best example thereof relates to the human rights implications of illiberal policies that have been adopted by a number of EU Member States (i.e. Hungary and Poland) in recent years (see, for example, Pech and Scheppele 2017). With these 'rule of law crises' it is the normative foundation of the EU that is now being put under threat. Issues of external coherence – the ability of the EU to promote its values across all EU foreign policies – have also negatively impacted the legitimacy and effectiveness of the EU's value promotion to China. A study published by the European Think-tank Network on China highlighted that "European countries differ to a large degree in the scope of their political action when dealing with issues of human rights with China" (ETNC 2018). At the multilateral level, these differences have been translated into a growing difficulty for the EU to speak with one voice in its critique against China's human rights violations in the framework of the UN Human Rights Council.[14] Even more fundamentally, the gap between the European and Chinese perspectives on human rights has consistently widened in recent years. Not only are values promoted by the EU with respect to China "dead on arrival" (Mattlin 2012), but China also increasingly assumes a "leadership role" in shaking the procedures, institutions, and norms at the heart of the global human rights regime (Chen 2019, p. 1197). This has led the EU to present China as a "systemic rival promoting alternative models of governance" in the joint communication (European Commission 2019c, p. 1).

The second important difference pertains to the diverging views on algorithmic citizenship, in general, and AI-enabled mass scoring of individuals in particular. Building upon the success of private sector-operated predictive algorithms and scoring systems, a number of governments now make use of AI-enabled technologies across a large range of policy fields (Dumbrava 2019). In general, AI can help governments process large amounts of data, making policies more targeted to the needs of end-users. However, the use of AI for governance purposes is not without significant risks, notably when it takes place in the absence of the right checks and balances mechanisms. Endorsing a quite dystopian perspective, McCarthy-Jones (2020) argues that "[A] government armed with AI could claim to know what its people truly want and what will really make them happy. At best it will use this to justify paternalism, at worst, totalitarianism".

As early as 2014, the Chinese State Council issued the Planning Outline for the Construction of a Social Credit System (2014–2020) (SCS) (State Council of the People's Republic of China 2014). According to this document, the Social Credit System, to be completed by 2020, constitutes an "important component part of the Socialist market economy system and the social governance system" and should help secure a culture of "sincerity and trustworthiness" (State Council of the People's Republic of China 2014). Far from the

---

[14] See for instance the Greek veto against an EU Resolution criticizing China's human rights record in 2017. Robin Emmott and Angeliki Koutantou, "Greece Blocks EU Statement on China Human Rights at U.N." (2017) (https://www.reuters.com/article/us-eu-un-rights-idUSKBN1990FP).

Orwellian integrated system that has sometimes been described in the press,[15] the SCS is rather to be seen as "an entire ecology of fragmented initiatives" taking place at both the local and corporate levels (Creemers 2018). The whole model (or rather models) of China's SCS is based on the vague concept of 'trust', thereby enabling the application of arbitrary and disproportionate punishments (Chen et al. 2018, p. 1).

Against the background of China's authoritarian system, the SCS aims to contribute to the creation of a new *Tianxia* and "align Chinese citizens with the ideology of the Chinese Communist Party (CCP) and to punish deviants and other destabilizing elements" (Devereaux and Peng 2020, p. 383). Digital transformation comes here to the service of a more general trend of "moralizing governance" under Xi Jinping, characterized by an "amalgamation of law and Socialist Core Values" (Lin and Trevaskes 2019, p. 46). Interestingly, and as a side note, research has demonstrated the "high degree of approval" of existing SCSs among the Chinese population: social rating is, in fact, considered primarily as beneficial for the socialist market economy more than a threat to privacy (Kostka 2019, p. 1565). More than providing a "counter-model" of social rating, the Chinese experience calls for a broader reflection on a more global trend that is a rising emphasis on quantification and reputation (Sithigh and Siems 2019, p. 1070).

The fear is clearly that innovations and developments in the area of AI in China can only reinforce what is already described as a 'surveillance state'. In this chapter, the definition of 'surveillance state' is provided by Wood et al.: "a society which is organised and structured using surveillance-based techniques" (Wood et al. 2006). While state surveillance is clearly not a novel phenomenon, it is nevertheless obvious that technology-enabled surveillance explains the increased salience and vivid debates surrounding this topic (Van der Meulen and Heynen 2019, p. 3).

Following this development, China is increasingly categorized as a surveillance state. Internally, the party-state has intensified its efforts to use digital transformation along with the development of AI technologies as tools of control and even sometimes repression (Qiang 2019, p. 53). In Xinjiang in particular, the party-state has deployed an "unprecedented surveillance assemblage" to enhance control over the Uighurs and other minority ethnic groups (Leibold 2020, p. 46). Externally, China is now heavily involved in exporting some of its surveillance technologies to a number of illiberal and authoritarian regimes around the world (Feldstein 2019, p.41), which *de facto* offers Beijing

---

[15] See for instance: S. Mosher, "China's New 'Social Credit System' is a Dystopian Nightmare", *New York Post*, 18 May 2019 (https://nypost.com/2019/05/18/chinas-new-social-credit-system-turns-orwells-1984-into-reality/).

access to foreign security and communication regimes (Harsano 2020). Under the label of 'Safe Cities', Huawei has now provided surveillance solutions to as many as 52 countries (with most of them located in Asia and Africa) (Hillman and McCalpin 2019). In sharp contrast with these circumstances in China, in the Policy and Investment Recommendations for Trustworthy Artificial Intelligence, the AIHLEG asks for a ban on "AI-enabled mass scale scoring of individuals" (European Commission 2019a). In the same way, the European Commission is now considering the reintroduction of legislation that would regulate the use of facial recognition within the EU, after initially backtracking on this idea in the AIWP (Stolton 2020).

A key issue seems to underpin the challenges listed above. As AI needs large amounts of data in order to be effective, data will increasingly become a currency, at the price of privacy. Therefore, stricter enforcement of privacy rules can lead to a decrease in data access and less effective AI systems. More than a decade ago, Ess warned that it would be "both mistaken and dangerous" to believe "privacy" in Asian contexts would be a simple translation of Western notions (2005, p. 5). In the EU, both the right to privacy and data protection are protected by the EU Charter of Fundamental Rights (Arts. 7 and 8) and have further been defined by the case law of the Court of Justice of the European Union (CJEU). Hence, it is to a great extent a rights-based approach that is endorsed by the EU today; such a level of protection in China is not a feasible reality. Both notions are clearly of secondary importance in an environment where cyber-governance remains largely state-centred and informed by a search for national security protection and social stability (Lee 2018, p. 58). Furthermore, from a private law perspective, the recognition of personality rights has arguably constituted "the most controversial issue in Chinese civil law" in recent years (Chen 2018, p. 103).

These normative differences explain why data transfer between the EU and China remains far from an easy process. In a report submitted to the European Parliament Committee on Civil Liberties, Justice, and Home Affairs, De Hert and Papakonstantinou (2015) highlighted that "[I]f a legalistic approach was adopted, then no common grounds could be found between two fundamentally different systems both in their wording and in their raison d'être". Nevertheless, ever since the release of that report, both EU law and the interpretation thereof have evolved significantly. The CJEU now imposes a very high threshold when assessing whether a third jurisdiction offers an adequate level of data protection in line with Art. 45 GDPR. In disputes over the transfer of data to the United States, the CJEU made it clear in *Schrems I* and *Schrems*

*II*[16] that a legalistic approach is necessary to establish whether a third country offers an adequate level of data protection for the transfer of data.[17] This adequate level of protection is not only defined by the existence of comprehensive data protection frameworks: data controllers also need to ensure no other laws impede the protection foreseen in data protection laws, as well as the existence of effective judicial remedies. *Schrems I* and *Schrems II* have established that data transfers from the EU to the US are still impeded by US surveillance laws and the absence of remedies available to EU citizens. The case law of the CJEU demonstrates how difficult it is, using the words of the Former European Data Protection Supervisor Peter Hustinx, to achieve "a reasonable degree of pragmatism in order to allow interaction with other parts of the world" (Hustinx 2017, p. 164) when establishing whether a third jurisdiction offers an adequate level of protection or not. Therefore, it appears highly unlikely that China will be considered at an adequate level of data protection in comparison to other countries, such as, for example, Japan that was recognized as having an adequate level of protection by the EU in an agreement signed in 2019.[18]

## CONCLUDING REMARKS

The AI revolution implicates the emergence of an AI global order, which involves state and non-state actors alike, both competing for power and influence in the development and regulation of AI in line with their own strategic priorities and values. The EU has set an objective for itself to take a leadership position within this global order, by creating its own version of AI and persuading other players to follow its example. To consolidate its position, the EU has made use of regulatory activism and pushed intensely to be the first to regulate this technology. It has come closer to this goal, especially with the publication of the AIA proposal. Moreover, it has highlighted the need for global cooperation and its intention to facilitate it. While collaborations with like-minded countries have already begun, the real obstacle in the EU's path to leadership in AI remains the cooperation with countries that have substantially different views on core concepts and values, such as China. The prospects of finding ways around this obstacle remain rather uncertain, especially when taking into

16 *Data Protection Commissioner v. Facebook Ireland Ltd and Maximillian Schrems* (Case C-311/18, "Schrems II").

17 *Maximillian Schrems v. Data Protection Commissioner* (Case C-362/14, "Schrems I").

18 Commission Implementing Decision (EU) 2019/419 of 23 January 2019 pursuant to Regulation (EU) 2016/679 of the European Parliament and of the Council on the adequate protection of personal data by Japan under the Act on the Protection of Personal Information (Text with EEA relevance).

account the diverging perspective on three key issues – human rights, algorithmic citizenship, data protection and privacy. Therefore, it remains difficult for the EU to attain the leadership position it currently hopes for.

## REFERENCES


Abbott, K. W. and Snidal, D. (2009) The Governance Triangle: Regulatory Standards Institutions and the Shadow of the State. In Mattli, W. and Woods, N. (eds), *The Politics of Global Regulation*. Princeton, NJ: Princeton University Press, 44–88.

Ala-Pietilä, P. and Smuha, N. A. (2021) A Framework for Global Cooperation on Artificial Intelligence and Its Governance. In Braunschweig B. and Ghallab M. (eds), *Reflections on Artificial Intelligence for Humanity*. Cham: Springer, 237–265.

Antonov, A. and Kerikmäe, T. (2020). Trustworthy AI as a Future Driver for Competitiveness and Social Change in the EU. In Troitiño, D. R., Kerikmäe, T., de la Guardia, R. and Pérez Sánchez, G. (eds), *The EU in the 21st Century*. Cham: Springer, 135–154.

BBC (2020) Facial Recognition to 'Predict Criminals' Sparks Row over AI Bias. https://www.bbc.com/news/technology-53165286.

Beijing Academy of Artificial Intelligence (BAAI) (2019) The Beijing AI Principles. https://www.baai.ac.cn/news/beijing-ai-principles-en.html#:~:text=For%20Humanity%3A%20The%20R%26D%20of,utilize%20or%20harm%20human%20beings.

Boranbay-Akan, S., König, T. and Osnabrügge, M. (2017) The Imperfect Agenda-Setter: Why Do Legislative Proposals Fail in the EU Decision-Making Process? *European Union Politics*, **18**(2), 168–187.

Bradford, A. (2020) *The Brussels Effect: How the European Union Rules the World*. New York: Oxford University Press.

Brattberg, E., Csernatoni, R. and Rugova, V. (2020) *Europe and AI: Leading, Lagging Behind, or Carving Its Own Way?* Carnegie Endowment for International Peace. https://carnegieendowment.org/2020/07/09/europe-and-ai-leading-lagging-behind-or-carving-its-own-way-pub-82236.

Buiten, M. C. (2019) Towards Intelligent Regulation of Artificial Intelligence. *European Journal of Risk Regulation*, **10**(1), 41–59.

Case C-311/18 *Data Protection Commissioner v. Facebook Ireland Ltd and Maximillian Schrems* ("Schrems II").

Case C-362/14 *Maximillian Schrems v. Data Protection Commissioner* ("Schrems I").

Cath-Speth, C. and Kaltheuner, F. (2020) Risking Everything: Where the EU's White Paper on AI Falls Short. *New Statesman*. https://tech.newstatesman.com/guest-opinion/eu-white-paper-on-artificial-intelligence-falls-short.

Chen, L. (2018) Codifying Personality Rights in China: Legislative Innovation or Scaremongering? In Oliphant, K., Pinghua, Z. and Lei, C. (eds), *The Legal Protection of Personality Rights: Chinese and European Perspectives*. Leiden: Brill, 103–137.

Chen, Y. J. (2019) China's Challenge to the International Human Rights Regime. *International Law and Politics*, **51**, 1179–1222.

Chen, Y. J., Lin, C. F. and Liu, H. W. (2018) Rule of Trust: The Power and Perils of China's Social Credit Megaproject. *Columbia Journal of Asian Law*, **32**(1), 1–36.

Commission Implementing Decision (EU) 2019/419 of 23 January 2019 pursuant to Regulation (EU) 2016/679 of the European Parliament and of the Council on the adequate protection of personal data by Japan under the Act on the Protection of Personal Information (Text with EEA relevance).

Council of Europe (2020) Recommendation of the Committee of Ministers to Member States on the Human Rights Impacts of Algorithmic Systems, CM/Rec(2020)1.

Creemers, R. J. E. H. (2017) Cyber China: Upgrading Propaganda, Public Opinion Work and Social Management for the Twenty-First Century. *Journal of Contemporary China*, **26**(103), 85–100.

Creemers, R. (2018) China's Social Credit System: An Evolving Practice of Control. *SSRN Electronic Journal*. https://papers.ssrn.com/sol3/papers.cfm?abstract_id=3175792.

De Hert, P. and Papakonstantinou, E. (2015). *The Data Protection Regime in China*. Brussels: European Parliament. https://cris.vub.be/ws/files/17639565/pdh15_vpThe_data_protection_regime_in_ChinaIPOL_IDA_2015_536472_EN.pdf.

Devereaux, A. and Peng, L. (2020) Give Us a Little Social Credit: To Design or to Discover Personal Ratings in the Era of Big Data. *Journal of Institutional Economics*, **16**(3), 369–387.

Directive 95/46/EC of the European Parliament and of the Council of 24 October 1995 on the protection of individuals with regard to the processing of personal data and on the free movement of such data.

Dumbrava, C. (2019) The Citizen, the Tyrant, and the Tyranny of Patterns. *Verfassungsblog on Matters Constitutional*. https://verfassungsblog.de/the-citizen-the-tyrant-and-the-tyranny-of-patterns/.

Emmott, R. and Koutantou, A. (2017) Greece Blocks EU Statement on China Human Rights at U.N. *Reuters*. https://www.reuters.com/article/us-eu-un-rights-idUSKBN1990FP.

Engler, A. (2022) The EU and U.S. are starting to align on AI regulation. *Brookings TechTank*. https://www.brookings.edu/blog/techtank/2022/02/01/the-eu-and-u-s-are-starting-to-align-on-ai-regulation/.

Erdélyi, O. J. and Goldsmith, J. (2018) Regulating Artificial Intelligence: Proposal for a Global Solution. *Proceedings of the 2018 AAAI/ACM Conference on AI, Ethics and Society*. AEIS, New Orleans, USA, 95–101.

Ess, C. (2005) "Lost in translation"? Intercultural Dialogues on Privacy and Information Ethics (Introduction to Special Issue on Privacy and Data Privacy Protection in Asia). *Ethics and Information Technology*, **7**(1), 1–6.

ETNC (2018) *Political Values in Europe-China Relations*. ETNC Report. https://merics.org/sites/default/files/2020-04/190108_ETNC_report_2018_updated_2019.pdf.

European Commission (2018) AI for Europe, COM 237 final.

European Commission (2019a) High-Level Expert Group on Artificial Intelligence, *Ethics Guidelines for Trustworthy AI*. https://ec.europa.eu/futurium/en/ai-alliance-consultation.

European Commission (2019b) High-Level Expert Group on Artificial Intelligence, *Policy and Investment Recommendations for Trustworthy AI*. https://ec.europa.eu/digital-single-market/en/news/policy-and-investment-recommendations-trustworthy-artificial-intelligence.

European Commission (2019c) *European Commission and HR/VP contribution to the European Council, EU-China – A Strategic Outlook*. https://ec.europa.eu/commission/sites/beta-political/files/communication-eu-china-a-strategic-outlook.pdf.

European Commission (2020a) *Shaping Europe's Digital Future*. https://ec.europa.eu/info/sites/info/files/communication-shaping-europes-digital-future-feb2020_en_4.pdf.

European Commission (2020b) White Paper – On Artificial Intelligence: A European Approach to Excellence and Trust, COM 65 final.

European Commission (2021a) High-Level Expert Group on Artificial Intelligence. https://ec.europa.eu/digital-single-market/en/high-level-expert-group-artificial-intelligence.

European Commission (2021b) Proposal for a Regulation of the European Parliament and of the Council Laying Down Harmonised Rules on Artificial Intelligence (Artificial Intelligence Act) and Amending Certain Union Legislative Acts, Brussels, 21.4.2021 Com(2021) 206 Final.

European Data Protection Supervisor (2021) *The History of the General Data Protection Regulation*. https://edps.europa.eu/data-protection/data-protection/legislation/history-general-data-protection-regulation_en#.

European External Action Service (2019) EU-China Legal Affairs Dialogue [Press Release]. https://eeas.europa.eu/delegations/china_en/60070/2019%20EU-CHINA%20LEGAL%20AFFAIRS%20DIALOGUE.

European Parliament (2017) Resolution of 16 February 2017 with recommendations to the Commission on Civil Law Rules on Robotics (2015/2103(INL)).

Ezrachi, A. and Stucke, M. (2019) *Virtual Competition: The Promise and Perils of the Algorithm-Driven Economy*. Cambridge, MA: Harvard University Press.

Feldstein, S. (2019) The Road to Digital Unfreedom: How Artificial Intelligence is Reshaping Repression. *Journal of Democracy*, **30**(1), 40–52.

Gless, S. (2020) AI in the Courtroom: A Comparative Analysis of Machine Evidence in Criminal Trials. *Georgetown Journal of International Law*, **51**(2), 195–253.

Global Partnership on Artificial Intelligence (2020) Joint Statement from Founding Members. Department for Digital, Culture, Media & Sport and Office for Artificial Intelligence. https://www.gov.uk/government/publications/joint-statement-from-founding-members-of-the-global-partnership-on-artificial-intelligence.

Google (n.d. a) Artificial Intelligence at Google: Our Principles. https://ai.google/principles/.

Google (n.d. b) Microsoft AI principles. https://www.microsoft.com/en-us/ai/responsible-ai?activetab=pivot1%3aprimaryr6.

Harsano, H. (2020) China's Surveillance Technology Is Keeping Tabs on Populations Around the World. *The Diplomat*. https://thediplomat.com/2020/06/chinas-surveillance-technology-is-keeping-tabs-on-populations-around-the-world/.

Hillman, J. and McCalpin, M. (2019) Watching Huawei's 'Safe Cities'. *CSIS Briefs*, 4 November. https://www.csis.org/analysis/watching-huaweis-safe-cities.

Hustinx, P. (2017) EU Data Protection Law: The Review of Directive 95/46/EC and the General Data Protection Regulation. In Cremona, M. (ed.), *New Technologies and EU Law*. New York: Oxford University Press, 123–173.

Jiang, R., Shi, H. and Jefferson, G. (2020) Measuring China's International Technology Catchup. *Journal of Contemporary China*, **29**(124), 519–534.

Kayser-Bril, N. (2020) EU Commission Publishes White Paper on AI Regulation 20 Days Before Schedule, Forgets Regulation. *Algorithm Watch*. https://algorithmwatch.org/en/ai-white-paper/.

Kostka, G. (2019) China's Social Credit Systems and Public Opinion: Explaining High Levels of Approval. *New Media & Society*, **21**(7), 1565–1593.

Lai, Y. C. (2019) Human Rights and Sustainability in EU-China Relations: The Limits of Normative Power. *European Foreign Affairs Review*, **24**(4), 555–576.
Lee, J. A. (2018) Hacking into China's Cybersecurity Law. *Wake Forest Law Review*, **53**, 57–104.
Leibold, J. (2020) Surveillance in China's Xinjiang Region: Ethnic Sorting, Coercion, and Inducement. *Journal of Contemporary China*, **29**(121), 46–60.
Lin, D. and Trevaskes, S. (2019) Creating a Virtuous Leviathan: The Party, Law, and Socialist Core Values. *Asian Journal of Law and Society*, **6**(1), 41–66.
Livingston, S. and Risse, M. (2019) The Future Impact of Artificial Intelligence on Humans and Human Rights. *Ethics and International Affairs*, **33**(2), 141–158.
Lozada-Pimiento, N. (2019) AI Systems and Technology in Dispute Resolution. *Uniform Law Review*, 24, 348–366.
Mattlin, M. (2012) Dead on Arrival: Normative EU Policy towards China. *Asia Europe Journal*, **10**, 181–198.
McCarthy-Jones, S. (2020) Artificial Intelligence is a Totalitarian's Dream – Here's How to Take Power Back. *The Conversation*, 12 August. https://theconversation.com/artificial-intelligence-is-a-totalitarians-dream-heres-how-to-take-power-back-143722.
Minsky, C. (2018) One Former Google Exec Says There's No Hope for Europe's Artificial Intelligence Sector. *Sifted*. https://sifted.eu/articles/interview-google-kaifu-lee-ai-artificial-intelligence/.
Moltzau, A. (2019) *National and International AI Strategies Around the World*. https://alexmoltzau.medium.com/national-and-international-ai-strategies-around-the-world-towards-2020-692b22b3c303.
Moore, M. (2016) *Tech Giants and Civil Power*. CMCP, Policy Institute, King's College London. https://doi.org/10.18742/pub01-027.
Mosher, S. (2019) China's New 'Social Credit System' is a Dystopian Nightmare. *New York Post*, 18 May. https://nypost.com/2019/05/18/chinas-new-social-credit-system-turns-orwells-1984-into-reality/.
OECD (2020) *AI Initiatives Worldwide*. https://www.oecd.org/going-digital/ai/initiatives-worldwide/.
Pech, L. and Scheppele, K. L. (2017) Illiberalism Within: Rule of Law Backsliding in the EU. *Cambridge Yearbook of International Legal Studies*, **19**, 3–47.
Qiang, X. (2019) The Road to Digital Unfreedom: President Xi's Surveillance State. *Journal of Democracy*, **30**(1), 53–67.
Raube, K. and Burnay, M. (2018) Coherence, Strategy, and Legitimacy: Variations of a Theme in the Case of EU-China Relations. *Global Affairs*, **4**(2–3), 291–304.
Regulation (EU) 2016/679 of the European Parliament and of the Council of 27 April 2016 on the protection of natural persons with regard to the processing of personal data and on the free movement of such data, and repealing Directive 95/46/EC (General Data Protection Regulation) (Text with EEA relevance).
Renda, A. (2020) Europe: Toward a Policy Framework for Trustworthy AI. In Dubber, M., Pasquale, F. and Das, S. (eds), *The Oxford Handbook of Ethics of AI*. New York: Oxford University Press, 651–666.
Scherer, M. (2016) Regulating Artificial Intelligence Systems: Risks, Challenges, Competencies and Strategies. *Harvard Journal of Law & Technology*, **29**(2), 353–400.
Sithigh, D. and Siems, M. (2019) The Chinese Social Credit System: A Model for Other Countries? *Modern Law Review*, **82**(6), 1034–1071.

State Council of the People's Republic of China (2014) State Council Notice concerning Issuance of the Planning Outline for the Construction of a Social Credit System (2014–2020).

Stolton, S. (2020) Commission Will 'Not Exclude' Potential Ban on Facial Recognition Technology. *Euroactiv*. https://www.euractiv.com/section/data-protection/news/commission-will-not-exclude-potential-ban-on-facial-recognition-technology/.

Stupp, C. (2018) Twenty-four EU Countries Sign Artificial Intelligence Pact in Bid to Compete with US and China. *Euractiv*. https://www.euractiv.com/section/digital/news/twenty-four-eu-countries-sign-artificial-intelligence-pact-in-bid-to-compete-with-us-china/.

Sullivan, A. (2018) AI: Government Pledges Billions Aimed at Bringing Germany Up to Speed. *DW Akademie*. https://www.dw.com/en/ai-government-pledges-billions-aimed-at-bringing-germany-up-to-speed/a-46296320.

The White House (2019) Executive Order on Maintaining American Leadership in Artificial Intelligence, E.O. 13859 of 11 February 2019, Executive Office of the President. https://www.whitehouse.gov/presidential-actions/executive-order-maintaining-american-leadership-artificial-intelligence/.

The White House (2020) Guidance for Regulation of Artificial Intelligence Applications. https://www.whitehouse.gov/wp-content/uploads/2020/01/Draft-OMB-Memo-on-Regulation-of-AI-1-7-19.pdf.

Van der Meulen, E. and Heynen, R. (2019) Unpacking State Surveillance: Histories, Theories, and Global Contexts. In Heynen, R. and Van der Meulen, E. (eds), *Making Surveillance States: Transnational Histories*. Toronto: University of Toronto Press, 3–30.

Von der Leyen, U. (2019) A Union that Strives for More, My Agenda for Europe: Political Guidelines for the next European Commission 2019–2024. https://op.europa.eu/en/publication-detail/-/publication/43a17056-ebf1-11e9-9c4e-01aa75ed71a1.

Von der Leyen, U. (2020) State of the Union 2020 – speech. https://ec.europa.eu/info/strategy/strategic-planning/state-union-addresses/state-union-2020_en.

Wood, D. M., Ball, K., Lyon, D., Norris, C. and Raab, C. (2006) *A Report on the Surveillance Society*. Summary report for the Information Commissioner, Surveillance Studies Network, UK.

Wouters, J. (2020) Revisiting Art. 2 TEU: A True Union of Values? *European Papers: A Journal on Law and Integration*, **5**(1), 255–277.

Yeung, K., Howes, A. and Pogrebna, G. (2020) AI Governance by Human Rights-Centered Design, Deliberation, and Oversight: An End to Ethics Washing. In Dubber, M., Pasquale, F. and Das, S. (eds), *The Oxford Handbook of Ethics of AI*. New York: Oxford University Press, 77–106.

# PART III

# Changing global trade order and European responses

# 16. Keep on trading in the Free World[1]

**Fernando Dias Simões**

## INTRODUCTION: HOW TRUMP AND BREXIT ROCKED THE WORLD OF FREE TRADE

In 2016 the world was rocked by two startling events: the election of Donald Trump in the United States and Brexit in the United Kingdom. While it would be imprudent to put forward simplistic, one-dimensional explanations, both outcomes seem to represent, to some extent, an electoral red card to the 'liberal internationalism' that shaped the world economy over the last decades. On both sides of the Atlantic, many citizens are voicing concerns over the drawbacks of free trade and the globalization process more broadly. This public disquiet is not unprecedented. What is new is how populist candidates used this anxiety with unexpected electoral success. Populist politicians condemn the 'liberal internationalism' that they associate with economic globalization, in particular the promotion of instruments of supranational integration and regulation, trade and investment treaties, etc. (Thompson 2017) Both Brexit and Trump's victory are linked to the conviction that internationally agreed upon rules, multilateralism, and globalization constrain and obstruct national interests (Harris 2016).

The electoral emergence of political groups that capitalize on citizens' feelings of economic insecurity has been portrayed as the largest threat to free trade since the Second World War (The Economist 2015). Trump made the protection of domestic interests the hallmark of his Administration, putting an end to a time-honored tradition of American internationalism. This inward

---

1 Title inspired by Neil Young's song *Rockin' in the Free World* (Reprise, 1989). Young wrote the song while touring with his band The Restless in 1989. When he learned that a planned concert in the Soviet Union had been canceled, he expressed his disappointment to the band's guitarist, Frank 'Poncho' Sampedro, who replied "we'll have to keep on rockin' in the free world" – see Andy Greene, "Flashback: Neil Young Unveils 'Rockin' in the Free World' at 1989 Seattle Gig", *Rolling Stone* (14 July 2015), https://www.rollingstone.com/music/music-news/flashback-neil-young-unveils-rockin-in-the-free-world-at-1989-seattle-gig-158334/.

shift may trigger a similar response from other governments, leading to retaliation and potentially threatening existing trade agreements. The rising wave of nationalism is especially dangerous for the post-sovereign, post-nationalist endeavor that is the European Union (EU) (Smith 2017).

It is plain to see that the EU–US relationship is at a nervous standstill. The negotiations for a Transatlantic Trade and Investment Partnership, which Barack Obama made energetic efforts to push forward until the last minute of his term, are paused until further notice. The dialogue is now narrowly focused on tariff liberalization for certain types of goods, regulatory standards, reform of the World Trade Organization (WTO), and other minor issues (European Commission 2019). Ambitious projects to strengthen trade and investment interactions across the Atlantic are no longer on the table. While the full impact of Trump's presidency on trade policy and global affairs more widely remains to be seen, one thing seems to be certain: the atmosphere surrounding the global trade policymaking arena is dramatically different. This has been recognized by Cecilia Malmström, European Commissioner for Trade, at a speech delivered in early 2019 in the American capital:

> We have moved from a period, beginning at the end of the last century, of hopeful optimism about benefits of international economic integration, leading to cooperation and the building of institutions. This optimism has now eroded, giving way to suspicion and distrust. Some of these shifts can be linked back to the pains of globalisation. Globalisation comes with many positive opportunities and is a force for good – but it has also transformed our economies in ways that were hard to predict. People saw their communities transforming; they saw jobs changing or disappearing. This made many feel insecure. And many also blamed trade for these changes. Some of those concerns were valid too – and … we have transformed our trade policy to face these challenges. (Malmström 2019)

This chapter starts by positing that Trump's victory and the Brexit result are symptoms of how trade policies are taking a central place in political discourses and electoral battles. In the third section, it focuses on three areas of concern for politicians and policymakers designing and implementing the EU's common commercial policy. The EU should play a leading role in restoring the credibility of the global trading system and promoting constructive consensus among political circles and the international community at large. The current backlash against free trade, multilateralism and global governance calls for fresh, creative policies. A more inclusive trade agenda is crucial to respond to the legitimate concerns of citizens. However, this can only be achieved if the policymaking process itself also becomes more inclusive: citizens need to feel confident about the benefits of trade and investment policies and reassure that any negative side effects are properly tackled.

## THE POLITICIZATION OF TRADE

Public opinion on the advantages and downsides of free trade policies has changed considerably over the last years (Blendon et al. 2017). The traditional consensus about the advantages of free trade has been eroded. While mainstream economists support the argument that free trade policy created more jobs than it destroyed, this assumption is increasingly being questioned.[2] Nowadays, a significant part of the population does not support traditional trade policies (Alden and Litan 2016).

Populist politicians spotted an opportunity to capitalize on citizens' concerns about the negative consequences of trade policies, particularly the growing unemployment rates. Anti-free trade rhetoric was deployed by Trump and Brexit supporters as an electoral weapon, and with resounding success.[3] Trump's inflamed speeches reverberated among many voters who resented trade policies and, more generally, considered themselves the losers of the globalization game (Chandy and Seidel 2016). In the words of former United States Trade Representative Michael Froman, "[y]ou don't really get to vote on globalization. ... You do get a vote on trade agreements. So trade agreements become the vessel into which people pour their very legitimate concerns about job security, wage stagnation, and income inequality" (The Wall Street Journal 2016).

Trump's anti-globalization statements played a decisive role in his election. He benefited from the anxiety of many American workers with the flooding of cheap imports and the destruction of jobs in some regions of the country, blaming them on traditional free trade policies (Brands 2017).

Social and political support for free trade cannot be taken for granted in the United States, Europe, or anywhere. Just like any other governmental decision, trade policies are inevitably and constantly subject to citizens' scrutiny. Trade measures cannot survive if they are not supported by both politicians and citi-

---

[2] See, e.g., Rodriguez, F. and Rodrik, D. (1999) *Trade Policy and Economic Growth: A Skeptic's Guide to the Cross-National Evidence*, National Bureau of Economic Research, Working Paper 7081 (http://www.nber.org/papers/w7081.pdf); Samman, E. (2005) *Openness and Growth: An Empirical Investigation*, United Nations Development Programme, Occasional Paper 2005/22 (http://hdr.undp.org/sites/default/files/hdr2005_samman_emma_22.pdf).

[3] See, e.g., CBC NEWS (2015) "NAFTA 'a Disaster' and I'll Renegotiate, Says Donald Trump" (25 September 2015, http://www.cbc.ca/news/business/nafta-a-disaster-and-i-ll-renegotiate-says-donald-trump-1.3 244280); Del Real, A. J and Sullivan, S. (2016) "Trump: TPP Trade Deal 'Pushed by Special Interests Who Want to Rape Our Country'", *The Washington Post*, 28 June 2016 (https://www.washingtonpost.com/news /post-politics/wp/2016/06/28/trump-tpp-trade-deal-pushed-by-special-interests-who-want-to-rape-our-country/?utm_term=.8257c8348bfb).

zens, otherwise they become illegitimate. Policymakers who still believe in the virtues of free trade should ask themselves whether conventional trade policies address the concerns of the common citizen. Trade policies cannot be designed in governmental offices without having due regard to the consequences of their implementation in real life. It is necessary to move beyond the technical consensus of experts and seek the legitimacy that only the popular vote can bring. If trade policies are blatantly disconnected from the reality of citizens' quotidian concerns, they easily become an electoral weapon in the hands of populist, demagogue politicians.

The current backlash against free trade calls for an assertive, effective response. Trade's legitimacy crisis is not a fleeting one – restoring the credibility of the global trading system is a long-term project (Harris 2016). It is necessary to devise and implement a "better trade agenda" able to restart the momentum toward liberalization that responds to the several legitimate concerns uttered by voters (Bergsten et al. 2017). European citizens need to feel confident about the benefits of free trade and reassured that its inevitable side effects are properly tackled.

## KEEP ON TRADING ... BUT NOT BUSINESS AS USUAL

In the face of mounting anti-globalization sentiment, the EU has repeatedly affirmed its open market strategy and commitment to free trade. The European Commission's latest trade and investment policy, released in 2015, bears a catchy title: *Trade for All: Towards a More Responsible Trade and Investment Policy* (European Commission 2015). While it was released a few months before the ascendance of Trump and Brexit, its focus on three plain principles – effectiveness, transparency, and values – already denotes the need to rethink and realign trade policymakers' traditional modus operandi. This new approach was not blessed by the gift of foretelling: the backlash against free trade is not a novel phenomenon and it was already abundantly clear that trade policy could no longer be conducted as business as usual.

At first glance, the slogan 'trade for all' denotes a concern with making trade policy a 'communal' affair or at least an issue where the community has a word to say. But is there a true commitment to making trade policy 'work for all'? After all, one of the pillars of the new trade and investment policy is 'effectiveness'. One may wonder whether the European Commission is ready to move from words to action. Answering that question would require a long-term assessment of the specific policies that have been adopted and their real-life consequences. Such an evaluation is beyond the scope of this chapter. More modestly, the following pages highlight three tools that the European Commission can use to fulfill its pledge, address the growing backlash against free trade policies, and revive public trust in and support for free trade policies.

## Making Trade Policy more Effective

One should not assume that people overwhelmingly support free trade. Many citizens around the world are having (to put it mildly) second thoughts about the overall benefits of free trade policies. European pro-trade politicians and policymakers need to increase public support for free trade, thus reinforcing the legitimacy of their policies. This requires a continuous effort to raise public awareness about the advantages of trade liberalization and the costs associated with protectionist measures. Protectionism is not a novel phenomenon and there are valuable lessons to learn from the past.

However, such a discussion should be frank and evidence-based, not a mere exercise of political persuasion. In the words of Dani Rodrik, "[w]e need to rescue globalization not just from populists, but also from its cheerleaders. Globalization evangelists have done great damage to their cause not just by underplaying the real fears and concerns on which the Trumps of this world thrive, but by overlooking the benefits of a more moderate form of globalization" (Rodrik 2016). Indeed, it is important to acknowledge that, despite its overall benefits, free trade policies have harmed some sectors of the economy. It is vital to launch a serious discussion about the impact of international trade on jobs and economic equality. Policies on trade liberalization have a profound impact on the national and global levels and cannot be based on erroneous assumptions.

Impact assessment studies may play an important role in this regard. These studies collect quantitative and qualitative information on the connection between proposed policies and their likely positive or negative consequences (Kirkpatrick and George 2008a). The ex-ante assessment of proposals offers data that negotiators can integrate into the negotiation process in order to address public concerns (Kirkpatrick and George 2014). Moreover, the ex-post appraisal of policies provides policymakers with figures on their actual effectiveness (George et al. 2011). This enables negotiators and governments to weigh the advantages and drawbacks of trade and investment policies and reshape them when they are not adequate. Impact assessment studies may also help to manage the expectations of varied stakeholders and reduce dissatisfaction with the regime (Franck 2013).

Trade impact assessment studies have been conducted over the last years by national governments, international organizations, and non-governmental organizations.[4] Within the EU, there are two types of studies concerning the

---

[4] See, e.g., United Nations Environment Programme (2001) *Reference Manual for the Integrated Assessment of Trade-Related Policies* (http://unep.ch/etb/etp/acts/manpols/refmania_final.pdf); Asian Development Bank (2008) *How to Design,*

impact of trade policies: Impact Assessments (IAs) (European Commission 2009) and Sustainability Impact Assessments (SIAs) (European Commission 2016). IAs are prepared by the European Commission services and accompany College of Commissioners' decision to request a negotiating authorization from the European Council, together with the draft negotiating directives to be issued by the latter. Once the Commission receives the negotiating mandate, a trade SIA is launched. While IAs are conducted before the negotiating mandate is granted, and analyze whether action should be taken, trade SIAs take place after the negotiation process has been initiated, discussing what actions to implement and their likely consequences. Another difference is that IAs are undertaken by Commission services, while SIAs are carried out by external consultants, with the Commission commenting on their findings via so-called 'position papers'.

The European Commission has been carrying out SIAs on all trade agreements negotiated since 1999. SIAs are defined by the European Commission as "a trade-specific tool developed for supporting major trade negotiations conducted under the aegis of the EU Commissioner for Trade. SIAs are a key tool for the conduct of sound, evidence-based and transparent trade negotiations" (European Commission 2016, p. 4). They complement the initial IA conducted by the Commission before negotiations are launched (European Commission 2016, pp. 3, 14). Despite the use of the term 'sustainability', SIAs go beyond the mere assessment of environmental impact, also gauging the economic, social, and human rights consequences of trade agreements, thereby offering important inputs on the nexus between these different dimensions (Gehring et al. 2017, pp. 163–165). Furthermore, these studies calculate the effect of trade agreements not only in the EU, but also in the partner country and developing countries (European Commission 2016, p. 5), thereby making a significant contribution to regional and global governance (Kirkpatrick and George 2006). The SIA mechanism signals an effort by the European Commission to adopt a new policymaking process that pursues diverse goals simultaneously: "evidence-based policymaking", "better governance", "sustainable development", and the need to "act globally" (Kirkpatrick and George 2003).[5] Do trade impact assessment studies help to make trade policies more effective?

---

*Negotiate, and Implement a Free Trade Agreement in Asia* (https://aric.adb.org/pdf/fta_manual.pdf); Organisation for Economic Co-operation and Development (2010) *Guidance on Sustainability Impact Assessment* (https://www.oecd.org/greengrowth/46530443.pdf).

[5] According to the European Commission (2016), SIAs are inspired by six key principles: they are "integrated, independent, evidence-based, transparent, participatory, and proportionate" (http://trade.ec.europa.eu/doclib/docs/2016/april/tradoc_154464.PDF).

The adoption by the Commission of trade SIAs was a strategic political decision aimed at reducing civil society opposition to trade liberalization policies (Kirkpatrick and George 2012). From an optimistic perspective, it can be argued that SIAs have a positive impact since they engage civil society in the consultation and dialogue process, thereby contributing to a greater consideration by the Commission of the impact of trade policies (Kirkpatrick and George 2012, p. 85). The Commission comments on the findings of these studies through 'position papers' defining points of agreement, responding to disagreements and considering further actions to be implemented (George et al. 2016). Civil society groups and parliamentarians in both the EU and its partner countries also make use of the findings of SIAs in their submissions to governments, thus seeking to influence the negotiation process (Kirkpatrick and George 2012, p. 84). These studies are also receiving increasing attention from the European Parliament (Kirkpatrick and George 2012, p. 75). By offering opportunities for greater transparency and public dialogue, these studies help to build capacity and increase cooperation, thus enhancing the credibility and legitimacy of trade and investment agreements (Zvelc 2012).

Some authors are less optimistic about any real-life effect of impact assessment studies. To start with, the Commission is not bound by the findings of these studies (Baxewanos and Raza 2013). Even if they recommend measures to mitigate the negative impact of proposed policies, there is no guarantee that they will be implemented (Baxewanos and Raza 2013, p. 12). Impact assessment studies have been criticized for focusing on justifying the Commission's proposals (European Commission 2007). Instead of being used by trade negotiators to develop and implement sustainable policies, trade SIA studies may simply provide an appearance of legitimacy that justifies pre-existing trade negotiations (Baxewanos and Raza 2013). These studies are not intended to influence policymaking directly, but rather indirectly through the promotion of public dialogue (Kirkpatrick and George 2008b).

The SIA process does not allow for sufficient consultation from non-corporate stakeholders and civil society organizations (Maes 2009). The choice of relevant stakeholders is often selective, with those consulted not having the necessary information to make their participation effectively (Baxewanos and Raza 2013). Some non-governmental organizations have revealed difficulties in devoting sufficient resources to commenting on the complex and lengthy process of SIAs, leading to a decrease in interest, attention, and resources devoted to this mechanism (Alf et al. 2008).

Improvements in terms of public participation are needed (von Homeyer et al. 2009). The creation of a proper legal framework on trade SIAs should include specific procedures for public participation (Gehring et al. 2017). New mechanisms to increase transparency and consultation should be implemented. The European Economic and Social Committee, for instance, has suggested the creation of a civil society monitoring mechanism including actors from business, trade unions, NGOs, academia and others (European Economic and Social Committee 2011).

## MAKING TRADE POLICY MORE TRANSPARENT

The European Commission, the leading negotiator of European trade agreements, has been facing criticism for an alleged lack of transparency.[6] The fact, however, is that transparency in diplomatic negotiations is a paradox (Delimatsis 2017). There is no rule of public international law prohibiting confidential negotiations between governments (Herrmann 2015). The privacy of trade and investment negotiations, be it at the bilateral, regional or multilateral level, is a time-honored practice (Herrmann 2015). The EU has also been following this praxis for a long time (Abazi 2016).

The EU is represented in the negotiation process by officials from the European Commission Directorate-General for Trade who meet with officers from partner countries in private. According to some commentators, the negotiation behind closed doors of an international agreement with tremendous economic and social impact undercuts democratic values (Monbiot 2013). The secrecy of the negotiations is perceived by others as a symbol of a hidden agenda against the interests of European citizens, directed at increasing the profit of multinational corporations (Pitlik 2016). The opacity or downright secrecy of trade and investment negotiations contributes to citizens' loss of trust in European trade policymaking.

In November 2014, the European Commission unveiled its 'Transparency Initiative' (European Commission 2014). This initiative was adopted to address the backlash regarding the Transatlantic Trade and Investment Partnership (TTIP). Different actions were advanced as part of a "fresh start" on the TTIP in order to "win public trust and support" (European Commission 2014). These measures were expected to "help to ensure greater access to trade documents by the general public and the European Parliament and legitimacy EU trade policy at large" (European Commission 2014, p. 2). The list of actions included the provision of more extensive access to documents, notably by making public all the negotiating texts that the Commission already shared

---

6 See, e.g. Garrido, M. V. (2013) "Business as Usual: On Untransparency, Lack of Participation, and Unaccountability in Free Trade Negotiations", in Cardoso, D., Mthembu, P., Venhaus, M. and Garrido, M. V. (eds), *The Transatlantic Colossus: Global Contribution to Broaden the Debate on the EU/US Free Trade Agreement*. Berlin Forum on Global Politics, Internet & Society Collaboratory and FutureChallenges.org; Stoczkiewicz, M. and Pica, E. (2013) "EU and US both Threatened by Secret Trade Talks", *EU Observer* (16 December 2013, https://euobserver.com/opinion/122467).

with the Member States and the European Parliament; the review of the classification of information related to TTIP; and the decision to keep such information classified only up to the point when it is shared with the other party.

The 'transparency initiative' goes beyond anything seen before in the EU (Hannah 2016). The Commission started to make available the EU's negotiating texts and position papers (European Commission 2018). This was the first time that this kind of document was made public at an early period of the negotiations and constituted a significant landmark in the Commission's efforts to promote the transparency of the negotiating process (Delimatsis 2017). The initiative was designed to give TTIP a 'fresh start', implicitly acknowledging that there was something wrong with the original approach. The negotiations started from the point of near absolute secrecy (Goyens and Auffret 2015), causing significant damage that had to be repaired (Novotna 2016). The Commission's new professed philosophy is that "[g]etting TTIP right means … being as open as possible about what we're negotiating".[7] On a dedicated webpage, the Commission makes available the EU's negotiating texts and position papers, chapter by chapter.[8]

A second impulse towards greater transparency took place in October 2015, when the European Commission presented its new trade and investment policy (European Commission 2015). The document starts with a sort of mea culpa by the EU Trade Chief, Cecilia Malmström:

> In recent years we have seen an intense debate about trade across the European Union which has some important lessons for EU trade policy. It is clear Europeans want … to know more about trade negotiations carried out in their name. In this new strategy … the Commission is adapting its approach to trade policy to take all of these lessons on board. As a result, trade policy will become more responsible, meaning it will be more effective, more transparent and will not only project our interests, but also our values. To make trade negotiations more transparent, the strategy commits to publishing key negotiating texts from all negotiations, as happens in the Transatlantic Trade and Investment Partnership (TTIP). (European Commission 2015, p. 5)

The document states that "[t]rade policy is more debated today than at any time in recent years, with many asking whether it is designed to support broad European interests and principles or the narrow objectives of large firms" (European Commission 2015, p. 18). The Commission claims to take "these concerns seriously. Policymaking needs to be transparent and the debate needs to be based on facts" (European Commission 2015, p. 5). The new trade and

---

7 See the European Commission website: "How We'll Make TTIP Happen" (http://ec.europa.eu/trade/policy/in-focus/ttip/about-ttip/process/#_transparency).

8 Ibid.

investment policy adds that "[l]ack of transparency undermines the legitimacy of EU trade policy and public trust. There is a demand for more transparency in trade negotiations, particularly when dealing with domestic policy issues like regulation. The Commission has taken unprecedented steps in response to this demand, in particular in publishing EU negotiating proposals" (European Commission 2015, p. 19) According to the document, "[t]ransparency should apply at all stages of the negotiating cycle from the setting of objectives to the negotiations themselves and during the post-negotiation phase" (European Commission 2015, p. 19). The Commission pledges to "actively engage with civil society and the public at large in the context of the civil society dialogues and citizens' dialogues" (European Commission 2015, p. 18) Besides, the Commission will "at launch, invite the Council to disclose all FTA negotiating directives immediately after their adoption; during negotiations, extend TTIP practices of publishing EU texts online for all trade and investment negotiations and make it clear to all new partners that negotiations will have to follow a transparent approach; and after finalizing negotiations, publish the text of the agreement immediately, as it stands, without waiting for the legal revision to be completed" (European Commission 2015, p. 19).

Is the current practice of the European Commission enough to make trade policy more transparent?

From an optimistic perspective, the new approach of the Commission to the negotiation process makes TTIP's transparency record unique (Delimatsis 2017). Naturally, the public clamor for greater access to negotiating documents and the ensuing involvement of the European Ombudsman played a decisive role in this change of attitude (Delimatsis 2017). Furthermore, the European Parliament has also increased its involvement in the negotiations, thanks to the TTIP's political prominence (Héritier et al. 2015). The transparency of the TTIP negotiations seems exceptional compared to the secrecy that traditionally marks intergovernmental negotiations (Rossi 2015). From this viewpoint, the TTIP represents a turning point towards a standard of transparency that is completely innovative in the panorama of intergovernmental negotiations (Rossi 2015, p. 21).

However, some commentators are not so enthusiastic. The initial release of a few negotiating texts was labeled by some as a sham since many of those documents had already been leaked online. The perception that the new posture of the Commission was nothing more than window dressing only contributed to fuel criticism (Winter 2016). While acknowledging that the Commission's efforts to publish its proposals are positive and even laudable, some authors believe that they are insufficient (Goyens and Auffret 2015). It has been argued that released documents on negotiating positions only contain general statements of intent that do not offer any meaningful information (Moody 2015). A higher level of transparency should be pursued, namely through the publication of consolidated negotiating texts as soon as possible.[9] However, since the United States refuse to disclose their proposals and consolidated negotiating texts, it seems impossible for the European Commission to elevate its transparency standard (Goyens and Auffret 2015). This is problematic. As the general public only has access to the initial position of one of the parties – the EU – there is the risk that, once texts are consolidated, the public is unaware of fundamental alterations.

Impact assessment studies, discussed above, also contribute to increasing the transparency of trade policymaking. In fact, the trade SIA program offers stakeholders in both the EU and its partner countries an opportunity to share their views with negotiators and policymakers. These studies also inform the general public about the potential effects of projected policies by including mechanisms for public participation and consultation (Berger 2008). Consultation with stakeholders and experts can shed light on relevant issues that are frequently overlooked during negotiations (Gehring and Segger 2015). This open, participatory debate about the consequences of international agreements might help policymakers to integrate societal concerns such as sustainable development more fully into trade policies (Abaza and Hamwey 2001).

While the direct influence of these studies on the decision-making process seems low, it can be said that they nevertheless contribute to raising public awareness about the broader consequences of trade policies (Kirkpatrick and George 2009). Impact assessment studies force policymakers to collate and evaluate evidence as they make decisions and produce a statement to explain their options. SIAs allow for a discussion between a broad range of stakeholders about a diversity of issues that would not be included in a traditional trade agenda (Harrison 2010). One should also take into account the power of public pressure. If concerns are raised by civil society groups that are refuted without proper justification, they may trigger significant public opposition (Alf et al. 2008). The existence of impact assessment studies requires policymakers to engage in discussion with the general public (Alf et al. 2008). Such studies are a significant, incremental step when compared with the secretive way trade negotiations were traditionally conducted.

The European Commission seems committed to a higher level of transparency in the negotiation of international trade agreements. This is a positive development that contributes to the democratization of a process that can significantly impact the lives of European citizens (Rossi 2015, p. 19). This

9 See, e.g., Transatlantic Consumer Dialogue (2015) "Letter to Ambassador Michael Froman and Commissioner Cecilia Malmström, of 30 January 2015" (http://tacd.org/wp-content/uploads/2015/01/TACD-letter-to-Froman-and-Malmstr%C3%B6m.pdf).

heightened standard of transparency is totally innovative in the panorama of intergovernmental negotiations, especially compared to the current situation on the other side of the Atlantic (Rossi 2015, p. 21).

Still, the European Commission also seems to be aware of the need to strike a balance between a high standard of transparency and the secrecy or privacy necessary to ensure a fruitful negotiation. Access to information regarding the negotiating process is generally limited to prevent the ultimate failure of negotiations (Puccio 2016). An excessive measure of transparency may cause delays, hamper the efficiency of the process, or even result in a breakdown in negotiations (Delimatsis 2017). Furthermore, restrictions to public access to documents might be necessary to safeguard a legitimate interest in the protection of strategic elements of the negotiations (Delimatsis 2017). Even if certain documents have already been transmitted to the other party, that does not mean that they should be made public, as disclosure can put the EU's interests regarding international relations at risk (Delimatsis 2017).

The benefits of transparency need to be balanced against its potential drawbacks, adopting a balanced approach to the secrecy/transparency dichotomy. Whereas a certain level of privacy ensures that negotiating parties have sufficient room for bargaining, negotiation results should be disclosed after every negotiation round to allow for public discussion and input (Janusch 2013). This methodology combines public and private stages of negotiation, depending on their timing and sensitiveness, and achieves a high level of transparency without compromising the need to create mutual trust between all the involved parties (Cottier and Temmerman 2013).

Finally, one should bear in mind that besides the two dimensions of transparency discussed above, there is a third, internal facet to the concept, referring to the exchange of information between the European Commission and the European Parliament. Under the EU's institutional architecture, the Commission has an obligation to report regularly to the Parliament on the progress of negotiations.[10] Where agreements between the EU and third countries or international organizations need to be negotiated and concluded, the Parliament shall be immediately and fully informed at all stages of the procedure.[11] Furthermore, consent by the Parliament is required before the conclusion of the agreement by the Council.[12] Being the chamber of European citizens, the European Parliament plays a decisive role in monitoring the nego-

---

10 Consolidated version of the Treaty on the Functioning of the European Union [2012], OJ C326/47, Art. 207(3).

11 Ibid., Art. 218(10).

12 Treaty on the Functioning of the European Union (n 104), Art. 218(6)a.

tiations and ensuring that they comply with high standards of transparency and democratic participation.

In its latest trade and investment policy, the European Commission states:

> As co-legislator alongside the Council, the European Parliament also has a central role in ensuring full democratic scrutiny and accountability of trade policy. The Parliament and the Commission have intensified their interaction, ensuring the close involvement of the Parliament at every step of the negotiations. The Commission will also step up its efforts to promote an informed debate in Member States and a deeper dialogue with civil society at large. This is an opportunity to raise people's awareness about ongoing and planned trade and investment negotiations, and to get feedback on issues from stakeholders concerned. (European Commission 2015)

European negotiators are well aware that consent by the European Parliament will be directly influenced by public opinion (Goyens and Auffret 2015). If accusations of secrecy and opacity of the negotiating process become unbearable, members of the Parliament may succumb to the pressure and reject the trade agreement. The European Parliament's rejection of ACTA in 2012 is a vivid example that lack of transparency leads to a reduction in public trust that may result in the failure of the agreement (Cottier and Temmerman 2013). Avoiding the repetition of this precedent requires paying greater attention to the issue of transparency in the conduct of the negotiations (Fabry et al. 2014).

Transparency should be a basic component of trade and investment negotiations. Taking into account the overall decline in trust, both in national governments and parliaments as well as in the EU, policymakers cannot conduct negotiations as they traditionally did (Dullien et al. 2015). The Commission's emphasis on transparency over the last few years is an auspicious step in the right direction (Winter 2016). The availability of relevant information pertaining to trade and investment agreements may diminish public criticism and help to restore the image of the EU as a credible institution that negotiates on behalf of all Europeans (Winter 2016). While the current practice can always be improved and fine-tuned, it already strikes a reasonable, sensible balance between the principles of transparency and democratic scrutiny; and the need to ensure orderly, fruitful international negotiations.

## Making Trade Policy Work for All

There is a rift between international trade policy and national concerns. Gardels and Berggruen (2017, p. 71) remind us that "[e]lites may think global, but people react local". The European Commissioner for Trade recently conceded that for globalization to succeed, it must work at both the global and local levels:

> [t]his is a way to try to spread the benefits of globalisation, across countries and across communities. To show that trade is good for people across countries, in different communities. It shows open trade is good for creating jobs, investment and growth all over. In this way, hand in hand with domestic measures, we work to address the backlash to trade at home. (Malmström 2019)

Overall, trade policies contribute to promoting global development. However, it is also true that occasionally they make victims at the domestic level (Lewis 2007). Free trade has helped to reduce inequality between countries considerably, but it also led to growing inequalities at the domestic level, particularly in developed nations (Rodrik 2017). Ironically, the global trading system benefits countries as a whole but makes some citizens richer and others poorer (Katz 2017).

Many voters facing financial difficulties blame liberalized trade for their predicaments (Meyer 2017). Academic reports reach contrasting conclusions on the precise contribution of factors such as technological evolution for growing unemployment rates in some sectors of the economy and rising inequality (Gardels and Berggruen 2017). Populist politicians blame free trade policies and liberal internationalism for all misfortunes that befall open economies, especially lost jobs. On balance, it does not seem fair to ascribe all the blame to trade rules. Trade policies and globalization more broadly are easy scapegoats for many structural changes that took place over the last decades (Irwin 2017). Many countries did not adjust to the new challenges of technological development, digitalization and automation of labor, which called for the implementation of new domestic measures (Tapp et al. 2017).

The unfairness of a system where only some citizens are benefited has been portrayed as "the international trade regime's Achilles' Heel" (Meyer 2017, p. 996). It should not cause any surprise that many see trade as the main source of job loss and economic inequality. Free trade advocates must acknowledge that trade policies have drawbacks and demonstrate their efforts to mitigate them (Bergsten et al. 2017). International trade agreements have hitherto failed to safeguard those citizens harmed by their policies (Meyer 2017). It is necessary to enhance the legitimacy of free trade policies among common citizens by dispelling the image that they only benefit large multinationals and the elite (Tucker 2017). Policymakers need to adopt new, effective measures that address citizens' legitimate anxiety about the economy and the job market (Irwin 2017). In a word, global trade governance cannot be disconnected from domestic policies (Gardels and Berggruen 2017).

## CONCLUDING REMARKS

European trade policy faces multiple challenges. Trump and Brexit rocked the foundations of the global trading system, turning trade policy into a highly politicized topic. While it is still early to assess the full consequences of the two electoral results on international politics, one thing seems to be certain: they were game-changers – the game of trade policymaking will never play in the same way.

If European policymakers wish to save the international trade system, they need to convince citizens of its overall benefits. Public discontent will not be properly tackled if trade policies are designed and implemented in a conventional, old-fashioned way; rather, the continuation of the trade liberalization project calls for new approaches and policies (Meyer 2017).

If European leaders firmly believe that globalization is "a force for good" (Malmström 2019), and that "trade is much more than money" (Malmström 2019), then they need to move from words to action and design measures that help citizens affected by globalization and the technological revolution (Katz 2017), ensuring that more citizens benefit from them (Tapp et al. 2017). In a word, trade policy needs to become more "inclusive" (Tapp et al. 2017, p. 628). One of the reasons that may explain the hostility of some Americans toward trade policies is the insufficiency of policies directly aimed at protecting those harmed by globalization (Tapp et al. 2017; Alden and Litan 2016). Public spending on worker retraining and replacement, for instance, is much lower in the United States than in most European countries (Alden and Litan 2016). The use of these measures may reduce social and political resistance to trade liberalization and the globalization process and build greater consensus around these policies (Tapp et al. 2017). The existence of adjustment programs for workers, for instance, seems to increase public favor about free trade policies (Scheve and Slaughter 2001). Advocating for the maintenance and expansion of free trade policies requires the creation of adequate compensation measures (Veeman 2017).

A more inclusive trade agenda also requires a rethinking of the policymaking process itself. Measures should be adopted to enhance public confidence in the discussion and the conclusion of international trade agreements (Tapp et al. 2017). Policymakers and politicians should create mechanisms that allow for greater public participation at the domestic and international levels (Tucker 2017). Well-informed citizens are more likely to support public policies when they feel engaged in their making.

# REFERENCES


Abaza, H. and Hamwey, R. (2001) Integrated Assessment as a Tool for Achieving Sustainable Trade Policies. *Environmental Impact Assessment Review*, **21**(6), 481–510.

Abazi, V. (2016) European Parliamentary Oversight Behind Closed Doors. *Cambridge Journal of International and Comparative Law*, **5**(1), 31–49.

Alden, E. and Litan, R. (2016) *A Winning Trade Policy for the United States*. New York: Council on Foreign Relations.

Alf, L., Assmann, C., Bauer, M. and Weinkopf, J. (2008) *Towards a Transatlantic Dialog on Trade and the Environment*. New York: Henry Luce Foundation.

Baxewanos, F. and Raza, W. (2013) *Human Rights Impact Assessments as a New Tool for Development Policy?* Vienna: Austrian Foundation for Development Research. https://www.econstor.eu/handle/10419/98807.

Berger, G. (2008) Sustainability Impact Assessment: European Approaches. In Organisation for Economic Co-operation and Development (ed.), *Conducting Sustainability Assessments*. Paris: OECD.

Bergsten, F. C., Truman, E. M. and Zettelmeyer, J. (2017) *G-7 Economic Cooperation in the Trump Era 4*. Peterson Institute for International Economics, Policy Brief 17-15.

Blendon, R. J., Casey, L. S. and Benson, J. M. (2017) Public Opinion and Trump's Jobs and Trade Policies. *Challenge*, **60**(3), 228–244.

Brands, H. (2017) U.S. Grand Strategy in an Age of Nationalism: Fortress America and its Alternatives. *The Washington Quarterly*, **40**(1), 73–94.

Chandy, L. and Seidel, B. (2016) Donald Trump and the Future of Globalization. *Brookings Up Front*. https://www.brookings.edu/blog/up-front/2016/11/18/donald-trump-and-the-future-of-globalization.

Cottier, T. and Temmerman, M. (2013) Transparency and Intellectual Property Protection in International Law. In Bianchi, A. and Peters, A. (eds), *Transparency in International Law*. Cambridge: Cambridge University Press, 197–220.

Delimatsis, P. (2017) TTIP, CETA, and TiSA Behind Closed Doors: Transparency in the EU Trade Policy. In Griller, S., Obwexer, W. and Vranes, E. (eds), *Mega-Regional Trade Agreements: CETA, TTIP, and TiSA – New Orientations for EU External Economic Relations*. New York: Oxford University Press, 216–245.

Dullien, S., Garcia, A. and Janning, J. (2015) *A Fresh Start for TTIP*. European Council on Foreign Relations. http://www.ecfr.eu/page/-/ECFR124_-_TTIP.pdf.

European Commission (2007) *The Evaluation Partnership: Evaluation of the Commission's Impact Assessment System*. Final Report. http://ec.europa.eu/smart-regulation/impact/key_docs/docs/tep_eias_final_report.pdf.

European Commission (2009) *Impact Assessment Guidelines*. http://ec.europa.eu/smart-regulation/impact/commission_guidelines/docs/iag_2009_en.pdf.

European Commission (2014) Communication to the Commission Concerning Transparency in TTIP Negotiations, C(2014) 9052 final.

European Commission (2015) *Trade for All: Towards a More Responsible Trade and Investment Policy*. http://trade.ec.europa.eu/doclib/docs/2015/october/tradoc_153846.pdf.

European Commission (2016) *Handbook for Trade Sustainability Impact Assessment*, 2nd ed. http://trade.ec.europa.eu/doclib/docs/2016/april/tradoc_154464.PDF.

European Commission (2018) *The EU's Position in the Negotiations*. http://ec.europa.eu/trade/policy/in-focus/ttip/documents-and-events/index_en.htm#eu-position.

European Commission (2019) *EU-US Relations: Interim Report on the Work of the Executive Working Group*. http://trade.ec.europa.eu/doclib/docs/2019/january/tradoc_157651.pdf.

European Economic and Social Committee (2011) Opinion of the European Economic and Social Committee on the Role of Civil Society in the Free Trade Agreement Between the EU and India. REX/316CESE1612/2011. http://www.eesc.europa.eu/?i=portal.en.rex-opinions.20331.

Fabry, E., Garbasso, G. and Pardo, R. (2014) *The TTIP Negotiations: A Pirandello Play*. European Policy Center and Jacques Delors Institute. http://www.notre-europe.eu/media/ttipnegotiationsfabrygarbassopardone-jdijan14.pdf?pdf=ok.

Franck, S. (2013) Managing Expectations: Beyond Formal Adjudication. In Echandi, R. and Sauvé., P. (eds), *Prospects in International Investment Law and Policy: World Trade Forum*. Cambridge: Cambridge University Press, 371–387.

Gardels, N. and Berggruen, N. (2017) Salvaging Globalization. *New Perspectives Quarterly*, **34**(1), 67–79.

Gehring, M. and Segger, M.-C. (2015) Overcoming Obstacles with Opportunities: Trade and Investment Agreements for Sustainable Development. In Schill, S., Tams, C. and Hofmann, R. (eds), *International Investment Law and Development: Bridging the Gap*. Cheltenham, UK and Northampton, MA, USA: Edward Elgar Publishing, 93–124.

Gehring, M., Stephenson, S. and Segger, M.-C. (2017) Sustainability Impact Assessments as Inputs and as Interpretative Aids in International Investment Law. *The Journal of World Investment & Trade*, **18**(1) 163–199.

George, C., Iwanow, T. and Kirkpatrick, C. (2011) Sustainability Impact Assessments Applied to Regional Integration. In Lombaerde, P., Flôres Jr., R., Iapadre, L., and Schulz, M. (eds), *The Regional Integration Manual: Quantitative and Qualitative Methods*. Abingdon: Routledge, 247–269.

George, C., Iwanow, T. and Kirkpatrick, C. (2016) EU Trade Strategy and Regionalism: Assessing the Impact on Europe's Developing Country Partners. In Lombaerde, P. and Schulz, M. (eds), *The EU and World Regionalism: The Makability of Regions in the 21st Century*. Abingdon: Routledge, 63–82.

Goyens, M. and Auffret, L. (2015) TTIP: What Is in It for Consumers? *Intereconomics*, **50**(6), 312–343.

Hannah, E. (2016) *NGOs and Global Trade: Non-State Voices in EU Trade Policymaking*. Abingdon: Routledge.

Harris, J. M. (2016) America, Europe and the Necessary Geopolitics of Trade. *Survival*, **58**(6), 63–92.

Harrison, J. (2010) *Human Rights Impact Assessments of Trade Agreements: Reflections on Practice and Principles for Future Assessments*. https://warwick.ac.uk/fac/soc/law/research/centres/chrp/governance/2010-hria-background-paper-harrison.pdf.

Héritier, A., Moury, C., Schoeller, M. G., Meissner, K. L. and Mota, I. (2015) *The European Parliament as a Driving Force of Constitutionalisation*. European Parliament, Directorate General for Internal Policies. http://www.europarl.europa.eu/RegData/etudes/STUD/2015/536467/IPOL_STU(2015)536467_EN.pdf.

Herrmann, C. (2015) Transleakancy. In Herrmann, C., Simma, B. and Streinz, R. (eds), *Trade Policy between Law, Diplomacy and Scholarship*. Cham: Springer, 39–46.

Irwin, D. A. (2017) The False Promise of Protectionism: Why Trump's Trade Policy Could Backfire. *Foreign Affairs*, **96**, 45–56.

Janusch, H. (2013) Public Protests and FTA Negotiations with the United States: Lessons for the TAFTA/TTIP. In Cardoso, D., Mthembu, P., Venhaus, M. and Garrido, M. V. (eds), *The Transatlantic Colossus: Global Contribution to Broaden the Debate on the EU/US Free Trade Agreement*. Berlin Forum on Global Politics, Internet & Society Collaboratory and FutureChallenges.org.

Katz, R. (2017) The Trade Debate (Continued) But Where to Go from Here? *The International Economy*, **31**(1).

Kirkpatrick, C. and George, C. (2003) *Sustainability Impact Assessment of World Trade Negotiations: Current Practice and Lessons for Further Development*. Impact Assessment Research Center Working Paper no. 2. https://ideas.repec.org/p/ags/idpmia/30587.html.

Kirkpatrick, C. and George, C. (2006) Methodological Issues in the Impact Assessment of Trade Policy: Experience from the European Commission's Sustainability Impact Assessment (SIA) Programme. *Impact Assessment and Project Appraisal*, **24**(4), 325–334.

Kirkpatrick, C. and George, C. (2008a) Assessing the Sustainability of Trade Policies and Agreements. In Organisation for Economic Co-operation and Development (ed.), *Conducting Sustainability Assessments*. Paris: OECD.

Kirkpatrick, C. and George, C. (2008b) Sustainability Impact Assessment of Trade Agreements: From Public Dialogue to International Governance. *Journal of Environmental Assessment Policy and Management*, **10**(1), 67–89.

Kirkpatrick, C. and George, C. (2009) Creation of Processes: Sustainability Impact Assessments. In Tussie, D. (ed.), *The Politics of Trade: The Role of Research in Trade Policy and Negotiation*. Leiden: Brill, 55–82.

Kirkpatrick, C. and George, C. (2012) Political Challenges in Policy-Level Evaluation for Sustainable Development: The Case of Trade Policy. In Von Raggamby, A. and Rubik, F. (eds), *Sustainable Development, Evaluation and Policy-Making: Theory, Practice and Quality Assurance*. Cheltenham, UK and Northampton, MA, USA: Edward Elgar Publishing, 73–90.

Kirkpatrick, C. and George, C. (2014) Trade and Development: Assessing the Impact of Trade Liberalisation on Sustainable Development. *Journal of World Trade*, **38**(3), 441–469.

Lewis, M. K. (2007) WTO Winners and Losers: The Trade and Development Disconnect. *Georgetown Journal of International Law*, **39**(1), 165–198

Maes, M. (2009) Civil Society Perspectives on EU-Asia Free Trade Agreements. *Asia Europe Journal*, **7**(1), 97–107.

Malmström, C. (2019) Speech at the Atlantic Council, 10 January, Washington DC. https://ec.europa.eu/info/news/trade-trends-2019-2019-jan-10_en.

Meyer, T. (2017) Saving the Political Consensus in Favor of Free Trade. *Vanderbilt Law Review*, **70**(3), 985–1026.

Monbiot, G. (2013) This Transatlantic Trade Deal is a Full-Frontal Assault on Democracy. *The Guardian*, 4 November. https://www.theguardian.com/commentisfree/2013/nov/04/us-trade-deal-full-frontal-assault-on-democracy.

Moody, G. (2015) European Commission Announces Major Transparency Initiative for TAFTA/TTIP. https://www.techdirt.com/articles/20150107/07102529619/european-commission-announces-major-transparency-initiative-taftattip.shtml.

Novotna, T. (2016) *EU View: Four Reasons Why TTIP May Fail and Why it Will Be Europe's Fault*. LSE Ideas Dahrendorf Forum – Debating Europe Special Report SR022 (May).

Pitlik, H. (2016) Lack of Trust, Campaigning and Opposition against the TTIP. In Gnan, E. and Kronberger, R. (eds), *Transatlantische Handels- und Investitionspartnerschaft zwischen der EU und den USA (TTIP)*. Vienna: Facultas, 221–232.

Puccio, L. (2016) *TTIP: Access to Consolidated Texts and Confidential Documents*. European Parliamentary Research Service. http://www.europarl.europa.eu/thinktank/en/document.html?reference=EPRS_BRI(2016)580909.

Rodrik, D. (2016) Put Globalization to Work for Democracies. *The New York Times*, 17 September. https://www.nytimes.com/2016/09/18/opinion/sunday/put-globalization-to-work-for-democracies.html.

Rodrik, D. (2017) *Is Global Equality the Enemy of National Equality?* John F. Kennedy School of Government, Harvard University, RWP 17-003.

Rossi, S. (2015) The TTIP: A New Generation Treaty. *The Federalist Debate*, **28**(2), 18–22.

Scheve, K. F. and Slaughter, M. J. (2001) *Globalization and the Perceptions of American Workers*. Washington, DC: Peterson Institute for International Economics.

Smith, K. E. (2017) The European Union in an Illiberal World. *Current History*, **116**(788), 83–87.

Tapp, S., Van Assche, A. and Wolfe, R. (2017) A Road Map for More Inclusive Canadian Trade Policy. In Tapp, S., Van Assche, A. and Wolfe, R. (eds), *Redesigning Canadian Trade Policies for New Global Realities*. Montreal: Institute for Research on Public Policy (IRPP), 593–633.

The Economist (2015) Playing with Fear. *The Economist*, 12 December. https://www.economist.com/news/leaders/21679792-america-and-europe-right-wing-populist-politicians-are-march-threat.

The Wall Street Journal (2016) Michael Froman: Where the TPP Stands. *The Wall Street Journal*, 19 June. https://www.wsj.com/articles/michael-froman-tells-where-the-tpp-stands-1466388124.

Thompson, G. F. (2017) Populisms and Liberal Democracy: Business as Usual? *Economy and Society*, **46**(1), 43–59.

Tucker, T. N. (2017) *The Sustainable Equitable Trade Doctrine: Building Progressive International Cooperation to Counter Right-Wing Economic Authoritarianism*. New York: Roosevelt Institute.

Veeman, M. (2017) North American Trade Policy for Agriculture and Forestry: Can Economics Trump Politics? *Canadian Journal of Agricultural Economics*, **65**(1), 43–68.

Von Homeyer, I., Collins, M. and Ingwersen, W. (2009) Improving Public Participation in Sustainability Impact Assessment of Trade Agreements. In Ekins, P. and Voituriez, T. (eds), *Trade, Globalization and Sustainability Impact Assessment: A Critical Look at Methods and Outcomes*. London: Earthscan, 189–208.

Winter, E. (2016) Trade for All or Unity at Stake? Reclaiming a Legitimate and Single Voice for EU Trade Policy. Transatlantic Policy Symposium 2016 at Georgetown University. http://tapsgeorgetown.com/wp-content/uploads/2016/02/Elisabeth-Winters-Trade-for-All-or-Unity-at-Stake.pdf.

Zvelc, R. (2012) Environmental Integration in EU Trade Policy: The Generalised System of Preferences, Trade Sustainability Impact Assessments and Free Trade Agreements. In Morgera, E. (ed.), *The External Environmental Policy of the European Union: EU and International Law Perspectives*. New York: Cambridge University Press, 174–203.

# 17. The EU and the US on investor-state dispute settlement reform

**Emily Gilson**

## INTRODUCTION

Both the European Union and the United States have joined the global chorus that investor-state dispute settlement (ISDS) drastically needs reform. The readouts from the United Nations Commission on International Trade Law (UNCITRAL) Working Group III on ISDS reform is proof enough that the EU, the US, and others in the international arbitration community agree there are several problems inherent to ISDS that must be solved to ensure investment disputes are more fairly adjudicated and multilateral in nature. The EU and the US have highlighted faults of the current ISDS system; a brief history of cases like *Philip Morris v. Uruguay* clearly demonstrates ways ISDS provisions can be misused or abused (Olivet and Villareal 2016).

Thus, the EU and the US have developed new approaches in reforming ISDS. The EU is pushing for ISDS mechanisms that are consistent with EU law and place ISDS within the purview of the EU, as seen in cases like *Achmea v. Slovakia*. The US, however, is advocating for ISDS reform by greatly reducing its use in future treaties, as seen in the US-Mexico-Canada Agreement's (USMCA) investment chapter. Both the EU and the US argue their approach would result in a more fair, transparent, and accountable ISDS system that benefits every sovereign nation – in other words, both claim their approach would achieve true multilateralism in the international arbitral system. Ultimately, both approaches use 'multilateralism' to disguise the fact that they put the EU or America first in their pursuit of a 'balanced' ISDS regime without jointly engaging with other countries.

Since *Achmea* was decided in March 2018 and the USMCA only entered into force on 1 July 2020, it is difficult to fully assess their respective impacts on investment law at this stage. Presumably, the effects of these ISDS approaches will be better understood when they have been active for a longer period. Therefore, the publicly available opinions of US and EU practitioners, scholars, and politicians in the international arbitration community are the best way to evaluate the implications of these respective positions. Through a two-year analysis of these differing perspectives, this chapter will highlight how the EU and the US's attempts to reform ISDS prioritize their own interests through manipulating legal doctrine – via autonomy of EU law for the EU and cherry-picking ISDS tools for the US – instead of indicating a real ambition to transform ISDS into a multilateral regime with committed rule of law principles.

## *ACHMEA* OVERVIEW

The *Achmea* case is the clearest example of the EU's modern approach to ISDS reform. In March 2018, for the first time, the Court of Justice of the European Union (CJEU) ruled in Slovak Republic v. Achmea BV (Case C-284/16) that an investor-state arbitration clause in a bilateral investment treaty (BIT) between two EU states was incompatible with EU law (Nichols and Tout 2018). To some Member States, this decision was considered surprising because past decisions, such as the *EU-Singapore* case, had clarified that the EU and its Member States would share competence regarding ISDS in relation to foreign direct investment and non-direct investment if the Member States were required to act as respondents in certain types of investment disputes (Grill 2017). Prior to their accession to the EU, 196 intra-EU BITs were concluded between Central and Eastern European states and older EU Member States, such as Germany and France (Gáspár-Szilágyi 2018). After these Central and Eastern European states acceded to the EU in 2004, 2007, and 2013, legal professionals wondered whether these BITs between former third party and current EU Member States would remain compatible with EU law (Gáspár-Szilágyi 2018). However, as far as the CJEU and the European Commission are concerned, there is no doubt about that compatibility (or rather incompatibility) after *Achmea*.

To understand the full weight of the *Achmea* case on ISDS within the EU, though, it is important to understand its rather convoluted background. The dispute originated from Slovakia's reversal of its reformed, liberalized healthcare system (Blanck 2018). After its accession to the EU in 2004, Slovakia opened its market for private medical insurance services (Blanck 2018). As a result, the Dutch insurance company Achmea established a subsidiary in Slovakia. Under the terms of a bilateral investment treaty the Netherlands and Slovakia had signed in 1991, Achmea began selling insurance services in Slovakia (Gáspár-Szilágyi 2018). In 2006, however, Slovakia partially reversed its 2004 reforms and prohibited the distribution of profits generated by insurance sales to shareholders, which prevented Achmea from operating in Slovakia (Nichols and Tout 2018; Gáspár-Szilágyi 2018; Blanck 2018; Jones 2018). In 2011, this prohibition was ruled as contrary to the Slovak

Constitution by Slovakia's Constitutional Court, once again allowing the distribution of profits for private insurers (Blanck 2018). That ruling was too late, however, as Achmea had already initiated an UNCITRAL arbitration against Slovakia under the terms of Article 8 of the Netherlands-Slovakia BIT (authorizing investor-state arbitration), alleging that "Slovakia's 2006 measures ... had caused damages to its investments in Slovakia" and had violated the terms of the BIT (Gáspár-Szilágyi 2018; Risse and Oehm 2018; Nichols and Tout 2018). As arbitration under the UNCITRAL rules is a form of ad hoc arbitration, and because Germany was chosen as the place of arbitration in the original BIT, the arbitration proceedings were governed by German law and the seat of the UNCITRAL tribunal was in Frankfurt, Germany (Carswell and Winnington-Ingram 2018). Slovakia objected to the UNCITRAL tribunal's jurisdiction by arguing that Article 8 of the BIT was incompatible with EU law and became invalid when Slovakia joined the EU in 2004 (Blanck 2018).

During this UNCITRAL arbitration, the European Commission intervened to support Slovakia's claim that the arbitral tribunal was improper under EU law (Nichols and Tout 2018). The UNCITRAL tribunal dismissed Slovakia's jurisdictional claims in 2010, and the case proceeded to a final award on the merits (Nichols and Tout 2018; Blanck 2018). In 2012, the UNCITRAL tribunal rendered its final award: Slovakia was ordered to pay 22.1 million euros plus interest in damages to the Achmea group for breaching the BIT's fair and equitable treatment standard, as well as for violating its "obligation to ensure the free transfer of payments" for Achmea's shareholders (Gáspár-Szilágyi 2018; Nichols and Tout 2018). As Frankfurt was the seat of arbitration, Slovakia challenged the arbitral award in the Higher Regional Court of Frankfurt in 2014, arguing again that the arbitral award violated "several provisions of EU law, in particular ... the Treaty on the Functioning of the European Union (TFEU)" because "the tribunal had lacked jurisdiction due to Article 8's incompatibility with EU law", but its action was dismissed (Risse and Oehm 2018; Blanck 2018; Nichols and Tout 2018). Slovakia immediately appealed that decision to Germany's highest civil court, the *Bundesgerichtshof* (Gáspár-Szilágyi 2018; Nichols and Tout 2018).

In 2016, the *Bundesgerichtshof* opined that "there was no incompatibility between EU law and the BIT", but referred the "compatibility" issue to the CJEU under Article 267 TFEU's preliminary reference procedure to determine "whether the arbitration agreement in the ... BIT was compatible with the TFEU" as a precaution (Gáspár-Szilágyi 2018; Nichols and Tout 2018). Article 267 is especially important in *Achmea* because it specifically authorized the CJEU to interpret the EU's foundational treaties, as well as to "interpret and determine the validity of acts of the institutions, bodies, offices or agencies of the EU" (Blanck 2018). When a question of interpretation is before a "court or tribunal of an EU member state", such as the *Bundesgerichtshof* in Achmea, Article 267 authorizes, but does not require the court or tribunal to request a ruling on the interpretive question from the CJEU in the form of a preliminary reference (Blanck 2018). This Article 267 procedure is extremely important for the EU judicial system, as it helps to produce uniform and consistent interpretations of EU law (Blanck 2018).

The three questions the *Bundesgerichtshof* posed to the CJEU as a preliminary reference to determine Article 8's adherence to EU law, specifically on "whether the application of the ISDS provisions in intra-EU BITs were precluded under EU law", were:

1. Whether Article 344 TFEU, which provides for exclusive CJEU jurisdiction "for disputes concerning the interpretation or application of EU treaties", precluded applying a provision that permitted investor-state arbitration under an intra-EU BIT;
2. If the first question was answered negatively, whether Article 267 TFEU, which provides the courts and tribunals of EU Member States with the mechanism to refer questions of EU law to the CJEU for a preliminary ruling, would preclude the application of an investor-state arbitration provision in an intra-EU BIT;
3. If the first two questions were both answered negatively, whether Article 18.1 TFEU, which provides anti-discrimination provisions, precluded the application of an investor-state arbitration provision in an intra-EU BIT because "the protections afforded by [intra-EU] BITs are not universally applicable to all EU Member States" (Nichols and Tout 2018; Carswell and Winnington-Ingram 2018).

Before the CJEU revealed its decision, one of the CJEU's advocates general (AG), Melchior Wathelet, provided an opinion which claimed "the [Netherlands-Slovakia] BIT's arbitration clause was not incompatible with EU law and was not discriminatory" (Nichols and Tout 2018; Risse and Oehm 2018). In responding to the *Bundesgerichtshof*, AG Wathelet concluded that intra-EU BITs were not in breach of EU law because:

1. The BIT was not discriminatory on nationality grounds that favored Dutch investors; thus, it did not violate Article 18 TFEU;
2. The arbitral tribunal created in the BIT was "a court or tribunal of a Member State" as defined by Article 267 TFEU, and thus could request the CJEU to issue preliminary rulings on questions of EU law if necessary; and
3. Investor-state disputes did not fall within the scope of Article 344 TFEU, and interpreting the obligations of intra-EU BITs would not concern "the interpretation or application of EU treaties" (Fouchard and Krestin 2018).

The CJEU, however, diverged from AG Wathelet's opinion on a key legal issue: the primacy of EU law. The CJEU first ruled on whether Articles 267 and 344 TFEU precluded a provision in an international agreement between EU Member States under which "an investor from one Member State may bring proceedings against another Member State before an arbitral tribunal, whose jurisdiction that Member State has undertaken to accept" (Power 2018). The CJEU ultimately held that the arbitration clause in *Achmea* was incompatible with EU law. The CJEU began its analysis by noting EU law had "primacy" over the law of the Member States (Blanck 2018). An international agreement, such as the Netherlands-Slovakia BIT, "could not affect the allocations of EU powers as set by the TFEU or the Treaty on the European Union (TEU)" (Blanck 2018). The CJEU then analyzed Articles 267 and 344 together under this "EU autonomy" framework (Blanck 2018):

1. First, an investment tribunal, in fulfilling its mandate under a BIT, could be required to interpret or apply EU law, which is contrary to Article 344 and past EU case decisions (Nichols and Tout 2018).
2. Second, the investment tribunal could not "be said to form part of the judicial system of either the Netherlands or Slovakia" and, as such, was not a "court" that could refer questions to the CJEU for a preliminary ruling, which is contrary to Article 267 (Nichols and Tout 2018). This arbitral tribunal was explicitly created by the BIT under UNCITRAL rules and was not a part of the judicial system of either Slovakia or the Netherlands; thus, the arbitral tribunal "has no power to make a reference to the CJEU for a preliminary ruling" (Fouchard and Krestin 2018; Gáspár-Szilágyi 2018). The CJEU could also not classify this arbitral tribunal as a court "common to several member states", like the Benelux Court of Justice, because it was expressly created by the ISDS provisions in a BIT (Gáspár-Szilágyi 2018). Furthermore, the CJEU determined that "the awards of such a tribunal [were] not subject to review by Member State courts to an extent that would allow them to refer a question to the CJEU on issues of EU law raised before the arbitral tribunal" (Gáspár-Szilágyi 2018). The Court also differentiated between commercial and investor-state arbitration awards, as ISDS "removes disputes from the judicial systems of the Member States and thus the EU" in a way commercial arbitration does not (Gáspár-Szilágyi 2018).
3. Finally, an arbitral tribunal's award was not subject to review by an EU Member State court, which is required by TEU Article 19, because of the "finality and one-sidedness" of investor-state arbitration (Nichols and Tout 2018; Fouchard and Krestin 2018). The arbitral tribunal also undermines the primacy of EU law because the tribunal may have to interpret or apply EU law, given that the arbitral tribunal must derive its ruling from

the law of the contracting state in the dispute as well as other international agreements between Slovakia and the Netherlands, which includes EU law; the arbitration clause in the BIT overall "removes disputes involving the interpretation or application of EU law from the mechanism of judicial review provided for by the EU legal framework" (Fouchard and Krestin 2018).

The CJEU also "criticized the absence of a universally applicable mechanism for judicial review of an arbitral award" because a review of any arbitral award within an EU member state will take place within, and be subject to, the national law of the country where the seat of arbitration is placed; according to the CJEU, these differences in jurisdiction will lead to inconsistent and unharmonious arbitral judgments and awards (Carswell and Winnington-Ingram 2018). *Achmea*, then, is clearly an attempt to put ISDS under the purview of EU authorities and to harmonize the EU legal order.

With EU autonomy in mind, *Achmea* was an immediate success for the European Union as an institution. As a direct consequence of the *Achmea* decision, EU Member States are now under an obligation to remove all intra-EU investor-state arbitration mechanisms that are like the one in Article 8 of the Netherlands-Slovakia BIT, even for Member States that have not yet terminated their intra-EU BITS and their sunset clauses. The CJEU "has interpreted this obligation to go as far as Member States having to denounce their prior international agreements" (Gáspár-Szilágyi 2018).

**Past Cases Involving BITs?**

It is important to note that until *Achmea*, arbitral tribunals "routinely rejected submissions that arbitration clauses in intra-EU BITs [were] incompatible with EU law" (Nichols and Tout 2018). This is also what inevitably led to the CJEU's decision in *Achmea*. In intra-EU BIT cases involving the Energy Charter Treaty (ECT) like *RREEF Infrastructure v Spain*, for example, the arbitral tribunal opined:

> Should it ever be determined that there existed an inconsistency between the ECT and EU Law … the unqualified obligation in public international law of any arbitration tribunal constituted under the ECT would be to apply the former. This would be the case even were this to be the source of possible detriment to EU law. EU law does not and cannot 'trump' public international law. (Schepel 2018)

In these past cases, arbitral tribunals rejected the idea of their "EU incompatibility" using a sort of conflicts-rules analysis: there was "no relevant material inconsistency or conflict" contained in the treaty's provisions; "no need to rule on matters of EU law" to solve the underlying dispute; no incompatibility of treaty obligations between the parties; and no BIT issue "that could not be solved by a 'harmonious interpretation'" of the BIT and any relevant EU obligations/treaties (Schepel 2018). Going from the CJEU's past decisions on unified market systems and the autonomy of EU law, a case-by-case or treaty-by-treaty analysis of this type by an ad hoc arbitral tribunal, which was unaffiliated with the EU court hierarchy, on whether a dispute settlement provision, applicable law clause, or award is compatible with EU law would inevitably be "unpredictable and lead to legal uncertainty" compared to a standardized, EU-stipulated court practice (Schepel 2018). *Achmea*, then, is not a surprising decision because the CJEU attempted to solve this conflicts law issue through developing a form of "field preemption", or "autonomy caselaw", based on TEU Article 19 (Schepel 2018). Via this field preemption analysis, the CJEU now "not only outlaw[s] the application of EU Law by any judicial body outside the European judicial hierarchy, but the application of any rules other than those of EU law in fields covered by EU law" – which is exactly the end result in *Achmea* (Schepel 2018).

## Consequences of *Achmea*

Opinions on whether *Achmea* actually resolved ISDS issues within the EU – or even if it was reasonable to adjust ISDS in the EU under an EU autonomy framework – are mixed. Some EU lawyers argue that the *Achmea* decision and its reformation of ISDS should not have come as a surprise, given that "the European Commission has consistently advocated against intra-EU BITs" (Nichols and Tout 2018). Since at least 2015, the European Commission has called on Member States to terminate their intra-EU BITs (Blanck 2018). The Commission viewed these BITs as arrangements that run contrary to the foundational principles of the EU single market because their provisions as applied can result in more favorable treatment for investors from certain Member States (Nichols and Tout 2018). Prior to *Achmea*, as noted by AG Wathelet in his opinion, the Commission had also regularly made submissions during arbitrations as 'amicus curiae' to investment tribunals, annulment committees, and national courts to argue that intra-EU arbitration clauses are contrary to the TFEU (particularly arguing a breach of Article 344 and Article 267, which were the primary questions posed by the *Bundesgerichtshof*) (Nichols and Tout 2018; Blanck 2018).

*Achmea*'s take on ISDS also cannot be found 'surprising' by many EU lawyers because it aligns with past case decisions that prioritize EU primacy and autonomy (Eckes 2018). For past intra-EU BIT decisions based on the ECT like *Electrabel*, for example, the arbitral tribunal determined that EU law "would prevail over the ECT in case of any material inconsistency (para. 4.191)" (Schepel 2018). "The autonomy of the EU legal order", according to

German lawyer and European law scholar Christina Eckes, can only be preserved by a judicial system that can "ensure the consistency and interpretation of EU law" (Eckes 2018). The EU legal system would be "undermined" if disputes were removed from the purview of the EU judicial system and taken to arbitral tribunals, which are not a part of the EU judicial system and thus cannot ask preliminary questions for interpretive guidance to the CJEU (Art. 267) (Eckes 2018). An infamous example of this line of thought as applied to EU case law is the CJEU's rejection of the EU's accession to the European Convention on Human Rights draft agreement in 2014 (Eckes 2018).

*Achmea* could ultimately be seen as a success for the EU in its reform of ISDS: on 5 May 2020, every EU Member State except for Austria, Ireland, Finland, and Sweden signed the Agreement for the Termination of Bilateral Investment Treaties between the Member States of the European Union ("the Agreement") to "implement … where the Court found that investor-State arbitration clauses in intra-EU bilateral investment treaties are incompatible with the EU Treaties" (Fermeglia and Mistura 2020). Following this agreement's entry into force, all intra-EU BITs and any incorporated 'sunset clauses' will be officially terminated (Fermeglia and Mistura 2020). Moreover, any intra-EU ISDS cases pending before intra-EU ISDS tribunals will either be: formally suspended or discontinued (Art. 7); subject to a settlement procedure that takes "into due account" national and CJEU case law (Art. 9); or brought before EU domestic courts, provided that an investor withdraws from the arbitration proceedings, renounces any award already issued but not yet enforced, and makes a claim based on national or EU law (Art. 10) (Fermeglia and Mistura 2020). Although this agreement is still subject to ratification, it is clear that Achmea is shaping the parameters of permissible investment protections and disputes within the EU.

Additionally, the *Achmea* decision has asserted its precedence when deciding intra-EU BIT cases with ISDS provisions in favor of EU autonomy. On 31 October 2018, the *Bundesgerichtshof* itself followed *Achmea*'s reasoning and set aside the Dutch insurer's (Achmea) favorable award (Jones 2018). According to the *Bundesgerichtshof*, the CJEU's ruling meant that there was no valid arbitration offer under the Netherlands-Slovakia BIT and the tribunal lacked the appropriate jurisdiction to hear it (Jones 2018). The court also ordered Achmea to cover the arbitral costs associated with the proceedings (Jones 2018). Achmea opposed the award by arguing that many tribunals in intra-EU arbitrations have subsequently adopted narrow interpretations of the judgment without going so far as to invalidate the entire BIT, such as in *Masdar*, *Vattenfall*, and *UP and CD Holdings v Hungary* (Jones 2018). Achmea also claimed that Slovakia "was prevented by German principles of good faith from … arguing that the offer to arbitrate was now invalid" because Slovakia had participated in the arbitration and had not attempted to terminate the BIT at any point (Jones 2018). The court rejected these arguments based on the primacy of EU law as delineated in *Achmea* (Jones 2018). The court also declined to transfer the case to Germany's Constitutional Court because it "concerned a principle of public international law" (Jones 2018).

On the other hand, some EU lawyers and scholars feel that the EU autonomy asserted in *Achmea* will result in more questions or problems than answers for awards rendered under ISDS. Some lawyers and legal scholars claim that *Achmea* will not affect investments made before a Member State acceded to the EU (as they would arguably not involve EU law), but will cause a lot of uncertainty if a measure that causes an investment dispute occurs after a Member State accedes to the EU (Newing et al. 2018). Even though the "substantive protections" of those BITs still exist for now (even post Agreement), an investor would have no way to effectively enforce them: as the arbitral tribunals composed by intra-EU BITs are incompatible with EU law, any award rendered by them will also be incompatible with EU law (Gáspár-Szilágyi 2018). Member States will also be prohibited from enforcing the awards from arbitral tribunals formed under intra-EU BITS, which means that these Member States could "breach their obligations under the ICSID Convention and the New York Convention" (Gáspár-Szilágyi 2018). Although claims in the remaining intra-EU BITs can instead be brought before a host State's courts and align with *Achmea*'s analysis of EU primacy, many investors do not find this alternative satisfactory (Newing et al. 2018). Their argument is that some Member State jurisdictions have court systems that are slower and less developed, and/or still have due process and partiality issues toward the actions of their governments even in the EU's "harmonized market system", which is why ISDS was an appealing alternative in the first place (Newing et al. 2018).

Furthermore, many current investors in the EU do not want the scrutiny of EU autonomy in their investments. After *Achmea*, some investors have been advised to restructure their intra-EU investments through holding companies outside the EU to escape the jurisdiction of the CJEU and to regain enforceable ISDS protections in their pre-existing BITs (Nichols and Tout 2018). In the past, investors favored Dutch or Luxembourg holding companies to "benefit from BIT protections" and their "more favorable tax arrangements" (Nichols and Tout 2018). According to multinational firms like Dentons, however, investors should "consider routing their investments through a non-EU jurisdiction such as Switzerland" so their EU-affiliated BITs will continue to be enforceable (Nichols and Tout 2018).

Another jurisdiction some investors may consider is the United Kingdom (UK) since exiting the EU in January 2020. The United Kingdom itself already has 12 BITs with Central and Eastern European countries and at least 55 other treaties that have investment provisions, so becoming a 'safe haven' for enforcing intra-EU BITs is not beyond the realm of possibility (Nichols and Tout 2018; Rogers et al. 2017). At the time of this writing, the EU and the UK are in a 'transition period' while the terms of the EU–UK relationship are being negotiated post-Brexit (Australian Government 2020). Until 31 December 2020, the UK was subject to EU rules and regulations – including those concerning free trade agreements (Australian Government 2020). After this date, however, the UK will no longer be subject to EU rules and regulations and will regain its ability to negotiate new investment treaties with other countries (Rogers et al. 2017). As the UK is subject to the primacy of EU law and the CJEU's supremacy until the end of the 'transition' period, any intra-EU BITs that existed pre-Brexit are still subject to the primacy and autonomy of EU law (Newing et al. 2018). Since the aforementioned Agreement will terminate every intra-EU BIT and related 'sunset clauses', the UK will not be able to rely on the arbitration provisions in any pre-Brexit EU BIT: these BITs and any provisions therein will effectively no longer exist (Fermeglia and Mistura 2020).

Given the EU's stance on intra-EU BITs historically, though, UK lawyers have hypothesized for some time that only intra-EU investments or their related disputes that occurred post-Brexit could bypass the CJEU (Newing et al. 2018). Any BITs negotiated post-Brexit, on the other hand, present unresolved questions for foreign investors. The UK could be used as a 'mailbox company' to circumvent the purview of the EU (Corporate Europe Observatory 2020). Since investors and investments from the UK will be considered 'foreign' to the EU by 2021, an EU member state could incorporate an entity or a subsidiary in the UK, let investments 'flow' through that UK entity to another EU member state, and then potentially be able to sue a fellow EU Member State in an ISDS proceeding outside of the EU without falling afoul of EU law (provided that the EU Member States in this hypothetical both have BITs with the UK in 2021) (Corporate Europe Observatory 2020). For investors who do not want the scrutiny of EU institutions in their investments and want to avoid domestic courts, therefore, Brexit could be a 'golden opportunity' (Corporate Europe Observatory 2020).

Since *Achmea* questions the validity and enforceability of previous ISDS awards under its EU autonomy analysis, it caused a 'ripple effect' for past ISDS cases decided on the basis of intra-EU BITs (Risse and Oehm 2018; Carswell and Winnington-Ingram 2018). The CJEU's *Achmea* decision specifically concerned an intra-EU bilateral investment treaty between two Member States, but the question of whether bilateral or multilateral agreements have 'EU law compatible' arbitration clauses or not when the EU itself is a member, like the Energy Charter Treaty (ECT), remains unanswered (Guerrero et al. 2018). The *Achmea* judgment's impact on multilateral investment treaties thus "remains uncertain", but the trend seems to be that such arbitration clauses are compatible in ECT investment disputes (Guerrero et al. 2018). In April 2018, for example, Germany requested the ICSID arbitral tribunal to dismiss its case against the Swedish investor Vattenfall (ICSID ARB 12/12) for a "lack of jurisdiction" following the CJEU's *Achmea* decision (Risse and Oehm 2018). Germany requested the ICSID tribunal to dismiss Vattenfall's claim as inadmissible based on the reasoning of the *Achmea* decision by the CJEU: "that arbitration proceedings between investors from the EU and an EU member state are *per se* inadmissible" (Risse and Oehm 2018; Reuters 2018). On 31 August 2018, the tribunal in *Vattenfall AB v. Germany* rejected Germany's jurisdictional argument (Goh 2018). The Vattenfall tribunal found no rule in the *Achmea* ruling that applied to interpreting the ECT, stating that an *Achmea* analysis "cannot be applied to multilateral treaties, such as the ECT, to which the EU itself is a party" (Goh 2018). According to ECT-based tribunals like Vattenfall thus far, the subject matter of the ECT does not involve questions of EU law. Even if an arbitral tribunal were required to interpret EU law under an ECT-based intra-EU BIT, it could request a preliminary reference from the CJEU because the EU itself is a party to the ECT (Goh 2018). Nevertheless, the Vattenfall tribunal stressed, that "ambiguity" in the *Achmea* judgment and in *Achmea's* application to the ECT still remains (Goh 2018). If "incompatibility" between ECT arbitration and EU law is ever found, the Vattenfall tribunal declared that it is up to the EU Commission, not the tribunal, to remedy such a situation (Goh 2018). Therefore, *Vattenfall* and other ECT-based intra-EU BIT disputes indicate there is still some uncertainty with regards to multilateral treaties under an *Achmea* analysis, but the general trend appears to be that multilateral treaties where the EU itself is a member are exempt from immediate nullification or cancellation (Goh 2018). This attitude towards the ECT seems to be supported many years past *Achmea*: despite the EU proclaiming that intra-EU ISDS claims are "incompatible" with EU law in the May 2020 Agreement for the Termination of Bilateral Investment Treaties between Member States of the European Union, intra-EU ISDS claims made under the ECT are specifically absent from this termination process (Fermeglia and Mistura 2020).

On the other hand, ICSID seems to have entirely rejected the CJEU's *Achmea* analysis – which goes against the EU's assertion that it should have primacy over intra-EU BIT matters. In November 2018, ICSID for the first time ruled that the CJEU's *Achmea* opinion "cannot defeat the jurisdiction of a [ICSID] tribunal constituted under an intra-EU BIT" in French checking company Up Groupe's claim against Hungary under the France-Hungary BIT (Bilbow 2018). In rejecting Hungary's objection to the arbitral tribunal under EU law, the tribunal decided "Achmea does not apply to an ICSID arbitration based on an intra-EU BIT" because the tribunal's jurisdiction already existed under the 1965 ICSID Convention (Bilbow 2018). Thus, any jurisdictional questions "should be viewed in a public international law context", instead of in a national or regional context – thus escaping the "primacy" of EU law analysis (Bilbow 2018). Moreover, the tribunal claimed it was "undisputed" that Hungary did not expressly terminate its participation in and submission to arbitration under the ICSID Convention when it joined the EU (Ross 2018). The tribunal also rejected the idea that acceding to the EU was an "implied withdrawal" from the ICSID Convention, as Hungary again made no direct denunciation of ICSID's applicability (Ross 2018). According to Up Groupe's representative, global law firm Quinn Emanuel Urquhart & Sullivan, "this case ... ruled that the Achmea decision has no impact whatsoever on an ICSID arbitration based on an intra-EU BIT, [and] endorses the principle that a state may not withdraw its consent to arbitration under international law simply by invoking its domestic or regional law" (Bilbow 2018).

For the time being, Up v. Hungary "appears to be the first case which is not based on the multilateral investment protection treaty (such as ECT), but still remained unaffected by the Achmea judgment" (Bilbow 2018). If ICSID cases remain 'immune' from Achmea, this could encourage investors to incorporate ICSID arbitration mechanisms into future investment treaty agreements with the EU (especially given that the ICSID Convention permits direct enforceability of ICSID awards without the New York Convention) (Bilbow 2018). The cases going before ICSID would probably not find their way in EU courts anyway, which means that ICSID's potential as a 'loophole' for *Achmea* analysis is still very limited (Bilbow 2018).

## *Achmea* and the Multilateral Investment Court

The uncertainty surrounding investments that fit under *Achmea's* analysis arguably strengthens the EU's push for an EU-wide investment court system (Newing et al. 2018). As the CJEU itself brought up the need for "a universally applicable" investment review mechanism in *Achmea*, the decision clearly signals the EU's intent to create an investment court system (Carswell and Winnington-Ingram 2018). As pending and future intra-EU BIT dispute cases no longer can be heard by independent ad hoc tribunals after *Achmea*, such cases must by necessity either go before a domestic court or be heard by an EU arbitration body, like the European Commission's long-proposed multilateral investment court (MIC). As the European Commission has strongly advocated for a MIC to resolve ISDS issues since 2015, it is reasonable to assume that *Achmea* was decided so all ISDS considerations in the EU fall under the purview of its judicial system (Grill 2017). Conveniently, former European Commissioner for Trade, Cecilia Malmström, had publicly stated that the best way to ensure consistency in ISDS is through an established court body like the MIC – thus indicating why *Achmea* was decided differently compared to past intra-EU BIT disputes (Malmström 2018). EU practitioners may differ on whether *Achmea* was appropriate, but most are in favor of moving towards a MIC. There are still differing opinions, however, about whether the MIC will be effective compared to the current ISDS model. According to some Member States, the MIC proposal announced in 2018 and 2019 does not address many of ISDS' shortcomings, like how costs, transparent proceedings, and judge appointments will be handled (Bilbow 2018). The explicit exclusion of intra-EU BITs in the EU since *Achmea* has only cemented some States' perception "that [the] CJEU (and ECJ before it) caselaw interfere[s] with national sovereignty", and the idea of an EU-led MIC does not exactly change that negative perception (Bilbow 2018).

Nevertheless, the CJEU cleared a "key legal hurdle" for the European Commission's version of ISDS reform through Opinion 1/17 on 30 April 2019 (Crevon-Tarassova et al. 2019). Opinion 1/17 officially concluded that the investment court system proposed in the EU and Canada's Comprehensive Economic and Trade Agreement (CETA) does not conflict with EU law (Crevon-Tarassova et al. 2019). CETA's hybrid court and arbitral tribunal framework, if implemented, will pave the way for similar dispute resolution mechanisms to be instituted in several agreements, like the EU-Singapore, EU-Vietnam, and EU Mexico treaties (Gouiffès et al. 2019). Thus, Opinion 1/17 should be considered a foundational step in the EU's pursuit of its version of ISDS reform. Although this decision could easily be the subject of its own chapter, understanding and comparing its major analytical points with those of *Achmea* illustrate how Opinion 1/17 is the next step in the EU's ISDS reform process.

As it did in *Achmea*, the CJEU addressed three main questions about CETA's investment court system:

1. Whether it was compatible with EU law;
2. Whether it was compatible with the general principle of equal treatment and the requirement of effectiveness; and
3. Whether it was compatible with the right to access an independent tribunal (Crevon-Tarassova et al. 2019).

The CJEU differentiates CETA from *Achmea* by stressing some key principles throughout its analysis; these include the principle of "mutual trust" and "sincere cooperation" between EU Member States, which would not be the case between an EU Member State(s) and non-Member States like Canada (Gouiffès et al. 2019; Syzszczak 2019). In AG Yves Bot's opinion from January 2019, for example, he argued that the European Union "might not be able to promote and encourage EU investors or attract foreign investment … without adequate and reciprocal substantive and procedural protection of investments" as seen in a neutral investment court (Declève and Van Damme 2019). Moreover, because CETA's drafters did not give it direct effect, both AG Bot and the CJEU affirm that investors "will not be able to invoke its provisions before domestic courts" (Gáspár-Szilágyi 2019). What neither analysis sufficiently explains is why the move to an investment court system is needed or is 'better' than traditional ISDS mechanisms in other treaties. As EU investment law scholar Szilárd Gáspár-Szilágyi pointedly argued in an analysis on AG Bot's opinion, "whether a [dispute resolution mechanism] is compatible with EU law is a different question than whether [such a dispute resolution mechanism] is needed" (Gáspár-Szilágyi 2019).

Another "key principle" to distinguish CETA from *Achmea* is the autonomy of EU law in CETA's investment court system (Batselé 2019). The CJEU noted "CETA tribunals could only apply the provisions of the relevant CETA sections" to any disputes heard and could only use EU law as a basis to establish facts (and not as interpretive guidance) (Batselé 2019). However, there is nothing to stop CETA from being applied indirectly at the domestic court level (Gáspár-Szilágyi 2019). Moreover, the enforcement of an award where the CETA Tribunal applies/reads EU law provisions that are not yet interpreted by the CJEU can indeed "affect the uniform application of EU law", as CETA's investment court system is not provided a preliminary reference system to ensure consistent interpretations (Gáspár-Szilágyi 2019).

The *Achmea* opinion is far from outdated, even in light of Opinion 1/17, and should still be discussed in terms of the EU's ISDS reform process. As previously mentioned, it is still unclear whether the CJEU can "review future decisions from an investment court for compliance with EU law", which could happen if an investment court decision applied or interpreted EU law that has not yet been authoritatively determined (or is contradictory) and a claimant is seeking enforcement of such an inconsistent decision (Crevon-Tarassova et al. 2019). This could also happen if a claimant successfully challenges, as attorneys in Dentons phrase it, "what may be defined as the 'public interest'" (Crevon-Tarassova et al. 2019). The overarching effect of the CETA opinion on the EU's preexisting bilateral investment treaties that do not contain CETA's specific provisions and language for "public interest", especially where Fair and Equitable Treatment provisions are concerned, is similarly unclear at this time (Crevon-Tarassova et al. 2019). Most importantly, CETA, even after Opinion 1/17, is not yet in force. For an investment court "… to begin to operate under CETA, Chapter 8 of the treaty (concerning the investment court system) needs to enter into application", which means the treaty must be (fully) ratified (Crevon-Tarassova et al. 2019; Gouiffès et al. 2019). As CETA is a mixed-competency agreement, it requires ratification with the investment court provisions at the domestic level by all EU countries; this has not happened at the time of this writing (Crevon-Tarassova et al. 2019).

Though the CJEU has clarified "the legal boundaries of ISDS mechanisms under EU law", the political concerns about ISDS are far from quelled (Batselé 2019).

Overall, the *Achmea* decision has serious implications for investment in Europe, especially where EU Member State sovereignty is concerned. To say that *Achmea* resolves ISDS issues under an 'EU autonomy' framework is still premature, however, as even a cursory review of the current scholarship on the decision indicates that the 'EU primacy' approach has several unresolved questions concerning applicability and jurisdiction (as seen in the discrepancies between the *Achmea* and CETA-ICS analyses). Mandating that all ISDS matters be subsumed by EU law is not a genuine commitment to multilateralism; the EU is unwilling to compromise its supremacy in this area, and there is little indication – other than Opinion 1/17 – about how the EU will align its ISDS autonomy with countries outside the EU.

## The US Approach in NAFTA

Does the EU's primacy approach over ISDS cases, as seen in *Achmea*, align with the US view on ISDS? In short: not really. If anything, the modern trend in US investment treaties is to curtail ISDS even more than in *Achmea*. This is clear in the changes the US required during the North American Free Trade Agreement's (NAFTA) renegotiation over the course of 2018, which created the current iteration of the US-Mexico-Canada Agreement (USMCA).

For some context on the US's changed position, it is important to understand what, exactly, NAFTA contained in terms of ISDS. NAFTA is considered one of the first comprehensive free trade agreements that joined developed and developing nations (i.e., Mexico at that time) (Hills 2013). The text of the NAFTA agreement served as a template for subsequent US-negotiated free trade agreements and established an enforceable dispute-resolution mechanism – which included a mechanism for ISDS – to give investors a 'fail-safe' when investing in riskier economies like Mexico (McBride and Aly Sergie 2017).

Former President Donald Trump, however, disparaged the ISDS provision in NAFTA, and his Administration strongly advocated for its removal during NAFTA's renegotiation process (Levy 2017). According to US Trade Representative Robert Lighthizer, protecting American companies against the risks of investing abroad "is effectively providing them with an unfair subsidy" and that administration should prioritize "America First" instead of encouraging investment abroad (Levy 2017). These types of comments ignore the fact that countries like Mexico used ISDS provisions "to reduce the riskiness of investment there" for US investors (Levy 2017). Since Mexico could offer foreign investors improved guarantees of fair treatment through ISDS mechanisms after NAFTA, the US was able to save several industries facing Chinese competition in the 1990s from failing, such as the auto industry, by taking advantage of Mexico's cheaper markets and manufacturing and developing more advantageous supply chains to compete with China in North America (Levy 2017). Notably, none of these are points that Donald Trump or Robert Lighthizer ever raised against US-affiliated ISDS mechanisms. Especially considering that the US heavily used NAFTA's ISDS system and never lost a case as a defendant in the 20+ years NAFTA existed, the US Administration did not appear to have a logical reason for eliminating NAFTA's dispute settlement provisions (Lavranos 2018).

## USMCA and ISDS

Despite all this, the US Administration succeeded in their goal of 'reforming' ISDS in NAFTA. After several months of negotiations for the USMCA, US investors in Canada will now have to arbitrate any violations of the USMCA in domestic, Canadian courts: ISDS stipulations between the US and Canada functionally no longer exist (Bernasconi-Osterwalder 2018). Mexico and the US, on the other hand, negotiated an annex that only allows ISDS in "well-defined circumstances" (Bernasconi-Osterwalder 2018). Within the terms of the annex, investors can bring expropriation and non-discrimination claims to ISDS; "fair and equitable treatment" claims are no longer permissible (Bernasconi-Osterwalder 2018). The US–Mexico dispute resolution annex also requires claimants to first attempt to resolve any dispute in the domestic courts of the US or Mexico before bringing dispute claims to ISDS (Bernasconi-Osterwalder 2018). This is notable because NAFTA originally permitted claimants to go directly to ISDS with a dispute claim (Bernasconi-Osterwalder 2018). Investors now cannot skirt around domestic courts, like they did under the original NAFTA's investment chapter: they must attempt to use local remedies for 30 months (Bernasconi-Osterwalder 2018). ISDS then becomes an option if local remedies do not reach a conclusion (Bernasconi-Osterwalder 2018). Notably, five defined sectors can use traditional investor-state provisions under the USMCA because they are "covered government contracts" with Mexico: oil and natural gas, power generation services, telecommunication services, transportation services, and ownership/ management of infrastructure (Bernasconi-Osterwalder 2018; Heilman Grier 2018). US investors in these sectors can still bring claims based on "most [USMCA] investor protections", even the "fair and equitable treatment" standard (Bernasconi-Osterwalder 2018). They also can initiate ISDS proceedings without exhausting local remedies (Bernasconi-Osterwalder 2018). Robert Lighthizer, who views ISDS "as a means for corporations to undercut [the] country's sovereignty", sees the "paring back" of ISDS in the USMCA as a major win for US interests. In reality, the US has carved out certain ISDS provisions to suit its economic interests instead of simply withdrawing from ISDS (Caporal and Reinsch 2018).

It is important to note that the changes to NAFTA via the USMCA are "mostly cosmetic" (Gertz 2018). With the exception of digital trade rights and the new ISDS stipulations, the USMCA kept most of NAFTA's "essential elements", which is notable for an agreement that Donald Trump once called "the worst trade deal ever approved in this country" (Baum 2018). By scaling-back ISDS provisions, the USMCA fails to protect US citizens and companies that choose to invest abroad, which is crucial for the US economy (Holwill 2018). Trump's claim that he is "keeping jobs at home" by doing away with ISDS, which in his view will eventually correct the US trade deficit, ignores the benefits of protected foreign investment (Holwill 2018). When US companies invest abroad, they actually establish more cost-effective supply chains and more jobs for US citizens through company growth (Holwill 2018). Moreover, using US protectionism to fix bilateral trade imbalances with Mexico and Canada without addressing the US government's spending habits will not reduce the aggregate US trade deficit long-term (Blackwill and Rappleye 2017). Importantly, the investment areas that involve the Mexican government have retained their ISDS protections; if the claim is that ISDS is 'harmful' to US interests, and if US investors would receive the same amount of protection in domestic courts, why has the US kept ISDS protections in the areas that are simultaneously the most profitable and risky for US interests (because of the Mexican government's history of expropriating US and foreign investments) (Mann 2018)? With this in mind, the USMCA's investment chapter conveniently cherry-picked ISDS provisions to keep them where it is obviously in the US's financial interest to do so, which fits very well within that administration's 'America First' rhetoric and the US-first approach to NAFTA renegotiation.

The Trump Administration's argument that ISDS is "not necessary" in Canada because it "has a fully developed legal system" also does not acknowledge several cases where US investors used ISDS in Canada to reverse discriminatory actions by Canadian provinces under the national treatment standard (Holwill 2018). Without ISDS, US investors must now rely on the US government to protect their investments without any guarantee that the government will take their case or make them 'whole' under the USMCA (Holwill 2018). In reality, it is the US investors who are harmed the most by removing ISDS, as Canada and Mexico still have ISDS protections available between them through their membership in the Comprehensive and Progressive Agreement for Trans-Pacific Partnership (CPTPP) (Heilman Grier 2018).

US investors are already having to consider whether they should assert their claims under NAFTA before they lose their access to ISDS. For example, US investor disputes that may arise from the COVID-19 pandemic – which would have been possible to pursue under Chapter 11 of NAFTA – will face additional hurdles and have fewer grounds for pursuing ISDS after the USMCA enters into force (Brown de Vejar et al. 2020). Canadian and Mexican investors will be able to bring investment claims between themselves under the CPTPP, but US investors will only have three years after 1 July 2020 to decide whether to bring claims (between 1 January 1994 and 1 July 2020) under NAFTA before their rights under that agreement are lost (Brown de Vejar et al. 2020).

Overall, the USMCA does not represent ISDS reform for North America. The ISDS stipulations in the USMCA are tailored to best suit US interests in high-profit and high-risk economic sectors. The only 'multilateralism' seen in the US approach to ISDS reform is that of 'America First': institutions or practices are only 'multilateral' if they serve US interests and reflect the 'America First' platform (Skinner 2018).

## CONCLUSION

The EU and the US have very different conceptions about what 'multilateralism' should entail in a new or modified ISDS system. The EU asserts any ISDS reform should ultimately lead to a MIC that is subject to the EU's authority, as the EU believes that an established court body is the only way ISDS awards can be decided consistently and transparently. Alternatively, the US wants to remove ISDS from investment treaties entirely under the presumption that any party would be treated more fairly under State–State arbitration or in the domestic courts. Both approaches, however, inevitably have the same intent: prioritizing their own interests over any other country or entity in the international arbitration community. Stipulating that any EU ISDS matter must be under the auspices of EU law, and not Member State law or country law (as said in *Achmea*), is incompatible with the 'multilateral' intent of the MIC. Similarly, carving out economic exceptions for only US parties in the USMCA is incompatible with the idea that any other country in North America (or elsewhere) will be treated fairly if US interests are at stake.

If countries accept that they will cede some sovereignty in their foreign investment policies to continue investing in the EU, creating a MIC and reforming ISDS in the EU's image under an *Achmea*-type (or CETA-type) analysis is a real possibility in the future. To approach multilateralism more earnestly, though, the EU should clarify the MIC's construction and how it would address modern ISDS concerns with a more definitive (instead of aspirational) proposal. This would show *Achmea* opponents and other countries that the EU's strict approach will still give any country's interests and concerns equal weight. Since the true motivation for reforming the USMCA was to 'rebrand' NAFTA as an agreement that puts the US first, the US has 'reformed' ISDS exactly as it planned: as ISDS 'à la carte' to best suit US economic interests (Lavranos 2018). To say that this is a 'multilateral approach', however, is disingenuous and should instead be called what it actually is: an 'America First' approach to ISDS. How sustainable this approach will be depends on the willingness of other countries to accept that the US will always maintain an aggressive bargaining position – with or without ISDS – in future investment treaties.

## REFERENCES


Australian Government (2020) UK Decision to Leave the EU – Brexit. Australian Government Department of Foreign Affairs and Trade (DFAT). https://www.dfat.gov.au/geo/united-kingdom/brexit#:~:text=On%2023%20June%202016%2C%20the,referred%20to%20as%20%E2%80%99Brexit%E2%80%99.

Batselé, F. (2019) European Investment Policy after the CETA Opinion. United Nations University Institute on Comparative Regional Integration Studies. http://cris.unu.edu/european-investment-policy-after-ceta-opinion.

Baum, C. (2018) Opinion: Trump's Trade and Investment Goals Don't Add Up. *MarketWatch.* https://www.marketwatch.com/story/trumps-trade-and-investment-goals-dont-add-up-2018-01-29.

Bernasconi-Osterwalder, N. (2018) USMCA Curbs How Much Investors Can Sue Countries – Sort Of. *International Institute for Sustainable Development Online.* https://www.iisd.org/library/usmca-investors.

Bilbow, A. (2018) Achmea Rejected. *Commercial Dispute Resolution (CDR) Online.* https://www.cdr-news.com/categories/disputes/8749-achmea-rejected.

Blackwill, R. and Rappleye, T. (2017) Unpacking Trump's 'Alternative Facts' on NAFTA. *Foreign Policy Online.* http://foreignpolicy.com/2017/09/15/unpacking-trumps-alternative-facts-on-nafta/.

Blanck, J. I. (2018) Slovak Republic v. Achmea BV: The Death Knell for Intra-EU BITs? *ASIL Insights Online*, **22**(8). https://www.asil.org/insights/volume/22/issue/8/slovak-republic-v-achmea-bv-death-knell-intra-eu-bits.

Brown de Vejar, K., Gans, K. S. and Westbrook, C. (2020) COVID-19 and investment Claims under NAFTA. *DLA Piper Publications.* https://www.dlapiper.com/en/us/insights/publications/2020/05/covid-19-and-investment-claims-under-nafta/.

Caporal, J. and Reinsch, W. A. (2018) From NAFTA to USMCA: What's New and What's Next? *Center for Strategic and International Studies Online.* https://www.csis.org/analysis/nafta-usmca-whats-new-and-whats-next.

Carswell, C. J. and Winnington-Ingram, L. M. (2018) The CJEU Preliminary Ruling in Slovak Republic v Achmea BV – What Does It Mean for Arbitration under Intra-EU BITs? *Reed Smith Client Alert 2018-080.* https://www.reedsmith.com/en/perspectives/2018/04/the-cjeu-preliminary-ruling-in-slovak-republic-v-achmea-bv.

Corporate Europe Observatory (2020) Post-Brexit EU-UK trade Deal Based on CETA Would Be Bad News. https://corporateeurope.org/en/2020/01/post-brexit-eu-uk-trade-deal-based-ceta-would-be-bad-news.

Court of Justice of the European Union (2018) The Arbitration Clause in the Agreement between the Netherlands and Slovakia on the Protection of Investments is Not Compatible with EU Law. Press Release No. 26/16 (Luxembourg). https://curia.europa.eu/jcms/upload/docs/application/pdf/2018-03/cp180026en.pdf.

Crevon-Tarassova, A., Honlet, J.-C., Howie, R., Lalonde, P., Legum, B. and Stephenson, S. (2019) Investment Court Clears Key Legal Hurdle with Court of Justice of the European Union (CJEU) Opinion 1/17. *Dentons Insights*. https://www.dentons.com/en/insights/articles/2019/may/13/investment-court-clears-key-legal-hurdle.

Declève, Q. and Van Damme, I. (2019) Opinion 1/17 on CETA: Advocate General Bot Finds Investment Court System in CETA Compatible with EU Law. *International Litigation Blog*. http://international-litigation-blog.com/opinion-1-17-ag-bot/.

Eckes, C. (2018) Don't Lead with Your Chin! If Member States Continue with the Ratification of CETA, They Violate European Union Law. *European Union Law Blog*. https://europeanlawblog.eu/2018/03/13/dont-lead-with-your-chin-if-member-states-continue-with-the-ratification-of-ceta-they-violate-european-union-law/.

European Commission (2015) *Investment in TTIP and Beyond – The Path for Reform*. Concept Paper. http://trade.ec.europa.eu/doclib/docs/2015/may/tradoc_153408.PDF.

European Commission Financial Stability and Capital Markets Union (2020) EU Member States Sign an Agreement for the Termination of Intra-EU Bilateral Investment Treaties. https://ec.europa.eu/info/publication/200505-bilateral-investment-treaties-agreement_en.

Fermeglia, M. and Mistura, A. (2020) Killing All Birds with One Stone: Is This the End of Intra-EU BITs (as we know them). *EJIL: Talk!* Blog of the European Journal of International Law. https://www.ejiltalk.org/killing-all-birds-with-one-stone-is-this-the-end-of-intra-eu-bits-as-we-know-them/.

Fouchard, C. and Krestin, M. (2018) The Judgment of the CJEU in Slovak Republic v. Achmea – A Loud Clap of Thunder on the Intra-EU BIT Sky! *Kluwer Arbitration Blog*. http://arbitrationblog.kluwerarbitration.com/2018/03/07/the-judgment-of-the-cjeu-in-slovak-republic-v-achmea/.

Gáspár-Szilágyi, S. (2018) The CJEU Strikes Again in Achmea. Is This the End of Investor-State Arbitration under intra-EU BITs? *Pluricourts Blog*. https://www.jus.uio.no/pluricourts/english/blog/szilard-gaspar-szilagyi/the-cjeu-strikes-again-in-achmea.html.

Gáspár-Szilágyi, S. (2019) AG Bot in Opinion 1/17. The Autonomy of the EU Legal Order v. the Reasons Why the CETA ICS Might Be Needed [AG Bot]. *PluriCourts Blog* (originally published on *European Law Blog*). https://www.jus.uio.no/pluricourts/english/blog/szilard-gaspar-szilagyi/autonomy-vs-reasons.html.

Gertz, G. (2018) 5 Things to Know about USMCA, the New NAFTA. *The Brookings Institution Online*, 2 October. https://www.brookings.edu/blog/up-front/2018/10/02/5-things-to-know-about-usmca-the-new-nafta/.

Goh, F. (2018) E-briefing: Arbitral Tribunal Rules that the ECJ Achmea Decision Is Not Applicable to Intra-EU ECT Arbitrations. *Eversheds-Harry Elias Online*. https://www.eversheds-harryelias.com/content/e-briefing-arbitral-tribunal-rules-ecj-achmea-decision-not-applicable-intra-eu-ect.

Gouiffès, L., Kendra, T., Ordonez, M. and Aubry, L (2019) *The CJEU Holds CETA's Dispute Resolution Mechanism to be Compatible with EU Law*. Hogan Lovells Publications. https://www.hoganlovells.com/en/publications/the-cjeu-holds-cetas-dispute-resolution-mechanism-to-be-compatible-with-eu-law.

Grill, A.-K. (2017) Towards a Post-Arbitration Age: The European Commission's Fast-Track Reform of Investment Dispute Settlement. *Kluwer Arbitration Blog*. http://arbitrationblog.kluwerarbitration.com/2017/12/11/towards-post-arbitration-age-european-commissions-fast-track-reform-investment-dispute-settlement/.

Guerrero, A., Badenes, F. and Namdar, A. (2018) Intra-EU Investment Arbitration in 2028: Will There Be Any BITs at All? *King & Wood Mallesons Online*. https://www.kwm.com/en/au/knowledge/insights/intra-eu-investment-arbitration-in-2028-will-there-be-any-bits-at-all-20181119.

Heilman Grier, J. (2018) USMCA Investor Dispute Settlement: NAFTA Minus. *Perspectives on Trade Blog of Djaghe LLC*. https://trade.djaghe.com/?tag=isds.

Hills, C. A. (2013) NAFTA's Economic Upsides: The View from the United States. *Foreign Affairs Online*. https://www.foreignaffairs.com/articles/canada/2013-12-06/naftas-economic-upsides.

Holwill, R. (2018) New NAFTA May Put 'America First', but it Puts US Investors Last. *The Hill*. https://thehill.com/opinion/finance/417170-new-nafta-may-put-america-first-but-it-puts-us-investors-last.

Jones, T. (2018) Germany's Top Court Shows Obedience to Achmea. *Global Arbitration Review Online*. https://globalarbitrationreview.com/article/1176731/germany%E2%80%99s-top-court-shows-obedience-to-achmea.

Judgment of the Court C/284-16, *Slowakische Republik v Achmea BV* [hereinafter *Achmea*], paras. 35, 50–52, 6 March 2018. http://curia.europa.eu/juris/document/document.jsf?text=&docid=199968&pageIndex=0&doclang=EN&mode=lst&dir=&occ=first&part=1&cid=2914694.

Lavranos, N. (2018) Beyond USMCA: ISDS à la carte. *Kluwer Arbitration Blog*. http://arbitrationblog.kluwerarbitration.com/2018/10/08/beyond-usmca-isds-la-carte/.

Levy, P. (2017) Critique of NAFTA Provision Highlights Team Trump's Misconceptions on Investment Abroad. *Forbes Online*. https://www.forbes.com/sites/phillevy/2017/10/23/should-team-trump-encourage-investment-in-mexico/#596e553970b4.

Malmström, C. (2018) A Multilateral Investment Court: A Contribution to the Conversation about Reform of Investment Dispute Settlement. European Commission: Speech by European Commissioner for Trade Cecilia Malmström, Belgian Minister of Foreign Affairs, Brussels. http://trade.ec.europa.eu/doclib/docs/2018/november/tradoc_157512.pdf.

Mann, H. (2018) Metalclad v. Mexico. *International Institute for Sustainable Development*. https://www.iisd.org/itn/2018/10/18/metalclad-v-mexico/.

McBride, J. and Aly Sergie, M. (2017) NAFTA's Economic Impact. *Council on Foreign Relations Online*, 4 October. https://www.cfr.org/backgrounder/naftas-economic-impact.

Newing, N., Alexander, L. and Meredith, L. (2018) What Next for Intra-EU Investment Arbitration? Thoughts on the Achmea Decision. *Kluwer Arbitration Blog*. http://arbitrationblog.kluwerarbitration.com/2018/04/21/what-next-for-intra-eu-investment-arbitration-thoughts-on-the-achmea-decision/.

Nichols, L. and Tout, L. (2018) European Investors Reconsider Their Position Following the ECJ's Decision in Achmea. *Dentons Online*. https://www.dentons.com/en/insights/alerts/2018/june/18/european-investors-reconsider-their-position-following-the-ecjs-decision-in-achmea.

Official Journal of the European Union (2020) Agreement for the Termination of Bilateral Investment Treaties between the Member States of the European Union, 20 May. https://eur-lex.europa.eu/legal-content/EN/TXT/PDF/?uri=CELEX:22020A0529(01)&from=EN.

Olivet, C. and Villareal, A. (2016) Who Really Won the Battle between Philip Morris and Uruguay? *The Guardian*. https://www.theguardian.com/global-development/2016/jul/28/who-really-won-legal-battle-philip-morris-uruguay-cigarette-adverts.

Power, R. (2018) OPINION: ECJ's Judgment Leaves Legal Questions for Energy Charter Treaty Claims. *Aberdeen Journals Limited – Energy Voice Online*. https://www.energyvoice.com/opinion/167925/opinion-ecjs-achmea-judgement-leaves-legal-questions-for-energy-charter-treaty-claims/.

Reuters (2018) Bundesreigierung hält Vattenfall-Schiedsgerichtsklage für unzulässig. *Reuters Deutschland*. https://de.reuters.com/article/deutschland-vattenfall-klage-idDEKBN1I916T.

Risse, J. and Oehm, M. (2018) The Aftermath of Achmea: Germany Requests Dismissal of Vattenfall Case after CJEU's Achmea Decision. *Global Arbitration Review*. https://globalarbitrationnews.com/aftermath-achmea-germany-requests-dismissal-vattenfall-case-cjeus-achmea-decision/.

Rogers, J., Goodall, S. and Dowling. C. (2017) *Brexit and Investor-State Dispute Settlement*. Norton Rose Fulbright Publications. https://www.nortonrosefulbright.com/en-us/knowledge/publications/e4e6cf5b/brexit-and-investor-state-dispute-settlement.

Ross, A. (2018) Achmea Does Not Apply to ICSID Cases, Tribunal Rules. *Global Arbitration Review Online*. https://globalarbitrationreview.com/article/1175480/achmea-does-not-apply-to-icsid-cases-tribunal-rules.

Schepel, H. (2018) From Conflicts-Rules to Field Preemption: Achmea and the Relationship between EU Law and International Investment Law and Arbitration. *European Law Blog*. https://europeanlawblog.eu/2018/03/23/from-conflicts-rules-to-field-preemption-achmea-and-the-relationship-between-eu-law-and-international-investment-law-and-arbitration/.

Skinner, K. (2018) Trump Defends the International Order. *The Wall Street Journal*. https://www.wsj.com/articles/trump-defends-the-international-order-11544573701.

Syszczak, E. (2019) Perils of a 'No Deal' Brexit: Opinion 1/17 and the Case of CETA. *UK Trade Policy Observatory Blog*. https://blogs.sussex.ac.uk/uktpo/2019/02/06/perils-of-a-no-deal-brexit-opinion-1-17-and-the-case-of-ceta/.

# 18. The European Union's global actorness in the climate change era: using Sustainable Development Goals to bring China and the US together

**Doga Ulas Eralp**

## INTRODUCTION

This chapter discusses the EU's global actorness in a period of US decline and Chinese emergence. Leveraging the UN's Agenda 2030 and specific objectives outlined in Sustainable Development Goals (SDGs) #13 on Climate Change, #14 on Life Below Water, and #16 Peace, Justice and Strong Institutions, the European Union has formulated a new global presence that responds to the global threat rather than projecting its normative framework to be reworked elsewhere. The SDGs provide a well-defined pathway for Brussels to encourage its longtime ally, the USA, and its new global partner China, to uphold and implement rules / legal frameworks for a sustainable planet. The chapter specifically evaluates global emergent regimes in climate change, fisheries, and conflict minerals and how EU's policies impact USA and China.

## CONCEPTUALIZING THE EU'S GLOBAL ACTORNESS

This chapter argues that Europe has a unique opportunity to remain relevant and expand beyond its traditional areas of engagement. In a period where the divergence and polarization between China and the USA becomes more clear regardless of who sits in the White House, Brussels can assume a constructive global mediator role. Europe's normative power to transform politics has often been criticized as being limited to its regional proves with little to no effect in global politics (Hennis 2001; Breslin and Higgott 2003). Global challenges articulated in the SDGs provide the correct fora for Brussels to refashion its benchmarks from Europe to the global stage. Mayer and Vogt (2006) foresaw as the only viable strategy to have global footprint suggesting that Europe's future global political identity should be the function of the global challenges. Europe needs a new narrative for its global strategic outreach and SDGs provide the perfect venue for that goal. The rise of China, Brexit, the global COVID-19 pandemic, and climate change among others signify a paradigmatic shift in global political order where Western domination may be coming to a close. European thinkers, such as Nicole Gnesotto (2007), point out that Europe's relative weight in global politics is declining and becoming more peripheral. Brussels should not shy away from officially recognizing its peripheral status and balance the expectations of the remaining members that it is willing to embrace a new narrative for its global role that could be useful in bridging the gap between China and the USA in the tumultuous global political economy of the climate change era. Only after such recognition may an honest discussion on power conversion start (Nicolaïdis and Howse 2002).

The first two decades of the twenty-first century proved to be a period of ambiguity and transition from unipolarity to a more multipolar world order. The rise of BRICS countries, emergence of global consumerism, and climate change suggest new ways to define stability and sustainability of global economic growth. A heightened sense of global security dilemma, growing xenophobia, the COVID-19 pandemic and the subsequent mistrust of governments' handling of the pandemic led to an authoritarian shift (Zhou et al. 2018). There are more non-democracies (Applebaum and Ignatieff 2020) since the end of the Cold War.

Scholarship on Europe's role in global politics is decoupled from the scholarship on globalization, global political economy, and international development, and it often times ignores the Global South. Academics working on EU foreign policy have very narrowly defined research agendas. These works examine the EU's external relations including the EU's institutional efficiency (Eralp 2012) and relations between the EU member states (Vimont 2015). Other research silos focus more on member states' national foreign policies and their interplay with the European Security and Defence Policy and European Political Cooperation (EPC) (Øhrgaard 2018). Another important research pillar on the EU focuses on the EU's agency as an actor measuring its capacity in different areas (Rhinard and Sjöstedt 2019). Moreover, this chapter measures the EU's effectiveness in supporting multilateralism in global trade, as well as promotion of democracy and human rights through different policy instruments (Meunier and Nicolaïdis 2005; Poletti and Sicurelli 2018). Other research is concerned with assessing the status of the EU in global power politics in an increasingly multipolar world versus during the unipolar hegemony of the US in the immediate post-Cold War era (Haas and Kupchan 2021), unpacking the legitimacy question of the EU's global presence (Lehne 2020; Bickerton 2011). A very popular area of research looks into how the EU sets, promotes, implements and adjusts norms at a global level (Manners 2002,

2006; Merlingen 2007). Previously, a popular research agenda used to explore the EU as a model for other regions.

According to Mayer (2008) and Salmon (2005) all of these approaches are Euro-centric and fail to capture the pace of global change. Instead, Mayer suggests a realistic assessment of Europe's place in a period of global shift of politics away from Western dominance. Embracing the advocacy for SDGs would work in favor of Europe on both domestic and global grounds. Ever since the conclusion of the 2004 enlargement there is a growing gap within Europe between citizens of member states and the Brussels bureaucracy. European electorates are growingly more insecure, nationalistic, and xenophobic and project a certain sense of fear on exterior challenges such as the refugees from North Africa and Syria, the COVID-19 pandemic, and the immediate disastrous impact of climate change. The EU's global standing does not make any significant changes in their daily lives. If the EU manages to leverage SDGs as the central piece of its global standing it may close that gap with its citizens.

Another contribution of setting the SDGs as a benchmark would allow Brussels to promote global policy objectives instead of giving the impression of pushing the EU's own normative agenda. This is an important distinction in reimagining the EU's normative power not as one projecting its normative framework, but rather as delivering visible hard policies that allow for the implementation of globally agreed sustainable development goals. The normative power of Europe has long been a central part of the studies on EU's global position. This started with Duchêne's work on Europe as a 'civilian power' (1973) and later Sjöstedt's (1977) work on Europe's actorness defined primarily through its capacity – the extent to which the EU is able to convert its normative agenda with achievable and measurable objectives to action. This framework more or less defined the confines of the scholarship on the EU's external actorness (Bretherton and Vogler 1999). Definitive works dealing with the value realities, and the capabilities of Europe include Manners' (2002) 'normative power Europe' and Sjursen's (2006) evaluation of the concept, Nye's (1990) classic 'soft power' definition, or Falkner's (2007) 'green normative power' and Meunier and Nicolaïdis' (2005, 2019) 'trade power' definitions, along with Grabbe's (2014) 'transformative power' projecting conditionalities and most interestingly the constructive ambiguity of the EU (Gasteiger 1996). Mayer (2008) problematizes all of these approaches as having a Euro-centric bias towards global responsibility as if the EU has something to teach the rest of the world. Instead, his argument suggests that the EU has to acknowledge that it should be the 'receiver of global obligations' by consideration of 'general morals' (Mayer 2008). SDGs do exactly that. They provide a model for global responsibility.

Mayer and Vogt (2006) identify six principles of global responsibility when they analyze the Euro-Atlantic relationship. These are: Contribution,

Beneficiary, Community, Capacity, Legitimate Expectation, and Consent Principles. Advocacy for SDGs satisfies a few of these principles. The Contribution principle suggests that an actor has a duty to mitigate a situation of harm or loss it may have contributed. The Beneficiary principle applies when an actor feels the obligation to mitigate the loss others experienced in a situation that benefited the actor. The Community principle suggests duties that arise from being a member to a community. The Capacity principle is about the moral obligation to act where one can. The Legitimate Expectation principle is an actor's duty to fulfill expectations to act. The Consent principle suggests an actor has to carry out its duty once it has consented to do so.

The bigger question (Jones and Van Genugten 2013) that needs to be answered is who the EU is responsible for. SDG advocacy would benefit not only the EU citizens, but all global citizens in a planetary perspective (Manners 2020). Terry O'Shaughnessy (2006), who examined the EU's responsibility as a trading global power, identified five different types of audiences in an order of priority. The first audience is the EU resident that is directly impacted by changes in the global trade regimes due to their sector of employment; second, residents across EU countries; third, former European colonies in the Global South; fourth, the sustenance of the global free trade regime principles; fifth, the global population. The EU's SDG advocacy between China and the USA allows for Brussels to uphold the interests of the global population over its domestic audiences in an attempt to satisfy the community principle of global responsibility.

This chapter evaluates how the European Union fulfills its global responsibility toward the world society through the promotion of Sustainable Development Goals on Fisheries (SDG #13), Climate Change (SDG #14) and Conflict Minerals (SDG #16) with the overall objective of consolidating the capacities of the multilateral trade regimes in the face of growing tensions between China and the USA. There are multiple political trends that impact the functional influence of global trade regimes. The first and most challenging of all is the consolidation of China as a global economic powerhouse with its manufacturing capacity and growing affluent consumerist middle class. Similarly, the return of Russia in geopolitical contest pushes for renewed competition over access and distribution of energy resources in the Eurasian landscape. In a parallel course of development, the rise of authoritarian regimes in emerging markets including South Africa, Brazil, and Turkey further feeds into the economic and political volatility in the Global South. In the US, confrontational and isolationist 'America First' policies embraced by the Trump Administration puts into question the US' role as the main leverage behind the Bretton Woods system.

The European Union, on the other hand, amidst its drive to sort out its finances in the wake of the Eurozone crisis and Brexit is strategically positioned to serve as a mediator between multilateral trade regimes and a declining United States and an emerging China. The EU's SDG advocacy on climate change, fisheries, and conflict minerals suggests that Brussels can indeed assume a global responsibility in reaction to the fulfillment of a global value system of sustainable human development through its balancing act.

## EU's Advocacy on Climate Change (SDG #13)

EU's positioning in its advocacy for SDG #13 on Climate Change fulfills the community principle for global responsibility with the global population on the receiving end. Brussels openly rejects prospects for new trade deals with countries that are not a party to the Treaty (Mathiesen 2018). The European Commission has made signing trade deals with the world's second biggest economy contingent on membership of the Paris Climate Agreement. As a result, EU trade agreements contain a chapter on sustainability.[1] For example, The Japan-EU Economic Partnership Agreement signed in December 2017 explicitly addresses climate change and commits the parties to implementing the Paris Agreement, to which they have made carbon emissions pledges.[2] Similarly, in December 2019, EU leaders at the European Council summit endorsed the objective of achieving a climate-neutral EU by 2050 with the exception of Poland.[3]

The European Court of Justice made it legal for the EU Commission to suspend parts of trade agreements if the other party was found to be in breach of the sustainability chapter of the Paris Agreement (Opinion 2/15 of the Court, 16 May 2017).[4] This decision theoretically allows the EU to penalize countries that did not live up to their commitments to the Paris deal. This is a very interesting case where the EU responded to a global policy objective, first adopting its trade policies and then later clearly enforcing the principle in its engagement with the third parties.

### Impact on the United States

Following his rather tumultuous election to the US Presidency, Joe Biden reversed almost all of the decisions of the previous administration on climate

---

1 See the website of the European Commission: http://trade.ec.europa.eu/doclib/press/index.cfm?id=1870.

2 See the website of the UNFCCC: https://unfccc.int/process-and-meetings/the-paris-agreement/d2hhdC1pcy.

3 See the European Council Conclusions: https://www.consilium.europa.eu/media/41768/12-euco-final-conclusions-en.pdf.

4 See the Opinion 2/15 of the Court, 16 May 2017, http://www.mlex.com/Attachments/2017-05-16_2CW21X23B07N046Z/C0002_2015%20EN.pdf.

change. The US is once again party to the Paris Climate Change Agreement. Furthermore, the Biden Administration pledged to adapt serious steps to turn the US economy totally carbon free by 2050 (Hengel 2021). Future uncertainty over the continued democratic control over two chambers of the US Congress along with the growing political polarization may hinder the pace of such decarbonization reforms as demanded by the progressives and democratic socialists in the form of a Green New Deal (Galvin and Healy 2020). The Biden Administration shares the same objectives with Brussels on climate change but has not cemented the legislation to push through with the reforms.

The EU has the capacity to support the Biden Administration's efforts in a number of ways. The COP26 Glasgow Summit on Climate Change that took place in November 2021 provided such an opportunity. Brussels could easily push Washington to take more concrete and practical steps on four different climate change topics: methane emissions, introducing a carbon tariff on imports, pushing for joint action on global climate change advocacy, and lastly supporting global financial institutions in their efforts to factor climate risk in their assessments.

On the issue of methane emissions, the European Commission can reach out to the US climate change envoy John Kerry's Cabinet to identify ways to cooperate under the auspices of the International Methane Emissions Observatory (IMEO). IMEO is responsible for data collection on methane emissions that escape energy supply chains including natural gas and oil pipelines. Currently there is a Methane Emissions Reduction Act of 2021 introduced in the US Senate that would, if enacted, force the US Treasury to levy a fee on methane emissions from oil and natural gas facilities, and for other purposes.[5] While there is a very little chance for the Bill to pass the Senate, the EU Commission could get the US involved in supporting the work of IMEO.

Concerning the carbon border adjustment mechanism, the EU boasts an effective Emissions Trading System that allows for a uniform carbon pricing across all EU member states. However, the US currently lacks a nationwide carbon pricing mechanism applicable to all 50 states and US territories. Currently there are 12 US states representing a third of the US GDP and quarter of the US population that have an active carbon trading scheme.[6] Brussels could reach out to individual states to link up their mechanisms with the EU's Emissions Trading System.

---

5 See Methane Emissions Reduction Act of 2021: https://www.congress.gov/bill/117th-congress/senate-bill/645?s=1&r=8.

6 See the Center for Climate and Energy Solutions website: https://www.c2es.org/content/market-based-state-policy/.

Brussels can coordinate with Washington to bring their positions closer on advocacy for climate waiver within the World Trade Organization that will encourage member countries to adapt climate change measures while sanctioning those who fail to take meaningful action. Another important initiative is the EU-led joint transatlantic campaign to support the global finance industry to include climate risk in their portfolio assessments and its mitigation. Investment in green industries and divestment from carbon-heavy industries may be a great catalyst for a green transition in the global economy.

### Impact on China

The EU applauded Beijing's verbal commitment to work together with the EU and other stakeholders to combat climate change, implement the 2030 Agenda for Sustainable Development, and promote global low greenhouse gas emissions, climate resilience and sustainable development. China and the EU agree that on climate finance, developed countries shall provide financial resources to assist developing countries with respect to both mitigation and adaptation in continuation of their existing obligations under the Convention. Prior to 2025 the Conference of the Parties serving as the meeting of the Parties to the Paris Agreement shall set a new collective quantified goal from a floor of USD 100 billion per year, taking into account the needs and priorities of developing countries.[7]

China pledges to follow its green, sustainable development concept strengthening measures to deal with climate change and would conscientiously follow the Paris Agreement in line with the SDGs.[8] Chinese President Xi refers to twenty-first century China as an "ecological civilization" with set goals of restoration of decimated forests, efforts to reverse desertification, the promotion of electric mobility and eco-friendly urbanization, as well as important investments in new technologies (Lent 2018).

There are obvious ecological challenges for Beijing, including widespread air pollution in urban centers, the impending water crisis, and possible flooding of China's most prosperous cities as sea levels rise. In 2015, the Chinese leadership published the 3rd Five Year Plan that identified low-carbon technologies as the technologies of the future. Beijing sees this as an opportunity to establish its dominance as an innovator as well as a manufacturer and exporter of these new frontier technologies (Dodwell 2018).

Another significant future ecological challenge is the water problems China will have to face at a global scale as it continues to pursue its global

---

7 Ministry of Foreign Affairs of the PRC: Joint statement of the 20th China-EU Summit Beijing, 16 July 2018.

8 See the UN website: https://sustainabledevelopment.un.org/memberstates/china.

trade efforts through its Belt and Road Initiative (Chihaia 2018). For China, the opportunities that tackling climate offered have begun to be seen as the engine of the next phase of prosperity. In 2016, China invested $102.9bn in renewable energy and installed half of the world's new wind power (Buckley and Nicholas 2017). Beijing is still highly dependent on coal, but its coal consumption has peaked and in decline, to be replaced over time by renewables, hydro, and nuclear power (IEA 2017).

The EU is already cooperating with Beijing in ICAO and in the IMO to ensure that aviation and shipping contribute to combating climate change, including through both domestic measures and international cooperation. Especially in the sub-sector of Emissions Trading, China and the EU agree on the importance of emissions trading as a cost-effective climate policy tool and agree to further enhance and reinforce bilateral cooperation activities on emissions trading in the context of reforming the EU Emissions Trading System and the launch of the national Emissions Trading System in China in 2021, allowing for the sharing of experience and expertise among the two largest carbon markets in the world.[9]

## EU Advocacy on SDG #14: Fisheries Policies

EU advocacy on SDG #14 on Fisheries is one of the most visible platforms to observe the EU's global actorness. The EU's position reflects a clear interpretation of how Brussels' global responsibility in advocating for the protection of the fisheries builds on its existing competences while reacting to a universally agreed upon need with accountability not only to the global community but also to the millions of people who make their livelihoods through non-industrial fishing. According to the UN's Food and Agriculture Organization (FAO) more than 30 percent of the world's marine fisheries are overfished – triple the volume in 1974 – and almost 60 percent are at the brink of sustainability.[10] An FAO report suggests that fish stocks in Africa and Southeast Asia are under-assessed and under-regulated. Furthermore, high seas fishing is not completely regulated – precisely the regions where the Chinese distant water fishing (DWF) fleet is highly active. Among the many reasons that lead to overfishing FAO cites subsidies imposed by governments as the main culprit.

---

[9] Ministry of Foreign Affairs of the PRC: Joint statement of the 20th China-EU Summit Beijing, 16 July 2018.

[10] See the Food and Agriculture Organization website: http://www.fao.org/news/story/en/item/1144274/icode/.

The EU has been at the forefront of the push to set up a responsible global fisheries regime. The 2017 WTO Buenos Aires Ministerial Conference (MC11), launched a work program that aims to complete the negotiations with the objective of finalizing an agreement on fisheries subsidies, at the 2019 Ministerial Conference that addresses the Sustainable Development Goal 14.6. Such a broad multilateral agreement will cover all 164 WTO members.[11]

The SDG 14.6 aims to prohibit "certain forms of fisheries subsidies which contribute to overcapacity and overfishing, [and] eliminate subsidies that contribute to illegal, unreported and unregulated fishing" (Thomson 2019). The European Commission has been the main actor behind this initiative. The EU has already been implementing its Common Fisheries Policy since 2014, which aims to ensure that all EU fish stocks are fished at a sustainable level by 2020 at the latest.[12]

The EU calls for a WTO regulation that clearly addresses the two most harmful types of subsidies. The first set of subsidies enhance the fleet capacity to catch fish which results in overfishing. Almost 60 percent of the subsidies are estimated to fund such capacity enhancement. The second set of subsidies are given to illegal, unregulated, and unreported (IUU) fishing. This type of fishing leads to the exhaustion of fish supplies and the destruction of natural habitats.[13] Brussels argues that least developed countries (LDCs) and developing countries should be allowed to build up their fleets, as long as the main objective of safeguarding sustainable global fisheries is protected, e.g., EU–Morocco Sustainable Fisheries Partnership negotiations.

**Impact on US policy**

The EU has traditionally cooperated better with the American Democrats on environmental issues than with Republicans. Brussels had worked out a joint statement with the Obama Administration in 2011 calling for joint action against IUU fishing. The Trump Administration became fixated on what was called a seafood trade deficit (USD 12bn). In 2018, after a serious crackdown on its staff, US officials forced the National Oceanic and Atmospheric Administration (NOAA) to reset its Fisheries' specific priorities to include expanding US seafood production, including wild-caught stocks and aqua-

---

[11] See the Word Trade Organization website: https://www.wto.org/english/tratop_e/rulesneg_e/fish_e/fish_e.htm.

[12] See fact sheet available from: https://www.pewtrusts.org/en/research-and-analysis/fact-sheets/2018/02/eu-still-far-from-ending-overfishing-in-its-waters.

[13] See the Food and Agriculture website: http://www.fao.org/3/y4773e/y4773e05.htm.

culture and deregulating limits set by states.[14] The overall objective of the Trump Administration was to introduce flexibility in the reauthorization of the Magnuson-Stevens Fishery Conservation and Management Act (MSA) set up in 1976 under President Ford. Fortunately, such a change did not materialize.

The new Biden Administration is much more enthusiastic in cooperating with the EU. At a White House summit, the US Administration voiced its commitment to work with the EU to protect oceans, including by combating marine litter. Washington also pledged to cooperate with the EU on designating new marine protected areas in the Southern Ocean, sustainable fishing, and the prevention of IUU fishing. Moreover, the US is willing to share scientific research with the EU through the EU-led All-Atlantic Ocean Research Alliance. Furthermore the Biden Administration proposed to formulate a joint US–EU position at the 2021 Fourth Session of the Intergovernmental Conference on Marine Biodiversity beyond National Jurisdiction, and later at the 2022 UN Ocean Conference in Lisbon. In May 2021, the Biden Administration published a new report titled "Conserving and Restoring America the Beautiful" that in complete reversal from the previous administration instructed NOAA to expand the National Marine Sanctuaries System and the National Estuarine Research Reserve System, to "help restore fish populations and better protect threatened and endangered species". This report is considered the administration's plan to meet the 30 percent of land and water protected by 2030 or '30 by 30' initiative put forth by Executive Order 14008 in January 2021 (Chase et al. 2021).

The EU's sustained commitment to uphold the global principles of sustainability of fisheries and SDG #14 seems to have worked in slowing the reversal under the Trump Administration and later facilitating possible cooperation with the Biden Administration.

### Impact on Chinese policy

When it comes to China, the EU found itself, at least on paper, a more than willing partner to cooperate on fisheries. China's commitment to maintain the oceans may well be an act of self-interest in an attempt to disguise the utter destructive impact of its fishing fleets on open seas. However, the EU seems to be satisfied with the official pledges Beijing so routinely announces. Subsequently, the EU Commission officials and the EU Council refrained from holding China accountable for the ongoing environmental abuses at the expense of alienating the emerging global power. The EU's global fisheries policy towards China lacks teeth and is built on praise for Chinese pledges

---

[14] See the National Oceanic and Atmospheric Administration website: https://www.fisheries.noaa.gov/national/aquaculture/us-aquaculture.

to comply with SDG #14. Global actorness requires responsibility to partners and the global community; however, the praise policy of the EU remains rather elusive and lacks effectiveness.

China currently is the world's largest producer and consumer of seafood products (70 MMT in 2017). The depletion of coastal fisheries has spurred rapid growth in fishing from more distant waters. China has the world's largest distant water fishing fleet, of 2,600 vessels (Damin 2018). In the 13th Fisheries Five Year Plan, China released a specific plan for the DWF industry that announced a cap of 3,000 fishing vessels by the year 2020 and a limit on the number of DWF enterprises at the 2016 level.[15] In 2016, the total reported DWF catch had fallen to 1.99 million tons (Mallory 2017).

Furthermore, high seas fishing is not completely regulated. China has been shifting production to the high seas, underscoring the need for a solid framework for fisheries management in these waters. Initiatives like the Arctic Council's decision to close the Arctic to fishing until more information is acquired about this potential resource is an example of a constructive policy (Gabbatiss 2017). Instead of expanding the DWF industry, China pledged to upgrade DWF production, increasing control over the industrial supply chain from point of capture, storage, shipping and processing to distribution, retail, marketing and branding (Feuling 2010). China has already launched 30 bases abroad and has over 100 global partnerships, including joint ventures, for this purpose (Mallory 2017). More Chinese mergers and acquisitions are likely to occur.

In 2017, the EU voiced its satisfaction with the China-EU Blue Year and agreed on a Blue Partnership for the Oceans as a means to improve cooperation aiming at better ocean governance and sustainable fisheries. In July 2018, the EU signed the Blue Partnership for the Oceans with China, applauded as an innovative tool that pledges to maintain and protect the marine ecology and implement SDG #14 on oceans. Each year both parties hold bilateral summits to monitor the implementation of the Partnership. The Blue Partnership encourages cooperation between Brussels and Beijing on areas such as the protection of marine biological diversity in the high seas and its sustainable use. The Partnership addresses the need to fight against expansion of marine pollution especially that of micro plastics and marine plastic litter. Parties pledge to mitigate and adapt to climate change impact on oceans with a particular focus on the Arctic Sea along with making a clear commitment to conserve marine living resources in the Antarctic. The Partnership also serves as a form of international oversight mechanism on governance of fisheries in regional

---

[15] See the State Council of the People's Republic of China website: http://www.gov.cn/xinwen/2017-12/08/content_5245275.htm.

and global platforms with the overall objective of preventing IUU fishing. The Agreement on Blue Partnership offers an inclusive orientation towards different stakeholders such as corporations, universities and research organizations, finance groups and trade associations. The Partnership calls for investment in the latest clean technologies for oversight and information sharing that would help build a blue economy.

## EU Advocacy on SDG #16 on Conflict Minerals

One of the more active arenas of the EU's global actorness is the advocacy on SDG #16 on Conflict Minerals. The EU has been spearheading the regulation of conflict minerals. Primarily on the issue of the diamond trade, the EU served as the chair of the Kimberly Process (KP) in 2018. The KP is a tripartite body consisting of government, civil society, and industry representatives with 54 state-based partners. The KP Certification Process claims to prevent 99.8 percent of the worldwide trade in 'conflict diamonds', defined as "rough diamonds used by rebel movements to finance wars against legitimate governments" (Makhetha 2016). Many EU member countries contributed to the implementation of the Organisation for Economic Co-operation and Development's Due Diligence Guidance for Responsible Supply Chains of Minerals from Conflict-Affected and High-Risk Areas – Tin, Tungsten, Tantalum, Gold (3TG).[16] On 1 January 2021 the EU Conflict Minerals Regulation came into force. The regulation covers more than 1,000 EU importers and their partners within the EU while setting thresholds for the amounts of tin, tantalum, tungsten and gold and of metals containing 3TG that are imported into the European Union. Importers are required to update their compliance tools to match the risk mitigation, due diligence, and audit requirements as mandated by the EU regulation. The regulation will have a significant impact on the direct and indirect supply chain providers.

### Impact on United States

One of the major challenges for the transatlantic cooperation on conflict minerals is the increasingly polarized nature of American politics. Reversals and abrupt changes in policies with the change of US administrations threaten the emergence of stable partnership across the ocean. As the EU's new conflict minerals regulation came into force in January 2021, the newly elected Biden Administration immediately ended the Trump Administration's plan to dismantle the DFA Section 1502. Trump's Executive Draft Order proposed that the Conflict Mineral Rule contained in section 1502 of the Dodd-Frank

[16] See the OECD website: http://www.oecd.org/corporate/mne/mining.htm.

Wall Street Reform and Consumer Protection Act should be suspended by the Securities and Exchange Commission.[17] It argued that there was "mounting evidence" that the rule has "caused harm to some parties in the Democratic Republic of the Congo and have thereby contributed to instability in the region and threatened the national security interest of the United States".[18] The draft order also argued that, "this Executive Order recognizes that humanitarian missions play an important role in the President's responsibility to defend the national security interests of the United States". As an alternative to the system in place, it directed the State Department and Treasury Department to come up with a plan in 180 days to "address such problems in the DRC and adjoining countries" that would more effectively target specific firms conducting illegal activities (Rathi 2017). The US Dodd-Frank Conflict Mineral Regulation applies to downstream companies, which are considered to be those that use minerals after the point of smelter and refinery – such as product assemblers, components manufacturers, and retailers (Young et al. 2019). The DFA Section 1502 not only affected US companies that traded on the US Stock Exchange, but also impacted the way European firms, as suppliers to US companies, operated their businesses due to strict disclosure requirements. The regulation requires further clarification. Minerals are imported to the EU in two ways: (1) in raw forms as ores and metals; and (2) as minerals inside components and products. Critics pointed out that the regulation seemed to suggest that only companies that import raw materials must comply with the new rule and those companies with products and components that contain the same minerals do not have this obligation. Larger companies often buy products from smaller companies, so if "all but the smallest EU firms" are subject to the rule, then those small companies' minerals will go unchecked and risk entering the larger companies' product supply chains (Ly 2017). The Biden Administration is taking important steps following the EU's initiatives on mining supply chain transparency for conflict minerals. The new Africa Intelligence Report (16 June 2021) makes recommendations for serious measures on how to better regulate and oversee the import of conflict minerals into the US.

### Impact on China

The EU's role in pushing the conflict mineral regulations may come across as yet another proof of its symbolic normative power (Partzsch 2018). Its content brings tangible oversight mechanisms to the trading of conflict minerals that

---

[17] See the South African Resource Watch statement: https://www.sec.gov/comments/statement-013117/cll2-typea.pdf.

[18] Ibid.

may significantly hurt the war economies in East Africa. The UN's Agenda 2030 and the SDG #16 contributed to the EU's taking up global responsibility.

## CONCLUSION

This chapter focused on EU's global actorness in a period of US decline and Chinese emergence. Normative power Europe has long been the overarching theme that described the EU's policy activism. However, an overwhelming majority of the normative power literature constructs this power as being projected from within the EU's own normative framework to do good. This chapter agrees with the dissenters and suggests that the EU can only become a global power in its own right when it responds to the global call for action. The UN's Agenda 2030 does exactly that. The EU's overall strategy in forging its global leadership role for supporting multilateralism runs in conjunction with the SDG Framework Vision 2030. SDGs provide a clear political framework, while the EU's support role focuses on encouraging partners, primarily the USA and China, to adopt and adhere to standards and rules/legal frameworks and implement it.

Sustainable Development Goals #13 on Climate Change, #14 on Life Below Water, and #16 Peace, Justice and Strong Institutions with their specific targets provide a very clear roadmap to assess the EU's achievements as a global actor living up to its global responsibility not only to its citizens and traditional and not-so-traditional partners, but also to the larger global community including its former colonies. There are two key takeaways. The EU has a natural partner in the US through the long tested and tried transatlantic partnership; however, this partnership seems to have waned during the changes of government in Washington, especially during the catastrophic four years under the Trump Administration. Secondly, almost paradoxically the EU has a long-term and forward looking relationship with the authoritarian Chinese government in the implementation of the mentioned SDGs. This is mainly due to continuity in the official language adapted by the Chinese Communist Party that overlaps on SDGs with the continuity in EU official language on the UN Agenda 2030. Although the lack of transparency is a significant issue when it comes to measuring the impact, Brussels seems to be satisfied with official declarations from Beijing.

The EU's advocacy on SDG #13 Climate Change allowed for both the US and China to recalibrate their positions in fulfilling a carbon neutral future. The Biden Administration is eager to catch up on climate change policies globally and sees the EU as the right partner for joint advocacy. Brussels can do a lot with Washington keeping in mind a possible change of government in Washington in 2024 and its effect on the transatlantic partnership. The low hanging fruit for both parties is to pressure the global finance industry to factor climate risk in their portfolio assessments and its mitigation. The Chinese government made serious overtures to Brussels during the four years of Trump presenting himself as a reliable global partner in pushing the agenda of the Paris Climate Change Summit with pledges of monetary compensation to developing nations trying to catch up with their stated objectives by 2030. The EU is keen to keep its partnership with Beijing growing as long as the vast monetary resources of the Chinese government are put to use.

SDG #14 covers life below water, and specifically the management of fisheries in open waters. The Biden Administration has pledged to work with the EU on designating new marine protected areas in the Southern Ocean, sustainable fishing, and the prevention of IUU fishing. Washington also pushed for a joint US–EU position at the Fourth Session of the Intergovernmental Conference on Marine Biodiversity beyond National Jurisdiction in 2021 and later at the 2022 UN Ocean Conference in Lisbon. These developments are a breath of fresh air after four years of the Trump Administration's efforts to relax the fishing regulations in favor of the fishing industry. However, Brussels should not bank on American support after the 2024 US Presidential elections.

In 2018, the EU signed the Blue Partnership for the Oceans with China. The partnership addresses the need to fight against expansion of marine pollution especially that of micro plastics and marine plastic litter. The Partnership also serves as a form of an international oversight mechanism on governance of fisheries in regional and global platforms with the overall objective of preventing IUU fishing. However, considering that China has the world's largest distant water fishing fleet with an ever-growing demand for seafood from its domestic consumer market, it is highly dubious that China will fulfill its pledges. The EU is very careful about pointing out this challenge to its partner in Beijing.

The EU's advocacy on SDG #16 on Conflict Minerals (3TG) is the most visible form of EU activism in global politics. The EU has already been at the forefront of ensuring the worldwide compliance with the Kimberly Process that regulates the global trade of 'blood diamonds'. Under the auspices of the World Trade Organization, Brussels has been advocating for a global standard of oversight and compliance across the supply chain of 3TG. The new EU Conflict Minerals Mechanism that came into full force in January 2021 is one of the most comprehensive oversight frameworks. The EU's new mechanism has largely been inspired by the Dodd-Frank Act's Section 1502 that came into force in 2012, thus is a great example of successful of transatlantic cooperation. However, reversals and abrupt changes in policies with the change of US administrations threaten the emergence of a stable partnership across the ocean. As we saw above, the newly elected Biden Administration immediately ended the Trump Administration's plan to dismantle the DFA Section 1502 and voiced its commitment to work with the EU for the advocacy on conflict minerals in different global fora. China, as always officially, is happy to collaborate with the EU and even move past the international expectations with no verifiable evidence on the implementation of the announced measures. In this particular case, while the new EU mechanism focuses on mineral *importers* only, China allegedly aligned its standards on conflict minerals with the OECD's Due Diligence Guidance for Responsible Supply Chains of Minerals from Conflict-Affected and High-Risk Areas. Again, Brussels voiced its satisfaction with the official pledge of compliance from Beijing.

## The Way Forward for the EU as a Responsible Global Actor

This chapter tackled how the EU could reimagine its global actorness not necessarily as a projection of its normative framework, but via the utilization of its innovative policy tools and normative continuity in response to global challenges. The decline of the United States and its liberal democratic model as the world's sole superpower coupled with the rise of authoritarian China as the next superpower has locked global politics into a new era of Cold War like tensions. The growing disastrous impact of climate change is further destabilizing the relationships between the center and the periphery. The UN's Agenda 2030 and the Sustainable Development Goals with their clearly defined objectives offer a path for forward for Brussels to seize the opportunity and contribute to the sustainable future of humanity. The EU's advocacy on SDGs such as climate change, fisheries, and conflict minerals offers a neutral ground that can bring the divergent global powers together with the wellbeing of the planet in mind.[19] Incorporating responsible minerals guidance into a national standard (called, the 'Standard'), as well as creating legally binding oversight and a supervision rule (called, the 'Rule') has been formulated in Beijing.[20] The Rule is meant to enforce the Standard of due diligence guidance for responsible supply chains of minerals from conflict-affected and high-risk areas. The rule is expected to apply to ores and concentrates containing the 'three T's': tin, tungsten, and tantalum from the Democratic Republic of Congo (DRC) and neighboring countries. The companies directly affected by the rule will be those importing, exporting, smelting, and refining these three substances in China (Nasr 2017).

The lack of transparency of Chinese politics make it impossible to verify the extent to which Beijing is able to rein in both the importers and exporters of conflict minerals. Both the Rule and the Standard serve to provide a national

---

19 See the OECD website: https://www.oecd.org/daf/inv/mne/GuidanceEdition2.pdf.

20 See the OECD website: https://www.oecd.org/china/42390089.pdf.

scale oversight; however, Beijing's performance on the matter needs to be supported by evidence. As is the case with fisheries, Brussels shies away from holding PRC accountable for lack of evidence, and instead chooses to applaud the official pledges. The EU's reluctance in pressing for more accountability from Beijing on conflict minerals damages its effectiveness as a global actor and more significantly its responsibility toward the people of Africa who suffered under European colonialism and still are impacted by the socio-political economic consequences of the colonial period. NGOs and activists within the EU may lobby for Brussels to press harder on Beijing to get past the rhetoric and bring measurable change in East Africa and elsewhere.

## REFERENCES

Applebaum, A. and Ignatieff, M. (2020) Keen on the Twilight of Democracy and the Rise of Authoritarianism [podcast].

Bickerton, C. J. (2011) Towards a Social Theory of EU Foreign and Security Policy. *JCMS: Journal of Common Market Studies*, **49**, 171–190.

Breslin, S. and Higgott, R. (2003) New Regionalism(s) in the Global Political Economy: Conceptual Understanding in Historical Perspective. *Asia Europe Journal*, **1**, 167–182.

Bretherton, C. and Vogler, J. (1999) *The European Union as a Global Actor*. London: Routledge.

Buckley, T. and Nicholas, S. (2017) *China's Global Renewable Energy Expansion*. Institute for Energy Economics and Financial Analysis. http://ieefa.org/wp-content/uploads/2017/01/Chinas-Global-Renewable-Energy-Expansion_January-2017.pdf.

Chase, A., O'Shea, H., Poole, K. and Smith, Z. (2021) Biden's Historic Action on 30x30. NRDC Expert Blog.

Chihaia, M. (2018) China's Belt and Road Initiative: A Project of Trade and Diplomacy. *New Eastern Europe*. http://neweasterneurope.eu/2018/04/18/chinas-belt-road-initiative-project-trade-diplomacy/.

Damin, T. (2018) Restoring China's Coastal Fisheries. *China Dialogue Ocean*. https://chinadialogueocean.net/1826-restoring-chinas-coastal-fisheries/.

Dodwell, D. (2018) Keep Calm and Relax: China's Tech Progress Is Only a National Security Challenge If We Make It So. *South China Morning Post*. https://www.scmp.com/business/global-economy/article/2159114/keep-calm-and-relax-chinas-tech-progress-only-national.

Duchêne, F. (1973) The European Community and the Uncertainties of Interdependence. In Kohnstamm, M. and Hager, W. (eds), *A Nation Writ Large? Foreign-Policy Problems before the European Community*. London: Macmillan, 1–21.

Eralp, D. U. (2012) *Politics of the European Union in Bosnia-Herzegovina*. Lanham, MD: Lexington Books.

Falkner, R. (2007) The Political Economy of 'Normative Power' Europe: EU Environmental Leadership in International Biotechnology Regulation. *Journal of European Public Policy*, **14**(4), 507–526.

Feuling, B. A. (2010) Developing China Sales and Distribution Capabilities. *China Business Review*. https://www.chinabusinessreview.com/developing-china-sales-and-distribution-capabilities/.

Gabbatiss, J. (2017) Arctic Ocean Fishing Ban Welcomed by Scientists and Environmentalists. *The Independent*. https://www.independent.co.uk/environment/arctic-ocean-fishing-ban-environment-scientists-populations-fish-a8091541.html.

Galvin, R. and Healy, N. (2020) The Green New Deal in the United States: What It Is and How to Pay for It. *Energy Research & Social Science*, **67**, 101529.

Gasteiger, C. (1996) *An Ambiguous Power*. Washington, DC: Bertelsmann Foundation.

Gnesotto, N. (2007) La sécurité dans un monde post-occidental. *Esprit*, May, 69–74.

Grabbe, H. (2014) Six Lessons of Enlargement Ten Years On. *JCMS: Journal of Common Market Studies*, **52**, 40–56.

Haas, E. and Kupchan, C. (2021) The New Concert of Powers: How to Prevent Catastrophe and Promote Stability in a Multipolar World. *Foreign Affairs*, 23 March.

Hengel, D. (2021) *Transatlantic Trends: Locking in U.S.-EU Cooperation to Combat Climate Change*. Washington, DC: German Marshall Fund of the United States.

Hennis, M. (2001) Europeanization and Globalization: The Missing Link. *JCMS: Journal of Common Market Studies*, **39**, 829–850.

IEA (2017) *World Energy Outlook 2017: China*. Paris: IEA. https://www.iea.org/reports/world-energy-outlook-2017-china.

Jones, E. and Van Genugten, S. (eds) (2013) *The Future of European Foreign Policy*. Abingdon: Routledge.

Lehne, S. (2020) *How the EU Can Survive in a Geopolitical Age*. Brussels: Carnegie Europe.

Lent, J. (2018) What Does China's 'Ecological Civilization' Mean for Humanity's Future? *EcoWatch*. https://www.ecowatch.com/china-ecological-civilization-2532760301.html.

Ly, P. (2017) Targeting the Conflict Minerals Trade: Corporate Social Responsibility Governance and the Multilateral System. *Willamette Journal of International Law and Dispute Resolution*, **25**(1), 25–55.

Makhetha, E. (2016) Small Scale Artisanal Diamond Mining and Rural Livelihood Diversification in Lesotho. University of Pretoria. https://repository.up.ac.za/bitstream/handle/2263/62649/Makhetha_Small_2017.pdf?sequence=1&isAllowed=y.

Mallory, T. (2017) Fishing for Sustainability. *Asia and the Pacific Policy Society*. https://www.policyforum.net/fishing-for-sustainability/.

Manners, I. (2002) Normative Power Europe: A Contradiction in Terms? *JCMS: Journal of Common Market Studies*, **40**, 235–258.

Manners, I. (2006) Normative Power Europe Reconsidered: Beyond the Crossroads. *Journal of European Public Policy*, **13**(2), 182–199.

Manners, I. (2020). Symbols and Myths of European Union Transnational Solidarity. In Krunke, H., Petersen, H. and Manners I. (eds), *Transnational Solidarity: Concept, Challenges and Opportunities*. Cambridge: Cambridge University Press, 76–100.

Mathiesen, K. (2018) EU Says No New Trade Deals with Countries Not in Paris Agreement. *Climate Change News*. https://www.climatechangenews.com/2018/02/02/eu-difficult-*imagine*-trade-deals-countries-not-paris-agreement/.

Mayer, H. (2008) Is It Still Called 'Chinese Whispers'? The EU's Rhetoric and Action as a Responsible Global Institution. *International Affairs*, **84**(1), 61–79.

Mayer, H. and Vogt, H. (eds) (2006) *A Responsible Europe? Ethical Foundations of EU External Affairs*. Basingstoke: Palgrave Macmillan.

Merlingen, M. (2007) Everything Is Dangerous: A Critique of 'Normative Power Europe'. *Security Dialogue*, **38**(4), 435–453.

Meunier, S. and Nicolaïdis, K. (2005) The European Union as a Trade Power. In Hill, C. and Smith, M. (eds), *International Relations and the European Union*. Oxford: Oxford University Press, 275–298.

Meunier, S. and Nicolaïdis, K. (2019) The Geopoliticization of European Trade and Investment Policy. *Journal of Common Market Studies*, **57**, 103–113.

Nasr, L. (2017). China Increases Focus on Conflict Minerals [blog]. https://blog.assentcompliance.com/index.php/china-increases-focus-on-conflict-minerals/.

Nicolaïdis, K. and Howse, R. (2002) 'This is my EUtopia …': Narrative as Power. *JCMS: Journal of Common Market Studies*, **40**, 767–792.

Nye, J. (1990) Soft Power. *Foreign Policy*, **80**, 153–171.

O'Shaughnessy, T. (2006) The European Union: A Responsible Trading Partner? In Mayer, H. and Vogt, H. (eds), *A Responsible Europe? Ethical Foundations of EU External Affairs*. Basingstoke: Palgrave Macmillan, 181–200.

Øhrgaard, J. C. (2018) International Relations or European Integration: Is the CFSP Sui Generis? In Tonra, B. and Christiansen, T. (eds), Rethinking European Union Foreign Policy. Manchester: Manchester University Press, 26–44.

Partzsch, L. (2018) The New EU Conflict Minerals Regulation: Normative Power in International Relations? *Global Policy*, **9**, 479–488.

Poletti, A. and Sicurelli, D. (2018) *The Political Economy of Normative Trade Power Europe*. Cham: Palgrave Macmillan.

Rathi, A. (2017) Renewed Digging: The US Coal Industry's Future Could Be to Mine Rare-Earth Metals for Wind Turbines. *Quartz Blog*. https://qz.com/1004718/the-us-coal-industrys-future-could-be-to-mine-metals-for-wind-turbines/.

Rhinard, M. and Sjöstedt, G. (2019) *The EU as a Global Actor: A New Conceptualization Four Decades after "Actorness"*. Stockholm: Swedish Institute for International Affairs.

Salmon, T. (2005) The European Security and Defence Policy: Built on Rocks or Sand? *European Foreign Affairs Review*, **10**(3), 359–379.

Sjöstedt, G. (1977) *The External Role of the European Community*. Farnborough: Saxon House.

Sjursen, H. (2006) The EU as a 'Normative' Power: How Can This Be? *Journal of European* Public *Policy*, **13**(2), 235–251.

Thomson, P. (2019). 2019: The Year to End Harmful Fisheries Subsidies. *International Institute for Sustainable Development*. https://sdg.iisd.org/commentary/guest-articles/2019-the-year-to-end-harmful-fisheries-subsidies/.

Vimont, P. (2015) *The Common Security and Defense Policy: National Perspectives*. Brussels: Carnegie Europe Analysis.

Young, S., Fernandes, S. and Wood, M. (2019). Jumping the Chain: How Downstream Manufacturers Engage with Deep Suppliers of Conflict Minerals. *Resources*, **8**(1), 26. http://dx.doi.org/10.3390/resources8010026.

Zhou, L., Wu, X., Xu, Z. and Fujita, H. (2018) Emergency Decision Making for Natural Disasters: An Overview. *International Journal of Disaster Risk Reduction*, **27**, 567–576.

# 19. Tackling labour rights and environmental protection through trade and Sustainable Development Chapters: the European approach

**Iulianna Romanchyshyna**[1]

## INTRODUCTION

Integrating non-economic objectives into the trade agenda has long been a contentious issue in the trade community. The World Trade Organization (WTO) to a certain extent addresses the linkages between trade and non-trade values through its general exception clauses (in terms of sustainable development these are the protection of the environment, morality, or prohibition of forced prison labour in Articles XX GATT and XIV GATS). However, it does not go further than ensuring that countries do not use these exceptions as a disguised protectionism. The multilateral forum, therefore, does not deliver significant results in terms of advancing the agenda of social and environmental protection. This could be explained by a variety of reasons. Among those reasons is a "deep-seated unease concerning the intrusion of international trade politics into areas that have hitherto been the preserve of national sovereignty", coupled with the inability to reach consensus among WTO Members adhering to contrasting values and priorities that has made collective action difficult (Melo Araujo 2016, p. 16).

However, given the urge to address the issues of sustainable development, countries seek to fill the governance gap by resorting to preferential trade agreements. The European Union (EU) is a prominent actor in framing its external trade agenda in pursuit of non-trade values, including sustainable development. The EU Commission's reflection paper on "Harnessing

[1] My gratitude goes to Prof. Roberto Caranta for his feedback and encouragement, as well as to the Leuven Çentre for Global Governance Studies, where I was a visiting researcher while writing this chapter. The usual disclaimer applies.

Globalisation" envisaged international trade as a means to reaffirm global social and environmental protection standards (European Commission 2017a). Likewise, a recent "Strategic Plan 2020–2024" of the EU Commission puts a particular emphasis on the trade policy's support for a broader push for sustainable development and internationally set standards (European Commission 2020). The EU external trade agenda is thus depicted as being about "much more than trade" (Larik 2011).

This chapter analyses the EU's current approach to trade and sustainable development (TSD) through a comparative analysis of the 'new generation' FTAs, as well as the reform proposals.[2] EU-Korea[3] as the first EU 'new generation' FTA was the first to include a specific TSD chapter so it provides a baseline for analysis of new trade objectives. While the ensuing 'new generation' free trade agreements with Colombia, Peru, and Ecuador,[4] Central America,[5] Singapore,[6] Canada (CETA),[7] Vietnam,[8] Japan[9] and Mexico[10] use a similar TSD template, there are some differences with regard to their substantive and procedural structure, which are discussed further in the chapter. To better

---

[2] The 'new generation' FTAs could be grouped into a separate category within the EU trade negotiating agenda, since their distinctive features in comparison to other types of agreements permit to find common benchmarks for a proper analysis that would identify the EU approach to this particular type of agreement. This approach also corresponds to the logic put into the 2016 report of the EU Commission on implementation of Free Trade Agreements, where it qualifies 'new generation' FTAs, DCFTAs and EPAs into separate groupings. See https://ec.europa.eu/transparency/regdoc/rep/1/2017/EN/COM-2017-654-F1-EN-MAIN-PART-1.PDF .

[3] Trade Agreement between the European Union and its Member States, of the one part, and the Republic of Korea, of the other part, L 127, 14.05.2011, p. 6–1344.

[4] Trade Agreement between EU and its Members, of the one part, and Colombia and Peru, of the other, OJ L 354, 21.12.2012, p. 3–2607; Protocol of Accession to the Trade Agreement between EU and its Members, of the one part, and Colombia and Peru, of the other part to take account of accession of Ecuador, OJ L 356, 24.12.2016, p. 3–1456.

[5] Agreement establishing an Association between the European Union and its Member States, on the one hand, and Central America on the other, OJ L 346, 15.12.2012, p. 3–2621.

[6] Free Trade Agreement between the European Union and the Republic of Singapore, OJ L 294, 14.11.2019, p. 3–755.

[7] Comprehensive Economic and Trade Agreement between Canada, the European Union and its Member States, OJ L 11, 14.1.2017, p. 23–1079.

[8] Free Trade Agreement between the European Union and the Socialist Republic of Viet Nam, OJ L186, 12.06.2020, p. 3–1400.

[9] Agreement between the European Union and Japan for an Economic Partnership. OJ L 330, 27.12.2018, p. 3–899.

[10] EU-Mexico Trade Agreement as part a modernized Global Agreement, agreement in principle was reached in April 2018, available at: http://trade.ec.europa.eu/doclib/press/index.cfm?id=1833.

understand the scope and the direction of the EU approach, this chapter draws upon the strategic EU Commission's non-papers on the development of TSD Chapters in FTAs (European Commission 2017b, 2018).

The chapter is structured as follows: the first section focuses on the substantive provisions, usually referring to the key multilateral environmental and labour rights agreements and conventions within the framework of FTAs; the second section discusses the enforcement mechanism, where the approach is essentially cooperative in nature ('cooperative model'), which does not include dispute settlement in a traditional sense. The third section discusses the institutional structure of cooperation. The final section concludes.

## SUBSTANTIVE PROVISIONS OF THE TSD CHAPTERS

A common feature of the TSD chapters in EU FTAs is that they refer to the parties' commitments under the international agreements and conventions. In the area of environmental protection, these are the Multilateral Environmental Agreements (MEAs) that the parties have ratified.[11] In the area of labour rights, the references are to the labour standards contained in the ILO Conventions ratified by the parties.[12] Although the exact list of the conventions is not usually mentioned, it is expected that the parties would at least respect the 'baseline' standards contained in the eight fundamental ILO Conventions.[13] The effective implementation of the four core labour standards contained in these conventions (elimination of forced labour, a right to collective bargaining, elimination of child labour and prohibition of discrimination) are explicitly spelled out in TSD chapters as an obligation of the parties.[14]

From the analysis of the substantive scope of TSD chapters, we could see some marginal advancements with regard to environment and labour. In the area of environment, for instance, this could be seen in climate change regulation. A common feature of TSD chapters in new generation FTAs is the enshrined commitment of the parties to effectively implement the United Nations Framework Convention on Climate Change (UNFCCC). In addition,

---

[11] See, e.g., Article 13.5.2 of the EU-Korea TSD Chapter.

[12] The only exception is the EU-Central America FTA, which lists eight fundamental ILO Conventions (Article 286.2).

[13] Freedom of Association and Protection of the Right to Organise Convention, 1948; Right to Organise and Collective Bargaining Convention, 1949; Forced Labour Convention, 1930; Abolition of Forced Labour Convention, 1957; Minimum Age Convention, 1973; Worst Forms of Child Labour Convention, 1999; Equal Remuneration Convention, 1951; Discrimination (Employment and Occupation) Convention, 1958.

[14] See, e.g., Article 13.4.3 of the EU-Korea TSD Chapter. EU-Central America FTA explicitly lists eight fundamental ILO Conventions (Article 286.2).

the agreements contain soft law provisions regarding the parties' cooperation in this area.[15] The most recent advancement was the inclusion of the Paris Agreement adopted under the auspices of the United Nations Framework Convention on Climate Change to the list of binding commitments in the agreements with Japan and Mexico. This development is significant especially given the EU Commission's intention to include Paris Agreement references into all future trade agreements.[16]

In the area of labour, in addition to the core labour standards, EU FTAs go further by referring to the ILO Decent Work Agenda, which makes them distinctive from labour provisions in US FTAs (Melo Araujo 2018). With regard to the Decent Work Agenda, it is especially relevant to note that CETA and EU-Mexico's FTA references extend beyond the previous FTAs' simple reaffirmation of commitments under the Ministerial Declaration on the UN Economic and Social Council on Generating Full and Productive Employment and Decent Work for All of 2006 ('Decent Work Agenda'). CETA and EU-Mexico expand this provision by including references to the ILO Declaration on Social Justice for a Fair Globalization of 2008 focusing on specific issue areas, such as occupational safety and health, compensatory schemes in case of injury, the establishment of certain non-discriminatory work condition standards or the maintenance of an effective labour inspection system.[17] Furthermore, CETA and EU-Mexico contain legally binding standards for domestic administrative and judicial proceedings in terms of labour law violations, seeking to enhance the transparency of the process and permitting effective action against infringement.[18] In this respect, CETA goes further than the EU-Mexico Global Agreement by extending a set of requirements for such proceedings.[19] However, it is worthwhile pointing out certain inconsistencies with regard to the EU approach on the Decent Work Agenda in the EU-Japan EPA, which not only fails to follow the CETA blueprint, but also enshrines a level of commitments that is even somewhat lower than in EU-Korea FTA.[20]

---

[15] See, e.g., Article 12.10 (f) of EU-Singapore FTA provides for cooperation on climate change, "including ways to address adverse effects of trade on climate, as well as means to promote low-carbon technologies and energy efficiency".

[16] Article 16.4.4 of the EU-Japan EPA and Article 5.2(a) of the EU-Mexico TSD Chapter.

[17] Article 23.3 of CETA, Article 3 of the EU-Mexico TSD Chapter.

[18] Article 23.5 of CETA and Article 3 para. 9 of EU-Mexico TSD Chapter.

[19] Article 23.5(2)(a)–(d) CETA.

[20] Article 13.4 (2) of the EU-Korea FTA reaffirms commitments under the 2006 Ministerial Declaration of the UN Economic and Social Council on Full Employment and Decent Work. The Decent Work Agenda references in EU-Japan are limited to a simple mention in the preamble to the TSD Chapter and a mere stipulation that parties

Legal scholarship has been critical of the material coverage of TSD chapters as too minimalistic. For example, Gruni (2018) argues that the EU ought to step up its level of commitment beyond "referring to an extremely basic international level of protection" and instead, use its social and environmental *acquis* as an external standard (Gruni 2018, p. 6).

A more country-specific approach with an emphasis on specific issue areas determined on a case-by-case basis with each trading partner could be a positive add-on to the current approach. Even if it does not go beyond the relevant international standards, it could play a role in reaffirming these standards in a more assertive manner, including further close cooperation between the partners. In this regard, the US-Peru Trade Promotion Agreement (TPA) might serve as an example. By recognizing the issue of illegal logging as a major point of concern in Peru, it specifically targets forests management.[21]

This goal is outlined in the Commission's 2018 non-paper on TSD which suggests that the EU seeks to adopt a more country-specific TSD approach in the future, which "may include further specific issues of relevance for a given partner" (European Commission 2018, p. 7). However, the EU non-paper lacks identification of material areas in which the level of protection must be strengthened.

## ENFORCEMENT

Without effective enforcement mechanisms even the most ambitious rules become a mere aspiration. Hence, enforcement is a cornerstone of TSD effectiveness. In their study, Marx et al. take stock of the existing mechanisms for enforcement focusing on various procedural aspects (Marx et al. 2017). In terms of possible outcomes the two main approaches that crystallized over time are the sanctions-based enforcement practised in the US and Canada where a breach of TSD clauses could either lead to a withdrawal of trade concessions or a monetary compensation, and a cooperative model of the European Union which is essentially based on increased political dialogue instead of sanctions.

A cooperative model in EU FTAs precludes the application of a traditional FTA's dispute settlement mechanism to TSD. Instead, there is a separate dispute settlement procedure with two levels – consultations and, in case they

---

may "cooperate on trade-related aspects of ILO's Decent Work Agenda" within the main text. In this regard, the EU-Japan EPA recedes to the level of protection enshrined in the EU-Vietnam and EU-Colombia, Peru and Ecuador FTAs (see Articles 1 and 14(e) of the EU-Vietnam TSD chapter; Articles 267 and 286 (k) of the EU-Colombia, Peru and Ecuador FTAs, which also only briefly mention the Decent Work Agenda).

[21] Annex 18.3.4 on forests sector governance, attached to Chapter 18 of the EU-Peru Trade Promotion Agreement, signed on 12 April 2006.

fail, evaluation of the case by the panel of experts, the recommendations of which have a non-binding force. Although over time, this mechanism has been supplemented with progressive instruments, for instance, installing a mandatory follow-up to the recommendations by a panel of experts[22] and giving the stakeholders a right to submit observations on the experts' recommendations,[23] it still remains a non-binding measure. It has never been used in practice until recently where it was applied to labour violations in Korea.

A lack of a legally binding enforcement mechanism in TSD chapters of EU FTAs continues to be a frequently voiced point of criticism.[24] For instance, the implementation report on the EU-Korea FTA found various shortcomings in the Republic of Korea with regard to implementation of labour standards, which even decreased during the period of evaluation (European Commission 2017c). The same applies to Peru and Colombia – as for the former, problems have been recorded in implementation of fundamental ILO Conventions, upholding the level of domestic labour protection and promoting the civil society dialogue (Orbie and Van den Putte 2016, p. 31); as for the latter, various interviews with stakeholders indicated that labour provisions under the TSD chapter have been "little more than lofty words" or "half-hearted exercise by the EU to tick the box on its treaty obligations" (Marx et al. 2016, p. 599). A need for a more vigorous approach to TSD enforcement was often pointed out by the European Parliament, which in its 2016 resolution called upon the Commission to "introduce TSD chapters with more effective deterrent mechanisms", including "in the form of monetary remedies", which could be implemented through "a temporary slowing down, reduction or even suspension of certain trade benefits provided by the agreement in the event of an aggravated, continuous breach of these standards".[25] Also, to enforce international climate change regulation, the French government issued a paper, where it proposed to treat the Paris Agreement as an essential clause of the CETA, for the violation of which a withdrawal of concessions may follow.[26]

---

[22] See, e.g., under EU-Colombia/Peru (Article 285), the parties shall present an action plan following the report of the Group of Experts. Also, according to CETA (Article 23.10(12)), "based on the final report of the Panel of Experts, the Parties shall endeavour within 3 months to identify appropriate measures to decide on a mutually acceptable plan".

[23] See, e.g., EU-Singapore (Article 12.7 (9)) and the subsequent agreement.

[24] See, e.g., Marx et al. (2016).

[25] See the European Parliament resolution of 5 July 2016 on implementation of the 2010 recommendations of Parliament on social and environmental standards, human rights and corporate responsibility (2015/2038(INI)), at 21(d).

[26] "Mise en œuvre du CETA: le plan d'action du gouvernement", available at: https://www.diplomatie.gouv.fr/IMG/pdf/plan_action_ceta_du_gouvernement_cle0c5b74.pdf, Axe 3, para. 4.

With a view to stepping up the enforcement of the TSD chapters, the European Commission in its non-paper of July 2017 initiated a discussion on whether it should continue the current approach or introduce a model with sanctions as practised by the US and Canada (European Commission 2017b). In its 2018 follow-up paper, however, the Commission expressed a clear preference for maintaining the current cooperative approach for several reasons (European Commission 2018). First, the Commission emphasized that the cooperative approach facilitates a broad design of TSD chapters, as trading partners would not be willing to undertake ambitious TSD commitments under the sanctions-based model. Second, the Commission argued that the US and Canada's sanction-based approach to TSD enforcement has not been practically effective. In *Guatemala – Issues Relating to the Obligations Under Article 16.2.1(a) of the CAFTA-DR*, which remains to date the only case concerning an alleged infringement of an FTA's TSD chapter, the US was unable to prove that Guatemala's failure to comply with certain labour rights standards guaranteed under the Dominican Republic – Central America FTA (CAFTA-DR) "constitute[d] a course of inaction that was in a manner affecting trade".[27] Ultimately, the rejection of the sanctions-based approach by the Commission is based on the premise that sanctions are simply punitive in nature and could ultimately hurt the vulnerable population, rather than remedy the existing TSD violations in a partner country.

It is relevant to mention, though, that the recently issued Opinion 2/15 of the European Court of Justice (CJEU) interpreting the EU-Singapore FTA authorized the use of sanctions for the breach of TSD clauses. The court classified these clauses as the "essential elements" of the agreement, the violation of which, based on the interpretation of Article 60(1) of the Vienna Convention of the Law of Treaties (VCLT), could be countered with suspension of execution of other provisions of the FTA.[28] The Court's decision, nevertheless, seems quite controversial in terms of legal reasoning purely based on the customary rules.[29] In fact, it does not correspond to the EU's current strategic position with regard to the TSD enforcement as mentioned before, which suggests that future withdrawal of concessions would still be highly unlikely, irrespective of the CJEU's authorization of sanctions.

---

[27] See the Final Report of the Arbitral Panel established pursuant to Chapter Twenty of the Dominican Republic – Central America – United States Free Trade Agreement in a Matter of Guatemala – Issues Relating to the Obligations Under Article 16.2.1(a) of the CAFTA-DR, 14 June 2017, para. 594.

[28] Opinion 2/15, *FTA with Singapore*, EU:C:2017:376, para. 156.

[29] See some criticism of the CJEU decision in Beaucillon, C. (2017), "Opinion 2/15: Sustainable Is the New Trade: Rethinking Coherence for the New Common Commercial Policy", *European Papers*, **2**(3), 825.

The position of the EU on the use of sanctions seems to be quite clear. Although this chapter is not aimed at advocating for either of the enforcement approaches, some of the Commission's arguments in favour of the cooperative model do not seem to be very convincing. Firstly, the TSD reform documents do not suggest substantial broadening of the scope of TSD chapters in future agreements, while a broad scope is the Commission's argument for non-application of sanctions. The analysis in the previous section shows only marginal improvements in the scope of 'new generation' FTAs. Secondly, an argument could be made that a mere possibility of trade sanctions improves the overall effectiveness of the TSD provisions. For instance, the threat of sanctions might itself act as a deterrence mechanism inducing the parties to comply with the TSD provisions (Marx et al. 2017, p. 53). Also, Vogt (2015) argued for the correlation between strict sanctions clauses and a strong review mechanism by pointing out that since the TSD clauses in EU FTAs are not subject to a binding dispute settlement, the EU Commission had little incentive to assess the labour law violations in partner countries sufficiently (Vogt 2015, p. 857).

Moreover, the outright rejection of sanctions closes the door to possible tailor-made solutions that could include certain elements of sanctions mechanisms – for instance, the application of sanctions to limited scope of TSD chapters that is of strategic significance. The French government suggested such an approach for the Paris Agreement violations.[30] The advantage of this approach might be that it would not prevent the overall broad scope of the TSD chapters, as the EU Commission fears, given that sanctions can exclusively be applied for specific violations. Meanwhile, it would give an opportunity to target violations of the especially significant strategic provisions in a more assertive manner, such as in those dealing with climate change. Another example of this tailor-made approach could be the application of sanctions directly to the violators – companies and individuals (the so-called 'targeted sanctions') (Portela 2018). One of the examples of this approach could be found in the US-Peru Trade Promotion Agreement, which provides for a possibility for the US to deny access to imports from those Peruvian exporters/producers who did not comply with relevant rules and regulations on forest management.[31] There have been other suggestions in academic literature on how to implement a more assertive TSD enforcement that could explore the benefits of a sanctions-based system (e.g. Marx et al. 2017).

---

[30] "Mise en œuvre du CETA: le plan d'action du gouvernement", available at: https://www.diplomatie.gouv.fr/IMG/pdf/plan_action_ceta_du_gouvernement_cle0c5b74.pdf, p. 50.

[31] Annex 18.3.4, para. 13 of the US-Peru TPA.

Effective enforcement, in any case, is not limited to the use of sanctions, which should be viewed as a measure of last resort. In fact, the US, while a sanctions-based approach proponent, increasingly uses a dialogue-based system, while arbitral initiation follows as a measure of last resort.[32] Its enforcement system largely relies on monitoring and review mechanisms. It maintains a special Monitoring and Enforcement of Trade Agreements Division in its Department of Labor that reviews the alleged inconsistencies with the FTA Labour Chapters and has been so far quite active. To date, it has issued recommendations for Guatemala, Bahrain, Peru, Mexico, Dominican Republic, Honduras, and Columbia.[33] The environmental reviews are performed by the United States Trade Representative (USTR) along with the Chair of the Council on Environmental Quality. Recently, following such a review, the USTR performed its inter-governmental consultations under the US-Peru Trade Promotion Agreement regarding management of forests, which proved to be successful.[34]

The EU does not have a comparable comprehensive periodic review mechanism, which, as has been mentioned above, could be correlated with its weaker enforcement mechanism. Instead, it has an annual FTAs review that addresses all free trade agreements, as well as ex-post in-depth evaluation reports for a particular FTA in terms of all issue areas (e.g. European Commission 2017c). In its non-paper of 2018, the European Commission draws attention to the needs for periodic reviews; however, it is still not quite clear how exactly this mechanism is going to be utilized with regard to the implementation of TSD chapters. Thus, an argument could be made that the review process might be one of the points where there is a room for improvement within the confines of the current EU cooperative model of enforcement.

The recent evidence, however, suggests that the EU is attempting to move towards a more assertive enforcement by exploring the possibilities of its current model. The intentions in the EU Commission's 2018 non-paper materialized recently when the EU non-binding dispute settlement was initiated with Korea for its non-compliance with two core labour principles: freedom of association and the right to collective bargaining, as well as failure to ratify four out of eight fundamental ILO Conventions. Since the consultations did

---

[32] See the summaries re labour consultations and review procedures: https://www.dol.gov/agencies/ilab/our-work/trade/fta-submissions. So far, consultations have been only held with Bahrain. As regards other countries, the US Department of Labor issued recommendations.

[33] Ibid.

[34] See the USTR Press Release of 4 September 2019 at: https://ustr.gov/about-us/policy-offices/press-office/press-releases/2018/april/ustr-successfully-resolves-concerns.

not bring settlement, in October 2020, the Panel of Experts heard the case and issued a number of recommendations with regard to implementations of labour standards by Korea. Pursuant to Article 13 of the EU-Korea FTA, Korea now has to "make best efforts" to take into considerations the panel's recommendations. In a way, this mechanism resembles consultations and recommendations under the US FTAs, but without a possibility to use sanctions. The final implementation of the panel recommendations by Korea will give an opportunity to test whether such a model without sanctions is a workable solution.

## INSTITUTIONAL STRUCTURE

Due to the non-adversarial nature of the cooperative approach to TSD enforcement in EU FTAs, it requires strong institutional cooperation – a platform for "learning and socialization", which can make improvements "through longer-term change in political norms and processes" (Harrison et al. 2019, p. 262). The importance of the institutional cooperation for the implementation of TSD clauses has been often emphasized by various studies. For instance, the ILO finds that one of the more successful aspects of trade agreements has been the multi-stakeholder institutions, leading to "increased public awareness of labour issues, enhanced social dialogue and a strengthened ability to place labour issues on the political agenda" (International Labour Organization 2017, p. 47). Also, the empirical analysis made by Carrère et al. (2017) concluded that deeper cooperation provisions could in practice be particularly effective as an enforcement tool.

The institutional structure of TSD implementation in EU FTAs is represented by a specific TSD Committee consisting of government representatives, as well as a structure for civil society participation – Domestic Advisory Groups (DAGs) at the country level and a joint Civil Society Forum (CSF) with participants from both parties.

The implementation report of the EU-Korea FTA has highlighted that the institutional mechanisms of the TSD chapter may deliver practical results (European Commission 2017c). For instance, continued and focused discussions at the TSD Committee led to a re-engagement of Korea with the ILO (European Commission 2017c). In addition, Korea unilaterally adopted an Emissions Trading Scheme in 2015 following the TSD Committee meeting where it was discussed extensively (Su 2018).

There are, however, certain drawbacks in EU FTAs when it comes to civil society involvement in TSD dialogue. As has been pointed out by Martens et al. (2018), who analysed the relevant provisions in the agreements starting from EU-Korea and concluding with CETA, there is considerable variation between civil society involvement in EU FTAs. Notably, taking into account various indicators such as membership and independence of DAGs, operation of CSF, interaction among civil society and interaction with the government(s), involvement in the dispute settlement mechanisms, both CETA and EU-Korea FTA turn out to be the most ambitious in terms of civil society involvement, whereas EU-Vietnam fits into the intermediate category and EU-Singapore along with EU-Colombia, Peru, and Ecuador scored the lowest (Martens et al. 2018).

The most recent agreements demonstrate considerable variation in terms of civil society engagement. On the one hand, the EU-Mexico trade agreement does add to the CETA blueprint by enhancing involvement of DAGs and the CFS in the implementation of TSD chapters. For example, both agreements create a framework for increased interaction between the TSD Committee and the CSF by setting up the obligation of the TSD Committee to present updates relating to the implementation of the TSD chapter to the CSF and grants the CSF the opportunity to express views and opinions on such updates.[35] The EU-Mexico FTA further obliges each party to "give due consideration" to such opinions.[36] Moreover, the EU-Mexico agreement provides a stronger role for DAGs in the TSD-specific dispute settlement procedure than any of its predecessors. It contains, for example, a binding obligation of the TSD sub-committee to seek advice of DAGs within the dispute settlement process[37] or a mandate to discuss implementing measures following the Panel of Experts' recommendations with the DAGs.[38] It should also be noted that the EU Commission has expressed intention to strengthen the role of DAG beyond the scope of the TSD Committee, allowing it to review the entire agreement in light of sustainability. The EU-Mexico trade agreement will be the first agreement to implement this approach (European Commission 2018). If the EU-Mexico's institutional and civil society provisions were to become a blueprint for future FTAs, the EU approach to civil society involvement will likely be a pioneer at the international stage, allowing for a more inclusive, regular and independent exchange on sustainability-related issues of the entire FTA with the broader public.

On the other hand, however, EU-Japan does not appear to demonstrate the same improvements in terms of civil society participation in the TSD Committee, as in CETA and EU-Mexico. For instance, it does not provide for exchanges between the civil society and the TSD Committee, but only mentions possible interactions.[39] In fact, even some of the provisions in EU-Korea are more ambitious than in EU-Japan, as EU-Korea foresees the participation

---

[35] Article 22.4.4(b) of CETA.

[36] Article 14.6 of the EU-Mexico TSD Chapter.

[37] Article 16.4 of the EU-Mexico TSD Chapter.

[38] Article 17.9 of the EU-Mexico TSD Chapter.

[39] Article 16.13 (2) (c).

of DAGs within the dispute settlement process, whereas this is not the case in the EU-Japan agreement.[40]

The fact that the EU-Japan falls outside the standard for civil society participation established in other 'new generation' FTAs illustrates that strengthening the participatory agenda is inconsistently applied across different FTAs. It is understandable that because of difference in negotiating leverage, as well as the domestic priorities of partner countries, the outcome of negotiations might differ across trading partners. However, it raises concerns that the EU is sending mixed messages when it comes to the institutional and civil society provisions, which are at the core of its cooperative TSD enforcement model.

## CONCLUSION

Despite a marginal improvement of the material coverage of the analysed EU 'new generation' FTAs and a positive trend towards a more assertive enforcement showcased in EU-Korea case, the EU approach to TSD has space for further development. Firstly, it relates to substantive commitments, especially considering that the advantage of the current cooperative approach without sanctions is that it allows maintaining a broader scope of commitments, which has been indicated by the EU Commission as one of its motivations for opting for this approach. As this chapter demonstrates, for the time being there appears to be no specific strategic endeavour to enhance the level of environmental and social protection under the TSD chapters, especially as going beyond MEAs or ILO Conventions. Secondly, the effective implementation of TSD standards under the existing approach might also be called into question. Although the EU Commission has clearly indicated that it does not seek to move from a 'cooperative' to a 'sanctions-based' TSD enforcement, there is also some room for improvement within the selected model, such as intensification of dialogue and review mechanisms. Pivotal for the current cooperative model is the institutional cooperation and the civil society engagement (backbone of the current 'cooperative' model). Despite such importance, this aspect is not consistently stepped up in all analysed trade agreements. In particular, the fact that the recently negotiated EU-Japan largely falls beyond the standards set by the EU-Korea, CETA or the EU-Mexico trade agreements as regards civil society engagement illustratively showcases that there is no consistent strengthening of the EU external TSD agenda in all material issue areas. In view of limited efforts to enhance the scope or enforcement of TSD chapters in EU FTAs, one might question whether the EU's current approach to TSD is sufficient to fulfil

---

40 Articles 13.14 (4) and 13.15 (1) of the EU-Korea TSD Chapter.

the objective to ensure sustainable development enshrined in Articles 3(5) and 21(2)(h) TEU.

## REFERENCES

Carrère, C., Olarreaga, M. and Raess, D. (2017) Labor Clauses in Trade Agreements: Worker Protection or Protectionism? CEPR Discussion Paper No. DP12251. https://ssrn.com/abstract=3031888.

European Commission (2017a) Reflection Paper on Harnessing Globalisation. https://ec.europa.eu/commission/sites/beta-political/files/reflection-paper-globalisation_en.pdf.

European Commission (2017b) Trade and Sustainable Development Chapters in EU Free Trade Agreements. Non-paper, 11 July.

European Commission (2017c) Civic Consulting and the IFO Institute, Evaluation of the Implementation of the Free Trade Agreement between the EU and its Member States and the Republic of Korea. http://trade.ec.europa.eu/doclib/docs/2017/june/tradoc_155673.pdf.

European Commission (2018) Feedback and Way Forward on Improving the Implementation and Enforcement of Trade and Sustainable Development Chapters in EU Free Trade Agreements. Non-paper, 26 February.

European Commission (2020) Strategic Plan 2020–2024.https://trade.ec.europa.eu/doclib/docs/2020/november/tradoc_159104.pdf.

Gruni, G. (2018) Towards a Sustainable World Trade: The Commercial Policy of the European Union After Opinion 2/15 CJEU. *Global Trade and Customs Journal*, **13**(1), 3–12.

Harrison, J., Barbu, M., Campling, L., Richardson, B. and Smith, A. (2019) Governing Labour Standards through Free Trade Agreements: Limits of the European Union's Trade and Sustainable Development Chapters. *JCMS: Journal of Common Market Studies*, **57**(2), 260–277.

International Labour Organization (2017) *ILO Handbook on Assessment of Labour Provisions in Trade and Investment Agreements*. Geneva: ILO.

Larik, J. (2011) Much More Than Trade: The Common Commercial Policy in a Global Context. In Evans, M. and Koutrakos, P. (eds.), *Beyond the Established Legal Orders: Policy Interconnections between the EU and the Rest of the World*. Oxford: Hart Publishing, 13–45.

Martens, D., Van den Putte, L., Oehri, M. and Orbie, J. (2018) Mapping Variation of Civil Society Involvement in EU Trade Agreements: A CSI Index. *European Foreign Affairs Review*, **23**(1), 41–62.

Marx, A., Ebert, F. and Hachez, N. (2017) Dispute Settlement for Labour Provisions in EU Free Trade Agreements: Rethinking Current Approaches. *Politics and Governance*, **5**(4), 49–59.

Marx, A., Lein, B. and Brando, N. (2016) The Protection of Labour Rights in Trade Agreements: The Case of the EU-Colombia Agreement. *Journal of World Trade*, **50**(4), 587–610.

Melo Araujo, B. (2016) *The EU Deep Trade Agenda: Law and Policy*. Oxford: Oxford University Press.

Melo Araujo, B. (2018) Labour Provisions in EU and US Mega-Regional Trade Agreements: Rhetoric and Reality. *International and Comparative Law Quarterly*, **67**(1), 233–253.

Orbie, J. and Van den Putte, L. (2016) Labour Rights in Peru and the EU Trade Agreement: Compliance with the Commitments under the Sustainable Development Chapter. ÖFSE Working Paper, Austrian Foundation for Development Research, Vienna.https://biblio.ugent.be/publication/8055501/file/8055504.pdf.

Portela, C. (2018) Enforcing Respect for Labour Standards with Targeted Sanctions. Singapore: Friedrich-Ebert-Stiftung Office for Regional Cooperation in Asia. http://library.fes.de/pdf-files/bueros/singapur/14689.pdf.

Su, C.-H. (2018) Regulatory Network Calibration in the EU-Korea Free Trade Agreement. *European Foreign Affairs Review*, **23**(1), 1–20.

UN General Assembly (1994) United Nations Framework Convention on Climate Change. Resolution adopted by the General Assembly, 20 January 1994, A/RES/48/189.

Vogt, J. (2015) The Evolution of Labour Rights and Trade: A Transatlantic Comparison and Lessons for the Transatlantic Trade and Investment Partnership. *Journal of International Economic Law*, **18**(5), 827–860.

# 20. Reform of international investment agreements and sustainable development: contrasting the EU and Global South approaches

**Gudrun Zagel**

## INTRODUCTION

In recent years, International Investment Agreements (IIAs) have become one of the most contested issues in global governance (UNCTAD 2018; UNCITRAL 2019). A particular challenge is the linkage between IIAs and the UN Sustainable Development Goals (UNSDGs).[1] The UNSDGs formulate various strategies to harmonize the three dimensions of sustainable development, namely economic growth, social inclusion, and environmental protection.[2] Whereas the UNSDGs stress the role of foreign investment in realizing sustainable development,[3] IIAs appear to impede rather than encourage their realization. While IIAs aim at promoting foreign investment through granting protection against undue host state conduct (Salacuse 2021, p. 142), they have recently faced intense criticism for affecting the host states' regulatory sovereignty to implement the environmental, social, climate, public health, and other sustainability policies required by the UNSDGs (Zagel 2020a, p. 4).

The IIA critique arose from several cases in which foreign investors have challenged sustainability-related host state measures affecting foreign investors – *Phillip Morris v. Australia* and *Uruguay* being prominent examples.[4] While foreign investors have not always won, the cases still show the weaknesses of traditional IIAs. Their lean provisions give arbitral tribunals

---

1 UNGA, *Transforming our World: The 2030 Agenda for Sustainable Development* (2015), A/Res/70/1.

2 UN 2030 Agenda, preamble, 3rd recital and paras 2 and 9.

3 UN 2030 Agenda, para 67, and SDGs 2a, 7a, 10b.

4 *Phillip Morris v. Australia*, PCA 2012-12; *Phillip Morris v. Uruguay*, ICSID Case No. ARB/10/7.

broad discretion to consider – or neglect – host state interests, thus preventing host states from predicting the cases' outcomes. Moreover, the investor-state dispute settlement (ISDS) system enshrined in IIAs is criticized for being unpredictable and biased towards host states. Finally, opponents criticize the unbalanced content of traditional IIAs that merely contain host state obligations towards investors but are silent on investor obligations towards host states and their public policies, notably their sustainable development policies (Traidcraft 2015; Mann 2013, p. 532).

The critique has induced a worldwide IIA reform process (UNCTAD 2018).. The EU is a predominant player. The investment chapters included in the EU's Trade and Investment Agreements (TIAs) refine the substantive protection standards, strengthen the host states' regulatory sovereignty, and include a reformed ISDS system (European Commission 2015). However, the controversies continue (Traidcraft 2015, p. 19). Extensive IIA reforms are also underway outside the EU in Africa, Asia, and the Americas. Prominent examples include Brazil,[5] India,[6] or the African continent.[7] The states pursue innovative approaches to reconcile investment protection and sustainable development that have gone mostly unnoticed in the European reform debates.

In light of the continuing critique of the EU's investment regime and the prospering IIA landscape outside Europe, the question arises of whether the EU responses are adequate to meet the contested IIA system's challenges. This chapter compares the reform approaches of EU IIAs and selected Global South IIAs to reconcile investment protection and sustainable development. The first section provides an overview of the IIA development in the EU and selected Global South states and the respective efforts to meet the IIAs' contestation. The second section compares the different techniques of integrating sustainable development in the reformed IIAs. The third section analyses the substantive IIA reforms to preserve the host state's regulatory authority to implement sustainable development policies. The fourth section explores the ISDS reforms to prevent arbitral proceedings from unduly affecting sustainable development. The conclusions examine which Global South reform approaches may constitute viable alternatives to the EU's IIA reforms to reconcile investment protection and sustainable development and provide possible answers to the current IIA regime's contestation.

---

5 Brazil Model-BIT 2015; all IIAs cited in this article are available at: https://investmentpolicy.unctad.org/international-investment-agreements.

6 India Model-BIT 2015.

7 E.g. Pan-African Investment Code (PAIC) 2016; BIT Morocco-Nigeria 2016.

# OVERVIEW OF THE IIA AND SUSTAINABLE DEVELOPMENT DEBATE IN EUROPE AND THE GLOBAL SOUTH

## European Union

Since the 1960s, many European states have concluded IIAs as Bilateral Investment Treaties (BITs) to provide an international legal framework for their investments in host states that were still struggling with forming and consolidating their state functions after independence (Salacuse 2021, p. 110). BITs establish substantive protection standards that host state conduct must meet, the most prominent being the rules on expropriation and fair and equitable treatment (FET) (Salacuse 2021, p. 168). BITs also enshrine an ISDS system that permits foreign investors to enforce their rights against host states and obtain compensation for breaches (Salacuse 2021, p. 493).

Since the Lisbon Treaty has vested the EU with the exclusive competencies to regulate foreign investment,[8] the EU has gradually taken over this task from its Member States and concluded several TIAs that include IIA chapters similar to BITs.[9] As long as IIAs were mainly concluded between Global North and Global South states, there was little discussion on these instruments. However, since the ISDS system has prospered in the mid-1990s (ICSID 2022, p. 7) and industrialized states increasingly became respondents to investors' claims, this perception has changed.

Controversial is particularly the impact of IIAs on the regulatory sovereignty of host states. Infamous cases, including *Eiser v. Spain*,[10] or *Philip Morris v. Australia*,[11] triggered concerns that IIAs and ISDS impede environmental, public health, or other sustainability measures required to implement the UNSDGs. The cases fuelled fears that IIAs require host states to compensate foreign investors for measures affecting their property, even if they serve sustainability purposes. Moreover, the ISDS rules frequently prevent host states from envisaging the case outcome, and the proceedings produce enormous costs even if a state wins the case.[12]

To remedy the shortcomings of IIAs, the EU has undertaken extensive reforms (European Commission 2015). Sustainable development plays a distinct role in this endeavour, as arts 21(2)(c) TEU and 205 TFEU require the

---

8 Art 207.4.2 TFEU.

9 CETA, TIA EU-Japan, TIA EU-Singapore, TIA EU-Vietnam, see also https://ec.europa.eu/trade/policy/countries-and-regions/negotiations-and-agreements/.

10 *Eiser v. Spain*, ICSID Case No. ARB/13/36.

11 *Phillip Morris v. Australia*, PCA 2012-12.

12 E.g. *Cortec v. Kenia*, ICSID Case No. ARB/15/29.

EU to pursue "sustainable economic, social and environmental development of developing countries" as a foreign policy goal that the EU must consider when regulating external trade and investment. Today, all EU TIAs with developed and developing countries alike contain distinct chapters addressing sustainable development and refine their IIA chapters to guide arbitrators on how to interpret IIA provisions affecting the implementation of host states' sustainability policies.[13] New elements to be discussed in the subsequent chapters include substantive obligations on sustainable development, the clarification of the host state's regulatory powers, and reforms of the ISDS system (European Commission 2015). Nevertheless, the European discussions on IIAs and their adverse effects on sustainable development continue (European Commission 2018).

## Global South

Until the end of the twentieth century, Global South states[14] were mainly the "junior partners" in IIAs that – despite being reciprocal – in practice primarily served to protect investments from industrialized countries in Global South host states (Salacuse 2021, pp. 110, 114). They also have been the primary respondents of investment claims, which frequently resulted in awards in favour of investors (ICSID 2022, p. 13). Although the adverse effects of IIAs on Global South host states are potentially worse than on industrialized states with politically stable systems and a high level of economic and social development, many Global South states continue to rely on IIAs to attract foreign investment and conclude IIAs with the Global North and increasingly also the Global South.[15] To address the potentially negative impact of IIAs on sustainable development, many Global South IIAs show reform approaches that hardly exist in EU IIAs.

A leading role in the IIA reform is played by the African continent, where the process started more than ten years ago.[16] African states have adopted several new instruments, including the SADC Protocol on Finance and

---

[13] See https://ec.europa.eu/trade/policy/policy-making/sustainable-development/; e.g. CETA; EU-Japan FTA, EU-Singapore FTA; EU-Vietnam FTA.

[14] Although the term 'Global South' is problematic, as it comprises numerous states with diverse states of political, economic, and social development, it will be used in this chapter for the group of states that have traditionally been the recipients of foreign investment, while they undertook little or no foreign investment activities.

[15] E.g. BIT Morocco-Nigeria, BIT Brazil-India.

[16] ECOWAS Supplementary Act A/SA.3/12/08 adopting community rules on investment and the modalities for their implementation with Economic Community of West African States, 12 December 2008.

Investment Amendment (2016)[17] or the BIT Morocco-Nigeria (2016).[18] The most ambitious project is the continent-wide Draft Pan-African Investment Code (PAIC) (2016),[19] which provides the basis for negotiating the AfCFTA Investment Protocol (Mbengue and Schacherer 2017). Likewise, Brazil, which refused to conclude IIAs for a long time, has adopted a Model-BIT in 2015 that shifts the focus from investment protection to investment promotion (Muniz et al. 2017).[20] Also, India has adopted a Model-BIT in 2015 that contains several elements to reconcile host state regulatory powers and investment protection (Zagel 2020b).[21]

The reformed IIAs are strongly influenced by the IIA reform proposals of UNCTAD and the IISD (UNCTAD 2018; IISD 2005), as e.g., the BIT Morocco-Nigeria exemplifies. Like in Europe, the reformed Global South IIAs aim at ensuring that IIA obligations do not prevent host states from pursuing the UNSDGs. The examined Global South IIAs integrate sustainable development and better balance host states' and investors' rights and obligations.[22] Several reform elements also exist in modern European IIAs, including the refined expropriation or FET provisions, the clarified host states' regulatory powers, or the ISDS reforms. However, there are also novel elements inexistent in European IIAs, such as the detailed specification of sustainable development objectives, the comprehensive establishment of the host state's right to regulate and corresponding investor obligations, and unique reforms of the ISDS system. Subsequently, these aspects will be discussed and compared to the EU approaches to assess their feasibility to counter the current IIA system's contestation.

## INTEGRATING SUSTAINABLE DEVELOPMENT IN IIAs

### EU Approach: Trade and Sustainable Development Chapters

The EU has a long tradition of promoting sustainable development through its external trade policy (Bartels 2013, p. 305). All TIAs concluded since

---

17 South African Development Community (SADC) Amendment 2016 to the SADC Protocol on Finance and Investment, 17 May 2017.

18 BIT Morocco-Nigeria, 3 December 2016.

19 Draft Pan-African Investment Code, 31 March–2 April 2016, revised December 2016 (PAIC).

20 Brazil Model-BIT 2015.

21 India Model-BIT 2020.

22 Cf. e.g. PAIC, preamble, 11th recital; Morocco–Nigeria BIT, preamble, 6th recital; Brazil Model-BIT, preamble, 3rd, 5th and 6th recital.

Lisbon contain "Trade and Sustainable Development" (TSD) chapters irrespective of whether the partners are industrialized or developing countries (Bartels 2013, p. 297).[23] The chapters are mostly uniform in their substantive content, implementing obligations, and monitoring mechanisms (NBTS 2019). However, it remains questionable whether and to what extent these EU foreign policy instruments contribute to realizing sustainable development (European Commission 2018).

The TSD chapters typically address sustainable development in its economic, social, and environmental dimensions.[24] For defining the substantive standards of sustainable development, they refer to relevant international environmental and labour agreements that the contracting parties should ratify and implement.[25] The implementing obligations in the TSD chapters reflect the implementing obligations in the respective international agreements, which are traditionally formulated weakly and constitute mainly best efforts obligations (Bartels 2013, p. 306; NBTS 2019, p. 25). Accordingly, the TSD chapters typically require to effectively implement the relevant international agreements through national measures, to cooperate in relevant international organizations, and to consult and cooperate on labour and social standards and environmental protection.[26]

Regarding implementation, the TSD chapters establish a mechanism that is entirely independent of the other TIA mechanisms.[27] They expressly exclude the general dispute settlement mechanism and ISDS.[28] Instead, they create a treaty body to conduct consultations, monitoring, and dispute settlement on disagreements arising from the TSD chapter only.[29] While government consultation and panel procedure are similar to the WTO dispute settlement process,[30] the implementation and outcome of the process resemble the monitoring processes of ILO conventions and MEAs (NBTS 2019, p. 25); for instance, the "enforcement" lacks sanctions but is limited to publishing the results of the

---

[23] See https://ec.europa.eu/trade/policy/policy-making/sustainable-development/, e.g. EU-Vietnam FTA, Chapter 13; EU-Japan FTA, Chapter 16, CETA, Chapters 22–24.

[24] See arts 21(2)(d) and 21(3) TEU; e.g. art 12.1.2 EU-Singapore FTA; art 16.1.2 EU-Japan FTA; art 22.1 CETA.

[25] E.g. arts 12.3 and 12.6 EU-Singapore FTA; arts 16.3, 16.4 and 16.6 EU-Japan FTA.

[26] E.g. arts 12.3, 12.4 and 12.6 EU-Singapore FTA; arts 16.3 and 16.4 EU-Japan FTA.

[27] E.g. arts 12.14ff EU-Singapore FTA.

[28] E.g. art 12.16 EU-Singapore FTA; arts 23.11 and 24.17 CETA.

[29] E.g. arts 12.14 and 12.15 EU-Singapore FTA.

[30] E.g. art 12.17.1ff EU-Singapore FTA.

consultations or panel decisions and the obligation to discuss their implementation (NBTS 2019, p. 23).[31]

A problem with the TSD chapters is that they do not specify their role in applying and interpreting the IIA chapters. For instance, the EU-Singapore IIA,[32] which was due to EU-internal legal reasons separated from the EU-Singapore FTA,[33] establishes in its preamble that foreign investment should promote sustainable development and refers to the "principles of sustainable development … reflected in the EU-Singapore FTA";[34] it lacks, however, details or binding obligations concerning sustainable development. The references in the EU-Singapore FTA's TSD chapter frequently address – in line with the title of the chapter – trade only,[35] whereas the references to investment are limited. The most explicit obligations regarding trade *and* investment are the obligations to implement a minimum of social, labour, and environmental standards, to introduce trade and investment-related environmental or social measures transparently, and the prohibition to reduce the levels of protection to attract foreign investment or trade.[36] Similarly, the CETA chapters 22–24 mainly focus on trade-related aspects of sustainable development. While the CETA chapters relating to sustainable development contain some references to investment, the CETA IIA chapter does not refer to the standards established in these chapters.

As the examples indicate, EU TIAs do not clarify how the substantive standards in the TSD chapters affect the IIA chapters' obligations. Although art 31(1) VCLT[37] requires the interpretation of the IIA chapters in their context, and the TSD chapters contain rules on sustainability measures affecting foreign investment, the lack of express reference in the IIA chapters creates uncertainty on whether and how arbitral tribunals will draw on these sustainability standards as relevant context when interpreting IIA rules. The fact that the implementation and monitoring mechanisms of the TSD chapters are entirely separate from the IIA chapter aggravates the problem.[38] Whereas ISDS jurisdiction is limited to claims arising under the IIA chapter,[39] and the IIA chapters provide enforcement and the adoption of sanctions for breaches of IIA

---

31 E.g. arts 12.16.6 and 12.17.8 EU-Singapore FTA; arts 23.9.5, 23.10.11, 24.14.5 and 24.15.10 CETA.

32 Cf. http://trade.ec.europa.eu/doclib/press/index.cfm?id=961.

33 CJEU, Opinion 2/15.

34 EU-Singapore FTA, preamble, 1st, 4th and 5th recital.

35 E.g. arts 12.1.2, 12.3.2, 12.4, 12.10 EU-Singapore FTA.

36 Arts 12.1.3, 12.12 and 12.13 EU-Singapore FTA; see also Bartels (2013, p. 306) with further reference.

37 Vienna Convention on the Law of Treaties (23 May 1969), 1155 UNTS 331.

38 See text accompanying nn. 27ff.

39 E.g. arts 1.18.5, 8.18.1, 23.11.1. and 24.16.1 CETA.

obligations,[40] the TSD monitoring process only provides soft mechanisms of monitoring. Due to these entirely separate regimes and their express limitation to the respective chapters, arbitral tribunals may be hesitant to consider the substantive sustainable development standards enshrined in the TSD chapters as a relevant context for interpreting the IIA obligations,[41] in particular, if this leads to a "de facto enforcement" of sustainable development standards, which contradicts the intention of the TSD chapters. In sum, the implementation of sustainable development into the EU's TIAs through TSD chapters appears insufficient to ensure that the IIA provisions are applied and interpreted in the light of the host states' sustainable development policies.

### Global South Approach: Extensive and Effective Reference to Sustainable Development in IIAs

Many Global South IIAs establish a clear link between sustainable development and foreign investment. Like many EU IIAs, many Global South IIAs expressly contain this objective in their preambles.[42] However, several Global South IIAs go one step further and integrate extensive reference to sustainable development in the substantive provisions of IIAs themselves. For instance, arts 1(1) and 4 PAIC establish the binding treaty objective that foreign investment must contribute to sustainable development and that only investment contributing to the sustainable development of the host state constitutes a protected investment (Mbengue and Schacherer 2017, p. 434). A different way to reinforce sustainable development is to specify host state regulatory powers and corresponding investor obligations to realize sustainable development (cf. the third section of this chapter). Such substantive obligations considerably strengthen the integration of sustainable development in IIAs.

Many Global South IIAs also pursue a broad sustainable development concept that exceeds the environmental and social standards contained in the TSD chapters and even specify the relevant standards. For instance, the BIT Morocco-Nigeria includes relevant international agreements to establish environmental, social, labour, and human rights obligations of investors and host states and combat corruption.[43] This approach makes the uncertain content of "sustainable development" tangible[44] and guides arbitrators on the substance

---

[40] E.g. arts 8.39 and 8.41 CETA.

[41] E.g. art 8.9 CETA; for details on host state regulatory authority under CETA see the third section of this chapter.

[42] Brazil Model-BIT, preamble, 4th recital; India Model-BIT, preamble, 2nd recital; PAIC, preamble, 7th and 17th recital.

[43] Cf. arts 13–15, 18, 19 and 24 BIT Morocco-Nigeria.

[44] Cf. FN2.

of sustainability measures the contracting parties intended to address. For instance, if ILO standards are an integral part of substantive IIA provisions, investor claims that host state regulatory measures implementing ILO obligations adversely affect their business conduct[45] may not be admissible, as the investment itself does not contribute to the sustainable development of the host state.[46] Alternatively, even if the claim is admissible, host state regulatory measures in line with the ILO standards are accepted measures to implement sustainable development that do not constitute indirect expropriation or a breach of the FET standard (see the third section of this chapter).

To conclude, introducing and clarifying sustainable development standards in IIAs is essential to reconcile sustainable development and investment protection. In contrast to EU IIAs, the examined Global South IIAs effectively integrate sustainable development in the substantive IIA provisions and specify the substantive sustainable development standards by referencing relevant international agreements. This approach ensures that arbitral tribunals apply and interpret IIA provisions in light of the envisaged standard of sustainable development.

## CLARIFYING HOST STATE REGULATORY POWERS

### EU Approach: Clarification of the Host State's Right to Regulate

Closely related to the lack of reference to sustainable development is that European IIAs unduly limit host states' regulatory powers to implement their sustainability policies. A host state's "police powers" are an essential element of a state's capability to perform its functions (UNCTAD 2012, p. 79).[47] They include the right to decide on the adoption and level of environmental, labour, and other sustainability measures, e.g., raising emission standards, regulating water prices, or increasing minimum wages. While states are free to choose the measures to implement their sustainability policies, they must comply with their IIA obligations to prevent responsibility.[48]

The substantive IIA provisions mostly perceived as impediments to the host state's regulatory powers are expropriation (Dolzer and Schreuer 2012, p. 98; Salacuse 2021, p. 380) and FET (Dolzer and Schreuer 2012, p. 130; Salacuse 2021, p. 289). Both provisions protect foreign investors against legal changes

---

45 E.g. *Veolia v. Egypt*, ICSID Case No. ARB/12/15.

46 Art 1 BIT Morocco-Nigeria.

47 *Tecmed v. Mexico* (Award), ICSID Case No. ARB(AF)/00/2 [119]; *Feldman v. Mexico* (Award, 2002), ICSID Case No. ARB(AF)/99/1 [83]; *ADC v. Hungary* (Award, 2006), ICSID Case No. ARB/03/16 [423].

48 *ADC* [423f]; *Tecmed* [120f].

in the host state affecting their businesses, and investors typically invoke them in investment disputes on regulatory measures to pursue public policies.[49] For instance, if environmental or social measures produce additional costs for foreign investors or even put them out of business, they may constitute indirect expropriation and require the host state to pay compensation (UNCTAD 2012, p. 63).[50] If not amounting to indirect expropriation, the measures may still require the host state to compensate foreign investors for a breach of the FET standard, if the legal changes are unexpected, do not follow the principles of transparency or the rule of law, or diminish the legitimately expected profits of an investor (Dolzer and Schreuer 2012, p. 145).[51]

The provisions on expropriation and FET in traditional IIAs are typically formulated in a lean manner and lack clauses exempting a host state's public policy measures from their scope of application. Therefore, arbitral tribunals have broad discretion to decide whether a host state's sustainability measure constitutes a legitimate exercise of the host state's regulatory sovereignty[52] or a measure interfering excessively or in bad faith with the investor's property.[53] Determining that threshold lies at the core of arbitral decisions,[54] but due to the limited guidance in IIAs, arbitral awards are hardly predictable (Mann 2013, p. 533).

Modern EU IIAs show different approaches to refine the line between a legitimate host state regulatory measure and a measure violating IIA obligations. Art 8.9 CETA provides the host state's right to regulate, preceding the provisions on expropriation and FET. Art 8.9.1 stresses the host state's right to regulate to achieve legitimate policy objectives, such as public health, environmental protection, or social protection. Following art 8.9.2, the mere fact that such regulations affect an investor's expectations does not amount to a breach of FET or expropriation. Art 8.10.2 specifies the meaning of FET and includes denial of justice, a fundamental breach of due process, manifest arbitrariness, targeted discrimination, or abuse of investors. Following art 8.10.4, FET only protects legitimate expectations if a host state made specific representations to the investor on which the investor relied and that the host state subsequently

---

49 E.g. cases cited in nn. 10–12.

50 E.g. *Tecmed*; *Metalclad v. Mexico* (Award, 2000), ICSID Case No. ARB(AF)/97/1 [103].

51 E.g. *CMS v. Argentina* (Award, 2005), ICSID Case No. ARB/01/8 [274ff]; *Sempra v. Argentina* (Award, 2007), ICSID Case No. ARB/02/16 [298] and [303].

52 *Tecmed* [119]; *Feldman* [103]; *El Paso v. Argentina* (Award, 2011) ICSID Case No. ARB/03/15 [367ff].

53 *ADC* [424].

54 *Feldman* [100] and [104f]; *El Paso* [348] and [402]; *Saluka v. Czech Republic* (Partial Award, 2006), UNCITRAL [302].

frustrated. Art 8.12 contains the classical rules on expropriation. However, it excludes in Annex 8-A non-discriminatory measures designed and applied to protect legitimate welfare objectives, such as health, safety, and the environment, from the scope of application of art 8.12 unless their impact on the investment is manifestly excessive.

An advantage of the detailed CETA rules is that they reaffirm the host states' right to adopt regulatory measures in the public interest. Yet, the rules still need interpretation regarding the conditions of a legitimate host state regulatory measure and its relationship with the substantive IIA protection standards. For instance, art 8.9 establishes the right to regulate in the public interest, and Annex 8-A provides that non-discriminatory measures in the public interest do not constitute indirect expropriation. However, it remains unclear whether such measures must meet due process and judicial review requirements specified in arts 8.12.1 and 8.12.4, as art 8.12 is not applicable. Whereas this deficit may be compensated by art 8.10.2 protecting against fundamental breaches of due process and denial of justice, the provisions still give ample scope for interpretation. As the Joint Interpretative Instrument on the CETA (JI) lacks further clarification, it lies again with the arbitral tribunals to determine the conditions of a legitimate host state regulatory measure.[55]

The perhaps most problematic issue for implementing sustainable development policies is that the CETA IIA chapter lacks any reference to sustainable development as an objective of host state regulatory measures, which raises the question of whether sustainability measures not mentioned in art 8.9 CETA are covered by the right to regulate – or rather trigger compensation claims. Arts 8.9.1, 8.12, and Annex 8-A(3) CETA only refer to measures to protect "public welfare" objectives, such as health, safety, and the environment. Additionally, art 8.9 permits the protection of public morals and social protection. However, a reference to other sustainable development policy areas, such as labour standards, is missing.[56] Although arts 23.5 and 24.5 CETA require the host state not to lower labour or environmental standards to attract foreign investment, the linkage between these rules and the IIA chapter is opaque.[57] Unclear also is how these provisions affect new standards or the increase in existing standards.[58] In sum, it is uncertain whether the clarifications in CETA cover the full range of host states' public policy measures necessary to implement all aspects of the UNSDGs.

---

[55] Joint Interpretative Instrument on the CETA (27 September 2017), 2017 OJ L 11/3, paras 2 and 6.

[56] See also CETA JI, paras 2 and 6.

[57] See the second section of this chapter.

[58] CETA JI, paras 7 and 8.

### Global South Approaches: Comprehensive Concept of Ensuring the Effective Implementation of Sustainable Development

Compared to EU IIAs, many Global South IIAs follow a broader reform approach. They pursue a comprehensive strategy of ensuring the effective implementation of sustainable development through foreign investment. Elements of this strategy include clarifying the expropriation and FET provisions and the host state's regulatory powers, as well as establishing corresponding investor obligations concerning sustainable development that complement the host state's efforts.

Many Global South IIAs refine the expropriation and FET standards to increase the host states' regulatory powers.[59] Whereas many provisions correspond to the EU approach, some Global South IIAs pursue a stricter line. For instance, art 7 Brazil Model-BIT exempts indirect expropriations entirely from the scope of the expropriation provision. Art 5.5 India Model-BIT exempts public policy measures from the scope of the expropriation provision if they are non-discriminatory.[60] Some IIAs delete the FET standard or replace it with provisions only granting specific treatment standards, such as transparency, the rule of law, or non-discriminatory treatment.[61] Clarifying substantive protection is, in principle, a feasible approach to limit the arbitral tribunals' discretion. However, maintaining fairness guarantees for investors and avoiding shifting the entire risk towards foreign investors is essential.

Like European IIAs, Global South IIAs specify the host state's regulatory powers to implement sustainable development policies. However, many Global South IIAs establish not only a *right* but comprehensive *obligations* of host states to regulate all elements of sustainable development. For instance, arts 13, 15, and 23 BIT Morocco-Nigeria oblige the host state to adopt environmental, social, and human rights measures following the relevant international conventions. Arts 15 and 16 Brazil Model BIT contain similar provisions. Moreover, many Global South IIAs pursue the broad concept of sustainable development provided by the UNSDGs and refer to sustainable development elements not mentioned in the EU context, such as human rights or measures against corruption.[62]

A novel element inexistent in European IIAs is investor obligations (Nowrot 2015, p. 1154; Zagel 2020a, p. 23). In many Global South IIAs, investor obligations form part of the overall strategy to achieve sustainable foreign

---

[59] E.g. art 11 PAIC; art 7 BIT Morocco-Nigeria.

[60] Art 5.5 India Model-BIT.

[61] PAIC, Brazil Model-BIT.

[62] E.g. art 15 Brazil Model-BIT; arts 15 and 17 BIT Morocco-Nigeria.

investment and complement the host states' efforts to implement sustainable development policies.[63] This element reflects the UNSDGs that stress the role of private businesses to realize sustainable development.[64] The scope of investor obligations varies. For instance, art 14 Brazil ModelBIT only contains an investor's general obligation to contribute to the host state's sustainable development and comply with the host state's corporate social responsibility standards. In contrast, arts 11ff ECOWAS Supplementary Act and arts 19ff PAIC enshrine a full chapter on investor obligations comprising substantive and procedural obligations and even remedies to enforce them.

Arts 13ff BIT Morocco-Nigeria constitute an example of a comprehensive set of investor obligations. Art 24(1) provides that "investors and their investments should strive to make the maximum feasible contribution to the sustainable development of the host state …". Arts 17–19 codify the investors' obligations on environmental protection, labour and social standards, human rights protection, and the fight against corruption, and refer to international treaties where appropriate. To implement environmental and social standards, arts 14 and 18 establish wide-ranging pre- and post-establishment impact assessment obligations, and arts 19 and 24 provide corporate governance obligations for foreign investors. Arts 13 and 15 on host state regulatory powers in the field of environment, human rights, and labour law clarify investors' sustainable development obligations.

To strengthen investor obligations, many Global South IIAs include remedies for breaches of investor obligations. For instance, arts 17 and 29 ECOWAS Supplementary Act or art 18 BIT Morocco-Nigeria provide jurisdictional rules that allow bringing breaches of investor obligations before the investor's host or home state's national courts. These rules close a jurisdictional gap resulting from the lack of national criminal or civil procedure rules of the host state or home state to permit the prosecution of acts occurring outside a state's territory. Some Global South IIAs also guide arbitrators on how to consider investor obligations in ISDS proceedings.[65]

Investor obligations not only enhance sustainable development but also contribute to mitigating the unbalanced content of IIAs, as they shift the IIA's objective from mere investment protection to a fair balance between host states' and investors' rights and obligations. Additionally, investor obligations contribute to regulating the conduct of TNCs that frequently are politically and economically in a much stronger position than their host states. Regulating

---

[63] E.g. arts 19ff, 30 and 34 PAIC; arts 11ff India Model-BIT; arts 11ff ECOWAS Supplementary Act.

[64] UN 2030 Agenda, paras 62 and 67.

[65] See the fourth section of this chapter.

the conduct of TNCs has been debated for decades.[66] A feasible approach to governing undesirable TNC behaviour may be to readjust the purpose of IIAs from mere investment protection to promoting sustainable foreign investment that regulates host states' *and* foreign investors' conduct (Zagel 2020b, p. 40).

To conclude, the comprehensive concept of implementing sustainable development in many Global South IIAs is an approach that may also be feasible in the European context. It guides arbitral tribunals on the scope and content of sustainable development and clarifies the host state sustainability measures that investors must accept without claiming a breach of IIA obligations. The corresponding investor obligations reinforce the sustainability policies of host states, help to overcome the IIA critique of the unfair distribution of rights and obligations between host states and investors, and constitute a possibility to govern the conduct of TNCs.

## DISPUTE SETTLEMENT

### EU Approach: Reform of the Traditional ISDS Process

A fundamental criticism of IIAs is the ISDS system that permits foreign investors to enforce substantive breaches of IIA standards against their host states (Salacuse 2021, p. 516). ISDS initially aimed to depoliticize investment disputes by replacing the time-consuming and highly political state-to-state dispute settlement by direct settlement between investor and host state (Dolzer and Schreuer 2012, p. 235). ISDS can avoid shortcomings of national courts, such as rule of law deficits or biases against foreign multinationals. However, critics oppose the ISDS system for its significant systemic deficiencies (Traidcraft 2015, p. 13).

ISDS raises structural questions about the composition of arbitral tribunals, their impartiality, the transparency of arbitral proceedings, and the lack of judicial review of arbitral awards (Tams 2014, pp. 587ff; UNCITRAL 2019). However, the most critical issue for sustainable development is that host states can hardly predict the outcome of arbitral tribunals' procedural decisions (Zagel 2020a, p. 41). IIAs lack procedural guidance leaving broad discretion for arbitral tribunals to pursue a case, decide a case, and determine indemnification. The resulting uncertainty significantly affects a host state's willingness to adopt sustainability measures, as the result of an award or the amount of compensation are uncertain.

---

[66] E.g. OHCHR, Guiding Principles on Business and Human Rights 2011, http://www.ohchr.org/Documents/Publications/GuidingPrinciplesBusinessHR_EN.pdf.

The EU has introduced numerous novel elements to improve arbitral tribunals' structural weaknesses and the arbitration procedure (Tams 2014, p. 595; European Commission 2015; Sardinha 2017, p. 628). Reform measures comprise strengthening the host states' influence on the arbitral proceedings, provisions on early dismissal, and rules on indemnification and costs. They clarify the arbitration procedure and directly prevent adverse effects of the ISDS system on sustainable development in the host state (Zagel 2020a, p. 42). Other measures include establishing a permanent investment court, an appeals procedure, and rules on transparency of proceedings (European Commission 2015, p. 7; Sardinha 2017, p. 633; European Parliament 2020). These elements introduce additional procedural steps that enhance the chances of considering sustainable development aspects in arbitral proceedings and awards, and the transparency rules permit increased public scrutiny for how the tribunals handle sustainability aspects of a case. Therefore, these reform elements have an indirect positive effect on a host state's willingness to adopt sustainability measures.

Arts 8.18ff CETA exemplify how the EU implements its reformed ISDS rules. First, the Committee on Services and Investment strengthens the contracting parties' role in the dispute settlement process by providing a forum for addressing issues arising from the IIA chapter (Sardinha 2017, p. 631).[67] Its tasks include consulting on difficulties arising from the IIA chapter's implementation, recommending the adoption of interpretations and amendments of the IIA chapter, and adopting amendments of the dispute settlement rules. The body permits the contracting parties to discuss the negative impacts of substantive IIA provisions on their powers to adopt sustainability measures and change procedural rules to reduce the adverse effects on sustainability policies. Second, art 8.18.3 CETA contains rules on the early dismissal of unfounded claims if investors undertook an investment through fraudulent misrepresentation, corruption, or conduct amounting to an abuse of process (Tams 2014, p. 605). Following arts 8.32 and 8.33 CETA, claims may also be dismissed at an early stage if they are manifestly without legal merits or unfounded as a matter of law. These provisions allow for shortening legal proceedings in cases with no reasonable chance, prevent the ISDS system's abuse, and save host states' resources and costs. Third, CETA addresses the calculation of damages and the distribution of costs. Following arts 8.31.3 and 8.44.3 CETA, damages shall not be greater than the loss suffered by the investors, punitive damages are prohibited, and the unsuccessful party shall bear the costs of the proceedings. The rules limit the financial burden for host states in case of unjustified or unsuccessful challenges of host state regulatory measures.

---

[67] Art 8.44 CETA.

In sum, the EU reforms are suitable to remedy many concerns against the traditional ISDS system. They enhance legitimacy, transparency, and consistency of arbitral decisions, at least within the respective TIA. Yet, while the large institutional setting may be manageable for the EU and Canada, it may constitute a challenge for smaller (developing) states with limited resources, like Vietnam or Peru. Moreover, the ISDS reforms evidently did not aim at preventing adverse effects on sustainable development specifically. Although the contracting parties can steer the interpretation of the substantive IIA provisions, and the new rules reduce the system's possible abuse and limit damages and costs, these elements improve the effects of ISDS on sustainable development only indirectly and to a limited extent.

### Global South Approach: Shifting the Parameters of Dispute Settlement from Traditional ISDS to a State-Centred System of Dispute Management

Like in the EU, the Global South ISDS reforms are not specifically directed at preventing adverse effects on sustainability policies. However, many Global South IIAs replace the classical ISDS model through a comprehensive dispute management system to reduce the resources needed in ISDS proceedings. A leading role in reforming the dispute settlement process is played by the Brazil Model-BIT and several African IIAs.[68] They focus on dispute prevention and dialogue and use dispute settlement proceedings only as a last resort. Several reform elements also contribute to mitigating the adverse impact of the traditional ISDS system on the host state's sustainable development.

Strengthening the contracting parties' role in the dispute settlement process is an essential element as it increases the possibility of host states to exercise influence in cases affecting the sustainability policies of host states. Reformed Global South IIAs use different approaches to facilitate host states' participation in the dispute settlement process. For instance, the Brazil Model-BIT and the BIT Morocco-Nigeria establish a "Joint Committee" with a leading role in the dispute settlement process. While the bodies have some powers similar to CETA, such as to issue joint statements on questions of interpretation of IIA rules or to amend IIA rules, they also hold powers to monitor the IIA's implementation and execution.[69]

The Joint Committees play a significant role in dispute prevention. Both the Brazil Model-BIT and the BIT Morocco-Nigeria provide that the contracting party whose nationality the investor holds must bring any dispute with the host

---

[68] E.g. PAIC, BIT Morocco-Nigeria, ECOWAS Supplementary Act.

[69] Art 4 BIT Morocco-Nigeria; art 17 Brazil Model-BIT.

state to the Joint Committee that assesses the conflict through consultations and negotiations.[70] The consultations take place in bilateral meetings of the contracting parties; the investor involved is invited to participate in these consultations.[71] The contracting parties' leading role in the consultations provides the opportunity to discuss the purpose of regulatory measures and negotiate solutions that may reconcile the sustainability interests of the contracting state involved and the investor's interests without getting arbitral tribunals involved in public policy choices. The state parties' involvement facilitates considering their common interests in implementing sustainable development policies in line with their international obligations.

The reformed Global South IIAs consider the traditional dispute settlement through arbitration as a last resort to solve investment disputes if preventive measures have failed. The approaches vary. Whereas the BIT Morocco-Nigeria provides for the traditional ISDS system,[72] the Brazil Model-BIT resorts to the classical public international law state-to-state dispute settlement to settle investment disputes.[73] In these proceedings, the investor's home state represents the investor's interests, but the BIT contains an obligation to pay any compensation awarded to the investor after deducing the costs.[74] To ensure that arbitral tribunals properly consider aspects of sustainable development, Global South IIAs contain several provisions to mitigate the adverse effects of arbitral proceedings on the host states' sustainable development that also exist in European IIAs (Zagel 2020a, p. 45). For instance, art 13.4 India Model-BIT restricts a claim's admissibility if the investment is not established correctly, e.g., if corruption is involved. Art 21 India Model-BIT prevents frivolous or abusive claims.[75] Such provisions prevent the ISDS system's abuse and save costs and resources that host states may better spend on implementing sustainability policies.

A novel feature inexistent in EU IIAs is to specify elements that may mitigate or offset compensation for breaches of substantive IIA obligations (Zagel 2020a, p. 52). This element addresses the uncertainty of how to calculate indemnification in traditional IIAs and guides arbitral tribunals to balance the host state's and investor's interests when determining compensation. For instance, art 12(2) PAIC introduces an element of proportionality and requires balancing public interest and the affected investor's interest when determining the amount of compensation. Art 5(2) SADC Investment Protocol Amendment

---

70 Art 26 BIT Morocco-Nigeria; art 23 Brazil Model-BIT.
71 E.g. art 26.2.c BIT Morocco-Nigeria; art 23(3)(c) Brazil Model-BIT.
72 Art 27 BIT Morocco-Nigeria.
73 Art 24 Brazil Model-BIT.
74 Art 24(13)(c) Brazil Model-BIT.
75 Art 21 India Model-BIT.

contains a similar provision and specifies the elements that arbitral tribunals must consider, including the purpose of the expropriation. Both provisions require arbitral tribunals to consider the host state's interests in implementing sustainability policies.

Some IIAs also introduce provisions on the mitigating and offsetting effects of investor conduct. The most comprehensive rule is arts 18 (2) and (4) ECOWAS Supplementary Act, which specifies the mitigating or offsetting effects of breaches of investor obligations. Similar but less extensive rules contain art 43 PAIC. These elements require arbitral tribunals to weigh the host states' interests in adopting sustainability measures against the investors' interests in protecting their property when determining the amount of compensation. This approach guides arbitral tribunals to consider public interest, such as sustainable development, when determining the amount of compensation. Together with the express purpose of IIAs to promote sustainable foreign investment, they effectively limit the possible negative impact of arbitral awards on sustainable development.

To conclude, in contrast to the European ISDS reforms, the examined Global South IIAs appear to include several elements that effectively reduce the potential adverse effects of ISDS on the sustainable development of host states. Whereas also the European IIAs provide for increased influence of the host states on ISDS, the examined Global South IIAs give host states a more influential role, in particular in the prevention of investment disputes, and allow them to shape sustainable investment policies in dialogue with all contracting parties and the relevant investors. Moreover, the procedural rules require considering the sustainability objectives and the investor conduct as reasons for mitigating or offsetting damages, which is a considerable improvement compared to the insufficient provisions on indemnification in traditional IIAs.

## CONCLUDING REMARKS

Notwithstanding considerable contestation, IIAs are still widely used to regulate foreign investment in Europe and worldwide. Despite the EU's large-scale IIA reforms to avoid undesired effects on sustainable development, EU IIAs continue to face widespread criticism. An exit to the dilemma may provide reformed Global South IIAs that use different approaches to shift the focus of IIAs from protecting investment to promoting sustainable foreign investment and improving the balance of host states' and investors' rights and obligations. While European and Global South IIAs share several reform approaches, three aspects hardly exist in European IIAs.

First, in contrast to European IIAs, many Global South IIAs expansively stress the purpose of sustainable development and clarify the role of sustainable development for the application and interpretation of the IIA. They specify the notion and scope of sustainable development by defining relevant policy areas, such as environmental protection, labour standards, social standards, human rights, and the fight against corruption. Some also refer to relevant international standards to clarify the substantive content of the respective policy areas. This clarification contributes to shifting the treaty purpose to sustainable foreign investment and guides arbitral tribunals on what standards to consider in disputes on host states' sustainability policies.

Second, in line with the UNSDGs, many Global South IIAs specify the host states' regulatory powers and obligations regarding sustainability measures and establish corresponding investor obligations to realize an all-encompassing strategy of implementing sustainable development policies. Whereas also European IIAs require investors to comply with the host state legal framework, the rules in Global South IIAs have teeth, as breaches of investor obligations may induce the inadmissibility of investment claims or the mitigation or offsetting of damages. This approach also improves the IIAs' balance between host state and investor rights and obligations.

Third, many Global South IIAs change dispute settlement from the traditional ISDS system to a dispute prevention and management system with a substantial influence of the contracting parties. This model facilitates addressing sustainable development issues that the reformed EU IIAs can only deal with to a limited extent. The preventative stage permits discussing the sustainable development aspects of investment disputes, and the participation of the contracting parties and the investors concerned facilitates solutions that are acceptable for investors and also comply with the contracting parties' sustainable development obligations. Furthermore, Global South IIAs strengthen the contracting parties' influence at the dispute settlement stage to prevent undesired results of arbitral proceedings. The Global South IIA reforms also minimize this risk of unpredictable procedural decisions by better procedural guidance to arbitral tribunals, particularly on the role of investor obligations and the calculation of costs and damages.

In the current controversies on IIAs in Europe, these Global South IIA reform approaches may provide new input to improve the acceptance of IIAs as instruments to regulate foreign investment and the implementation of the UNSDGs alike. The approaches may help to overcome the unwanted and at times undue influence of foreign investors on their host states' regulatory sovereignty and prevent unfavourable outcomes of investment disputes – problems that are relatively recent in Europe, but that most states belonging to the Global South have had to cope with for decades. Whether the Global South reform approaches succeed in promoting sustainable foreign investment while adequately protecting investors remains to be seen. As most IIAs applicable in investment disputes still follow the traditional IIA model with no specific provisions on sustainable development, and most reformed IIAs have not even entered into force, the international community must be patient.

## REFERENCES

Bartels, L. (2013) Human Rights and Sustainable Development Obligations in EU Free Trade Agreements. *Legal Issues of Economic Integration*, **40**, 297–314.

Dolzer, R. and Schreuer, C. (2012) *Principles of International Investment Law*, 2nd edition. Oxford: Oxford University Press.

European Commission (2015) Investment in TTIP and Beyond – the Path for Reform. http://trade.ec.europa.eu/doclib/docs/2015/may/tradoc_153408.PDF.

European Commission (2018) Feedback and Way Forward on Improving the Implementation and Enforcement of Trade and Sustainable Development Chapters in EU FTAs. http://trade.ec.europa.eu/doclib/docs/2018/february/tradoc_156618.pdf.

European Parliament (2020) *Multilateral Investment Court, Overview of the Reform Proposals and Prospects*. Briefing. https://www.europarl.europa.eu/RegData/etudes/BRIE/2020/646147/EPRS_BRI(2020)646147_EN.pdf.

ICSID (2022) The ICSID Case-Load – Statistics (Issue 2022-2). https://icsid.worldbank.org/sites/default/files/publications/The_ICSID_Caseload_Statistics_2022-2_ENG.pdf.

IISD (2005) Model International Agreement on Investment for Sustainable Development. https://www.iisd.org/system/files/publications/investment_model_int_agreement.pdf.

Mann, H. (2013) Reconceptualizing International Investment Law: Its Role in Sustainable Development. *Lewis & Clark Law Review*, **17**, 521–544.

Mbengue, M. and Schacherer, S. (2017) The "Africanization" of International Investment Law: The Pan-African Investment Code and the Reform of the International Investment Regime. *Journal of World Investment & Trade*, **18**, 414–448.

Muniz, J., Duggal, K. A. N. and Peretti, L. A. S. (2017) The New Brazilian BIT on Cooperation and Facilitation of Investments: A New Approach in Times of Change. *ICSID Review – Foreign Investment Law Journal*, **32**, 404–417.

National Board of Trade Sweden (NBTS) (ed.) (2019) *TSD Handbook, Implementation of the Chapter on Trade and Sustainable Development in the Trade Agreement between EU and Ecuador*. https://www.kommerskollegium.se/globalassets/publikationer/guider/2019/handbook-tsd-en.pdf.

Nowrot, K. (2015) Obligations of Investors. In Bungenberg, M., Griebel, J., Hobe, S. and Reinisch, A. (eds.), *International Investment Law*. Baden Baden: Nomos, 1154–1185.

Salacuse, J. (2021) *The Law of Investment Treaties*, 3rd edition. Oxford: Oxford University Press.

Sardinha, E. (2017) The New EU-Led Approach to Investor-State Arbitration: The Investment Tribunal System in the Comprehensive Economic Trade Agreement (CETA) and the EU-Vietnam Free Trade Agreement. *ICSID Review – Foreign Investment Law Journal*, **32**, 625–672.

Tams, C. (2014) Procedural Aspects of Investor-State Dispute Settlement: The Emergence of an European Approach? *Journal of World Investment & Trade*, **15**, 585–611.

Traidcraft (ed.) (2015) *International Investment Agreements under Scrutiny: Bilateral Investment Treaties, EU Investment Policy and International Development*. https://www.tni.org/files/download/iias_report_feb_2015.pdf.

UNCITRAL (2019) Possible Reforms of ISDS, A/CN.9/WG.III/WP.166 and Addendum A/CN.9/WG.III/WP.166. Add.1.

UNCTAD (ed.) (2012) *Expropriation*. New York: United Nations.

UNCTAD (2018) *UNCTAD's Reform Package for the International Investment Regime*. https://investmentpolicy.unctad.org/publications/1190/unctad-s-reform-package-for-the-international-investment-regime-2018-edition-.

Zagel, G. (2020a) Achieving Sustainable Development Objectives in International Investment Law. In Chaisse, J., Choukroune, L. and Jusoh, S. (eds), *Handbook of International Investment Law and Policy*. Singapore: Springer, 1–55.

Zagel, G. (2020b) India's International Investment Agreements (IIAs) and Sustainable Development: Friends or Foes? *Indian Journal of International Economic Law*, **12**, 1–39.

# 21. The 'object and purpose' and incrementalism of investment treaties: can international investment law reinvent its identity?

**Güneş Ünüvar**

## INTRODUCTION

This chapter provides an overview of how changes in treaty drafting and language affect the prescribed objectives and identity of the international investment law (IIL) regime. It generally argues that, despite occasional arbitral backlash (manifesting as traditional interpretations of newer agreements), current trends favoring further clarity, specificity, and inclusivity, represented *inter alia* by a series of new free trade agreements (FTAs) negotiated by the European Union (EU) in particular, have begun to alter the exclusively investor-centric identity of IIL. It chiefly argues that through gradual additions to treaty preambles and provisions in international investment agreements (IIAs) concerning environment, health, general public interest, sustainable development, labor rights as well as investor obligations and responsibilities, new generation IIAs are increasingly becoming informed political-legal declarations. The emerging tendencies and patterns in treaty and policymaking indicate that unqualified, ambiguous international protections extended to foreign investors by earlier generation IIAs have lost their appeal, and IIAs that are assertive in their objective of protecting public interest goals such as health and environmental protection are becoming more and more common (albeit still rather limited). They might even attest substantial responsibilities for foreign investors to that end, breaking the asymmetrical foreign investment protection centerpiece that dominated the IIL regime for its hitherto existence.

IIL is a legal field which has constructed its identity and normative discourse on the idea that a particular stakeholder – foreign investor – needs protection vis-à-vis the state. This simple yet extremely controversial presupposition has driven the discourse and paradigms in the field. Treaties that govern and drive the system are IIAs that emphasize the 'promotion and protection of foreign investments' and 'fair' treatment of investors. Some treaties adopt less targeted language and emphasize the 'development of economic relations' between signatories.

There has been an observable trend towards concluding IIAs (and domestic Model BITs) that highlight states' regulatory prerogatives, as well as sustainable development, vis-à-vis the protection of foreign investment (UNCTAD 2020). These newer features are often incorporated in preambles and other substantive provisions. They aim to introduce more explicit and nuanced caveats to ambiguous and broad object and purpose formulations in earlier generation IIAs. This trend is particularly visible in the new EU FTAs. These treaties, in addition to incorporating a so-called Investment Court System (ICS) to replace arbitration as a dispute settlement method, include an emphasis on the protection of health, promotion of sustainable development, and the prohibition of a regulatory rollback in labor, health and environmental standards in new IIAs. While these FTAs and their investment chapters do not radically alter the investor-centric discourse dominant in most treaties in force today, they stand out from the earlier generation treaties by paying closer attention to exceptions to the protection of foreign investors. Even though they still primarily outline a protection framework, they are enriched by qualifications and exceptions[1] to said protection to complement the objective of promoting foreign investments, and potentially serve as interpretative tools for clarifying the extent of protection afforded to them. This being said, some recent arbitral awards (not stemming from EU FTAs), as will be detailed below, demonstrate that despite the existence of such clarifications, tribunals can still find controversial ways to sidestep and discard them.

This focus still necessitates a multi-faceted, legal-political understanding of treaty interpretation: the role of preambles, the Vienna Convention on the Law of Treaties (VCLT), arbitral experience (through incremental interpretation of substantive principles) as well as national and international policy considerations, modifications and adjustments to laws, regulations and treaties governing the domain of foreign investment law and protection. Understanding treaty interpretation is crucial, for both drafting treaties (including preambles), and of course correctly interpreting these treaties. Indeed, one particularly challenging issue for this chapter is identifying precisely how the object and purpose of a treaty, in this case an IIA, can be determined. While preambles are helpful and greatly affect the overall interpretation of specific provisions, they are not the only place in a treaty from which such 'object and purpose' can be discerned. In addition to clarifications introduced by preambles, elements of

1 For instance, see Comprehensive and Economic Trade Agreement between the EU and Canada (CETA), Article 8.12 on Expropriation and subsequent Annex 8-A.

this object and purpose can be found in special provisions, which indicate that the object and purpose of IIAs is not the protection of foreign investment or investors per se, at least not without qualifications, exceptions or balancing of interests. As this chapter illustrates, some more recent FTAs and BITs, through their preambles and negotiated provisions, reflect a more explicit approach.

## WHY DO INVESTMENT LAW (AND INVESTMENT TREATIES) EXIST?

IIAs have been mostly vague, unspecific, short instruments for most of their existence. Especially since late 1990s, many IIA-based arbitral claims have been lodged by foreign investors against their host states. As these cases proliferated, a somewhat clearer picture of how these IIAs in force functioned when applied to concrete disputes emerged. It has also become apparent that they transcended above being basic and ambiguous texts promising better protection in order to attract investment without any (or negligible) consequences and responsibility for host states (Poulsen 2015). In some cases, states came to realize that the vague nature of these IIAs allowed for interpretations broader, or narrower, than what they had intended (assuming, of course, that they had intended any actual dispute to arise from these IIAs in the first place) – often at the expense of their sovereign competences and authority. This initial 'epiphany phase' lasted roughly from 1997 to the mid-2000s, resulting in a backlash (Franck 2005). Subsequently, these 'lessons learned' manifested in future IIAs through clarifications or omissions, prompting the creation of a newer generation of IIAs, sometimes by way of streamlining of how IIAs should be read by contracting states. It could also be said that this initial epiphany and subsequent backlash against IIL and investor-state dispute settlement (ISDS) eventually lead to calls for reform. UNCITRAL's Working Group III and its multilateral effort to reform ISDS (ongoing as of September 2021) is a direct result of these calls, despite critics pointing out that the scope of reform is too narrow as it does not delve into substantive, policy-related issues such as climate change (Polonskaya 2020).

One fundamental reason for this shift is that the seemingly bilateral relationship between a foreign investor and the host state envisaged by IIAs has a plethora of spillover effects. This phenomenon has come under the limelight in the context of some ISDS disputes. Among them were the cases lodged against Argentina after its 2001–2002 economic crisis (Alvarez and Khamsi 2009), by the *Philip Morris* arbitrations against Uruguay and Australia, and the *Vattenfall* dispute against Germany, to name a few. This spillover occurs, in particular, when the public is affected by the actions or negligence of a foreign investor (or the state vis-à-vis the foreign investor) in cases concerning public services or resource extraction, or when a state takes measures ostensibly in public interest but to the detriment of a foreign investor. As a regime expressly geared towards protecting foreign investment from state intervention through specific or regulatory acts, IIL inevitably seeks to balance the interests of a foreign investor on the one hand, and *everyone else* (the state, communities, residents, citizens) on the other. Thus, one key question pertaining to the *raison d'être* of IIL is the following: If there is to be an agreement between two countries concerning foreign investment, why should it asymmetrically protect only one stakeholder of this multi-dimensional interaction among the host state, foreign investor, and public?

The investor-centric nature alluded to above is therefore well-embedded in the history of IIL. If one extends the inquiry of *why foreign investments were granted such generous international protection* to the broader issue of *why, and how, foreign property is protected in a host country*, the examination of IIAs would extend well beyond the last three centuries (Newcombe and Paradell 2009; Miles 2013; Ünüvar forthcoming). The historical and conceptual link between earlier forms of protection of foreign property on the one hand, and the contemporary instruments (i.e., IIAs) to protect foreign investments, on the other, has had a profound impact on the current form and context of the IIL regime.

The historic-political presupposition has always been that the private actors (in this case foreign investors) are inherently vulnerable vis-à-vis the governing, regulating and legislating sovereign state – therefore its protection must be ensured, particularly in colonized, or otherwise controlled territories in the nineteenth and twentieth centuries. This rationale ultimately culminated in the creation of the specialized legal field often referred to as IIL, which ensures the extraterritorial application of the law and influence of the home state (Miles 2013). For the purposes of this chapter, it is also noteworthy to point out that the phrase 'law of foreign investment protection' or similar varieties are used synonymously with IIL – a stark reminder as to the scope and current purpose of the legal system and its instruments. The very existence of these rights and remedies is indeed contested (Sornarajah 2014) – to this day, IIL regime is struggling to "normatively justify [...] the way it aims to provide a better and more effective legal protection for foreign investors" than remedies available in domestic laws (Alvik 2020, p. 312). To that end, the existence of ISDS and IIL has gained a lot of public attention with their *raison d'être* constantly challenged. Moreover, it was argued that IIL has greatly hindered the fulfillment of international human rights obligations and transitional justice efforts (Van Ho 2016).

Generally speaking, the IIAs that are in force today contain provisions on fair and equitable treatment (FET), full protection and security (FPS), and protection against government takings in the form of expropriation (direct/indirect expropriation). They further ensure foreign investors the treatment extended to domestic investors, as well as the treatment accorded to the 'most favored' third country investors (National Treatment (NT) and the Most-Favored-Nation Treatment (MFN)) (OECD 2004). It is extremely rare to see substantial responsibilities attested to foreign investors in IIAs, and virtually all obligations belong to the state hosting foreign investment (Choudhury 2020, p. 88). Most of these provisions outlining state responsibility are infamously vague and have been thoroughly examined over time regarding their content and scope (Dolzer and Bloch 2003; Kläger 2011). The real consequences of these vague provisions manifest themselves in the phase of dispute resolution, as discretion left to arbitrators on disputes between host states on the one hand, and foreign investors on the other, has led to meanings previously unforeseen by the creators of these IIAs.

Another main controversy stems from the nature of disputes that arise in ISDS, as some of these foreign investors are multinational corporate enterprises (MNCs) that undertake public services such as sanitation, telecommunication, or energy production; or operations such as resource extraction. Such activities and their sheer infrastructural and financial extent in the twenty-first century are incomparable to the circumstances that led to the historic presupposition that the investor is inherently vulnerable. Even if this assumption were true in retrospect, it is extremely challenging to justify it in a world globalizing and interconnecting at an unprecedented pace. The fact of the matter remains that some MNCs have higher net worth than entire countries' gross domestic product (Foreign Policy 2016).

## Preambles and the 'Object and Purpose' of an IIA: Identifying the Missing Links and Affected Parties

Since this chapter focuses on how IIAs are worded, formulated, and subsequently interpreted at the core of its discourse (as opposed to generally discussing paradigms and shifts in policy choices in states' foreign investment policies), it is of utmost importance to reiterate the legal tools that inevitably direct the interpretation of IIAs. Pursuant to Article 31(1) Vienna Convention on the Law of Treaties (VCLT), a treaty "shall be interpreted in good faith and in accordance with the ordinary meaning to be given to the terms of the treaty in their context and in the light of its object and purpose [...]". In law, it is common to refer to the preambles of a treaty to identify its objectives (Bjorge 2014, p. 85). According to Dothan (2019), this provision recalls textual (ordinary meaning of the text), subjective (pursuant to the intentions of the parties), as well as teleological (focusing on the object and purpose of the treaty) elements of interpretation (Dothan 2019, p. 766). It gives limited guidance to adjudicators, and leaves some discretion as to what the ordinary meaning, the intentions of the parties or the object and purpose of the treaty may be.

It is common to refer to a treaty's preamble to identify its object and purpose. Dörr and Schmalenbach (2011) note that "a preamble can thus be of both contextual and teleological significance. There are many examples in international jurisprudence of reference being made to the preamble of a treaty in order to elucidate the meaning of a particular provision" (Dörr and Schmalenbach 2011, p. 544). Virtually all IIAs have such preambles, and as noted by Dolzer and Schreuer (2012), while interpreting IIAs, "the object and purpose is often sought in [these] preambles" (Dolzer and Schreuer 2012, p. 29). For instance, the Contracting Parties of the Argentina – Netherlands BIT note, in the preamble of the agreement, the following:

> Desiring to strengthen the traditional ties of friendship between their countries, to extend and intensify the economic relations between them, particularly with respect to investments by the investors of one Contracting Party in the territory of the other Contracting Party,
>
> Recognizing that agreement upon the treatment to be accorded to such investments will stimulate the flow of capital and technology and the economic development of the Contracting Parties and that fair and equitable treatment of investments is desirable [...]

Still, a holistic reading of an agreement is often necessary to pinpoint its object and purpose, as they are not necessarily confined to the preamble. The text, title, as well as the annexes of an IIA, will also be considered. For instance, majority of IIAs make direct references to 'promotion and protection of investments' in their titles.[2] This choice of wording, combined with preambles supporting such reading, could *prima facie* mean that these agreements in fact exist only – or at least, mainly – to promote and protect foreign investments – and do not concern themselves with anything beyond that. The *SGS v. Philippines* tribunal, which interpreted and applied the Philippines – Switzerland BIT of 1997, expressed this approach as follows:

> The object and purpose of the BIT supports an effective interpretation of Article X (2). The BIT is a treaty for the promotion and reciprocal protection of investments. According to the preamble it is intended 'to create and maintain favourable conditions for investments by investors of one Contracting Party in the territory of the other'. It is legitimate to resolve uncertainties in its interpretation so as to favour the protection of covered investments.

When compared to the above Argentina – Netherlands BIT preamble, what stands out in the applicable BIT in this dispute is the explicit reference to

---

[2] For instance, the Argentina – Jamaica BIT (1995) is officially called "Agreement between the Government of Jamaica and the Government of the Argentine Republic on the Promotion and Reciprocal Protection of Investments".

the maintenance of "favourable conditions by investors". Similarly, in *Noble Ventures v. Romania*, the Tribunal adopted an interpretation that was "exclusively in favour of investors", since according to the Tribunal, the object and purpose as distilled from the preamble of US – Romania BIT of 1992 justifies such interpretation. The said preamble refers to reciprocal encouragement and protection of investment, as well as maintaining a stable framework. None of these preambles, and many others in IIAs beyond those that are mentioned above, include a reference to public interest as a balancing factor vis-à-vis creating favorable conditions for investors and protecting investments.

Other Tribunals have adopted more assertive positions. In *Saluka v. Czech Republic*, the Tribunal interpreted and applied the Czech Republic – Netherlands BIT. Like the Argentina – Netherlands BIT, the preamble in this BIT refers to Contracting Parties' desire to "extend and intensify the economic relations between them particularly with respect to investments", and "stimulate the flow of capital and technology and the economic development" in the two countries. It does not refer to, or in any way emphasize, creating favorable conditions for investors. In this light, the Tribunal noted that:

> This is a more subtle and balanced statement of the Treaty's aims than is sometimes appreciated. *The protection of foreign investments is not the sole aim of the Treaty*, but rather a necessary element alongside the overall aim of encouraging foreign investment and extending and intensifying the parties' economic relations. That in turn *calls for a balanced approach to the interpretation of the Treaty's substantive provisions* for the protection of investments, since an interpretation which exaggerates the protection to be accorded to foreign investments may serve to dissuade host States from admitting foreign investments and so undermine the overall aim of extending and intensifying the parties' mutual economic relations. (Emphasis added)

Arbitral interpretations that focus on the exclusive protection of investments can give rise to excessive, or generally unintended, interpretations. These results can be in the form of excessive restrictions on regulatory space, even exceeding those that exist under respective domestic laws (Van Harten 2008, p. 150). If a regulation, or another form of governmental measure affected a foreign investment, then the foreign investor could claim damages – creating a situation in which a state has to compensate for the loss of a private investor, simply for performing its sovereign prerogatives and international duties which could benefit the public.

The current system is constructed, in all directions, upon two interconnected and traditional centerpieces: protection of (a) foreign investor; and (b) foreign investment. While admittedly a distant possibility within the current international political and legal climate, the trend of 'tipping the balance' in favor of non-investor stakeholders might eventually transform IIL into an international legal realm focused on delivering what some call 'civil justice' (Steinitz 2019) – a notion, in this context, which can mean to hold all those accountable – and protect all those in need of protection – foreign investor, public, or otherwise – from adverse effects directly arising out of the investment relationship.

Whether IIAs exist in order to promote and protect foreign investment, or they also have the multi-faceted role of protecting public good, has therefore emerged as a highly contentious issue among commentators (Baetens 2013). This scrutiny has occasionally led to the contention that IIL has a systemic bias favoring foreign investors (Chung 2007), and that this obligation of protecting foreign investments with little or no reservation comes at the expense of the public and sovereign interests on matters such as health, environment, and more generally, the right to regulate.

Treaty preambles, perhaps more than the individual provisions in a treaty, adopt a general declaratory tone and role regarding important aspects and considerations of the parties of a treaty. In IIAs, the tendency seems to be to incorporate broadly defined goals that eventually affect interpretations of substantive principles to varying degrees. Therefore, the preambles relate to what types of 'checks and balances' a treaty seeks to implement. As such, these limitations and clarifications give direction to individual provisions and contextualize them. Several new FTAs, IIAs and Model BITs demonstrate the tendency towards further clarity in preambles to give direction on how provisions such as FET should be interpreted. Unlike earlier generation IIAs, these treaties all include relatively elaborate preambles regarding different stakeholders and interests.

Take, for instance, the gradual expansion and transformation of the Indian Model BIT preambles from 2003 to 2016. According to the 2003 model, the treaty builds upon the desire "to create conditions favourable for fostering greater investment by investor of one State in the territory of another State". Furthermore, the preamble recognizes that "the encouragement and reciprocal protection [...] will be conductive to the stimulation of individual business initiative and will increase prosperity". However, aside from a few broad and vague endorsements of fostering economic development through favorable treatment of foreign investors, the preamble is silent on virtually any other stakeholder involved. In its 2015 draft model (which was the precursor to the eventual 2016 model), a short preamble underscores "bilateral cooperation between the Parties". In addition, the model preamble reaffirms "the right of Parties to regulate Investments in their territory in accordance with their Law and policy objectives including the right to change the conditions applicable to such investments". It adds that the treaty would seek "to align the objectives of Investment with sustainable development and inclusive growth of the Parties". The emphasis on bilateral cooperation is nothing new. However, the two latter declarations concerning the right to regulate and the explicit aim to balance or align investment promotion and protection on the one hand, and sustainable development and inclusivity on the other, demonstrate the shifting priorities as unanimously declared by India. However, while the 2015 draft can be read as a desired scope for future IIAs, the model was eventually watered down in its entirety. Yet, similar declaratory provisions can be found under the final preamble. In its final version, the preamble refers to "bilateral cooperation", "stimulation of mutually beneficial business activity, to the development of economic cooperation between [the Parties] and to the promotion of sustainable development", and a reference to the reaffirmation of "the right [...] to regulate investments in their territory in accordance with their law and policy objectives". While sustainable development and right to regulate remain novel features in 2015 and 2016 versions vis-à-vis earlier generation BITs of India, the final version arguably adopts a somewhat cautious tone when compared to the 2015 draft. Despite the softening of its tone, the fact remains that India seeks to pursue a less investor-centric phase of its new generation IIAs, nuanced with protection of other policy objectives vis-à-vis the foreign investor.

The Indian example does not occur in a vacuum, and it resonates in different parts of the world. Particularly since the Treaty of Lisbon, the European Commission and different Union institutions have focused on a fundamentally altered investment protection system embodied by the ICS (and, eventually the Multilateral Investment Court). This new regional policy adopted by the EU generally stems from alleged investor-centrism or systemic bias towards foreign investment, lack of transparency and a perceived inconsistency in awards delivered by arbitral tribunals (Brown 2018). The general framework has hinted at a broader and multi-faceted politico-legal coverage with regard to relevant stakeholders and actors in a potential foreign investment dispute. For instance, the preamble for the EU – Singapore Investment Protection Agreement (EUSIPA) includes a relatively lengthy (two pages) preamble with similar emphases. The preamble notes that the economic, trade and investment relations would be strengthened with regard to "the objective of sustainable development, in its economic, social and environmental dimensions". It further notes that the parties seek to "promote investment in a manner mindful of high levels of environmental and labour protection and relevant internationally-recognized standards" to that end. Subsequent paragraphs reaffirm the Parties' commitment to "the principles of sustainable development and transparency" as well as their right "to pursue legitimate policy objectives such as social, environmental, security, public health and safety, promotion and protection of cultural diversity". An explicit reference to the Charter of the United Nations and the Universal Declaration of Human Rights is followed by another emphasis on the importance of transparency in investment and trade relations "to the benefit of all stakeholders", and not just foreign investors/investments that the system has traditionally protected.

There are interesting differences between the preambles of EUSIPA and its contemporary, EU – Vietnam Investment Protection Agreement (EUVIPA). While they are generally similar in content and format, it is also evident that they shift in accordance with their parties' priorities with regard to economic and social expectations tied to these deals. One striking example is the absence of any underscoring of the right to regulate in the EUVIPA preamble. Instead, the preamble notes that the parties desire "to raise living standards, promote economic growth and stability, create new employment opportunities and improve the general welfare and, to this end, reaffirming their commitment to promoting trade and investment liberalization". Another difference in the EUVIPA preamble is the additional emphasis on the parties' contention that "EUVIPA will create [...] a stable and predictable environment for trade and investment, thus enhancing the competitiveness of their firms in global markets".

The 2018 Model BIT of the Netherlands contains similar emphases. In addition to traditional objectives, such as extending and intensifying economic relations between the parties, the Model also makes references to "sustainable economic development", "open and transparent policy environment", sustainable development "and to enhancing the contribution of international trade and investment to sustainable development", as well as recognizes the parties' "right [...] to regulate within their territories through measures necessary to achieve legitimate policy objectives, such as the protection of public health, safety, environment, public morals, labor rights, animal welfare, social or consumer protection or for prudential financial reasons".

These goals and considerations focusing on different stakeholders are virtually absent in the 1997 Model BIT of the Netherlands. One important aspect of this Model BIT is the explicit contention that "fair and equitable treatment of investment is desirable". The 2004 Model BIT represents a middle ground between the 1997 and 2018 models: while not as outright as 2018 Model, it makes references to, *inter alia*, "internationally accepted labour standards" in addition to the desirability of fair and equitable treatment of investments.

Another remarkable addition to the BIT network in this regard is the Iran – Slovakia BIT, which entered into force in 2017. It stands out from the rest of BITs in force for several reasons. It is one of the few BITs in force that includes investor obligations and responsibilities at any degree, and an explicit recognition of the respondent state's right to counterclaim on some of these grounds (i.e. corruption, fraud, compliance with the host state law) under its Articles 10 and 14. The preamble recognizes that investment is critical for sustainable development, and notes that "the promotion of investment requires *co-operative efforts by investors and both Contracting Parties*". It further states that the parties expect investments to be "consistent with and facilitative of the protection of health, safety and the environment, the promotion and protection of [...] labor rights". What is noteworthy about this BIT is its express aim "to secure *an overall balance of rights and obligations between investors and the Host State*", as well as "to prevent and combat corruption, including bribery, in international cooperation and investment and to promote corporate social accountability". Overall, the preamble allows for arbitrators to take into account additional considerations vis-à-vis the protection of investment/investor and other general objectives, such as stimulation of economic activities.

While the above examples do not suffice or aim to definitively assert any pattern or systemic divergence attached to specific preambular wordings, it reveals how preambles, to the extent that they are considered to be expressions of the object and purpose of IIAs, can affect the overall analysis of an arbitral tribunal significantly. It illustrates the importance of the wording used even in 'less substantial' sections of an IIA. It should therefore not come as a surprise that different wordings will be attested different meanings by different arbitrators within the context of different factual and legal information being available. In other words, an IIA with an explicit reference to actively creating favorable conditions to investors can be, and has been, applied in a manner more favorable to investors than an IIA that, for instance, simply underlines "fostering economic cooperation between the Contracting Parties". This interpretative divergence could be better justified, especially if the IIA does not contain any further limitations on how substantive principles, such as FET, should be interpreted. It is probable that an arbitral tribunal, tasked with assessing the fairness of a given state measure, might interpret the factual, legal and overall contextual background of the dispute differently due to an emphasis on legitimate policy objectives, promotion of sustainable investment, or the responsible behavior expected from the foreign investor. Taken together with more detailed and articulated substantive provisions, accurately worded preambles can reinforce the intended balance between different stakeholders while protecting a foreign investor from unjust or unlawful interventions of host states.

IIL is a system established on the premise that foreign investors need a legal system essentially dedicated to facilitating their international remedies against host states, a need particularly stark when dealing with countries with a poor rule of law record, corrupt and politically motivated judiciaries, and undemocratic polities. This exchange resulted in the surge of thousands of IIAs, equipped with volatile provisions more than capable of producing substantial pecuniary burden for states. Most IIAs were, and generally still are, historically based on the same or similar model treaty texts, which emphasized one aspect (the possible need for protection of foreign investors) of this multi-dimensional network of relationships among the public, foreign investor, and the state created at the time of a foreign investor's entry into a national market through its investment.

While IIL and twentieth-century policymakers sought to remedy one perceived problem (i.e., the vulnerable position of foreign investors vis-à-vis host states' arbitrary conduct) in a swiftly globalizing world, they could not or did not extend this effort to designing IIL so as to protect and preserve the interests of all possible stakeholders. Accepting this (incidental, intended, or negligent) investor-centric rationale of IIL also calls for admitting that these foundational premises are dated, incomplete and inadequate to address all evident effects and consequences of this multi-dimensional relationship.

## Implementing the Object and Purpose: Substantive Principles, Regulatory Carve-Outs and (More) Symmetrical Protection

Beyond the question of the object and purpose of IIAs lies the challenge of implementing these reflected objectives in the form of substantive protection principles. In other words, understanding what Contracting States intended (and specifically how they articulated these intentions in an agreement) is only the prelude to the question of how these objectives are implemented in such agreements, in the form of substantive and enforceable obligations. It is beyond doubt that IIAs, no matter what counter-balancing elements might come into play, chiefly contain provisions only on *how to protect foreign investors*, and the overarching goal is the prevention of 'unfair', arbitrary, and destructive interventions by home states. The so-called counter-balancing elements (or carve-outs and exceptions to these obligations) are shaped in accordance with policy choices and identified shortcomings of earlier generation IIAs put to test through international arbitration. For instance, in its 2015 Model BIT, Norway has included a provision on "The Right to Regulate", in addition to traditional protection principles such as National Treatment (Article 3), Most-Favoured-Nation Treatment (Article 4), FET (Article 5), and Expropriation (Article 6). The provision (Article 12) arguably reframes the scope of these protection principles vis-à-vis states' right to regulate as a policy concern and functions as a limitation on Contracting Parties' obligations towards foreign investors. It reads that:

> Nothing in this Agreement shall be construed to prevent a Party from adopting, maintaining or enforcing any measure otherwise consistent with this Agreement that it considers appropriate to ensure that investment activity is undertaken in a manner sensitive to health, safety, human rights, labour rights, resource management or environmental concerns.

This provision attempts to clarify the language of protection principles to be included in future Norwegian IIAs by curbing the arbitral discretion in regulatory matters relating to public policy areas such as health and environment. This provision is supported by the recognition of other policy considerations in the preambles, such as corporate social responsibility, sustainable investments, prevention of corruption, transparency, and environment, among others.

Besides such general qualifications and exceptions in separate provisions or preambles of agreements, treaty-makers might inject specific clarifications and qualifications under individual provisions. These clarifications aim at channeling the wording and language of individual protection principles in a specific direction, thereby giving guidance to adjudicators on how these provisions should be read.

As mentioned above, through arbitral practice, states have come to realize that certain vague provisions created unanticipated, unfair results. Such lack of anticipation eventually prompted claims that the IIL regime was inconsistent, thus inadequate to address disputes with direct consequences on the public; and as demonstrated through arbitral awards which failed to recognize *inter alia* states' right to regulate, even biased towards the protection of investors vis-à-vis states' sovereign prerogatives. This realization is arguably the starting point of what could be called the first phase of the transformation of investment law from a law of protection of foreign investment to a system of governance.

Parallel to this, the broad, divergent, or unanticipated arbitral awards have a directly observable impact on how these countries revised their IIAs. One salient illustration is the Comprehensive Economic and Trade Agreement (CETA) between Canada and the EU, and it has one of the most elaborate Fair and Equitable Treatment (FET) provisions to date, a protection principle traditionally vague and difficult to define. Its Article 8.10, entitled "Treatment of Investors and Covered Investments", states that "[e]ach Party shall accord in its territory to covered investments of the other Party and to investors with respect to their covered investment fair and equitable treatment [...] in accordance with paragraphs 2 and 6". Paragraph 2 contains a negative list of acts, formulated as follows:

> A Party breaches the obligation of fair and equitable treatment [...] where a measure or series of measures constitutes:
> **Denial of justice** in criminal, civil or administrative proceedings;
> **Fundamental breach of due process**, including a fundamental breach of transparency, in judicial and administrative proceedings;
> **Manifest arbitrariness**;
> **Targeted discrimination** on manifestly wrongful grounds, such as gender, race or religious belief;
> **Abusive treatment** of investors, such as coercion, duress and harassment; or
> A breach of any further elements of the [FET] obligation adopted by the parties [...]

This provision model is unique to some recent EU FTAs. It makes no references to customary international law or international law as a yardstick, nor does it leave the provision unqualified and, therefore, 'autonomous' – a difference often voiced, but never clarified. Instead, it creates a 'checklist', to which members of tribunal would have to refer when assessing whether a measure is unfair. This, again, would be done vis-à-vis the distilled object and purpose of the treaty. One potential shortcoming is, while it introduces a certain degree of clarity to the previous vagueness of the principle, some elements (such as 'manifest arbitrariness') of the checklist might still fall short of establishing a stable yardstick for FET and whatever its Parties anticipated as its scope.

On expropriatory measures, the disagreement between disputing parties in *Pope & Talbot*, an early NAFTA claim, on the meaning of the term 'tantamount to expropriation' is relevant to the analysis on future IIAs. In that dispute, Canada argued that the challenged measure by the claimant was "an exercise of regulatory power". It further claimed that states were not "required to compensate an investment for any loss sustained by the imposition of *a non-discriminatory, regulatory measure*" and that "liability is possible *only if the measure is discriminatory*" (emphasis added). The Tribunal ultimately disagreed. It noted that "creeping expropriation could be conducted by regulation, and a blanket exception for regulatory measures would create a gaping loophole in international protections against expropriation". While there is nothing in the NAFTA text to support the Canadian argument, the Tribunal seems to have erroneously interpreted Canada's argument to mean a *complete* exception for all regulatory measures.

The Canadian position in *Pope & Talbot* has been subsequently explicitly incorporated in several North American instruments, in line with the policy objective of retaining regulatory competences. Under the Annex B.13 (Canada Model BIT) and Annex B (US Model BIT), the treaty-makers have laid forth a detailed test which not only outlines the elements of consideration (*inter alia* economic impact of the measure, the extent of interference or the character of the measure), they further carve out "non-discriminatory regulatory actions by a Party that are designed and applied to protect legitimate public welfare objectives, such as health, safety, and the environment". The US revised its Model BIT further in 2012, but these features remained the same. Likewise, the post-2004 US and Canadian IIAs are, to a significant extent, based on these models. Adjudicatory elaborations on how to differentiate between indirect expropriation and non-compensable state acts have thus found more concrete and elaborate clarifications. As of 2021, for instance, all new EU FTAs follow the same carve-out model, excluding measures that are non-discriminatory and have a legitimate public purpose from the scope of indirect expropriation.

This analysis above reveals an important fact about the interaction between the arbitral practice and treaty-making: Arbitral practice, through elaborations on meanings based on wording, has a significant role in attesting context to prescribed, yet untested, rules. It remarkably alters the rules and their meaning, as well as their anticipated results and implications. The alteration of meaning eventually results in the adjustment of its wording, complemented with the learned arbitral experience. Ultimately, the transformation of these rules creates an aggregate understanding of their functioning vis-à-vis foreign investors and the public. It also puts their degree of fairness to the test and reveals when it is necessary to allow adjudicators to use discretion or adhere to written rules and preset policy objectives pursued by signatory states in a manner respectful to all affected parties and stakeholders involved in an investment relationship. This is a defining aspect of arbitral process – it not only clarifies the present objectives of IIL, but also sheds light on its future.

While states try to prevent unintended or unwanted interpretative outcomes through novel and more explicit wordings, it is far from granted that arbitral practice will immediately evolve alongside such broader clarifications themselves. More recently, provisions analogous to Article 12 of the Norwegian Model BIT which contain so-called 'general exceptions' to the protections extended to foreign investors, have come under scrutiny and criticism. *Eco Oro v. Colombia*, an award rendered in September 2021, is a stark illustration of how such general exceptions can still be sidestepped by arbitral tribunals. The applicable IIA to the case was the Canada – Colombia FTA of 2008, which includes, *inter alia*, a general exception clause (Article 2201(3)). It denotes that "nothing in this Agreement shall be construed to prevent a Party from adopting or enforcing measures necessary […] [t]o protect human, animal or plant life or health, which the Parties understand to include environmental measures necessary to protect human, animal or plant life and health". In its analysis and interpretation of this provision, the Tribunal first referred to the preamble of the FTA and determined that, since it seeks to "ensure a predictable commercial framework for business planning and investment in a manner that is consistent with environmental protection and conservation" (Paragraph 828, *Eco Oro* Award), the parallel goals of ensuring a predictable commercial framework and environmental protection are not 'subservient' to another, and neither takes precedence over the other. The Tribunal then noted that while a state, pursuant to Article 2201(3), cannot be precluded to enact measures to protect environment:

> there is no provision in Article 2201(3) permitting such action to be taken without the payment of compensation [...] had it been the intention of the Contracting Parties that a measure could be taken pursuant to Article 2201(3) without any liability for compensation, the Article would [make it] explicit that the taking of such a measure would not give rise to any right to seek compensation under Chapter Eight.
> [...]
> 830. The Tribunal therefore construes Article 2201(3) such that whilst a State may adopt or enforce a measure pursuant to the stated objectives in Article 2201(3) without finding itself in breach of the FTA, this does not prevent an investor claiming under Chapter Eight that such a measure entitles it to the payment of compensation.

This reading, whereby a state is seemingly allowed to regulate to protect environment without automatically absolving it from the obligation to compensate, is controversial. The Tribunal compares the lack of any explicit provision in Article 2201(3) concerning compensation to that found under Annex 811(2)(b), according to which expropriation would not exist if the challenged measure is adopted in good faith, in a non-discriminatory manner and to protect legitimate public welfare objectives. If Article 2201(3) were drafted as Annex 811(2)(b), the Tribunal contended, then the former would also not entail a compensation.

This conundrum is directly linked to an earlier award, *Bear Creek v. Peru*, where the Tribunal maintained that Peru's actions constituted indirect expropriation. The applicable IIA in *Bear Creek* was Canada – Peru FTA of 2009 with an expropriation provision (Article 812), which includes Annex 812.1. This Annex contains a virtually identical clause to aforementioned Annex 811(2)(b), whereby "nondiscriminatory measures of a Party that are designed and applied to protect legitimate public welfare objectives, such as health, safety and the environment, do not constitute indirect expropriation". This provision is designated to preserve a state's prerogatives to regulate for public policy by excluding a measure fulfilling these preconditions from the scope of expropriation which, by consequence, means the measure is non-compensable. Instead of handling Peru's argument that its measures constituted police powers (and were therefore non-compensable state acts), it appears that the Tribunal erroneously evaluated this defense under Article 2201.1 of the FTA, including a general exceptions clause analogous to 2201(3) of the Canada –

Colombia FTA above. Consequently, the Bear Creek Tribunal erroneously ignored Annex 812.1 and its carve-out, then contended that no such police powers exception existed under Article 2201.1. It then found a violation of the FTA.

This creates an interpretative loop difficult to break, perpetuated by erroneous readings of the general exceptions provisions on the one hand, and the expropriation carve-outs on the other. In *Eco Oro*, the Tribunal contended that *precisely* because a general exception clause was not drafted akin to an expropriation carve-out, liability and duty to compensate remained – in *Bear Creek*, the Tribunal *precisely* ignored such a carve-out and still found the state liable for compensation, going back to a general exception clause. It is also noteworthy that the Eco Oro tribunal heavily relies on the preamble to reach its conclusion, whereby it places environmental protection and investment protection on the same pedestal. While these provisions are put in place to streamline arbitral interpretations and give guidance to arbitral tribunals, it is striking that such interpretative mishaps occur. Still, one should be cautious to generalize these readings and assume that such interpretations, clearly controversial if not erroneous, would dominate awards rendered pursuant to new IIAs. It does, however, mean that the interaction between treaty-making and arbitral practice is dynamic and continuous, and treaty-makers should take note of such sidesteps.

## CONCLUSION

This chapter sought to provide an overview of the ongoing policy shifts in IIL from the perspective of its *raison d'être*, borne out of the interaction between investment arbitration practice and the wording/phrasing preferences in IIAs. This interaction has a decisive influence on the framework that governs the international legal regime on the protection of foreign investment. Thousands of IIAs have invoked hundreds of claims to date – the vast majority after the late 1990s. Most of the IIAs that were invoked were signed during the 1980s and 1990s, with only scarce claims to test their application at the time. The shortcomings (as well as divergences between intended and actual functioning of these IIAs) were only visible after the accumulation of claims and arbitral elaborations – and awards such as *Bear Creek* and *Eco Oro* show that there is still a long way to go.

As this chapter shows, more elaborate preambles, rules, exceptions, and carve-outs injected into newer IIAs vis-à-vis their predecessors indicate that the seemingly singular purpose of the IIL regime is changing and enhancing itself. Amid fierce criticism targeted at the ISDS regime, many states sought to remedy their national, as well as regional, investment policies. Most reforms indicate broader policy space for states on matters concerning and affecting public interest. Many foreshadow broader responsibilities and obligations for investors vis-à-vis the state and public.

By using accurately worded objects, clearly set-out purposes, and eloquent counter-balancing measures (such as exceptions and carve-outs conceived in line with expected or desired goals) that are set to direct or limit arbitrators (or members of the ICS tribunals), states, as well as investors, IIAs can become legal tools governing investment relations more inclusively rather than in the asymmetrical bilateral manner to which it is currently confined. With such clarity in their wording and attested meanings, they can act as clear policy declarations that address factual disputes with a broader outlook, and not only the formalistic boundaries that currently govern the system.

## REFERENCES

1997 Netherlands Model BIT.
2003 India Model Text of BIPA.
2004 Canada Model BIT.
2004 Netherlands Model BIT.
2004 US Model BIT.
2015 Draft India Model BIPA.
2015 Norway Model BIT: https://www.regjeringen.no/contentassets/e47326b61f424d4c9c3d470896492623/draft-model-agreement-english.pdf.
2016 India Model BIPA.
2018 Netherlands Model BIT.
Alvarez, J. E. and Khamsi, K. (2009) The Argentine Crisis and Foreign Investors: A Glimpse into the Heart of the Investment Regime. In Sauvant, K. P. (ed.), *The Yearbook on International Investment Law and Policy 2008/2009*. New York: Oxford University Press, 379–478.
Alvik, I. (2020) The Justification of Privilege in International Investment Law: Preferential Treatment of Foreign Investors as a Problem of Legitimacy. *European Journal of International Law*, **31**(1), 289–312.
Argentina–Netherlands BIT (1994): http://investmentpolicyhub.unctad.org/Download/TreatyFile/107.
Baetens, F. (ed.) (2013) *Investment Law within International Law*. Cambridge: Cambridge University Press.
*Bear Creek Mining Corporation v. Republic of Peru* (2017), ICSID Case No. ARB/14/21.
Bjorge, E. (2014) *The Evolutionary Interpretation of Treaties*. New York: Oxford University Press.
Brown, C. (2018) The European Union's Approach to Investment Dispute Settlement. 3rd Vienna Investment Arbitration Debate. https://trade.ec.europa.eu/doclib/docs/2018/july/tradoc_157112.pdf.
Canada – Colombia Free Trade Agreement (2008).
Canada – Peru Free Trade Agreement (2009).
Choudhury, B. (2020) Investor Obligations for Human Rights. *ICSID Review*, **35**. 82–104.

Chung, O. (2007) The Lopsided International Investment Law Regime and Its Effect on the Future of Investor-State Arbitration. *Virginia Journal of International Law*, **47**, 953–976.

Comprehensive Economic and Trade Agreement (CETA 2014). http://trade.ec.europa.eu/doclib/docs/2014/september/tradoc_152806.pdf.

Czech Republic – Netherlands BIT (1992).

Dolzer, R. and Bloch, F. (2003) Indirect Expropriation: Conceptual Realignments? *International Law Forum du droit international*, **5**, 155–165.

Dolzer, R. and Schreuer, C. (2012) *Principles of International Investment Law*, 2nd edition. Oxford: Oxford University Press.

Dörr, O. and Schmalenbach, K. (2011) Article 31: General Rules of Interpretation. In Dorr, O. and Schmalenbach, K. (eds), *Vienna Convention on the Law of Treaties: A Commentary*. Heidelberg: Springer, 521–570.

Dothan, S. (2019) The Three Traditional Approaches to Treaty Interpretation: A Current Application to the European Court of Human Rights. *Fordham International Law Journal*, **42**, 765.

*Eco Oro Minerals Corp. v. Republic of Colombia* (2021), ICSID Case No. ARB/16/41.

EU – Singapore Investment Protection Agreement (EUSIPA 2019).

EU – Vietnam Investment Protection Agreement (EUVIPA 2020).

European Commission (2019) Press Release, Trade: European Court of Justice Confirms Compatibility of Investment Court System with EU Treaties (30 April). https://europa.eu/rapid/press-release_IP-19-2334_en.htm.

Foreign Policy (2016) These 25 Companies Are More Powerful Than Many Countries (15 March). https://foreignpolicy.com/2016/03/15/these-25-companies-are-more-powerful-than-many-countries-multinational-corporate-wealth-power/.

Franck, S. (2005) The Legitimacy Crisis in Investment Arbitration: Privatizing Public International Law through Inconsistent Decisions. *Fordham Law Review*, **73**, 1521–1625.

Kläger, R. (2011) *'Fair and Equitable Treatment' in International Investment Law*. Cambridge: Cambridge University Press.

Miles, K. (2013) *The Origins of International Investment Law: Empire, Environment and the Safeguarding of Capital*. Cambridge: Cambridge University Press.

Newcombe, A. and Paradell, L. (2009) *Law and Practice of Investment Treaties: Standards of Treatment*. Alphen aan den Rijn: Kluwer.

*Noble Ventures, Inc. v. Romania* (2005), ICSID Case No. ARB/01/1, Award, par. 52.

OECD (2004) *Most-Favoured-Nation Treatment in International Investment Law*. Working Papers on International Investment 2004/02. https://www.oecd.org/daf/inv/investment-policy/WP-2004_2.pdf.

*Philip Morris Asia Limited v. Australia*, UNCITRAL, PCA Case No. 2012-12.

*Philip Morris Brands Sarl and others v. Uruguay*, ICSID ARB/10/7.

Polonskaya, K. (2020) Metanarratives as a Trap: Critique of Investor-State Arbitration Reform. *Journal of International Economic Law*, **23**, 949–971.

*Pope & Talbot v. Canada* (2001) UNCITRAL, NAFTA (Award on the Merits Phase II).

Poulsen, L. (2015) *Bounded Rationality and Economic Diplomacy: The Politics of Investment Treaties in Developing Countries*. Cambridge: Cambridge University Press.

*Saluka Investments B.V. v. Czech Republic* (2006) UNCITRAL, par. 300.

*SGS Société Générale de Surveillance S.A. v. Philippines* (2004), ICSID Case No. AR/02/6, Decision of the Tribunal on Objections to Jurisdiction, par. 116.

Slovakia – Iran BIT (2016): https://investmentpolicy.unctad.org/international-investment-agreements/treaties/bilateral-investment-treaties/3633/iran-islamic-republic-of---slovakia-bit-2016-.

Sornarajah, M. (2014) *The International Law on Foreign Investment*, 3rd edition. Cambridge: Cambridge University Press.

Steinitz, M. (2019) *The Case for an International Court of Civil Justice*. Cambridge: Cambridge University Press.

Treaty between the Federal Republic of Germany and Pakistan for the Promotion and Protection of Investments (1959; entry into force 1962). http://investmentpolicyhub.unctad.org/Download/TreatyFile/1387.

UNCTAD (2020) The Changing IIA Landscape: New Treaties and Recent Policy Developments. *IIA Issues Note*, Issue 1 (July). https://unctad.org/system/files/official-document/diaepcbinf2020d4.pdf.

United Nations, Vienna Convention on the Law of Treaties, 23 May 1969, United Nations, Treaty Series, vol. 1155.

Universal Declaration of Human Rights, UN General Assembly (10 December 1948).

Ünüvar, G. (forthcoming) The Vague Meaning of Fair and Equitable Treatment Principle in Investment Arbitration and New Generation Clarifications. In Jemielniak, J. and Kjær, A. L. (eds), *Legal Interpretation in the Practice of International Courts and Tribunals*. Oxford: Oxford University Press.

Van Harten, G. (2008) *Investment Treaty Arbitration and Public Law*. Oxford: Oxford University Press.

Van Ho, T. (2016) Is It Already Too Late for Colombia's Land Restitution Process? The Impact of International Investment Law on Transitional Justice Initiatives. *International Human Rights Law Review*, **5**(1), 60–85.

*Vattenfall AB and others v. Germany*, ICSID ARB/12/12.

# Index